United Nations Environment Programme
Environmental
Data Report

United Nations Environment Programme

Environmental Data Report

Prepared for UNEP by the

GEMS Monitoring and Assessment Research Centre, London, UK

in co-operation with the

World Resources Institute, Washington DC
UK Department of the Environment, London

Blackwell Reference

For bibliographic and reference purposes this publication should be referred to as:
UNEP 1991 United Nations Environment Programme
Environmental Data Report, 3rd edition,
Basil Blackwell, Oxford.

1st edition published 1987.
2nd edition published 1989.

Basil Blackwell Ltd
108 Cowley Road, Oxford OX4 1JF, UK

Basil Blackwell Inc.
3 Cambridge Center, Massachusetts 02142, USA

British Library Cataloguing-in-Publication Data
  Environmental Data Report.
  1. Environment
  I. United Nations. Environment Programme.   II. GEMS Monitoring and
  Assessment Research Centre.   III. World Resources Institute.   IV. Great Britain.
  Department of the Environment
  333.7021
  ISBN 0–631–18083–4
  ISSN 0956–9324

Library of Congress Cataloging-in-Publication Data
  Environment data report/prepared for UNEP by the GEMS Monitoring and
  Assessment Research Centre London UK, in co-operation with the World Resources
  Institute, Washington DC, UK Department of the Environment, London.—3rd ed.
  At head of title: United Nations Environment Programme.
  1. Pollution.   2. Environmental monitoring.   I. United Nations Environment
  Programme.   II. GEMS Monitoring and Assessment Research Centre.
  III. World Resources Institute.
  TD 174.E576 1991   363.7—dc20   91–9393 CIP
  ISBN 0–631–18083–4   69695
  ISSN 0956–9324

Typeset in Times Roman by GEMS MARC, London
Printed in Great Britain at The Alden Press, Oxford

This book is printed on acid-free paper.

Contents

Foreword

All too often we have cared little for our environment. Chronic air pollution and contamination of fresh water are increasingly exposing millions of people to decidedly unhealthy living. Our lands and forests are being damaged by acid deposition while excessive pesticide and fertilizer misuse continue. Deforestation continues almost unabated and, when coupled with greenhouse gas emissions from industrial sources, has raised the spectre of global change. The world's soils are no less in danger than its forests. We still treat our rivers and oceans like dustbins. How we treat our fellow animals is often scandalous, endangering species and thus destroying our children's heritage.

Yet environmental awareness, particularly in the past few years, is beginning to capture our imagination as more and more people from all nations see the need to preserve biological diversity, to develop strict controls on pollution and to call for statesmanship of the highest order to resolve such problems. The United Nations Environment Programme (UNEP), working as a catalyst in association with its partner organizations within the UN system, has done much to improve matters. The Convention on International Trade in Endangered Species of Wild Fauna and Flora (CITES), the Basel Convention on the Control of Transboundary Movements of Hazardous Wastes and their Disposal, the Vienna Convention for the Protection of the Ozone Layer and its Montreal Protocol, the Intergovernmental Panel on Climate Change (IPCC) and negotiations under way for a global convention on climate change are such examples. Governments and people everywhere have several success stories. They are not many, but they show that this destruction can be stopped.

All these far-reaching actions require accurate, precise and reliable environmental data, without which we may well follow false leads and divert scarce resources into dead ends. To meet such challenges, biennial editions of the 'UNEP Environmental Data Report' are produced to bring together in one series the best available data on the global environment. Explanations accompany the data tables in order to aid interpretation, highlight trends, pin-point challenging issues and provide referenced sources for detailed regional and global assessment purposes.

As no one volume can contain all the necessary information, other sources of reliable data are highlighted providing a concise library of contemporary information.

The gathering of data from monitoring stations worldwide, from regional programmes and from national studies is a huge task. It relies on the views and judgements of hundreds of scientists throughout the world, from within the UN system and in international and regional organizations, from governmental and non-governmental organizations, and from industries and universities. I should like to thank all our advisers and contributors and to request them to continue to work with UNEP on this major task.

Despite the wealth of environmental data, particularly from developed countries, reliable data on some major problems, such as rates of deforestation, land degradation and toxic waste dumping to mention but a few, are still lacking. To counteract this, UNEP is committed to supporting a number of major global projects which are designed to address such issues. These efforts are highlighted in this edition of the 'UNEP Environmental Data Report' and will provide important new data sets for forthcoming volumes. The unprecedented changes sweeping across Eastern Europe are offering opportunities for these countries to join GEMS monitoring and other international networks, to plug outstanding gaps in data coverage and so to work towards improvement of the environment for all citizens.

Despite increasing environmental awareness and improved data gathering, the challenges of massive ecological change, burgeoning population growth and decreasing natural resources, still remain awesome. The analysis of available data must be translated into effective environmental management, and into action plans to stimulate the transfer of efficient and clean industrial technology to countries where the need is greatest.

The preservation of our global heritage relies upon the successful interpretation and assessment of accurate and reliable environmental data. I hope the 'UNEP Environmental Data Report' will meet those requirements.

Mostafa K. Tolba
Executive Director
United Nations Environment Programme

Notes to all Tables

To the extent possible, a consistent notation scheme has been used in the data listings:

Blank space	data not available or not applicable
–	negligible quantity, i.e., usually less than one-half the unit indicated
0	none, magnitude nil or zero

Countries are not listed when: (i) they have not submitted data to a data base or (ii) no data are available under the selected data headings.

Totals may not represent the sum of individual values due to rounding.

For ease of reference, countries have been listed in alphabetical order within the following continental groupings: Africa, North America, South America, Asia, Europe, USSR and Oceania. In some cases, however, some special regional groupings are maintained from source documents. Designations "developed" and "developing" countries, as assigned in source documents, are intended for statistical convenience and do not represent judgements about the stage reached by a particular country or area in the developing process.

As far as possible, SI units (the International System of Units) have been used throughout. Multiplying prefixes are used to indicate decimal multiples or fractions:

10^{15}	peta	P	10^{-1}	deci	d
10^{12}	tera	T	10^{-2}	centi	c
10^{9}	giga	G	10^{-3}	milli	m
10^{6}	mega	M	10^{-6}	micro	μ
10^{3}	kilo	k	10^{-9}	nano	n
10^{2}	hecto	h	10^{-12}	pico	p
10	deka	da	10^{-15}	femto	f

Introduction

Publication of the third edition of the 'UNEP Environmental Data Report' builds upon the now generally accepted philosophy that world-wide accurate and reliable environmental monitoring data form the basis of sound environmental policies and management. The three editions in the continuing series contain a wealth of up-to-date information at regional, national and local levels which is carefully selected in order to illustrate all major environmental issues of current concern.

Each edition of the 'UNEP Environmental Data Report' contains the same 10 recurrent parts describing major environmental themes: environmental pollution, climate, natural resources, population/settlements, human health, energy, transport/tourism, wastes, natural disasters and international co-operation. Each edition of the report contains a set of "core" data tables which are retained and updated in each published volume. The core data sets are supplemented with additional information which may comprise either data which reflect new world-wide monitoring activities, national or regional data sets illustrating topical issues and/or specific local studies deemed of significance in the wider context. This edition focuses on, for example, refugees, renewable energy resources and tourism. A section on the use of sediment cores and ice cores for reconstructing past environmental conditions and depositional history is also included for the first time (Part 1: Environmental Pollution, Historical Monitoring).

All parts of the 'UNEP Environmental Data Report' include brief explanatory texts which aid interpretation of the data sets and assist in the cross-linking, where appropriate, of one environmental variable with another. Comments are also made on the reliability and representativeness of the data. These allow users of the data to look for comparable information collected on a sound scientific basis and presented in a uniform manner.

The information presented in the 'UNEP Environmental Data Report' series is compiled from a great many diverse sources. Specific data holdings and data bases have been consulted from the World Meteorological Organization (WMO), Food and Agriculture Organization (FAO), United Nations Economic Commission for Europe (UN-ECE), Organisation for Economic Co-operation and Development (OECD), World Data Centers (WDC), the World Conservation Union (IUCN) and the World Conservation Monitoring Centre (WCMC) to mention only a few organizations. National activities in countries world-wide within the 30 international monitoring programmes implemented via GEMS and associated organizations have also been consulted in the preparation of this report.

The assessment of environmental trends, both temporally and spatially, is often hampered by a lack of comparable data at regional and global scales. National data cannot always be integrated readily into regional or international data sets because of, for example, the lack of agreement on the analytical measurement procedures, or on the definition of descriptive criteria, or, because of the variations in frequency of measurements or data collection. Such difficulties have arisen because the driving force for gathering of environmental information has been the need to deal with specific problems rather than the need to produce co-ordinated integrated data sets.

Since inception, GEMS has been working with some 142 countries in one or more activities to help to standardize working methods, data handling and assessment procedures. The UNEP/GEMS-Harmonization of Environmental Measurements Centre (HEM), established in 1989, has been developed to assist this process. Similarly, international and regional associations including the UN-ECE European Statisticians working group, the EEC's CORINE (Co-ordinated Information System on the State of the Environment and Natural Resources) and the International Standards Organization (ISO) continue to develop recommendations to standardize data collection and handling. A close integration of national monitoring systems seems an inevitable consequence of the need for international comparability and compatibility of data.

Despite the quantity of environmental data now available, surprising gaps still exist in data gathering. Increasing concerns over such issues as hazardous wastes, desertification, forest destruction and habitat loss are widely reported, yet reliable and comprehensive data are generally unavailable. The lack of co-ordinated methods of classification and definition of waste materials, for example, has severely hampered the collection of statistics on this issue. Recent advances within the OECD are, however, helping to resolve such problems.

Some of the major gaps in environmental monitoring, particularly with respect to desertification and deforestation, have also been receiving attention. The UNEP/FAO tropical forest assessment has alerted decision makers to the need for international action. A Global Assessment of Soil Degradation (GLASOD) is being undertaken by UNEP's Soils Group through the International Soil Reference and Information Centre (ISRIC), FAO and others, and in association with UNEP's Global Resource Information Database (GRID). The results will be reported in detail in future issues of the 'UNEP Environmental Data Report'. Another gap now being addressed is the need for an early warning network to improve awareness of impending changes of climate and natural resources. This new UNEP/GEMS programme will be highlighted in forthcoming editions of the report.

Increasingly, a wide range of industrial chemical substances are being detected in areas far removed from their manufacture and use. Some of these areas are in remote parts of the world where recent analytical studies have recorded their presence, thus advancing the concept of global contamination. With some metals and organic substances, global contamination is now accepted as a reality. Efforts to analyse the background levels of chemical substances in remote areas are reported in this edition.

Detailed information on specific chemicals and hazardous wastes is routinely compiled by UNEP's International Register of Potentially Toxic Chemicals (IRPTC). The International Programme on Chemical Safety (UNEP/WHO/ILO) Environmental Health Criteria reports provide overviews of the toxicity and health effects of many industrial chemicals. The point has been reached, however, where the 10 millionth chemical substance, namely cis-(±)-4,6,7,8,8a,8b-hexahydro-6,6,8b-trimethyl-4-H-naphtho (1,8-bc)furan, has been registered by the American Chemical Society's Chemical Abstract Service. Thus it must be realised that only a few substances of major concern to wildlife and exposure to chemical substances by people can be mentioned in the 'UNEP Environmental Data Report'.

In association with the 'UNEP Environmental Data Report', GEMS MARC is enlarging and updating the computerized data base which houses all the data contained in the report series. The function of the data base in the longer term is to facilitate provision of a query-response service and to enable more complicated indicators to be calculated by linking data from one section or environmental compartment with data from another. Moreover, it is the intention to make extracts from the data base available in diskette form.

Other associated computer data bases, comprising UNEP's information system, include the three WHO/UNEP GEMS health-related programme data bases – namely the US EPA urban air pollution data base, the Canada Centre for Inland Waters data base on global water quality and the WHO(HQ) data base housing food contamination data – and UNEP's GRID. GRID is the major source for georeferenced data on the world's environment and natural resources. Through its world-wide network of centres, it holds extensive georeferenced environmental data sets at global, regional and national scales and thus forms a bridge between monitoring and assessment and environmental management. Its main task at present is to provide reliable data handling and analytical capabilities to help in the assessment of deforestation, climate change, desertification, ozone depletion and many other important environmental issues.

A great many individuals and organizations have contributed to the compilation of data for this report, via GEMS MARC and its co-operating organizations the World Resources Institute, Washington DC, and the UK Department of the Environment. This invaluable support is acknowledged in Appendix 1. UNEP is grateful for all the advice and comments received in shaping this edition. The pooling of knowledge and resources internationally provide the basis for understanding environmental problems, proposing solutions at the national and international level and seeing through the resolutions.

Part 1
Environmental Pollution

Human activities, either directly or indirectly, have resulted in the introduction of numerous chemical contaminants into the global environment. Many contaminants, for example halocarbons and pesticides, are man-made and have no natural sources. Others, including trace metals and the oxides of carbon, sulphur and nitrogen, are naturally occurring, but industrial activities have markedly modified their global biogeochemical cycles.

Contamination of the environment has now reached global proportions; data presented in this section of the 'UNEP Environmental Data Report' illustrate that trace metal and organic pollutants have been detected in remote locations far removed from the major industrial centres of the Northern Hemisphere. Moreover, environmental contamination problems are no longer only of local or even regional concern. Issues such as climate change and ozone layer depletion serve to emphasize the global scope of the impact of environmental contamination.

In order to formulate sound environmental management policies, it is of vital importance to have reliable data on the concentrations of pollutants in the various environmental compartments – air, precipitation, soils/sediments, water and biota. There is now an enormous amount of data of this type available from individual local-scale research projects, national surveys and regionally and globally co-ordinated monitoring programmes. This section of the 'UNEP Environmental Data Report' provides an overview of significant spatial and temporal trends in concentrations of a range of contaminants in all the environmental compartments, including man. Where possible data from global or regional-scale monitoring programmes, such as those co-ordinated by UNEP's Global Environment Monitoring System (GEMS), have been selected for presentation. Such programmes are subject to analytical quality control procedures and intercalibration exercises and therefore are able to provide internationally comparable data sets. In order to expand the scope and coverage of this section it has, however, been necessary to include results from national monitoring programmes and individual studies. Although the data obtained may not necessarily be directly comparable between locations, some valuable insights regarding trends in environmental quality may be gained from this type of approach.

For logistical reasons, data are presented in sub-sections according to individual environmental compartments. However, where possible, pollutant inputs to the various environmental media are considered and cross-references are made to related information presented in other sections of the report so as to facilitate a more complete understanding of the issues.

In recent years there has been a growing awareness of the need to adopt an "integrated" or "ecosystem" approach to environmental monitoring, especially in remote areas. It is anticipated that this type of approach will provide more information about baseline levels of contaminants and also, by measuring pollutant concentrations in all media at the same location, improve understanding of interactions between variables in different compartments. Brief mention of ongoing integrated monitoring initiatives, most of which are in pilot phases, was made in the previous edition of this report. As little new information is available at the present time, this topic will not be covered in this edition of the 'UNEP Environmental Data Report' but will be re-introduced in a subsequent edition. In its place a section on Historical Monitoring, i.e., the use of palaeoecological records for the reconstruction of past environmental conditions, has been included.

Atmosphere

Gases and particulates are emitted to the atmosphere from a wide range of sources, both natural and man-made. Emissions of gaseous and particulate pollutants, predominantly from anthropogenic combustion sources, have given rise to a host of environmental problems on global, regional and local scales. Issues such as global warming, ozone layer depletion, acid deposition and urban air pollution have received considerable attention in recent years and have been the focus of major international research projects and collaborative monitoring programmes.

In this section of the report trends in atmospheric concentrations of greenhouse gases, ozone (stratospheric and tropospheric) and selected urban air pollutants are reviewed. As far as possible observed trends in concentrations are related to trends in emissions of atmospheric contaminants.

Greenhouse Gases

The atmospheric abundance of naturally occurring, radiatively active trace gases (i.e., greenhouse gases) plays a significant role in determining the earth's climate. Greenhouse gases, such as water vapour, carbon dioxide (CO_2), methane (CH_4), chlorofluorocarbons (CFCs), nitrous oxide

(N$_2$O) and tropospheric ozone (O$_3$), are for the most part transparent to incoming short-wave solar radiation but absorb and trap long-wave radiation emitted by the earth's suface; their presence in the atmosphere thus exerts a warming effect on the earth. It is generally accepted that continuing increases in atmospheric concentrations of selected greenhouse gases due to human activities will lead to an enhanced greenhouse effect and global climatic change (WMO/UNEP, 1990).

Routine monitoring of CO$_2$ and other greenhouse gases is conducted primarily in remote regions of the world, removed from distorting influences of major industrial centres. The Climate Monitoring and Diagnostics Laboratory (CMDL) of the US National Oceanic and Atmospheric Administration (NOAA), formerly Geophysical Monitoring for Climatic Change (GMCC), has maintained a number of observatory sites since the early 1970s, two of which date back to the 1950s. A range of parameters, including greenhouse gases, are monitored at these sites. More recently a global flask sampling network has been established for more spatially extensive trace gas monitoring.

Additional greenhouse gas monitoring programmes include the Global Atmospheric Gases Experiment (GAGE), and that co-ordinated by the Institute of Atmospheric Sciences at the Oregon Graduate Center (OGC) in the USA. The Background Air Pollution Monitoring Network (BAPMoN), initially established by the World Meteorological Organization (WMO) in 1969, includes the measurement of CO$_2$ at 23 of its sites. The United Nations Environment Programme provides support for the BAPMoN programme which in turn contributes data to GEMS. In 1989 the BAPMoN network was integrated into the WMO's new Global Atmospheric Watch (GAW) programme. The new programme will provide a framework for improved monitoring and assessment of trends in air quality in background areas by expanding the existing network of permanent observatories (WMO, 1989).

Carbon Dioxide As the primary contributor to the enhanced greenhouse effect, CO$_2$ has been the most intensively studied of the greenhouse gases to date. Atmospheric concentrations of CO$_2$ have been monitored at Mauna Loa, Hawaii, since 1958. During the 1970s and 1980s networks for the monitoring of atmospheric concentrations of CO$_2$ expanded; global networks are currently operated by NOAA/CMDL and by the WMO (as part of BAPMoN). A number of NOAA/CMDL stations also serve as BAPMoN sites.

CMDL monitors CO$_2$ on a continuous basis using non-dispersive infra-red gas analysers at its four observatory sites located at Barrow (Alaska), Mauna Loa (Hawaii), Cape Matatula (American Samoa) and at the South Pole. Results of measurements made since 1973, expressed as monthly and annual mean values, are given in Table 1.1. Figure 1.1 illustrates the growth in atmospheric CO$_2$ since 1958, as recorded at Mauna Loa, Hawaii. The observed

seasonality in the CO$_2$ record is attributed to the annual withdrawal and production of CO$_2$ by the terrestrial biota.

In order to gain a more detailed picture of the spatial distribution of selected atmospheric trace gases, including CO$_2$, NOAA/CMDL have established a global flask sampling network. The first site, based at Niwot Ridge, Colorado, became operational in 1968; the network has since expanded and now comprises 30 sites world-wide. Samples of air are collected weekly (or twice-weekly) in 0.5 litre glass flasks and are returned to the CMDL for analysis for CO$_2$, carbon monoxide (CO) and CH$_4$. The results for CO$_2$ during the period 1981–1984 were summarized in the 1989 edition of the 'UNEP Environmental Data Report' (UNEP, 1989). A more detailed description of the flask sampling programme for CO$_2$ and assessment of results has been published by Conway et al. (1988). CMDL data for CO$_2$ (and CH$_4$) are also available from the Carbon Dioxide Information Analysis Center (CDIAC) in Oak Ridge, USA, in both published form (Boden et al., 1990) and computerized format.

Available data from the NOAA/CMDL networks confirm that atmospheric concentrations of CO$_2$ are increasing globally. At present, levels average around 353 ppmv; flask data indicate that during the 1980s (1981–1989) CO$_2$ levels have risen, on average, by 1.4 ppmv per year (Tans, 1990). Concentrations are higher in the Northern Hemisphere due to the greater density of emissions sources (see below). Past concentrations of CO$_2$ have been inferred from measurements made in air trapped in polar ice. Compilation of available results suggests that in pre-industrial times atmospheric CO$_2$ averaged 280 ppmv (UNEP, 1989; WMO/UNEP, 1990). The ice-core record also provides evidence of strong correlations between atmospheric CO$_2$ and temperature over the glacial-interglacial cycle (see Part 1: Environmental Pollution, Historical Monitoring).

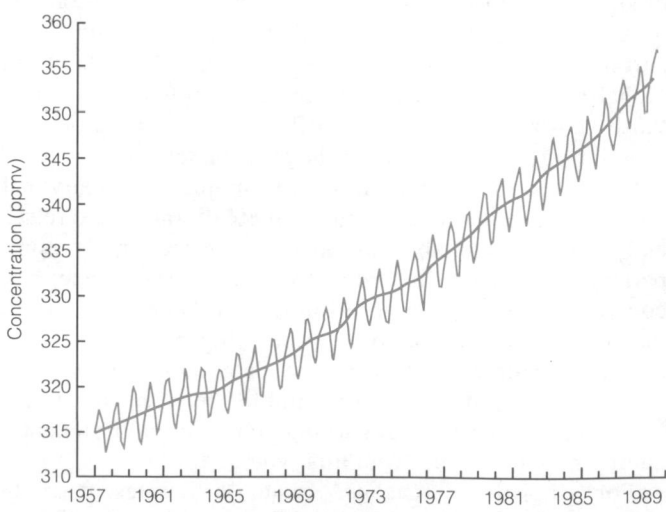

Figure 1.1 Monthly mean concentrations of atmospheric CO$_2$ at Mauna Loa, 1958–1989
Source: figure provided by NOAA/CMDL

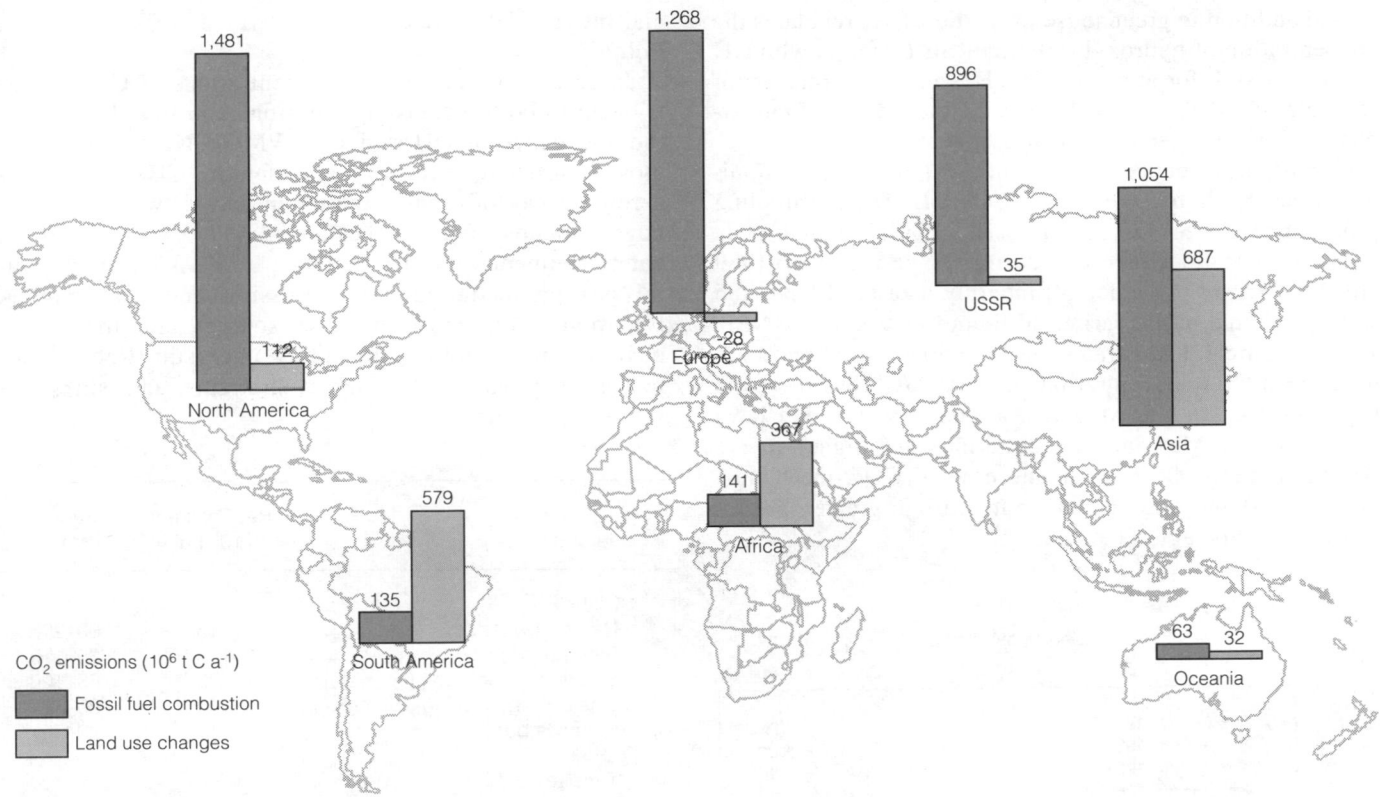

Figure 1.2 Emissions of CO_2 to the atmosphere from human activities, 1980 (the negative value for land use changes in Europe indicates a net sink for CO_2)
Source: data from Table 1.3

Atmospheric CO_2 has both natural and man-made emission sources; of the latter, emissions from fossil fuel combustion and deforestation are the most significant. Combustion of fossil fuels currently releases nearly 6 Gt C a^{-1} and land use changes, although estimates are less certain, produce a net emission to the atmosphere of between 1–2 Gt C a^{-1}. A small amount of CO_2 is released during the manufacture of cement.

Estimates of CO_2 emissions from fossil fuel combustion and cement manufacture are prepared by CDIAC. Global and national emissions inventories are calculated from UN fuel production and consumption data, to which appropriate emission factors are applied according to the procedures developed by Marland and Rotty (1983). Inventories are updated annually and are available in both published form and as machine-readable data files (Marland et al., 1989; Boden et al., 1990).

Global emissions of CO_2 from fossil fuel combustion and cement manufacture have more than trebled since 1950 (Table 1.2). On a regional basis, emissions in the more developed world regions (North America, Europe) have stabilized since the 1970s, but continue to increase steadily in the less developed regions (Africa, Asia, South America) and in eastern Europe (Marland et al., 1989; UNEP, 1989).

National emissions of CO_2, spanning 1960–1988, are given in Table 1.3, together with per capita and per unit GNP (Gross National Product in US$) values for 1988. Estimates of the net CO_2 emission to the atmosphere from land use changes, compiled by Houghton et al. (1987) for 1980, are also included in Table 1.3. Emissions of CO_2 from fossil fuel combustion and land use changes are compared on a regional basis in Figure 1.2. Emissions from fossil fuel burning in the Northern Hemisphere clearly dominate the global flux of CO_2 to the atmosphere; CO_2 emissions from land use changes exceed those from fossil fuels only in Africa and South America.

Assuming that the annual input of CO_2 to the atmosphere from fossil fuel burning and deforestation is currently about 7.0 ± 1.1 Gt C, and that CO_2 is accumulating in the atmosphere at a rate of 3.4 ± 0.2 Gt C a^{-1}, some 3.6 Gt C a^{-1} are available for uptake by other sinks of CO_2. Carbon cycle models estimate that the oceans (the major sink for atmospheric CO_2) absorb around 2.0 ± 1.0 Gt C a^{-1}. The remaining 1.6 ± 1.5 Gt C a^{-1} are at present unaccounted for and represent an imbalance in current knowledge of the global carbon budget. Uptake by terrestrial biota has been suggested as a possible additional sink for CO_2 (WMO/UNEP, 1990; Tans et al., 1990).

Methane Methane is an important atmospheric constituent. In addition to greenhouse properties, CH_4 regulates the concentration of hydroxyl (OH) radicals (reaction with OH is a major sink for atmospheric CH_4) and the formation of O_3, both of which are involved in the breakdown of numerous trace gases present in the atmosphere.

Atmospheric concentrations of CH_4 have been monitored as part of the NOAA/CMDL flask sampling programme since 1983 (Steele et al., 1987). Annual mean CH_4 concentrations recorded during the period 1984–1989 are summarized in Table 1.4; monthly data for 1983–1985 were presented in the earlier edition of this report (UNEP, 1989). Figure 1.3 illustrates the latitudinal variation in annual mean CH_4 concentrations at NOAA/CMDL sites; the high altitude sites at Mauna Loa and Niwot Ridge have been omitted. Methane concentrations are higher in the Northern Hemisphere; as in the case of CO_2, the hemispheric gradient may be attributed to a greater source strength in this region (see below).

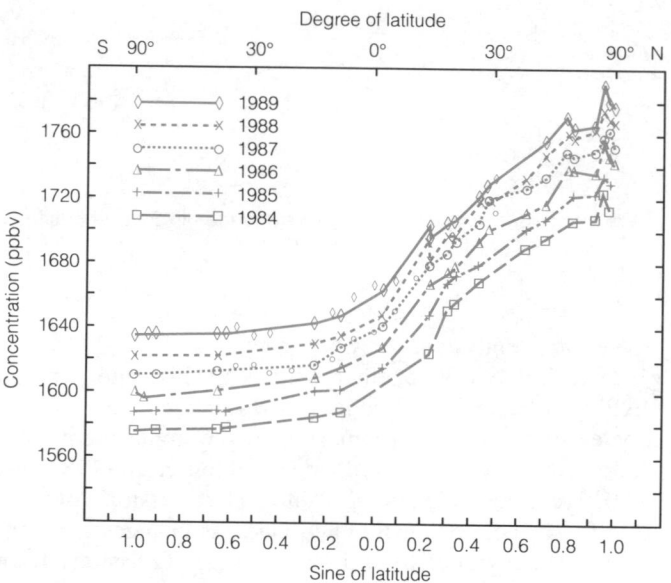

Figure 1.3 Latitudinal distribution of atmospheric CH_4 concentrations, 1984–1989 (the smooth curves are cubic spline fits to the points shown as large symbols; the small symbols represent measurements made during ship cruises)
Source: figure provided by NOAA/CMDL

Measurements of atmospheric CH_4 have been made by a number of other research groups, details of which were included in earlier editions of this report (UNEP, 1989). Data collectively indicate that levels of CH_4 have increased from around 1.51 ppmv in 1978 to 1.72 ppmv in 1989, equivalent to an average rate of increase in the range 0.8–1.0 per cent per year (or 14–17 ppbv per year). Pre-industrial and earlier atmospheric concentrations have been obtained through analysis of ancient air trapped in polar ice. Results show that CH_4 concentrations have more than doubled since the 1700s. As in the case of CO_2, con-

centrations of atmospheric CH_4 correlate well with glacial-interglacial cycles (see Part 1: Environmental Pollution, Historical Monitoring).

Increases in atmospheric concentrations of CH_4 are attributed to both increasing emissions and to a decrease in the abundance of OH radicals (WMO/UNEP, 1990). The most significant sources of atmospheric CH_4 are the anaerobic decay of organic matter in natural wetlands (e.g., bogs, swamps amd marshes), rice paddies and landfills, enteric fermentation in ruminants, biomass burning, natural gas production and transmission and coal mining. Emissions from most of these sources are difficult to quantify and therefore are highly uncertain. Recent estimates of global CH_4 source strengths and sinks are summarized below:

Sources/sinks	Best estimate (10^6 t a^{-1})	Range (10^6 t a^{-1})
SOURCES		
Natural wetlands	115	100–200
Rice paddies	110	25–170
Enteric fermentation (animals)	80	65–100
Gas drilling, venting, transmission	45	25–50
Biomass burning	40	20–80
Termites	40	10–100
Landfills	40	20–70
Coal mining	35	19–50
Oceans	10	5–20
Fresh waters	5	1–25
CH_4 hydrate destabilization	5	0–100
SINKS		
Removal by soils	30	15–45
Reaction with OH	500	400–600
ATMOSPHERIC INCREASE	44	40–48

Source: WMO/UNEP, 1990

Since the publication of the second edition of this report, some progress has been made with respect to quantifying the magnitude of CH_4 emissions from natural wetlands. Earlier estimates had indicated that natural wetlands in the high latitudes represented the greater source of CH_4 emissions; new data suggest that wetlands in tropical regions are both more abundant and that the CH_4 flux from these ecosystems is more important than previously assumed (Aselmann and Crutzen, 1989; WMO/UNEP, 1990). Recent estimates of CH_4 emissions from natural wetlands and rice paddies, according to latitude, are illustrated in Figure 1.4.

Although estimates are uncertain, it is likely that emissions of CH_4 have increased since pre-industrial times as a result of human activities. In particular, the area under rice cultivation, livestock numbers (see Part 3: Natural Resources, Agriculture), biomass burning (forest clearing), coal mining and natural gas production have grown steadily

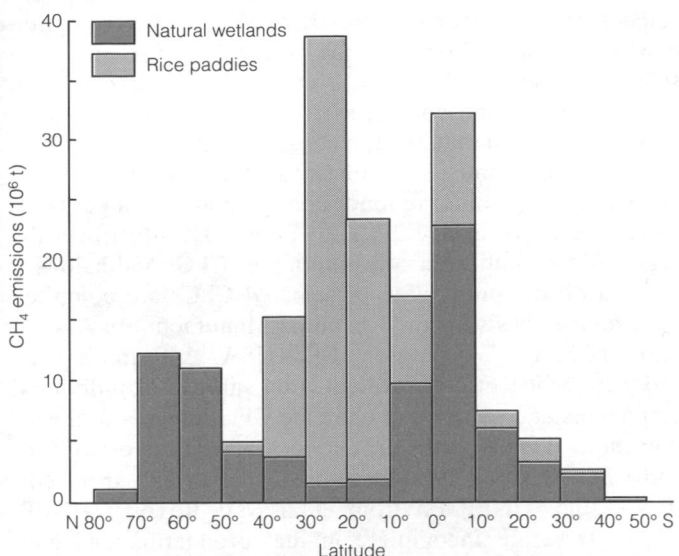

Figure 1.4 Latitudinal distribution of CH₄ emissions from natural wetlands and rice paddies
Source: Aselmann and Crutzen, 1989

over the past 40–50 years. It has been estimated that CH$_4$ emissions have risen, on average, by 3.5×10^6 t a^{-1} (or 1 per cent per year) between 1940 and 1980 (Bolle et al., 1986; UNEP, 1989).

Halocarbons In recent years rising atmospheric concentrations of CFCs and halons have caused considerable concern in view of their contribution to both the greenhouse effect and ozone layer depletion. Many halocarbons, in particular the fully halogenated compounds, are resistant to the physical and chemical removal processes that operate in the troposphere and consequently have long atmospheric lifetimes. In the mid-upper stratosphere, however, halocarbons are photodecomposed by ultraviolet (UV) radiation. Photodissociation of CFCs and halons pro-

duces reactive chlorine and bromine atoms which can then participate in ozone-depleting catalytic cycles (see 'Ozone' below). The non-fully halogenated halocarbons typically have shorter atmospheric lifetimes as they are primarily removed in the troposphere by reaction with OH radicals.

On a percentage basis, atmospheric concentrations of the more common halocarbons are increasing more rapidly than are the other principal greenhouse gases. Routine monitoring of the more abundant halocarbons, including CFC-11 (CCl_3F), CFC-12 (CCl_2F_2), CH_3CCl_3 and CCl_4, has been conducted by a number of groups and organizations, some of which have been described in an earlier edition of this report (UNEP, 1989). The Institute of Atmospheric Sciences based at the OGC, for example, has been monitoring levels of CFC-11, CFC-12, CCl_4 and CH_3CCl_3 since 1975.

Since 1977 concentrations of CFC-11 and CFC-12 have been measured at five sites located throughout both hemispheres by NOAA/CMDL. Monthly mean concentrations of CFC-11 and CFC-12 are given in Table 1.5 for the five sites; trends in atmospheric CFC-11 at three sites are illustrated in Figure 1.5. During the 13-year period for which data are available concentrations of CFC-11 and CFC-12 have risen on average by 10 pptv per year and 17 pptv per year, respectively.

Atmospheric concentrations of other CFCs and halons are generally less well documented, partly because these gases occur at very low concentrations and their measurement presents a number of technical difficulties. Present concentrations and growth rates for a range of CFCs and halons, as assessed by the WMO/UNEP-sponsored Intergovernmental Panel on Climate Change (IPCC) in 1990, are listed below:

Halocarbon	Mixing ratio 1990 (pptv)	Annual rate of increase (pptv)	Annual rate of increase (%)	Lifetime (years)
CFC-11	280	9.5	4	65
CFC-12	484	16.5	4	130
CFC-13	5			400
CFC-113	60	4–5	10	90
CFC-114	15			200
CFC-115	5			400
CCl₄	146	2.0	1.5	50
HCFC-22	122	7	7	15
CH₃Cl	600			1.5
CH₃CCl₃	158	6.0	4	7
Halon-1211	1.7	0.2	12	25
Halon-1301	2.0	0.3	15	110
CH₃Br	10–15			1.5

The 1990 mixing ratios have been based upon an extrapolation of measurements reported in 1987 or 1988, assuming that the recent trends remained approximately constant.
Source: WMO/UNEP, 1990

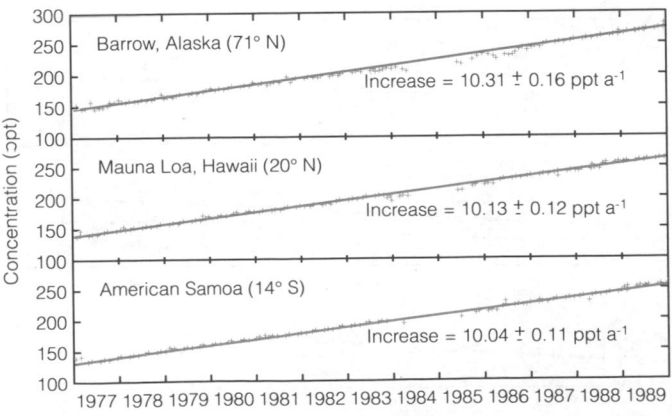

Figure 1.5 Monthly mean concentrations of CFC-11 at three NOAA/CMDL baseline sites, 1977–1989
Source: figure provided by NOAA/CMDL

The majority of halocarbons (with the exception of CH₃Cl) are man-made chemicals and have no natural sources. Observed increases in the atmosphere can therefore be attributed to human activity alone. Production of CFCs and halons began in the 1930s and since then these compounds have found increasing applications as refrigerants (CFC-12; CFC-114 ($C_2Cl_2F_4$); HCFC-22 ($CHClF_2$)), aerosol propellants (CFC-11; CFC-12; CFC-114), foam blowing agents (CFC-11; CFC-12), solvents (CFC-113 ($C_2Cl_3F_3$); CH_3CCl_3; CCl_4) and fire retardants (Halon-1211 ($CBrClF_2$); Halon-1301 ($CBrF_3$)). At present the significant imbalance in the sources and sinks of halocarbons is resulting in a relatively rapid rise in atmospheric concentrations (WMO/UNEP, 1990).

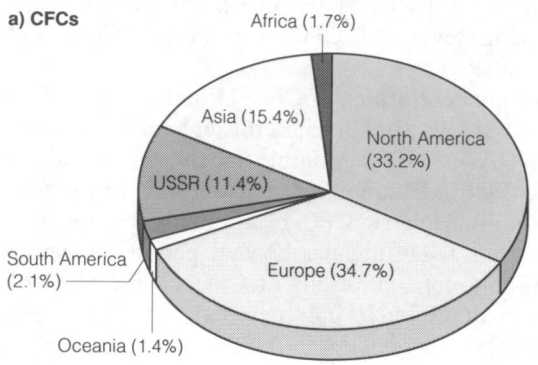

a) CFCs

Africa (1.7%)
Asia (15.4%)
North America (33.2%)
USSR (11.4%)
South America (2.1%)
Europe (34.7%)
Oceania (1.4%)

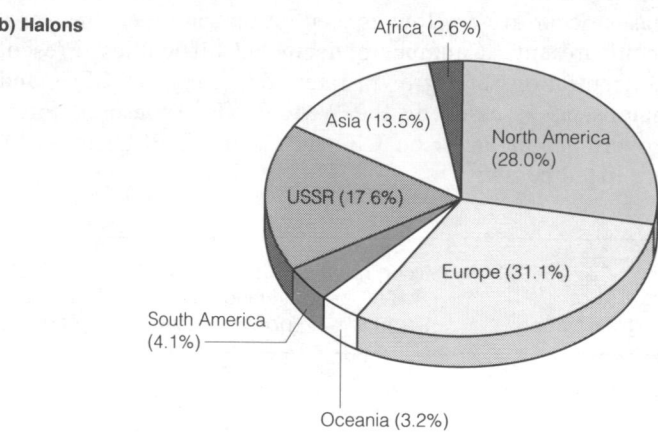

b) Halons

Africa (2.6%)
Asia (13.5%)
North America (28.0%)
USSR (17.6%)
South America (4.1%)
Europe (31.1%)
Oceania (3.2%)

Figure 1.6 Percentage consumption of CFCs and halons by world region, 1986
Source: data from Table 1.6

Recognizing the deleterious effects of halocarbons in the atmosphere, many countries have committed themselves to future reductions in consumption of selected CFCs and halons by becoming signatories to UNEP's Montreal Protocol on Substances that Deplete the Ozone Layer (see Part 10: International Co-operation). Substances currently controlled by the Protocol include the so-called Group I compounds, CFC-11, CFC-12, CFC-113 CFC-114 and CFC-115, and the Group II compounds, Halon-1211, Halon-1301 and Halon-2402.

Under the terms of the Montreal Protocol, Parties are required to submit data on their production, consumption and trade (imports/exports) of the eight controlled substances to the Ozone Secretariat, UNEP. Consumption data for 1986, which provide a baseline for reduction schemes under the Montreal Protocol, have recently been designated as non-confidential data and are published here. Aggregated data for the consumption (a reliable indicator of actual emissions) of Group I compounds (CFCs) and Group II (halons) in tonnes per year and on a per capita basis are given in Table 1.6. Figure 1.6 illustrates the regional distribution in consumption of CFCs and halons.

Data on the production of selected CFCs are compiled on a routine basis by the Chemical Manufacturers Association (CMA), Washington DC, USA. Information on production of CFCs are collected by surveys of individual companies and are used to estimate CFC releases to the atmosphere. Trends in the production and release of CFC-11 and CFC-12 since 1930 were presented in an earlier edition of the 'UNEP Environmental Data Report' (UNEP, 1987). Data are incomplete in that production and consumption statistics from several major users are not included.

Nitrous Oxide Like the halocarbons, N_2O is both a greenhouse gas and potential contributor to stratospheric O_3 depletion. Photodissociation of N_2O and reaction with excited oxygen atoms (O^1D) in the stratosphere produces nitric oxide (NO), which in turn plays an important role in regulating O_3 concentrations.

Atmospheric concentrations of N_2O are currently around 310 ppbv and are rising at a rate of about 0.6–1.0 ppbv (or 0.2–0.3 per cent) per year. Monthly mean concentrations of N_2O measured at NOAA/CMDL sites during 1977–1989 are given in Table 1.7 and shown graphically in Figure 1.7. Ice-core records for N_2O, which were presented in some detail in the 1989 edition of this report (UNEP, 1989), suggest that levels have risen by almost 10 per cent since the 1600s.

Nitrous oxide has natural and man-made sources, both of which are highly uncertain. Microbial processes in

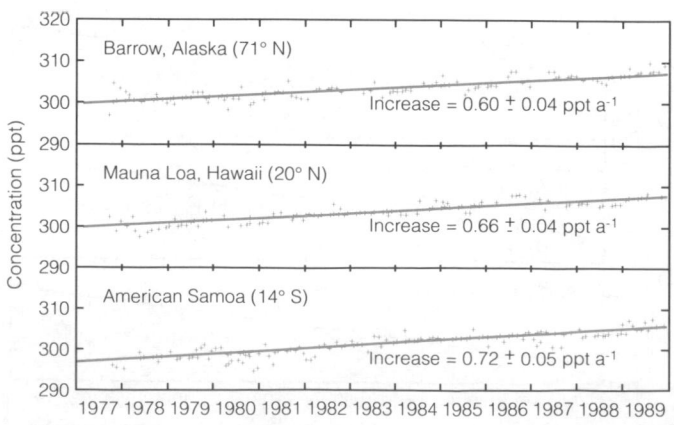

Barrow, Alaska (71° N)
Increase = 0.60 ± 0.04 ppt a⁻¹

Mauna Loa, Hawaii (20° N)
Increase = 0.66 ± 0.04 ppt a⁻¹

American Samoa (14° S)
Increase = 0.72 ± 0.05 ppt a⁻¹

Concentration (ppt)

1977 1978 1979 1980 1981 1982 1983 1984 1985 1986 1987 1988 1989

Figure 1.7 Monthly mean concentrations of N_2O at three NOAA/CMDL baseline sites, 1977–1989
Source: figure provided by NOAA/CMDL

natural soils (i.e., denitrification) are generally considered to be the dominant source of N_2O, followed by emissions from oceans. A number of man-made sources have also been identified; these include biomass burning and fossil fuel combustion. In addition, the application of nitrogenous fertilizers to land and the conversion of forest to agricultural land are considered to enhance the flux of N_2O from soils (Bolle et al., 1986; WMO/UNEP, 1990). Current estimates of global N_2O source strengths and sinks, based on the conclusions of the IPCC, are given below:

Sources/sinks	Range (10^6 t N a^{-1})
SOURCES	
Oceans	1.4–2.6
Soils (tropical forests)	2.2–3.7
Soils (temperate forests)	0.7–1.5
Fossil fuel combustion	0.1–0.3
Biomass burning	0.02–0.2
Fertilizer (including ground water)	0.01–2.2
SINKS	
Removal by soils	Unknown
Photolysis in the stratosphere	7–13
ATMOSPHERIC INCREASE	3–4.5

Source: WMO/UNEP, 1990

The above inventory takes into account new information regarding emissions of N_2O from fossil fuel and biomass burning. Previous estimates for combined flux from these sources, which were in the range 2–5 x 10^6 t N a^{-1}, have been revised downwards (to 0.1–0.5 x 10^6 t N a^{-1}) in light of evidence that the earlier results had been based on erroneous measurements of N_2O (WMO/UNEP, 1990).

It is estimated that photodissociation removes 7–13 x 10^6 t N of N_2O from the stratosphere per year. A global source strength for N_2O in the range 10–17.5 x 10^6 t N a^{-1} is therefore required to account for the observed accumulation of N_2O in the atmosphere at a rate of 3–4.5 x 10^6 t N a^{-1}. These estimates suggest that known sources of N_2O have been underestimated or that there are some as yet unidentified sources of N_2O (WMO/UNEP, 1990).

References

Aselmann, I. and Crutzen, P. J. 1989 Global distribution of natural freshwater wetlands and rice paddies; their net primary productivity, seasonality and possible methane emissions, *Journal of Atmospheric Chemistry* **8**, 307–358.

Boden, T. A., Kanciruk, P. and Farrel, M. P. 1990 *Trends '90: A Compendium of Data on Global Change*, ORNL/CDIAC-36, The Carbon Dioxide Information Analysis Center, Oak Ridge National Laboratory, Oak Ridge.

Bolle, H. J., Seiler, W. and Bolin, B. 1986 Other greenhouse gases and aerosols. In: *The Greenhouse Effect, Climatic Change and Ecosystems*, SCOPE Report No. 29, B. Bolin, B. R. Döös, J. Jäger and R. A. Warrick (Eds), John Wiley and Sons, Chichester, 157–203.

Conway, T. J., Tans, P. P., Waterman, L. S., Thoning, K. W., Masarie, K. A. and Gammon, R. H. 1988 Atmospheric carbon dioxide measurements in the remote global troposphere, *Tellus* **40B**, 81–115.

Houghton, R., A., Boone, R. D., Fruci, J. R., Hobbie, J. E., Melillo, J. M., Palm, C. A., Peterson, B. J., Shaver, G. R., Woodwell, G. M., Moore, B., Skole, D. L. and Myers, N. 1987 The flux of carbon from terrestrial ecosystems to the atmosphere in 1980 due to changes in land use: geographic distribution of the global flux, *Tellus* **39B**, 122–139.

Marland, G. and Rotty, R. M. 1983 *Carbon Dioxide Emissions from Fossil Fuels: A Procedure for Estimation and Estimates for 1950-1981*, DOE Report No. TR003, US Department of Energy, Washington DC.

Marland, G., Boden, T. A., Griffin, R. C., Huang, S. F., Kanciruk, P. and Nelson, T. R. 1989 *Estimates of CO2 Emissions from Fossil Fuel Burning and Cement Manufacturing Based on the United Nations Energy Statistics and the US Bureau of Mines Cement Manfacuring Data*. ORNL/CDIAC-25, NDP-030, Oak Ridge National Laboratory, Oak Ridge.

Steele, L. P., Fraser, P. J., Rasmussen, R. A., Khalil, M. A. K., Conway, T. J., Crawford A. J., Gammon, R. H., Masarie, K. A. and Thoning, K. W. 1987 The global distribution of methane in the troposphere, *Journal of Atmospheric Chemistry* **5**, 125–171.

Tans, P. P. 1990 Personal communication, Climate Monitoring and Diagnostics Laboratory, National Oceanic and Atmospheric Administration, Boulder, Colorado, USA.

Tans, P. P., Fung, I. Y. and Takahashi, T. 1990 Observational constraints on the atmospheric CO2 budget, *Science* **247**, 1431–1438.

UNEP 1987 *United Nations Environment Programme Environmental Data Report*, Basil Blackwell, Oxford.

UNEP 1989 *United Nations Environment Programme Environmental Data Report*, Basil Blackwell, Oxford.

WMO 1989 *The Global Atmosphere Watch*, Fact Sheet No. 3, World Meteorological Organization, Geneva.

WMO/UNEP 1990 *Scientific Assessment of Climate Change*, Report prepared for the Intergovernmental Panel on Climate Change by Working Group 1, World Meteorological Organization, Geneva, and United Nations Environment Programme, Nairobi.

Ozone

Approximately 90 per cent of atmospheric O_3 is found in the stratosphere, with maximum concentrations occurring at altitudes of 25 km over the equator and at 15 km over the poles. The so-called ozone layer in the stratosphere provides protection from harmful solar UV radiation; it also plays an important role in controlling the temperature structure of the stratosphere. At lower altitudes O_3 exhibits greenhouse gas properties, is a potent respiratory irritant and can adversely affect plant growth.

Continuous monitoring of total column O_3 has been conducted by the WMO's Global Ozone Observing System (GO3OS) since the 1960s. The network of ground-based Dobson spectrophotometers, currently numbering 140 world-wide, has been complemented in more recent decades by satellite-based instrumentation. Data are held in computerized form at the Atmospheric Environment Service in Downsview, Canada, and are available in published form as 'Ozone Data for the World'.

Stratospheric Ozone The concentrations of stratospheric O_3 are controlled by a series of dynamic and photochemical processes. It is now widely accepted that single Cl atoms, derived from man-made halocarbons, participate in catalytic chain reactions which result in the net destruction of stratospheric O_3 (Solomon, 1990). The most pronounced losses occur over the Antarctic during the Southern Hemisphere spring (September–October).

Measurements of total column O_3 (which reflect changes in stratospheric O_3) made by both ground-based and satellite-based instruments were reviewed in detail in the previous edition of the 'UNEP Environmental Data Report' (UNEP, 1989) and are not extensively covered again here. However, monthly mean total O_3 amounts recorded at the NOAA/CMDL observatory at the South Pole since the early 1960s indicate that a severe depletion in springtime O_3 again occurred in 1990 (Figure 1.8).

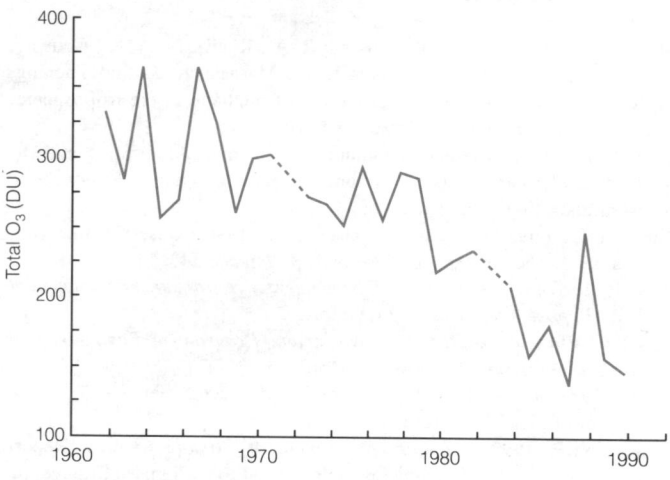

Figure 1.8 Trends in October (15–31) mean total O_3 at the South Pole
Source: figure provided by NOAA/CMDL

Under present conditions, depletion in stratospheric O_3 is not expected to occur over the Arctic to the same extent or rate as that observed over the Antarctic, largely because of the differences in meteorological conditions between the North and South Poles. However, a recent series of experiments have indicated that a degree of O_3 loss occurred in the stratosphere over Arctic regions in January–February 1990 (Hofmann and Deshler, 1991).

Tropospheric Ozone In the troposphere O_3 arises from two sources: the downwards mixing of stratospheric O_3 and the photolysis of nitrogen dioxide (NO_2) in the presence of reactive hydrocarbons.

Until relatively recently, systematic monitoring of tropospheric O_3 in rural and remote locations has been limited. Available data, collected over the last 20 years, have shown that concentrations of tropospheric O_3 vary markedly with latitude, longitude, altitude and season. Notable features include the existence of a pronounced spring–summer maximum (monthly mean concentrations in the range 30–600 ppbv) in the mid-latitudes of the Northern Hemisphere. The observed maximum is linked to enhanced photochemical oxidation of O_3 precursors during the summer months. In other latitudes, tropospheric O_3 levels are generally lower and exhibit a winter maximum. In some tropical regions, however, emissions of O_3 precursors from biomass burning may provide a significant photochemical source of tropospheric O_3 (WMO/UNEP, 1990).

Most significantly there is good evidence to suggest that average concentrations of tropospheric O_3 have increased by a factor of 2–3 in the mid-latitudes of the Northern Hemisphere since the early 1900s. This trend is attributed to increases in O_3 precursor emissions, particularly the nitrogen oxides and hydrocarbons, from man-made sources (Penkett, 1988; WMO/UNEP, 1990).

References

Hofmann, D. J. and Deshler, T. 1991 Evidence from balloon measurements for chemical depletion of stratospheric ozone in the Arctic winter of 1989–90, *Nature* (London) **349**, 300–305.
Penkett, S. A. 1988 Indications and causes of ozone increase in the troposphere. In: *The Changing Atmosphere*, F. S. Rowland and I. S. A. Isaksen (Eds), John Wiley & Sons, Chichester, 91–103.
Solomon, S. 1990 Progress towards a quantitative understanding of Antarctic ozone depletion, *Nature* (London) **347**, 347–354.
UNEP 1989 *United Nations Environment Programme Environmental Data Report*, Basil Blackwell, Oxford.
WMO/UNEP 1990 *Scientific Assessment of Climate Change*, Report prepared for the Intergovernmental Panel on Climate Change by Working Group I, World Meteorological Organization, Geneva, and United Nations Environment Programme, Nairobi.

Urban Air Pollutants

Air pollutants that are prevalent in cities world-wide include the oxides of sulphur (SO_x), the nitrogen oxides (NO_x), CO, O_3, trace organics (aldehydes, benzene and polyaromatic hydrocarbons (PAHs)), selected trace metals, most notably lead (Pb), and suspended particulate matter (SPM). Many countries, in both the developed and less developed world, have now established nation-wide urban air quality networks for the monitoring of pollutant levels in their major cities.

Since 1974, standardized data on concentrations of sulphur dioxide (SO_2) and SPM from selected cities world-wide have been submitted to the World Health Organization (WHO) as part of the WHO/UNEP-GEMS Urban Air Quality Monitoring Project (GEMS/Air). The project currently extends to nearly 80 cities in over 50 countries. Most cities report data from three sites, which are classified as either city centre or suburban and as either commercial, industrial or residential. Regular quality assurance exercises have been conducted to ensure comparability of all data. Data are stored, in computerized form, at the GEMS/Air data centre located at the US EPA's Atmospheric Research Exposure Assessment Laboratory in North Carolina. Since commencement of the programme, a number of assessments of global trends in

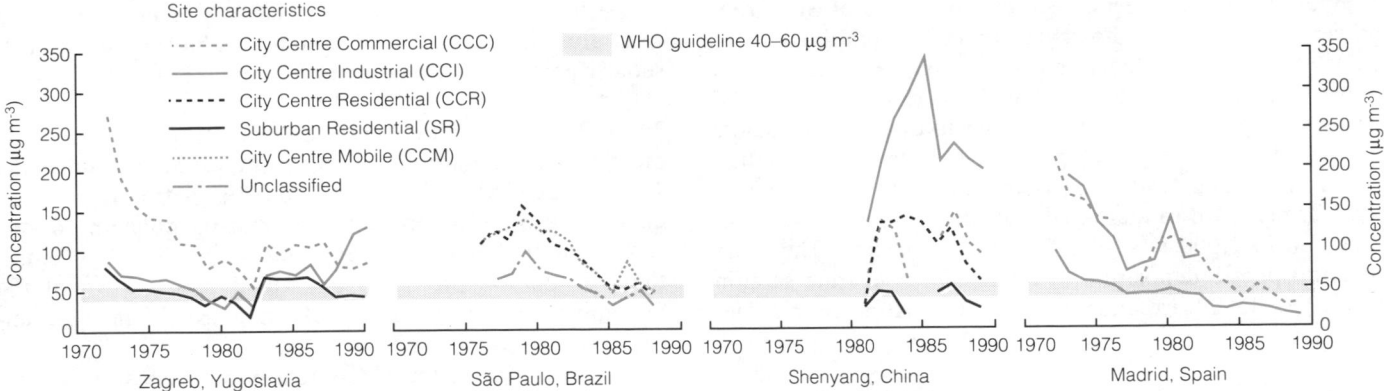

Figure 1.9   Trends in annual mean concentrations of SO₂ in Zagreb, São Paulo, Shenyang and Madrid
Source: data from Table 1.8

urban air quality which draw on data collected by the GEMS/Air project, have been prepared (UNEP/WHO 1984, 1988). An ongoing work, which is examining air quality conditions in 20 "megacities" (cities having populations of around 10 million or over), is scheduled for publication in 1991.

Sulphur Dioxide   Sulphur dioxide is a potent respiratory tract irritant and thus potentially harmful to human health. A summary of data on annual mean concentrations of SO₂, as reported to the GEMS/Air project, is given in Table 1.8. Trends in annual mean SO₂ concentrations in selected cities are shown in Figure 1.9. WHO recommended guideline values for SO₂ are also shown.

Declining trends in urban SO₂ concentrations are evident in many cities, especially in those of the more developed regions (UNEP/WHO, 1988). In North America and Europe, improvement in air quality conditions with respect to SO₂ has been achieved by reducing emissions of SO₂, in particular from low level emission sources within populated areas (Table 1.9). Although countries vary in their emissions control policies, typical strategies have included fuel switching (from high sulphur coal and oil to low sulphur fuels, such as natural gas), increased use of electricity and natural gas for domestic heating and improved energy efficiency. Although the data base for SO₂ emissions in developing countries is limited, there are indications that emissions are increasing (Table 1.9).

Trends in emissions of SO₂ in the UK are shown in Figure 1.10a. Total emissions of SO₂ have declined by over 40 per cent over the 1970–1988 period; the most pronounced reductions have been achieved in the industrial,

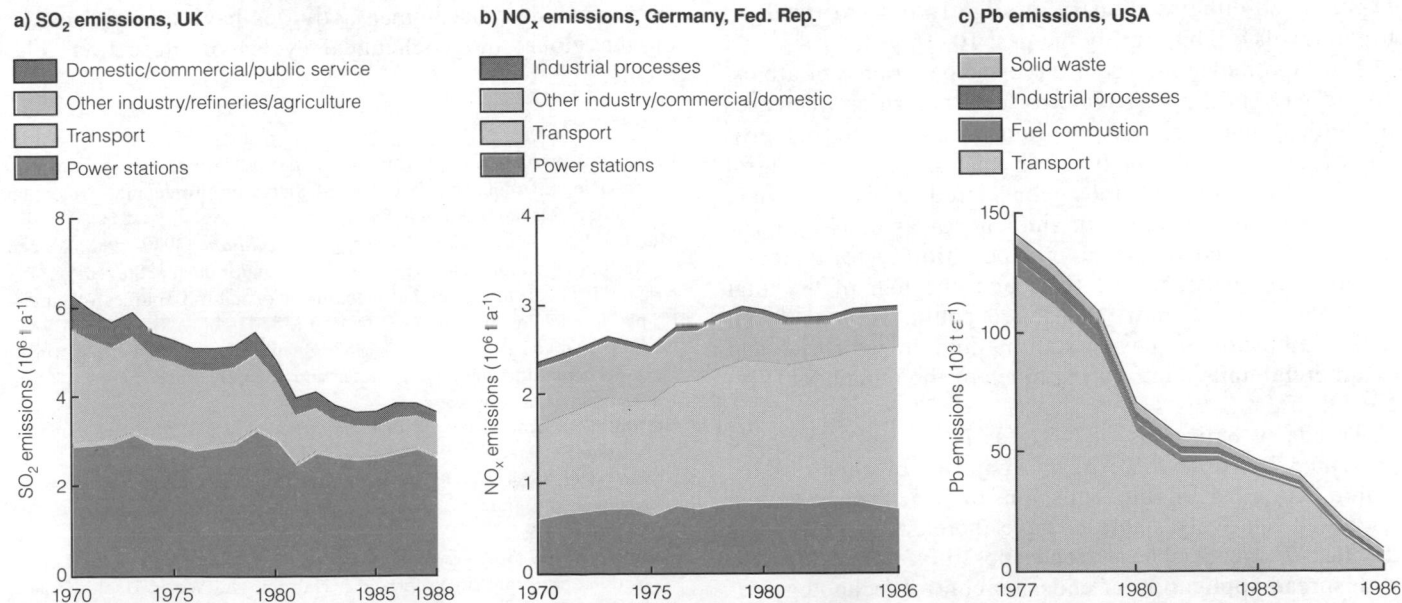

Figure 1.10   Trends in national emissions of a) SO₂ in the UK, b) NOₓ in Germany, Fed. Rep., and c) Pb in the USA
Sources: Munday, 1989; Umweltbundesamt, 1989; EPA, 1988

commercial and domestic sectors. Emissions of SO_2 from power stations have, however, remained relatively constant. Much of the local impact of SO_2 emissions from power stations has been reduced by discharging waste gases through tall chimneys in order to disperse pollutants over a wider area. The adoption of the "tall stack" policy in European and North American countries has, however, inadvertently led to increased deposition of acidic gases in areas up to 1,000 km from the original source. The issue of atmospheric deposition is treated in a separate section (see Part 1: Environmental Pollution, Atmospheric Deposition).

Nitrogen Oxides   Combustion of fossil fuels produces two oxides of nitrogen, nitric oxide (NO) and nitrogen dioxide (NO_2), which are collectively termed NO_x. Nitric oxide is generally produced in the first instance but, once in the atmosphere, photochemical oxidation may occur to produce NO_2. Ambient concentrations of NO_2 are generally too low to pose a significant threat to human health. Nevertheless, NO_x, together with hydrocarbons, are important precursors to the formation of tropospheric O_3 and other photochemical oxidants including peroxyacetyl nitrate (PAN).

Many national urban air quality networks incorporate monitoring of NO_2, although monitoring is perhaps less extensive compared with that for SO_2. At present, data on urban NO_2 levels are not submitted to GEMS/Air. However, it is likely that in the future the GEMS/Air programme will be extended to include other urban air pollutants such as NO_2, O_3 and CO.

Selected data on NO_2 levels have been compiled and assessed as part of the most recent GEMS/Air assessment of global urban air quality (UNEP/WHO, 1988). Given the rather limited amount of systematic data on urban NO_2, generalizations are difficult. Nevertheless, it appears that a number of cities in both Europe and North America have experienced either stationary or slightly upward trends in urban levels of NO_2 during the past 10–15 years.

Motor vehicles represent the principal source of atmospheric NO_x in the vast majority of large cities. Increases in vehicle numbers, despite improvements in fuel efficiency and the introduction of exhaust emission control technologies, are generally considered to be the main cause of observed trends in ambient levels of NO_2. On a national basis, however, the transportation sector typically accounts for between one third and one half of the total NO_x emissions in most developed countries, with fossil fuel combustion in power stations and in industrial and commercial units contributing much of the remainder (Figure 1.10b).

Trends in emissions of NO_x (as NO_2) since 1970 are presented in Table 1.10; in the majority of countries for which data are available, emissions of NO_x appear to have remained relatively stable or have increased slightly over the last 20 years. These trends possibly reflect the less widespread application of emission control technology for NO_x compared with that for SO_2. Although some countries have introduced compulsory fitting of catalytic converters to cars, for example, USA, Canada, Japan and Australia, increases in vehicle numbers have tended to offset any potential national emission reductions.

Trace Metals   Of the heavy metals, Pb is generally the most widely monitored in urban atmospheres. Since the 1930s, tetraethyl lead has been added to petrol as an "anti-knock" agent. More recently, increasing concern for the risk to public health from exposure to elevated concentrations of Pb has prompted a gradual phase-down of the maximum permissible Pb levels in petrol in many countries.

The reduction of the Pb content in petrol has resulted in a marked decrease in the ambient concentrations of Pb in urban centres. In the USA for example, where legislation to reduce the Pb content of petrol was first introduced in the mid-1970s, emissions of Pb fell from 141,200 t in 1977 to 8,600 t in 1986 (Figure 1.10c). During a similar time period, a concomitant decrease in airborne Pb levels in urban areas was reported (EPA, 1988). Similar trends are evident in urban centres in other countries (UNEP/WHO, 1988).

National emissions inventories for Pb and other trace metals are, for the most part, not widely available and therefore not included here. Estimates of global emissions from both natural and man-made sources of a range of metals and metalloids have been reported (Nriagu and Pacyna, 1988; Nriagu, 1989). These estimates, which are based on production data and a series of emission factors, are subject to a substantial degree of uncertainty and are therefore reported as ranges. Table 1.11 provides emission estimates for eight metals; estimates for manganese, molybdenum, tin, selenium, titanium, and vanadium were also calculated. The estimates suggest that for many of the metals, including Pb, mercury and cadmium, emissions from industrial sources exceed those from natural sources. It is concluded that human activities have a major impact on the global biogeochemical cycles of these trace elements.

References

EPA 1988 *National Air Quality and Emissions Trends Report 1986*, Report No. EPA450/4 88 001, United States Environmental Protection Agency, Research Triangle Park.

Munday, P. K. 1989 *UK Emissions of Air Pollutants 1970–1988*, Warren Spring Laboratory, Department of Trade and Industry, Stevenage.

Nriagu, J. O. 1989 A global assessment of natural sources of atmospheric trace metals, *Nature* (London) **338**, 47–49.

Nriagu, J. O. and Pacyna, J. M. 1988 Quantitative assessment of worldwide contamination of air, water and soils by trace metals, *Nature* (London) **333**, 134–139.

Umweltbundesamt 1989 *Daten zür Umwelt 1988/89*, Erich Schmidt Verlag, Berlin.

UNEP/WHO 1984 *Urban Air Quality 1973–1980*, United Nations Environment Programme, Nairobi, and World Health Organization, Geneva.

UNEP/WHO 1988 *Assessment of Urban Air Quality Worldwide*, United Nations Environment Programme, Nairobi, and World Health Organization, Geneva.

Table 1.1 Monthly and annual mean atmospheric concentrations of carbon dioxide at NOAA/CMDL observatory sites, 1973–1989 (ppm by mole fraction in dry air)

Site/year	Jan.	Feb.	Mar.	Apr.	May	Jun.	Jul.	Aug.	Sep.	Oct.	Nov.	Dec.	Annual
POINT BARROW, ALASKA													
1973								321.95	323.36	327.78	332.73	333.50	(327.86)
1974	336.47	336.02	336.66	337.09	336.85	335.94	328.70	323.45	324.21	328.76	331.98	335.17	332.61
1975	336.79	336.58	337.14	337.72	337.92	335.37	330.10	324.39	324.58	329.25	334.33	336.45	333.39
1976	336.98	336.70	337.73	338.04	337.80	336.77	331.04	323.47	325.09	329.78	334.07	336.57	333.67
1977	336.83	336.91	338.23	339.15	339.43	337.74	330.12	325.38	326.84	331.96	334.69	338.78	334.67
1978	339.13	340.23	341.49	340.98	340.78	339.39	332.61	327.72	327.43	332.14	338.78	339.40	336.67
1979	340.09	341.33	342.50	342.35	342.87	342.04	333.63	327.74	329.32	333.12	338.14	341.51	337.89
1980	341.92	342.44	343.36	343.30	343.26	342.61	337.29	331.77	331.35	337.87	340.52	342.59	339.86
1981	344.27	345.48	344.55	345.79	346.79	344.40	338.22	331.77	333.28	338.76	342.20	344.86	341.70
1982	345.75	347.18	348.27	348.39	347.99	345.70	339.15	333.16	333.16	337.85	342.11	344.47	342.77
1983	347.14	346.95	348.00	348.13	348.30	346.90	340.38	333.75	335.35	340.47	346.54	346.66	344.05
1984	350.97	350.74	350.04	349.77	350.66	348.30	341.34	335.92	338.30	342.18	345.00	348.52	345.98
1985	349.69	349.51	350.53	351.52	352.49	350.07	343.77	337.83	338.62	343.25	346.92	349.66	346.99
1986	350.21	351.63	353.42	353.09	353.33	351.43	344.51	339.45	342.03	345.03	348.70	351.09	348.66
1987	352.36	352.72	353.90	353.85	354.44	352.19	346.45	340.40	340.37	348.71	349.62	352.71	349.81
1988	354.87	356.23	356.56	357.40	356.83	355.27	348.43	343.10	345.87	350.59	354.28	357.86	353.11
1989	360.88	358.16	359.15	359.27	358.74	357.04	349.34	344.48	346.18	351.19	355.81	358.29	354.88
MAUNA LOA, HAWAII													
1973													
1974					333.15	332.07	330.99	329.17	327.39	327.25	328.26	329.51	(329.72)
1975	330.69	331.41	331.84	333.26	333.92	333.39	331.81	329.90	328.56	328.45	329.29		(331.14)
1976	331.65	332.66	333.53	334.80	334.80	334.14	332.88	330.64	329.01	328.62	330.13	331.63	332.04
1977	332.74	333.23	334.91	336.01	336.82	336.13	334.75	332.53	331.27	331.21	332.36	333.47	333.79
1978	334.74	335.22	336.52	337.77	338.00	338.04	336.39	334.33	332.35	332.33	333.77	334.80	335.35
1979	336.20	336.65	337.79	338.95	339.03	339.22	337.58	335.51	333.83	334.05	335.26	336.70	336.73
1980	337.81	338.26	340.07	340.87	341.48	341.30	339.36	337.84	335.98	336.07	337.22	338.33	338.72
1981	339.35	340.47	341.73	342.47	343.02	342.46	340.78	338.61	337.04	337.13	338.49	339.85	340.12
1982	340.93	341.67	342.78	343.71	344.31	343.41	341.96	339.79	337.91	338.10	339.27	340.67	341.21
1983	341.45	342.69	343.42	345.17	345.79	345.40	343.99	342.00	340.02	340.16	341.39	343.01	342.87
1984	343.92	344.64	345.18	347.10	347.45	346.80	345.44	343.24	341.25	341.49	342.84	344.37	344.48
1985	345.03	345.89	347.47	348.02	348.73	348.11	346.59	344.59	343.01	342.88	344.19	345.64	345.85
1986	346.48	346.98	347.94	349.60	350.40	349.74	347.80	345.89	344.80	344.31	345.67	346.87	347.21
1987	348.23	348.50	349.58	351.10	351.87	351.46	349.80	347.73	346.38	346.49	347.71	348.93	348.98
1988	350.19	351.50	352.11	353.51	354.16	353.60	352.61	350.32	348.81	348.96	350.09	351.32	351.43
1989	352.72	353.16	353.68	355.29	355.54	355.02	353.70	351.30	349.89	350.19	351.42	352.76	352.89
CAPE MATATULA, AMERICAN SAMOA													
1973													
1974													
1975													
1976	332.24	331.90	331.32	331.09	330.67	331.17	331.14	331.15	331.29	331.45	332.03	331.93	331.45
1977	331.82	331.95	332.05	332.09	332.60	332.67	332.23	333.03	332.82	333.16			(332.44)
1978		334.76	335.15	335.33	335.00	335.15	335.00	335.76	335.75				(335.24)
1979		336.13	335.86	336.57	335.81	336.03	336.28	336.33	336.32	336.62	336.73	336.87	(336.32)

Continued over

Table 1.1 Continued

Site/year	Jan.	Feb.	Mar.	Apr.	May	Jun.	Jul.	Aug.	Sep.	Oct.	Nov.	Dec.	Annual
1980	337.44	337.60	337.89	337.34	337.77	337.99	338.39	338.30	338.19	338.11	338.54	338.83	338.03
1981	339.04	339.25	338.98	339.51	338.72	339.27	338.99	339.09	339.11	338.90	339.42	339.83	339.18
1982	340.39	340.38	340.33	340.20	339.99	339.87	340.55	340.71	340.36	339.90	340.31	340.23	340.27
1983	340.41	340.61	340.82	340.67	341.20	341.70	341.94	342.05	342.05	342.18	342.53	342.75	341.58
1984	343.08	343.39	343.45	343.37	342.47	342.85	343.20	343.33	343.39	343.37	343.46	344.07	343.29
1985	344.05	344.50	344.56	344.41	344.74	344.41	344.77	344.69	344.41	344.39	344.76	345.23	344.58
1986	345.56	345.71	345.76	345.85	345.55	346.29	346.23	345.89	345.98	346.06	346.05	346.21	345.93
1987	346.58	346.94	346.80	346.44	347.89	347.83	348.24	347.76	347.93	348.06	348.23	348.79	347.62
1988	349.24	349.70	349.35	350.27	349.63	349.66	349.94	349.81	348.94	349.26	349.72	350.58	349.67
1989	351.29	351.62	351.38	351.40	351.66	350.73	351.04	351.07	350.62	350.21	350.63	350.60	351.02

SOUTH POLE, ANTARCTICA

Site/year	Jan.	Feb.	Mar.	Apr.	May	Jun.	Jul.	Aug.	Sep.	Oct.	Nov.	Dec.	Annual
1973													
1974													
1975	329.10	328.80	328.47	328.32	328.60	328.64	329.37	329.80	330.10	330.30	330.20	330.25	329.33
1976	330.05	329.76	329.64	329.64	329.70	329.91	330.29	330.70	331.01	331.12	331.09	331.14	330.34
1977	330.89	330.32	330.27	330.64	331.00	331.39	331.81	332.24	332.70	332.98	332.98	332.74	331.66
1978	332.56	332.38	332.29	332.51	332.95	333.31	333.84	334.44	334.93	335.02	334.87	334.70	333.65
1979													
1980	336.13	335.96	336.00	336.22	336.60	336.93	337.38	337.65	337.90	338.09	338.04	338.03	337.08
1981	337.84	337.77	337.88	337.91	338.07	338.29	338.72	338.95	339.17	339.13	338.93	338.50	338.43
1982	338.45	338.60	338.37	338.56	338.88		339.24	339.24	339.61	339.86	339.77	339.52	339.09
1983	339.67	339.61	339.71	340.05		340.88	341.15	341.85	342.08	342.16	342.23	342.04	(341.04)
1984	341.90	341.86	341.65	341.73	341.88	342.08	342.52	343.05	343.35	343.44	343.24	343.02	342.48
1985	343.13	342.94	342.81	342.96	343.27	343.58	344.06	344.53	344.76	344.78	344.84	344.58	343.85
1986	344.53	344.41	344.39	344.47	344.60	344.89	345.37	345.77	346.03	346.23	345.98	345.76	345.20
1987	345.72	345.55	345.54	345.72	345.95	346.41	346.92	347.47	347.94	348.02	348.17	348.10	346.79
1988	348.06	347.92	347.98	348.18	348.28	348.50	348.89	349.33	349.59	349.70	349.53	349.23	348.77
1989	349.03	348.99	348.90	348.98	349.75	350.20	350.55	350.96	351.04	351.08	350.42	349.89	349.98

Continuous measurements of atmospheric CO_2 are made by non-dispersive infra-red analysers at NOAA/CMDL observatory sites. Air samples are dried before analysis; measurements are calibrated against standard gases and concentrations of CO_2 are expressed in ppm relative to the WMO 1985 mole fraction scale (X85). A digital-filtering technique has been applied to the continuous CO_2 data in order to separate the seasonal cycle from the longer-term trend signals.
Bracketed values indicate that annual means have been calculated from less than 12 monthly mean values.

Measurements of CO_2 have been made at the Mauna Loa site since 1958. During the period 1958–1974, measurements were made by C. D. Keeling of the Scripps Institution of Oceanography; NOAA/CMDL assumed responsibility for the Mauna Loa measurements in 1974.

Source:
Tans, P. P. 1990 Personal communication, Climate Monitoring and Diagnostics Laboratory, National Oceanic and Atmospheric Administration, Boulder, Colorado, USA.

Table 1.2 Global emissions of carbon dioxide from fossil fuel combustion and cement manufacture, 1950–1988

Year	Solid fuels 10^6 t C a^{-1}	%	Liquid fuels 10^6 t C a^{-1}	%	Natural gas 10^6 t C a^{-1}	%	Natural gas flaring 10^6 t C a^{-1}	%	Cement manufacture 10^6 t C a^{-1}	%	Total 10^6 t C a^{-1}	Growth rate (%)[a]
1950	1,077	66	423	26	97	6	23	1	18	1	1,638	
1951	1,137	64	479	27	115	6	24	1	20	1	1,775	8.4
1952	1,127	63	504	28	124	7	26	1	22	1	1,803	1.6
1953	1,132	61	533	29	131	7	27	1	24	1	1,848	2.5
1954	1,123	60	557	30	138	7	27	1	27	1	1,871	1.2
1955	1,215	59	625	30	150	7	31	2	30	1	2,050	9.6
1956	1,281	59	679	31	161	7	32	1	32	1	2,185	6.6
1957	1,317	58	714	31	178	8	35	2	34	1	2,278	4.3
1958	1,344	57	732	31	192	8	35	1	36	2	2,338	2.6
1959	1,390	56	790	32	214	9	36	1	40	2	2,471	5.7
1960	1,419	55	850	33	235	9	39	2	43	2	2,586	4.7
1961	1,356	52	905	35	254	10	42	2	45	2	2,602	0.6
1962	1,358	50	981	36	277	10	44	2	49	2	2,708	4.1
1963	1,404	49	1,053	37	300	11	47	2	51	2	2,855	5.4
1964	1,442	48	1,138	38	328	11	51	2	57	2	3,016	5.6
1965	1,468	47	1,221	39	351	11	55	2	59	2	3,154	4.6
1966	1,485	45	1,325	40	380	11	60	2	63	2	3,314	5.1
1967	1,455	43	1,424	42	410	12	66	2	65	2	3,420	3.2
1968	1,456	40	1,552	43	445	12	73	2	70	2	3,596	5.1
1969	1,494	39	1,674	44	487	13	80	2	74	2	3,809	5.9
1970	1,571	38	1,838	45	515	13	87	2	78	2	4,090	7.4
1971	1,571	37	1,946	46	553	13	88	2	84	2	4,241	3.7
1972	1,587	36	2,056	47	582	13	95	2	89	2	4,409	4.0
1973	1,594	34	2,240	48	607	13	110	2	95	2	4,647	5.4
1974	1,591	34	2,244	48	616	13	108	2	96	2	4,655	0.2
1975	1,686	36	2,131	46	620	13	95	2	95	2	4,628	-0.6
1976	1,723	35	2,313	47	644	13	111	2	103	2	4,894	5.7
1977	1,786	35	2,390	47	645	13	105	2	108	2	5,034	2.9
1978	1,802	35	2,383	47	673	13	107	2	116	2	5,082	1.0
1979	1,899	35	2,535	47	713	13	100	2	119	2	5,365	5.6
1980	1,921	37	2,409	46	724	14	89	2	120	2	5,263	-0.9
1981	1,930	38	2,272	44	734	14	72	1	121	2	5,129	-2.6
1982	1,993	39	2,178	43	732	14	70	1	121	2	5,093	-0.7
1983	1,998	39	2,163	43	735	14	63	1	125	2	5,084	-0.2
1984	2,088	40	2,191	42	796	15	57	1	128	2	5,260	3.5
1985	2,196	41	2,172	40	826	15	55	1	130	2	5,379	2.3
1986	2,253	41	2,277	41	842	15	53	1	136	2	5,561	3.4
1987	2,313	41	2,290	40	888	16	48	1	142	3	5,680	2.1
1988	2,385	40	2,392	41	919	16	48	1	150	3	5,893	3.8

[a] Annual growth rate, i.e., the percentage increase in emissions with respect to the previous year.

Note that emissions are in units of 10^6 t a^{-1} as carbon; for emissions in 10^6 t a^{-1} as carbon dioxide, multiply by 3.67.

Global annual emissions of CO_2 from fossil fuel combustion sources are derived from emission factors applied to United Nations fuel production data (UN 1990 *Energy Statistics Yearbook 1988*, United Nations, New York) and gas flaring data compiled by Rotty (for 1950–1970) and the US Department of Energy (after 1970). Emissions from cement manufacturing are calculated from cement production data given in the US Bureau of Mines Yearbooks.

The uncertainty of the total emissions estimates is ± 8 per cent. Full details of the procedures for calculating emissions are given in the source document. Percentage distribution of CO_2 emissions may not necessarily total 100 per cent due to rounding.

Source:
Marland, G., Huang, S. F., Boden, T. A., Kanciruk, P., Griffin, R. C. and Nelson, T. R. 1989 *Estimates of CO_2 Emissions from Fossil Fuel Burning and Cement Manufacturing, Based on the United Nations Energy Statistics and the US Bureau of Mines Cement Manufacturing Data*, ORNL/CDIAC-25, NDP-030, Oak Ridge National Laboratory, Oak Ridge.

Table 1.3 National emissions of carbon dioxide from anthropogenic sources, 1960–1988

| Region/country | Fossil fuel combustion and cement manufacturing | | | | Per capita (t C a^{-1}) 1988 | Per unit GNP (kg C a^{-1}) 1988 | Land use changes (10^3 t C a^{-1}) 1980 |
| | Total (10^3 t C a^{-1}) | | | | | | |
	1960	1970	1980	1988			
WORLD	2,490,500	3,850,368	5,037,102	5,669,775			1,782,600
AFRICA	39,845	81,962	141,142	169,605			367,400
Algeria	1,717	4,126	18,063	15,630	0.66	0.27	
Angola	151	966	1,449	1,300	0.14		5,500
Benin	44	78	133	150	0.03	0.09	2,500
Botswana	0	0	272	449	0.38	0.37	700
Burkina Faso	12	39	116	131	0.02	0.07	
Burundi		13	30	46	0.01	0.04	0
Cameroon	74	174	1,057	1,532	0.14	0.14	15,600
Cape Verde	6	10	33	19	0.05	0.08	
Cent. African Rep.	24	55	29	53	0.02	0.05	3,600
Chad	15	35	58	56	0.01	0.06	4,200
Comoros	3	7	11	14	0.03	0.07	
Congo	61	149	105	482	0.26	0.25	3,400
Côte d'Ivoire	126	663	1,403	1,590	0.14	0.19	100,500
Djibouti	11	28	58	76	0.20		
Egypt	4,388	5,783	12,329	20,469	0.40	0.62	
Equatorial Guinea	6	10	15	19	0.05		300
Ethiopia	96	428	493	688	0.02	0.12	7,800
Gabon	36	318	1,223	1,382	1.26	0.43	2,200
Gambia	5	13	43	51	0.06	0.31	7,700
Ghana	399	717	662	919	0.07	0.16	8,800
Guinea	112	209	257	270	0.04		
Guinea-Bissau	5	18	29	37	0.04	0.21	3,000
Kenya	663	760	1,691	1,282	0.06	0.15	1,700
Liberia	45	373	531	209	0.09		7,800
Libya	189	8,807	7,347	8,543	2.02	0.37	
Madagascar	110	248	436	373	0.03	0.18	23,200
Malawi		115	194	171	0.02	0.13	15,700
Mali	33	55	107	114	0.01	0.06	2,100
Mauritania	10	117	167	853	0.45	0.93	
Mauritius	49	135	162	246	0.23	0.13	
Morocco	995	1,928	4,354	5,558	0.23	0.28	
Mozambique	518	791	874	329	0.02	0.22	7,000
Niger	8	59	156	209	0.03	0.10	1,600
Nigeria	934	5,855	18,588	15,548	0.15	0.50	59,500
Réunion	20	75	188	199	0.35		
Rwanda		16	70	104	0.02	0.05	300
São Tomé & Príncipe	3	4	9	9	0.09		
Senegal	226	340	762	604	0.09	0.13	2,900
Seychelles	0	8	26	34	0.51	0.13	
Sierra Leone	195	198	161	181	0.05		1,000
Somalia	23	59	166	260	0.04	0.26	1,000
South Africa	26,907	40,795	58,230	77,484	2.30	1.00	
St Helena	0	0	0	1	0.11		
Sudan	372	1,302	900	916	0.04	0.08	26,600

Continued opposite

Table 1.3 Continued

Region/country	Fossil fuel combustion and cement manufacturing						Land use changes (10^3 t C a^{-1}) 1980
	Total (10^3 t C a^{-1})				Per capita (t C a^{-1}) 1988	Per unit GNP (kg C a^{-1}) 1988	
	1960	1970	1980	1988			
Swaziland	9	101	129	117	0.16	0.20	
Tanzania		482	494	574	0.02	0.14	4,900
Togo	18	71	161	132	0.04	0.11	700
Tunisia	471	995	2,580	3,663	0.47	0.38	
Uganda	114	385	192	229	0.01	0.05	2,200
Western Sahara		19	44	51	0.30		
Zaire	644	750	941	1,066	0.03	0.19	35,000
Zambia		1,036	967	753	0.10	0.34	4,200
Zimbabwe		2,247	2,652	4,428	0.49	0.72	4,200
NORTH AMERICA	881,447	1,308,159	1,481,192	1,543,745			111,600
Antigua & Barbuda	10	126	39	77	0.91	0.27	
Bahamas	112	703	2,179	365	1.44	0.14	
Barbados	47	114	184	253	0.98	0.17	
Belize	12	34	52	49	0.28	0.18	600
Bermuda	43	62	116	174	3.00		
Br. Virgin Is.	0	5	7	13	0.90		
Canada	52,700	90,610	115,820	119,388	4.58	0.27	
Cayman Is.	3	10	28	61	2.78		
Costa Rica	134	339	672	687	0.24	0.15	9,400
Cuba	3,751	5,075	8,369	9,492	0.94		100
Dominica	3	7	10	15	0.19	0.11	
Dominican Rep.	284	848	1,738	1,843	0.27	0.37	100
El Salvador	168	384	581	616	0.12	0.13	200
Greenland	61	104	152	65	1.17		
Grenada	6	12	13	20	0.20	0.12	
Guadeloupe	43	83	162	298	0.88		
Guatemala	368	618	1,225	1,054	0.12	0.13	10,000
Haiti	78	106	205	194	0.03	0.08	100
Honduras	168	358	560	510	0.11	0.12	10,100
Jamaica	401	1,362	2,304	1,408	0.58	0.55	100
Martinique	46	99	213	282	0.85		
Mexico	17,223	28,914	71,001	83,733	0.99	0.57	33,400
Montserrat	0	4	3	7	0.52		
Neth. Antilles[a]	3,025	4,524	2,863	1,332			
Nicaragua	146	378	554	617	0.17		16,900
Panama	345	710	951	794	0.34	0.16	5,500
Puerto Rico	1,972	3,179	3,832	3,980	1.10		
St Christopher & Nevis				18	0.36	0.16	
St Lucia	4	18	30	44	0.33	0.20	
St Pierre & Miquelon	10	10	10	31	4.43		
St Vincent & Grenadines	3	8	10	14	0.13	0.11	
Trinidad & Tobago	704	2,285	4,552	5,003	4.02	1.20	100
US Virgin Is.	34	1,597	3,475	1,160	10.45		
USA	799,544	1,165,477	1,259,281	1,310,248	5.34	0.27	

Continued over

Table 1.3 Continued

Region/country	Fossil fuel combustion and cement manufacturing				Per capita (t C a^{-1}) 1988	Per unit GNP (kg C a^{-1}) 1988	Land use changes (10^3 t C a^{-1}) 1980
	Total (10^3 t C a^{-1})						
	1960	1970	1980	1988			
SOUTH AMERICA	52,485	90,720	134,584	152,533			578,500
Argentina	13,325	22,156	29,336	32,400	1.03	0.41	
Bolivia	274	672	1,233	1,171	0.17	0.30	6,800
Brazil	12,808	23,622	48,178	55,247	0.38	0.18	336,100
Chile	3,702	6,703	7,356	7,278	0.57	0.38	
Colombia	4,511	6,952	10,724	14,438	0.47	0.39	123,300
Ecuador	492	1,132	3,666	4,574			39,900
Falkland Is.	53	3	4	11	3.70		
French Guiana	6	26	100	98	1.10		300
Guyana	180	431	483	276	0.27	0.82	400
Paraguay	83	197	403	459	0.11	0.10	8,400
Peru		4,798	6,423	6,138	0.29	0.23	45,000
Suriname	118	439	648	376	0.96	0.36	400
Uruguay	1,179	1,556	1,576	1,287	0.42	0.17	
Venezuela	15,755	22,033	24,456	28,780	1.53	0.47	17,900
ASIA	360,794	620,670	1,054,139	1,463,107			686,600
Afghanistan	117	460	486	1,744	0.12		
Bahrain	157	248	1,795	3,252	6.47		
Bangladesh			2,085	3,670	0.03	0.20	2,100
Bhutan		1	6	9	0.01	0.04	300
Brunei	91	2,238	1,871	1,307	5.23		2,700
Cambodia	65	320	78	123	0.02		4,800
China	215,295	211,607	406,440	609,858	0.56	1.65	69,000
Cyprus	242	465	873	1,174	1.71	0.27	
Hong Kong	808	2,264	4,489	8,060	1.42	0.15	
India	33,193	53,261	95,547	163,757	0.20	0.59	33,000
Indonesia[b]	5,843	9,047	25,825	37,774	0.22	0.49	191,900
Iran	10,199	23,991	31,682	43,803	0.82		
Iraq	2,254	6,352	11,997	13,419	0.76		
Israel	1,764	4,521	5,768	8,576	1.93	0.22	
Japan	63,907	202,454	254,881	269,766	2.20	0.10	
Jordan	203	403	1,290	2,504	0.64	0.42	
Korea	3,455	14,230	34,314	55,838	1.31	0.37	
Korea, Dem.	6,520	20,173	34,269	40,759	1.86		
Kuwait	2,128	6,951	6,752	8,501	4.38	0.32	
Laos	22	152	50	56	0.01		84,700
Lebanon	705	1,078	1,684	2,313	0.82		
Macau	14	56	136	262	0.59		
Malaysia	1,148	3,934	7,636	11,886	0.72	0.36	49,900
Maldives		0	12	23	0.12		
Mongolia	348	750	1,829	2,587	1.24		
Myanmar q.v. Burma	744	1,120	1,308	1,250	0.03		51,200
Nepal	22	63	148	272	0.02	0.09	6,900
Oman		65	1,594	2,524	1.83	0.36	
Pakistan			8,648	15,938	0.14	0.43	1,100
Philippines	2,303	6,733	9,970	10,817	0.18	0.29	56,700

Continued opposite

Table 1.3 Continued

Region/country	Total (10^3 t C a^{-1})				Per capita (t C a^{-1}) 1988	Per unit GNP (kg C a^{-1}) 1988	Land use changes (10^3 t C a^{-1}) 1980
	1960	1970	1980	1988			
Qatar	48	2,063	3,518	4,172	12.24		
Saudi Arabia	731	9,831	35,685	46,057	3.52	0.53	
Singapore	380	4,964	8,217	11,937	4.51	0.50	
Sri Lanka	618	981	930	949	0.06	0.14	1,700
Syria	880	1,663	5,274	8,279	0.71	0.42	
Thailand	1,012	4,190	10,922	17,876	0.33	0.33	94,500
Turkey	4,587	11,504	20,741	32,645	0.61	0.47	
United Arab Em.	3	4,158	9,897	11,867	9.71	0.62	
Viet Nam		7,696	4,593	5,054	0.08		36,100
Yemen	16	46	326	949	0.13	0.18	
Yemen, Dem.	975	639	579	1,500	0.65	1.51	
EUROPE	732,237	1,076,354	1,268,038	1,180,202			-28,000
Albania	277	932	2,639	2,705	0.86		
Austria	8,394	13,729	14,247	14,209	1.90	0.12	
Belgium	25,033	34,396	34,860	25,066	2.53	0.18	
Bulgaria	5,956	21,777	30,332	33,908	3.77		
Czechoslovakia	35,394	54,341	66,094	63,714	4.09		
Denmark	8,146	16,957	17,285	15,512	3.03	0.16	
Faeroe Is.	16	70	115	133	2.77		
Finland	4,132	10,987	15,036	13,793	2.79	0.15	
France[c]	74,791	116,177	132,129	87,274	1.56	0.10	
German Dem. Rep.	71,940	73,845	83,678	89,262	5.36		
Germany, Fed. Rep.	148,614	200,858	208,021	182,704	3.01	0.16	
Gibraltar	13	12	18	10	0.34		
Greece	2,545	4,602	14,031	18,024	1.80	0.38	
Hungary	12,208	19,568	22,964	21,832	2.06	0.84	
Iceland	331	379	509	581	2.32	0.12	
Ireland	3,039	4,916	6,845	7,982	2.19	0.29	
Italy[d]	30,143	77,955	101,564	98,105	1.71	0.13	
Luxembourg	3,175	3,755	2,883	2,362	6.42	0.28	
Malta	93	178	270	421	1.21	0.23	
Netherlands	20,173	34,813	41,364	32,603	2.23	0.15	
Norway	3,583	6,846	10,948	10,333	2.47	0.12	
Poland	55,049	82,783	125,436	125,342	3.30	1.78	
Portugal	2,248	3,716	7,396	8,828	0.86	0.24	
Romania	14,585	32,599	54,489	60,183	2.61		
Spain	13,424	30,194	54,546	51,535	1.32	0.17	
Sweden	13,455	25,179	19,416	14,885	1.78	0.09	
Switzerland	5,346	10,780	11,169	11,049	1.69	0.06	
UK	160,770	175,397	160,551	152,520	2.67	0.21	
Yugoslavia	9,368	18,616	29,205	35,328	1.50	0.60	
USSR	396,057	628,209	895,504	1,086,000	3.82	0.43	35,000
OCEANIA	27,635	44,294	62,503	74,583			31,500
American Samoa	9	38	116	129	3.39		
Australia	24,060	38,884	55,348	65,825	4.02	0.32	

Continued over

Table 1.3   Continued

Region/country	Fossil fuel combustion and cement manufacturing				Per capita (t C a^{-1}) 1988	Per unit GNP (kg C a^{-1}) 1988	Land use changes (10^3 t C a^{-1}) 1980
	Total (10^3 t C a^{-1})						
	1960	1970	1980	1988			
Christmas Is.		19	27				
Cook Is.		3	159	165	7.85		
Fiji	53	142	213	149	0.21	0.13	
French Polynesia	10	50	77	145	0.83		
Guam	35	336	557	334	2.78		
Kiribati	0	6	8	6	0.09		
Nauru		18	34	34	3.81		
New Caledonia	238	651	540	437	2.72		
New Zealand	3,167	3,884	4,802	6,599	1.98	0.20	
Niue		1	1	1	0.21		
Pacific Is. Tr. Tr.	4	37	42	44	0.26		
Papua New Guinea	49	189	499	601	0.16	0.20	3,500
Samoa	4	8	27	31	0.18	0.30	
Solomon Is.	3	11	28	42	0.14	0.22	
Tonga	3	7	11	22	0.19	0.27	
Vanuatu	0	11	17	20	0.13	0.16	

[a]   Includes Aruba.
[b]   Includes East Timor.
[c]   Includes Monaco.
[d]   Includes San Marino.

Note that emissions are in units of 10^3 t a^{-1} and kg a^{-1} as carbon; for emissions in 10^3 t a^{-1} and kg a^{-1} as carbon dioxide multiply by 3.67.
National CO_2 emissions are based on estimates of net consumption of gas, liquid and solid fuels and cement (derived from UN international energy trade statistics) and appropriate emission factors. Full details of the procedures for calculating emissions are given in the source document. World and regional totals include only those countries listed; trends in regional totals may overestimate real trends in CO_2 emissions, as data for the earlier years (1960 and 1970) may be missing for some countries.
Per capita emissions use population data as compiled by the UN Demographic and Social Statistics Branch. Emissions per unit GNP (Gross National Product) are based on GNP data (in US$) compiled by the World Bank.
Net CO_2 emissions from land use changes (mainly deforestation) are derived from model computations of the annual change in the carbon content of

terrestrial ecosystems following land-use disturbances that has been developed by Houghton et al. (1987). Full details of the model calculations are given in the source document. The regional total for North America includes an estimate of combined net CO_2 emissions from USA and Canada of 25 x 10^6 t C a^{-1}. The regional total for Oceania includes an estimate of combined net CO_2 emissions from Australia and New Zealand of 28 x 10^6 t C a^{-1}. In Europe, the terrestrial biosphere is estimated to provide a net sink for CO_2 of 28 x 10^6 t C a^{-1}.

Sources:
Houghton, R. A., Boone, R. D., Fruci, J. R., Hobbie, J. E., Melillo, J. M., Palm, C. A., Peterson, B. J., Shaver, G. R., Woodwell, G. M., Moore, B., Skole, D. L. and Myers, N.   1987 The flux of carbon from terrestrial ecosystems to the atmosphere in 1980 due to changes in land use: geographic distribution of the global flux, *Tellus* **39B**, 122–139.
Marland, G., Huang, S. F., Boden, T. A., Kanciruk, P., Griffin, R. C. and Nelson, T. R.   1989 *Estimates of CO$_2$ Emissions from Fossil Fuel Burning and Cement Manufacturing, Based on the United Nations Energy Statistics and US Bureau of Mines Cement Manufacturing Data*, ORNL/CDIAC-25, NDP-030, Oak Ridge National Laboratory, Oak Ridge.

Table 1.4 Annual mean concentrations of methane at NOAA/CMDL flask sampling network sites, 1984–1989 (ppbv in dry air)

Site	Latitude	1984	1985	1986	1987	1988	1989
Alert, North West Territories	82°27'N			1,742	1,752	1,767	1,777
Mould Bay, North West Territories	76°14'N	1,714	1,730	1,746	1,761	1,769	1,780
Point Barrow, Alaska	71°19'N	1,724	1,733	1,755	1,759	1,774	1,791
Ocean Station M, N. Atlantic	66°00'N	1,708	1,723	1,736	1,749	1,763	1,765
Cold Bay, Alaska	55°12'N	1,707	1,722	1,738	1,747	1,758	1,763
Shemya Is., N. Pacific	52°43'N			1,739	1,750	1,760	1,771
Olympic Penisula, Washington	48°15'N						
Cape Meares, Oregon	45°00'N	1,696	1,707	1,717	1,734	1,747	1,756
Niwot Ridge, Colorado	40°03'N	1,673	1,683	1,691	1,707	1,720	1,724
Azores (Terceira Is.), N. Atlantic	38°45'N	1,690	1,701	1,711	1,727	1,733	
Bermuda, East	32°22'N						
Bermuda, West	32°16'N						
Sand Islet (Midway), N. Pacific	28°13'N			1,701	1,720	1,717	1,730
Key Biscayne, Florida	25°40'N	1,669	1,679	1,693	1,705	1,718	1,722
Mauna Loa, Hawaii	19°32'N	1,637	1,649	1,661	1,673	1,684	1,697
Cape Kumukahi, Hawaii	19°31'N	1,659	1,673	1,679	1,694	1,698	1,707
St Croix, Virgin Is.	17°45'N	1,652	1,668	1,674	1,686	1,697	1,704
Guam (Marianas Is.), N. Pacific	13°26'N	1,624	1,647	1,667	1,680	1,681	1,696
Ragged Point, Barbados	13°10'N					1,695	1,702
Christmas Is., Pacific	2°00'N		1,615	1,628	1,641	1,648	1,663
Seychelles (Mahe Is.), Indian Ocean	4°40'S						
Ascension Is., S. Atlantic	7°55'S	1,589	1,602	1,615	1,628	1,635	1,647
American Samoa, S. Pacific	14°15'S	1,585	1,600	1,609	1,617	1,630	1,634
Amsterdam Is., Indian Ocean	37°57'S	1,578	1,588				1,636
Cape Grim, Tasmania	40°41'S	1,577	1,588	1,601	1,612	1,622	1,635
South Georgia Is., S. Atlantic	54°00'S						
Palmer Station, Antarctica	64°55'S	1,576	1,588		1,610		1,634
Syowa, Antarctica	69°00'S						1,634
Halley Bay, Antarctica	75°40'S						
South Pole, Antarctica	89°59'S	1,575	1,587	1,599	1,610	1,622	1,634

Weekly flask samples, taken in pairs, are analysed for CH_4 at the NOAA/CMDL laboratory at Boulder, Colorado, by gas chromatography with flame ionization detection. Two aliquots are extracted for CH_4 analysis from a single flask prior to analysis of both flasks for CO_2. All samples, including calibration gases, are dried before analysis. All measurements are traceable to the original pair of standards obtained at the time the programme was started in 1983. The annual means represent 12-month running means, calculated from the flask data.

Blank spaces in the above table indicate that there are insufficient data to calculate a representative annual mean. Sites are listed according to latitude, beginning with the most northern.

Source:
Dlugokencky, E. J. and Lang, P. M. 1990 Personal communication, Climate Monitoring and Diagnostics Laboratory, National Oceanic and Atmospheric Administration, Boulder, Colorado, USA.

Table 1.5 Monthly mean atmospheric concentrations of CFC-11 and CFC-12 at NOAA/CMDL sites, 1977–1989 (ppt)

CFC-11

Site/year	Jan.	Feb.	Mar.	Apr.	May	Jun.	Jul.	Aug.	Sep.	Oct.	Nov.	Dec.
POINT BARROW, ALASKA												
1977	155.2	152.7	148.2	149.9	159.9	147.8		151.6	152.7	159.4	160.4	162.7
1978	160.8	159.4	162.4	164.2	161.9	162.3	163.5	164.7	168.3	168.9	173.9	171.2
1979	168.5	171.1	173.9	173.1	172.3	171.9	172.7	171.9	175.5	178.8	177.3	181.6
1980	182.6	181.3	183.4	181.8	181.4	182.9	182.2	187.9	185.8	183.9	192.2	188.8
1981	188.2	192.7	187.3	191.3	190.1	191.4	191.6	201.0	191.0	195.8	198.8	200.6
1982	198.6	201.3	202.1	200.4	198.6	197.4	200.6	200.7	202.5	203.9	205.6	206.8
1983	208.5	207.8	208.6	209.7		210.9	213.4	209.5	210.4	213.5	216.2	213.5
1984	216.9	216.3	214.9	211.2								
1985					225.5	223.4			229.6	233.4	235.7	236.1
1986	236.8	236.6	233.9	244.6	238.5	238.4	237.9	240.4	240.5	248.9	246.5	250.5
1987	248.9	249.8	250.2	253.3	257.6	253.1	255.1	256.5	259.4	262.7	265.5	265.9
1988	263.5	266.8	266.1	268.5	268.0	266.1	265.6	267.3	273.2	271.9	277.6	275.8
1989	274.6	276.7	278.3	278.5	276.6	275.6	279.0	274.9	277.6	283.5	290.0	288.2
NIWOT RIDGE, COLORADO												
1977	157.3	154.0	147.8	151.0	152.0	144.2	148.3	158.6	149.3	156.4	153.3	159.9
1978	154.6	159.4	156.6		166.6	157.6	163.5	165.7	170.8	165.3	167.5	164.6
1979	164.3	163.5	173.4	166.6	166.1	168.9	168.7	171.8	169.1	174.0	176.1	174.5
1980	175.0	174.8	184.4	178.6	182.9	179.6	181.6	194.6	184.1	181.7	184.8	180.7
1981	184.0	183.7	186.0	183.3	188.1	188.1	187.6	189.4	190.6	192.6	190.1	191.0
1982	192.3	190.8	195.7	196.9	196.2	196.6	199.9	197.0	198.4	198.5	203.1	203.4
1983	201.1	204.4	207.0	208.4	209.1	207.1	208.0	208.1	208.7	210.6	209.8	212.7
1984	210.3	207.4	212.5	209.7								
1985					223.6	221.9			230.6	229.6	230.3	229.0
1986	228.3	226.2	227.2	231.9	234.2	234.8	231.7	236.9	233.9	240.6	243.8	239.9
1987	240.4	243.5	243.9	242.8	247.4	249.6	247.7	251.4	254.5	260.8	258.0	260.0
1988	260.3	258.5	263.5	262.1	269.4	263.8	266.3	270.0	264.5	263.8	272.6	271.5
1989	269.5	270.9	267.6	270.8	271.1	272.4	285.7	277.1	279.6	275.9	280.7	276.7
MAUNA LOA, HAWAII												
1977	145.4	148.1	143.0	141.4	142.2	145.0	143.6	147.4	149.9	147.7	149.4	149.8
1978	155.9	152.9	149.0	154.1	154.5	154.8	153.9	158.1	160.3	158.2	159.7	159.6
1979	162.6	164.1	164.1	163.4	162.6	162.9	165.5		169.2	175.2	170.8	171.3
1980	173.3	172.9	175.6	177.4	172.0	176.6	178.9	179.1	176.1	181.1	182.5	177.9
1981	178.5	182.1	183.2	184.1	183.7	186.1	187.5	186.7	189.8	189.7	189.1	191.3
1982	189.0	189.2	190.6	191.3	193.5	191.9	191.2	194.7	196.4	197.4	196.6	196.0
1983	197.8	198.8	200.3	201.3	202.9	207.7	206.9	206.1	204.0	207.1	206.3	200.4
1984	205.6	207.7	206.1	206.6								
1985					216.9	218.5			224.1	226.7	224.9	231.1
1986	223.5	227.2	228.4	234.0	232.6	235.4	234.1	232.4	239.4	240.4	240.2	239.9
1987	239.4		243.3	244.5		244.9	242.2	246.2	249.8	252.0	252.7	249.3
1988	248.8	245.4	250.3	259.1	256.9	257.9	257.7	259.1	261.8	262.0	266.9	
1989	266.6	264.3	265.5	269.6	268.8	270.1	268.4	271.3	273.7	273.8	272.2	276.3
CAPE MATATULA, AMERICAN SAMOA												
1977	138.7	141.5	130.8	136.4	135.5	135.1	134.8	137.8	138.3	139.2	137.7	137.7
1978	142.3	141.8	144.0	146.3	146.8	145.7	145.5	147.9	147.8	149.4	152.3	151.2
1979	154.3	157.9	154.3	156.2	155.3	155.1	156.6	158.7	155.7	162.0	157.1	160.7

Continued opposite

CFC-12

Jan.	Feb.	Mar.	Apr.	May	Jun.	Jul.	Aug.	Sep.	Oct.	Nov.	Dec.
					266.4			251.3		274.3	284.2
269.9	289.5	282.5	260.2	267.4		273.7		285.7	290.6	293.8	292.4
287.6	290.0	296.1	289.2	289.1	293.0	294.4	293.3	300.0	297.1	296.0	304.1
306.2	301.7	303.5	309.0	309.0	306.9	303.2	307.1	312.3	311.1	319.8	327.9
315.1	315.4	319.0	331.3	326.8	328.0	327.1	337.5	327.4	332.8	332.7	335.4
339.6	343.0	336.6	339.8	340.0	334.6	340.3	341.6	343.2	348.1	351.2	350.9
353.4	353.9	352.8	353.2	355.3	352.3	353.1	355.4	361.0	367.6	370.0	359.7
367.2	377.9	364.3	375.3								
	389.3	387.8	389.7	392.5	394.6	388.1	393.4	400.8	404.0	406.8	408.3
407.0	408.4	409.6	410.7	407.7	407.8	406.7	404.3	406.4	413.7	415.5	419.4
417.0	417.5	424.9	422.6	432.9	429.0	434.4	433.1	441.7	443.5	445.4	444.9
443.9	446.6	448.0	447.8	445.2	446.8	446.8	448.6	457.0	456.7	469.6	462.0
459.5	460.0	460.8	461.6	463.1	459.8	468.1	464.1	467.1	471.0	477.1	478.0
						260.2	268.3	258.2			286.9
		279.9			298.6	302.5	301.0		296.5	293.8	
283.9	292.5		316.4	297.7	297.7	295.1	300.1	311.6	296.9	301.8	306.5
314.2	305.5	309.0	304.1	310.8	301.6	301.3	301.6	309.7	304.6	305.0	308.8
309.5	307.5	315.5	316.6	318.4	320.0	323.3	324.8	325.9	331.2	322.3	325.4
329.3	326.5	330.6	339.9	333.0	337.1	345.3	339.8	339.3	343.1	343.5	343.2
344.1	347.1	349.1	349.5	353.2	352.7	365.9	349.2	357.2	362.2	363.2	366.9
365.0	361.8	360.1	368.4								
		380.0	379.9	384.8	385.0	386.1	393.4	406.6	401.6	403.7	397.1
396.7	396.1	398.4	397.2	404.2	404.5	400.3	405.5	399.2	406.3	405.2	406.8
409.0	406.7	418.9	418.3		433.0	430.7	431.6	438.4	441.2	439.7	438.9
440.9	437.2	441.8	445.4	445.8	445.6	454.4	455.4	450.9	448.5	459.1	451.2
453.6	455.8	447.0	455.2	459.1	461.4	475.4	468.3	467.5	464.2	470.8	468.1
				249.8		250.5		255.8	262.3	262.8	272.7
275.3	267.6	275.1	277.9		282.3	280.6	279.2	277.6	277.6	281.6	291.0
290.4	283.3	286.6	283.2	289.3	293.9	293.3		298.0	320.3	298.1	299.5
309.6	310.4	298.8	304.2	292.8	309.2	316.8	300.6	301.2	310.9	309.3	306.0
303.8	310.6	310.2	320.8	324.3	332.1	329.5	333.8	330.4	333.4	328.2	339.5
332.6	336.6	329.9	330.1	332.6	330.9	330.4	334.1	337.9	339.3	339.7	342.5
337.1	342.3	343.1	343.6	343.3	346.1	357.9	345.4	355.6	356.6	362.1	357.0
358.8	367.0	353.4	368.8								
	377.3	379.5	375.4	382.4	390.5	382.7	384.5	396.0	398.6	392.3	398.3
395.1	400.0	398.4	400.2	399.5	401.1	397.2	402.1	403.0	412.1	409.7	400.8
410.5	401.9	421.5	416.6		423.1	422.2	426.5	435.8	435.9	436.0	428.9
428.3	432.9	430.9	439.5	438.3	438.6	442.8	442.0	445.7	446.0	449.2	435.7
453.6	447.4	450.9	454.1	452.8	461.9	453.8	458.4	460.6	464.1	467.2	459.7
			245.8	238.2	234.0	215.4	235.9	237.5	239.4	240.0	246.5
250.1	251.9	245.1	261.0	255.4	255.6	253.1	254.4	257.8	258.5	262.1	262.0
269.3	268.5	268.1	269.0	267.5	268.3	271.2	275.1	275.2	275.3	269.8	275.1

Continued over

Table 1.5 Continued

Site/year	Jan.	Feb.	Mar.	Apr.	May	Jun.	Jul.	Aug.	Sep.	Oct.	Nov.	Dec.
	CFC-11											
1980	163.6	164.5	164.5	165.5	165.5	167.6	166.2	166.4	170.1	167.9	168.2	168.9
1981	170.7	176.5	171.7	174.6	175.1	174.8	176.1	177.5	180.4	179.6	181.6	181.8
1982	183.9	184.3	182.7	185.8	185.4	186.8	186.3	188.0	188.0	189.1	189.4	188.6
1983	193.8	190.7	194.9	194.2	193.8	195.5	195.7	194.4	196.1	198.9	196.6	200.9
1984	201.7	202.6	197.2	201.2								
1985					212.2	210.7			214.4	215.1	214.3	218.0
1986	217.2	216.2	218.6	225.7	233.9	226.1	225.6	226.6	228.9	227.4	225.7	229.9
1987	229.6	236.4		232.8		232.0	232.9		239.1	236.5	239.9	241.1
1988	242.7	243.9	238.0	246.1	243.7	245.5	246.2	249.2	245.8	249.9	251.5	257.7
1989	260.4	257.1	258.9	258.4	258.7	254.2	258.9	263.3	262.1	263.5	263.8	266.2
SOUTH POLE, ANTARCTICA												
1977	137.6	29.6										
1978							156.5					
1979	150.9	157.6									165.3	154.6
											154.3	169.5
1980	161.8	160.9		167.1	174.4	162.9				176.5	165.0	167.8
1981	169.6				184.8					194.1	173.1	185.7
1982											201.0	
1983	202.0					177.3						200.6
1984		195.3										193.1
1985												
1986											214.6	220.9
1987	228.2										227.1	
1988											238.9	237.4
1989											246.9	244.3
												259.8

Air samples are collected on a weekly basis in pairs of 0.3 litre stainless steel flasks at the four NOAA/CMDL baseline observatories and Niwot Ridge, Colorado. Flasks are returned to the NOAA/CMDL laboratory in Boulder, Colorado, for analysis for CFC-11, CFC-12 (and N_2O) by electron-capture gas chromatography. Samples are dried prior to analysis. Measurements are calibrated against the Oregon Graduate Center Scale and corrected for drift where necessary. Monthly mean values are calculated from the weekly flask data. Data are provisional, pending final calibrations.

Pairs of flask samples are usually collected at the South Pole only during the Antarctic summer (November–January).

CFC-12

Jan.	Feb.	Mar.	Apr.	May	Jun.	Jul.	Aug.	Sep.	Oct.	Nov.	Dec.
279.6	279.1	279.3	282.5	281.1	283.7	284.5	283.6	288.1	287.4	286.7	290.5
291.5	298.3	298.3	300.5	303.8	307.8	306.7	307.0	305.5	309.4	311.3	312.9
317.8	322.0	317.3	320.4	320.2	318.5	321.0	322.5	323.3	325.7	235.0	325.2
330.1	330.9	334.5	333.7	332.9	333.1	327.5	335.8	341.6	345.9	348.0	349.6
349.5	357.0	352.2	360.8								
	369.8	368.0	369.4	373.0	373.5	375.7	373.7	379.8	381.5	375.6	383.6
383.9	388.8	386.5	387.1	387.7	393.5	388.9	391.7	392.6	392.4	390.8	394.1
396.0	398.4	404.5	406.8		400.5	408.0			409.1	413.0	413.5
415.7	418.8	415.4	424.1	421.3	419.2	426.9	426.8	426.6	433.5	437.6	434.0
437.4	440.5	435.0	437.8	440.5	432.2	443.1	442.3	445.2	448.4	448.1	451.5
	230.2				227.8						248.2
									249.7	251.4	257.5
258.9	253.4								298.1	275.1	274.5
275.0	271.8		276.9	277.3	281.8	279.6		300.6	286.2	284.3	286.9
286.2	291.8			294.9				324.0	329.5		311.2
308.4										337.6	
340.0					345.6						334.2
	347.8										
										375.1	377.6
381.0										385.2	387.3
390.5										407.8	410.9
405.1										423.4	423.1
427.4											445.6

Source:
Thompson, T. M. and Elkins, T. W. 1990 Personal communication, Climate Monitoring and Diagnostics Laboratory, National Oceanic and Atmospheric Administration, Boulder, Colorado, USA.

Table 1.6 Consumption of chlorofluorocarbons and halons in selected countries, 1986 (t a^{-1})

Region/country	CFCs[a] (t a^{-1})	Halons[b] (t a^{-1})	Total (t a^{-1})	% of global consumption	Per capita consumption (kg a^{-1})
WORLD			1,171,884	100	
AFRICA	18,485	746	26,456	2.26	
Algeria[c]			2,200	0.19	0.10
Côte d'Ivoire[c]			980	0.08	0.10
Egypt[d]	5,042		5,042	0.43	0.10
Gabon[c]			115	0.01	0.10
Kenya[d]	136	1	137	0.01	0.01
Madagascar	49	0	49	–	–
Morocco[c]			2,200	0.19	0.10
Rwanda	8	0	8	–	–
Senegal[c]			600	0.05	0.09
South Africa[d]	12,500	695	13,195	1.13	0.40
Togo			300	0.03	0.10
Tunisia[d]	750	50	800	0.07	0.11
Zimbabwe[c]			830	0.07	0.10
NORTH AMERICA	353,680	8,132	365,108	31.18	
Belize[c]			16	–	0.09
Canada[d]	20,670	501	21,171	1.81	0.83
Cuba			620	0.05	0.06
Dominica			2	–	0.03
Dominican Rep.[c]			620	0.05	0.10
El Salvador[c]			480	0.04	0.10
Guatemala[d]	1,800	80	1,880	0.16	0.23
Honduras[c]			160	0.01	0.04
Jamaica			1,098	0.09	0.46
Mexico[d]	8,355	8	8,363	0.71	0.11
Nicaragua[c]			300	0.03	0.09
Panama[d]	303	1	304	0.03	0.14
USA[d]	322,552	7,542	330,094	28.19	1.37
SOUTH AMERICA	22,618	1,178	27,666	2.36	
Argentina	5,015	1,076	6,091	0.52	0.20
Bolivia[c]			650	0.06	0.10
Brazil[d]	11,194	50	11,244	0.96	0.08
Chile[d]	733	8	741	0.06	0.06
Colombia[c]			2,900	0.25	0.10
Ecuador[d]	618	0	618	0.05	0.06
Paraguay[c]			320	0.03	0.08
Peru	832	0	832	0.07	0.04
Uruguay	330	0	330	0.03	0.11
Venezuela[d]	3,896	44	3,940	0.34	0.22
ASIA	163,637	3,913	214,109	18.24	
Bahrain[d]	98	10	108	0.01	0.26
China[c]			18,000	1.54	0.02
Cyprus[c]			500	0.04	0.74
India	4,600	700	5,300	0.45	0.01
Indonesia	2,489	5	2,494	0.21	0.01

Continued opposite

Table 1.6 Continued

Region/country	CFCs[a] (t a^{-1})	Halons[b] (t a^{-1})	Total (t a^{-1})	% of global consumption	Per capita consumption (kg a^{-1})
Iran[c,d]			4,400	0.38	0.10
Iraq[c]			1,590	0.14	0.10
Israel			5,000	0.43	1.16
Japan[d]	130,551	1,769	132,320	11.30	1.09
Jordan[d]	302	13	315	0.03	0.09
Korea	9,244	150	9,394	0.8	0.23
Kuwait	981	84	1,065	0.09	0.59
Malaysia[d]	2,327	270	2,597	0.22	0.16
Pakistan[c]			10,000	0.85	0.10
Philippines	2,439	0	2,439	0.21	0.04
Saudi Arabia			5,181	0.44	0.43
Singapore[d]	4,423	400	4,823	0.41	1.87
Sri Lanka[d]			258	0.02	0.02
Syria[d]	925	484	1,409	0.12	0.13
Thailand[d]	2,500	20	2,520	0.22	0.05
Turkey	2,758	8	2,766	0.24	0.05
United Arab Em.[d]			1,630	0.14	1.18
EUROPE	369,939	9,013	395,451	33.81	
EEC Members[d,e]	311,072	6,818	317,890	27.15	0.99
Austria[d]	7,800	200	8,000	0.68	1.06
Bulgaria[c]			2,000	0.17	0.22
Czechoslovakia[d]	6,996	24	7,020	0.60	0.45
Denmark[d]	5,656	146	5,802	0.50	1.13
Finland[d]	3,395	85	3,480	0.30	0.71
German Dem. Rep.[d]	15,515	223	15,738	1.34	0.95
Hungary[d]	3,061	2	3,063	0.26	0.29
Luxembourg[d]	170	4	174	0.01	0.48
Malta[d]			499	0.04	1.30
Netherlands[d]	8,675	445	9,120	0.78	0.63
Norway[d]	1,411	145	1,556	0.13	0.37
Poland[c,d]			10,000	0.85	0.27
Romania[c]			4,000	0.34	0.17
Spain[d]	20,145	600	20,745	1.77	0.54
Sweden[d]	5,140	201	5,341	0.46	0.64
Switzerland[d]	8,300	175	8,475	0.72	1.30
Yugoslavia	7,249	1,140	8,389	0.72	0.36
USSR[d]	121,784	5,100	126,884	10.84	0.45
OCEANIA	15,200	940	16,210	1.38	
Australia[d]	13,100	800	13,900	1.19	0.87
Fiji[c,d]			70	0.01	0.10
New Zealand[d]	2,100	140	2,240	0.19	0.69

a   Group I compounds: CFC-11; CFC-12; CFC-113; CFC-114 and CFC-115.
b   Group II compounds: Halon-1301; Halon-1211 and Halon-2402.
c   UNEP estimate.
d   Parties to the Montreal Protocol.
e   EEC member states (Belgium, Denmark, France, Germany, Fed. Rep., Greece, Ireland, Italy, Luxembourg, Netherlands, Portugal, Spain and the UK) reported consumption data collectively. Some member countries also provided national data; these data are included where available.

Data on consumption of CFCs (Group I) and halons (Group II) are based on offical reports submitted to the Ozone Secretariat, UNEP, under the terms of the Montreal Protocol. Out of all the countries, Parties and non-Parties, 56 countries and the EEC reported data and a further 19 countries reported zero or negligible consumption or that data are unavailable. UNEP estimates of total consumption still stand for 23 countries. For other countries, consumption is registered as 0.

Source:
Ozone Secretariat 1991 Secretariat for the Vienna Convention for the Protection of the Ozone Layer and its Montreal Protocol on Substances that Deplete the Ozone Layer, United Nations Environment Programme, Nairobi.

Table 1.7 Monthly mean atmospheric concentrations of nitrous oxide at NOAA/CMDL sites,1977–1989 (ppb by mole fraction in dry air)

Site/year	Jan.	Feb.	Mar.	Apr.	May	Jun.	Jul.	Aug.	Sep.	Oct.	Nov.	Dec.
POINT BARROW, ALASKA												
1977									298.5	306.0	302.1	305.0
1978	304.1	303.5	301.7	301.9	302.2	302.2	302.5	301.9	303.4	302.1	301.7	301.7
1979	301.2	301.5	302.1	302.6	303.0	302.9	304.1	303.9	304.0	302.6	301.7	303.1
1980	302.7	303.0	302.0	299.8	302.3	302.7	302.5	305.4	303.0	301.0	301.6	303.9
1981	302.9	302.5	303.1	304.0	303.7	304.0	303.8	306.7	303.2	302.8	302.5	303.3
1982	302.1	304.2	304.0	304.7	304.7	305.1	305.0	305.3	304.7	303.7	304.1	304.3
1983	304.2	305.0	304.4	303.7	303.5	304.2	306.1	305.1	302.7	304.6	303.7	304.0
1984	304.1	304.0	303.8	304.5	305.2	305.5	305.1	306.5	305.2	305.4	306.5	306.1
1985	307.9	305.7	305.1	305.6	306.9	306.0	303.3	304.5	305.6	305.8	305.5	305.1
1986	305.2	305.3	305.2	306.1	307.1	307.9	309.1	308.8	307.2	306.5	306.5	305.6
1987	306.8	307.0	307.3	306.6	309.1	308.8	307.8	308.0	308.0	308.2	307.0	308.3
1988	307.5	307.3	308.7	307.5	307.4	307.0	306.6	306.1	308.4	307.5	307.7	308.4
1989	308.5	309.7	307.8	309.2	309.4	308.6	310.9	309.2	309.0	308.4	310.4	309.4
NIWOT RIDGE, COLORADO												
1977									303.0	300.3	299.7	301.8
1978		302.3	301.9	302.8	302.6	302.2	301.7	302.0	302.9	302.5	302.9	303.6
1979	303.4	301.5	304.1	302.2	302.7	303.0	303.7	303.8	301.0	302.5	305.0	304.1
1980	307.0	304.4	303.3	303.8	303.7	305.8	302.8	306.2	304.7	302.9	304.4	303.1
1981	304.2	303.2	304.5	304.9	303.7	304.5	303.5	305.2	304.0	303.6	303.6	303.6
1982	304.7	303.4	303.6	306.1	305.6	305.8	306.8	307.9	305.8	304.9	306.3	305.9
1983	305.9	306.5	306.4	305.2	306.7	305.8	308.1	308.6	305.5	305.8	304.8	306.1
1984	305.2	305.0	304.1	305.2	306.0	307.7	308.5	309.0	307.1	307.0	307.3	307.8
1985	308.1	308.8	304.9	305.9	307.5	305.5	306.8	306.1	306.7	306.4	306.7	305.9
1986	306.0	306.0	306.0	306.4	306.4	306.5	308.0	307.0	306.8	307.4	306.8	307.0
1987	307.5	306.6	307.9	307.2	307.7	308.2	306.4	307.4	305.4	307.9	309.5	310.8
1988	309.6	308.0	309.8	306.7	307.5	307.0	309.6	309.8	307.6	308.7	309.7	308.8
1989	308.8	311.5	308.4	309.4	310.6	311.6	309.8	311.5	310.0	310.6	309.6	309.4
MAUNA LOA, HAWAII												
1977									304.0	301.4	300.4	302.8
1978	302.2	301.7	303.8	300.4	299.2	301.5	300.1	300.4	301.5	301.0	301.2	300.8
1979	301.4	303.1	301.4	302.5	302.3	301.6	302.4	301.7	302.1	305.1	302.6	303.5
1980	303.0	302.8	304.3	301.6	303.3	303.0	301.9	301.5	303.0	304.0	301.8	301.5
1981	301.8	302.1	303.4	304.7	303.5	305.0	303.7	304.0	303.2	304.6	303.8	303.0
1982	304.3	303.8	305.0	304.6	304.4	305.0	304.6	307.0	304.7	306.0	305.0	304.2
1983	304.2	304.9	305.1	304.8	305.2	304.2	303.9	305.2	305.4	304.6	304.2	304.9
1984	305.2	304.5	304.3	306.4	305.6	304.9	307.8	306.3	305.6	306.7	307.8	306.3
1985	307.5	307.4	306.4	305.8	305.1	306.9	304.8	304.9	307.1	307.6	307.7	307.6
1986	306.8	306.2	308.0	306.9	307.5	307.0	309.0	308.5	309.0	309.0	308.6	307.6
1987	307.2	307.7	308.2	305.8	308.3	307.1	307.3	307.9	306.5	307.7	307.2	307.9
1988	306.9	308.0	306.4	308.1	307.3	306.5	308.2	307.1	307.0	307.9	309.0	307.2
1989	308.1	309.1	308.6	309.7	308.8	309.4	308.4	309.3	309.7	309.7	308.4	309.5
CAPE MATATULA, AMERICAN SAMOA												
1977										298.0	297.5	
1978	297.2	298.9	300.1	299.7	301.0	300.1	299.6	298.9	299.1	298.9	300.1	299.5
1979	301.4	299.8	298.6	299.0	300.0	299.4	300.2	301.7	302.3	302.8	299.6	301.5

Continued opposite

Table 1.7 Continued

Site/year	Jan.	Feb.	Mar.	Apr.	May	Jun.	Jul.	Aug.	Sep.	Oct.	Nov.	Dec.
1980	302.0	302.8	300.5	298.1	298.8	300.5	299.2	298.5	300.2	300.0	296.6	297.2
1981	301.0	302.8	300.0	298.3	300.9	301.0	301.8	300.3	301.7	301.3	302.5	300.6
1982	299.2	299.1	300.0	302.5	302.9	303.1	301.8	302.1	303.3	302.6	302.6	302.3
1983	303.7	302.9	302.7	303.0	301.1	302.7	304.6	304.4	302.4	304.0	302.8	303.6
1984	304.1	303.9	306.3	303.6	303.8	303.8	303.7	303.8	304.2	304.3	303.2	304.8
1985	304.3	304.8	303.7	304.7	303.7	304.8	303.9	304.5	306.5	304.7	304.1	304.9
1986	302.8	305.4	304.5	304.8	304.1	305.6	305.1	306.2	305.5	304.8	305.9	305.1
1987	304.5	303.0	304.0	306.4		302.5	305.8	302.3	305.6	305.9	306.1	306.3
1988	306.9	306.4	304.2	304.7	304.9	305.2	304.8	305.8	305.2	305.3	307.0	308.0
1989	305.9	309.0	307.9	306.5	306.5	308.5	306.6	309.2	308.2	306.9	307.8	308.0
SOUTH POLE, ANTARCTICA												
1977						303.3		303.6		301.5			300.5
1978	299.1	302.3	302.4	298.6	301.4	301.9	301.7		299.5		300.5	300.9
1979	300.9	301.2								300.9	301.6	301.5
1980	302.1	302.6	301.8	301.5	303.2	300.0	299.1	304.3		300.1	301.1	300.2
1981	299.9	301.4	303.6	304.9	302.5	303.8	304.0	303.0	303.7	305.3	303.2	302.9
1982	304.0										302.8	303.5
1983	303.4					303.6			304.3			303.4
1984	303.5	303.8									304.7	305.7
1985	308.7										304.5	305.3
1986	306.5										305.8	304.9
1987	307.2										306.5	306.1
1988	307.0	307.2										306.1
1989	307.1											308.1

Air samples are collected on a weekly basis in a pair of 0.3 litre stainless steel flasks at the four NOAA/CMDL observatory sites and at Niwot Ridge, Colorado. Flasks are returned to the NOAA/CMDL laboratory in Boulder, Colorado for analysis for N_2O (and CFC-11, CFC-12) by electron-capture gas chromatography. Samples are dried prior to analysis. Measurements of N_2O are calibrated against the National Bureau of Standards SRM scale which is prepared using gravimetric techniques. Monthly mean values are calculated from the weekly flask data. Data are provisional, pending final calibrations.

Pairs of flask samples are generally only collected at the South Pole during the Antarctic summer (November–January).

Source:
Thompson, T. M. and Elkins, T. W. 1990 Personal communication, Climate Monitoring and Diagnostics Laboratory, National Oceanic and Atmospheric Administration, Boulder, Colorado, USA.

Table 1.8 Concentrations of sulphur dioxide at selected GEMS/Air sites, 1972–1989 (average mean annual values, µg m^{-3} and number of observations)

Region/country	City	Site	1972–73	1974–75	1976–77	1978–79	1980–81	1982–83	1984–85	1986–87	1988–89
NORTH AMERICA											
Canada	Hamilton	SR			50.5 (696)	31.5 (705)	35.5 (696)	28.0 (704)	42.0 (259)[a]	19.5 (690)	24.0 (360)[a]
		CCC			58.0 (726)	43.0 (725)	30.5 (727)	36.5 (716)	31.5 (702)		
	Montreal	SR			23.0 (720)	24.5 (638)	27.5 (557)	23.0 (629)	23.0 (597)	14.0 (299)[a]	
		CCC			56.5 (646)	46.5 (638)	43.5 (614)	24.0 (640)	25.0 (360)		
	Toronto	SI		36.0 (347)	24.5 (652)	19.5 (689)	16.0 (645)	7.0 (662)	12.0 (351)[a]	8.0 (704)	8.0 (684)
		SR			33.5 (695)	19.5 (674)	20.0 (695)	4.5 (346)	3.5 (339)		
	Vancouver	CCR	27.5 (414)	17.0 (548)	19.0 (330)	20.5 (502)	17.0 (614)	18.0 (335)[a]			
USA	New York City	SR				42.5 (156)	40.0 (728)	35.0 (716)	31.0 (725)	27.0 (361)[a]	
		CCR				90.5 (170)	70.5 (725)	64.5 (730)	61.0 (724)	52.0 (364)[a]	
		CCI				65.5 (60)	50.5 (726)	47.0 (723)	45.0 (729)	40.0 (350)[a]	
SOUTH AMERICA											
Brazil	São Paulo	CCR			116.5 (729)	142.0 (728)	120.0 (729)	97.0 (728)	62.0 (727)	54.5 (120)	55.0 (61)[a]
		CCM			121.0 (731)	137.5 (730)	127.0 (723)	99.0 (723)	60.0 (725)	73.0 (120)	50.0 (61)[a]
Chile	Santiago	CCC			67.0 (665)	74.0 (574)	67.5 (659)	89.5 (628)	79.5 (691)		
		CCR			45.5 (619)	53.5 (591)	37.0 (587)	43.5 (679)	46.0 (360)[a]		
Venezuela	Caracas	CCC			20.5 (528)	27.5 (525)	29.5 (397)	34.0 (500)	27.0 (471)	21.0 (458)	21.0 (270)[a]
ASIA											
China	Beijing	SI					38.0 (104)[a]	60.5 (365)	79.0 (76)[a]	61.5 (297)	53.5 (336)
		CCC					66.0 (113)[a]	101.5 (374)	130.0 (86)[a]	112.5 (326)	103.0 (351)
		SR					6.0 (93)[a]	15.0 (349)	27.0 (80)[a]	28.5 (324)	29.5 (326)
		CCR					98.0 (110)[a]	147.0 (368)	161.0 (78)[a]	125.0 (293)	114.5 (330)
	Guangzhou	SR					140.0 (93)[a]	101.5 (326)	40.0 (324)	11.0 (345)	20.5 (350)
		CCR					66.0 (97)[a]	56.0 (345)	123.5 (337)	104.5 (338)	99.0 (346)
		CCC					117.0 (76)[a]	93.5 (349)	67.5 (336)	59.5 (345)	58.5 (353)
		CCI					12.0 (55)[a]	14.5 (333)	113.0 (317)	122.0 (333)	135.5 (354)
	Shanghai	CCI					23.0 (88)[a]	52.5 (341)	49.0 (86)[a]	40.5 (357)	55.5 (338)
		CCR					52.0 (87)[a]	69.0 (354)	84.5 (353)	98.0 (351)	104.0 (294)
		CCC					65.0 (85)[a]	57.5 (355)	51.0 (358)	77.5 (358)	69.0 (343)

Continued below

Table 1.8 Continued

Region/country	City	Site	1972–73	1974–75	1976–77	1978–79	1980–81	1982–83	1984–85	1986–87	1988–89
	Shenyang	CCR					29.0 (73)[a]	130.5 (288)	135.0 (288)	115.5 (290)	70.0 (288)
		CCI					136.0 (72)[a]	238.5 (288)	320.0 (288)	223.0 (288)	207.5 (288)
		CCC					72.0 (72)[a]	130.5 (288)	58.0 (72)[a]	134.0 (288)	101.5 (288)
		SR					27.0 (72)[a]	46.0 (287)	17.0 (72)[a]	49.0 (288)	29.0 (276)
	Xian	SR					22.0 (98)[a]	30.0 (383)	29.5 (313)	31.0 (276)	37.0 (252)
		CCR					108.0 (119)[a]	118.0 (396)	100.5 (324)	118.0 (289)	97.5 (288)
		CCC					160.0 (120)[a]	104.5 (397)	120.5 (323)	92.5 (288)	95.5 (286)
		SI					46.0 (117)[a]	66.5 (394)	52.0 (321)	66.5 (287)	79.5 (288)
Hong Kong	Hong Kong	CCC		14.0 (357)[a]	7.0 (720)	27.5 (722)	40.0 (731)	46.0 (716)	32.0 (208)[a]		
		SI		100.0 (364)[a]	33.0 (730)	60.5 (730)	85.5 (731)	31.5 (714)	15.0 (208)[a]		
Iran	Tehran	CCC			74.0 (124)	47.0 (147)	169.5 (172)	145.5 (122)	97.5 (115)	90.0 (49)	211.0 (42)
		SI			82.5 (67)	41.5 (130)	137.5 (154)	161.5 (135)	87.5 (94)	120.5 (31)	149.0 (28)
		SR			85.5 (65)	46.0 (133)	140.0 (160)	111.0 (125)	47.5 (98)	45.5 (33)	81.5 (30)
Israel	Tel Aviv	CCC	24.0 (337)[a]	29.5 (664)	25.5 (419)	22.0 (324)	4.0 (433)	9.5 (164)	53.0 (179)[a]		
Japan	Osaka	CCC		73.0 (273)[a]	72.0 (707)	49.0 (715)	34.5 (724)	31.0 (724)	27.0 (724)	27.5 (720)	27.0 (366)[a]
		CCI		74.0 (365)[a]	57.5 (725)	39.5 (718)	35.5 (719)	31.0 (725)	29.5 (731)	28.5 (730)	25.0 (366)[a]
		SR		63.0 (330)[a]	57.5 (706)	45.5 (729)	32.0 (730)	27.5 (729)	25.5 (731)	24.5 (729)	24.0 (363)[a]
		CCI		62.0 (362)[a]	55.0 (343)[a]	46.0 (705)	41.0 (731)	33.0 (729)	32.5 (730)	34.0 (728)	34.0 (366)[a]
	Tokyo	CCC	60.0 (729)	66.5 (726)	67.5 (724)	55.0 (727)	42.0 (719)	25.5 (719)	24.0 (731)	20.5 (730)	19.0 (360)[a]
		SR	47.5 (723)	47.0 (707)	50.0 (730)	46.5 (730)	40.0 (722)	37.0 (726)	31.0 (727)	21.5 (729)	18.0 (366)[a]
		CCI	88.5 (723)	78.0 (722)	79.5 (731)	64.5 (717)	48.5 (724)	31.0 (724)	31.0 (731)	29.5 (730)	26.0 (366)[a]
Thailand	Bangkok	SR					14.0 (155)	18.0 (310)	14.0 (166)	14.5 (121)	13.0 (190)
EUROPE											
Belgium	Brussels	CCC	185.0 (341)	97.0 (679)	101.5 (583)	93.5 (626)	67.5 (706)	70.5 (655)	36.5 (644)	32.0 (323)[a]	
		SR	124.5 (380)	86.0 (560)	77.0 (661)	72.0 (598)	59.5 (689)	43.0 (695)	37.5 (686)	43.0 (323)[a]	
		SI	136.0 (322)	101.0 (652)	86.5 (612)	72.0 (647)	51.5 (715)	40.0 (615)	46.0 (686)	38.0 (355)[a]	
		CCC			104.0 (422)	105.5 (681)	72.5 (727)	45.5 (722)			
Finland	Helsinki	CCC				25.0 (709)	20.5 (690)	28.0 (56)[a]		29.0 (354)[a]	30.0 (683)
Germany, Fed. Rep.	Frankfurt	SI	87.0 (316)[a]	81.5 (592)	66.5 (326)	49.0 (424)	35.5 (378)	40.0 (245)[a]	59.5 (642)	54.5 (644)	26.0 (421)
		CCC	107.0 (321)[a]	104.5 (641)	85.5 (613)	79.5 (630)	70.5 (625)	58.5 (582)			
Greece	Athens	SI				51.5 (354)	49.5 (262)	30.5 (569)	26.0 (362)	27.0 (130)[a]	
		CCC				48.0 (540)	44.5 (539)	58.0 (397)	33.0 (614)	35.0 (122)[a]	

Continued over

Table 1.8 Continued

Region/country	City	Site	1972–73	1974–75	1976–77	1978–79	1980–81	1982–83	1984–85	1986–87	1988–89
Ireland	Dublin	CCR			49.0 (364)a	49.5 (729)	65.5 (722)	47.0 (725)	40.0 (726)	49.0 (671)	28.5 (704)
		CCI			49.0 (364)a	38.5 (727)	41.5 (727)	42.5 (712)	22.5 (543)	45.0 (656)	23.0 (720)
		SR			26.0 (347)a	26.0 (726)	37.0 (725)	39.0 (704)	28.0 (696)	36.5 (620)	18.0 (578)
Netherlands	Amsterdam	CCC	75.0 (366)	38.0 (684)	34.0 (659)	39.0 (646)	28.0 (636)	26.5 (595)	21.5 (644)	30.0 (87)a	
		SI	79.0 (369)	34.5 (697)	32.0 (683)	35.5 (645)	27.0 (600)	26.5 (613)	22.0 (596)	33.0 (85)a	
Poland	Warsaw	CCR				31.0 (321)	31.5 (305)	29.0 (332)	37.5 (397)	11.5 (342)	19.5 (409)
		CCI				40.5 (358)	39.0 (367)	46.5 (388)	45.5 (544)	16.0 (445)	29.5 (527)
		CCC				41.5 (371)	46.0 (367)	34.5 (422)	42.5 (538)	14.0 (516)	23.5 (574)
	Wroclaw	CCC				45.5 (588)	39.0 (577)	40.5 (583)	62.5 (565)	35.0 (488)	53.0 (564)
		CCI				32.0 (575)	27.5 (583)	34.5 (563)	48.5 (547)	26.0 (445)	34.5 (542)
		CCR				29.0 (555)	31.5 (558)	31.0 (527)	44.0 (522)	32.0 (446)	40.0 (506)
Spain	Madrid	CCC	192.0 (351)	149.5 (588)	68.0 (139)	80.0 (369)	111.5 (578)	80.5 (566)	47.5 (499)	50.5 (667)	31.5 (663)
		SR	86.5 (379)	61.5 (635)	48.5 (645)	45.0 (482)	46.0 (653)	33.5 (654)	27.5 (582)	25.5 (680)	17.5 (658)
		CCI	193.0 (320)a	155.5 (578)	91.5 (501)	81.5 (395)	113.5 (310)	91.0 (208)a			
UK	Glasgow	CCC	175.0 (220)a	133.0 (606)	94.0 (365)a	84.0 (359)a	75.5 (730)	57.0 (730)	49.5 (731)		
		CCI	172.0 (162)a	91.0 (339)	86.0 (357)a	76.5 (729)	64.5 (731)	40.5 (730)	46.0 (687)		
	London	CCC	235.0 (366)	151.0 (708)	114.0 (727)	93.0 (730)	55.0 (730)	55.0 (724)	42.5 (673)		
		SI	73.5 (354)	53.5 (711)	78.0 (279)	66.0 (661)	56.5 (678)	35.0 (719)	33.5 (727)		
Yugoslavia	Zagreb	CCC	85.5 (357)	69.0 (720)	128.5 (727)	96.0 (668)	87.5 (671)	85.0 (716)	104.5 (727)	110.0 (703)	82.5 (694)
		SR			48.5 (721)	37.5 (724)	41.5 (730)	42.5 (712)	64.5 (694)	63.0 (725)	44.0 (637)
		CCI			64.5 (721)	47.0 (730)	41.5 (731)	53.0 (705)	75.0 (721)	73.0 (679)	102.0 (698)
OCEANIA											
Australia	Melbourne	CCC		16.0 (292)a	16.0 (651)	7.5 (562)	7.5 (585)	5.0 (432)	10.0 (157)a		
	Sydney	SI		31.0 (340)a	28.5 (595)	24.0 (658)	35.0 (692)	21.5 (725)	13.0 (697)		
New Zealand	Auckland	SI		20.0 (78)a	20.0 (498)	23.5 (659)	20.5 (698)	7.5 (716)	3.0 (583)	3.0 (674)	3.0 (682)
		CCC		16.0 (280)a	12.0 (700)	20.0 (633)	11.0 (710)	3.5 (702)			
	Christchurch	SR			30.0 (319)	18.5 (653)	21.0 (646)	18.5 (660)	14.5 (679)	20.5 (442)	
		SI				27.5 (563)	35.5 (674)	45.0 (472)	43.0 (347)	43.0 (97)a	
		SC			18.0 (72)a	28.5 (672)	28.0 (646)	12.5 (665)	10.0 (629)	16.0 (193)a	

a Based on one year of measurements only.

CCC = City Centre Commercial.
CCI = City Centre Industrial.
CCM = City Centre Mobile.
CCR = City Centre Residential.
SI = Suburban Industrial.
SR = Suburban Residential.

Annual mean concentrations of SO_2 are based on data for two years, except where indicated. The total number of observations made during each two-year period is given in parentheses in order to provide an indication of the level of completeness of the data. Although many sites make observations on a daily basis, at some locations measurements are made less frequently, e.g., once every six days. Thus the use of the number of observations to assess data completeness must be viewed with some caution.

Station data presented above have been extracted from the GEMS/Air data base; stations reporting less than five two-year values during the 1972–1989 period have been excluded.

Source:
WHO 1990 Personal communication, Division of Environmental Health, World Health Organization, Geneva, Switzerland.

Table 1.9 Emissions of sulphur dioxide from man-made sources in selected countries, 1970–1989 (10^3 t a^{-1} as SO_2)

Region/country	1970	1975	1980	1981	1982	1983	1984	1985	1986	1987	1988	1989	Source(s)
NORTH AMERICA													
Canada	6,678	5,322[a]	4,650	4,328	3,567	3,608	3,938	3,670					1
USA	28,200	26,030	23,900	23,500	22,000	21,500	22,100	21,600	21,200		20,700		1,2,3
ASIA													
China				14,210	13,270	12,570				14,120			4,5
Israel			268				239	213	223	246	241		6
Japan		1,682[b]	1,259			1,079							1
Malaysia										268	236		7
Turkey							276	322	354	398			8
EUROPE													
Austria			370			218	182	178		136	114		8
Belgium			828	712	694	560	500	452	474	414			8
Czechoslovakia			3,100					3,150	3,020	2,960	2,800		8
Denmark	574	418	452	363	368	312	296	339	278	248	241		1,8
Finland	515	535	584	536	488	374	368	382	332	328	302		8,9
France			3,338	2,588	2,490	2,094	1,866	1,470	1,342	1,288	1,216	1,272	8
German Dem. Rep			4,264		4,551		5,039	5,339	5,358	5,559	5,208		10
Germany, Fed. Rep.	3,750	3,350	3,200	3,050	2,850	2,700	2,650	2,450	2,300		1,300		3,11
Hungary			1,632				1,460	1,404	1,370	1,292	1,218	1,084	8
Ireland		186	217	189	155	140	129	138		160	148		8
Italy			3,800			3,150	2,656	2,504	2,370	2,410			8
Netherlands	772	386	465	454	395	331	289	260	276	282	278	254	1,8
Norway			142	128	112	104	96	98	90	76	66	66	8
Poland			4,100					4,300	4,200	4,200	4,180	3,910	8
Portugal	116	178	266			305		198	234	218	204		8
Spain			3,250					2,877					12
Sweden	930	690	502	409	348	289	275	273	253	225	199		1,13
Switzerland	125	109	126				95		63				1,8
UK	6,330	5,310	4,850	4,390	4,160	3,820	3,670	3,680	3,860	3,860	3,664	3,552	8,14
Yugoslavia			1,300	1,300	1,300	1,400	1,450	1,500	1,500	1,550	1,600	1,650	8
USSR				19,530	19,830	20,260	19,740	19,550	18,680	18,600	17,650		15

Continued over

Table 1.9 Continued

a 1976.
b 1977.

Methods for estimating emissions vary between countries. Trends observed within each country may be more reliable than comparisons between countries.

Sources:

1 OECD 1989 *OECD Environmental Data Compendium 1989*, Organisation for Economic Co-operation and Development, Paris.

2 EPA 1988 *National Air Quality and Emissions Trends Report 1986*, Report No. EPA 450/4-88-001, United States Environmental Protection Agency, Research Triangle Park.

3 French, H. F. 1990 *Green Revolutions: Environmental Reconstruction in Eastern Europe and the Soviet Union*, Worldwatch Paper 99, Worldwatch Institute, Washington DC.

4 State Statistical Bureau 1985 *Materials on Chinese Social Statistics*, Zhongguo Tongi Chubanshe, Beijing.

5 State Statistical Bureau 1988 *China Statistical Yearbook 1988*, International Centre for the Advancement of Science and Technology Ltd, Hong Kong and China Statistical Information and Consultancy Service Centre, Beijing.

6 Central Bureau of Statistics 1989 *Statistical Abstract of Israel 1989*, No. 40, Central Bureau of Statistics, Jerusalem.

7 DOE 1989 *Environmental Quality Report 1988*, Department of the Environment, Ministry of Science, Technology and the Environment, Kuala Lumpur.

8 Iversen,T., Halvorsen, N. E., Saltbones, J. and Sandnes, H. 1990 *Calculated Budgets for Airborne Sulphur and Nitrogen in Europe*, EMEP/MSC-W Report 2/90, The Norwegian Meteorological Institute, Oslo.

9 Central Statistical Office 1987 *Environment Statistics 1987*, Central Statistical Office of Finland, Helsinki (in Finnish with English titles).

10 Institut fur Umweltschutz 1990 *Umweltbericht der DDR*, Verlag Visuell, Berlin (in German).

11 Umweltbundesamt 1989 *Daten zur Umwelt 1988/89*, Erich Schmidt Verlag, Berlin (in German).

12 UN-ECE 1987 *Environment Statistics in Europe and North America: An Experimental Compendium*, United Nations, New York.

13 SCB 1990 *Utsläpp till luft i Sverige av Svaveldioxid (SO_2), Kväveoxider (NO_x) och Koldioxid (CO_2) 1988*, Statistiska Centralbyrån, Stockholm (in Swedish with English titles).

14 Munday, P. K. 1989 *UK Emissions of Air Pollutants 1970–1988*, Warren Spring Laboratory, Department of Trade and Industry, Stevenage.

15 Rovinsky, F. Ya. 1990 Personal communication, Natural Environment and Climate Monitoring Laboratory, LAM, Moscow.

Table 1.10 Emissions of nitrogen oxides from man-made sources in selected countries, 1970–1989 (10^3 t a^{-1} as NO_2)

Region/country	1970	1975	1980	1981	1982	1983	1984	1985	1986	1987	1988	1989	Source(s)
NORTH AMERICA													
Canada	1,364	1,756[a]	1,942	1,886	1,881	1,863	1,854	1,940					1
USA	18,100	19,100	20,300	20,300	19,500	19,100	19,700	19,700	19,300		19,800		1,2,3
ASIA													
China				4,401	4,138								4
Israel		86	74				104	106	111	123	131		6
Japan		1,550[b]	1,339			1,416							1
Malaysia										96	74		7
EUROPE													
Austria								230		218	212		8
Belgium			317		297	271		281	292	297			8
Czechoslovakia		182		212				1,127	1,060	965	950		8
Denmark			245		228	223	230	258	266	262	249		8
Finland								251	256	270	276		8
France								1,615	1,618	1,605	1,655	1,761	8
German Dem. Rep									955	1,001	1,008	1,005	8
Germany, Fed. Rep.	2,350	2,550	2,950	2,850	2,850	2,850	2,950	2,950	3,000	2,900	2,850	2,720	3,8,11
Hungary								262	268	276	259	249	8
Ireland		60	71	68	68	67	67	68		77	77		1,8
Italy								1,595	1,607	1,700			8
Netherlands	430	447	553	547	537	533	550	544		559	552	552	1,8
Norway		192	203	196	198	209	226	224	244	232	227	226	1,8
Poland								1,500	1,530	1,520	1,550	1,480	8
Portugal								96	110	116	122		8
Spain								950					8
Sweden	302	310	332	327	321	307	314	327	330	325	316		13
Switzerland								214	187		194	189	8
UK	2,400	2,370	2,420	2,330	2,320	2,230	2,160	2,280	2,350	2,430	2,480	2,513	8,14
Yugoslavia								400	420	440	480		8
USSR				5,290	5,790	5,880	5,650	5,680	6,080	6,260	6,290		15

a 1976.
b 1977.

Methods for estimating emissions vary between countries. Trends observed within each country may be more reliable than comparisons between countries.

Sources:
See Table 1.9.

Source category	As	Cd	Cr	Cu	Hg	Ni	Pb	Zn
MAN-MADE SOURCES	12,000–25,630	3,100–12,040	7,340–53,610	19,860–50,870	910–6,200	24,150–87,150	288,700–376,000	70,250–193,500
Median value	18,820	7,570	30,480	35,370	3,560	55,650	332,350	131,880
Coal combustion								
Power plants	232–1,550	77–387	1,240–7,750	930–3,100	155–542	1,395–9,300	775–4,650	1,085–7,750
Industry and domestic	198–1,980	99–495	1,680–11,880	1,390–4,950	495–2,970	1,980–14,850	990–9,900	1,485–11,880
Oil combustion								
Power plants	5.8–29	23–174	87–580	348–2,320	–	3,840–14,500	232–1,740	174–1,280
Industry and domestic	7.2–72	18–72	358–1,790	179–1,070	–	7,160–28,640	716–2,150	358–2,506
Pyrometallurgical non-ferrous metal production								
Mining	40–80	0.6–3	–	160–800	–	800	1,700–3,400	310–620
Pb production	780–1,560	39–195	–	234–312	7.8–16	331	11,700–31,200	195–468
Cu and Ni production	8,500–12,750	1,700–3,400	–	14,450–30,600	37–207	7,650	11,050–22,100	4,250–8,500
Zn and Cd production	230–690	920–4,600	–	230–690	–	–	5,520–11,500	46,000–82,800
Secondary non-ferrous metal production	–	2.3–3.6	–	55–165	–	–	90–1,440	270–1,440
Steel and iron manufacturing	355–2,480	28–284	2,840–28,400	142–2,840	–	36–7,100	1,065–14,200	7,100–31,950
Refuse incineration								
Municipal refuse[a]	154–392	56–1,400	98–980	980–1,960	140–2,100	98–420	1,400–2,800	2,800–8,400
Sewage sludge[b]	15–60	3–36	150–450	30–180	15–60	30–180	240–300	150–450
Phosphate fertilizers	–	68–274	–	137–685	–	137–685	55–274	1,370–6,850
Cement production	178–890	8.9–534	890–1,780	–	–	89–890	18–14,240	1,780–17,800
Wood combustion	60–300	60–180	–	600–1,200	60–300	600–1,800	1,200–3,000	–
Mobile sources	–	–	–	–	–	–	248,030[c]	–
Miscellaneous	1,250–2,800	–	–	–	–	–	3,900–5,100	1,724–4,783
NATURAL SOURCES	860–23,000	150–2,600	4,500–83,000	2,300–54,000	100–4,900	3,000–57,000	970–23,000	4,000–86,000
Median value	12,000	1,300	44,000	28,000	2,500	30,000	12,000	45,000
TOTAL	13,000–49,000	3,200–15,000	12,000–137,000	22,000–105,000	1,000–11,000	27,000–144,000	290,000–399,000	74,000–280,000
Median value	31,000	8,900	74,000	63,000	6,100	86,000	344,000	177,000

a It is assumed that 25 per cent of municipal refuse generated annually is incinerated.

b It is assumed that 10 per cent of the estimated global production of sewage sludge (30×10^6 t a^{-1}) is incinerated; a further 20 per cent is dumped or discharged to water bodies with the remainder deposited on land.

c It is assumed that 45 per cent of total leaded petrol in the world has a Pb content of 0.15 g l^{-1}, the remaining 55 per cent is assumed to contain 0.40 g l^{-1}.

Sources:
Niragu, J. O. 1989 A global assessment of natural sources of atmospheric trace metals. Nature (London) 338, 47–49.
Niragu, J. O. and Pacyna, J. M. 1988 Quantitative assessment of worldwide contamination of air, water and soils by trace metals. Nature (London) 333, 134–139.

Atmospheric Deposition

Increases in anthropogenic emissions of acidic pollutant gases, including sulphur dioxide (SO_2) and the nitrogen oxides (NO_x), have led to concomitant increases in atmospheric deposition fluxes of these species. The resultant acidification of terrestrial ecosystems has been most noticeable in the acid-sensitive regions of North America and Europe. Atmospheric deposition is also a significant source of many trace metals to terrestrial ecosystems; trace metals such as cadmium (Cd), mercury (Hg) and lead (Pb), which are toxic at relatively low levels, are known to be accumulating in the biosphere.

Acidic Species

Globally, emissions of acid deposition precursor gases have increased substantially since the advent of industrial activity. Man-made emissions of SO_2, derived largely from fossil fuel combustion sources, are now similar in magnitude to those from natural sources (biogenic sources and volcanic activity) and total some 80×10^6 t S a^{-1}. Similarly, global emissions of NO_x are divided equally between anthropogenic (fossil fuel combustion and biomass burning) and natural sources (microbial sources and lightning). Current estimates for global NO_x emissions are in the range 55–60×10^6 t N a^{-1} (WMO/UNEP, 1990). Sulphur and nitrogen oxides are transported by prevailing winds for distances up to 1,000 km from their original source before returning to the earth's surface as either wet or dry deposition.

Monitoring networks for the measurement of precipitation chemistry and wet deposition have been established on global, regional and national scales. Sites are generally located in remote or rural areas which are, as far as possible, unaffected by local pollution sources. In the absence of a suitable measurement technique, dry deposition is not widely monitored on a systematic basis.

World-wide monitoring of precipitation chemistry has clearly established that extensive areas of North America and Europe currently receive fluxes of sulphur and nitrogen up to 10 times the estimated natural flux (Rodhe et al., 1988). Adverse effects on the environment, including acidification of fresh waters and terrestrial ecosystems, are well documented in these regions. At the present time, regional scale acidification due to man-made emissions of sulphur and nitrogen is not considered to be a significant problem in other world regions. Although rainfall pH appears to be consistently low (pH 4.5–5.0) in many tropical forest regions, it is likely that naturally occurring organic acids are largely responsible for the low pH observed in such areas. Elsewhere, particularly in mid-continental regions of northern China and India, rainfall acidity is well-buffered by ammonia and alkaline soil dusts. Here, the pH of rainfall is typically above 6.0. Nevertheless, there are indications that certain tropical regions, for example, southern China, south-western India, south-

eastern Brazil and northern Venezuela, may experience problems relating to acidification in the future if current trends in urbanization and industrialization continue into the 21st century (Rodhe et al., 1988).

Measurement of precipitation chemistry on a global scale is conducted as part of the work of the WMO's Background Air Pollution Monitoring Network (BAPMoN). First established in 1969, the BAPMoN network currently comprises some 196 stations, 152 of which have the capability for carrying out sampling for measurements of precipitation chemistry. The US Environmental Protection Agency (EPA) in North Carolina acts as the data centre for the BAPMoN network; here station data are processed, validated and stored in computerized form. Previous editions of the 'UNEP Environmental Data Report' have presented summary data obtained from BAPMoN stations (UNEP 1987, 1989).

Regional-scale precipitation chemistry networks are now well established in both North America and Europe. Within the USA and Canada, precipitation chemistry monitoring is conducted by five networks which submit their data to a single Acid Deposition System (ADS) data base, maintained at the US EPA's Pacific Northwest National Laboratory. Raw daily measurements are processed and validated prior to publication in the form of seasonal and annual data summaries (Olsen et al., 1990). In the USA, research into all aspects of acid deposition is co-ordinated by the National Acid Precipitation Assessment Program (NAPAP); details of a range of monitoring activities were provided in the previous edition of this report (UNEP, 1989).

Monitoring and assessment of regional air pollution in the European region is the remit of the UN-ECE Co-operative Programme for Monitoring and Evaluation of Long-range Transmission of Air Pollution in Europe (EMEP). First established in 1977, as a joint UN-ECE/WMO/UNEP venture, the EMEP programme is now in its fifth phase. The first phase of EMEP covered the period 1978–1980, the second 1981–1983, the third 1984–1986 and the fourth phase 1987–1989. Discussion of the results of the fourth phase of the EMEP programme forms the focus of the section on atmospheric deposition in this edition of the 'UNEP Environmental Data Report'. Future editions of this report will describe acidic deposition monitoring activities and related issues in other world regions.

The activities of EMEP have two principal components: a chemical component and a meteorological component. The former is responsible for the co-ordination of routine measurements of air and precipitation quality at a network of 102 sites located throughout the European region. The range of parameters measured at EMEP sites include, in air, gaseous SO_2, nitrogen dioxide (NO_2), ozone (O_3) and nitric acid (HNO_3) and particulate sulphate (SO_4^{2-}), nitrate (NO_3^-), nitric acid (HNO_3) and ammonium (NH_4^+). Parameters measured in precipitation include pH, conductivity, the major cations – ammonium (NH_4^+), sodium (Na^+), potassium (K^+), magnesium (Mg^{2+}) and calcium

(Ca^{2+}) – and the major anions – SO_4^{2-}, NO_3^- and chloride (Cl^-).

In the initial stages of the EMEP programme, monitoring was limited to the sulphur oxides in air and precipitation. However, in more recent years monitoring capabilities of participating stations, which are generally selected from existing national networks, have expanded. During the fourth phase of EMEP, 79 stations reported both precipitation and air quality data, 10 provided only precipitation chemistry data and 13 stations recorded only air data. During the lifetime of the programme, new stations have been added to the network and others relocated. A number of EMEP stations are also BAPMoN stations.

Stations participating in the EMEP network submit air quality and precipitation chemistry data to the Chemical Co-ordinating Centre (CCC) at the Norwegian Institute for Air Research (NILU) for processing and archiving. Routine data quality assurance exercises are also co-ordinated by the CCC in order to ensure maximum comparability of results reported by participating stations.

Data summaries are routinely prepared by the CCC and published as annual reports. An analysis of data compiled during the five-year period 1983–1987 has also been prepared (Hanssen et al., 1990). Five-year average volume weighted arithmetic mean, minimum and maximum concentrations of SO_4^{2-} and NO_3^- in precipitation at selected EMEP sites are given in Table 1.12. Average annual mean wet deposition rates of SO_4^{2-} and NO_3^- are also provided. Earlier data have been presented in previous editions of this report (UNEP 1987, 1989).

Results show that much of central and eastern Europe receives rainfall containing SO_4^{2-} in excess of 1 mg S l^{-1}. The highest concentrations, over 1.5–2.0 mg S l^{-1}, are recorded in eastern Europe. However, in 1983–1987 the size of the area receiving precipitation with SO_4^{2-} concentrations over 1.5 mg S l^{-1} was reduced compared with that for the period 1978–1982 (Hanssen et al., 1990).

Nitrate in precipitation is greatest (i.e., in excess of 0.7 mg N l^{-1}) over northern Poland, eastern Germany and the Baltic Sea. Concentrations of NH_4^+ in precipitation, not tabulated here, exhibit two maxima; concentrations exceed 1.0 mg N l^{-1} in rainfall over parts of France, Belgium and the Netherlands and also over an area in eastern Europe (the Poland-Czechoslovakia-USSR border).

Some EMEP stations have unbroken records of precipitation chemistry measurements for 10 years or more. Trends in SO_4^{2-} and NO_3^- concentrations in precipitation have been assessed at those stations having continuous

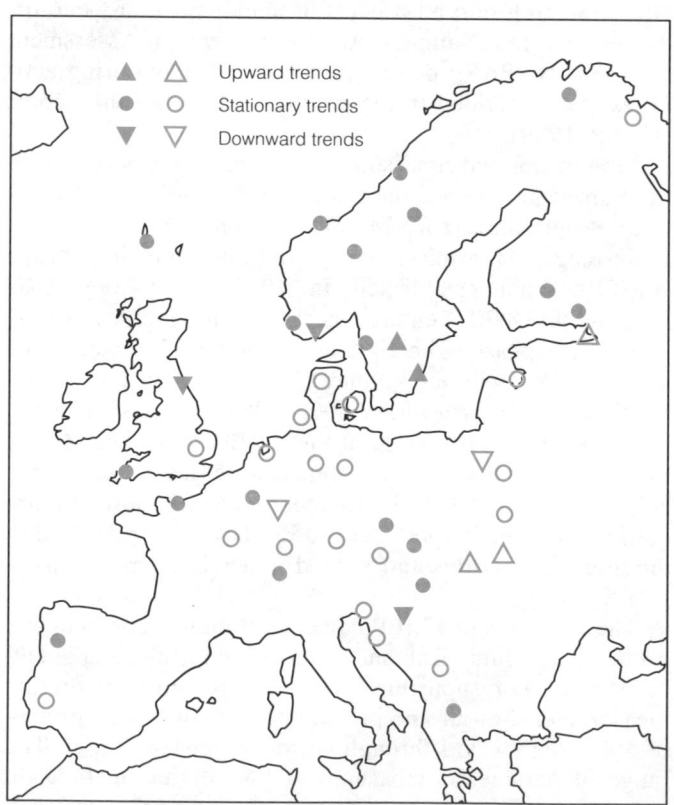

Figure 1.11 Trends in SO_4^{2-} concentrations in precipitation, 1979–1988 (trends shown as filled symbols are based on records of a minimum of eight years in length; trends shown by open symbols are based on slighter shorter records, a minimum of six years)
Source: adapted from Hannsen et al., 1990

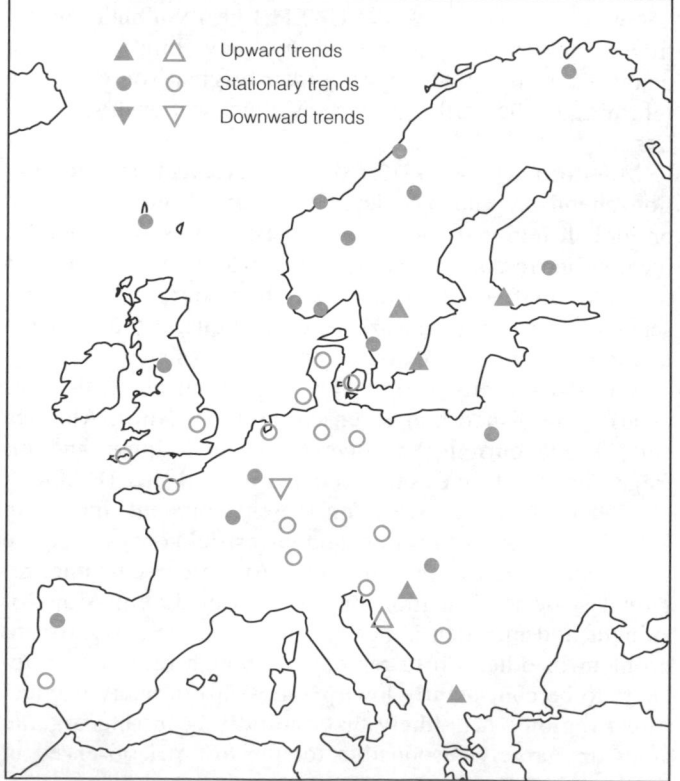

Figure 1.12 Trends in NO_3^- concentrations in precipitation, 1979–1988 (trends shown as filled symbols are based on records of a minimum of eight years in length; trends shown by open symbols are based on slighter shorter records, a minimum of six years)
Source: adapted from Hannsen et al., 1990

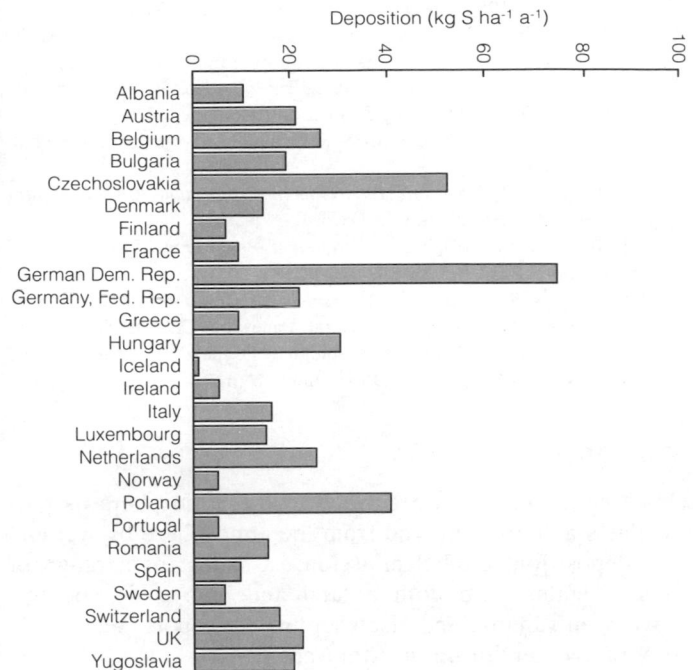

Figure 1.13 Annual deposition of sulphur in Europe, 1988
Source: data from Table 1.13

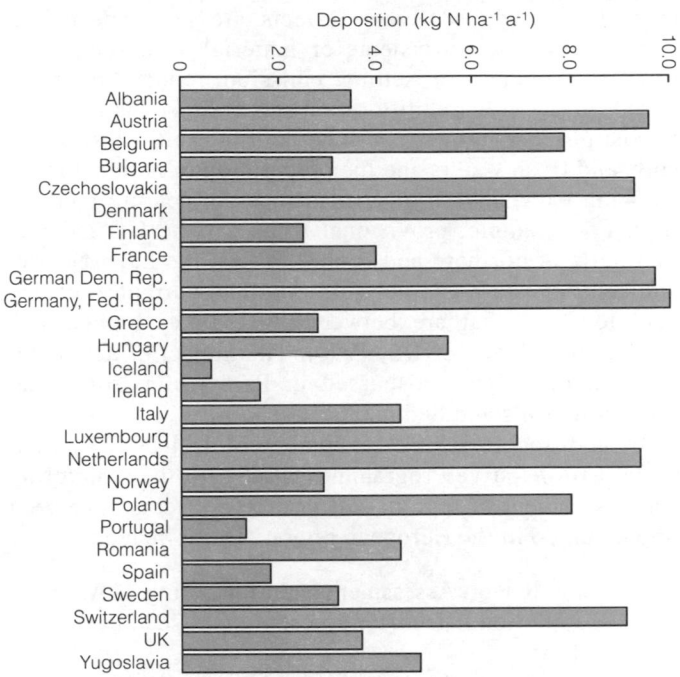

Figure 1.14 Annual deposition of oxidized nitrogen in Europe, 1988
Source: data from Table 1.14

records for a minimum length of six years. Figure 1.11 shows that at most locations there are no significant trends in SO_4^{2-} in precipitation. Figure 1.12 indicates a similar situation for NO_3^- in precipitation.

In addition to air quality and precipitation chemistry monitoring, the WMO under the EMEP programme co-ordinates two Meteorological Synthesizing Centres, MSC-West (in Norway) and MSC-East (in Moscow). Dispersion models, which simulate the emission and deposition of acidic components in the European region, have been developed by both MSC-W and MSC-E. The MSC-W Langrangian model is receptor-oriented and calculates the concentration and deposition (by source country or area) for 10 chemical species including SO_2, NO, NO_2, HNO_3, particulate SO_4^{2-} and particulate NO_3^-. Model validation is provided by means of comparison of calculated concentrations of SO_2 and particulate SO_4^{2-} in air with observations made by the EMEP CCC. A more detailed description of the MSC-W model and results for 1988 and 1989 are given by Iversen et al. (1990).

Since publication of the second edition of this report, significant improvements have been made in the MSC-W model. The area covered by the model has been extended to cover neighbouring sea areas. Emissions from sea areas, primarily from ships and biogenic sources (as dimethylsulphide), have been included in the model computations. Additional modifications include a more realistic representation of precipitation scavenging processes and background concentrations of sulphur and nitrogen species (Sandnes, 1990). Modelled sulphur deposition budgets presented in the previous edition of this report for earlier

years (1980, 1983 and 1985) were based on the older version of the model.

As input, the model requires data on emissions of sulphur and nitrogen species from both natural and man-made sources, background concentrations of atmospheric constituents and basic meteorological data. The latter are provided by the Norwegian Meteorological Institute. As far as possible, the model calculations use official emission estimates for man-made SO_2, NO_x and NH_3 that are submitted by participating countries to the UN-ECE under the terms of the 1985 and 1988 Protocols to the 1979 Convention on Long-range Transboundary Air Pollution (see Part 10: International Co-operation). In instances where official data are not available, emissions are estimated by EMEP. The majority of the national data for NH_3 emissions are based on the estimates of Buijsman et al. (1987) as very few countries submit official emissions data.

Emissions and model calculations for sulphur deposition in 1988 are presented in Table 1.13. Levels of sulphur deposition within the European region vary from less than 10 kg S ha^{-1} a^{-1} in Scandinavia to over 50 kg S ha^{-1} a^{-1} in eastern European countries (Figure 1.13). Tables 1.14 and 1.15 give calculated budgets for oxidized nitrogen and reduced nitrogen, respectively. Figure 1.14 illustrates the range in levels of nitrogen deposition (oxidized species) in European countries.

EMEP estimates of transboundary fluxes and deposition of acidic pollutants provide input information essential to the development of future European emission reduction policies based on the concept of "critical loads". Critical loads are quantitative estimates of the deposition of pollutants below which adverse effects are not expected to occur to plants, ecosystems or materials. As such, they provide a means of setting emission reduction targets based on the vulnerability of various ecosystems to acidic deposition. Preliminary work on defining critical loads for soils and fresh waters and the preparation of national maps showing exceedances of critical loads is nearing completion. For example, provisional maps for the UK indicate that parts of northern and central Wales, the Lake District and south-western and northern Scotland currently receive acid loadings that are between 5–10 times higher than their critical load (ENDS, 1990). The impact of acidic deposition on soils is discussed in Part 1: Environmental Pollution, Soils and Sediments.

In addition to EMEP, a number of UN-ECE International Co-operative Programmes (ICPs) for the monitoring and assessment of regional air pollution effects have been implemented in the European region. These include:

(a)   the ICP on Assessment and Monitoring of Air Pollution Effects on Forests, established in 1985;

(b)   the ICP on Assessment and Monitoring of Acidification in Rivers and Lakes, established in 1986;

(c)   the ICP on Effects on Materials, including Historic and Cultural Monuments, established in 1986;

(d)   the ICP for Research on Evaluating Effects of Air Pollution and other Stresses on Agricultural Crops, established in 1987.

In 1988 a fifth programme on Integrated Monitoring was established. This activity is currently in its pilot phase. A brief description of the activities of four ICPs for monitoring and assessment of regional air pollution effects was given in the 1989 edition of this report (UNEP, 1989). Further details of the ICP for forests, including presentation of UN-ECE/UNEP-GEMS forest damage survey results for 1986–1989, are included in Part 1: Environmental Pollution, Biological Monitoring of this edition of the 'UNEP Environmental Data Report'.

References

Buijsman, E., Maas, H. F. M. and Asman, W. A. H.   1987 Anthropogenic NH_3 emission in Europe, *Atmospheric Environment* **21**(5), 1009–1022.

ENDS   1990 Acid deposition in parts of the UK exceeds critical loads, *ENDS Report* **185**, 8–9,

Hanssen, J. E., Pederson, U., Schaug, J., Dovland, H., Pacyna, J. M., Semb, A. and Skjelmoen, J. E. 1990 *Summary Report from the Chemical Co-ordinating Centre for the Fourth Phase of EMEP*, EMEP/CCC - Report 2/90, Norwegian Institute for Air Research, Lillestrøm.

Iversen, T., Halvorsen, N. E., Saltbones, J. and Sandnes, H. 1990 *Calculated Budgets for Airborne Sulphur and Nitrogen in Europe*, EMEP/MSC-W Report 2/90, The Norwegian Meteorological Institute, Oslo.

Olsen, A. R., Voldner, E. C., Bigelow D. S., Chan, W. H., Clark, T. L., Lusis, M. A., Misra, P. K., Vet, R. J. 1990 Unified wet deposition data summaries for North America: data summary procedures and results for 1980–1986, *Atmospheric Environment* **24A**(3), 661–672.

Rodhe, H., Cowling, E., Galbally, I. E., Galloway, J. N. and Herrera, R. 1988 Acidification and regional air pollution in the tropics. In: *Acidification in Tropical Countries*, SCOPE Report No. 36, H. Rodhe and R. Herrera (Eds), John Wiley & Sons, Chichester.

Sandnes, H. 1990 The EMEP/MCS-W European acid deposition model, *Monitair* **5**, 5–12.

UNEP 1987 *United Nations Environment Programme Environmental Data Report*, Basil Blackwell, Oxford.

UNEP 1989 *United Nations Environment Programme Environmental Data Report*, Basil Blackwell, Oxford.

WMO/UNEP 1990 *Scientific Assessment of Climate Change*, Report prepared for the Intergovernmental Panel on Climate Change by Working Group I, World Meteorological Organization, Geneva, and United Nations Environment Programme, Nairobi.

Trace Metals

Most heavy metals are emitted to the atmosphere as particulates and are removed from the atmosphere by wet and dry deposition. Global emission estimates for a range of trace metals, from both natural and man-made sources, have been summarized elsewhere in this report (see Part 1: Environmental Pollution, Atmosphere).

Owing to the technical difficulties in measuring low concentrations of trace metals in precipitation, wet deposition fluxes of trace metals are generally poorly characterized. Pre-1970 data on trace metal levels in precipitation are viewed with caution because of suspected contamination problems (Barrie et al., 1987). More recent data, which are believed to reflect typical trace metal concentrations in precipitation in remote and rural areas, have been summarized by Barrie et al. (1987). Concentrations of Cd, for example, are reported to range from 0.002–0.7 μg l^{-1} in rural and remote locations in North America and Scandinavia. Lead levels in similar locations tend to lie in the range 0.1–15 μg l^{-1}.

In the absence of comprehensive and reliable data on trace metal deposition from precipitation analyses, use of biomonitoring techniques has been made in a number of countries to estimate deposition fluxes of trace metals. Metal deposition has been routinely studied by moss surveys since 1968 in Sweden. Surveys are now conducted every five years and there are plans to extend this work, as a co-ordinated effort, in a number of other north European countries (Ross, 1990). (See also Part 1: Environmental Pollution, Biological Monitoring). Palaeoecological records have also provided a useful means of reconstructing histories of trace metal deposition. Examples of this type of work are discussed elsewhere in this report (see Part 1: Environmental Pollution, Historical Monitoring).

References

Barrie, L. A., Lindberg, S. E., Chan, W. H., Ross, H. B., Arimoto, R. and Church, T. M. 1987 On the concentration of trace metals in precipitation, *Atmospheric Environment* **21**, 1133–1135.

Ross, H. 1990 On the use of mosses (*Hylocomium splendens* and *Pleurozium schreberi*) for estimating atmospheric trace metal deposition, *Water, Air and Soil Pollution* **50**, 63–76.

Table 1.12 Precipitation chemistry at selected EMEP sites, 1983–1987 (mean annual values)

Country/site	Non-sea salt SO_4^{2-} Concentration in precipitation				NO_3^- Concentration in precipitation			
	Mean (mg S l^{-1})	Min. (mg S l^{-1})	Max. (mg S l^{-1})	Deposition (mg S m^{-2})	Mean (mg N l^{-1})	Min. (mg N l^{-1})	Max. (mg N l^{-1})	Deposition (mg N m^{-2})
Austria								
Illmitz					0.67	0.02	5.81	1,589.4
Belgium								
Offagne	1.21	0.13	20.96	4,041.2	0.53	–	7.31	1,784.0
Denmark								
Færøern-Akraberg	2.31	-20.93	546.47	8,649.3	0.30	–	20.80	1,107.2
Keldsnor	1.37	-0.96	12.40	2,874.7	0.83	0.03	12.00	1,751.2
Tange	1.00	-0.96	18.64	3,178.1	0.58	–	6.75	1,825.1
Finland								
Ähtari	0.64	-0.01	13.65	2,014.6	0.32	0.01	7.11	995.6
Utö	1.20	-1.34	12.07	3,224.6	0.72	0.06	10.09	1,943.7
Virolahti	1.36	0.08	22.84	5,148.7	0.49	0.01	9.95	1,862.3
France								
Vert-le-Petit	1.27	0.00	46.75	3,531.9	0.76	0.02	34.66	2,093.2
German Dem. Rep.								
Arkona	2.27	0.63	8.51	3,109.6	0.76	0.29	3.77	1,034.1
Neuglobsow	2.59	0.00	11.92	7,445.8	0.75	0.20	4.47	2,154.9
Germany, Fed. Rep.								
Brotjacklriegel	1.20	0.20	15.19	5,788.4	0.68	0.10	9.99	3,309.8
Deuselbach	0.97	0.13	17.11	3,539.8	0.53	0.02	16.30	1,933.3
Langenbrügge	1.44	0.17	18.38	4,520.5	0.76	0.02	5.39	2,382.3
Schauinsland	0.66	0.07	8.78	5,806.8	0.37	0.02	6.42	3,268.0
Westerland	1.15	-4.14	15.39	3,707.4	0.75	0.02	10.44	2,402.6
Hungary								
K-puszta	1.77	0.00	14.11	4,272.1	0.63	0.12	5.76	1,529.8
Iceland								
Irafoss	0.41	-2.25	22.55	3,400.8				
Ireland								
Valentia	0.30	0.01	9.70	2,226.1				
Norway								
Birkenes	0.95	0.04	17.74	7,126.2	0.53	–	9.40	3,997.9
Jergul	0.44	0.01	7.75	741.2	0.13	–	1.74	211.5
Kårvatn	0.20	0.00	6.68	1,391.8	0.07	–	5.92	507.2
Narbuvoll	0.40	0.03	4.54	1,320.4	0.18	–	1.60	579.6
Skreådalen	0.49	0.00	7.97	5,173.0	0.26	–	5.60	2,719.1
Tustervatn	0.22	0.00	5.52	1,406.1	0.08	–	3.23	490.6
Poland								
Suwalki	1.83	0.23	20.12	5,341.1	0.60	0.04	3.97	1,753.4
Portugal								
Braganca					0.13	0.03	0.78	124.8
Romania								
Fundata	3.01	0.11	16.42	7,884.5	0.50	0.01	3.21	1,309.2
Paring	2.03	-0.03	9.50	5,518.4	0.80	–	3.98	2,162.6
Rarau	2.61	-0.02	5.57	9,293.5	0.43	0.05	2.00	1,525.1

Continued over

Table 1.12 Continued

Country/site	Non-sea salt SO_4^{2-}				NO_3^-			
	Concentration in precipitation				Concentration in precipitation			
	Mean (mg S l^{-1})	Min. (mg S l^{-1})	Max. (mg S l^{-1})	Deposition (mg S m^{-2})	Mean (mg N l^{-1})	Min. (mg N l^{-1})	Max. (mg N l^{-1})	Deposition (mg N m^{-2})
Semenic	3.85	0.12	8.37	6,983.1	0.46	0.05	4.55	837.9
Stina de Vale	2.60	0.00	4.81	19,182.8	1.05		3.15	7,789.6
Turia	1.74	-0.03	5.58	2,937.6	0.46	–	3.91	782.4
Sweden								
Bredkälen	0.59	-0.12	7.71	2,122.6	0.19	–	1.36	668.1
Hoburg	1.64	-0.04	34.51	3,375.1	0.85	–	10.14	1,750.7
Rörvik	1.20	-5.25	34.84	4,462.2	0.70	–	36.44	2,610.5
Velen	1.06	-0.02	9.26	3,224.7	0.48	–	5.64	1,462.2
Switzerland								
Jungfraujoch	0.36	0.00	8.99	1,963.1	0.14	–	4.20	781.2
Payerne	0.73	0.11	21.56	1,801.8	0.37	0.05	8.80	897.7
UK								
Eskdalemuir	0.55	-0.10	28.47	4,033.1	0.22	0.01	10.20	1,623.1
Goonhilly	0.60	-0.10	62.65	2,681.5	0.26	0.01	11.09	1,172.2
Ludlow	1.19	0.07	23.72	2,091.4	0.54	0.02	7.30	952.3
Stoke Ferry	1.41	0.12	55.87	3,901.1	0.61	0.06	24.93	1,685.9
USSR								
Beregovo	2.25	-0.39	20.34	7,620.7				
Lesogorsky	1.35	-4.72	51.60	4,977.0				
Nida	1.33	-2.02	6.51	1,800.1	0.80[a]	–[a]	5.01[a]	1,278.5[a]
Rava-Russkaya	1.80	-0.22	22.82	5,161.3				
Rayakosky	0.50	-0.40	8.11	1,118.9				
Svityaz	1.33	-0.03	16.89	2,893.7				
Syrve	0.90	-0.75	11.84	2,057.8	0.56[a]	–[a]	4.30[a]	1,284.7[a]
Vysokoe	1.85	-1.76	24.22	5,030.8	0.78[a]	–[a]	7.83[a]	2,109.4[a]
Yugoslavia								
Ivan Sedlo	1.28	-0.28	6.68	6,967.6	0.29	–	8.96	1,599.7
Lazaropole	1.59	-0.14	25.41	8,530.0	0.27	0.01	2.15	1,459.2
Masun	0.82	-0.15	19.67	7,051.7	0.31	0.02	13.90	2,695.3
Puntijarka	1.64	-0.02	11.73	9,600.1	0.39	0.01	16.92	2,290.6
Zavizan	1.44	-0.44	18.72	13,145.0	0.46	–	14.69	4,234.0

[a] Between 50–75 per cent data completeness.

Data in the above table are five-year averages of measurements made during the period, 1983–1987. Only sites which were operational throughout the entire five-year period have been included.
Five-year values given in the above table are based on data having at least 75 per cent level of completeness, unless otherwise indicated. A blank space indicates a less than 50 per cent level of data completeness.

Concentrations of SO_4^{2-} and NO_3^- in precipitation are volume weighed.
Wet deposition of sulphur of 1 g S m^{-2} is equivalent to deposition of 10 kg S ha^{-1}.

Source:
Dovland, H. 1990 Personal communication, EMEP-Chemical Co-ordinating Centre, Norwegian Institute for Air Research, Lillestrøm, Norway.

Table 1.13 Emission and deposition of sulphur in European countries, 1988

Country	Emissions (10^3 t a^{-1})	Deposition		Deposition source		
		Total (10^3 t a^{-1})	Density (kg ha^{-1} a^{-1})	Domestic (%)	Foreign (%)	Indeterminate (%)
Albania	25[a]	28.5	10.4	13	67	19
Austria	57	176.4	21.3	7	85	8
Belgium	208[a]	86.7	26.4	47	48	5
Bulgaria	515	213.0	19.3	57	35	8
Czechoslovakia	1,400	658.0	52.5	53	44	3
Denmark	121	60.9	14.4	22	69	9
Finland	151	202.2	6.6	23	60	17
France	608	514.1	9.3	39	47	14
German Dem. Rep.	2,629	786.4	74.7	81	17	2
Germany, Fed. Rep.	650	538.5	22.0	36	58	6
Greece	250[a]	122.5	9.4	37	45	18
Hungary	609	280.3	30.4	54	41	4
Iceland	3[a]	9.8	1.0	5	46	49
Ireland	74	35.5	5.2	43	42	15
Italy	1,205[a]	473.7	16.1	60	29	11
Luxembourg	6[a]	3.9	15.1	26	67	8
Netherlands	139	86.3	25.4	24	71	6
Norway	33	151.2	4.9	5	73	21
Poland	2,090	1,241.7	40.8	54	43	4
Portugal	102	45.0	4.9	46	41	13
Romania	100[a]	351.9	15.3	9	80	11
Spain	1,570[a]	478.5	9.6	81	12	8
Sweden	107	259.7	6.3	12	73	16
Switzerland	37	70.4	17.7	13	75	12
Turkey[b]	199[a]	220.7	4.5	25	42	33
UK	1,832	541.2	22.4	88	8	3
USSR[b]	5,062	3,570.8	9.8	62	24	14
Yugoslavia	800	525.0	20.6	47	44	9
Baltic Sea	37[a]	507.6	11.9	2	88	10
North Sea	87[a]	694.6	9.4	4	86	9
Atlantic Ocean[b]	159[a]	1,195.1	1.8	6	67	27
Mediterranean[c]	6[a]	1,039.3	5.3	–	81	19
Black Sea		284.8	6.4	–	78	22
Remaining areas[b]		183.4	1.7	33	34	33

[a]   EMEP estimates
[b]   Land and ocean regions within the EMEP area of calculation.
[c]   Includes only the area in the vicinity of Gibraltar.

Emissions are official estimates submitted to EMEP, unless otherwise indicated. Emissions from ocean regions represent emissions from ships engaged in international trade. Emissions of sulphur from biogenic sources totalling 755 x 10^3 t a^{-1} as S are also included in the sulphur budget model. Estimates of sulphur deposition are derived from MSC-W model calculations, further details of which are given in the source document. Percentage distribution of deposition sources may not necessarily total 100 per cent due to rounding.

Sources:
Iverson, T. 1991 Personal communication, Meteorological Synthesizing Centre-West, The Norwegian Meteorological Institute, Oslo, Norway.
Iverson, T., Halvorsen, N. E., Saltbones, J. and Sandnes, H. 1990 *Calculated Budgets for Airborne Sulphur and Nitrogen in Europe*, EMEP/MSC-W Report 2/90, The Norwegian Meteorological Institute, Oslo.

Table 1.14 Emission and deposition of oxidized nitrogen in European countries, 1988

Country	Emissions (10^3 t a^{-1} as NO$_2$)	Deposition Total (10^3 t a^{-1})	Density (kg ha^{-1})	Deposition source Domestic (%)	Foreign (%)	Indeterminate (%)
Albania	9[a]	9.6	3.5	1	80	19
Austria	212	79.6	9.6	4	89	7
Belgium	298[a]	25.8	7.9	10	83	7
Bulgaria	150	34.5	3.1	7	77	16
Czechoslovakia	950	116.3	9.3	18	76	6
Denmark	249	28.3	6.7	6	86	8
Finland	276	75.3	2.5	16	70	14
France	1,655	220.3	4.0	35	54	11
German Dem. Rep.	1,008	101.9	9.7	17	75	6
Germany, Fed. Rep.	2,850	245.0	10.0	41	54	6
Greece	746[a]	36.0	2.8	36	44	20
Hungary	259	51.0	5.5	12	80	8
Iceland	12[a]	5.8	0.6	3	50	47
Ireland	77	10.8	1.6	8	72	20
Italy	1,700[a]	132.0	4.5	36	51	13
Luxembourg	17[a]	1.8	6.9	–	94	6
Netherlands	552	32.0	9.4	16	78	6
Norway	227	88.5	2.9	7	79	14
Poland	1,550	245.2	8.0	24	70	7
Portugal	122	12.3	1.3	23	46	31
Romania	390[a]	102.9	4.5	13	75	11
Spain	950[a]	89.8	1.8	41	40	19
Sweden	390	133.1	3.2	12	69	11
Switzerland	194	36.0	9.1	8	91	9
Turkey[b]	175[a]	73.1	1.5	10	54	36
UK	2,480	89.1	3.7	64	28	8
USSR[b]	4,190	846.6	2.3	40	43	17
Yugoslavia	480	124.7	4.9	13	75	12
Baltic Sea	80[a]	169.2	4.0	2	89	9
North Sea	192[a]	244.1	3.3	3	88	9
Atlantic Ocean[b]	349[a]	376.1	0.6	7	56	37
Mediterranean[c]	13[a]	281.6	1.4	–	79	21
Black Sea		59.8	1.3	–	78	22
Remaining areas[b]		72.6	0.7	5	49	46

[a] EMEP estimates.
[b] Land and ocean regions within the EMEP area of calculation.
[c] Includes only area in the vicinity of Gibraltar.

Emissions are official estimates submitted to EMEP, unless otherwise indicated. Emissions from ocean regions represent emissions from ships engaged in international trade.
Estimates of nitrogen deposition are derived from MSC-W model calculations, further details of which are given in the source document.
Note that emissions are given in units of 10^3 t a^{-1} as NO$_2$; deposition of oxidized nitrogen species are in units of 10^3 t a^{-1} as N.

The percentage distribution of deposition sources may not necessarily total 100 per cent due to rounding.

Sources:
Iverson, T. 1991 Personal communication, Meteorological Synthesizing Centre-West, The Norwegian Meteorological Institute, Oslo, Norway.
Iverson, T., Halvorsen, N. E., Saltbones, J. and Sandnes, H. 1990 *Calculated Budgets for Airborne Sulphur and Nitrogen in Europe*, EMEP/MSC-W Report 2/90, The Norwegian Meteorological Institute, Oslo.

Table 1.15 Emission and deposition of reduced nitrogen in European countries, 1988

Country	Emissions (10^3 t a^{-1} as NH$_3$)	Deposition		Deposition source		
		Total (10^3 t a^{-1})	Density (kg ha^{-1})	Domestic (%)	Foreign (%)	Indeterminate (%)
Albania	24.0	13.4	4.9	57	30	12
Austria	85.0	76.9	9.3	42	52	6
Belgium	94.0	50.1	15.2	64	33	3
Bulgaria	147.0	80.6	7.3	63	31	6
Czechoslovakia	200.0	120.6	9.6	60	36	4
Denmark	129.0	58.5	13.8	76	21	3
Finland	43.0	61.8	2.0	32	51	17
France	841.0	474.0	8.6	85	10	5
German Dem. Rep.	242.0	120.1	11.4	71	26	3
Germany, Fed. Rep.	380.0	270.6	11.1	60	36	4
Greece	112.0	50.9	3.9	65	23	12
Hungary	151.0	77.7	8.4	69	26	5
Iceland	3.0	4.2	0.4	24	31	45
Ireland	139.0	59.9	8.6	90	7	3
Italy	426.0	204.9	6.9	77	16	7
Luxembourg	6.0	2.9	11.2	55	39	3
Netherlands	218.0	92.9	27.3	81	17	2
Norway	41.0	55.6	1.8	31	51	18
Poland	478.0	285.5	9.3	69	26	5
Portugal	55.0	23.0	2.5	78	15	7
Romania	350.0	213.7	9.2	66	28	6
Spain	273.0	134.6	2.7	78	15	7
Sweden	62.0	87.3	2.1	30	56	14
Switzerland	61.0	49.1	12.3	48	47	5
Turkey[a]	699.0	229.0	5.0	36	54	10
UK	478.0	221.6	9.2	88	10	2
USSR[a]	3,180.0	1,802.1	4.9	17	75	8
Yugoslavia	235.0	152.7	6.0	60	31	9
Baltic Sea		114.8	2.7	–	87	13
North Sea		162.5	2.2	–	88	12
Atlantic Ocean[a]		241.9	0.4	–	60	40
Mediterranean[b]		171.2	0.9	–	72	28
Black Sea		87.2	1.9	–	82	18
Remaining areas[a]		44.9	0.4	37	27	36

[a] Land and ocean regions within the EMEP area of calculation.
[b] Includes only the area in the vicinity of Gibraltar.

Emissions of NH$_3$ are EMEP estimates with the exception of Switzerland.
Estimates of nitrogen deposition are derived from MSC-W model calculations, further details of which are given in the source document.
Note that emissions are given in units of 10^3 t a^{-1} as NH$_3$: deposition of reduced nitrogen species are in units of 10^3 t a^{-1} as N.
The percentage distribution of deposition sources may not necessarily total 100 per cent due to rounding.

Sources:
Iverson, T. 1991 Personal communication, Meteorological Synthesizing Centre West, The Norwegian Meteorological Institute, Oslo, Norway.
Iverson, T., Halvorsen, N. E., Saltbones, J. and Sandnes, H. 1990 *Calculated Budgets for Airborne Sulphur and Nitrogen in Europe*, EMEP/MSC-W Report 2/90, The Norwegian Meteorological Institute, Oslo.

Soils and Sediments

Soils

Soils have been subjected to multiple uses over thousands of years ranging from production of food, fodder and timber, to sources of raw materials such as minerals and coal, and to infra-structural use for housing, industrial premises, roads and waste disposal. All too often, soil degradation has arisen from such intense pressure on limited local resources. Indeed, Lal and Stewart (1990) consider that soil degradation, whether from leaching of nutrients, build-up of toxic substances, erosion or salinization, is one of the greatest challenges facing mankind.

Since 1975, UNEP and the Food and Agriculture Organization (FAO) have been working together to elucidate a method of assessing soil degradation (FAO, 1977). A Global Assessment of Soil Degradation (GLASOD) and the World Soils and Terrain Digital (SOTER) Database are being developed through the International Soil Reference and Information Centre (ISRIC), FAO and others and in co-operation with UNEP's Global Resource Information Database (GRID) (see Part 3: Natural Resources). Three world map sheets on the status of human-induced soil degradation (1:10 million scale) have recently been published by UNEP/ISRIC for the GLASOD project (Oldeman et al., 1990). The GLASOD maps are being digitized so it will be possible to update the map and accompanying data base in the future.

Intensive agricultural practices, atmospheric deposition from industrial emissions, inappropriate irrigation and salt build-up, sewage sludge disposal to land and effluent discharges to waste sites, can all lead to overt soil contamination, particularly by chemicals and acidic substances. The real extent to which land has been contaminated by potentially toxic substances is largely unknown on a global basis. Nriagu and Pacyna (1988) and Nriagu (1989) have estimated global trace metal emissions from natural as well as industrial sources, thus illustrating the significant part played by human activities in both dispersion of metals on global scales and consequential deposition to soil.

The need for monitoring soil contamination is crucial. Even in Europe most countries have not made a thorough assessment of the problems of soil protection despite the identification of the need for a European community-wide strategy (Blum, 1990). In one of the few studies available, it has been calculated that approximately 185,000 ha or 0.2 per cent of the total land area of Denmark, the Netherlands, Federal Republic of Germany, UK and France is seriously contaminated. When the potentially contaminated areas are considered, some 330,000 ha or 0.4 per cent of the land area in these five countries is affected (Haines, 1988).

Remote sensing and associated geological studies on soil and vegetation have been undertaken at some locations, including areas polluted by industrial discharge.

Estimates of national, regional and global areas of mineralized and anthropogenically polluted soils have yet to be compiled. Several major soil topics including acidification, contamination by potentially toxic trace elements and organic substances, are discussed in greater detail below.

Acidification Excess soil acidity, manifested by low pH, high concentrations of aluminium (Al) (and sometimes manganese (Mn)) and low levels of exchangeable base cations (Ca, Mg and potassium (K)) can markedly reduce soil fertility and crop growth. Reduced growth is particularly marked when the pH falls below approximately 4.5 and is associated with mobilization of the hydrated Al ion, $Al(H_2O)_6^{3+}$, written as Al^{3+} for simplicity (Logan, 1990). Soil acidity can be produced by four different mechanisms: inputs of strong acids from the atmosphere ("acid rain"); formation of soil organic matter including humic acids; oxidation of reduced sulphur compounds in the soil; and removal of base cations by crops and inorganic fertilizer applications.

Widespread areas of naturally acidic soils occur throughout the world. For example, acid sulphate soils, found primarily in tropical regions, occupy an estimated 12.5×10^6 ha world-wide (Prasittikhet and Gambrell, 1989). Acidic conditions are also found in the spodosols of humid tropic regions. Oxisols (lateritic soils) generally have high Al saturations and are poorly buffered. Cultivation of soils in the humid tropics can lead to rapid leaching losses and pH decreases. For example, Lal (1985) has reported a decrease in pH in a forest soil on an alfisol in Nigeria from 6.1 to 4.4 as well as loss of major nutrients, following six years of cultivation.

Anthropogenic acidification no doubt began during the Iron Age when large-scale deforestation brought about major changes in land use. Acidification by strong acids from combustion of fossil fuels and use of inorganic fertilizers did not, however, occur on a large scale until after the Industrial Revolution.

Soil acidification over more than 100 years has been measured at both permanent grasslands and woodland at Rothamsted Experimental Station, Harpenden, UK. Soil samples had been collected and stored from the Geescroft Wilderness area which had been fenced off and left unattended since 1886. Trends in pH, measured in samples collected from three depths in 1883, 1904, 1965 and again in 1983, are illustrated in Figure 1.15. The results show a fall of 2.9 pH units over the 100 years (Johnston et al., 1986). The acidifying inputs from the atmosphere were calculated to be approximately 1.05, 1.67 and 3.90 Keq $H^+ha^{-1}a^{-1}$ in 1850, 1920–1930 and 1984, respectively.

Many studies have been undertaken on acidification in soils where a decrease in pH, a decrease of Ca/Al ratio and an increase in inorganic Al concentrations have been recorded (Ulrich et al., 1980; Hallbäcken and Tamm, 1986; Bergkvist, 1987; Tyler, 1987). Soil pH in beech (*Fagus sylvatica*) and hornbeam (*Carpinus betulus*) forests of southern Sweden has decreased by up to 1.5 units over 35 years (average decrease 0.8 units) (Figure 1.16). During 1949–1970, 75 per cent of soil samples had a pH of 5.0 and above, whereas only 20 per cent attained this level in the mid-1980s. Soil profiles down to 1 m also reflect the decrease in pH over the 35-year period.

Acidification of soils can lead to increased mobility of selected heavy metals including cadmium (Cd), lead (Pb) and mercury (Hg) (Jones, 1991). Soil acidification studies in a forested catchment area in the Harz mountains in the Federal Republic of Germany concluded that depletion of cations in the soil was also of major importance. The trees were reported to show symptoms of Mg deficiency (Hauks and Bramke, 1989).

The concept of critical loads has been developed in order to evaluate the capacity of particular ecosystems to withstand and buffer the effects of acidic deposition. This concept is based on the assumption of a threshold response in terms of the onset of harmful effects and is thus soil, site and ecosystem specific. A critical load is defined as "a quantitative estimate of an exposure to one or more pollutants below which significant harmful effects on specified sensitive elements of the environment do not occur according to prior knowledge" (UN-ECE, 1988). Hence, if the input of acid substances to the soil and the removal of base cations is balanced by the release of exchangeable base cations from chemical weathering, or other processes, no harmful effects or long-term acidification will take place. Critical loads of 20 Keq $km^{-2}a^{-1}$ for sensitive Scandinavian soils and up to 80 or more for less sensitive soils have been estimated (Nilsson and Grennfelt, 1988).

A number of countries have produced maps of sensitive soils and/or ecosystems based on their susceptibility to acidification. Figure 1.17 shows the susceptibility of soils

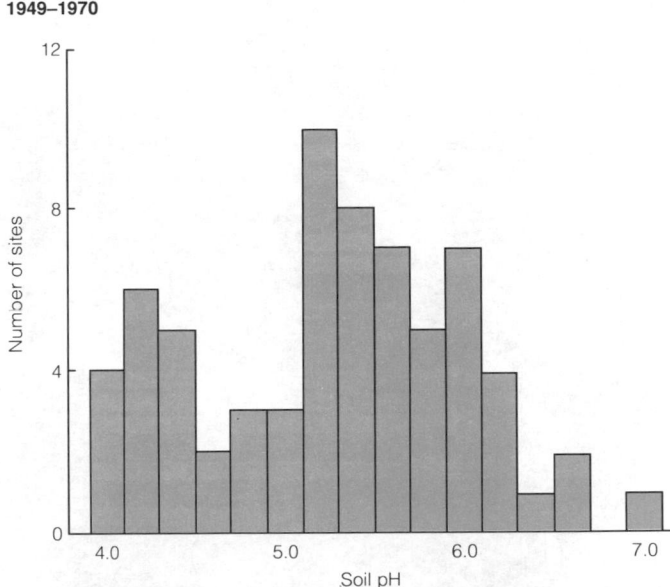

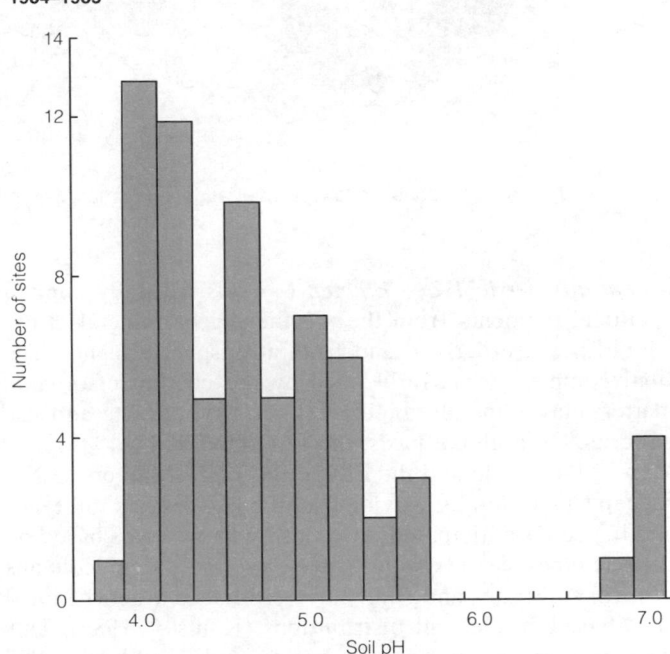

Figure 1.16 Distribution of soil pH (humus layer) at forested sites (*Fagus sylvatica, Carpinus betulus*) in Sweden, 1949–1970 and 1984–1985
Source: Falkengren-Grerup, 1989

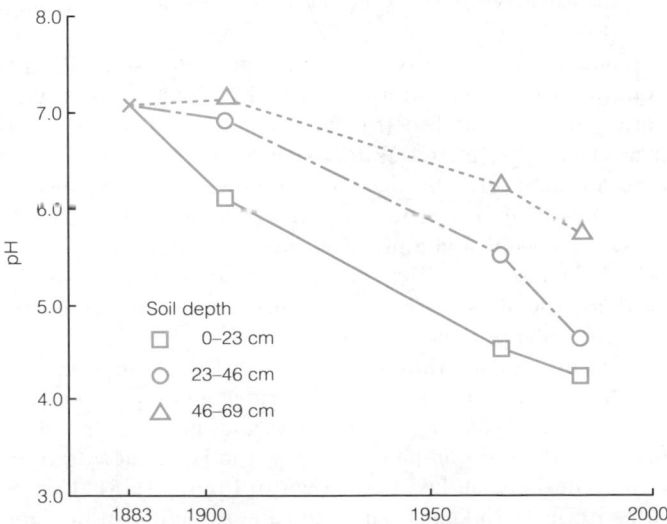

Figre 1.15 Decrease in soil pH at three different depths at the Geescroft Wilderness area, UK, 1883–1983
Source: Johnston et al., 1986

in Hungary to acidification based on six classification classes.

Anthropogenic acidification of soils in Hungary and other European countries has been reported to be increasing. Soils at risk throughout the world include, for example, those in Venezuela, south-east Brazil, Nigeria, south India, southern China and much of South-east Asia (Rodhe and Herrera, 1988).

Acid soils
Highly susceptible
Susceptible
Moderately susceptible
Slightly susceptible
Unsusceptible

Figure 1.17 Susceptibility of soils to acidification in Hungary (simplified, schematic version of the original 1:500,000 map)
Source: Várallyay, 1990

Potentially Toxic Trace Elements   Soils naturally contain chemical elements from the weathering of minerals from which they are derived and from atmospheric inputs. The final composition is influenced by the content of organic matter, clay minerals, biological activity, climate and use patterns. On a global basis, the FAO/UNESCO (1981) Soil Map of the World and the EEC (1985) Soil Map of the European Communities provide useful basic data on soil types and hence on anticipated levels of trace elements based on generic types. Some countries have produced detailed maps of rural soil types and some have published a geochemical atlas based on element distributions (Kantsky, 1986). This type of approach was reported in an earlier edition of this report (UNEP, 1989).

Concentrations of elements in soils, although examined in some countries, cannot easily be compared on a regional or global basis in view of the lack of agreed systematic sampling and analytical methods and uncertain analytical quality control. Nevertheless, such basic data sets are necessary before anthropogenic inputs can be said to give rise to elevated element concentrations (Jones, 1991).

Base-metal mining and smelting, secondary metal smelters, incinerators, coal-fired power plants and electroplating industries, for example, release trace elements which contaminate the soil directly, or via atmospheric deposition, alluvial or fluvial transport (Nriagu, 1989).

Numerous reports of the case-history type have been published on local situations. Some countries have recorded soil contamination on a national basis, e.g., heavy metals in soils of Japan (Kitagishi and Yamane, 1981). More usually, soil contamination is reported by individual elements (Hutchinson and Meema, 1987), although some volumes deal with many heavy metals in soils (Alloway, 1990).

Thousands of reports have appeared in the scientific literature on the concentrations of many elements in a wide variety of plants and their respective soils but few generalizations can be made. With the global variations in soil type, climatic effects, the large numbers of plant species involved, their differences in growth stages, and possible presence of soil contamination, the compilation of meaningful data sets is difficult. Plant : soil correlations for particular local situations may, however, provide useful data for some purposes (Alloway, 1990).

Mercury concentrations in Swedish forest soils (mor or raw humus layer) have been examined in some 363 samples collected during 1983–1984 and are illustrated in Figure 1.18 (the companion figure for Hg concentrations in pike in Swedish lakes is shown in Figure 1.25). The results reflect linkages to atmospheric deposition and sources of emission on a Europe-wide basis (Håkanson et al., 1990). Input-output budget calculations in catchment areas show that the Hg input from precipitation still ex-the European Community has been discussed by Laville-Timsit (1987). Mine-lands in the eastern USA are extensive and have destroyed more than 1.5 x 10⁶ ha of arable land (Arnold et al., 1990). Pyritic (FeS_2) mine spoils occur throughout the world and are characterized as having a low pH (<4), high levels of iron and non-ferrous metals and low available nutrients. Extensive soil leaching and contamination of rivers and ground waters occur on such sites following atmospheric oxidation of the pyrite.

Land has long been used for the disposal of wastes without regard for the assimilation capacity of soils. Disposal of municipal sewage sludges to land for recircu-

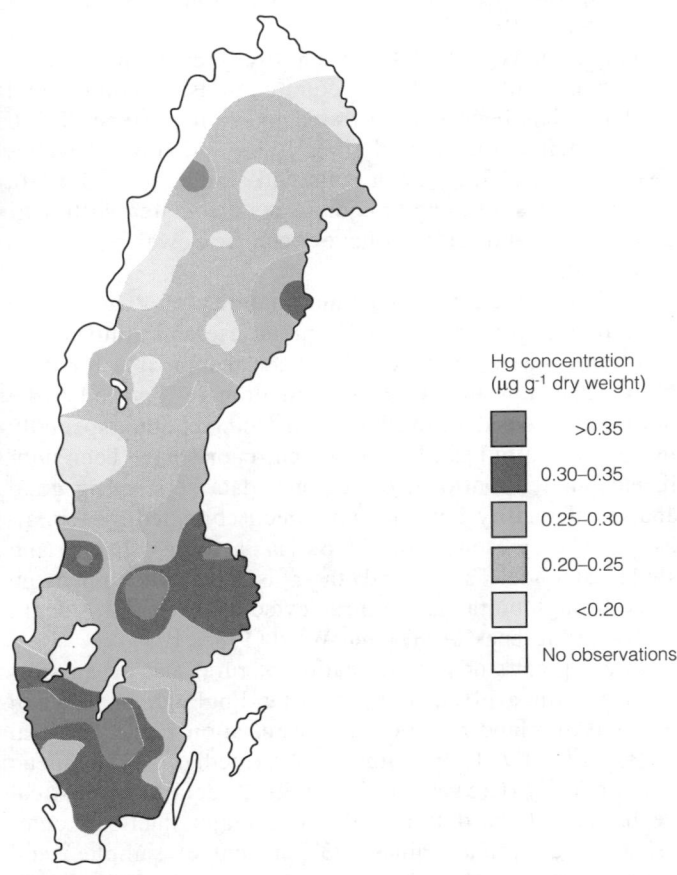

Figure 1.18 Concentrations of Hg in soil (raw humus layer) in Sweden, 1983–1984
Source: Håkanson et al., 1990

ceeds the Hg run-off from the soil systems to the lakes. Acidification processes have also led to the increasing mobility of Hg in soils.

Urban soils have been examined to determine human habitation effects. Heavy metals in soils have been shown to be elevated around 100 cities in the USSR (Rovinsky, 1990). In the UK, Pb, zinc (Zn), copper (Cu) and Cd in garden soils in the major cities London and Birmingham are reported to be elevated compared with suburban and rural soils (Davies et al., 1979; Davies and Houghton, 1984; Moir and Thornton, 1989). In Britain, some 4,650 garden soils and household dusts have been analysed for Pb and other elements at 53 locations (Culbard et al., 1988). The results, illustrated in Figure 1.19, show the wide range of Pb concentrations recorded in UK soils. The highest values occurred in the Derbyshire mining villages, followed by several inner London boroughs where contamination from habitation and industrial activity is pronounced.

Abandoned mine-lands, metal smelter sites and associated contaminated lands occur throughout all regions of the world although data on a global scale are not available. The effects of metal mines and smelters on soils in

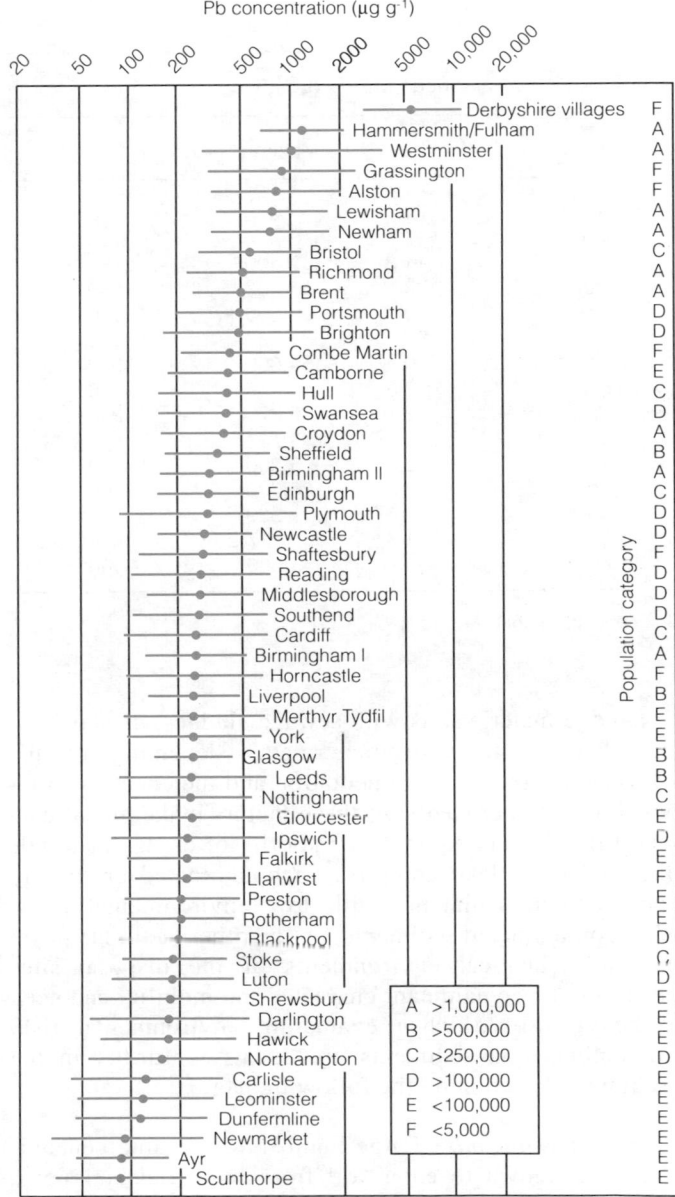

Figure 1.19 Range of Pb concentrations in garden soils for England, Scotland and Wales (geometric mean ± S.D., 100 households in each location)
Source: Culbard et al., 1988

lation of organic constituents is increasing in some countries as bans on ocean dumping reduce this option (Sauerbeck, 1987). In Britain alone, some 70 per cent of the 1×10^6 dry tonnes of sewage sludge produced each year is disposed of on land (see Part 8: Wastes). Element composition of sewage sludge varies extensively depending on the presence or absence of industrial discharges which are, in many cases, treated along with domestic wastes. National guidelines and regional directives are often established to set limits on the concentrations permitted in sewage sludges added to land, and on the annual rates of application (CEC, 1986). The table below illustrates the ranges of trace elements commonly encountered in sewage sludge:

| Element | Concentrations (μg g^{-1} dry sludge) | | |
	Minimum	Maximum	Median
As	1.1	230	10
Cd	1	3,410	10
Co	11.3	2,490	30
Cu	84	17,000	800
Cr	10	99,000	500
F	80	33,500	260
Fe	1,000	154,000	17,000
Hg	0.6	56	6
Mn	32	9,870	260
Mo	0.1	214	4
Ni	2	5,300	80
Pb	13	26,000	500
Sn	2.6	329	14
Se	1.7	17.2	5
Zn	101	49,000	1,700

Source: Logan, 1990

Dredge materials, as with sewage sludges, display considerable variations in trace metals depending on the industry upstream of sedimentation and the chemical composition of the eroded soil; these factors make global data sets difficult to compile. The majority of dredge materials disposed of to land comprise uncontaminated or slightly contaminated sediments with low environmental risks. With contaminated sediments, on the other hand, the physical and chemical environments of the disposal sites influence the contaminant character and mobility and need to be considered when evaluating environmental risk. Contaminants in sediments are discussed further in the 'Sediments' section on the following page.

Organic Compounds Large numbers of organic contaminants are known to enter soil from industrial emissions, sewage sludge and dredge spoil materials. Of these, the polychlorinated biphenyls (PCBs) and polyaromatic hydrocarbons (PAHs) are generally regarded as the most important (Sauerbeck, 1987). In this edition of the 'UNEP Environmental Data Report' attention will be given to PCBs in soil. The PAHs were considered in the second edition (UNEP, 1989).

The ubiquity of PCBs, a group of 209 congeners which can be present in different combinations in commercial products, has been demonstrated by their presence in all environmental media including living organisms, water, peat, snow and ice and in soils and sludges (Waid 1986, 1987). Early studies and major issues associated with their distribution and effects have been reviewed by Waid (1986, 1987).

The prolonged environmental stability of PCBs, taken in conjunction with their widespread use and atmospheric and hydrospheric transport, has been responsible for their global distribution. PCB contamination is reported to be more pronounced in the Northern Hemisphere, especially in the mid-latitudes. Many research reports have been published but few national or regional data sets, using good analytical quality control, have been collected systematically. The presence of PCBs in sewage sludge and sludge-amended soils and their biomagnification from soils through biota has been reviewed by Tarradellas et al., (1987), Sauerbeck (1987) and Waid (1986, 1987).

In a typical study, examination of rural and urban soils from 50 km grid squares covering England, Wales and lowland Scotland revealed a concentration range for total PCBs of 1.7–1,199 μg kg^{-1} (median 6.5, mean 31.8 μg kg^{-1}) (Creaser et al., 1989). A detailed statistical evaluation of the data revealed two major data sets comprising background values (93 per cent of samples) and outliers representing highly contaminated sites. Background values were reported to range from 1.7–32 μg kg^{-1} (median 6.1 and mean 9.5 μg kg^{-1}) which agree with earlier data by the same authors. Samples showing elevated levels of total PCBs were collected from industrial areas in south Wales, the English Midlands and industrial north of England.

The concentrations of six selected PCB congeners – 28, 52, 101, 153, 138 and 180 – analysed in 19 soil samples are presented in Table 1.16. Concentrations of individual congeners range from 0.03 to 8.76 μg kg^{-1} and from 0.48 to 22.77 μg kg^{-1} for the sums of the six congeners. Congeners 52, 153 and 138 are present at higher concentrations in soils than the others. The sums of the concentrations of the six individual congeners show good agreement with the total PCBs but individual congener concentrations correlate poorly with the total PCBs. Data from the congener analyses can also be used to identify commerical products. For example, samples 10, 15, 44 and 88 where the isomer 180 was not detectable, are characteristic of Aroclor 1260 demonstrating the relatively lower contamination of this commercial mixture in these samples (Table 1.16).

References

Alloway, B. J. 1990 *Heavy Metals in Soils*, Blackie and Son Ltd, Glasgow and London.
Arnold, R. W., Szaboles, I. and Targulian, V. O. 1990 *Global Soil Change: Report of an IIASA-ISSS-UNEP Task Force on the Role of*

Soil in Global Change, International Institute for Applied Systems Analysis, Laxenburg.

Bergkvist, B. 1987 Leaching of metals from forest soils as influenced by tree species and management, *Forest Ecology and Management* **22**, 29–56.

Blum, W. E. H. 1990 The challenge of soil protection in Europe, *Environmental Conservation* **17**, 72–74.

CEC Directive 1986 Council Directive of 12 June 1986 on the protection of the environment, and in particular of the soil, when sewage sludge is used in agriculture, *Official Journal of the European Commission*, No. L181, 4 July 1986, 6–12.

Creaser, C. S., Fernandes, A. R., Harrad, S. J. and Hurst, T. 1989 Background levels of polychlorinated biphenyls in British soils – II, *Chemosphere* **19**, 1457–1466.

Culbard, E. B., Thornton, I., Watt, J., Wheatley, M., Moorcroft, S. and Thompson, M. 1988 Metal contamination in British urban dusts and soils, *Journal of Environmental Quality* **17**, 226–234.

Davies, B. E. and Houghton, N. J. 1984 Distance-decline patterns in heavy metal contamination of soils and plants in Birmingham, England, *Urban Ecology* **8**, 285–294.

Davies, B. E., Conway, D. and Holt, S. 1979 Lead pollution in London soils: a potential restriction on their use for growing vegetables, *Journal of Agricultural Science* **93**, 749–752.

EEC 1985 *Soil Map of the European Communities (1:1,000,000)*, Directorate-General for Agriculture, Commission of the European Communities, Luxembourg.

Falkengren-Grerup, U. 1989 Soil acidification and its input on ground vegetation, *Ambio* **18**, 179–183.

FAO 1977 Assessing soil degradation, *FAO Soils Bulletin* No. 34, Food and Agriculture Organization, Rome.

FAO-UNESCO 1981 *Soil Map of the World*, Food and Agriculture Organization, Rome, and the United Nations Educational Scientific and Cultural Organization, Paris.

Haines, R. C. 1988 Contaminated land: the scale of the problem in Europe, costs of clean up and application of novel techniques to reduce clean up costs. In: *Contaminated Soil '88*, K. Wolf, W. J. van den Brink, F. H. Colon (Eds), Kluwer, Dordrecht, 481–485.

Håkanson, L., Nilsson, A. and Andersson, T. 1990 Mercury in the Swedish mor layer – linkages to mercury deposition and sources of emission, *Water, Air and Soil Pollution* **50**, 311–329.

Hallbäcken, L. and Tamm, C. O. 1986 Changes in soil acidity from 1927 to 1982–84 in a forest area of south-west Sweden, *Scandinavian Journal of Forest Research* **1**, 219–232.

Hauks, M. and Bramke, L. 1989 An ecosystem study of a forested catchment. In: *Advances in Environmental Science: Acidic Precipitation, Volume 1, Case Studies*, D. C. Adriano and M. Havas (Eds), Springer-Verlag, New York, 137–180.

Hutchinson, T. C. and Meema, K. M. 1987 *Lead, Mercury, Cadmium and Arsenic in the Environment*, SCOPE Report No. 31, John Wiley & Sons, Chichester.

Johnston, A. E., Goulding, K. W. T. and Poulton, P. R. 1986 Soil acidification during more than 100 years under permanent grassland and woodland at Rothamstead, *Soil Use and Management* **2**, 3–10.

Jones, K. C. 1991 Contaminant trends in soils and crops, *Environmental Pollution* **69**. In press.

Kantsky, G. 1986 *Geochemical Atlas of Northern Fennoscandia*, Geological Survey of Sweden, Uppsala.

Kitagishi, K. and Yamane, I. 1981 *Heavy Metal Pollution in Soils of Japan*, Japan Scientific Societies Press, Tokyo.

Lal, R. 1985 Mechanized tillage systems effects on properties of a tropical alfisol in watersheds cropped with maize, *Soil and Tillage Research* **6**, 149–161.

Lal, R. and Stewart, B. A. 1990 Soil degradation: a global threat. In: *Advances in Soils Science, Vol. 11*, R. Lal and B. A. Stewart (Eds), Springer-Verlag, New York, XIII–XVII.

Laville-Timsit, L. 1987 Impacts on soils related to industrial activities: Part III – effect of metal mines on soil pollution. In: *Scientific Basis for Soil Protection in the European Community*, H. Barth and P. L'Hermite (Eds), Elsevier Applied Science, London and New York, 281–297.

Logan, T. J. 1990 Chemical degradation in soil. In: *Advances in Soils Science, Vol. 11*, R. Lal and B. A. Stewart (Eds), Springer-Verlag, New York, 187–220.

Moir, A. M. and Thornton, I. 1989 Lead and cadmium in urban allotment and garden soils and vegetables in the United Kingdom, *Environmental Geochemistry and Health* **11**, 113–119.

Nilsson, J. and Grennfelt, P. (Eds) 1988 Critical loads for sulphur and nitrogen, *Miljörapport 1988*, Volume 15, Nordic Council of Ministers, Copenhagen.

Nriagu, J. O. 1989 A global assessment of natural sources of atmospheric trace metals, *Nature* (London) **338**, 47–49.

Nriagu, J. O. and Pacyna, J. M. 1988 Quantitative assessment of worldwide contamination of air, water and soils by trace metals, *Nature* (London) **333**, 134–139.

Oldeman, L. R., Hakkeling, R. T. A. and Sombroek, W. G. 1990 *World Map of the Status of Human-induced Soil Degradation*, International Soil Reference and Information Centre, Wageningen, and the United Nations Environment Programme, Nairobi.

Prasittikhet, J. and Gambrell, R. P. 1989 Acidic sulphate soils. In: *Advances in Environmental Science: Acidic Precipitation, Volume 4, Soils, Aquatic Processes and Lake Acidification*, S. A. Norton, S. E. Lindberg and A. L. Page (Eds), Springer-Verlag, New York, 207–266.

Rodhe, H. and Herrera, R. (Eds) 1988 *Acidification in Tropical Countries*, SCOPE Report No. 36, John Wiley and Son, Chichester.

Rovinsky F. Ya. 1990 Personal communication, Natural Environment and Climate Monitoring Laboratory, LAM, Moscow.

Sauerbeck, D. 1987 Effects of agricultural practices on the physical, chemical and biological properties of soils, Part II - use of sewage sludge and agricultural wastes. In: *Scientific Basis for Soil Protection in the European Community*, H. Barth and P. L'Hermite (Eds), Elsevier Applied Science, London and New York, 181–210.

Tarradellas, J. Muntau, H. and Beck, H. 1987 Abundance and analysis of PCBs in sewage sludge. In: *Polychlorinated Biphenyls (PCB)*, R. Leschber, J. Tarradellas and P. L'Hermite (Eds), Commission of the European Communities, Brussels, 11–42.

Tyler, G. 1987 Acidification and chemical properties of south Sweden beech (*Fagus sylvatica L.*) forest soils, *Swedish Journal of Forest Research* **2**, 263–271.

Ulrich, B., Mayer, R. and Khanna, P. K. 1980 Chemical changes due to acid precipitation in a loess derived soil in Central Europe, *Soil Science* **130**, 193–199.

UN-ECE 1988 *ECE Critical Levels Workshop*, Final Draft Report of the Bad Hartzburg Workshop, Umweltbundesamt, Berlin.

UNEP 1989 *United Nations Environment Programme Environmental Data Report*, Basil Blackwell, Oxford.

Várallyay, G. 1990 Soil quality and land use. In: *State of the Hungarian Environment*, D. Hinrichsen and G. Enyedi (Eds), Hungarian Academy of Sciences, Budapest, Ministry for Environment and Water Management, Budapest and Hungarian Central Statistical Office, Budapest.

Waid, J. S. (Ed.) 1986 *PCBs and the Environment*, Vols 1 and 2, CRC Press, Boca Raton.

Waid, J. S. (Ed.) 1987 *PCBs and the Environment*, Vol. 3, CRC Press, Boca Raton.

Sediments

Quantities of fine particles originating from weathering and erosion of soils, along with deposited wind-blown particles, are transported by rivers and dispersed into lakes, reservoirs, estuaries, coastal embayments and the open sea.

These fine particles, depending on chemical composition, accumulate elements and organics and sediment by a series of natural processes. Sediment properties of the original material may be modified by subsequent transport and deposition. Adsorption of anthropogenic substances can also take place during transport. Sediments can provide a record of depositional history of anthropogenic impacts on the surrounding area (see Part 1: Environmental Pollution, Historical Monitoring). Data on sediment loads from selected rivers world-wide have been summarized in the second edition of the 'UNEP Environmental Data Report' (UNEP, 1989). Marine sediments are highlighted in the present third edition.

Fowler (1990) has reviewed available data on concentrations of selected heavy metals and chlorinated hydrocarbons in sediments from a wide range of marine locations. Little information is available on both groups of substances in deep-sea surface sediments from the open ocean waters. However, there is a considerable amount of information on sediments in coastal waters.

Selected data summarizing typical concentrations of Hg, Cd and Pb in surface layers of estuarine sediments from around the world are summarized in Table 1.17. High concentrations of Hg, Cd and Pb have been reported from Minimata Bay, Bay of Naples and the Mediterranean, respectively.

Sediments show large variations in contaminant concentrations because of major differences in mineralogy, grain size, organic matter, water content and sources of anthropogenic inputs. This makes the interpretation of contaminant concentrations difficult. In addition, the variations of concentrations reported are enhanced by the different analytical methodologies adopted and the different extraction systems used by some researchers.

In this edition, national monitoring programmes in the USA are used to illustrate the type of data collected on contaminants in sediments. The second edition of the 'UNEP Environmental Data Report' (UNEP, 1989) presented results for the Mediterranean. The Dredged Material Research Programme, which deals with all sediments dredged from navigable US waters, has been conducted by the US Army Engineer Waterways Experimental Station since the early 1970s. A comprehensive, nation-wide study to detail the open-water (subaqueous), inter-tidal and upland methods for the disposal of dredged materials has been developed (Gambrell et al., 1978). The influence of the disposal environment on the availability and plant uptake of potentially toxic elements in dredged material has been examined (Folsom et al., 1981) and comprehensive management strategies have been formulated (Palermo et al., 1989). The extent of sediment contamination across the USA, methods for its classification, risks to human health and to the ecosystem, sediment resuspension and contaminant mobilization, remedial strategies and technologies for handling contaminated sediments have recently been the subject of a major symposium (NRC, 1989).

The National Oceanic and Atmospheric Administration's (NOAA) National Status and Trends Program is involved in the routine analysis of surface sediments collected from approximately 200 coastal and estuarine sites throughout the USA (NOAA, 1988). It includes the analysis of 12 potentially toxic elements as well as various organics including PCBs, PAHs and chlorinated pesticides. Analyses of bivalve molluscs and sediments at Mussel Watch sites have also been included in the programme. Quality assurance programmes and several laboratory inter-calibration exercises were undertaken to ensure that accurate, reliable and reproducible data were collected. Results revealed that regardless of what was sampled, or when, the highest levels of contamination were associated with sediments collected near urban areas. Representative data as well as the most contaminated locations ("hot spots") were reported. Data illustrating the range of total PCBs analysed in 159 US surface sediments from coastal and estuarine sites sampled during the NOAA National Status and Trends Program are illustrated in Figure 1.20. Further work is ongoing to try to relate sediment

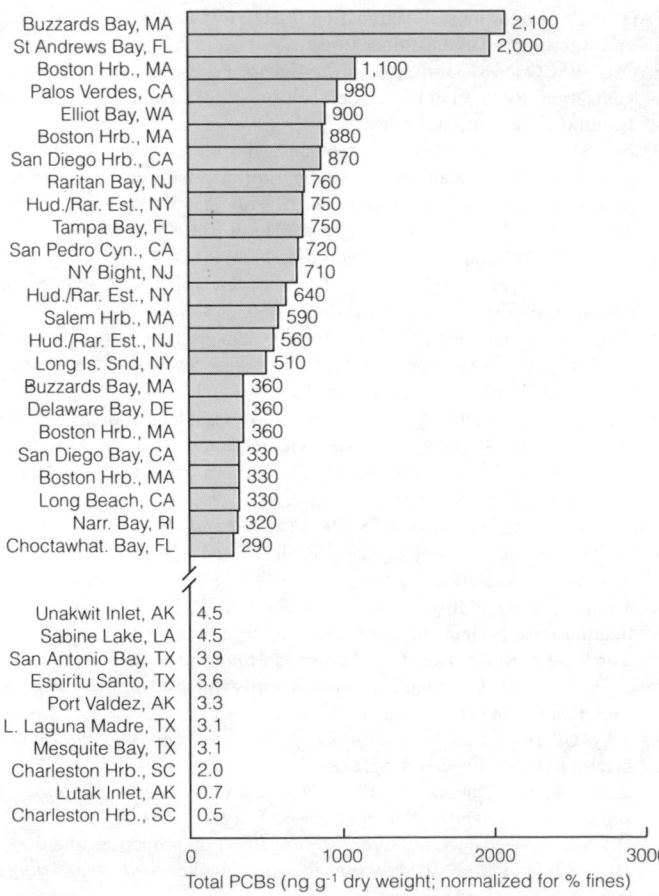

Figure 1.20 Total PCB concentrations in sediments from coastal and estuarine sites in the USA
Source: NOAA, 1988

contamination with the presence of possible biological effects (NOAA, 1988).

Total PCBs, along with HCB and various chlorinated hydrocarbons, have also been analysed in surface sediments from the Gulf of Mexico during 1986–1987 to define the geographic distribution of contaminants (Sericano et al., 1990). The range of PCB concentrations from the 30 samples extended from <0.02 to 189 ng g^{-1} (mean ± S.D. and median were 9.84 ± 20.6 and 4.20 respectively) for 1986, whilst for 1987 the range was <0.02 to 3,730 ng g^{-1} (55.7 ± 328 and 5.40 ng g^{-1} respectively for the mean ± S.D. and median). The PCB congeners were nearly equally dominated by hexa- and pentachlorobiphenyls (27.8 and 25.1 per cent respectively) and to a lesser extent by tetra- and heptachlorobiphenyls (19.5 and 16.5 per cent respectively) representing more than 89 per cent of the total sediment burden. In oysters collected from the same sites, PCBs were largely dominated by pentachlorobiphenyls (46.8 per cent) with some hexa- and tetrachlorobiphenyls (22.3 and 21.0 per cent respectively). Individual PCB congeners in sediments and oysters were also reported.

As part of the NOAA Status and Trends Mussel Watch Program, sediments and bivalves have been analysed for tributyltin (TBT) and its degradation products, dibutyltin and monobutyltin. TBT, frequently used in anti-fouling paints, was found in 75 per cent of the sediments analysed and accounted for, on average, 79 per cent of the total butyltins (Wade et al. 1988, 1990). The two degradation products occurred at lower concentrations and were found in only 30 per cent of the sediments analysed and then usually where TBT occurred at high concentrations. Although the mean bivalve concentrations of TBT were 18 times higher than sediment concentrations, there was no correlation between the two. Data for TBT in US coastal sediments are given in Table 1.18.

A pilot survey of TBT in sediments from 35 stations in the Alexandria (Egypt) coastal area of the Mediterranean was undertaken in 1988 as part of a larger Mediterranean Action Plan Pollution Monitoring and Research Programme (MEDPOL). All samples contained TBT with concentrations ranging from 30 to 1,375 ng Sn g^{-1} dry weight (Gabrielides et al., 1990).

References

Folsom, B. L. Jr., Lee, C. R. and Bates, D. J. 1981 *Influence of Disposal Environment on Availability and Plant Uptake of Heavy Metals in Dredged Material*, Technical Report EL-81-12, US Army Engineer Waterways Experimental Station, CE, Vicksburg, Mississippi.

Fowler, S. W. 1990 Critical review of selected heavy metal and chlorinated hydrocarbon concentrations in the marine environment, *Marine Environmental Research* **29**, 1–64.

Gabrielides, G. P., Alzieu, C., Readman, J. W., Bacci, E., Dahab, O. A. and Salihoglu, I. 1990 MEDPOL survey of organotins in the Mediterranean, *Marine Pollution Bulletin* **21**, 233–237.

Gambrell, R. P., Khalid, R. A. and Patrick, W. H. Jr. 1978 *Disposal Alternatives for Contaminated Dredged Material as a Management Tool to Minimize Adverse Environmental Effects*, Technical Report DS-78-8, US Army Engineer Waterways Experimental Station, CE, Vicksburg, Mississippi.

NRC 1989 *Contaminated Marine Sediments – Assessment and Remediation*, National Academy Press, Washington DC.

NOAA 1988 *A Summary of Selected Data on Chemical Contaminants in Sediments Collected During 1984, 1985, 1986 and 1987: A Progress Report*, National Status and Trends Program, Technical Memorandum No. 5, OMA 44, US Department of Commerce, Rockville.

Palermo, M. R., Lee, C. R. and Francingues, N. R. 1989 Management strategies for disposal of contaminated sediments. In: *Contaminated Marine Sediments – Assessment and Remediation*, National Academy Press, Washington DC, 200–220.

Sericano, J. L., Atlas, E. L., Wade, T. L. and Brooks, J. M. 1990 NOAA's Status and Trends Mussel Watch Programme: Chlorinated pesticides and PCBs in oysters (*Crassostrea virginica*) and sediments from the Gulf of Mexico, 1986–1987, *Marine Environmental Research* **29**, 161–203.

UNEP 1989 *United Nations Environment Programme Environmental Data Report*, Basil Blackwell, Oxford.

Wade, T. L., Garcia-Romero, B. and Brooks, J. M. 1988 Tributyltin contamination in bivalves from United States coastal estuaries, *Environmental Science and Technology* **22**, 1488–1493.

Wade, T. L., Garcia-Romero, B. and Brooks, J. M. 1990 Butyltins in sediments and bivalves from US coastal areas, *Chemosphere* **20**, 647–662.

Table 1.16 Concentrations of total PCBs and individual PCB congeners (isomers) in rural and urban soils of England, Wales and lowland Scotland ($\mu g\ kg^{-1}$)

| Sample number | Total PCBs | Isomers | | | | | | Sum of individual isomers |
		28	52	101	153	138	180	
3	6.5	0.04	0.13	0.12	0.28	0.25	0.23	1.05
5	4.1	0.06	0.47	0.15	0.17	0.22	0.35	1.42
10	55.0	1.55	8.76	8.06	2.13	2.27	ND	22.77
15	4.7	0.06	0.21	0.11	0.12	0.17	ND	0.67
23	5.4	0.04	0.24	0.17	0.14	0.17	0.17	0.93
26	2.3	0.03	0.13	0.10	0.16	0.13	0.12	0.67
30	2.4	0.03	0.21	0.11	0.13	0.16	0.17	0.81
35	3.4	0.03	0.19	0.11	0.11	0.10	0.15	0.69
38	16.6	0.18	0.67	1.01	0.98	0.88	1.73	5.45
44	3.2	ND	0.21	0.12	0.15	ND	ND	0.48
46	7.3	0.12	0.80	0.52	0.32	0.46	0.24	2.46
50	3.3	0.06	0.25	0.12	0.20	0.18	0.17	0.98
58	4.6	0.07	0.20	0.18	0.16	0.18	0.10	0.89
62	16.8	0.41	2.04	1.43	0.66	0.62	0.49	5.65
63	15.8	0.22	1.31	0.82	0.77	0.86	0.55	4.53
75	31.0	0.34	1.13	2.02	2.90	2.44	1.28	10.11
88	22.0	0.26	1.84	1.76	0.70	0.87	ND	5.43
96	6.0	0.06	0.31	0.15	0.28	0.29	0.15	1.24
98	3.5	0.03	0.22	0.09	0.21	0.14	0.15	0.84
Mean	11.25	0.19	1.02	0.90	0.56	0.55	0.32	3.53
Median	5.4	0.06	0.25	0.15	0.21	0.22	0.17	1.05
Range	2.3–55	ND–1.55	0.13–8.76	0.09–8.06	0.11–2.90	ND–2.44	ND–1.73	0.48–22.77
Std dev.	13.22	0.35	1.96	1.84	0.75	0.69	0.45	5.33

ND = Not detected.

Source:
Creaser, C. S., Fernandes, A. R., Harrad, S. J., Hurst, T. and Cox, E. A. 1989 Background levels of polychlorinated biphenyls in British soils, *Chemosphere* **19**, 1457–1466.

Table 1.17 Reported concentrations of mercury, cadmium and lead in surface layers of nearshore sediments ($\mu g\ g^{-1}$ dry weight)

Region/country	Location	Hg	Cd	Pb
AFRICA				
Côte d'Ivoire	North-east Atlantic	0.004–2.3		7–250
Nigeria	North-east Atlantic	0.04–0.16	1.84–2.8	48–87
West Africa	North-east Atlantic	0.002–1.4	0.1–2.8	2–87
NORTH AMERICA				
Bermuda	North-west Atlantic		<0.25–0.99	6.4–230
Canada	North-west Atlantic	0.61 ± 0.33	0.10–0.47	
Costa Rica	North-east Pacific	0.022 ± 0.029	0.12 ± 0.08	5.3 ± 3.0
Mexico	North-west Atlantic		0.1–2.4	10–91
Trinidad	North-west Atlantic		0.05–4.5	6.7–29
USA	Puget Sound	0.276	0.367	43.8
	Southern California Bight[a]	0.13–4.4	0.4–140	10–540
	Southern California Bight[a]		1.1–6.0	32–130
	New York Bight	0.12–4.9	<0.47–9.6	5–270
	South Carolina		0.01–0.46	0.3–30
SOUTH AMERICA				
Argentina	South-west Atlantic		0.24–0.44	5.3–19.9
Brazil	South-west Atlantic	0.2–1.4	0.3–1.3	15–70
Chile	South-east Pacific	0.11–0.49	1.05–9.16	8.6–7.4
ASIA				
China	North-west Pacific			21.6 ± 3.8
India	Bay of Bengal	0.95–5.3		
	Bombay	0.038–0.08	10 ± 2	48 ± 7
	Cauvery Estuary	0.118	1.85	38
	Karwar	0.05–1.32		
Iraq	Gulf		0.14–0.23	5.6–25.6
Israel	Mediterranean	0.2–0.5		15–28
Japan	Minimata Bay	23.5–32.4		
	Seto Inland Sea		0.14–0.88	14 43
Jordan	Red Sea		2–18	83–225
Korea	North-west Pacific			25–120
Kuwait	Gulf		0.75–3.0	10–40
Malaysia	North-west Pacific		ND–1.21	6.5–32
Oman	Gulf	0.012–0.023	2.5–4.7	49–63

Continued over

Table 1.17 Continued

Region/country	Location	Hg	Cd	Pb
Philippines	North-west Pacific		0.0005–0.11	
Thailand	North-west Pacific		0.1–0.4	11–18
EUROPE				
France	North-east Atlantic	0.08–0.12	0.15–0.21	31–45
Greece	Saronikos Gulf	0.3–10		
	Thermaikos		0.2–5.1	18–246
Ireland	Irish Sea	0.07–3.3		
Italy	Adriatic Sea	<0.1–16.9	<0.05–5.6	5.3–96
	Bay of Naples	0.1–1.75	5–200	
	Ligurian Sea		0.3–7.0	36–180
	Sicily[a]	0.03–2.0		7.5–20
	Sicily[a]		2.5–4.6	4.5–17
Portugal	Tagus Estuary	0.02–9.4		
Spain	Mediterranean	0.06–16.5	0.03–4.0	4.8–550
UK	Plymouth Estuary	0.02–2.6		
OCEANIA				
Australia	Albany		0.26–7.6	13–180
	Darwin		0.8–3.1	18.3–91
	Port Phillip Bay		0.15–9.9	4.6–180
New Zealand	Auckland			98–247
	Estuaries and harbours			43 ± 19
	Fjords and sounds			35 ± 10
	Manukau Harbour			98–247

[a] Data from different references.

Data presented here represent a compilation of data from a number of different published sources, full details of which are given in the source document. Consequently data are not strictly comparable between locations.

Source:
Fowler, S. W. 1990 Critical review of selected heavy metal and chlorinated hydrocarbon concentrations in the marine environment, *Marine Environmental Research* **29**, 1–64.

Table 1.18 Concentrations of tributyltin in sediments from coastal locations of the USA (ng Sn g^{-1} dry weight)

Region/state	Location	Concentration
EAST COAST		
Maine	Boston Harbor, Deer Island	41
Richmond	Narragansett Bay, Dyer Island	7
New York	Long Island Sound, Hempstead Harbor	35
	Long Island Sound, Throgs Neck	28
	Hudson-Raritan Estuary, Lower Bay	40
Maryland	Chesapeake Bay, Mountain Point Bar	33
South Carolina	Charleston Harbor, Fort Johnson	5
Florida	St Johns River, Chicopit Bay	87
MEXICO GULF		
Florida	Naples Bay	48
	Charlotte Harbor, Bird Island	6
	Tampa Bay, Papys Bayou	<5
	St Andrew Bay, Watson Bayou	36
	Pensacola Bay, Indian Bayou	<5
Mississippi	Mississippi Sound, Biloxi Bay	18
Louisiana	Breton Sound, Sable Island	<5
	Barataria Bay, Bayou St Denis	<5
	Terrebonne Bay, Lake Felicity	<5
	Joseph Harbor Bayou, Joseph Harbor Bay	<5
Texas	Galveston Bay, Confederate Reef	6
	Galveston Bay, Hanna Reef	11
	Galveston Bay, Todd's Dump	7
	Galveston Bay, Yacht Club	13
	Matagorda Bay, Gallinipper Point	<5
	Corpus Christi, Neuces Bay	9
	Lower Laguna Madre, South Bay	<5
WEST COAST		
California	San Diego Bay, Harbor Island	30
	San Pedro Harbor, Fishing Pier	187
	San Fransisco Bay, Dunbarton Bridge	13
Oregon	Yaquina Bay, Oneatta Point	10
	Tillamook Bay, Hobsonville Point	6
Washington	Sinclair Inlet, Waterman Point	9
	Bellingham Bay, Squalicum Marina Jetty	12
PACIFIC OCEAN		
Hawaii	Honolulu Harbor, Keehi Lagoon	29

Source:
Wade, T. L., Garcia-Romero, B. and Brooks, J. M. 1990 Butyltins in sediments and bivalves from US coastal areas, *Chemosphere* **20**, 647–662.

Water Quality

Water is essential for life and clean, unpolluted water is necessary to maintain human health and the quality of the environment. Fresh-water and marine pollution occurs as a result of surface run-off, direct discharges, waste disposal, accidental releases and atmospheric deposition.

As the world's demands on fresh-water resources increase, so does the need for extensive monitoring in order to optimize the efficient use of fresh water. Demands for fresh-water quantity as well as quality must be met bearing in mind that the activities of some users may restrict the activities of others. Monitoring of water resources usually takes place for one of three reasons. Firstly, the quality of the water needs to be known before it can be used for certain purposes (e.g., drinking-water supplies, irrigation, industry); secondly, the quality of water may be affected by a particular activity, such as an industrial discharge or agricultural run-off; or thirdly, baseline information may be required to detect trends in water quality over time.

Basic physical, chemical and biotic measurements are made to determine natural water quality before any additional impact from anthropogenic sources can be assessed. With the increasing number of chemicals being released into the environment by human activity, the possible number of variables which can be monitored in both fresh and marine waters is constantly growing. For this reason, water quality monitoring programmes usually make a selection of variables to be measured based on national and international lists of "priority pollutants", such as the European Community Directive 76/464/EEC on the identification of priority aquatic pollutants and the "red list" implemented by the UK Department of the Environment and other comparable national schemes.

Data quality cannot always be assured as not all monitoring programmes are subjected to analytical quality control. Moreover, data presented in this section of the 'UNEP Environmental Data Report' have been extracted from a range of national and international water quality monitoring programmes and are selected to reflect some of the current concerns with respect to water quality. However, data may have been derived from a variety of analytical methods of differing sensitivity and accuracy thus making direct comparisons within data sets difficult.

Of the relatively few global freshwater quality monitoring programmes, the GEMS global water quality monitoring project (GEMS/Water) remains the most comprehensive. Initiated in 1976 and implemented by WHO with the support of UNEP, UNESCO and WMO, GEMS/Water forms part of the GEMS health-related monitoring activities. At present, the GEMS/Water network extends to some 450 sampling stations on rivers, lakes and ground waters in 59 countries on all continents. It is, however, more developed with regard to rivers than for lakes and ground waters. Analytical quality control programmes have been conducted on the GEMS/Water network by the US Environmental Protection Agency (EPA) in 1983 and 1990. An assessment of global fresh-water quality, based on data submitted to the GEMS/Water project, was published in 1989 (WHO/UNEP, 1989). The data centre for GEMS/Water is located at the National Water Research Institute (NWRI), Canada Centre for Inland Waters (CCIW), Burlington, Ontario.

The first phase of the GEMS/Water project was designed to strengthen national water monitoring efforts. In the 1990s the project is now moving into a second phase; its objectives have been revised, with a shift in emphasis from monitoring to interpretation of data and assessment of water quality issues and trends (UNEP/WHO/UNESCO/WMO, 1990). A restructured global network comprising 40–50 "baseline stations", 300–400 "trend monitoring stations" and 60–70 "global river flux stations" for the monitoring of fluxes of potentially toxic chemicals, nutrients and other pollutants from major river basins to the continent/ocean interfaces is envisaged. The focus on certain aspects of monitoring, particularly of ground waters where there has been much recent concern about point source and diffuse pollution by pesticides and bacterial contamination, will be sharpened. Additional ground-water stations will begin operation in the mid-1990s to monitor trends in contamination of major aquifers by toxic chemicals, salts, nutrients and municipal and industrial effluents.

References

UNEP/WHO/UNESCO/WMO 1990 *GEMS/Water 1990–2000: The Challenge Ahead,* United Nations Environment Programme, Nairobi; World Health Organization, Geneva; United Nations Educational and Scientific Cultural Organization, Paris, and World Meteorological Organization, Geneva. Draft report.

WHO/UNEP 1989 *Global Freshwater Quality: A First Assessment,* M. Meybeck, D. Chapman and R. Helmer (Eds), Basil Blackwell, Oxford.

Fresh Waters

Anthropogenic inputs to fresh waters generally have fairly local impacts and concentrations of pollutants decrease with increasing distance from point sources of pollution. Data for pollution indicators in selected rivers world-wide are presented in Table 1.19. Data are mean values, 10th and 90th percentiles for the period 1984–1988 thus giving a "snap-shot" view of the water quality during this period. The data were extracted from the GEMS/Water data base and selected to include only those sites from which at least 30 samples were analysed during the five-year period. Data for stations not included in the table can be obtained from the published GEMS/Water data summaries (UNEP/WHO/UNESCO/WMO 1983, 1987, 1990). Extensive data summaries from the GEMS/Water data base concerning rivers, lakes and ground waters were presented in the previous editions of this report (UNEP 1987, 1989). Trends for certain variables in different rivers have been identified by studying the GEMS data since 1978 and selected examples were also presented in the second edition of this report (UNEP, 1989).

Due to the high population densities in European countries the degree of surface water pollution in Europe is high in certain regions. The rivers Rhine and Meuse are considered to be two of the most polluted in Europe (Dethlefsen, 1988). The Rhine carries pollution loads from four countries; Switzerland, France, Germany and the Netherlands. However, the progressive introduction and implementation of pollution prevention measures during the 1980s have resulted in a steady decrease in concentration of some pollutants in recent years. Table 1.20 shows concentrations of selected heavy metals in the rivers Rhine and Meuse since 1975; estimates of heavy metal loads are also given. The values for metal loads are only of limited accuracy as concentrations differ considerably within one cross-section of a river. Owing to tidal movements it is not possible to calculate the load at the mouth of the rivers.

The problem of acidification of fresh waters has long been recognized in many parts of the world, especially in Scandinavia and north-eastern North America. A number of national and international monitoring programmes concerned with acidification are now well established in both these regions. An International Co-operative Programme (ICP) on Assessment and Monitoring of Acidification in Rivers and Lakes has been set up under the auspices of the UN-ECE 1979 Convention on Long-range Transboundary Air Pollution. Data from the first three years of this monitoring programme, which commenced in 1987, will be published in 1991. Results for 1988 have recently been published (NIVA, 1990). The Programme Co-ordinating Centre for this assessment is the Norwegian Institute for Water Research (NIVA) whose own extensive survey of the extent of acidification in 1,005 Norwegian lakes was discussed in the second edition of this report (UNEP, 1989).

In the USA, the National Surface Water Survey (NSWS), which was designed by the US EPA and forms an integral part of the National Acid Precipitation Assessment Program (NAPAP), includes a National Stream Survey and a National Lake Survey. Data for 1985 from the first phase of the National Stream Survey were presented in the second edition of this report (UNEP, 1989). Table 1.21 shows a summary of data from the National Lake Survey conducted in 1986. The results indicate that the regions of greatest acidification are the south-east, where the relative proportion of acidic lakes (i.e., those with no acid neutralizing capacity (ANC)) in Florida is 22.1 per cent, and in the north-east where 4.6 per cent of the lakes in the region as a whole are acidic (EPA, 1986). No acidic lakes were found in the west of the USA that were not associated with hot springs (EPA, 1987).

Acidification of ground waters is closely linked with the buffering capacity of soils in the area concerned and the residence time of water in soils and bedrock. Ground-water acidification is therefore most likely in areas where soils have low buffering capacities, in ground waters with short residence times (which may be due to abstraction), and in shallow ground waters (Bromssen, 1989). Table 1.22 shows long-term acidification trends in public

ground-water supplies in Sweden. The decreasing pH values, increasing sulphate concentrations and the increasing ratio of total hardness to alkalinity all indicate anthropogenic inputs of mineral acids. Table 1.23 shows annual mean concentrations of selected water quality parameters in four aquifers of southern Norway where soils are known to have very limited buffering capacities. The ground-water chemistry is similar to that of the surface water in the region, particularly with respect to low pH values and high sulphate concentrations (SFT, 1986).

One of the major environmental concerns related to lakes is the problem of eutrophication. This enrichment of the lake with nutrients is a natural phenomenon which has, in recent decades, been enhanced by the use of fertilizers (via run-off from agricultural land) and the discharge of waste water into rivers and lakes. Water quality data have been collected by the Organisation for Economic Co-operation and Development (OECD) member countries and published in the OECD Environmental Data Compendium (OECD, 1989). Table 1.24 shows concentrations of phosphorus and nitrogen in selected lakes in OECD countries from 1970–1987, indicating related degrees of eutrophication. Comparisons between countries must be made with caution as the methods of measurement vary from country to country and the treatment of samples in each case has not been made clear.

Since the publication of the second edition of this report, the International Lake Environment Committee (ILEC) have produced a second volume on the 'Survey of the State of World Lakes'. The two volumes together contain detailed information on 109 lakes and reservoirs. This collection of scientific and socio-economic data on the present status of world lakes and their catchments is expected to aid decision makers and technical experts involved in lake management, particularly in developing countries (UNEP/ILEC, 1989).

References

Bromssen, U. von 1989 Acidification Trends in Swedish Groundwaters: Review of Time Series 1950–85, National Swedish Environmental Protection Board, Report 3457, Solna.

Dethlefsen, V. 1988 Status report on aquatic pollution problems in Europe, Aquatic Toxicology 11, 259–286.

EPA 1986 Characteristics of Lakes in the Eastern United States, Volume 1, Population Descriptions and Physico-Chemical Relationships, EPA/600/4-86/007a, United States Environmental Protection Agency, Office of Research and Development, Washington DC

EPA 1987 Characteristics of Lakes in the Western United States, Volume 1, Population Descriptions and Physico-Chemical Relationships, EPA/600/3-86/054a, United States Environmental Protection Agency, Office of Acid Deposition, Environmental Monitoring and Quality Assurance, Washington DC.

NIVA 1990 Convention on Long-range Transboundary Air Pollution, International Co-operative Programme on Assessment and Monitoring of Acidification in Rivers and Lakes: Data Report 1988, Norwegian Institute for Water Research, Oslo.

OECD 1989 OECD Environmental Data Compendium 1989, Organisation for Economic Co-operation and Development, Paris.

SFT 1986 The Norwegian Monitoring Programme for Long-range Transported Air Pollutants, The Norwegian State Pollution Control Authority, Oslo.

UNEP 1987 *United Nations Environment Programme Environmental Data Report*, Basil Blackwell, Oxford.

UNEP 1989 *United Nations Environment Programme Environmental Data Report*, Basil Blackwell, Oxford.

UNEP/WHO/UNESCO/WMO 1983 *GEMS/Water Data Summary 1979–1981*, World Health Organization Collaborating Centre for Surface and Groundwater Quality, Canada Centre for Inland Waters, Burlington, Ontario.

UNEP/WHO/UNESCO/WMO 1987 *GEMS/Water Data Summary 1982–1984*, World Health Organization Collaborating Centre for Surface and Groundwater Quality, Canada Centre for Inland Waters, Burlington, Ontario.

UNEP/WHO/UNESCO/WMO 1990 *GEMS/Water Data Summary 1985–1987*, World Health Organization Collaborating Centre for Surface and Groundwater Quality, Canada Centre for Inland Waters, Burlington, Ontario.

UNEP/ILEC 1989 *Data Book of World Lake Environments*, Survey of the State of World Lakes (2) Interim Report, Lake Biwa Research Institute and International Lake Environment Committee (Eds), Otsu, Japan.

Seas, Coastal Waters and Estuaries

Conditions in coastal waters are becoming a major focus of environmental research and monitoring in many countries. In some seas which are common to several countries, such as the North Sea and the Mediterranean, international co-operative monitoring programmes have been established. Selected data from one such programme co-ordinated by the International Council for the Exploration of the Sea (ICES), which monitors the North Sea and North Atlantic through collaboration between participating laboratories in a number of countries, were given in the second edition of this report (UNEP, 1989). A description of MED POL, the monitoring and research programme of the Mediterranean Action Plan (MAP) which is one of the 10 UNEP Regional Seas Programmes, was also given. Trends in concentrations of heavy metals and dissolved/dispersed hydrocarbons were highlighted (UNEP, 1989).

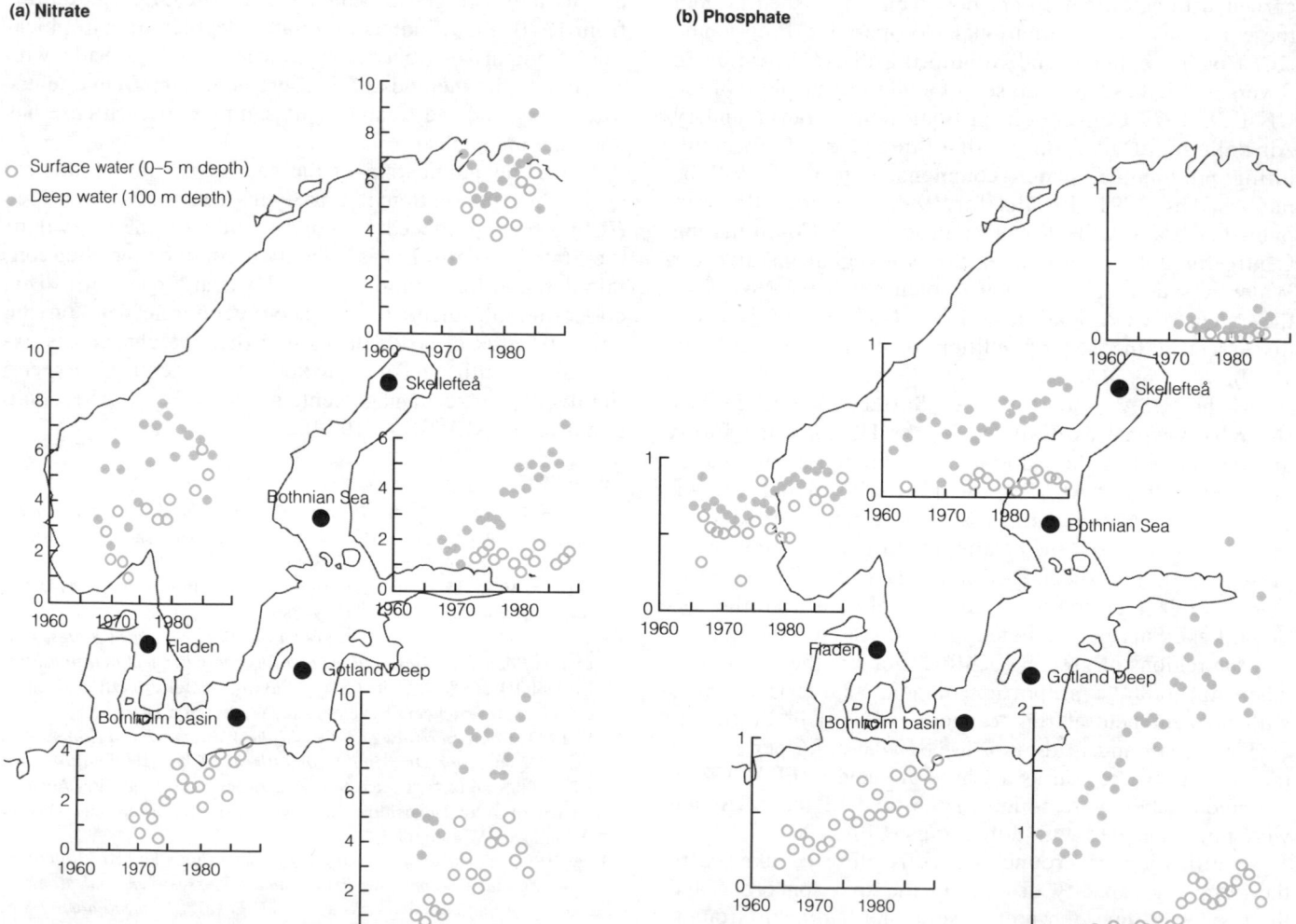

(a) Nitrate

(b) Phosphate

Figure 1.21 Change in nitrate and phosphate levels in the Baltic Sea and the Kattegat (μmol l⁻¹)
Source: Rosenberg et al., 1990

In some countries, biomonitoring surveys have been conducted in order to supplement information on coastal water quality obtained from direct measurements. Programmes conducted by ICES and the US National Oceanic and Atmospheric Administration (NOAA), using fish and shellfish species as indicators of pollution by heavy metals and organochlorine compounds, are discussed in Part 1: Environmental Pollution, Biological Monitoring.

In recent years there has been growing awareness of the problem of marine eutrophication which is now apparent in many coastal regions. Many estuaries and bays are already among the most intensively fertilized environments and there are good reasons to believe that the fluxes of nutrients, especially nitrogen, into coastal waters will continue to increase (Nixon, 1990).

Nutrients are known to be present in substantial quantities in sewage effluents and run-off from agricultural land. As such, elevated nutrient levels may indicate anthropogenic activity. For this reason, and because of concern over eutrophication, it has been traditional to monitor nutrient levels in the fresh-water environment. There is now a need for similar monitoring of nutrient levels in the marine environment.

One region where the marine eutrophication is apparent is the Baltic Sea and neighbouring waters around the coasts of Scandinavia. However, the problem also exists around the rim of the Mediterranean, and in an increasing number of bays and estuaries along the coasts of North and South America, Africa, India, South-east Asia, Australia, China and Japan.

The 1980s saw a dramatic increase in nutrient enrichment in the Baltic Sea area. During this decade, inputs of nitrogen and phosphorus to the Baltic proper increased by a factor of approximately 4–6 and by a factor of more than 8 in the Kattegat (Rosenberg et al., 1990). Table 1.25 shows the amounts of nitrogen and phosphorus supplied to different sub-basins of the Baltic Sea area in the 1980s. Figure 1.21 shows changes in nitrate and phosphate levels in surface and deep waters of the Baltic and Kattegat since 1960. The most notable increases in nitrate and phosphate concentrations during this period have been in surface waters of the Baltic, although increasing concentrations in surface waters of the Kattegat and in deep waters of both the Baltic and Kattegat have been observed.

The quality of coastal bathing waters has also been the cause of some concern in recent years. The increasing use of the sea as a recreational amenity has led to increased human exposure to pollutants discharged into coastal waters. Of primary concern is the deterioration in bacteriological quality of bathing waters which is caused by sewage emissions. National and international monitoring programmes, particularly in developed countries, are increasingly necessary in order to ensure that bathing waters meet required standards.

Table 1.26 presents data on the bacteriological quality of coastal waters for selected OECD countries from 1975–1985. Table 1.27 shows compliance with standards of coastal bathing water quality sites with the European Community microbiological water quality directive (76/160/EEC) in selected countries.

References

Nixon, S. W. 1990 Marine eutrophication: A growing international problem, *Ambio* **19**(3), 101.

Rosenberg, R., Elmgren, R., Fleischer, S., Jonsson, P., Persson, G. and Dahlin, H. 1990 Marine eutrophication case studies in Sweden, *Ambio* **19**(3), 102–108.

UNEP 1989 *United Nations Environment Programme Environmental Data Report*, Basil Blackwell, Oxford.

Table 1.19 Global water quality – pollution indicators for selected rivers, 1984–1988 (mean values, 10th and 90th percentiles)

Region/country	Site	Biological Oxygen Demand (BOD) (mg l⁻¹ O₂)			Chemical Oxygen Demand (COD) (mg l⁻¹ O₂)		
		P_{10}	Mean	P_{90}	P_{10}	Mean	P_{90}
NORTH AMERICA							
Canada	Saskatchewan River						
	Fraser River						
	Churchill River						
	Mackenzie River						
Mexico	Rio Colorado	0.84	2.10	4.00	2.73	14.01	29.20
	Rio Conchos		5.33			14.96	
	Rio Bravo	1.18	2.61	4.45	7.95	35.05	85.70
	Rio Blanco	1.23	11.58	20.80	10.00	68.15	131.50
	Rio Lerma	5.62	41.18	94.31	59.84	356.99	626.20
	Rio Usumacinta	1.00	1.80	3.00	2.90	20.62	41.10
	Rio Grijalva	1.00	5.06	10.00	12.00	22.20	34.80
	Rio Panuco	0.72	2.81	4.40	1.24	21.05	19.72
	Rio Coatzacoalcos	0.43	20.26	37.50	14.84	436.93	1,292.60
	Rio Balsas		5.10			130.25	
	Rio Atoyac	10.00	45.04	95.00	49.32	112.54	226.00
SOUTH AMERICA							
Argentina	Rio de la Plata Buenos Aires	0.50	1.28	2.00			
	Rio Parana Corrientes	0.20	0.50	0.90			
Brazil	Rio Sao Francisco-Petrolandia	1.01	2.21	2.96			
	Rio Paraiba do Sul-aparecida	1.00	2.23	4.00	9.00	15.86	23.00
	Rio Guandu-Tomada D'agua	0.40	1.36	2.40	4.30	12.55	18.60
	Rio Paraiba do Sul-barra Mansa	0.58	1.65	2.80	5.10	13.14	18.60
	Rio Jacui,ja 042	1.00	2.33	2.00			
	Rio Capibaribe	2.00	21.73	53.40			
	Rio Velhas - Honorio Bicalho	2.00	2.69	4.05			
	Rib. Serra Asul-Faz Sobradinho	2.00	2.27	2.70			
Chile	Rio Maipo En El Manzano	0.40	1.05	1.60	3.00	4.72	8.00
	Rio Mapocho En Los Almendros	0.50	0.89	1.10	2.80	4.19	4.00
ASIA							
China	Huanghe (Yellow River)	0.81	1.91	3.38			
	Changjiang (Yangtze River)	0.30	0.88	1.48			
	Zhujiang (Pearl River)	0.20	0.58	0.97			
India	Bhima River near Takali	2.30	6.52	11.20	14.40	27.30	48.80
	Mahi River near Sevalia	1.00	2.21	4.20	4.80	8.49	11.93
	Tungabhadra River at Ullanuru	1.00	1.22	2.00	12.00	34.40	52.40
	Cauveri River near Musiri	1.10	3.89	5.80	8.00	38.03	71.50
	Cauveri River D/s K.R.S. Res.	1.00	1.08	1.00	9.60	28.92	40.40
	Cauveri River near Satyagalam	1.00	1.32	2.00	12.00	28.21	44.20
	Krishna River near Karad	2.84	5.57	8.30	12.00	26.66	46.40
	Krishna River at Honnali Town	1.00	1.14	2.00	9.20	22.97	44.00
	Krishna River at Gadwal	2.50	3.50	4.12	18.30	26.17	35.00
	Kallada River at Panamthottam Kad	0.40	2.40	3.53	5.80	17.62	37.20
	Narmadh River at Sethani Ghat	0.95	2.95	5.00	10.00	20.25	30.00
	Tapti River at Kathore	1.32	3.24	5.03	6.55	14.70	20.00

Continued opposite

Total Cd (mg l⁻¹)			Total Hg (mg l⁻¹)			Total Pb (mg l⁻¹)			Faecal coliforms (No. per 100 ml)		
P_{10}	Mean	P_{90}	P_{10}	Mean	P_{90}	P_{10}	Mean	P_{90}	P_{10}	Mean	P_{90}
			0.020	0.020	0.020	0.001	0.001	0.002			
			0.020	0.022	0.021	0.001	0.002	0.003			
			0.013	0.020	0.020	0.001	0.001	0.001			
						0.001	0.002	0.004			
									3	224	464
									0	1,315	0
									9,030	95,471	240,000
									24	222,458	930,000
									1	10,091	19,500
									1	44,681	240,000
	0.050			0.001					6	1,018	2,400
									15	83,125	240,000
									1,180	107,192	240,000
									91,499	567,448	999,999
									60	1,959	3,450
									0	157	230
0.001	0.010	0.035	0.020	0.346	0.720				180	890	1,390
	0.005			0.100			0.100		1,700	24,239	74,100
0.002	0.002	0.002							1	1,252	4,900
0.002	0.004	0.002							8	13,024	36,000
	0.002			0.029					21	1,535	5,000
0.000	0.030	0.054	0.009	0.305	0.620				92	9,015	3,300
0.000	0.001	0.002	0.430	1.148	1.920				120	2,113	2,400
0.000	0.001	0.001	0.360	1.744	3.400				23	1,447	2,400
									139	722	1,400
									2	12	13
									112	4,793	15,547
									146	759	1,700
				0.100					38	653	1,565
									2	776,645	1,042,000
									114	1,393	2,400
									0	194	365
									9	762	1,800
									30	1,010	2,400
									75	1,307	2,400
									9	16	28
									17	762	1,600
									0	19,787	8,400

Continued over

Table 1.19 Continued

Region/country	Site	Biological Oxygen Demand (BOD) (mg l⁻¹ O₂)			Chemical Oxygen Demand (COD) (mg l⁻¹ O₂)		
		P_{10}	Mean	P_{90}	P_{10}	Mean	P_{90}
	Subernarekha River at Mango Bridge	0.95	3.67	3.35	20.00	49.32	68.00
	Chaliyar River at Kalpalli	0.28	2.28	3.64	4.00	23.40	37.59
	Subarnarekha River D/s Ranchi	1.65	6.55	13.60	18.00	42.89	84.80
	Sabarmati River near Dharoi Dam	0.67	1.89	3.02	4.00	7.02	12.20
	Sabarmati River in Ahmedabad	11.60	62.47	106.00	33.80	180.94	289.40
	Godavari River near Polavaram	2.00	3.11	4.00	15.40	22.71	28.20
	Mahi River at Vasad, Baroda	0.94	1.90	3.50	4.88	8.56	11.60
	Narmada River near Garudeshwar	0.58	2.01	3.96	4.98	12.35	26.45
	Tapti River near Nepanagar	0.76	1.33	2.00	4.00	11.47	20.00
	Tapti River near Burhanpur	1.14	2.06	3.20	11.16	22.85	38.60
	Wainganga River near Ashti	2.24	6.16	9.65	14.80	33.15	44.80
	Godavari River near Dhalegaon	2.40	5.68	10.00	16.00	30.29	47.20
	Godavari River near Mancherial	2.98	3.71	4.20	22.40	31.44	40.20
	Periyar River near Kaladi	0.30	1.43	2.40	5.80	12.58	24.00
	Periyar River near Alwaye	0.56	2.12	4.62	5.60	20.69	44.00
	Subernarekha River at Jamshedpur	1.06	1.90	2.50	18.00	35.33	60.00
	Chaliyar River at Koolimadu	0.26	1.52	2.62	6.32	13.76	24.00
	Krishna River near Vijayawada	2.00	3.35	4.00	20.00	29.93	40.60
Indonesia	River Sunter	5.26	9.35	13.00	14.00	23.23	35.00
	River Surabaya	3.30	14.79	22.10	6.98	21.98	47.10
	River Citarum	3.08	6.88	11.10	13.80	28.03	48.50
	River Banjir Kanal	5.06	10.40	16.20	13.20	23.49	34.60
	Barito River, South Kalimantan	0.90	1.34	1.86	5.68	9.10	12.50
Japan	Kiso River at Inuyama	0.50	1.00	1.41			
	Tone River at Tone-Ozeki	0.80	1.40	1.81			
	Yodo River at Hirakata Bridge	1.40	3.69	5.47			
	Kiso River at Asahi	0.40	0.82	1.29			
	Shinano River at Zuiun Bridge	0.78	1.76	2.80	2.70	7.63	14.98
	Sagami River at Samukawa	1.10	1.95	2.79			
	Toyohira River At Shiraikawa	0.62	1.35	2.20			
	Kiso River at Shimo-Ochiai	0.19	0.69	1.00			
	Ohta River at Hesaka	0.50	0.68	0.90			
Korea	Han River	0.60	1.45	2.30	4.98	8.85	11.74
Malaysia	Klang River	3.55	6.79	9.58	20.91	50.76	55.90
	Kelantan River	0.60	1.55	2.76	5.68	17.39	34.30
	Muda River	0.00	0.92	1.00	10.00	16.43	20.00
Pakistan	Ravi River, downstream Lahore	2.00	5.88	9.30	13.6	24.73	36.00
	Indus River at Kotri	2.00	4.76	8.00	8.00	15.20	25.60
	Lower Chenab River/Gujra Branch	1.00	2.57	5.30	7.00	19.38	26.60
	Ravi River, upstream Lahore	1.00	2.33	4.60	7.00	13.77	22.60
Philippines	Cagayan River	0.20	0.73	1.30	1.94	16.58	32.20
Turkey	Porsuk River, Agackoy	0.61	1.53	2.84		16.80	
	Cark Suyu, Beskopruler	0.80	1.35	1.98		23.80	
	Sakarya River, Adatepe	0.94	2.64	5.42	22.40	31.42	39.20

Continued opposite

Total Cd (mg l⁻¹)			Total Hg (mg l⁻¹)			Total Pb (mg l⁻¹)			Faecal coliforms (No. per 100 ml)		
P_{10}	Mean	P_{90}	P_{10}	Mean	P_{90}	P_{10}	Mean	P_{90}	P_{10}	Mean	P_{90}
									49	505	1,600
									940	25,519	54,000
									700	22,403	46,000
									20	148	330
									100,000	1,724,783	3,430,000
									0	2	5
									2	522,527	244,000
									2	630,430	1,220,000
									9	93	213
									28	173	460
									0	7	13
									31	436	958
									24	480	1,600
									421	7,103	19,800
									23	534	1,600
									4	8	11
0.000	0.002	0.005		0.200					142,000	865,789	999,999
0.003	0.039	0.060									
0.001	0.004	0.007							26,100	637,567	999,999
	0.002			0.200					230,000	884,999	999,999
0.000	0.000	0.000							4,000	5,130	5,993
0.001	0.001	0.001	0.001	0.461	0.500				140	2,729	2,400
0.005	0.005	0.005	0.500	0.750	0.500		0.010		50	3,994	3,480
0.001	0.008	0.010	0.001	0.255	0.500				20,600	165,196	290,000
0.001	0.002	0.005	0.500	0.781	0.500				49	457	909
0.002	0.004	0.005		0.500							
0.001	0.001	0.001	0.100	0.100	0.100	0.005	0.009	0.010	330	2,512	4,900
			0.500	0.500	0.500	0.010	0.010	0.010	40	451	1,262
0.001	0.001	0.001	0.001	0.450	0.500			0.000	110	832	2,310
	0.001		0.500	0.500	0.500	0.005	0.005	0.005	220	1,458	3,480
0.002	0.002	0.002	0.500	0.500	0.500				0	147	350
	0.001		0.000	0.000	0.001				0	810,000	0
									170	4,537	9,000
									140	1,291	1,530
									70	110	190
									98	396	600
									90	407	999
									100	502	1,000
									17	145	340
			0.400	0.590	0.900				4,000	39,960	90,000

Continued over

Table 1.19 Continued

Region/country	Site	Biological Oxygen Demand (BOD) (mg l^{-1} O$_2$)			Chemical Oxygen Demand (COD) (mg l^{-1} O$_2$)		
		P_{10}	Mean	P_{90}	P_{10}	Mean	P_{90}
EUROPE							
Belgium	Meuse River at Heer/Agimont	2.00	4.13	7.00	4.40	16.74	24.00
	Escaut River at Bleharies	2.00	3.73	6.00	30.00	45.45	61.00
	Lys River at Warneton	2.50	5.04	8.50	42.00	77.60	118.00
	Sure River at Martelange	2.00	3.73	6.00	6.00	15.29	24.00
	Meuse River at Lanaye/Ternaaien	2.00	3.85	5.56	11.40	22.33	31.20
	Scheldt River at Doel	2.00	3.19	4.00	38.00	57.59	81.80
	Sambre River at Erquelinnes	2.00	4.93	8.05	13.20	27.28	40.80
	Zelzate River at Ghent/Terneuzen	2.80	5.36	9.00	28.00	59.98	91.00
Hungary	Tisza River at Szolnok	1.20	2.58	3.80	5.76	11.42	15.82
	Danube River at Budapest	3.56	5.99	8.66	14.40	18.75	23.50
Netherlands	Rhine River at German frontier	1.60	3.52	6.30	16.00	21.00	26.90
	Maas River at Belgian frontier	2.00	3.34	5.00	14.00	22.00	29.80
Norway	River Glama at Askim						
	River Glama at Haslemoen						
Portugal	River Tejo at Santarem	0.85	1.61	2.54			
Sweden	Dalalven River						
	Morrumsan River						
	Rane Alv River						
UK	River Carron				5.42	8.19	10.37
	River Trent						
	River Exe		1.43				
	River Tweed above Galafoot						
	River Thames				14.28	21.84	29.33
	River Avon						
	River Mersey				30.50	45.00	60.00
	River Leven						
	River Dee						
OCEANIA							
Australia	River Murray, Mannum						
	Murray River						
	La Trobe River						
	Mitta Mitta River						
	Yarra River						
Fiji	Waimanu River	0.60	0.87	1.14			
New Zealand	Waikato River at Mercer Bridge	0.70	1.39	2.29	7.60	11.37	14.11

Values presented are means, 10th and 90th percentiles of the data collected during the 1984–1988 period. Only those stations which have analysed at least 30 samples during this period are included.

Data for BOD and COD have been quoted to two decimal places and to three decimal places for Cd, Hg and Pb, but reporting accuracy in the GEMS/Water data base may differ. For further information see the GEMS/Water data summaries for 1982–1984 and those for 1985–1987.

Total Cd (mg l^{-1})			Total Hg (mg l^{-1})			Total Pb (mg l^{-1})			Faecal coliforms (No. per 100 ml)		
P$_{10}$	Mean	P$_{90}$	P$_{10}$	Mean	P$_{90}$	P$_{10}$	Mean	P$_{90}$	P$_{10}$	Mean	P$_{90}$
0.000	0.000	0.001		0.007							
0.000	0.001	0.001	0.000	0.015	0.034						
0.001	0.002	0.005		0.008							
0.000	0.001	0.001		0.003							
0.000	0.001	0.001	0.000	0.013	0.030						
0.000	0.001	0.002		0.004							
0.000	0.001	0.002	0.000	0.002	0.001						
0.000	0.001	0.001	0.000	0.018	0.050						
0.000	0.000	0.001							0	254	640
0.000	0.001	0.001									
0.000	0.000	0.000	0.040	0.072	0.106				990	52,877	30,300
0.000	0.001	0.001	0.030	0.110	0.170				2,280	9,050	17,000
0.000	0.000	0.001							2	64	192
0.000	0.000	0.001							10	110	300
0.000	0.192	0.300	0.020	0.129	0.530						
0.000	0.387	0.737									
0.001	0.576	0.700									
0.500	0.691	1.000	0.100	0.426	0.500						
0.000	0.168	0.400									
0.000	0.187	0.379	0.060	0.161	0.198						
0.500	0.527	0.500									
1.000	1.15	2.000									
0.000	0.001	0.001									
									240	5,109	11,000
									50	459	1,100

Recommended sampling frequencies and analytical methods are given in the 'GEMS/Water Operational Guide'. Further information on the GEMS/Water network coverage and reporting experience can be obtained from WHO, Geneva.

Source:
Data supplied by the National Water Research Institute, Canada Centre for Inland Waters, Burlington, Ontario.

Table 1.20 Heavy metal concentrations and metal loads at selected locations of the rivers Rhine and Meuse, 1975–1985

Metal	Year	Rhine, Lobith		Rhine, Maassluis			Meuse, Eijsden			Meuse, Keizersveer	
		Mean (μg l^{-1})	Maximum (μg l^{-1})	Load (10^6 kg a^{-1})	Mean (μg l^{-1})	Maximum (μg l^{-1})	Mean (μg l^{-1})	Maximum (μg l^{-1})	Load (10^6 kg a^{-1})	Mean (μg l^{-1})	Maximum (μg l^{-1})
As	1975	4.5	9.0	0.3	3.9	5.5	11.0	21	0.04	7.5[a]	9.5[a]
	1980	3.0	7.0	0.2			14.0	34	0.08		
	1983	3.6	18.0	0.4	3.4	9.0	3.1	11	0.03		
	1984	0.3	4.0	0.2	1.9	3.0	2.4	10	0.04	2.0[b]	2.0[b]
	1985	1.8	2.7	0.1	1.9	3.0	1.9	3	0.01	1.6	1.9
Cd	1975	2.3	5.0	0.2	0.9[c]	2.2	3.2	9.9	0.1	0.9	2.1
	1980	1.6	4.0	0.1	0.9	1.5	3.4	11.0	0.02	1.6	7.0
	1983	0.4	0.8	0.04	0.5	1.7	1.4	8.1	0.01	0.4	0.9
	1984	0.2	0.8	0.02	0.2	0.7	0.9	7.2	0.03	0.3	0.9
	1985	0.1	0.2	0.01	0.3	3.0	0.4	0.9	0.003	0.2	0.6
Cr	1975	35	76	2.2	21	54	14.0	104	0.1	6.7	16
	1980	20	40	1.6	10	20	10.0	38	0.1	8.0	24
	1983	11	35	1.0	6	17	9.0	57	0.1	4.8	18
	1984	5	30	0.7	4	8	9.4	60	0.1	3.4	5
	1985	8	13	0.4	6	21	6.5	17	0.04	3.1	5
Cu	1975	20	37	1.3	10	37	16.0	104	0.1	7	18
	1980	14	37	1.5	12	17	11.0	29.0	0.07	7	14
	1983	10	22	0.8	6	10	8.0	26.0	0.07	6	11
	1984	5	19	0.7	6	17	10.0	68.0	0.2	4	6
	1985	6	10	0.4	5	21	5.5	7.3	0.04		
Hg	1975	0.4	1.0	0.03	0.2	1.4	0.3	0.5	0.002	0.2	0.6
	1980	0.2	0.6	0.02	0.1	0.2	0.3	1.7	0.002	0.2	0.5
	1983	0.1	0.2	0.009	0.02	0.3	0.1	0.7	0.001	0.06	0.1
	1984	0.07	0.2	0.006	0.05	0.1	0.1	0.6	0.002	0.06	0.2
	1985	0.07	0.2	0.005	0.05	0.08	0.06	0.12	0.001	0.06	0.2
Pb	1975	22	59	2.2	13	26	17	49	0.1	13	29
	1980	15	53	1.3	11	20	23	94	0.2	13	47
	1983	7	24	0.7	2	11	12	60	0.1	6	13
	1984	6	36	0.5	4	18	14	81	0.3	5	19
	1985	4	7	0.2	2	5	6	13	0.1	4	8
Ni	1975	10	23	0.5	7	10	6.0	12.0	0.2	9	12
	1980	9	19	0.7	10	15	8.0	30.0	0.05	6	9
	1983	5	12	0.4	4	6	4.0	14.0	0.04	6	9
	1984	5	8	0.4	4	9	5.0	20.0	0.09	5	7
	1985	5	9	0.3	5	11	3.1	4.3	0.02		

Continued below

Table 1.20 Continued

Metal	Year	Rhine, Lobith Mean (µg l⁻¹)	Rhine, Lobith Maximum (µg l⁻¹)	Load (10⁶ kg a⁻¹)	Rhine, Maassluis Mean (µg l⁻¹)	Rhine, Maassluis Maximum (µg l⁻¹)	Meuse, Eijsden Mean (µg l⁻¹)	Meuse, Eijsden Maximum (µg l⁻¹)	Load (10⁶ kg a⁻¹)	Meuse, Keizersveer Mean (µg l⁻¹)	Meuse, Keizersveer Maximum (µg l⁻¹)
Zn	1975	135	220	13.2	93	190	368	1,972	13.2	95	247
	1980	102	175	8.4	79	126	305	1,345	2.2	152	445
	1983	57	108	4.8	36	66	77	310	0.9	51	98
	1984	37	197	4.4	35	62	102	519	2.0	51	118
	1985	50	100	2.9	47	301	69	151	0.6	53	81

a Data for the third quarter of the year.
b Only one measurement.
c Unfiltered sample.

Source:
CBS 1987 Environmental Statistics of the Netherlands 1987,
Netherlands Central Bureau of Statistics, The Hague.

Table 1.21 US National Lake Survey; distribution of lake water pH and other water quality parameters by sub-region, 1986

Region/sub-region	No. of lakes	Median pH	Percentage of lakes with pH			Median ANC (μeq l^{-1})	Percentage of lakes with ANC[a]			Median DOC (mg l^{-1})	Percentage of lakes with DOC[b]	
			≤5.0	≤5.5	≤6.0		≤0	≤50	≤200		≤2	≥6
THE NORTH EAST	7,096	6.9	3.4	8.6	12.9	158.1	4.6	19.2	60.0	4.3	8.1	26.4
Adirondacks	1,290	6.7	10.0	19.9	26.6	111.8	10.7	35.6	70.5	4.1	7.4	14.9
Poconos/Catskills	1,479	7.0	0.8	5.7	7.8	297.4	5.3	13.1	38.7	3.8	5.5	18.6
Central New England	1,483	6.8	1.7	7.8	12.9	119.9	2.4	17.7	67.6	4.4	6.2	27.5
Southern New England	1,318	6.8	5.0	10.0	14.6	161.8	5.0	21.6	57.3	4.0	18.0	27.0
Maine	1,526	6.9	0.5	1.6	4.8	148.4	0.5	10.8	66.8	5.2	4.4	42.1
THE UPPER MID-WEST	8,502	7.1	1.5	3.6	9.6	359.5	0.0	15.4	41.4	7.5	1.3	62.9
Northeastern Minnesota	1,457	6.9	0.0	0.0	1.4	184.9	9.8	4.2	57.0	9.2	0.2	76.0
Upper Peninsula of Michigan	1,050	7.1	9.4	13.6	17.7	283.6	3.1	18.9	41.7	6.8	4.4	56.7
Northcentral Wisconsin	1,480	6.7	2.1	11.1	27.7	93.9	0.0	41.4	56.7	4.6	4.1	34.2
Upper Great Lakes Area	4,515	7.4	0.0	0.1	4.5	801.7	1.7	9.8	31.3	8.8	0.0	69.6
THE SOUTH EAST												
Southern Blue Ridge	258	7.0	0.0	0.0	0.4	250.2	0.0	1.4	34.3	1.9	53.6	6.1
Florida	2,098	6.6	12.4	20.6	32.7	83.5	22.1	35.3	55.1	8.6	11.5	68.9
THE WEST	10,392	7.2			1.0	119.4		16.8	66.6	1.2	69.7	5.4
California	2,401	6.9			1.3	62.6		36.7	86.6	1.0	80.7	3.0
Pacific Northwest	1,706	7.0			2.4	139.8		19.5	71.6	1.3	68.1	2.7
Northern Rockies	2,379	7.4			0.0	195.2		12.7	50.7	1.2	70.8	8.2
Central Rockies	2,299	7.2			1.3	104.9		6.9	77.8	1.3	67.3	4.0
Southern Rockies	1,609	7.6			0.0	317.0		4.6	39.4	1.5	56.5	9.8

Continued below

Table 1.21 Continued

Region/subregion	No. of lakes	Median SO$_4^{2-}$ (µeq l^{-1})	Percentage of lakes with SO$_4^{2-}$		Median extractable Al (µg l^{-1})	Percentage of lakes with extractable Al		
			≥50	≥150		≥50	≥100	≥150
THE NORTH EAST	7,096	115.4	99.4	26.0	4.6	5.2	3.0	2.0
Adirondacks	1,290	118.7	99.8	12.8	7.1	14.4	12.1	9.9
Poconos/Catskills	1,479	159.3	99.5	56.1	3.0	6.0	2.9	0.3
Central New England	1,483	101.2	100.0	15.7	6.5	1.8	0.0	0.0
Southern New England	1,318	141.1	88.5	45.8	2.9	4.0	0.8	0.8
Maine	1,526	74.6	97.3	1.1	4.5	0.0	0.0	0.0
THE UPPER MID-WEST	8,502	57.1	61.1	7.1	3.0	0.5	0.0	0.0
Northeastern Minnesota	1,457	62.5	73.7	1.9	1.9	0.0	0.0	0.0
Upper Peninsula of Michigan	1,050	77.7	79.1	6.6	3.0	2.1	0.4	0.4
Northcentral Wisconsin	1,480	56.9	69.5	1.0	2.6	0.9	0.0	0.0
Upper Great Lakes Area	4,515	50.1	50.1	11.0	3.3	0.0	0.0	0.0
THE SOUTH EAST								
Southern Blue Ridge	258	31.8	23.1	8.5	1.9	0.0	0.0	0.0
Florida	2,098	93.7	68.1	40.3	4.5	7.4	4.4	1.5
THE WEST	10,392	18.9	13.5		2.8	0.2		
California	2,401	6.6	7.8		2.7	0.2		
Pacific Northwest	1,706	14.7	17.1		5.6	0.6		
Northern Rockies	2,379	15.6	10.7		3.3	0.0		
Central Rockies	2,299	24.4	5.6		1.1	0.0		
Southern Rockies	1,609	34.6	33.7		2.5	0.0		

a Acid neutralizing capacity.
b Dissolved organic carbon.

Water chemistry data are based on the results of the Eastern and Western Lake Surveys (phase 1) which were conducted in 1984 and 1985, respectively. A total of 1,592 lakes (more than 4 and less than 2,000 ha) from three regions of the eastern USA and one region of the western USA were sampled. The lakes were selected in such a way so as to allow statistically reliable estimates of the total number of lakes, i.e., target population, and their chemical characteristics within the study area to be made. Data in the table refer to the target population.

Sources:
US EPA 1986 *Characteristics of Lakes in the Eastern United States, Volume 1, Population Descriptions and Physico-Chemical Relationships,* EPA/600/4-86/007a, United States Environmental Protection Agency, Office of Research and Development, Washington DC.
US EPA 1987 *Characteristics of Lakes in the Western United States, Volume 1, Population Descriptions and Physico-Chemical Relationships,* EPA/600/3-86/054a, United States Environmental Protection Agency, Office of Acid Deposition, Environmental Monitoring and Quality Assurance, Washington DC.

Table 1.22 Acidification trends in public groundwater supplies in three counties of Sweden, 1950–1986

Location	Period	Trend[a] (range of concentrations)				
		pH	SO_4^{2-} (mg l^{-1})	$Ca^{2+} + Mg^{2+}$ (mg l^{-1})	HCO_3^- (mg l^{-1})	$(Ca^{2+} + Mg^{2+})$ + alkalinity
VÄRMLAND COUNTY						
Eda, Köla	1968–86	− (6.0–6.8)	0 (5–10)	0 (10–20)	0 (20–30)	+
Filipstad, Nordmarkshyttan	1964–86	− (5.8–6.4)	+ (2–12)	+ (1–10)	− (5–20)	+
Kil, Gunnita	1964–86	− (7.3–7.8)	+ (2–12)	0 (40–60)	+ (170–210)	+
GÖTEBORG and BOHUS COUNTY						
Munkedal, Hensbacka	1970–86	0 (5.5–5.9)		− (10–20)	− (10–15)	−
Uddevalla, Backamo	1970–86	− (6.0–6.6)	(1–5)	0 (10–20)	− (10–25)	+
Tanum, Heestrand	1960–81	− (6.8–7.5)		+ (10–20)	+ (35–45)	+
Tanum, Östad	1971–80	− (6.2–6.8)		+ (10–20)	− (15–35)	+
Stenungssund, Gategård	1960–81	− (6.0–6.7)		+ (20–50)	− (20–70)	+
Stenungssund, Ucklum	1964–81	− (6.0–7.0)		+ (10–30)	− (25–60)	+
Uddevalla, Gullmarsberg	1962–86	− (6.0–7.0)		+ (10–20)	− (20–30)	+
KALMAR COUNTY						
Kalmar, Råbäcks källa	1950–86	− (6.0–7.0)	+ (10–30)	+ (10–30)	+ (10–30)	+
Kalmar, Vassmolösa	1950–86	− (6.0–7.0)	+ (10–30)	+ (10–20)	+ (20–40)	+
Kalmar, Ölvingstorp	1950–86	0 (6.0–7.0)	+ (10–30)	+ (10–20)	+ (20–30)	+

a Trends are assessed on the basis of the period as a whole and are expressed as: +, − or 0 corresponding to rising, falling or stationary trends respectively.

Source:
Bromssen, U. von 1989 *Acidification Trends in Swedish Groundwaters*, Report Number 3457, National Swedish Environmental Protection Board, Solna.

Table.1.23 Annual mean concentrations of selected water quality parameters in aquifers of southern Norway ($\mu eq\ l^{-1}$)

Parameter	Birkenes				Amli				Langtjern				Evje	
	1981	1982	1983	1984	1981	1982	1983	1984	1981	1982	1983	1984	1983	1984
pH	5.24	5.16	5.17	5.19	5.58	5.34	5.34	5.35	5.3	5.24	5.13	5.07	5.22	5.28
Conductivity[a]	4.77	5.27	4.36	3.85	2.46	2.61	2.22	2.46	2.12	2.27	2.27	2.18	2.43	2.44
Ca^{2+}	99	126	78	54	56	55	48	55	54	62	63	60	31	31
Mg^{2+}	50	54	46	37	26	29	22	25	19	22	21	20	23	20
Na^+	151	154	148	145	83	78	66	75	49	53	53	53	75	77
K^+	9	9	9	9	5	9	7	8	2	2	2	2	5	3
Cl^-	169	157	152	157	59	61	49	57	21	23	25	18	68	71
SO_4^{2-}	129	134	112	108	74	85	66	70	100	112	114	113	93	85
NO_3^-	46	86	63	10	11	21	27	24	1	1	1	1	2	2
HCO_3^-	14	18	12	5	47	23	19	27	17	17	9	6	19	16
Al^{3+}	48	56	45	39	12	21	18	20	80	69	75	79	61	51
Fe^{3+}	2	6			3	9			23	23				
Mn^{2+}	0.7	0.8			0.3	0.5			1	1				
Turbidity[b]	0.24	0.73	0.38	0.28	0.37	0.97	1.17	0.46	2.70	1.75	1.79	1.20	4.20	0.90
TOC[c]	0.5	0.6			0.5	0.6			6.6	6.6	6.7	6.9	0.5	

a $mS\ cm^{-1}$.
b   ITU units.
c   Total organic carbon ($mg\ l^{-1}$).

Source:
SFT 1986 *The Norwegian Monitoring Programme for Long-range
.Transported Air Pollutants*, TA-606 Report 230/86, The Norwegian
State Pollution Control Authority, Oslo.

Table 1.24 Nutrient concentrations in selected lakes in OECD countries, 1970–1987

Region/country	Lake	Total phosphorus (mg l⁻¹ as P)					Total nitrogen (mg l⁻¹ as N)				
		1970	1975	1980	1985	1987	1970	1975	1980	1985	1987
NORTH AMERICA											
Canada	Ontario	0.022	0.022	0.017	0.013	0.011[a]	0.226	0.283[b]	0.308	0.572	
	Erie	0.017	0.023[b]	0.011[c]	0.012			0.278[b]	0.163[c]		
USA	Cayuga (NY)	0.020[d]	0.020[e]				0.37[f,d]	0.51[f,e]			
	West Twin (Ohio)	0.150[g]	0.100[h]				1.93[f,g]				
ASIA											
Japan	Biwa (North)	0.012[g]	0.008	0.010	0.009	0.010[a]	0.190	0.290	0.290	0.270	0.270[a]
	Biwa (South)	0.027[g]	0.027	0.027	0.027	0.024[a]	0.450	0.530	0.410	0.410	0.370[a]
	Kasumigaura		0.040	0.080	0.060	0.060[a]		1.200	1.000	1.200	1.300[a]
Turkey	Kurtbogazi			0.110	0.200	0.190			0.430[f]	0.360[f]	0.660[f]
	Sapanca			0.030	0.030	0.030			0.942[f]	0.617[f]	0.809[f]
	Altinapa			0.030	0.150	1.060			1.550[f]	0.549[f]	0.957[f]
EUROPE											
Austria	Zeller-See		0.017	0.018	0.015[j]	0.010[j]					0.010[j]
Denmark	Knud Soe		0.060[k]	0.050	0.042	0.025[a]		2.000[k]	3.000	2.900	3.000[a]
Finland	Paeijaenne	0.010	0.011	0.009	0.008	0.009	0.500	0.460	0.460	0.510	0.510
France	Aydat		0.053					0.694			
	Pavin		0.282								
Germany, Fed. Rep.	Bodensee	0.061	0.099	0.099	0.071	0.088	0.755	0.763	0.856	0.875	1.013
Ireland	Ennel		0.089	0.029	0.032			0.270[l]	0.470[l]	0.388[l]	
	Derg		0.025	0.020	0.058[l]			0.840[l]	1.200[l]	1.04[l,l]	
Italy	Maggoire		0.026	0.036	0.019				0.77[f,m]		
	Como		0.068	0.078	0.052		0.640	0.710	0.800	0.800	
	Garda		0.009	0.020	0.011		0.310	0.300	0.390	0.350	
	Orta			0.011	0.006		13.000	9.620	9.500	7.110	
Netherlands	Ijssel		0.350	0.350	0.290	0.210		4.025	4.385	4.140	4.450
Norway	Mjoesa	0.010	0.008	0.009	0.007	0.008[a]	0.400	0.400	0.500	0.432	0.459[a]
Portugal	Ria de Aveiro			0.015	0.026						

Continued below

Table 1.24 Continued

Region/country	Lake	Total phosphorus (mg l⁻¹ as P)					Total nitrogen (mg l⁻¹ as N)				
		1970	1975	1980	1985	1987	1970	1975	1980	1985	1987
Spain	Alcantara		0.387^h	2.570^n				1.341^h	2.864^n		
Sweden	Malaren	0.029	0.024	0.034	0.031	0.026	0.918	0.735	0.708	0.859	0.785
	Vaettern	0.008	0.009	0.009	0.006	0.005	0.594	0.562	0.625	0.681	0.704
Switzerland	Leman	0.104	0.082	0.090	0.073	0.068		0.861	0.660	0.730	0.713
	Constance	0.055	0.078	0.077	0.065^i	0.058			0.900	0.920^i	0.940
UK	Neagh		0.095	0.107	0.114	0.940		1.180	1.580	1.920	1.500
	Lomond			0.009	0.009	0.005			0.300	0.290	0.230
OCEANIA											
Australia	Gordon							0.270	0.200		

a 1986.
b 1978.
c 1979.
d 1972.
e 1973.
f Total inorganic nitrogen.
g 1971.

h 1974.
i 1984.
j Upper limit reading.
k 1976.
l Only nitrates and nitrites (as nitrogen).
m 1981.
n 1977.

The values given are annual mean concentrations.
Sampling methodologies may vary according to year and location.

Source:
OECD 1989 *OECD Environmental Data Compendium 1989,*
Organisation for Economic Co-operation and Development, Paris.

Table 1.25 External supply of nitrogen and phosphorus to different sub-basins of the Baltic Sea area, 1980s

Area of Baltic	Total nitrogen $(t\ a^{-1})$	Percentage of total	Total phosphorus $(t\ a^{-1})$	Percentage of total
BOTHNIAN BAY				
Sweden	19,000	28	1,000	29
Finland	32,000	47	2,000	57
Deposition	17,000	25	500	14
TOTAL	68,000	100	3,500	100
BOTHNIAN SEA				
Sweden	35,500	30	1,600	37
Finland	22,100	19	1,660	38
Deposition	60,000	51	1,100	25
TOTAL	117,600	100	4,360	100
GULF OF FINLAND				
Finland	16,300	21	860	16
USSR	57,700	76	399	76
Deposition	2,100	3	410	8
TOTAL	76,100	100	5,260	100
BALTIC SEA[a]				
Sweden	44,300	6	1,780	5
USSR	72,600	10	1,890	5
Poland	109,900	15	19,100	52
German Dem. Rep.	3,600	1	380	1
Germany, Fed. Rep.	16,400	2	2,370	6
Denmark	51,000	7	7,860	22
Deposition	289,900	41	3,420	9
N_2-fixation	130,000	18		
TOTAL	717,700	100	36,800	100
KATTEGAT				
Sweden	37,000	46	900	29
Denmark	18,000	22	1,900	61
Deposition	26,000	32	300	10
TOTAL	81,000	100	3,100	100

[a] Includes Gulf of Riga, The Sound and The Belt Sea.

Values shown are mean inputs for one or several years during the period 1982–1987.

Source:
Rosenberg, R., Elmgren, R., Fleischer, S., Jonsson, P., Persson, G. and Dahlin, H. 1990 Marine eutrophication case studies in Sweden, *Ambio* **19**(3), 102–108.

Table 1.26   Bacteriological quality of coastal waters of selected OECD countries, 1975–1985

Year	Region	Country	N[a]	Percentage of samples in categories				
				A	B	C	D	A+B
1975	NORTH AMERICA	Canada	112	92	6	0	2	98
	EUROPE	Belgium	20	0	45	45	10	45
		France[b]	669	45	30	20	5	75
		Italy	231	54	36	6	4	90
		Netherlands	14	21	14	14	50	36
		Norway	9	0	0	100	0	0
		Portugal	55	29	35	15	22	64
		Yugoslavia	122	47	36	12	5	83
	OCEANIA	Australia	19	37	53	5	5	89
1980	NORTH AMERICA	Canada	140	88	5	0	7	93
	EUROPE	Belgium	15	0	40	53	7	40
		Finland[c]	5	100	0	0	0	100
		France	922	31	33	29	7	64
		Germany, Fed. Rep.[d]	202	91	8	1	0	99
		Italy	231	56	33	7	3	89
		Netherlands	18	17	22	44	17	39
		Norway	9	0	0	100	0	0
		Portugal	18	0	28	33	39	28
		UK	27	19	48	22	11	67
		Yugoslavia	125	47	35	14	4	82
	OCEANIA	Australia	19	47	53	0	0	100
1985	NORTH AMERICA	Canada	43	79	5	0	16	84
	EUROPE	Belgium[e]	18					96
		Denmark[f]	1,220	79	14	7	0	93
		Finland	5	100	0	0	0	100
		France[g]	1,152	38	41	20	1	79
		Germany, Fed. Rep.[d]	205	87	12	1	0	99
		Italy[h]	441	60	23	17	0	83
		Netherlands	27					73
		UK	27	22	56	19	4	78

[a]   Total number of sample points from three major coastal zones.
[b]   Data refer to 1976.
[c]   Data refer to 1982.
[d]   Data refer to two coastal zones only.
[e]   Data refer to 1986.
[f]   Data refer to 1987.
[g]   Values for categories A and C refer to A+B and C+D totals respectively.
[h]   Value for category C refers to C+D total.

Category A: At least 95 per cent of the samples are under the following
thresholds:
10,000 total coliforms per 100 ml.
2,000 faecal coliforms per 100 ml.
and: At least 80 per cent of the samples are under:
500 total coliforms per 100 ml.
100 faecal coliforms per 100 ml.

Category B: At least 95 per cent of the samples are under:
10,000 total coliforms per 100 ml.
2,000 faecal coliforms per 100 ml.
and: Less than 80 per cent of the samples are under:
500 total coliforms per 100 ml.
100 faecal coliforms per 100 ml.

Category C: Between 5 and 33 per cent of the samples are above:
10,000 total coliforms per 100 ml.
2,000 faecal coliforms per 100 ml.

Category D: More than 33 per cent of the samples are above:
10,000 total coliforms per 100 ml.
2,000 faecal coliforms per 100 ml.

Source:
OECD 1989 *OECD Environmental Data Compendium 1989*, Organisation for
Economic Co-operation and Development, Paris.

Table 1.27 Compliance of coastal bathing water quality sites with the microbiological water quality directive (76/160/EEC) in selected European Community countries, 1983–1988

Country	Year	Total number of sampling points	Parameters[a]	Number of sampling points	
				Conforming	Not conforming
Belgium	1983	15	1,2,4	2	13
	1984	15	1,2,4	4	11
	1985	15	1,2,4	4	11
	1986	18	1,2,4	9	9
	1987	18	1,2,4	8	10
	1988	39	1,2,4	31	8
Denmark[b]	1983	1,314	1,2	1,073	241
	1984	1,346	1,2	1,092	254
	1985	1,374	1,2	1,017	357
	1986	1,327	1,2	1,121	206
	1987	1,351	1,2	1,080	271
	1988	1,369	1,2	1,139	230
France	1983	1,717	1,2,3	1,312	405
	1984	1,553	1,2,3	1,243	310
	1985	1,555	1,2,3	1,301	254
	1986	1,710	1,2,3	1,465	245
	1987	1,704	1,2,3	1,419	285
	1988	1,713	1,2,3	1,456	257
Italy	1986	3,525	1,2,3,4	2,161	1,364
Spain	1988	1,020	1,2	828	192
UK	1986	479	1,2	212	267
	1987	547	1,2	323	224
	1988	440	1,2	295	145

[a] 1 = Total coliforms; limit 10,000 per 100 ml.
   2 = Faecal coliforms; limit 2,000 per 100 ml.
   3 = Faecal streptococci; limit 0 per 100 ml.
   4 = Salmonella; limit 0 per 100 ml.
[b] Includes both coastal and inland bathing areas.

Source:
CEC 1990 *Quality of Bathing Water 1988*, Commission of the European Communities, Luxembourg.

Biological Monitoring

The term "biological monitoring" can broadly be defined as the measurement of the response of living organisms to changes in their environment. It encompasses both the measurement of effects on growth and metabolism and the measurement of concentrations of contaminants in a wide range of living organisms.

Although the word "monitoring" suggests measurements made on a systematic basis to ensure compliance with standards of environmental quality, the proportion of biological monitoring surveys carried out for this purpose is very small; the vast majority of surveys are designed to investigate particular aspects of localized contamination in affected areas (Burton, 1986). However, it is now apparent that biological monitoring techniques are increasingly assuming a greater importance in national monitoring programmes, especially in some developing countries (Samiullah, 1990).

This section presents selected data from both national and international biological monitoring programmes, some of which update information published in previous editions of this report (UNEP 1987, 1989). Data from individual studies, published either in reports or in scientific journals, are also included in order to expand coverage of the subject. In this section, examples of monitoring programmes using plants and animals from the terrestrial, the freshwater and the marine environments are discussed independently.

References

Burton, M. A. S. 1986 *Biological Monitoring of Environmental Contaminants: Plants*, MARC Report Number 32, Monitoring and Assessment Research Centre, London.

Samiullah, Y. 1990 *Biological Monitoring of Environmental Contaminants: Animals*, MARC Report Number 37, Monitoring and Assessment Research Centre, London.

UNEP 1987 *United Nations Environment Programme Environmental Data Report*, Basil Blackwell, Oxford.

UNEP 1989 *United Nations Environment Programme Environmental Data Report*, Basil Blackwell, Oxford.

Terrestrial Wildlife

Studies relating to trace contaminant concentrations in terrestrial wildlife are diverse and are generally designed to highlight regional differences in pollutant levels in biota at the time of study. The few national long-term monitoring programmes that do exist have tended to concentrate on metal concentrations in terrestrial birds. Extracts or summaries of data from such programmes were reported in the previous editions of this report (UNEP 1987, 1989). The scarcity of long-term data sets concerning metals in terrestrial wildlife species means that no new information has been included in the current edition of the 'UNEP Environmental Data Report'.

Concentrations of organochlorine residues in the adult woodcock (*Philohela minor*) from eastern Canada were monitored closely from 1971 to 1980 by the Canadian Wildlife Service of Environment Canada (Peakall, 1990).

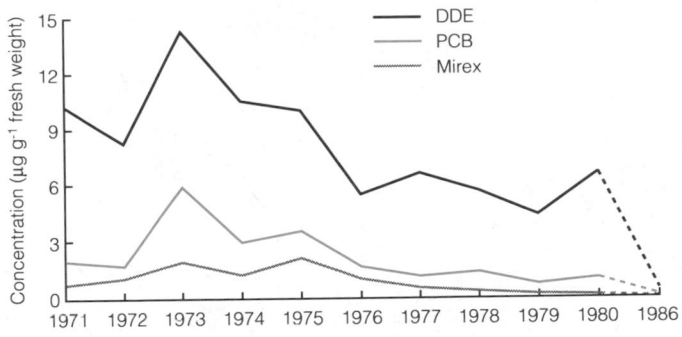

Figure 1.22 Mean concentrations of organochlorine residues in adult woodcock (*Philohela minor*), 1971–1980 and 1986
Source: figure provided by D. B. Peakall, Canadian Wildlife Service, Environment Canada

Figure 1.22 shows the decrease of concentrations of polychlorinated biphenyls (PCBs) and the pesticide compounds banned since the mid-1970s – DDE (a metabolite of dichlorodiphenyltrichloroethane (DDT)) and mirex – in woodcock from the New Brunswick Province. Table 1.28 presents data for a wider range of organochlorine compounds measured in woodcock sampled in four eastern Canadian provinces in 1986. In the previous edition of this report, similar downward trends in DDE residues were reported in starlings (*Sturnus vulgaris*) from the USA (UNEP, 1989).

References

Peakall, D. B. 1990 Personal communication, Canadian Wildlife Service, Environment Canada, Canada.

UNEP 1987 *United Nations Environment Programme Environmental Data Report*, Basil Blackwell, Oxford.

UNEP 1989 *United Nations Environment Programme Environmental Data Report*, Basil Blackwell, Oxford.

Terrestrial Plants

Data from the use of terrestrial plants as biomonitors have, for the most part, been reported in such a way as to indicate the environmental impact of point sources of pollution. Terrestrial (and aquatic) bryophytes have been used in this way in urban and industrial habitats (Burton, 1990).

Mosses and lichens have a high capacity for inception and retention of airborne (and waterborne) contaminants and therefore have been widely used for monitoring purposes. Since the late 1960s, levels of contaminants in mosses have been systematically monitored on a nationwide basis in Sweden in order to assess spatial and temporal variations in trace metal atmospheric deposition. Extracts of data from the Swedish surveys of heavy metal deposition were presented in the second edition of this report (UNEP, 1989). This programme has now been joined by the UN-ECE Co-operative Programme for Monitoring and Evaluation of the Long-range Transmission of Air Pollutants in Europe (EMEP) and has been extended to

analysed for DDT and other organochlorine contaminants following the discovery in 1986 that a forest spraying programme (implemented in 1984 in the southern part of the German Democratic Republic) was using large amounts of DDT (Eriksson et al., 1989). Figure 1.23 shows the sampling site locations for the survey.

Systematic monitoring of forest damage in Europe has been conducted since 1986 as part of the UN-ECE and UNEP-GEMS International Co-operative Programme (ICP) for the Monitoring and Assessment of Air Pollution Effects on Forests. The forest damage survey programme is one of five ICPs that have been recently established under the auspices of the 1979 UN-ECE Convention on Long-range Transboundary Transport of Air Pollutants.

Surveys of tree health are conducted in participating countries by trained observers according to a standardized methodology. In 1989 surveys were conducted in 26 countries comprising 23 national surveys and 10 in selected regions only. Nearly 370,000 individual trees on 26,000 sample plots covering approximately 116 million hectares (or 66 per cent) of the 176 million hectares of forest in Europe were assessed (UN-ECE/UNEP-GEMS, 1990).

The survey assesses defoliation (the loss of leaves or needles) as an indicator of tree health. Both broadleaved and coniferous trees are included in the survey. Results are reported for all species, broadleaved species and coniferous species, and also for some individual tree species (oak, common beech, silver fir, pine and Norway spruce). The survey specifies that defoliation of sample trees, due to biotic or abiotic causes, is classified as follows:

Class	Needle/leaf loss (%)	Tree health
0	0–10	no defoliation
1	11–25	slight defoliation, warning stage
2	26–60	moderate defoliation
3	61–99	severe defoliation
4	100	dead

Figure 1.23 Pine needle sampling stations
Source: Eriksson et al., 1989

include Iceland, Norway, Finland, the Baltic States of the USSR, Poland, Germany, Czechoslovakia, Switzerland, Portugal, Spain, Italy, Hungary and Austria. First results of this extended survey are expected in mid-1991 (Rühling, 1990). Other components of the EMEP programme are discussed in Part 1: Environmental Pollution, Atmospheric Deposition.

In addition to mosses and lichens, pine needles are widely recognized as useful biomonitors. A biomonitoring study in Poland which used analyses of sulphur, fluorine and metals in pine needles (*Pinus sylvestris*) to show different zones of contamination throughout the country, was outlined in the second edition of this report (UNEP, 1989). The present edition also highlights the suitability of the pine needle as a biomonitor. Table 1.29 shows mean concentrations of organochlorines in pine needles sampled from selected locations in Europe during 1984–1986. Samples were collected at sites throughout Europe and

Table 1.30 compares the percentage of sample trees with defoliation of greater than 25 per cent (i.e., trees in classes 2, 3 and 4) for each of the years 1986 to 1989 and for each country participating in the survey. The table also compares the percentage changes between 1988 and 1989 for each country for which data for these two years are available. Figure 1.24 shows the results of the 1989 forest damage survey. Figure 1.24 and Table 1.30 do not include results from regional surveys of forest health.

Surveys of forest health have also been conducted in the USA. The National Acid Precipitation Assessment Program (NAPAP) is an umbrella organization under which the Forest Research Programme (FRP) and the Forest Service Forest Inventory and Analysis (FIA) programme operate. The FRP surveys forest health and searches for spatial or temporal patterns that may be related to environmental factors such as air quality and

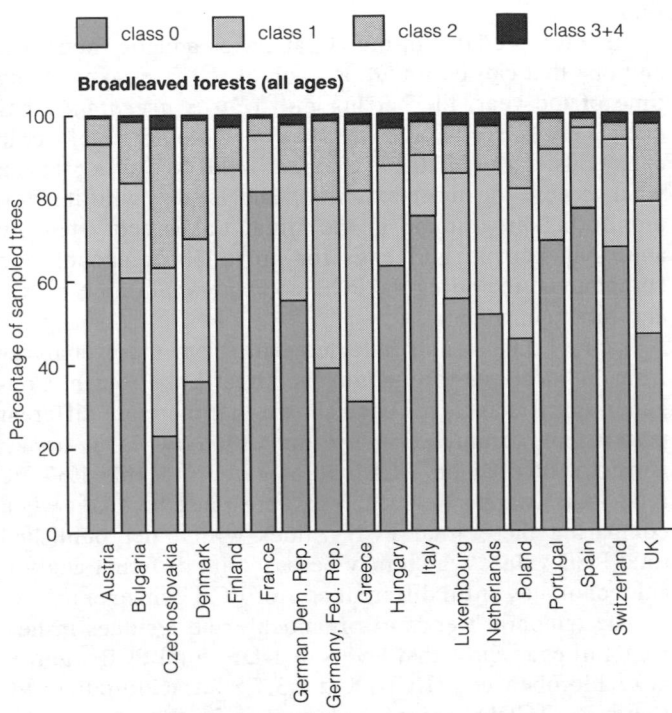

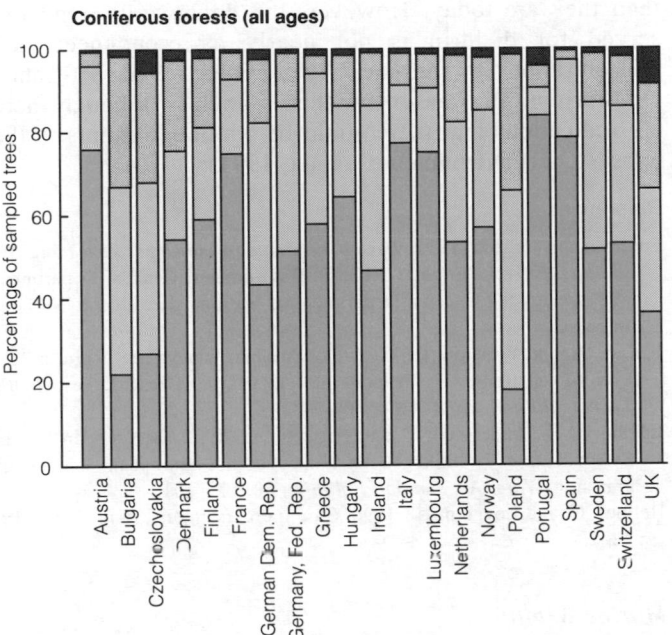

Figure 1.24 Results of the 1989 European forest damage survey (percentage distribution of sample trees according to defoliation class)
Source: UN-ECE/UNEP-GEMS, 1990

atmospheric deposition in five main regions across the USA. Recent regional surveys of forest damage in the USA have been concentrated in the north-east of the country (Vogelmann et al., 1988; Miller-Weeks et al., 1989).

References

Burton, M. A. S. 1990 Terrestrial and aquatic bryophytes as monitors of environmental contaminants in urban and industrial habitats, *Botanical Journal of Linnean Society* **104**, 267–280.

Eriksson, G., Jensen, S., Kylin, H. and Strachan, W. 1989 The pine needle as a monitor of atmospheric pollution, *Nature* (London) **341**(6239), 42–44.

Miller-Weeks, M., Spruce, J., Levesque, B., Smoronk, D., Cooke, R., Cox, S. and Millers, I. 1989 Monitoring of red spruce and balsam fir decline in the northeastern United States: symptomatology and mortality mapping. In: *Air Pollution and Forest Decline*, J. B. Bucher and I. Bucher-Wallin (Eds), Birmensdorf, 483–485.

Rühling, A. 1990 Personal communication, University of Lund, Sweden.

UN-ECE/UNEP-GEMS 1990 *Forest Damage and Air Pollution: Report of the 1989 Forest Damage Survey in Europe*, prepared by the Programme Co-ordinating Centres with the assistance of the United Nations Environment Programme, Nairobi, and the Secretariat of the United Nations Economic Commission for Europe, Geneva. In press.

UNEP 1989 *United Nations Environment Programme Environmental Data Report*, Basil Blackwell, Oxford.

Vogelmann, H. W., Perkins, T. D., Badger, G. J. and Klein, R. M. 1988 A 21-year record of forest decline on Camels Hump, Vermont, USA, *European Journal of Forest Pathology* **18**, 240–249.

Freshwater Wildlife

Biomonitoring programmes have been conducted in the North American Great Lakes since the early 1970s, initially to support the Canada-USA Agreement on Great Lakes Water Quality (Fox and Weseloh, 1987). These programmes have enabled managers to assess the effects of remedial measures in cases of environmental pollution and have been instrumental in the identification of various metal and organochlorine contaminants within the Great Lakes ecosystem.

Various biomonitoring programmes continue in the Great Lakes and there are now some long time-trend data sets available for a wide range of contaminants and freshwater species. Available data, some of which are presented here, are published in an extensive review of the status of the Great Lakes (Environment Canada, 1991).

Fish can be excellent biomonitors of ecosystem health. Tables 1.31 and 1.32 show annual mean concentrations of organochlorine residues and mercury in whole body tissues of three forage species common throughout the Great Lakes ecosystem, namely, rainbow smelt (*Osmerus mordax*), walleye (*Stizostedion vitreum*) and lake trout (*Salvelinus namaycush*). The data show that concentrations of most of the organochlorine contaminants in the fish have decreased between the late 1970s and early 1980s reflecting improved industrial practices and regulatory bans or restrictions on the manufacture and use of compounds such as DDT, mirex and certain PCBs. However, the period since the mid-1980s has seen an equilibrium in the concentrations of residues in the forage species. This is attributed to either inputs from remaining anthropogenic sources, cycling of contaminants within the aquatic ecosystem and/or re-mobilization from lake sediments rather than to any onset of bioaccumulation or bioconcentration or to major new inputs to the ecosystem.

The equilibrium in concentrations of DDT, mirex and total PCBs in the Great Lakes is considered to be due to sediment re-mobilization alone as historical sources have now been largely eliminated. However, atmospheric deposition of metabolites of DDT (principally p,p'-DDE) may still occur across the Great Lakes basin (Environment Canada, 1991).

Once released into the environment, mercury can be converted into methyl mercury; this form of mercury is more readily absorbed by living organisms, especially fish. The observed levels of mercury in the three fish species have decreased since the late 1970s across the Great Lakes region (Tables 1.31 and 1.32). These concentrations, however, are significantly lower than those observed in pike (*Esox lucius*) in Swedish lakes. Figure 1.25 shows that concentrations of mercury in pike from lakes across Sweden can exceed 1.0 mg kg^{-1} in some areas. Although discharges from paper and pulp mills in Sweden have in the past contributed significantly to high concentrations of mercury in Swedish freshwater bodies, today atmospheric deposition of mercury emissions from other European countries are considered to be the main source of this metal in Sweden (Hellner and Lovgren,

1990). Bioaccumulation of methyl mercury in pike in Swedish lakes may be enhanced as a result of acidification.

As a top predator in the Great Lakes aquatic food web, and one that can be found on each of the five lakes at any time of the year, the herring gull (*Larus argentatus*) has been very successfully used as a biomonitor of toxic chemicals. In 1974, the Canadian Wildlife Service began what is now the most extensive and largest wildlife biomonitoring programme in the Great Lakes ecosystem by analysing herring gull eggs for up to 70 organochlorine compounds, including 41 PCB congeners and nine dioxin and furan congeners.

Table 1.33 presents selected data from these analyses from 11 locations throughout the Great Lakes basin. Congener-specific analyses have shown that there are different patterns of accumulation for individual PCBs in organisms; for this reason, PCB values given in Table 1.33 are total PCB values. Nevertheless, care must be taken when comparing these total PCB values with other published total PCB values which may be based on different analytical techniques or on different sets of PCB congeners.

The temporal trends of organochlorine residues in herring gull eggs show that levels of DDE, total PCBs, mirex, hexachlorobenzene (HCB) and 2,3,7,8 tetrachlorodibenzo-*p*-dioxin (TCDD) were much higher in the early 1970s than they are today. However, the downwards trend observed for dieldrin is not nearly as pronounced and concentrations in the late 1980s appear to have reached equilibrium. The reason for this is unclear although there are indications that there could be continued inputs to the ecosystem (Environment Canada, 1991).

References

Environment Canada 1991 *Toxic Chemicals in the Great Lakes and Associated Effects, Volumes 1 and 2*, Environment Canada, Department of Fisheries and Oceans, Department of National Health and Welfare. In press.

Fox, G. A. and Weseloh, D. V. 1987 Colonial waterbirds as bio-indicators of environmental contamination in the Great Lakes, *ICBP Technical Publication* No. 6, 209–216.

Håkanson, L., Andersson, T. and Nilsson, A. 1990 Mercury in fish in Swedish lakes – linkages to domestic and European sources of emission, *Water Air and Soil Pollution* **50**, 171–191.

Hellner, C. and Lovgren, K. 1990 Stop mercury inputs, *Acid Enviro* **10**, 22–23.

Marine Wildlife

This edition of the 'UNEP Environmental Data Report' presents selected data on seabirds, fish, shellfish and mammals as biomonitors of the state of the marine environment throughout the Northern Hemisphere (with the exception of the Arctic for which few data are available). At present, there are few biomonitoring programmes in the Southern Hemisphere. In Antarctica, biomonitoring programmes have concluded that, at present, it is unlikely that the low levels of contaminants recorded in marine biota have adverse effects on the ecosystem (Stromberg et al., 1990). However, recent data from analyses of penguin (*Pygoscelis*

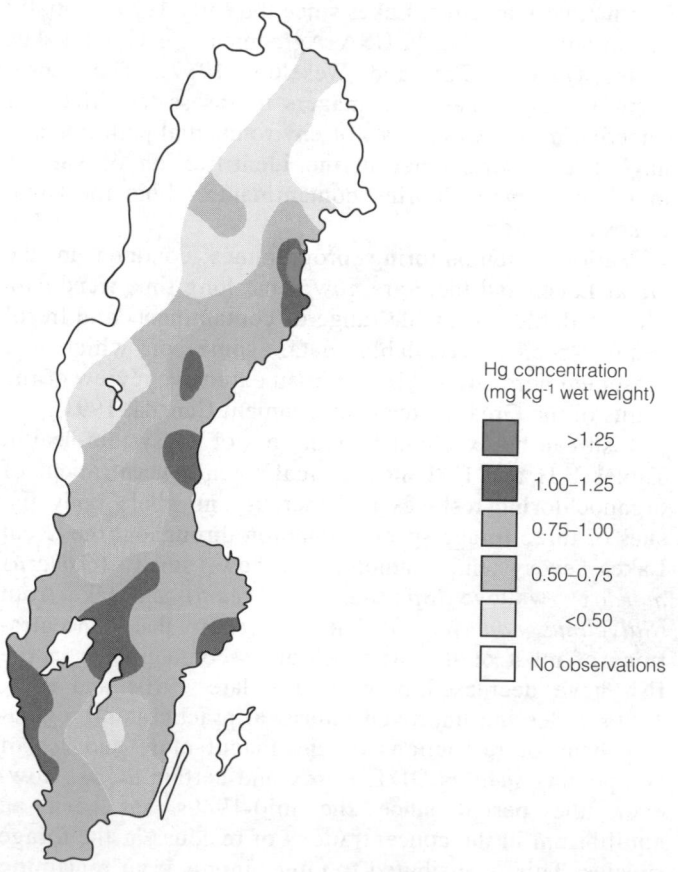

Hg concentration
(mg kg^{-1} wet weight)

- >1.25
- 1.00–1.25
- 0.75–1.00
- 0.50–0.75
- <0.50
- No observations

Figure 1.25 Mean mercury concentrations in pike from Swedish lakes, 1980s
Source: Håkanson et al., 1990

sp.) tissues (the preen gland lipid is suitable for monitoring the body burden of organochlorine compounds) suggest that such programmes are needed in order to provide more detailed baseline data (Luke et al., 1989). The series of recently published reports from the UNEP Regional Seas programmes includes useful information of contaminants in marine organisms (e.g., Stromberg et al., 1990).

Data presented in Table 1.34 show long-term trends in the concentrations of organochlorine residues in eggs of three species of seabird: the double crested cormorant (*Phalacrocorax auritus*), Leach's storm petrel (*Oceanodroma leucorhoa*) and Atlantic puffin (*Fratercula arctica*) from the eastern coast of Canada. Colonial seabirds are good biomonitors because, like the herring gull in fresh water, they feed relatively high in the food chain and can conveniently be sampled at their breeding sites. In addition, as they are long-lived animals, there is a greater probability that they will show subtle chronic effects of toxic substances (Noble and Burns, 1990). The data show significant decreases in concentrations of p,p'-DDE, mirex, PCBs and dieldrin in each species. Figure 1.26 compares data from analyses of seabird eggs of the same, or ecologically similar species, from the east and west coasts of Canada sampled during 1984–1985. Organochlorine residue concentrations are generally higher in eggs from the east coast, with the exception of DDE levels in petrel and Rhinocerus auklet (*Cerorhinca monocerata*). DDE levels were higher on the west coast, suggesting atmospheric inputs of DDT from the Gulf of Mexico and from Asia where it is still heavily used (Elliott et al., 1989).

The International Council for the Exploration of the Sea (ICES), which is engaged in regular marine biomonitoring programmes, has published the results of its 1985 baseline study of contaminants in fish and shellfish in the North Atlantic, the North Sea and the Baltic Sea (ICES, 1988). The study was the first attempt to conduct a unified biomonitoring exercise on such a wide geographical scale. Thirty-three participating laboratories from 16 countries were involved in the survey and more than 10,000 contaminant concentration values for trace metals and organochlorine residues were submitted from the 670 samples that were collected. The fish and shellfish species used as biomonitors in the study were: cod (*Gadus morhua*), plaice (*Pleuronectes platessa*), flounder (*Platichthys flesus*), dab (*Limanda limanda*), herring (*Clupea harengus*), blue mussel (*Mytilus edulis*), Mediterranean mussel (*Mytilus galloprovincialis*) and oysters (*Crassostrea gigas* and *Crassostrea virginica*).

The results of the study reflect known sources of contamination and, where general contamination is indicated,

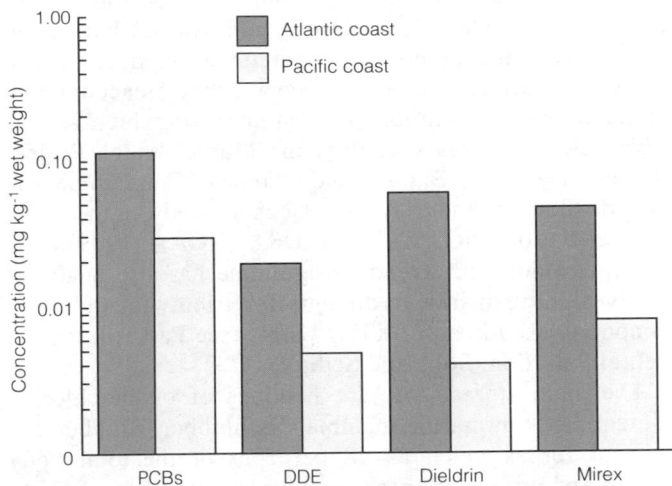

a) **Double crested cormorant**

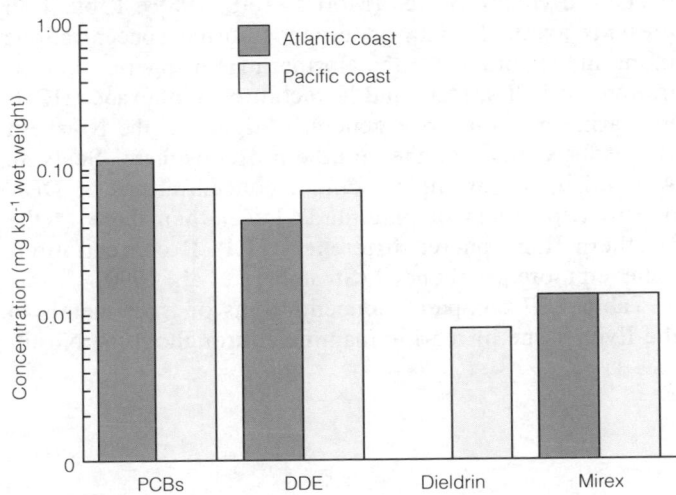

b) **Leach's storm petrel**

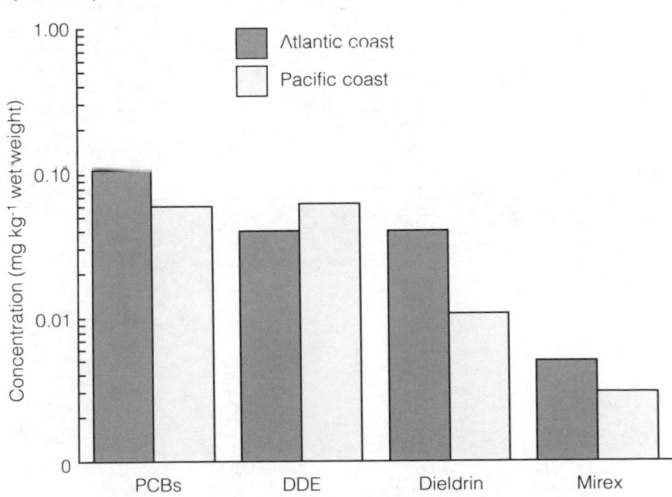

c) **Alantic puffin (Atlantic coast)/Rhinoceros auklet (Pacific coast)**

Figure 1.26 Organochlorine concentrations in eggs of the double crested cormorant, Leach's storm petrel, Atlantic puffin and Rhinoceros auklet from the east and west coasts of Canada, 1984–1985 (concentrations are plotted on a logarithmic scale)
Source: Elliott et al., 1989

it is in coastal areas that are clearly associated with major centres of population and/or industrial activity (ICES, 1988). The results for cod, herring and blue mussel are presented in Table 1.35. Mussels (and oysters) have been widely used for monitoring contamination in estuarine ecosystems because, as filter feeders, they bioaccumulate contaminants. A similar programme using bivalves as biomonitors of estuary quality, the Mussel Watch Project of the National Status and Trends Programme, is co-ordinated by the National Oceanic and Atmospheric Administration (NOAA) in the USA (NOAA, 1989). The National Status and Trends Programme has also analysed bivalves and estuarine sediments for tributyltin (TBT), a compound used in anti-fouling paints (see Part 1: Environmental Pollution, Soils and Sediments).

The main storage site for residues of organochlorine contaminants in marine mammals is blubber. Blubber can account for as much as 98 per cent of the total body burden of organochlorine residues (Stromberg et al., 1990). Although methods of measurement may vary between individual studies (Morris et al., 1989), Table 1.36 presents available data on organochlorine concentrations in marine mammals for the Northern Hemisphere. Concentrations of PCBs, DDT and hexachlorocyclohexane (HCH) in marine mammals are generally higher in the Northern Hemisphere than in the Southern Hemisphere. Seals in Antarctica, for example, contain concentrations of DDT one to two orders of magnitude lower than those of the Northern Hemisphere; differences in PCB concentrations are even more pronounced (Stromberg et al., 1990).

Table 1.37 compares concentrations of trace metals in the liver tissue of marine mammals throughout the North-ern Hemisphere. Concentrations of mercury are the highest of the trace metals. Mercury concentrations are particularly high in the liver tissues, and such concentrations tend to increase with age. The limit of tolerance for mercury in mammalian hepatic tissues is considered to lie within the range 100–400 $\mu g \ g^{-1}$ (Morris et al., 1989).

References

Elliott, J. E., Noble, D. G. and Norstrom, R. J. 1989 Organochlorine contaminants in seabird eggs from the Pacific coast of Canada, 1971–1986, *Environmental Monitoring and Assessment* **12**, 67–82.

ICES 1988 *Results of 1985 Baseline Study of Contaminants in Fish and Shellfish*, Co-operative Research Report 151, International Council for the Exploration of the Sea, Copenhagen.

Luke, B. G., Johnstone, G. W. and Woehler, E. J. 1989 Organochlorine pesticides, PCBs and mercury in Antarctic and sub-Antarctic seabirds, *Chemosphere* **19**(12), 2007–2021.

Morris, R. J., Law, R. J., Allchin, C. R., Kelly, A. and Fileman, C. F. 1989 Metals and organochlorines in dolphins and porpoises of Cardigan Bay, West Wales, *Marine Pollution Bulletin* **20**(10), 512–523.

NOAA 1989 *A Summary of Data on Tissue Contamination from the First Three Years (1986–1988) of the Mussel Watch Project*, National Status and Trends Program for Marine Environmental Quality Progress Report, NOAA Technical Memorandum NOS OMA 49, National Oceanic and Atmospheric Administration, Rockville.

Noble, D. G. and Burns, S. P. 1990 *Contaminants in Canadian Seabirds: A State of the Environment Fact Sheet*, Environment Canada, Ottawa.

Stromberg, J. O., Anderson, L. G., Bjork, G., Bonner, W. N., Clark, A. C., Dick, A. L., Ernst, W., Limbert, D. W. S., Peel, D. A., Priddle, J., Smith, R. I. L. and Walton, D. W. H. 1990 *State of the Marine Environment in Antarctica*, UNEP Regional Seas Reports and Studies No. 129, United Nations Environment Programme, Nairobi.

Table 1.28 Mean concentrations of organochlorine residues in adult woodcock[a] from eastern Canada, 1986 ($\mu g\ kg^{-1}$ fresh weight)

Province	Total DDT	DDE	Mirex	Total PCBs	Dieldrin
Nova Scotia	0.008	0.040	0.026	0.110	0.009
New Brunswick	0.018	0.448	0.055	0.118	0.018
Quebec	0.023	0.172	0.048	0.172	0.014
Ontario	0.034	0.104	0.355	0.300	0.013

[a] *Philohela minor.*

Mean concentrations are based on analyses of 4 pooled samples of 25 wings (without feathers) from each province.

Source:
Peakall, D. B. 1990 Personal communication, Canadian Wildlife Service, Environment Canada, Canada.

Table 1.29 Mean concentrations of organochlorines in pine needles from selected locations in Europe, 1984–1986 ($ng\ g^{-1}$ fresh weight)

Residue	Region[a]	1984	1985	1986
Total DDT	Northern Sweden (1)	0.30	0.31	0.25
	Central Sweden (11)	0.25	0.25	0.19
	East coast of Sweden (8)	0.43	0.26	0.25
	Norwegian foothills (2)	0.19	0.18	0.12
	Northern Germany and Denmark (7)	0.65	0.63	0.30
	Switzerland and southern Germany (4)	0.55	0.50	0.31
	Southern France (7)	0.47	0.29	0.25
	South-western Poland (2)		2.48	1.74
	South-eastern Poland (2)		0.59	0.30
Total PCBs	Northern Sweden (1)	7.9	5.9	4.4
	Central Sweden (11)	4.5	6.2	5.6
	East coast of Sweden (8)	5.8	6.7	5.8
	Norwegian foothills (2)	4.6	6.3	5.6
	Northern Germany and Denmark (7)	6.8	8.1	6.8
	Switzerland and southern Germany (4)	6.2	7.3	4.8
	Southern France (7)	8.1	7.9	5.6
	South-western Poland (2)		10.1	6.5
	South-eastern Poland (2)		1.1	2.0
PCP[b]	Northern Sweden (1)	1.36	1.39	0.85
	Central Sweden (11)	1.23	1.08	1.00
	East coast of Sweden (8)	1.07	1.08	0.85
	Norwegian foothills (2)	0.59	0.75	0.77
	Northern Germany and Denmark (7)	0.48	0.53	0.42
	Switzerland and southern Germany (4)	0.46	0.43	0.39
	Southern France (7)	0.23	0.25	0.51
	South-western Poland (2)		0.45	0.54
	South-eastern Poland (2)		0.09	0.16
HCH[c]	Northern Sweden (1)	5.9	4.1	2.4
	Central Sweden (11)	2.8	2.6	2.1
	East coast of Sweden (8)	2.8	2.9	2.1
	Norwegian foothills (2)	2.2	2.7	1.4
	Northern Germany and Denmark (7)	2.0	1.8	2.7
	Switzerland and southern Germany (4)	2.7	2.6	1.4
	Southern France (7)	2.6	3.3	2.9
	South-western Poland (2)		2.5	3.0
	South-eastern Poland (2)		0.3	0.7

[a] Numbers in parentheses are the number of sites sampled within each region per year.
[b] Pentachlorophenol.
[c] γ-hexachlorocyclohexane and α-hexachlorocyclohexane.

Source:
Eriksson, G., Jensen, S., Kylin, H. and Strachan, W. 1989 The pine needle as a monitor of atmospheric pollution, *Nature* (London) **341**, 42–44.

Table 1.30 European forest damage survey results, 1986–1989

Country	Conifers (all ages) Percentage of defoliated trees[a]					Broadleaves (all ages) Percentage of defoliated trees[a]				
	1986	1987	1988	1989	Change 1988–89	1986	1987	1988	1989	Change 1988–89
Austria	4.5	3.5	4.0	4.1	+0.1	5.5	7.8	5.5	6.7	+1.2
Bulgaria	4.7	3.8	7.6	32.9	+25.3	4.0	3.1	8.8	16.2	+7.4
Czechoslovakia	16.4	15.6	27.0	32.0	+5.0			29.1	37.0	+7.9
Denmark		24.0	21.0	24.0	+3.0		20.0	14.0	30.0	+16.0
Finland		13.5	17.0	18.7	+1.7		4.7	7.9	12.6	+4.7
France	12.5	12.0	9.1	7.2	-1.9	4.8	6.5	5.3	4.8	-0.5
German Dem. Rep.	9.2	10.3	15.5	17.5	+2.0	1.6	2.8	9.0	12.9	+3.9
Germany, Fed. Rep.	19.5	15.9	14.0	13.2	-0.8	16.8	19.2	16.5	20.4	+3.9
Greece			7.7	6.7	-1.0			28.5	18.4	-10.1
Hungary			9.4	13.3	+3.9			7.0	12.5	+5.5
Ireland			4.8	13.2	+8.4					
Liechtenstein	22.0	27.0	23.0			10.0	7.0	5.0		
Luxembourg	4.2	3.8	11.1	9.5	-1.6	5.6	10.1	12.3	13.9	+1.6
Netherlands	28.9	18.7	14.5	17.7	+3.2	13.2	26.5	25.4	13.1	-12.3
Norway			20.8	14.8	-6.0					
Poland			24.2	34.5	+10.3			7.1	17.7	+10.6
Portugal			1.7	9.8	+8.1			0.8	8.6	+7.8
Spain	18.2	10.7	7.3	3.5	-3.8	13.7	13.7	6.8	3.2	-3.6
Sweden	11.1	5.6	12.3	12.9	+0.6			5.2		
Switzerland	16.0	14.0	15.0	14.0	-1.0	8.0	15.0	7.0	6.0	-1.0
UK		23.0	27.0	34.0	+7.0		20.0	20.0	21.0	+1.0
Yugoslavia	23.0	16.1				20.0	7.3			

a Percentage of sampled trees in defoliation classes 2–4 inclusive; i.e., those with more than 25 per cent defoliation.

Data represented are those from national surveys only.

Source:
UN-ECE/UNEP-GEMS 1990 Forest Damage and Air Pollution, Report of the 1989 Forest Damage Survey in Europe, prepared by the Programme Co-ordinating Centres with the assistance of the United Nations Environment Programme, Nairobi, and the Secretariat of the United Nations Economic Commission for Europe, Geneva. In press.

Table 1.31 Mean concentrations of organochlorine residues and mercury in whole body tissue of rainbow smelt[a] from the Great Lakes, 1977–1988 (mg kg^{-1} wet weight)

Residue	Lake	1977	1978	1979	1980	1981	1982	1983	1984	1985	1986	1987	1988
Total DDT	Erie	0.06	0.06	0.10	0.12	0.06	0.07	0.04	0.03	0.03	0.02	0.05	0.07
	Huron			0.07	0.07	0.10	0.12	0.10	0.09	0.07	0.01	0.03	0.07
	Ontario	0.60	0.39	0.39	0.25	0.49	0.43	0.53	0.33	0.18	0.24	0.24	0.30
	Superior					0.07	0.09	0.06	0.04	0.04	0.03	0.03	0.02
p,p'-DDE	Erie	0.04	0.04	0.05	0.06	0.03	0.03	0.02	0.01	0.01	0.02	0.05	0.03
	Huron			0.05	0.05	0.07	0.08	0.07	0.07	0.06	0.01	0.03	0.04
	Ontario	0.44	0.33	0.33	0.21	0.33	0.34	0.41	0.25	0.15	0.22	0.22	0.23
	Superior					0.10	0.08	0.06	0.05		0.08	0.07	0.01
Mirex	Ontario	0.11	0.05	0.05	0.04	0.04	0.02	0.05	0.01	0.01	0.01	0.02	0.03
Total PCBs	Erie	0.18	0.27	0.38	0.26	0.23	0.30	0.32	0.00	0.00	0.06	0.11	0.28
	Huron			0.19	0.11	0.13	0.29	0.18	0.09	0.16			0.21
	Ontario	1.50	1.74	0.80	1.12	0.90	1.66	1.48	1.01	0.55	0.61	0.68	2.15
	Superior			0.11		0.11	0.16	0.23	0.12	0.30	0.13		1.03
Dieldrin	Ontario	0.02	0.05	0.04	0.04	0.06	0.05	0.03	0.03	0.02	0.03	0.02	0.02
	Superior					0.02	0.02	0.01					
Hg	Erie	0.05	0.05	0.04	0.03	0.04	0.03						0.01
	Huron			0.06	0.07	0.06	0.05						0.03
	Ontario	0.08	0.06	0.06	0.09	0.07	0.09						0.03
	Superior					0.10	0.08	0.06	0.05				0.02

a *Osmerus mordax.*

Analyses are performed on pooled samples, each pool comprising five fish. The total number of fish sampled however vary with year and lake.

Source:
Environment Canada 1991 *Toxic Chemicals in the Great Lakes and Associated Effects, Volume 1: Contaminant Levels and Trends,* Environment Canada, Department of Fisheries and Oceans, Department of National Health and Welfare. In press.

Table 1.32   Mean concentrations of organochlorine residues and mercury in whole body tissue of lake trout and walleye from the Great Lakes, 1977–1988 (mg kg⁻¹ wet weight)

Residue	Species[a]	Lake	1977	1978	1979	1980	1981	1982	1983	1984	1985	1986	1987	1988
Total DDT	Walleye	Erie			0.59	0.52	0.10	0.28	0.24	0.17	0.13	0.12	0.15	0.19
	Lake trout	Huron				0.46	0.91	0.66	0.53	0.88	0.88	0.87	0.94	0.42
	Lake trout	Ontario		1.27	1.99	0.81	1.51	1.13	1.56	1.33				1.21
	Lake trout	Michigan	6.34	4.58	6.91	4.74	3.22	2.74						
	Lake trout	Superior				0.35	0.38	0.29	0.15	0.13	0.08	0.09	0.15	0.22
p,p'-DDE	Walleye	Erie	0.39	0.20	0.23	0.21	0.04	0.12	0.11	0.08	0.06	0.10		0.10
	Lake trout	Huron				0.34	0.50	0.44	0.35	0.56				0.30
	Lake trout	Ontario		1.01	1.50	0.64	0.89	0.8	1.02	0.78	0.59	0.75	0.80	0.88
	Lake trout	Superior				0.29	0.26	0.17	0.16	0.18	0.09	0.14	0.23	0.11
Mirex	Lake trout	Ontario		0.15	0.25	0.14	0.15	0.16	0.21	0.08	0.13	0.06	0.11	0.20
Total PCBs	Walleye	Erie			3.60	1.70	1.26	1.72	1.58	0.83	0.80	1.88	1.30	1.72
	Lake trout	Huron				0.75	1.96	1.82	1.21	0.98				1.76
	Lake trout	Ontario		5.06	4.73	4.77	3.67	5.87	6.44	5.91	2.80	2.87	3.49	3.39
	Lake trout	Michigan	11.58	8.18	8.82	9.93	6.49	5.63						
	Lake trout	Superior				0.90	0.45	0.38	0.52	0.86	0.51	0.16	0.42	1.96
Dieldrin	Walleye	Erie		0.05	0.11	0.06	0.01	0.06	0.01	0.04	0.05	0.04	0.04	0.01
	Lake trout	Huron			0.07	0.13	0.08	0.04	0.11					0.05
	Lake trout	Ontario		0.21	0.23	0.12	0.11	0.15	0.14	0.15	0.11	0.14	0.13	0.12
	Lake trout	Michigan	0.40	0.44	0.58	0.34	0.26	0.21						
	Lake trout	Superior				0.04	0.07	0.05	0.03	0.03	0.01	0.02	0.02	0.03
Hg	Walleye	Erie		0.17	0.16	0.19	0.13	0.13	0.13	0.16				0.10
	Lake trout	Huron				0.12	0.22	0.17	0.1					0.09
	Lake trout	Ontario		0.18	0.20	0.20	0.16	0.17	0.22	0.14	0.14	0.11	0.13	0.11
	Lake trout	Superior				0.29	0.26	0.17	0.16	0.18	0.09	0.14	0.23	0.13

[a]   Lake trout *Salvelinus namaycush*; Walleye *Stizostedion vitreum*.

Analyses are performed on pooled samples, each pool comprising five fish. The total number of fish sampled however vary with year and lake.

Source:
Environment Canada 1991 *Toxic Chemicals in the Great Lakes and Associated Effects, Volume 1: Contaminant Levels and Trends*, Environment Canada, Department of Fisheries and Oceans, Department of National Health and Welfare. In press.

Table 1.33 Organochlorine residues in herring gull[a] eggs from the Great Lakes, 1974–1989 (mg kg^{-1}, unless otherwise indicated)

Compound	Lake	Location	1974	1975	1976	1977	1978	1979	1980	1981	1982	1983	1984	1985	1986	1987	1988	1989
DDE	Erie	Port Colborne Lighthouse	8.7	7.9		7.6	5.6	3.4	3.4	4.7	7.5	3.1	4.4	3.6	3.2	1.7	1.9	3.1
		Middle Island	5.6	6.9		7.4	3.0	2.8	2.6	3.1	2.6	1.7	2.0	2.0	2.3	1.7	2.2	2.2
	Huron	Channel/Shelter Island	21.0	12.0		13.0	6.0	2.5	8.9	7.3	8.1	6.1	5.6	4.80	6.0	4.0	4.5	7.0
		Chantry Island	14.0	16.0		19.0	7.0	2.1	2.8	4.0	5.0	2.2	2.5	2.5	2.0	1.0	1.1	0.8
		Double Island							2.6	3.6	3.8	3.2	2.6	3.1	2.1	1.6	1.7	2.4
	Ontario	Mugg's Island	23.0	22.0		13.0	11.0	9.0	8.2	10.0	11.0	4.5	5.3	4.90	4.0	2.3	3.3	5.3
		Snake Island	21.0	24.0		17.0	10.0	8.8	7.1	12.0	8.7	5.1	7.2	7.2	4.7	2.9	5.2	5.2
	Michigan	Big Sister Island			33.0		22.0	11.8	11.0		18.0	6.8	9.3	7.9	7.1	12.0	6.1	4.7
		Gull Island					23.0		13.0		14.0	6.2	6.4	5.9	7.9	4.0		5.0
	Superior	Agawa Rock	14.0	22.0		12.0	8.5	7.3	3.7	6.3	5.8	3.5	2.5	3.0	3.1	2.2	2.7	2.6
		Granite Island	19.0	24.0		12.0	9.6	6.4	3.6	5.2	6.7		3.4	3.3	3.3	2.9	3.2	2.4
Total PCBs	Erie	Port Colborne Lighthouse	32.70	24.19		26.43	20.61	17.02	17.02	19.71	26.88	16.58	20.16	13.44	10.75	11.70	7.96	16.68
		Middle Island	32.26	31.81		34.94	18.82	26.43	24.19	30.91	26.43	17.02	21.06	21.06	19.26	21.91	16.95	20.73
	Huron	Channel/Shelter Island	41.88	18.99		31.17	15.58	15.10	34.09	31.66	35.06	23.86	26.79	23.38	22.40	22.34	33.49	27.82
		Chantry Island	27.27	22.40		37.50	16.07	12.66	1.20	13.64	18.51	8.28	10.71	6.82	5.84	3.98	5.40	3.10
		Double Island							8.28	11.20	15.10	9.74	8.77	9.74	5.84	4.54	5.74	7.08
	Ontario	Mugg's Island	77.17	49.68		40.37	35.87	35.55	27.82	33.63	30.04	18.18	22.77	17.04	11.67	6.85	9.32	15.80
		Snake Island	65.24	83.88		55.92	33.09	29.36	24.70	40.08	28.43	21.44	24.70	16.31	13.51	8.78	12.32	14.37
	Michigan	Big Sister Island			54.94						31.09	12.99	15.78	17.17	12.53	22.27	10.21	9.87
		Gull Island									29.70	15.31	13.46	12.53	12.99	8.29		9.40
	Superior	Agawa Rock	22.65	31.71		25.37	16.76	26.27	10.87	16.31	13.59	9.51	7.25	5.44	6.34	5.45	5.47	6.81
		Granite Island	33.98	37.15		24.92	20.39	26.73	12.23	14.04	18.12		8.15	9.06	6.34	5.76	7.19	7.18
Mirex	Erie	Port Colborne Lighthouse	0.84	0.42		0.51	0.38	0.25	0.28	0.42	0.60	0.29	0.38	0.24	0.25	0.21	0.18	0.33
		Middle Island	0.44	0.22		0.39	0.02	0.10	0.09	0.07	0.08	0.04	0.05	0.05	0.03	0.01	0.03	0.03
	Huron	Channel/Shelter Island	2.20	0.48		0.33	0.24	0.20	0.20	0.06	0.23	0.07	0.03	0.08	0.13	0.05	0.09	0.09
		Chantry Island	0.52	0.55		0.55	0.16	0.17	0.16	0.35	0.58	0.16	0.49	0.14	0.13	0.11	0.07	0.05
		Double Island							0.06	0.17	0.38	0.15	0.20	0.29	0.11	0.06	0.07	0.14
	Ontario	Mugg's Island	7.40	3.40		2.10	1.40	1.80	1.70	2.50	3.70	1.40	1.70	1.30	1.00	0.50	0.70	1.20
		Snake Island	6.60	6.00		2.90	1.70	2.00	1.60	2.80	2.50	1.50	2.00	1.70	1.20	0.90	0.90	1.10
	Michigan	Big Sister Island			0.36		0.26	0.31	0.07		0.07	0.04	0.13	0.18	0.05	0.10	0.04	0.03
		Gull Island					0.16		0.14		0.11	0.06	0.06	0.04	0.09	0.06		0.05

Continued over

Table 1.33 Continued

Compound	Lake	Location	1974	1975	1976	1977	1978	1979	1980	1981	1982	1983	1984	1985	1986	1987	1988	1989
	Superior	Agawa Rock	0.76	1.30		0.42	0.27	0.33	0.17	0.20	0.51	0.15	0.19	0.12	0.12	0.16	0.09	0.09
		Granite Island	1.30	0.62		0.24	0.39	0.19	0.09	0.09	0.22		0.05	0.09	0.09	0.03	0.03	0.05
Dieldrin	Erie	Port Colborne Lighthouse	0.37	0.38		0.50	0.28	0.24	0.27	0.24	0.36	0.17	0.34	0.16	0.20	0.14	0.18	0.23
		Middle Island	0.34	0.28		0.31	0.21	0.27	0.16	0.20	0.24	0.24	0.32	0.22	0.26	0.14	0.17	0.11
	Huron	Channel/Shelter Island								0.18	0.32	0.16	0.23	0.21	0.18	0.19	0.19	0.15
		Chantry Island	0.47	0.31		0.57	0.24	0.28	0.23	0.25	0.29	0.20	0.19	0.29	0.24	0.10	0.21	0.15
		Double Island	0.53	0.41		0.51	0.22	0.32	0.24	0.23	0.26	0.25	0.25	0.32	0.17	0.33	0.24	0.25
	Ontario	Mugg's Island	0.46	0.24		0.28	0.25	0.22	0.18	0.28	0.29	0.14	0.13	0.13	0.14	0.11	0.12	0.30
		Snake Island	0.47	0.35		0.50	0.28	0.19	0.20	0.27	0.27	0.21	0.28	0.18	0.18	0.15	0.18	0.14
	Michigan	Big Sister Island			0.82		0.90	0.54	0.65		0.75	0.53	0.64	0.54	0.28	0.85	0.58	0.53
		Gull Island					0.83		0.75		0.88	0.68	0.41	0.40	0.49	0.33	0.55	
	Superior	Agawa Rock	0.42	0.32		0.40	0.40	0.56	0.35	0.49	0.34	0.33	0.34	0.36	0.32	0.13	0.37	0.33
		Granite Island	0.61	0.44		0.35	0.39	0.64	0.33	0.38	0.44		0.37	0.28	0.37	0.26	0.31	0.34
HCB[b]	Erie	Port Colborne Lighthouse	0.21	0.16		0.19	0.09	0.10	0.08	0.08	0.08	0.06	0.06	0.05	0.05	0.03	0.03	0.05
		Middle Island	0.38	0.23		0.19	0.09	0.12	0.09	0.10	0.08	0.05	0.06	0.07	0.06	0.04	0.06	0.05
	Huron	Channel/Shelter Island								0.14	0.17	0.14	0.09	0.09	0.07	0.07	0.08	0.08
		Chantry Island	0.47	0.18		0.33	0.13	0.10	0.08	0.07	0.08	0.05	0.07	0.05	0.05	0.02	0.04	0.03
		Double Island	0.30	0.24		0.21	0.09	0.10	0.06	0.07	0.07	0.05	0.06	0.07	0.04	0.02	0.04	0.04
	Ontario	Mugg's Island	0.60	0.45		0.34	0.28	0.21	0.20	0.23	0.16	0.07	0.11	0.06	0.07	0.03	0.05	0.06
		Snake Island	0.56	0.22		0.50	0.35	0.22	0.15	0.26	0.16	0.09	0.14	0.08	0.07	0.05	0.09	0.07
	Michigan	Big Sister Island			0.14		0.12	0.13	0.08		0.07	0.03	0.06	0.05	0.07	0.07	0.06	0.04
		Gull Island					0.12		0.10		0.12	0.07	0.06	0.05	0.08	0.04		0.05
	Superior	Agawa Rock	0.22	0.12		0.12	0.11	0.14	0.08	0.14	0.10	0.05	0.06	0.05	0.05	0.04	0.05	0.04
		Granite Island					0.14	0.15	0.08	0.09	0.07		0.05	0.06	0.05	0.04	0.05	0.06
TCDD[c]	Erie	Port Colborne Lighthouse								25	20	9	32	17	32	15	17	19
		Middle Island											12	15	16	21	12	16
	Huron	Channel/Shelter Island											99	87	88	137	86	78
		Chantry Island								155	214	141	30	24	22	14	14	12
		Double Island								45	61	15	28	37	31	27	19	18

Continued below

Table 1.33 Continued

Compound	Lake	Location	1974	1975	1976	1977	1978	1979	1980	1981	1982	1983	1984	1985	1986	1987	1988	1989
	Ontario	Hamilton Harbour																
		Mugg's Island											50		44	49	44	55
		Scotch Bonnet Island	923		489	518	261	169	170	229	204	90	60	39	49	45	40	
		Snake Island								185	129		101	67	65	80	47	91
	Michigan	Big Sister Island	40		54	60			24	58	45	10	18	14	17	26	10	10
		Gull Island									23		12	12		17	14	11
	Superior	Agawa Rock								79	51	13	18	16	28	37	19	19
		Granite Island											14	19	18		16	16

a Larus argentatus.
b Hexachlorobenzene.
c 2,3,7,8-tetrachlorodibenzo-p-dioxin (ng kg^{-1}).

With the exception of TCDD, data for 1974–1986 are mean, wet-weight values based on samples of 9–11 eggs. TCDD data are all based on a 10-egg pool. Data for 1987–1989 are mean, wet-weight values based on one analysis of a 10-egg pool.

Source:
Environment Canada 1991 *Toxic Chemicals in the Great Lakes and Associated Effects, Volume 1: Contaminant Levels and Trends*, Environment Canada, Department of Fisheries and Oceans, Department of National Health and Welfare. In press.

Table 1.34 Mean concentrations of organochlorine residues in eggs of seabirds from the east coast of Canada, 1972–1988 (mg kg^{-1} wet weight)

Residue	Species[a]	1972	1976	1980	1984	1988
p,p'-DDE	Double crested cormorant	2.85	2.18	1.34	1.85	1.05
	Leach's storm petrel	2.91	0.74	0.46	0.44	0.86
	Atlantic puffin	0.64	0.59	0.54	0.40	0.19
Mirex	Double crested cormorant			0.047	0.046	0.019
	Leach's storm petrel			0.026	0.014	0.019
	Atlantic puffin			0.015	0.005	0.005
PCB[b]	Double crested cormorant	14.0	17.1	10.2	11.4	7.6
	Leach's storm petrel	3.7	2.6	1.6	1.2	2.6
	Atlantic puffin	1.9	2.4	2.5	1.1	0.8
Dieldrin	Double crested cormorant	0.12	0.07	0.05	0.06	0.03
	Atlantic puffin	0.05	0.04	0.04	0.04	0.06

[a] Cormorant *Phalacrocorax auritus;* Petrel *Oceanodroma leucorhoa*; Puffin *Fratercula arctica.*
[b] PCB as Aroclor 1254:1260,1:1.

Cormorant eggs were collected from Ile-aux-Pommes, Quebec; petrel and puffin eggs from Great Island, Newfoundland.

Sources:
Peakall, D. B. 1990 Personal communication, Canadian Wildlife Service, Environment Canada, Canada.
Pearce, P. A., Elliott, J. E., Peakall, D. B. and Norstrom, R. J. 1989 Organochlorine contaminants in eggs of seabirds in the north-west Atlantic, 1968–1984, *Environmental Pollution* **56**, 217–235.

Table 1.35 Mean organochlorine and trace metal concentrations in selected fish and shellfish species from marine locations in northern and western Europe, 1985

Country[a]	Sample location	Species[b]	Tissue	p,p'-DDT (μg kg^{-1})	p,p'-DDE (μg kg^{-1})	PCBs[c] (μg kg^{-1})	Hg (mg kg^{-1})	Cd (mg kg^{-1})	Pb (mg kg^{-1})
Belgium	Belgian Coast	Cod	Liver			5,620	0.034	0.008	0.103
		Cod	Muscle			31	0.108		0.090
		Mussel	Whole soft body			193	0.039	0.162	0.378
Denmark	Kattegat-Ringhals	Mussel	Whole soft body				0.002	0.164	0.317
	Kiel	Mussel	Whole soft body				0.005	0.130	0.183
	Sassnitz	Mussel	Whole soft body				0.019	0.408	0.438
Finland	Aland Islands	Cod	Liver	114	220				
		Cod	Muscle				0.033	0.014	0.024
	Hanko	Cod	Liver	152	236				
		Cod	Muscle				0.039	0.039	0.062
	Pori	Cod	Liver	120	205			0.017	0.033
		Cod	Muscle				0.048		
France	St Nazaire	Mussel	Whole soft body			147	0.022	0.255	0.500
German Dem. Rep.	Kiel	Cod	Liver			2,540			
		Cod	Muscle				0.061	0.002	0.015
	Southern Bight North Sea	Cod	Liver			3,120			
Germany, Fed. Rep.	Ems Estuary	Mussel	Whole soft body	0.5	1.5			0.138	0.523
	Kiel	Herring	Liver	24.5	30.5				
		Herring	Muscle	5.8	14.6		0.026	0.002	0.017
	Malmo	Cod	Liver			51		0.049	0.043
		Cod	Muscle				0.029		
		Herring	Liver	16.5	13.5				
Ireland	Boyne Estuary	Mussel	Whole soft body	6.9	4.4				
	Cork Harbour	Mussel	Whole soft body	13.5	1.2				
	Shannon Estuary	Mussel	Whole soft body	15.4	0.7				
	Waterford Harbour	Mussel	Whole soft body	1.1	5.2				
Netherlands	Heligoland	Cod	Liver	28.5	140		0.040	0.013	0.080
		Cod	Muscle	0.7	1.2		0.060	0.006	0.060
	Netherlands Coast	Mussel	Whole soft body				0.030	0.140	0.320
	North Sea	Cod	Liver	19.5	87.0		0.020	0.028	0.090
		Cod	Muscle	1.6	2.0		0.030	0.008	0.006
	Scheldt Estuary (East)	Mussel	Whole soft body				0.030	0.074	0.590
	Scheldt Estuary (West)	Mussel	Whole soft body				0.043	0.754	0.693
	Waddenzee	Mussel	Whole soft body				0.030	0.060	0.620
Norway	Barents Sea	Cod	Liver	180	161	549			
		Cod	Muscle	0.4	0.5	3	0.010	0.019	
	Bay of the White Sea	Cod	Liver	214	140	1,063			
		Cod	Muscle	0.6	0.5	4	0.016	0.003	

Continued over

Table 1.35 Continued

Country[a]	Sample location	Species[b]	Tissue	p,p'-DDT (μg kg^{-1})	p,p'-DDE (μg kg^{-1})	PCBs[c] (μg kg^{-1})	Hg (mg kg^{-1})	Cd (mg kg^{-1})	Pb (mg kg^{-1})
	North Sea	Cod	Liver	326	152	642	0.024	0.027	
		Cod	Muscle	0.3	0.2	4	0.030	0.004	
	Orkdals Fjord	Cod	Liver			380	0.025	0.214	0.323
	Oslo Fjord	Mussel	Whole soft body			44			
		Cod	Liver		414	4,305	0.099	0.068	
		Cod	Muscle				0.030		
	Trondheim Fjord	Mussel	Whole soft body		50.0	31	0.052	0.261	0.254
		Cod	Liver					0.100	
		Cod	Muscle						
		Mussel	Whole soft body				0.013	0.293	0.263
Poland	Gdansk Bay	Cod	Liver	264	614	1,375	0.026	0.028	0.203
		Cod	Muscle	2.5	4.7		0.025	0.033	0.304
		Herring	Liver	39.1	80.0	118	0.025	0.470	0.830
		Herring	Muscle	1.6	2.8	5	0.017	0.025	
		Mussel	Whole soft body					0.068	
	Karlskrona	Cod	Liver	471	568	1,553	0.009	0.026	0.243
		Cod	Muscle	1.4	1.0	5	0.008	0.543	0.323
		Herring	Liver	37.3	55.3	96	0.028	0.032	0.463
		Herring	Muscle				0.011	0.033	
	Sassnitz	Cod	Liver	243	397	827	0.025	0.025	0.200
		Cod	Muscle	3.6	4.5	13	0.019	0.543	0.197
		Herring	Liver	40.7	61.7	113	0.028	0.047	0.463
		Herring	Muscle				0.011		
Spain	Ria de Arosa	Mussel	Whole soft body	1.7	1.8		0.071	0.134	0.457
	Ria de Pontevendra	Mussel	Whole soft body	3.9	2.1				
	Ria de Vigo	Mussel	Whole soft body				0.115	0.112	0.524
	Santander	Mussel	Whole soft body	10.0	4.9				
Sweden	Gotland	Cod	Liver	397	749	2,160	0.024	0.051	0.036
		Cod	Muscle						
	Kattegat-Ringhals	Cod	Liver	99.8	348	2,030	0.066	0.105	0.051
		Herring	Muscle						
	Lulea	Herring	Liver	2.0	5.1	23	0.023	0.169	0.517
		Herring	Muscle						
	Norrkoping	Herring	Liver	7.3	10.7	52	0.037	0.519	0.048
		Herring	Muscle	12.9	37.4	115	0.034	0.548	0.087
UK	Eastbourne	Mussel	Whole soft body				0.030	0.100	1.000
	Farne Isles	Mussel	Whole soft body				0.029	0.120	
	Humber Estuary	Cod	Liver			1,500	0.080		
		Cod	Muscle			6	0.030		
		Mussel	Whole soft body	4.0	2.8	42		0.650	

Continued below

Table 1.35 Continued

Country[a]	Sample location	Species[b]	Tissue	p,p'-DDT (µg kg^{-1})	p,p'-DDE (µg kg^{-1})	PCBs[c] (µg kg^{-1})	Hg (mg kg^{-1})	Cd (mg kg^{-1})	Pb (mg kg^{-1})
	Liverpool Bay	Cod	Liver	39	580	8,100	0.230	0.070	
		Mussel	Whole soft body	1.0	2.0		0.179	0.651	
	Lough Swilly	Mussel	Whole soft body	4.4	5.9	48	0.069	0.225	0.605
	Mersey Estuary	Mussel	Whole soft body			32	0.054	0.353	1.090
	Morcambe Bay	Mussel	Whole soft body		2.5	30	0.019	0.090	0.590
	Selsey Bill	Mussel	Whole soft body		4.0	36	0.034	0.724	2.050
	Severn Estuary	Mussel	Whole soft body	2.5		10	0.060	0.913	0.693
	Solway Firth	Mussel	Whole soft body	1.5	2.0	45	0.036	0.250	2.100
	Southampton Water	Cod	Liver			1,635	0.075		
	Southern Bight North Sea	Cod	Muscle				0.025		
		Mussel	Whole soft body			10	0.100	0.131	0.633
	St Austell Bay	Cod	Liver	160	170	3,400	0.150		
		Cod	Muscle						
	St Ives Bay	Mussel	Whole soft body			30	0.030	0.246	3.390
	Swansea Bay	Mussel	Whole soft body		1.5	24	0.031	0.179	3.190
		Mussel	Whole soft body			10	0.032	0.242	0.707
	Thames Estuary	Cod	Liver	6.0	97.5		0.080	0.040	
		Cod	Muscle				0.034		
	The Wash	Mussel	Whole soft body	1.0	1.4	40	0.015	0.285	0.600
		Mussel	Whole soft body		1.3	9	0.030	0.109	
	Tremadoc Bay	Mussel	Whole soft body			23	0.032	0.274	2.590
	Tyne Estuary	Cod	liver			540	0.050		
		Cod	Muscle				0.020		
		Mussel	Whole soft body			17		0.110	3.010

a   Country refers to the country in which the laboratory analysis was performed.

b   Cod *Gadus morhua*; Herring *Clupea harengus*; Mussel *Mytilus edulis*.

c   Data for PCBs were supplied on formulation bases which vary.

All analyses were conducted on wet material; results are as wet weight.

Source:
ICES 1988 *Results of 1985 Baseline Study of Contaminants in Fish and Shellfish*, Co-operative Research Report 151, International Council for the Exploration of the Sea, Copenhagen.

Table 1.36 Mean concentrations of organochlorine residues in the blubber of marine mammals from the Northern Hemisphere, 1971–1988 (μg g^{-1} wet weight)

Species[a]	Region	Country	Location	Year(s)
Grey seal	NORTH AMERICA	Canada		1976
	EUROPE	UK	Cardigan Bay, Wales	1988[b]
			Farne Islands, England	1988
Common (harbour) seal	EUROPE	Denmark	Schleswig-Holstein	1975–76
		Netherlands		1975–76
		UK	Eastern England	1988
Arctic ringed seal	EUROPE	Norway	Spitzbergen	1986
Common (harbour) porpoise	NORTH AMERICA	Canada		1971–77
		USA		1971–75
	EUROPE	Denmark		1972–73
		Germany, Fed. Rep.	Baltic Sea	1976
		Netherlands		1978[b]
				1971[b]
		UK	Cardigan Bay, Wales	1988
Bottlenose dolphin	NORTH AMERICA	USA		1983–86[d]
	EUROPE	UK	Cardigan Bay, Wales	1988[b]
Striped dolphin	NORTH AMERICA	USA		1971–75
	ASIA	Japan		1979
		Japan		1979
		Japan		1978–79
	EUROPE	France		1972–77
		UK	Cardigan Bay, Wales	1988[b]
White-beaked dolphin	NORTH AMERICA	Canada		
Pacific white-sided dolphin	ASIA	Japan		1981
Killer whale	ASIA	Japan		1986[b]
White whale (beluga)	NORTH AMERICA	Canada		1982–85
		Canada		1971[b]

[a] Grey seal *Halichoerus grypus*; Common (harbour) seal *Phoca vitulina*; Arctic ringed seal *Pusa hispida*; Common (harbour) porpoise *Phocoena phocoena*; Bottlenose dolphin *Tursiops truncatus*; Striped dolphin *Stenella coeruleoalba*; White-beaked dolphin *Lagenorhynchus albirostris*; Pacific white-sided dolphin *Lagenorhynchus obliquidens*; Killer whale *Orcinus orca*; White whale (beluga) *Delphinapterus leucas*.

[b] Individual specimen.
[c] μg g^{-1} fat weight.
[d] Melon samples (no blubber analyses conducted). The melon is an acoustic organ, located in the forehead of the Cetacea, consisting of fatty tissue resulting from the breakdown of lipid.

Sex	HCB	Total HCH	Dieldrin	p,p'-DDE	p,p'-DDT	Total DDT	Total PCBs
				7.6	5.30	13.0	12
	0.006	0.020	0.260	1.1	0.26	1.4	17
	0.130	0.017	0.160	2.6	1.50	4.2	18
				5.0	2.00	8.5	76[c]
			0.400	27.0	12.00	47.0	700[c]
	0.004	0.027	0.230	3.1	1.60	4.7	23
	0.022	0.140	0.071	1.2	0.39		
Male	0.230					100.0	79
Female	0.250					39.0	47
			1.500	20.0	28.00	58.0	74
			6.100	16.0	18.00	49.0	78
			3.200	18.0	8.60	38.0	120
	0.100		2.500	9.2	13.00	25.0	59
	1.300		17.000	20.0	20.00	49.0	190
	0.430	0.310	6.200	3.5	2.50	12.0	49
Male			5.900	11.0	11.00	24.0	91
Female			0.920	1.8	2.10	4.1	20
	0.650	0.800	74.000	55.0	23.00	150.0	290
Male			1.400	48.0	18.00	71.0	39
Female			2.400	140.0	68.00	230.0	69
	0.130	0.470		28.0	4.30	33.0	23
		0.410				29.0	21
Male		0.470				33.0	23
Female		0.150				2.2	2.5
				248.0	71.00	340.0	270[c]
	0.710	0.300	4.900	12.0	17.00	50.0	22
Male	1.100	0.810	0.730	25.0		43.0	53
Female	0.900	0.820	0.210	16.0		28.0	29
		14.000				76.0	38
Male							410
Female							360
				29.0	11.00	50.0	150
				440.0	260.00	830.0	800

This table represents a compilation of data from different sources, full details of which are given in the source document.

Source:
Morris, R. J., Law, R. J., Allchin, C. R., Kelly, C. A. and Fileman, C. F. 1989 Metals and organochlorines in dolphins and porpoises of Cardigan Bay, West Wales, *Marine Pollution Bulletin* **20**(10), 512–523.

Table 1.37 Mean trace metal concentrations in the livers of marine mammals from the Northern Hemisphere, 1969–1990 (μg g^{-1} wet weight)

Species	Region	Country	Location	Year(s)	Sex	Cu	Zn	Cd	Hg	Pb
Grey seal[a]	EUROPE	Germany, Fed. Rep.	Coastal waters	1975	Male	21.0	61	0.02	20	0.31
		UK	Eastern England	1988	Male	22.0	25	0.06	110	<0.60
			Eastern England	pre-1975				1.20	120	8.00
			North-eastern England	pre-1978				0.31	43	<2.50
			Eastern Scotland	1975–78	Female	13.0	60	0.91	142	<2.50
					Male			0.89	25	<0.50
			Northern Ireland	1988–89	Female			0.57	36	<0.50
					Female			0.85[b]	28	<0.60
Common (harbour) seal[c]	NORTH AMERICA	Canada	East coast	1971					13	
		USA	California	1971					270	
	EUROPE	Denmark	Schleswig-Holstein	1975–76					210	
		Germany, Fed. Rep.	Wadden Sea	1974–76		9.1	34	0.31	83	0.23
		Netherlands	Wadden Sea	1975–76					290	
		UK	Eastern England	1988	Male	8.1	42	0.08[b]	30	<0.70
					Female	7.8	49	0.20[b]	56	<0.80
			Northern Ireland	1969–70		15.0	57	1.20	60	2.30
				pre-1975		14.0	51	0.26[b]	51	10.00
				1988–89						<0.60
Ringed seal[d]	NORTH AMERICA	Canada		1971		20.0	56	10.00	8.7	0.02
Common (harbour) porpoise[e]	NORTH AMERICA	Canada		1969–71	Male				0.8	
					Female				1	
	EUROPE	Belgium	Coastal waters	1987–88		4.5	59	0.03	0.7	3.50
		Denmark		1972–73		4.0	34	0.11	22	0.43
		Germany, Fed. Rep.		pre-1978	Male	11.0	50	0.47[b]	2.5	0.26
		UK	Scotland	1988–89	Female	59.0	39	0.15	15	<0.70
			Eastern Scotland	1974	Male	7.3	43	0.27	2.2	
					Female	7.2	44	0.15	3.4	
			Northern Ireland	1988–89		10.0	80	0.15	6	<0.70
			Cardigan Bay, Wales	1988–89		13.0	58	<0.07	14	<0.70
									1.3	
Dall's porpoise[f]	ASIA		North-west Pacific Ocean	pre-1988	Male	5.4	28	3.90	6.4	<0.40
					Female	8.6	46	21.00		<0.04
Common dolphin[g]	EUROPE	Belgium		1986					30	
		UK	Carmarthen Bay, Wales	1990	Female	4.2	26	0.34	11	1.00
White-beaked dolphin[h]	NORTH AMERICA	Canada		1982		20.0	100	2.40	3	0.38
	EUROPE	Denmark		1972	Female	6.4	24		19	4.50
		UK	Wirral, England	1989	Female	6.8	27	0.11	27	3.80

Continued below

Table 1.37 Continued

Species	Region	Country	Location	Year(s)	Sex	Cu	Zn	Cd	Hg	Pb
Striped dolphin[i]	ASIA	Japan		1977–80		8.1	45	6.30	205	0.22
	EUROPE	UK	Wales	1990	Male	11.0	56	9.70	11	<0.70
Atlantic bottlenose dolphin[j]	NORTH AMERICA	USA	East coast	1987–88		8.3	76	ND	22	0.23
	EUROPE	UK	Cardigan Bay, Wales	1989	Male	8.3	42	0.12	21	<0.60
			Tenby, Wales	1989	Female	5.7	32	<0.07	20	<0.70

a   Halichoerus grypus.
b   "Less than" values treated as half of the limit of detection.
c   Phoca vitulina.
d   Pusa hispida.
e   Phocoena phocoena.
f   Phocoenoides dalli.
g   Delphinus delphis.
h   Lagenorhynchus albirostris.
i   Stenella coeruleoalba.
j   Tursiops truncatus.

ND = Not detected, no limit of detection given.

This table represents a compilation of data from a collection of sources, full details of which are given in the source document.

Source:
Law, R. J., Fileman, C. F., Hopkins, A. D., Baker, J. R., Harwood, J., Jackson, D. B., Kennedy, S., Martin, A. R. and Morris, R. J. 1991 Concentrations of trace metals in the livers of marine mammals (seals, porpoises and dolphins) from waters around the British Isles, Marine Pollution Bulletin. In press.

Human Exposure

In order to protect human health and to assess the impact of control measures, monitoring of the level and duration of human exposure to environmental contaminants is essential. Two approaches to measuring exposure are available. In the first approach, the concentrations of contaminants in potential pathways (air, water and food) are used as source-orientated indicators of human exposure. However, source-orientated monitoring provides little information on how much of a contaminant humans are actually exposed to at the individual level. The second approach, which involves taking measurements of the concentrations of contaminants in human tissue (such as blood and adipose tissue), secreta (e.g., breast milk) and excreta (e.g., urine, faeces), provides an index of integrated exposure.

Chemical Contaminants in Food and Dietary Intake

Food contamination is a major problem which poses serious threats to food security and sustainable development world-wide (FAO, 1988). The GEMS/Food project, a collaborative effort of WHO/UNEP/FAO, was established in 1976 to evaluate food contamination around the world and to promote the adoption of measures to prevent and control such contamination (UNEP/FAO/WHO, 1988). Data have been collected on the concentrations of 18 contaminants including metals, chemicals and toxins in over 1,200 individual foods and in the typical diets of the populations of the 39 countries participating in the programme (UNEP, 1990). Comparisons between dietary intake levels and levels assessed to be toxicologically-tolerable (i.e., PTWIs, Provisional Tolerable Weekly Intakes) can be used to determine the risks to consumers (Galal-Gorchev, 1990a).

Current estimates of national average adult dietary intakes of lead (Pb), cadmium (Cd) and mercury (Hg) for selected countries are presented in Table 1.38. All countries which have submitted data to GEMS/Food have levels below the PTWI established by the Joint FAO/WHO Expert Committee on Food Additives (JECFA) for both Cd and Hg. However, the PTWI for Pb is exceeded by samples from three countries and closely approached by one other.

Sources of contamination of food by Pb include canned foods and beverages, plumbing, atmospheric deposition on crops, and the use of sewage sludge containing Pb on agricultural land (Galal-Gorchev, 1990a). The contribution of individual foods to the total intake of Pb depends on the quantity of the food consumed and the concentration of the contaminant in that food (Galal-Gorchev, 1990b). Based on the theoretical "global diet" and "typical" concentrations found in food, the major contributors to Pb intake from food are (in descending order) canned beverages, drinking water, cereals, root and tuber vegetables and fruit (Table 1.39). Lead levels in fresh and canned produce as reported to GEMS/Food were presented in a previous edition of this report (UNEP, 1987).

In addition to outright food losses, mould growth on food can lead to contamination by a range of mycotoxins presenting major health hazards (WHO, 1979). Aflatoxins produced by strains of *Aspergillus flavus* and *A. parasiticus*, are a group of potent hepatotoxic and hepatocarcinogenic fungal metabolites. Concentrations of aflatoxins reported to GEMS/Food are shown in Table 1.40 for several countries. Many countries have adopted routine procedures to monitor and control aflatoxin concentrations and in many cases these have proved effective.

Within the GEMS/Food project, analytical quality assurance studies on aflatoxins (WHO, 1988) have been in operation since 1980 as part of a wider mycotoxin check sample programme currently covering 50 countries and 203 laboratories and co-ordinated by WHO's International Agency for Research on Cancer (IARC).

References

FAO 1988 *Report of the Second Joint FAO/WHO/UNEP International Conference on Mycotoxins*, Bangkok, Thailand, 28 September–2 October 1987, Food and Agriculture Organization, Rome.

Galal-Gorchev, H. 1990a Dietary intake, levels in food and estimated intake of cadmium, lead and mercury. Paper presented at the Symposium on Food Contamination, Cairo, 4–15 November 1990. Unpublished paper.

Galal-Gorchev, H. 1990b Global overview of dietary lead exposure. Paper presented at the Symposium on the Bioavailability and Dietary Uptake of Lead, Chapel Hill, 24–27 September 1990. Unpublished paper.

UNEP 1987 *United Nations Environment Programme Environmental Data Report*, Basil Blackwell, Oxford.

UNEP 1990 *GEMS: Global Environment Monitoring System*, United Nations Environment Programme, Nairobi.

UNEP/FAO/WHO 1988 *Assessment of Chemical Contaminants in Food*, United Nations Environment Programme, Nairobi, Food and Agriculture Association, Rome, and World Health Organization, Geneva.

WHO 1979 *Mycotoxins*, Environmental Health Criteria, Number 11, World Health Organization, Geneva.

WHO 1988 *Joint UNEP/FAO/WHO Food Contamination Monitoring Programme: Analytical Quality Assurance Studies III, 1985–1987*, World Health Organization, Geneva.

Contaminants in Human Excreta, Secreta and Tissues

The concentration of chemical contaminants in human tissues is used as an indicator of total exposure to chemicals in the environment. This approach to human exposure monitoring is particularly suited to the monitoring of environmentally persistent and metabolic-resistant chemicals including, for example, organochlorine compounds (UNEP, 1987). The concentration of organochlorine contaminants is greatest in fat-rich tissues such as adipose tissue and in breast milk. Lactation is the most important elimination route for such contaminants and as a result studies of this type have focused on analyses of breast milk (Jensen, 1989). In this section data on concentrations of Pb and aflatoxins in urine; polychlorinated biphenyls (PCBs), polychlorinated dibenzo-*p*-dioxins (PCDDs), some pesticides and arsenic (As) in breast milk; and organochlorine compounds in adipose tissue are presented. With the exception of As, elevated concentrations tend to occur in human populations from industrialized countries (Jensen, 1989). The second edition of this report contained data showing trends of Pb concentrations in human blood (UNEP, 1989).

As source-orientated monitoring provides little information on exposure to contaminants at the individual level, UNEP and WHO are developing the Human Exposure Assessment Locations (HEALs) project as part of the health-related monitoring component of UNEP/GEMS. HEALs has been developed to encourage international co-operation in pooling information and resources and to ensure good quality control so results can be compared within and between countries. Pilot phase studies have been recently completed for Pb, Cd, nitrogen dioxide (NO_2), dichlorodiphenyltrichloroethane (DDT) and hexachlorobenzene (HCB) in China, India, Japan, Sweden, USA and Yugoslavia.

Contaminants in Excreta Results from the HEALs pilot phase study on Pb, based on a sample of non-smoking women, are illustrated in Figure 1.27. The figure illustrates the different contributions to total intake of Pb (indicated by the amount excreted through faeces) made by diet and air. In Zagreb, Yugoslavia, for example, three times more Pb is excreted than is found in the typical diet thus indicating the existence of a more important source of ingested Pb than food and water.

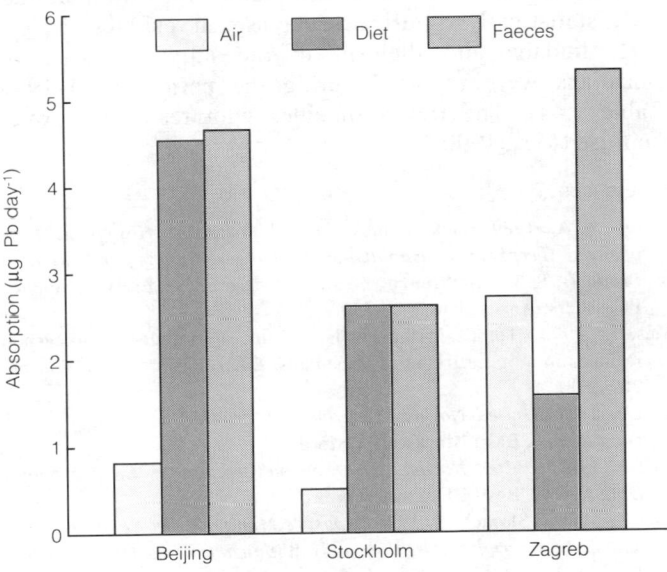

Figure 1.27 Daily absorption of Pb estimated from the measured amounts in air, diet and faeces in selected cities
Source: Vahter and Slorach, 1990

In recent years, analytical methods for measuring the concentrations of aflatoxins, their metabolites or macro-molecular-aflatoxin adducts in human body fluids (such as milk, blood and urine) have become available. Results from this type of analysis accurately reflect the exposure of individuals to such compounds (Wild et al., 1990).

Ingested Aflatoxin B_1 may be metabolically degraded to Aflatoxin M_1 which can be measured in urine. For example, immunoassays of urinary aflatoxin M_1 have shown that the methods are sensitive enough to measure short-term environmental exposure to as little as 1 µg of aflatoxin B_1 (14 ng aflatoxin B_1 kg^{-1} body weight). Figure 1.28 illustrates the range of values recorded. Although the results presented reflect the suitability of the methods used to measure aflatoxin B_1 exposure, larger trials are required to establish relative ranges of national exposures and related epidemiological interpretations of the data.

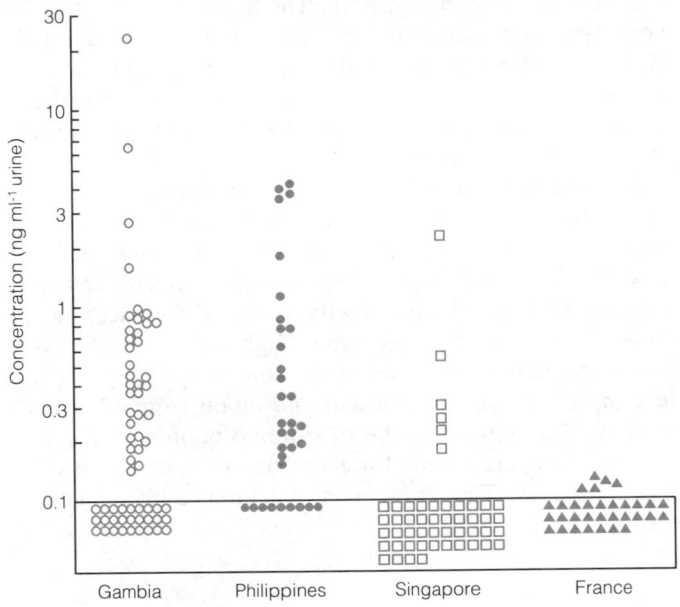

Figure 1.28 Aflatoxin levels in human urine
Source: Wild et al., 1988

Contaminants in Breast Milk Contaminants in human milk are very important in the context of dietary intake of contaminants by infants. Part of the WHO's strategy for 'Health for All by the Year 2000' consists of promoting the benefits to infants of breast-feeding (data reflecting global trends in the prevalence of breast-feeding are given in Part 5: Human Health).

Reports of elevated concentrations of selected contaminants in breast milk prompted the WHO Regional Office for Europe (WHO/EURO), in collaboration with the Regional Government of Venice, to assess the health risks to infants of exposure to some organochlorine compounds. Four hundred samples of breast milk were collected from women in 19 countries between 1986 and 1988. One of the conclusions of the study was that the levels of contaminants to which infants were exposed in breast milk were too low to negate the nutritional benefits gained from a diet of breast milk. However, the expert group warned that the margin of safety was small and that infants may have a higher sensitivity to contaminants in breast milk than is currently known (Yrjänheikki, 1989).

Table 1.41 presents data on the concentrations of two extremely toxic congeners of PCDDs in human breast milk (2,3,7,8 tetrachlorodibenzo-*p*-dioxin or 2,3,7,8-TCDD and octachlorodibenzo-*p*-dioxin or OCDD). The largest values for 2,3,7,8-TCDD, the most toxic congener of dioxins, were recorded in two cities in Viet Nam. Agent Orange, a defoliant, has been suggested as a possible source of exposure to dioxins amongst the Vietnamese population. Levels of OCDD were highest in Japan. Generally, the levels in more densely populated and industrial areas tend to be higher than those in rural areas. These differences are, however, not statistically significant (Yrjänheikki, 1989).

Table 1.42 illustrates the range of concentrations of PCBs measured in breast milk. The highest levels of PCBs were typically found in the most developed countries. There were no significant differences for populations in industrial versus rural areas. The results are not directly comparable between all countries as two different analytical methods were used.

A study of trace and minor elements in breast milk conducted by the WHO and the International Atomic Energy Agency (IAEA) found that exposure to As varies considerably by geographic region (Figure 1.29). Arsenic levels in tissues and body fluids directly reflect differences in the dietary intake of this element. High values of As were found in samples of breast milk from the Philippines and in samples of body tissue, hair and blood from other parts of Asia. The dietary intake of Filipino babies is 12 μg As per day compared with 1 μg per day or less in the other five countries. The provisional tolerable daily intake for As is 12 μg per day.

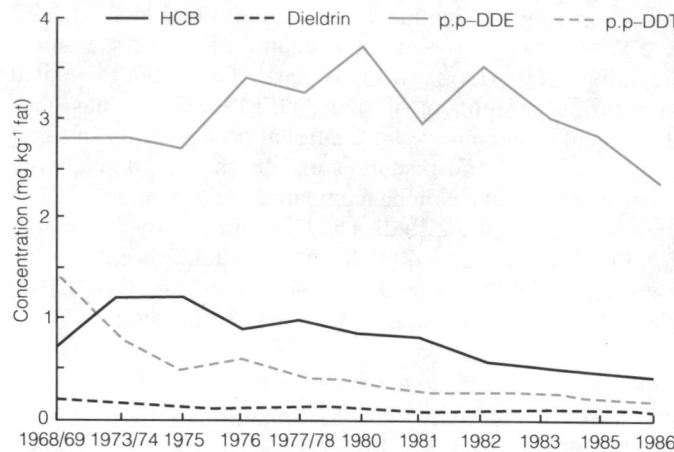

Figure 1.30 Trends in the levels of organochlorine pesticide residues in human adipose tissue of Dutch citizens, 1968–1988
Source: data from Table 1.43

stricted in the Netherlands and other developed countries since the early 1970s. Small decreases in concentration are observed for the other chemicals (Table 1.43). In a similar study, statistically significant decreases in residues of p,p'-DDT, lindane and dieldrin in the adipose tissue of Canadians were reported during the period 1969–1985 (Table 1.44). The trend coincides with restrictions over their use (Mes, 1990).

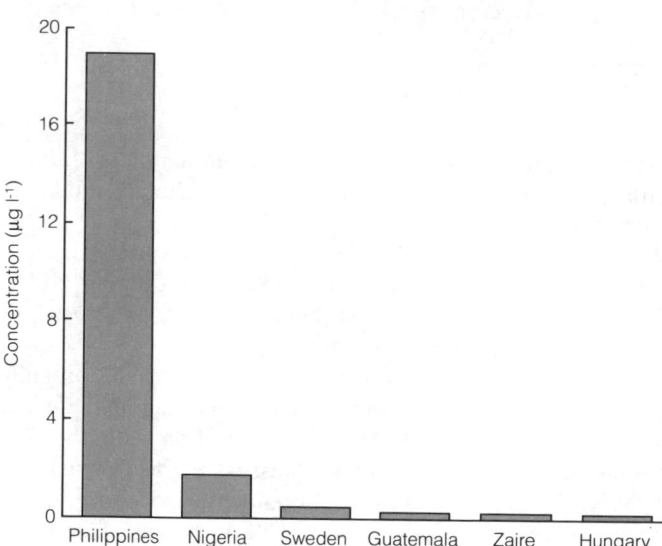

Figure 1.29 Levels of As in human breast milk in selected countries
Source: WHO/IAEA, 1989

Contaminants in Adipose Tissue Concentrations of organochlorine chemicals in human tissues have been under intense investigation since it was discovered that DDT, a metabolic-resistant compound, accumulates in human fat and is not readily eliminated. Figure 1.30 illustrates the persistence of 1,1'-(2,2-dichlorethenylidene)-bis[4-chlorobenzene] (p,p'-DDE); the levels of p,p'-DDE, a metabolite of DDT, have remained relatively constant in adipose tissue of Dutch citizens even though the use of DDT has been re-

References

Jensen, A. A. 1989 Background levels in humans. In: *Halogenated Biphenyls, Terphenyls, Naphthalenes, Dibenzodioxins and Related Products*, R. D. Kimbrough and A. A. Jensen (Eds), Elsevier Science Publishers, Amsterdam, 345–380.

Mes, J. 1990 Trends in the levels of some chlorinated hydrocarbon residues in adipose tissue of Canadians, *Environmental Pollution* **65**, 269–278.

UNEP 1987 *United Nations Environment Programme Environmental Data Report*, Basil Blackwell, Oxford.

UNEP 1989 *United Nations Environment Programme Environmental Data Report*, Basil Blackwell, Oxford.

Vahter, M. and Slorach, S. 1990 *Exposure Monitoring of Lead and Cadmium: An International Pilot Study Within the WHO/UNEP Human Environmental Assessment Location (HEAL) Programme*, World Health Organization, Geneva, and United Nations Environment Programme, Nairobi.

WHO/IAEA 1989 *Minor and Trace Elements in Breast Milk*, Report of a Joint WHO/IAEA collaborative study, World Health Organization, Geneva, and International Atomic Energy Agency, Vienna.

Wild, C. P., Chapot, E., Scherer, E., Den Engelse, L. and Montesano, R. 1988 Application of antibody methods to the detection of aflatoxin in human body fluids. In: *Methods of Detecting DNA Damaging Agents in Humans: Applications in Cancer Epidemiology and Prevention*, H. Bartsch, K. Hemminki and I. K. O'Neill (Eds), IARC Scientific Publications No. 89, International Agency for Research on Cancer, Lyon, 67–74.

Wild, C. P., Jiang, Y. Z., Sabbioni, G., Chapot, B. and Montesano, R. 1990 Evaluation of methods for quantification of aflatoxin-albumin adducts and their application to human exposure assessment, *Cancer Research* **50**, 245–251.

Yrjänheikki, E. J. 1989 *Levels of PCBs, PCDDs and PCDFs in Breast Milk*, World Health Organization, Geneva.

Exposure to Ionizing Radiation

The compilation of human exposure data and radiation effects from natural and man-made sources of radiation is centred on the United Nations Scientific Committee on the Effects of Atomic Radiation (UNSCEAR) (UNSCEAR, 1988).

The average person receives a radiation dose of 2.421 millisievert (mSv) per year (UNEP, 1985). Nearly 83 per cent of this dose arises from natural sources of radiation, mainly terrestrial radiation. Other sources of radiation include medicine (16 per cent), nuclear fall-out (1 per cent) and nuclear power generation (0.04 per cent).

tween "indoors" and "outdoors" include the choice of building materials and ventilation systems. In tropical countries there is probably little difference between exposure levels indoors and outdoors (UNEP, 1985).

Inhalation of radon (Rn) and of its decay products, particularly indoors, are the most important sources of exposure to terrestrial radiation (UNEP, 1985). Approximately half the average annual dose of terrestrial radiation comes from Rn. Radon concentrations can be quite high in homes constructed with materials containing radionuclides such as granite, pumice stone and phosphogypsum. However, the greatest route of exposure to Rn is the diffusion of the gas through the soil and into the basements of

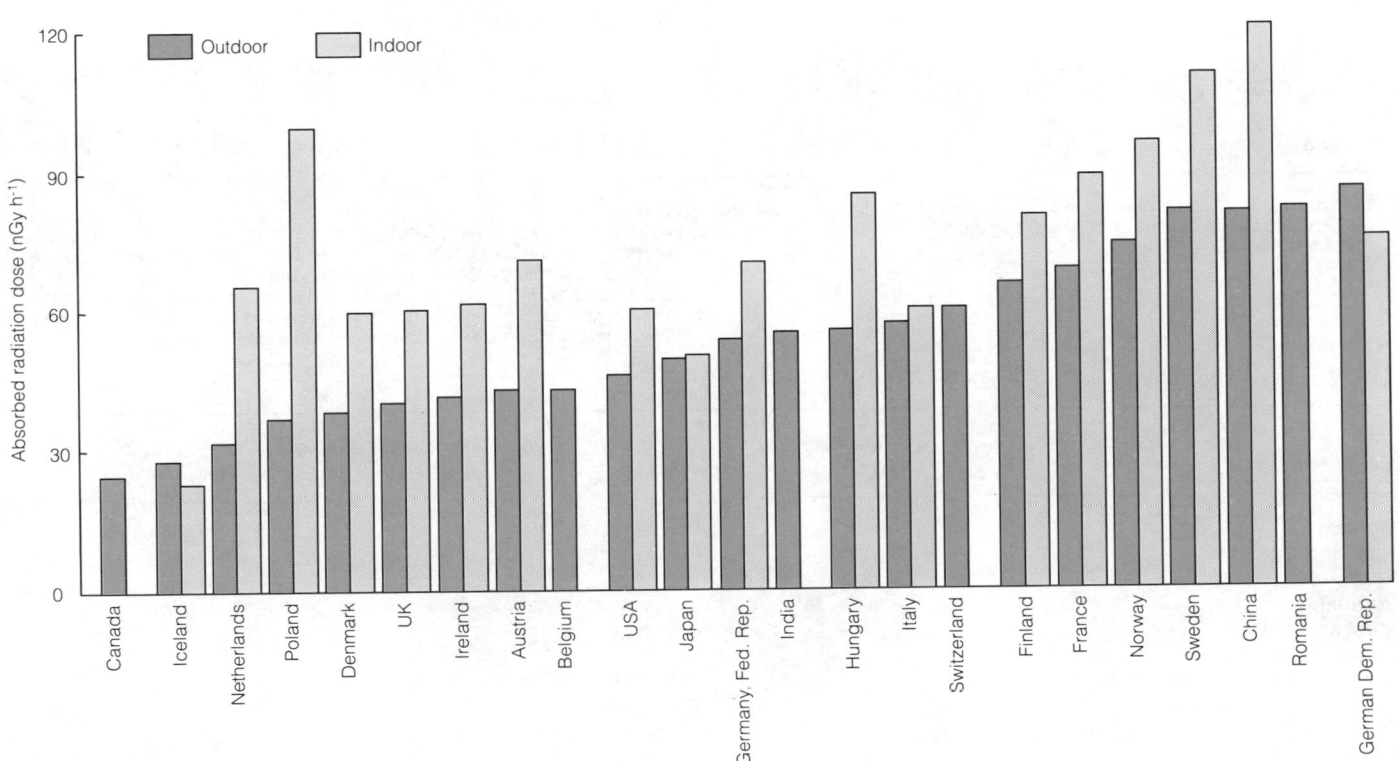

Figure 1.31 Exposure to terrestrial radiation, "indoors" and "outdoors"
Source: data from Table 1.45

Table 1.45 summarizes the results of large-scale surveys undertaken by individual countries to determine their population's level of exposure to terrestrial radiation. Terrestrial radiation is classified as either internal or external. Internal sources of natural radiation include radionuclides inhaled or ingested through water or food. Approximately two-thirds of the natural dose of radiation received by the general population is of the internal type. External radiation includes cosmic radiation and radiation from radionuclides present in building materials.

In most countries a higher radiation dose is received via exposure to terrestrial sources "indoors" than "outdoors" (Figure 1.31). Factors which influence the differential be-

homes. Radon is trapped in homes by insulation and concentrates in basements because it is heavier than air. Table 1.46 illustrates the range of levels of Rn measured in homes in selected countries. The data in Tables 1.45 and 1.46 may not be strictly comparable as survey design and sampling procedures may vary between countries. Exposure to Rn is linked to several forms of cancer (see Part 5: Human Health).

References

UNEP 1985 *Radiation: Doses, Effects, Risks*, United Nations Environment Programme, Nairobi.

UNSCEAR 1988 *Sources, Effects and Risks of Ionizing Radiation*, 1988 Report to the General Assembly, United Nation, New York.

Table 1.38 Adult dietary intake of selected metals, 1980–1988 ($\mu g\ kg^{-1}$ body weight per week)

Country	Pb	Cd	Hg	Country	Pb	Cd	Hg
PTWI[a]	50	7	5	Germany, Fed. Rep.	26.8	3.1	2.6
				Hungary	11.1	0.6	
AMERICAS				Italy	59.5	3.4	1.1
				Ireland	15.2		
Canada	5.7	1.5	1.0	Netherlands	10.5	2.1	0.6
Cuba	63.3						
Guatemala	32.3	2.0	1.4	Poland	18.2	4.3	
USA	0.9	1.5	0.3	Sweden	2.6	1.0	
				Switzerland	3.5		
SOUTH EAST ASIA				Turkey	6.4		
				UK	7.1	1.9	0.4
India	60.0			Yugoslavia	1.8		
Thailand	48.1		0.8				
				WESTERN PACIFIC			
EUROPE							
				Australia	3.8	1.0	0.3
Belgium	31.5	5.4	1.5	China	5.4		
Denmark	7.0	2.8	1.3	Japan	9.9	3.4	
France	19.8	3.5	1.2	New Zealand	25.0	4.6	0.6
Finland	1.7	1.2	0.2				

[a] Provisional Tolerable Weekly Intakes as established by the Joint Food and Agriculture Organization/World Health Organization Expert Committee on Food Additives.

Sources:
Galal-Gorchev, H. 1990 Global overview of dietary lead exposure. Paper presented at the Symposium on the Bioavailability and Dietary Uptake of Lead, Chapel Hill, 24–27 September 1990. Unpublished paper.
Galal-Gorchev, H. 1990 Dietary intake, levels in food and estimated intake of cadmium, lead and mercury. Paper presented at the Symposium on Food Contamination, Cairo, 4–15 November 1990. Unpublished paper.

Table 1.39 Estimated global daily dietary intake of lead

Commodity	Global diet (g day^{-1})	Typical lead levels (mg kg^{-1})	Estimated intake (μg day^{-1})	Percentage of total daily intake
Cereals	405	0.06	24	9.9
Root and tuber	301	0.05	15	6.1
Fruit	236	0.05	12	4.8
Vegetables	182	0.05	9	3.7
Meat and poultry	105	0.05	5	2.1
Sugar and honey	58			
Milk (solids) and products	55	0.03	6	2.3
Vegetable oils and fats	38	0.02	1	0.3
Fish	33	0.10	3	1.3
Pulses	22	0.04	1	0.4
Eggs	17	0.02		0.1
Nuts and oilseeds	16	0.04	<1	0.3
Crustaceans and molluscs	6	0.20	1	0.5
Offal	6	0.20	1	0.5
Animal oils and fats	5			
Spices and herbs	3	0.30	1	0.4
Coffee, cocoa, miscellaneous	12			
TOTAL FOOD	1,500		80	32.7
Drinking water	2,000	0.02	40	16.2
Canned beverages	600	0.20	120	48.7
Canned food[a]	30	0.20	6	2.4
TOTAL DIET			246[b]	100.0

[a] Assumes canned food consumption contributes 2 per cent of the total.
[b] Equivalent to 29 $\mu g\ kg^{-1}$ body weight per week. The provisional tolerable weekly intake is 50 $\mu g\ kg^{-1}$ body weight per week.

The global diet is a representative of an "average" adult based on the Food and Agriculture Organization's surveys.

Source:
Galal-Gorchev, H. 1990 Global overview of dietary lead exposure. Paper presented at the Symposium on the Bioavailability and Dietary Uptake of Lead, Chapel Hill, 24–27 September 1990. Unpublished paper.

Table 1.40 Aflatoxin concentrations in selected foods as reported to GEMS/Food, 1988 ($\mu g\ kg^{-1}$ food as its basis)

Country	Foods	Food origin	No. of samples	Type of aflatoxin	Concentration Minimum	Maximum	Median
Brazil	Groundnuts	Domestic	222	B_1	4	520	
	Groundnuts	Domestic	117	B_2	19	689	189.0
	Groundnuts	Domestic	222	G_1	15	489	175.0
	Groundnuts	Domestic	117	G_2	21	437	118.0
Canada	Groundnuts	Domestic and imported	23	B_1	<0.3[a]	2.1	<0.5
	Brazil nuts	Imported	17	B_1	<0.5[a]	25	1.2
	Pistachios	Imported	16	B_1	<0.4[a]	28.3	<0.5
	Figs (dehydrated)	Imported	13	B_1	<0.5[a]	15.5	<0.5
Cuba	Groundnuts[b]	Domestic	43	B_1	<5.0[a]	3,500	<5.0
Guatemala	Groundnuts	Domestic	35	Residue	<3.0[a]	900	9.0
Ireland	Groundnuts	Imported	18	B_1	<1.0[a]	1,940	20.0
	Figs (fresh)	Imported	13	B_1	<1.0[a]	<1.0	<1.0
USA	Groundnuts	Domestic	10,612	Residue	<4.0[a]	970	<4.0
	Pistachios	Domestic	56	Residue	<4.0[a]	119	<4.0

[a] Limit of detection.
[b] Dry basis.

Source:
Galal-Gorchev, H. 1990 Personal communication, International Programme on Chemical Safety, Division of Environmental Health, World Health Organization, Geneva, Switzerland.

Table 1.41 Levels of selected dioxins in human breast milk

Region/country	Location	Number of mothers	Fat content of milk (%)	Mean concentration (ng kg^{-1} fat) 2,3,7,8 TCDD	OCDD
AMERICAS					
Canada	British Columbia	23	4.5	3.4	160
	Maritimes	19	3.6	2.5	148
	North & Eastern Ontario	32	4.0	2.2	143
	Prairies	31	3.9	2.7	143
	Quebec	34	3.9	2.8	152
	Toronto & SW Ontario	44	4.0	2.2	137
USA	Binghamton	22	2.6	3.5	163
	Los Angeles	21	3.9	3.1	303
SOUTH EAST ASIA					
India	Bombay	7	2.4	<1.0	
Thailand	Bangkok	3	3.2	<1.0	
EUROPE					
Austria	Tulln	51	4.0	2.7	141
	Vienna	54	3.9	2.9	159
Belgium	Industrial area		2.8	10.2	283
	Rural area		3.3		555
	Urban area		2.8	9.1	517
Denmark		42	3.4	2.1	210
Finland	Helsinki	38	3.8	2.0	154
	Kuopio	31	4.1	1.8	113
Germany, Fed. Rep.	Recklinghausen	23	3.6	3.8	170
	West Berlin	40	3.2	3.3	210
Hungary	Budapest	100	5.3	3.4	210
	Szentes	50	4.2	3.7	271
Netherlands	Rural area	13	2.9	5.2	627
	Urban area	13	2.8	5.4	545
Norway	Hamar	10	3.9	2.5[c]	150[c]
	Skien/Porsgrunn	10	3.4	2.7[c]	156[c]
	Tromsø	11	3.5	2.9[c]	153[c]
Poland	Bytom	5	4.2	3.6[c]	250[c]
Sweden	Borlänge	10	3.4	2.8[c]	184[c]
	Gothenburg	10	3.0	3.2[c]	237[c]
	Sundsvall	10	2.6	3.3[c]	209[c]
	Uppsala	10	2.8	2.9[c]	255[c]
UK	Birmingham		2.8	6.5	303
	Glasgow		3.4	4.6	271
Yugoslavia	Krk	14	3.4	1.6	101
	Zagreb	41	4.1	1.9	90

Continued opposite

Table 1.41   Continued

Region/country	Location	Number of mothers	Fat content of milk (%)	Mean concentration (ng kg^{-1} fat)	
				2,3,7,8 TCDD	OCDD
WESTERN PACIFIC					
Japan	Fukuoka Prefecture	3	2.6	2.4	1300
New Zealand	Auckland	2	4.9	1.4[c]	141c
Viet Nam	Gan Gio	3	2.5	9.0	61
	Hanoi	28	2.1	2.2	68
	Ho Chi Minh	38	2.1	7.1	231
	Ho Chi Minh 2	15	3.0	9.9	283
	Ho Chi Minh 3	8	2.2	5.0	178
	Long Xuyen	2	2.2	2.0	28
	Song Be	12	2.2	17.0	185
	Tan Uyen	2	2.2	2.9	210
	Tan Uyen 2	2	4.8	5.2	120
	Tan Uyen 3	2	3.8	11.0	99

[a]   2,3,7,8 tetrachlorodibenzo-*p*-dioxin.
[b]   Octachlorodibenzo-*p*-dioxin.
[c]   Mean of individual samples.

Data represent mean values of pooled samples unless otherwise indicated.

Source:
Yrjänheikki, E. J. 1989 *Levels of PCBs, PCDDs and PCDFs in Breast Milk,* World Health Organization, Geneva, 71–75.

Table 1.42 Levels of PCBs in human breast milk

Region/country	Location	Number of mothers	Fat content of milk (%)	Mean (µg kg^{-1} fat)
AMERICAS				
USA	Binghamton	13	2.6	220[a]
	Los Angeles	24	3.9	202[a]
SOUTH EAST ASIA				
Thailand	Bangkok	3	3.5	62[a]
EUROPE				
Belgium	Antwerp area	18	2.8	663
	Brabant area	12	3.2	558
	East Flanders	32	3.0	655
	Liege area	21	3.2	609
	Limburg	30	2.7	604
	Northern part	114	2.9	615
	Northern part – rural	50	2.9	617
	Northern part – urban	38	3.0	525
	Northern part – industrial	26	2.8	734
	West Flanders	22	3.0	557
Denmark		10		830
Finland	Helsinki	38	3.8	150[a]
	Kuopio	31	4.1	203[a]
Germany, Fed. Rep.	North Rhine – Westphalia	143	3.5	762
Netherlands	Rural area	10		416
	Urban area	10		392
Norway	Hamar	10		507
	Skien	8		533
	Tromsoe	10		562
Sweden	Borlänge	10		1,000
	Gothenburg	10		1,200
	Sundvall	10		1,100
	Uppsala	10		1,100
Yugoslavia	Krk	14		420
	Krk	14		500[a]
	Zagreb	41		450[a]
WESTERN PACIFIC				
Viet Nam	Hanoi	28	2.1	103[a]
	Ho Chi Minh	15	2.2	129[a]
	Song Be	12	2.2	93[a]

[a] Mean of pooled samples.

Data represent mean values of individual samples unless otherwise indicated.

Source:
Yrjänheikki, E. J. 1989 *Levels of PCBs, PCDDs and PCDFs in Breast Milk,* World Health Organization, Geneva, 71–75.

Table 1.43 Organochlorine pesticide residues in adipose tissues of Dutch citizens, 1968–1986 (mg kg^{-1} fat)

Year	HCB	α-HCH	β-HCH	γ-HCH	HEPO	Dieldrin	p,p'-DDE	TDE	o,p'-DDT	p,p'-DDT
1968–69	0.7	<0.1	0.4	<0.1	0.1	0.2	2.8	0.6	0.1	1.4
1973–74	1.2	<0.1	0.6	<0.1	0.2	0.2	2.8	0.1	0.1	0.8
1975	1.2	0.01	0.32	0.04	0.12	0.11	2.7	0.08	0.04	0.47
1976	0.86	0.01	0.38	0.02	0.12	0.09	3.4	0.03	0.03	0.56
1977–78	0.98	<0.01	0.4	0.01	0.14	0.11	3.2	0.03	0.02	0.4
1980	0.85	0.01	0.37	<0.01	0.12	0.1	3.7	0.01	0.01	0.32
1981	0.80	<0.01	0.27	<0.01	0.08	0.07	2.9	<0.01	<0.01	0.25
1982	0.58	<0.01	0.35	<0.01	0.09	0.07	3.5	<0.01	<0.01	0.23
1983	0.49	<0.01	0.29	<0.01	0.1	0.06	3.0	<0.02	<0.02	0.22
1985	0.42	<0.01	0.26	<0.01	0.12	0.07	2.8	0.03	0.01	0.17
1986	0.38	<0.01	0.27	<0.01	0.1	0.05	2.3	0.04	<0.01	0.14

HCB = Hexachlorobenzene.
α-HCH = Isomer of hexachlorocyclohexane.
β-HCH = Isomer of hexachlorocyclohexane.
γ-HCH = Isomer of hexachlorocyclohexane.
HEPO = Heptachlor epoxide.
p,p'-DDE = 1,1'-(2,2-dichloroethenylidene)-bis[4-chlorbenzene].
TDE = 1,1'-(2,2-dichloroethylidene)-bis[4-chlorbenzene].
o,p'-DDT = 1-chloro-2-[2,22-trichloro-1-(4-chlorophenyl)ethyl]benzene.
p,p'-DDT = 1,1'-(2,2,2-trichloroethylidene)-bis(4-chlorobenzene).

Source:
Greve, P. A. and van Zoonen, P. 1990 Organochlorine pesticides and PCBs in tissues from Dutch citizens (1968–1986), *International Journal of Environmental Analytical Chemistry* **38**, 265–277.

Table 1.44 Organochlorine residues in the adipose tissue of Canadians, 1969–1985 (mg kg^{-1} fat)

Residue	1969	1972	1976	1985
HCB		0.062	0.095	0.030
α-HCH		0.004	0.004	0.002
β-HCH		0.054	0.151	0.043
γ-HCH	0.015	0.007	0.003	0.002
Oxychlordane		0.055	0.055	0.036
t-Nonachlor		0.065	0.056	0.056
HEPO	0.040	0.043	0.037	0.011
Dieldrin	0.122	0.069	0.049	0.002
o,p'-DDT	0.049	0.031	0.032	0.007
PCBs		0.907	0.944	0.490
p,p'-DDE	3.430	2.095	1.721	1.330
μ,μ'-DDT	1.017	0.439	0.311	0.059

Footnotes as Table 1.43.

Source:
Mes, J. 1990 Trends in the levels of some chlorinated hydrocarbon residues in adipose tissue of Canadians, *Environmental Pollution* **65**, 269–278.

Table 1.45   Exposure to terrestrial radiation in selected countries, (n Gy h^{-1})

Region/country	Outdoors[a]			Indoors[b]				Average absorbed dose rate in air	Population weighted absorbed dose rate in air
	Year of survey	Number of measurements	Absorbed dose rate in air	Year of survey	Number of dwellings	Type of building			
NORTH AMERICA									
USA	1972	25 areas[c]	46	1985	2,300	Various		60	
ASIA									
China	1986	38,661	80	1986	53,952	Various			120
India	1986	2,800	55						
Japan	1980	1,127	49	1984	135	Various			50
EUROPE									
Austria	1980	>1,000	43	1980	1,900	Brick	110		
						Concrete	81		71
						Wood	75		
						Natural stone	110		
Belgium	1987	272	43						
Denmark	1980	14 sites	38	1985	82	Brick	60[d]		
						Concrete	50		60
						Wood	30		
Finland	1980		65	1983			80[e]		
France	1985	5,142	68	1980	946	Various	88[d]		
					5,798	Various	75		
German Dem. Rep.	1969	1,005	85[f]	1969	667	Various	74		
Germany, Fed. Rep.	1978	24,739	53	1978	29,996	Solid	70		
						Frame	71		70
						Prefabricated	40		
						Wood	45		
Hungary	1987	123 sites	55	1987	123	Various	84		
Iceland	1982		28	1982		Concrete	23		
Ireland	1980	264	42	1985	223	Various	62[d]		
Italy	1972	1,365	57	1984	600	Various	~60[d]		
Netherlands	1985	1,049	32	1955	399	Various	64		
Norway	1977	234	73	1965	2,026	Brick	120		
				1977		Concrete	105		95
Poland[g]	1980	352 sites	37	1984	1,351	Coal-by-product prefabricate	77–120		
						Red brick	57–100		
						Gravel-sand prefabricate	54–68		
						Wood	42–51		
Romania	1979	2,372	81						
Sweden	1979		80	1980	1,282	Brick	92		
						Concrete	120		110
						Aerated concrete	170		
						Wood	53		
Switzerland	1964		60[h]						
UK	1984	1,400	40	1985	2,300	Various	60		60

[a]   Estimates of absorbed dose rate in air, 1 metre above ground level obtained from large-scale surveys.
[b]   Gamma radiation absorbed dose rate in air obtained from large-scale surveys.
[c]   Inhabited by approximately 30 per cent of the country's population.
[d]   The cosmic-ray contribution has been subtracted from the reported value.
[e]   Estimated.
[f]   A contribution of 1.0 µR per hour from nuclear weapons fallout was subtracted from the total exposure rate.
[g]   The study covered about 10 per cent of the country.

[h]   A contribution of 3.1 µR per hour from nuclear weapons fallout was subtracted from the total exposure rate.

The above table is a compilation of results from a number of individual surveys, further details of which are included in the source document.

Source:
UNSCEAR 1988 *Sources, Effects and Risks of Ionizing Radiation,* 1988 Report to the General Assembly, United Nations, New York.

Table 1.46 Exposure to indoor radon in selected countries[a] (Bq m^{-3})

Region/country	Year of survey	Number of dwellings	Type of dwellings	Rn concentration Median	EEC[b]
NORTH AMERICA					
Canada	1980	13,413	Houses	33[c]	7
Port Hope	1976	2,960	Homes	36	11
Uranium City	1976	632	Homes		48
Elliot Lake	1976	1,921	Homes		30
Bancroft	1977	1,162	Homes		26
Saskatchewan	1980	155	Homes		11
	1980	74	Homes		47
	1980	438	Homes		28
	1980	175	Homes		65
	1980	770	Homes		13
	1980	961	Homes		16
USA	1984	552	Single-family homes	35	
SOUTH AMERICA					
Argentina	1985	112	Homes	37	
ASIA					
China	1983	896		120[c]	80[c]
Beijing	1987	537	364 houses and 173 apartments	30[c]	
Japan	1988	250	Houses	10[c]	
EUROPE					
Austria, Salzburg	1980	729	Homes	15	9
Belgium[d]	1984	79	73 houses and 6 apartments	41	
Denmark	1985	400	Homes	50	
Germany, Fed. Rep.	1984	5,970	Homes	40	13
Finland	1982	8,150	Homes	64	
France[d]	1985	765	Houses	44	
Hungary	1972	833	Houses		12[c]
Ireland[d]	1987	736	Houses	37	
Italy[d]	1984	1,000	Houses	43	
Netherlands	1985	1,000	Houses	24	10
Norway	1985	1,500	Houses	90[c]	
Poland	1978	201	Apartments	9	4[c]
Sweden		315	Detached houses built before 1975	65	
	1982	191	Apartments built before 1975	46	
		96	Detached houses built 1978–1980	59[c]	
	1986	46,268	38,260 detached houses and 8,008 apartments built before 1982		~100
Switzerland	1982	123	Homes	60	
	1983	105	Homes	22–5,500	
UK	1985	2,300	Homes: living rooms	17	
			main bedrooms	12	
Cornwall and other uraniferous regions	1985	700	Homes: living rooms	140	14

a   Data obtained through large-scale indoor surveys.
b   Equilibrium equivalent concentrations.
c   Mean of measurements.
d   Preliminary results.

The above table is a compilation of results from a number of individual surveys, further details of which are included in the source document.

Source:
UNSCEAR 1988 *Sources, Effects and Risks of Ionizing Radiation*, 1988 Report to the General Assembly, United Nations, New York.

Historical Monitoring

The collection and analysis of retrospective or historical samples, accurately dated, can constitute a record of past environmental conditions. Such a record provides a major perspective of the impact of human activities and industrial developments on natural processes. Three main types of depositional media are commonly used in historical monitoring, namely lake sediments, peat, and polar ice and snow. Media profiles are sampled by coring methods and dated by a variety of techniques. Unlike sediment cores, which are often taken from industrial areas and thus represent local conditions, ice cores are generally obtained from remote locations and may reflect regional and global scale changes. Other materials, including tree-rings, archived samples and museum specimens, preserved human remains such as hair, teeth and skeletal materials and bat guano have also been examined in historical context. All aspects of historical monitoring have been critically reviewed by MARC (1985).

Of crucial importance in historical monitoring is the dating technique. The radioisotope ^{210}Pb is used routinely and over long time periods. ^{137}Cs, which first appeared in measurable quantities in the environment as a result of nuclear weapons testing in 1954 (and reached a peak in 1963), is also commonly used for dating purposes. However, its use for recent sediment dating from soft-water lakes has been reported to be a failure (Davis et al., 1984). Pollen markers are often used as a second dating technique; for example, pollen from the growth of ragweed (*Ambrosia*) following forest clearance.

Historical monitoring techniques have been incorporated into several international programmes. For example, tree-rings and ice cores are utilized in the European Science Foundation's 18-nation study, initiated in 1989, on The European Palaeoclimate and Man since the Last Glaciation. The International Geosphere-Biosphere Programme's (IGBP) Past Global Changes (PAGES) is co-ordinating and integrating existing national and international palaeo-projects and implementing new activities to obtain information on pre-industrial climate variations.

References

Davis, R. B., Hess, C. T., Norton, S. A., Hanson, D. W., Hoagland, K. D. and Anderson, D. S. 1984 ^{137}Cs and ^{210}Pb dating of sediments from soft-water lakes in New England (USA) and Scandinavia, a failure of ^{137}Cs dating, *Chemical Geology* **44**, 151–185.

MARC 1985 *Historical Monitoring*, MARC Report Number 31, Monitoring and Assessment Research Centre, London.

Sediments

Lake sediments, and to a lesser extent marine sediments, provide a unique medium from which past environmental conditions can be reconstructed. Heavy metals, organic pollutants and radionuclides have been examined in sediment profiles from a variety of lake types including hard- and soft-water lakes, shallow and deep lakes and small water bodies (Alderton, 1985; WHO/UNEP, 1989). Ana-

lyses of this type have been conducted predominantly in North American and European lakes but are increasingly finding applications in lakes in other countries (Mao et al., 1989). Contaminants in sediments are also discussed in Part 1: Environmental Pollution, Soils and Sediments but not from a historical perspective.

There is striking uniformity between a variety of research results of the finding of the historical rise in lead (Pb), copper (Cu), zinc (Zn), cadmium (Cd) and mercury (Hg) concentrations in sediments associated with industrial and human activities (Alderton, 1985; Norton et al., 1990). Recent decreases in Pb emissions in particular are now reflected in the decreased concentrations in surface lake sediments from a number of countries. With organic

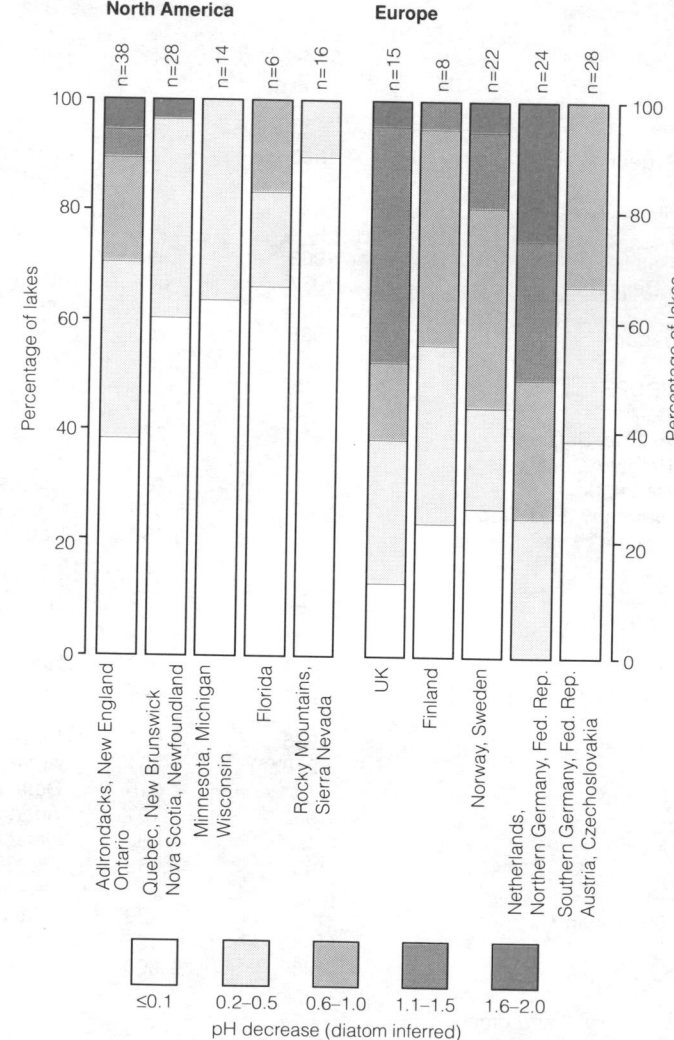

Figure 1.32 Decrease of diatom-inferred pH in lakes in 10 different regions (the length of each graph is 100 per cent with the number of lakes sampled in each region shown at the right-hand side; lakes are graded into five classes of pH decrease from pre-industrial times until about 1980–1985)
Source: Charles et al., 1990

pollutants, especially hexachlorobenzene (HCB), dichlorodiphenyl-trichloroethane (DDT) and polychlorinated biphenyls (PCBs), their appearance in sediment cores is related to their production and release dates into the environment (WHO/UNEP, 1989).

Deposition of acidic substances, in addition to metals and organics, has been clearly recorded in lake sediments (Charles et al., 1990; Sullivan et al., 1990). Fossilized diatom assemblages in lake sediments are good indicators of past lake pH as the taxa are common and correlate well with pH. Changes in the long-term natural acidification processes over 10,000 or so years have been documented using this technique; chemical methods were used as well as pollen and diatom assemblages to determine retrospective pHs (Ford, 1990).

The ability of existing predictive equations to infer pH from diatom assemblages agrees well with current measured pHs in surface sediments (Charles et al., 1990). Figure 1.32 and Table 1.47 show that extensive regional-scale lake acidification has occurred in low alkalinity lakes of North America and Europe. Results collected by Charles et al. (1990) show that sensitive water bodies in Europe are affected more by acidification than are those in North America. At least 30 per cent of the lakes studied in Europe had a diatom-inferred pH decrease of 0.6 pH units, whereas only one region in North America had more than 20 per cent of its lakes in this category.

Concentrations of polycyclic aromatic hydrocarbons (PAHs), carbonaceous particles (soot), and magnetic particles in sediments are also used to interpret atmospheric deposition of substances derived from the combustion of fossil fuels. Remains of littoral crustaceans (*Chydorids*) and midge larvae (*Chironomids*) can also be of value in establishing changes in aquatic biota with acidification (Charles et al., 1990).

References

Alderton, D. H. M. 1985 Sediments. In: *Historical Monitoring*, MARC Report Number 31, Monitoring and Assessment Research Centre, London, 1–95.

Charles, D. F., Battarbee, R. W., Renberg, I., Van Dam, H. and Smol, J. P. 1990 Palaeoecological analysis of lake acidification trends in North America and Europe using diatoms and chrysophytes. In: *Acid Precipitation, Volume 4, Soils, Aquatic Processes and Lake Acidification*, S. A. Norton, S. E. Linberg and A. L. Page (Eds), Springer-Verlag, Berlin, 207–276.

Ford, M. S. 1990 A 10,000 year history of natural ecosystem acidification. *Ecological Monographs* **60**, 57–89.

Mao, M. Z., Lin, J. Y., Bertine, K. K., Koide, M. and Goldberg, E. D. 1989 Atmospheric pollution in Beijing, China, as recorded in sediments of the Summer Palace Lake, *Environmental Conservation* **16**, 233–236.

Norton, S. A., Dillon, P. J., Evans, R. D., Mierle, G. and Kahl, J. S. 1990 The history of atmospheric deposition of Cd, Hg and Pb in North America: evidence from lake and peat bog sediments. In: *Acidic Precipitation: Volume 3, Sources, Deposition and Canopy Interactions*, S. E. Lindberg, A. L. Page and S. A. Norton (Eds), Springer-Verlag, Berlin, 73–102.

Sullivan, T. J., Charles, D. F., Smol, J. P., Cumming, B. F., Selle, A. R., Thomas, D. R., Bernert, J. A. and Dixit, S. S. 1990 Quantification of changes in lake water chemistry in response to acidic deposition, *Nature* (London) **345**, 54–58.

WHO/UNEP 1989 *Global Freshwater Quality: A First Assessment*, M. Meybeck, D. Chapman and R. Helmer (Eds), Basil Blackwell, Oxford.

Snow and Ice

The permanently ice-covered regions of the world have presented a unique and datable record of the past composition of the Earth's atmosphere. Falling snow scavenges aerosols and gases from the atmosphere so the deposition of snow on the ice sheets provides a stratified record which is superficially analogous to that found in lake sediments. For chemical species that are well mixed in the global troposphere, such as long-lived trace gases, ice-core records provide the best indication of past atmospheric concentrations which pre-date the instrumental records. For other chemical substances, such as metals and pesticides, the remoteness of the polar ice sheets means that concentrations in ice reflect the extent of long-range transport of pollutants. In addition, snow and ice may contain traces of contamination due to emissions from human activity within the polar regions themselves. The use of snow and ice cores has been reviewed by Alderton and Coleman (1985) and more recently in the Dahlem Workshop volume edited by Oeschger and Langway (1989) and by Wolff (1990).

Considerable effort has been made over the last 20 or so years to obtain profiles of heavy metals from polar snow formed from pre-industrial times to the present day in order to examine the extent to which metals have become global pollutants. Metal concentrations in ice and snow from the Arctic and Greenland are generally higher than those found in Antarctica. The reliability of the early data, particularly for Antarctica, has been questioned because of possible external and laboratory contamination and the difficulties of chemical analysis at the pg g^{-1} level (Alderton and Coleman, 1985). Nevertheless, it is generally accepted that recent increases in Pb concentrations in Antarctic ice and snow are real; i.e., from about 0.4 pg Pb g^{-1} during pre-industrial times to 2 pg Pb g^{-1} today (Boutron and Patterson, 1987). Data on possible increases of other metals arising from the pre-industrial period remain limited (Batifol et al., 1989).

Low levels of a number of organic compounds, including the chlorinated compounds DDT, hexachlorocyclohexane (HCH) and PCBs, have been measured in Arctic and/or Antarctic snow. The most probable source for these compounds is long-range atmospheric transport and subsequent deposition (Gregor and Gummer, 1989). More research is needed, however, before trends can be interpreted and possible contamination problems resolved (Wolff, 1990).

Relatively high concentrations of nitrate (NO_3^-) and sulphate (SO_4^{2-}) have been reported in Greenland snow by several groups of researchers (Mayewski and Legrand, 1990). Results show that the increase in sulphate concentrations started around the 1920s and that for nitrate had begun by the 1950s. These findings are in broad agreement with trends in emissions of SO_2 and NO_x in the industrial Northern Hemisphere. Smaller increases in con-

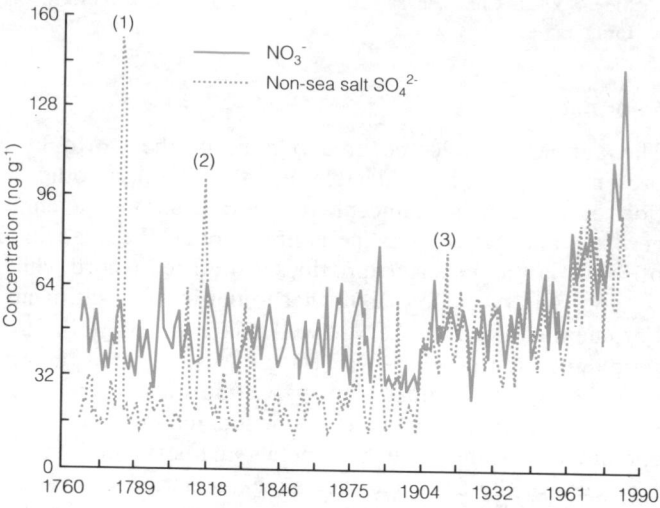

Figure 1.33 Time series of non-sea salt SO_4^{2-} and NO_3^- concentrations in an ice core from southern Greenland (volcanic events are at (1) 1783, (2) 1815 and (3) 1912)
Source: Mayewski et al., 1990

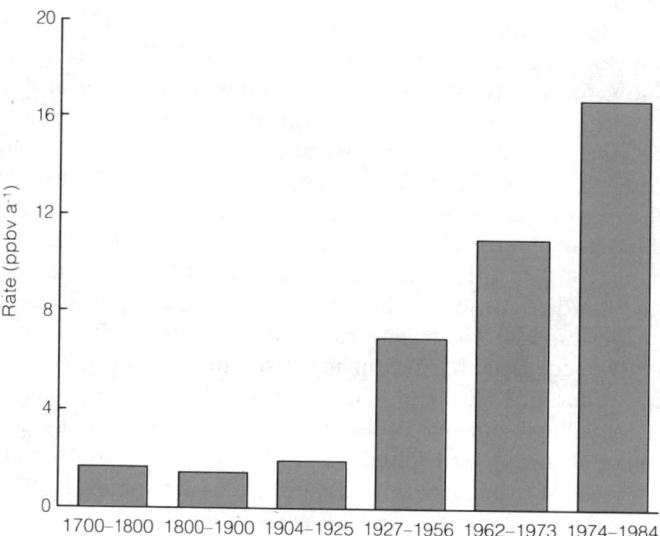

Figure 1.34 Rate of change in atmospheric methane, 1700–1984 (from measurements in air trapped in polar ice)
Source: Khalil and Rasmussen, 1987

centrations in snow in Antarctica were expected in view of the lower quantities of industrial emissions in the Southern Hemisphere and the limited inter-hemispheric exchange. Biomass burning in the Southern Hemisphere has been suggested as a source of NO_x (Mayewski and Legrand, 1990). Figure 1.33, which illustrates the time series for non-sea sulphate and nitrate, highlights the natural variability in background concentrations and the occurrence of volcanic events (Mayewski et al., 1990).

Several research groups have established concentration profiles of methane from bubbles of air trapped in ice

from sites in Greenland and Antarctica. Results for two sites, one in Greenland (Dye 3) and one in Antarctica (Bryd Station), which extend back to 10,000 years BP are summarized in Table 1.48. Data for a greater range of locations were reported in the 1989 edition of this report (UNEP, 1989).

Available ice-core data show that the concentration of methane, after being constant for perhaps 20,000 years or more, started to increase rapidly about 100 or 200 years ago (Khalil and Rasmussen, 1987). Rate of change over the more recent past is illustrated in Figure 1.34. Between 1700 and 1900 methane increased slowly at an average rate of about 1.5 ppbv per year, compared with about 17 ppbv per year for the past decade. Most recent data show that atmospheric methane concentrations are now over 1.6 ppmv, more than double the pre-industrial value (see also Part 1: Environmental Pollution, Atmosphere).

Carbon dioxide (CO_2) concentrations have also been measured in enclosed air bubbles in polar ice (Siegenthaler and Oeschger, 1987). The data show that atmospheric concentrations of CO_2 have risen by 25 per cent since pre-industrial times, from 280 ppmv to the present-day value of about 353 ppmv (Figure 1.35). More detailed information on CO_2 in polar ice was included in the previous edition of this report (UNEP, 1989).

Increases in atmospheric CO_2 are attributed to increases in CO_2 emissions from fossil fuel combustion and deforestation. Supporting evidence comes from measurements of the $^{13}C/^{12}C$ ratio in carbon dioxide in air bubbles (Friedli et al., 1986). Fossil fuel and biospheric carbon dioxide emissions are depleted in ^{13}C compared with the atmosphere; this is reflected in the data from the air in ice cores which show that ^{13}C has decreased by 1.14 ± 0.15‰ in the last two centuries.

Methane and carbon dioxide concentrations have also been measured in ice from the Vostok core (East Antarctica) back to approximately 160,000 years BP. This represents one glacial-interglacial cycle (Chappelaz et al.,

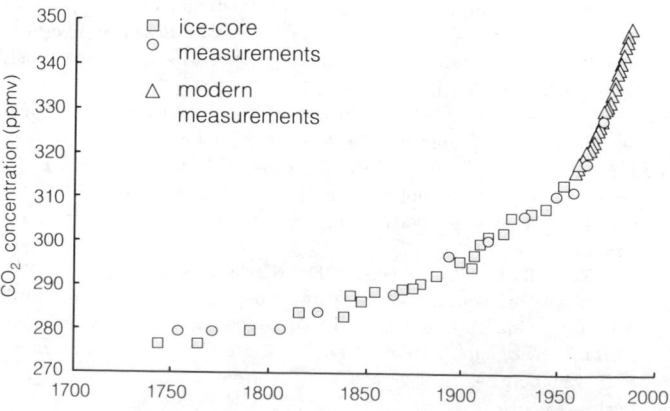

Figure 1.35 Trends in atmospheric concentrations of carbon dioxide during the past 230 years
Source: UNEP, 1989

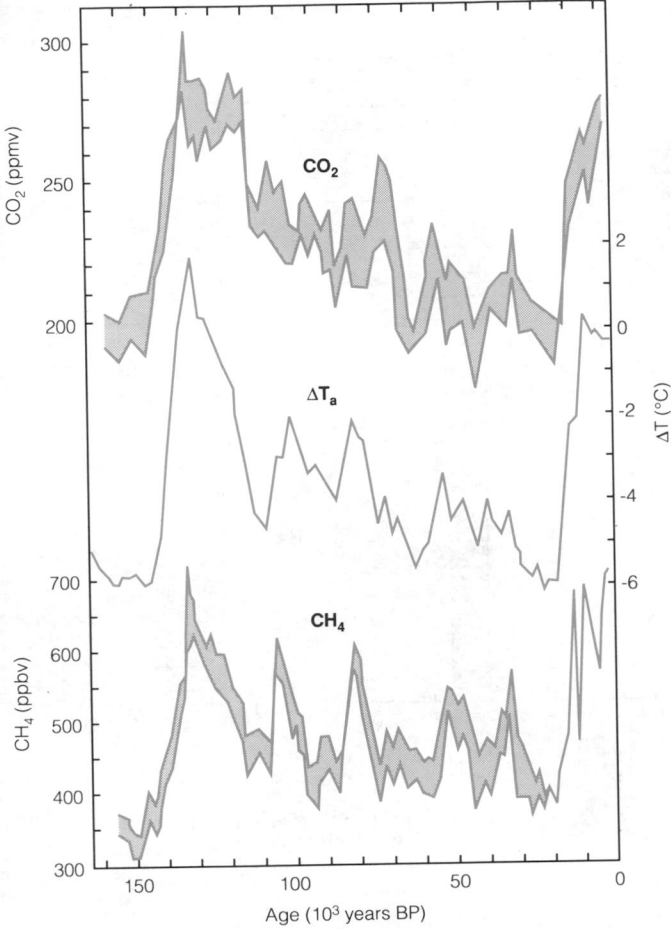

Figure 1.36 Vostok ice-core records from 160,000 years BP (carbon dioxide and methane are measured in air bubbles trapped in ice and illustrated as an envelope taking uncertainties of measurements into account; temperature is derived from measurements of hydrogen and oxygen isotope ratios and is expressed as deviations from the modern surface temperature value of -55.5°C
Source: Chappellaz et al., 1990

1990). The data show substantial changes in concentrations which correlate with temperature fluctuations (Figure 1.36). The results point to changes in the sources of methane and also suggest that methane has probably contributed, like carbon dioxide, to glacial-interglacial temperature change.

References

Alderton, D. H. M. and Coleman, D. O. 1985 Ice cores and snow. In: *Historical Monitoring*, MARC Report Number 31, Monitoring and Assessment Research Centre, London.

Batifol, F., Boutron, C. and de Angelis, M. 1989 Changes in copper, zinc and cadmium concentrations in Antarctica ice during the past 40,000 years, *Nature* (London) **337**, 554–546.

Boutron, C. F. and Patterson, C. C. 1987 Relative levels of natural and anthropogenic lead in recent Antarctic snow, *Journal of Geographical Research* **92**, 8454–8464.

Chappelaz, J., Barnola, J. M., Raynaut, D., Korotkevich, Y. S. and Lorius, C. 1990 Ice-core record of atmospheric methane over the past 160,000 years, *Nature* (London) **345**, 127–131.

Friedli, H., Lotscher, H., Oeschger, H., Siegenthaler, U. and Stauffer, B. 1986 Ice-core record in the $^{13}C/^{12}C$ ratio of atmospheric CO2 in the past two centuries, *Nature* (London) **324**, 237–238.

Gregor, D. J. and Gummer, W. D. 1989 Evidence of atmospheric transport and deposition of organochlorine pesticides and polychlorinated biphenyls in Canadian Arctic snow, *Environmenal Science and Technology* **23**, 561–565.

Khalil, M. A. K. and Rasmussen, R. A. 1987 Atmospheric methane: trends over the last 10,000 years, *Atmospheric Environment* **21**, 2445–2452.

Mayewski, P. A. and Legrand, M. R. 1990 Recent increase in nitrate concentrations of Antarctic snow, *Nature* (London) **346**, 258–260.

Mayewski, P. A., Lyons, W. B., Spencer, M. J., Twickler, M. S., Buck, C. F. and Whitlow, S. 1990 An ice-core record of atmospheric response to anthropogenic sulphate and nitrate, *Nature* (London) **246**, 554–556.

Oeschger, H. and Langway, C. C. Jr. (Eds) 1989 *The Environmental Record in Glaciers and Ice Sheets*, John Wiley & Sons, Chichester.

Siegenthaler, U. and Oeschger, H. 1987 Biospheric CO2 emissions during the past 200 years reconstructed by deconvolution of ice-core data, *Tellus* **39B**, 140–154.

UNEP 1989 *United Nations Environment Programme Environmental Data Report*, Basil Blackwell, Oxford.

Wolff, E. W. 1990 Signals of atmospheric pollution in polar snow and ice, *Antarctic Science* **2**, 189–205.

Peat

The use of peat cores for historical monitoring is based on the premise that peat can contain a record of atmospheric pollution input. This input is retained both as particulate matter within the profile and incorporated into or absorbed on the plants and their remains. Most analyses of this type have been performed on ombrotrophic peat bogs, i.e., those that receive almost all their nutrients and water via the atmosphere (MARC, 1985). Peat cores can record at least qualitative trends in the past deposition of pollutants and are particularly suited to recording local sources of pollution. Cores can be dated by ^{210}Pb, radiocarbon and pollen analysis.

In a typical study the elements Pb, Cu, Zn, iron (Fe) and chromium (Cr) have been shown to increase in concentration from pre-settlement days to the present (Figure 1.37). Some metal concentrations increased by orders of magnitude from around 1940 (Cole et al., 1990). Other elements, such as manganese, aluminium, nickel and cadmium show only small increases up to the present day whereas strontium, a mobile element, accumulates in the oldest peat deposits. Several reports have shown that atmospheric deposition rates of metals derived from lake sediments are comparable with those from peat bogs (Norton and Kahl, 1987; Norton et al., 1990).

Atmospheric deposition of organic compounds in ombrotrophic peat bogs has also been described (Rapaport and Elsenreich, 1988). The onset of accumulation rates in peat of PCBs, HCB, HCH and DDT was shown to be consistent with production data. This demonstrated a rapid response time of the atmosphere and the ecosystem to changes in input.

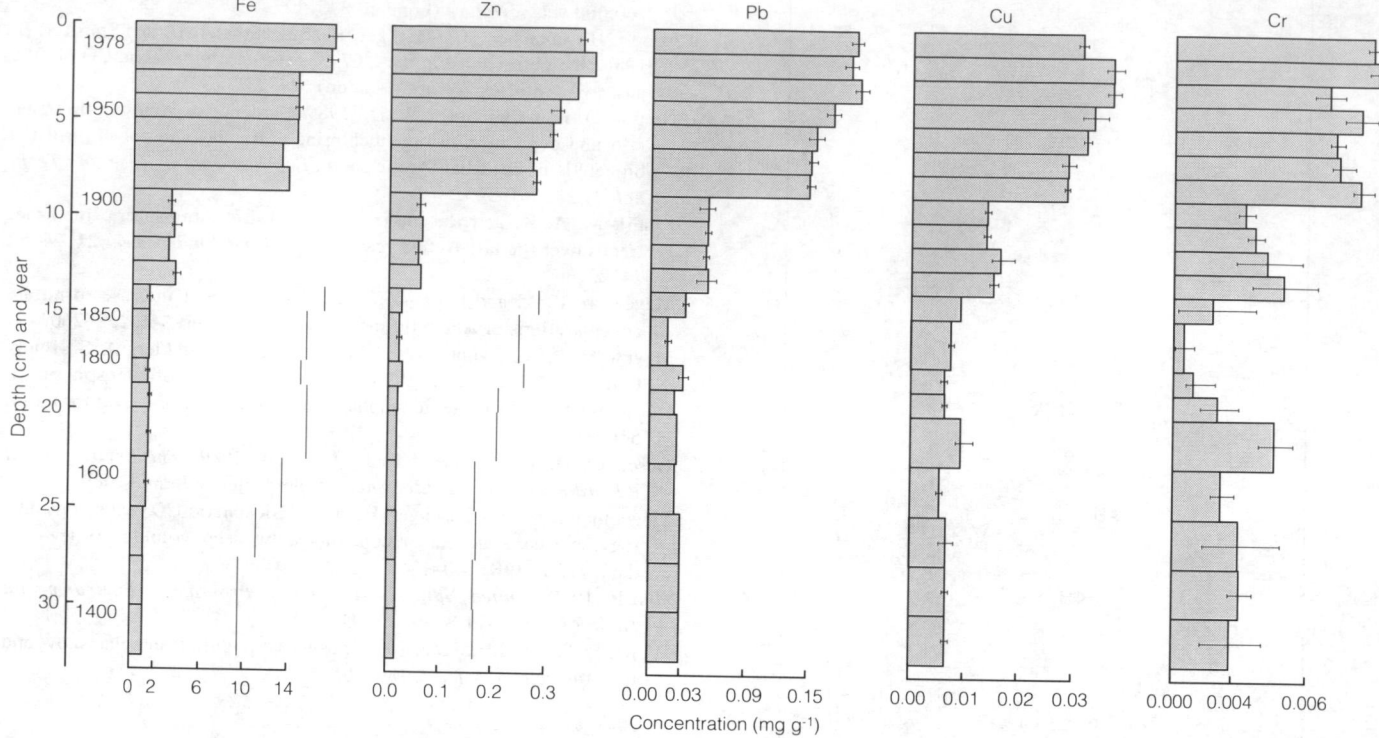

Figure 1.37 Metal concentrations vs depth in Cowles peat bog, USA (metals are arranged from left to right depending upon the percentage increase from pre-settlement values to peak values; error bars show the range between two samples)
Source: Cole et al., 1990

References

Cole, K. L., Engstrom, D. R., Futyma, R. P. and Stottlemyer, R. 1990 Past atmospheric deposition of metals in a peat core from Cowles Bog, *Environmental Science and Technology* **24**, 543–549.

MARC 1985 *Historical Monitoring*, MARC Report Number 31, Monitoring and Assessment Research Centre, London.

Norton, S. A. and Kahl, J. S. 1987 A comparison of lake sediments and ombrotrophic peat deposits as long-term monitors of atmospheric pollution. In: *New Aproaches to Monitoring Aquatic Organisms*, T. P. Boyle (Ed.), ASTM STP 940, American Society for Testing and Materials, Philadelphia, 40–57.

Norton, S. A., Dillon, P. J., Evans, R. D., Mierle, G. and Kahl, J. S. 1990 The history of atmospheric deposition of Cd, Hg and Pb in North America: Evidence from lake and peat bog sediments. In: *Acidic Precipitation, Volume 3, Sources, Deposition and Canopy Interactions*, S. E. Lindberg, A. L. Page and S. A. Norton (Eds), Springer-Verlag, Berlin, 73–102.

Rapaport, R. A. and Elsenreich, S. J. 1988 Historical atmospheric inputs of high molecular weight chlorinated hydrocarbons to Eastern North America, *Environmental Science and Technology* **22**, 931–941.

Tree-Rings

Compared with lake sediments, ice- and peat cores, which are sources of data covering a wide time-span, tree-rings are used for monitoring a relatively short historical record of environmental damage being restricted to the life of the tree. Tree-ring analyses have frequently been used to assess the input around point sources although their application at the regional scale is still the subject of controversy. Samples can be accurately dated, although some continuing metabolic processes may modify the chemical composition of constituents of particular rings laid down in earlier years.

The usefulness of tree-rings as pollution monitors for local emissions over time has been reviewed by Burton (1985) and more recently for North America by Chevone and Linzon (1988). A number of papers have appeared in recent years addressing the reported decline in parts of the USA in the growth of red spruce (*Picea rubens*) as shown by decreasing tree-ring widths and wood density (Conkey, 1988; Chevone and Linzon, 1988; Innes and Cook, 1989). Other forest tree species in the USA and in Europe have also been examined to try to establish whether climatic fluctuations account for the decline, or whether anthropogenic factors such as air pollutants are involved.

Standardized chronologies of ring widths and maximum late wood densities from cores of red spruce are illustrated in Figure 1.38. When the data are plotted as 20-year segments (or as 25-year moving increments) the results show substantial decreases in growth over the past two decades, 1965–1984 (Figure 1.39). This finding agrees with that of some other authors (Chevone and Linzon, 1988). A number of factors are probably involved in these declines.

a) Ring width

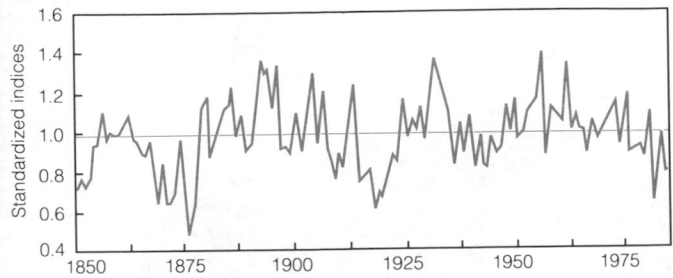

b) Maximum density

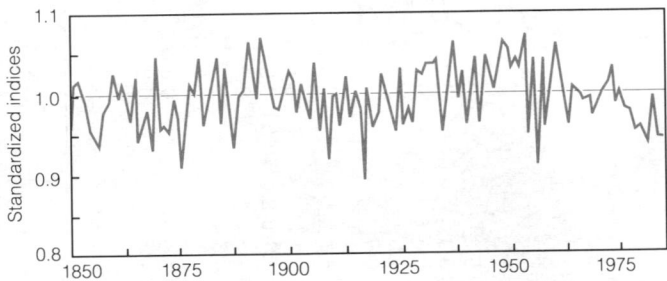

Figure 1.38 Standardized chronologies of tree-ring widths and maximum late wood densities of red spruce from Maine, USA, (the horizontal line shows the mean value for the period 1850–1984)
Source: Conkey, 1988

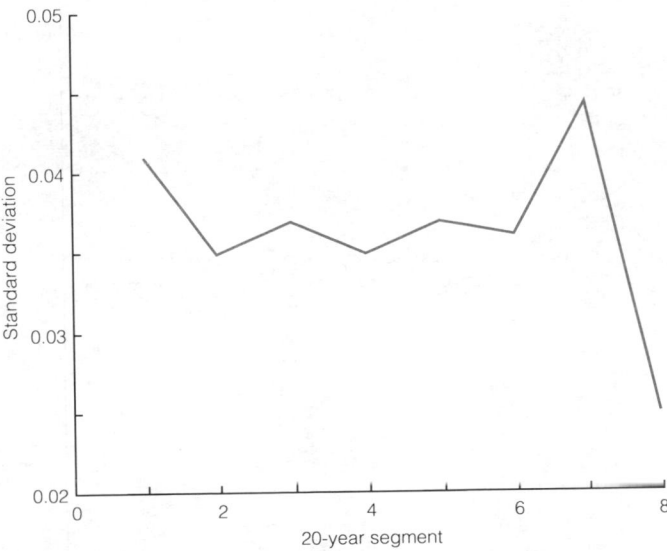

Figure 1.39 Standard deviations of 20-year segments of the maximum density indices, chronologically ordered from red spruce, (segment 1 is 1822–1841, segment 2 is 1842–1861, etc., up to segment 8, which is 1965–1984)
Source: Conkey, 1988

Time series of absolutely-dated, tree-ring width indices have also been used to reconstruct quantitative climatic records, particularly at higher latitudes where temperature can yield a clear signal (Jacoby and D'Arrigo, 1989). Three tree species, white spruce (*Picea glauca*), eastern larch (*Larix laricina*) and northern white cedar (*Thuja occidentalis*), were used to reconstruct Northern Hemisphere and Arctic annual temperature departures from 1671 to 1973. Results show the partial amelioration of temperature after the Little Ice Age in the early 1700s; an abrupt, severe renewal of cold in the early 1800s and a prolonged warming since approximately 1840. Comparable tree-ring indices were reported from 1635 AD to the present in northern North America by Diaz et al. (1989). Tree-ring reconstructions from AD 500 to the present day have been reported from Scots pine (*Pinus sylvestris*) for northern Fennoscandia (Briffa et al., 1990). The temperature inferences were less clear-cut in this region.

References

Briffa, K. R., Bartholin, T. S., Eckstein, D., Jones, P. D., Karlén, W., Schweingruber, F. H. and Zetterberg, P. 1990 A 1,400-year tree-ring record of summer temperatures in Fennoscandia, *Nature* (London) **346**, 434–439.

Burton, M. A. S. 1985 *Biological Monitoring: Plants*. MARC Report Number 32, Monitoring and Assessment Research Centre, London.

Chevone, B. I. and Linzon, S. N. 1988 Tree decline in North America, *Environmental Pollution* **50**, 87–99.

Conkey, L. E. 1988 Decline in old-growth red spruce in western Maine: an analysis of wood density and climate, *Canadian Journal of Forest Research* **18**, 1063–1068.

Diaz, H. F., Andrews, J. T. and Short, S. K. 1989 Climatic variations in northern North America (6000 BP to present) reconstructed from pollen and tree-ring data, *Arctic and Alpine Research* **21**, 45–59.

Innes, J. L. and Cook, E. R. 1989 Tree-ring analysis as an aid to evaluating the effect of pollution on tree growth, *Canadian Journal of Forest Research* **19**, 1174–1189.

Jacoby, G. C. Jr. and D'Arrigo, R. 1989 Reconstructed northern hemisphere annual temperature since 1671 based on high-latitude tree-ring data from North America, *Climatic Change* **14**, 39–59.

Table 1.47 Extent and timing of pH changes for selected lakes in North America and Europe

Region/country	Location/lake	Year of core	Current lake water pH	Surface sediment inferred pH	Inferred pH (pre-1850)	Inferred pH change[a]	Approximate date of first pH change	Primary cause of pH change
NORTH AMERICA								
USA								
	Adirondack Park							
	Bear Pond	1983	5.0	5.5	5.9	-0.4	1920–1940	A
	Big Moose Lake	1982	4.6–5.1	5.0	6.0	-1.0	1920–1940	A
	Clear Pond (Elk Lake)	1982	7.0	7.0	7.0	–		
	Deep Lake	1983	4.7	4.8	5.4	-0.6	1940–1950	A
	Holmes Lake[b]	1984	5.0[c]		5.3	–		
	Honnedaga Lake	1976	4.7–4.8	5.2	6.1	-1.1		A
	Lake Arnold	1982	4.8	4.7	5.1	-0.4		A
	Little Echo Pond	1982	4.8	4.5	4.6	–	du	A
	Merriam Lake	1982	4.9	5.1	5.4	-0.3	1910–1930	A
	Panther Lake	1980	7.2	6.9	7.5	-0.6	post-1960	A
	Queer Lake	1983	5.3	5.4	6.4	-1.0	1930–1950	A
	Sagamore Lake	1978	6.0	6.3	6.8	-0.5	1940s	A
	Seventh Lake	1976	6.4–7.0	6.5	6.6	–		
	Upper Wallface Pond	1983	5.0	4.9	5.3	-0.4	1910–1930	A
	West Pond	1982	5.5	5.7	5.6	–		
	Windfall Pond	1982	6.5	6.9	6.8	–		
	Woods Lake	1980	4.9	4.8	5.2	-0.4	1930s	A
	Woodhull Lake	1976	5.1–5.3	6.0	6.1	–		
EUROPE								
Norway								
	Blåvatn	1978	5.1	5.1	5.2	-0.1	1930	A
	Botnavatn	1978	5.7	5.7	5.9	-0.2	1920	A
	Bråvatn	1979	5.2	5.2–5.3	5.6–6.3	-0.7	1900	A
	Dorsvatn	1978	5.0	5.0	5.0	–		
	Grönlivatn	1978	6.5	6.5	6.5	–		
	Gulspettvatn	1985	4.9	4.8	5.6	-0.8	du	A
	Holetjorn	1986	4.6	4.6	5.1	-0.5	du	A
	Holmvatn	1978	4.7	4.6	4.9–5.2	-0.5	1930	A
	Hovvatn	1978	4.4		4.8–5.4	-0.7	1918	A
	Langtjern	1975	4.7–5.2	3.9–4.4	4.3–6.2	–		
	Ljosvatn	1986	4.5	4.6	5.2	-0.6	du	A
	Nedre Målmesvatn	1979	4.6	4.4–4.5	4.9–5.3	-0.6	1890	A
	Oppljosvatn	1979	5.8	5.8	5.8	–		
	Övre Målmesvatn	1977	4.5		4.4–6.5	-0.5	1930	A

Continued below

Table 1.47 Continued

Region/country	Location/lake	Year of core	Current lake water pH	Surface sediment inferred pH	Inferred pH (pre-1850)	Inferred pH change[a]	Approximate date of first pH change	Primary cause of pH change
	Röyrtjörna	1987	6.5	6.0	6.0	—	du	A
	Skomakarvatn	1987	4.6	4.5	5.1	-0.6	du	A
	Verevatn	1986	4.4	4.4	5.1	-0.7	1950	A
Sweden	Gardsjön	1979	4.6	4.5	6.0	-1.5	du	A
	Härsvatten	1979	4.4	4.2	5.9	-1.7	du	A
	Lilla Öresjön	1986	4.5	4.6	6.1	-1.5	du	A
	Lysevatten	1979	5.9	5.2[d]	6.1	-0.9[d]	du	A
	Stora Skarsjön	1971	4.5	4.5	6.0	-1.5	du	A

a   Surface sediment pH minus pre-1850 diatom-inferred pH.
b   Holmes Lake has been limed; it is therefore not possible to infer a pH change.
c   Data refer to 1980.
d   Affected by liming in 1974.

A dash signifies that the pH change is not significant, i.e., less than, or equal to, 0.2 pH units.

The entry "du" in the column "Approximate date of first pH change" indicates that dating of the core is uncertain or that the core was not dated.
The entry "A" in the column "Primary cause of pH change" indicates that acidic deposition is considered to be the primary cause of the observed pH change.

Source:
Charles, D. F., Battarbee, R. W., Renberg, J., van Dam, H. and Smol, J. P. 1990 Palaeoecological analysis of lake acidification trends in North America using diatoms and crysophytes. In: Acidic Precipitation. Volume 4. Soils Aquatic Processes and Lake Acidification. S. A. Norton, S. E. Lindberg and A. L. Page (Eds). Springer Verlag, New York. 207–276.

Table 1.48　Atmospheric concentration of methane, 100,000 years BP–present (measurements made in air trapped in polar ice)

Sampling location (and date)	Age of air (years BP)	CH₄ concentration (ppbv)	Sampling location (and date)	Age of air (years BP)	CH₄ concentration (ppbv)
ARCTIC			ANTARCTICA		
Dye 3 (1979–81)[a]	32	1,310	Byrd Station (1967–68)[b]	550	667
	33	1,210		600	647
	70	1,090		7,100	615
	169	980		10,600	638
	324	800		14,300	460
	2,166	650		22,400	341
	3,466	710		27,900	360
	9,776	760		33,500	385
	27,116	650		46,600	457
				51,100	505
Dye 3 (1979–81)[b]	3,400	627	Byrd Station (1971)[c]	334	650
	7,700	663		424	700
	7,800	680		544	660
	7,900	645		644	640
	10,800	477		844	700
	14,000	650		1,024	700
	16,000	389		1,114	700
	19,000	327		1,224	800
	21,000	358		1,324	670
	39,800	561		1,564	680
	40,500	411		1,834	820
	41,000	427			
	73,000	468			
	100,000	468			

[a]　Data originally reported by Craig, H. and Chan, C. C. 1982 Methane: record in polar ice cores, *Geophysical Research Letters* **9**, 1221–1224.

[b]　Data originally reported by Stauffer, B., Lochbronner, E., Oeschger, H. and Schwander, J. 1988 Methane concentration in the glacial atmosphere was only half that of the pre-industrial Holocene, *Nature* (London) **332**, 812–814.

[c]　Data originally reported by Rasmussen, R. A. and Khalil, M. A. K. 1984 Atmospheric methane in recent and ancient atmospheres: concentrations, trends and interhemispheric gradient, *Journal of Geophysical Research*, **89**(D7), 11599–11605.

The data presented here represent a compilation of measurements of methane in air extracted from ice cores reported by a number of workers. Data from the individual studies have been adjusted in order to make the results comparable with each other.

For further details regarding gas extraction and ice core dating techniques, please refer to the source documents.

Source:
Khalil, M. A. K. 1989 Personal communication, Institute of Atmospheric Sciences, Oregon Graduate Center, Oregon, USA.

Part 2
Climate

The presence of naturally occurring infra-red absorbing gases in the earth's atmosphere means that the global mean surface temperature is around a habitable 15°C. However, there is a growing concern that observed increases in atmospheric concentrations of greenhouse gases due to human activities will profoundly alter the global climate within the next century.

Complex ocean-atmosphere coupled general circulation models of the earth's climatic system have been developed in order to assess the likely effects of increases in atmospheric concentrations of greenhouse gases. A synthesis of current model results has been prepared for the Intergovernmental Panel on Climate Change (IPCC), a research effort jointly co-ordinated by the World Meteorological Organization (WMO) and UNEP. Assuming a "business-as-usual" emissions scenario, it is predicted that global mean temperatures will rise by an average rate of about 0.3°C per decade (with an uncertainty range of 0.2–0.5°C) during the next century. This will result in an increase in global mean temperature of about 2°C above that in pre-industrial times by 2025, and about 4°C by 2100. Global warming of this magnitude is expected to lead to an increase in global average precipitation by a few per cent by 2030. Areas of sea ice and snow cover are also likely to diminish. In addition, a rise in global mean sea level of 20 cm by 2030, and 65 cm by the end of the next century, is predicted. The "business-as-usual" emissions scenario for greenhouse gases assumes a continued reliance on coal and oil, a modest improvement in energy efficiency, limited controls on emissions of carbon dioxide (CO_2), continued deforestation, uncontrolled emissions of methane (CH_4) and nitrous oxide (N_2O) from agricultural sources and a reduction of chlorofluorocarbon (CFC) emissions in line with the Montreal Protocol (WMO/UNEP, 1990).

Regional-scale climatic changes cannot reliably be predicted at this time, although some continental-scale changes are consistently predicted by a number of current climate models. It is probable, for example, that warming will be most pronounced in the mid-high latitudes of the Northern Hemisphere during winter months. Precipitation is also expected to increase in the mid-high latitude continental areas during winter, whereas reduced precipitation is predicted during summer months in southern Europe and central North America. At the present time there is no clear evidence for increased climate variability or greater frequency of extreme events in a warmer world. However, with an increase in global mean temperatures, episodes of high temperatures are likely to become more frequent and cold episodes less frequent (WMO/UNEP, 1990).

The aim of this section is to provide a brief overview of the existing climate monitoring activities. In addition, analyses of selected long-term instrumental records of key climatic variables of particular relevance to the question of the detection of global warming will be presented. Data on emissions and atmospheric concentrations of greenhouse gases are given in Part 1 (Environmental Pollution, Atmosphere) of this report.

The detection of a greenhouse gas-induced climatic change in the observational record represents an important part of climate research and, in recent years, has become a high priority issue. In order to claim detection of climatic change it is necessary not only to identify a change in one or more climatic variable(s), but also to attribute this change to increased atmospheric concentrations of greenhouse gases. Although analyses of the observational records indicate that global mean surface air temperatures have increased by approximately 0.5°C over the past 100 years (see below), an unequivocal cause-and-effect relationship has not been proven. This is in part due to the inherent large variability of the global climate which, at the present time, appears to mask any signal of an enhanced greenhouse effect. It is thus the view of the IPCC that it is not yet possible to attribute all (or even part) of the observed global mean warming to increases in atmospheric concentrations of greenhouse gases on the basis of the observational data currently available (WMO/UNEP, 1990).

Detection of an enhanced greenhouse effect in the observational record will provide a means of validating computer models of the climate system. For the purposes of making comparisons between model results and observations, hemispheric and global average trends in selected climatic variables are computed from individual station data. Changes in surface air temperatures are expected to provide the clearest signal of climatic change, and thus have received the greatest attention to date. Analyses of hemispheric and global temperature trends over the past century will be updated in each edition of the 'UNEP Environmental Data Report'. This edition also highlights changes in the cryosphere (snow and ice) whereas the focus of the previous edition of this report was on past fluctuations in precipitation and cloud cover (UNEP, 1989).

References

UNEP 1989 *United Nations Environment Programme Environmental Data Report*, Basil Blackwell, Oxford.

WMO/UNEP 1990 *Scientific Assessment of Climate Change*, Report prepared for the Intergovernmental Panel on Climate Change by Working Group 1, World Meteorological Organization, Geneva, and United Nations Environment Programme, Nairobi.

Climate System Monitoring

In order to improve our understanding of the earth's climatic system and to assess the extent of man's influence on the global climate, systematic long-term observations of climatic variables are essential. However, the bulk of information that is currently available on climate change has been derived from measurements which were designed to monitor the weather rather than climate change.

Compilation of global data on basic meteorological parameters, including surface air temperature, sea-surface temperature (SST), upper air temperature, precipitation, wind speed and direction, atmospheric pressure and relative humidity, is the function of the World Weather Watch (WWW) system of the WMO. Established in 1963, the WWW has three principal components:

(a) the Global Observing System;
(b) the Global Telecommunications System; and
(c) the Global Data Processing System.

The Global Observing System (GOS) currently comprises a global network of about 9,500 ground-based observation stations operated by national meteorological services and a space-based observing system of five geostationary and four polar orbiting satellites. Information is also gathered from around 7,000 ships, 3,000 aircraft, over 600 radar stations and 280 fixed and drifting buoys (WMO, 1989a).

Meteorological observations from both ground-based stations and satellites are relayed via the Global Telecommunication System (GTS) to designated Meteorological Centres for processing. At the Meteorological Centres the WWW Global Data Processing System analyses the raw weather data and provides short- and medium-range forecasts, which are transmitted back to collaborating national meteorological services, again via the GTS (WMO, 1989a).

Monthly summary data for selected climatic variables including, for example, surface air temperature and precipitation reported by a sub-set of national meteorological stations via the GTS are published as the 'World Weather Records' on a regular basis. This data set is currently stored in digitized form by the National Center for Atmospheric Research (NCAR) and by the National Climatic Data Center, both in the USA.

An extensive catalogue of existing national meteorological networks, station histories and available climatic data sets is also published by the WMO. The catalogue, which is prepared by WMO's INFOCLIMA service (the World Climate Data and Information Referral Service), has recently been updated to include information on satellite-derived and palaeoclimatic data sets (WMO, 1989b). Synthesized information of the current state of the climatic system, focusing on significant large-scale anomalies in climatic patterns, is published on a monthly basis. The 'Climatic System Monitoring Monthly Bulletin' has been issued since July 1984. The third in a series of biennial reviews of significant meteorological anomalies has also been published recently (WMO, 1990a).

Recent advances in microcomputer technology have facilitated the development of the CLICOM system (Transfer of Technology in Climate Data Management and User Services) for the processing, analysis, archiving and exchange of meteorological data among participating countries in a standardized computer format. By mid-1990 CLICOM systems were operational in 89 WMO member countries (Figure 2.1); a further 30 countries plan to install such systems in the near future. Some countries have more than one installation; the USA, for example, currently has 40 operational CLICOM systems.

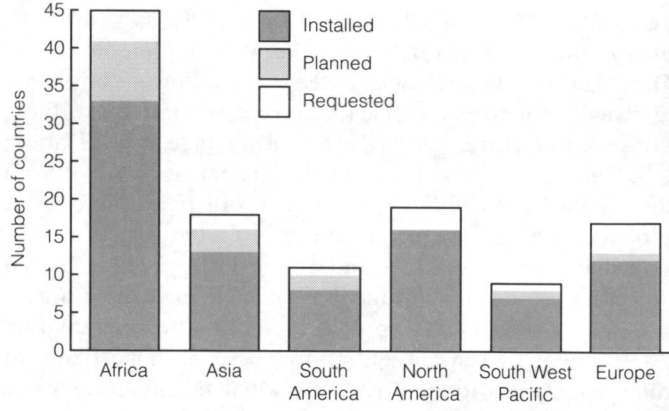

Figure 2.1 Status of the CLICOM system network in WMO member countries, as of the end of May 1990
Source: WMO, 1990b

Despite such improvements for data transfer, the existing WWW system is inadequate to support the growing need for comprehensive and reliable climatic data sets required by the international scientific community for the study of global climatic change. Although over 9,500 land-based meteorological stations are currently making routine weather observations, only about 1,200 stations submit monthly averaged surface air temperature records via the GTS. Data from only 2,000 stations are being published each decade as the 'World Weather Records' (WMO, 1990c).

In addition to problems of geographical coverage, existing instrumental records for the majority of climatic variables suffer from poor temporal resolution, biases, lack of adequate supporting "metadata" (data about data) and an inadequate infrastructure for the distribution of available data sets to the scientific community. Daily measurements of surface air temperature, for instance, although housed within numerous national meteorological data centres world-wide are not readily available to climatic scientists in a usable computerized format. Future efforts of the WMO will therefore be directed towards improving activities such as the WWW in order to develop a comprehensive global observing system for climate monitoring (WMO, 1990c).

In addition to improved routine monitoring, a programme of climatic research, involving unprecedented international co-operation, is required to increase understanding of the earth's climatic system and to improve predictive capabilities of climate models. Under the auspices of the WMO's World Climate Research Programme (WCRP) and the International Geosphere-Biosphere Programme (IGBP), several major internationally co-ordinated projects are currently under way or planned. A number of these are listed below:

Body[a]	Research Programme
Ongoing Programmes	
IGBP	The International Global Atmospheric Chemistry Programme (IGAC)
IGBP	The Joint Global Ocean Flux Study (JGOFS)
IGBP	Past Global Changes (PAGES)
WCRP	Global Energy and Water Cycle (GEWEX)
WCRP	The Tropical Ocean – Global Atmosphere Programme (TOGA)
WCRP	The World Ocean Circulation Experiment (WOCE)
Proposed Programmes	
IGBP	Biospheric Aspects of the Hydrological Cycle (BAHC)
IGBP	Climate Change Impacts on Agriculture and Forestry
IGBP	Geosphere-Biosphere Models
IGBP	Global Change and Terrestrial Ecosystems (GCTE)
IGBP	Global Ocean Euphotic Zone Study (GOEZS)
IGBP	Land-Ocean Interactions in the Coastal Zones
IGBP	Modelling Global Biogeochemical Cycles

[a] Co-ordinating body.
IGBP = International Geosphere-Biosphere Programme.
WCRP = The World Climate Research Programme.

Many of the above programmes rely heavily on satellite-based monitoring instruments. Satellite remote-sensing of the earth, by virtue of its superior temporal and spatial coverage, will play an increasingly important role in the study of global climatic change in the future. An overview of existing satellite systems for environmental monitoring is given elsewhere in this report (see Part 10: International Co-operation). Although some satellite-based instruments are already yielding useful information (see

Snow and Ice below), many satellite-derived data sets are still of insufficient length for trend assessment. Furthermore, satellite measurements are beset with problems relating to calibration stability and interpretation.

References

WMO 1989a *World Weather Watch: Fourteenth Status Report on Implementation,* WMO Publication No. 714, World Meteorological Organization, Geneva.

WMO 1989b *INFOCLIMA: Catalogue of Climate Data Sets 1989 Edition,* WMO/TD-No. 293, World Meteorological Organization, Geneva.

WMO 1990a *The Global Climate System: Climate System Monitoring, June 1986–November 1988,* World Meteorological Organization, Geneva.

WMO 1990b *CLICOM News,* Issue No. 5, World Climate Programme, World Meteorological Organization, Geneva.

WMO 1990c *Report of the Expert Group on Global Baseline Datasets,* WCDP-11, WMO/TD-No. 359, World Meteorological Organization, Geneva.

Indicators of Climatic Change

Temperature

Land-based Records Sources of meteorological station data include the 'World Weather Records' (published since the 1920s) and the 'Monthly Climatic Data for the World', compiled and published by the Climatic Analysis Center, USA. Both data sets are available in digitized form from the NCAR, USA. These observations, together with the historical land-based surface air temperature records compiled by Bradley et al. (1985), comprise the raw data set from which hemispheric and global temperature trends are derived.

Analyses of hemispheric and global temperature trends are hampered by several major deficiencies in the available records. Although the available data base extends back to the mid-1800s, the earlier records have limited geographical coverage and are biased towards Europe. In addition, changes in measurement procedures, station relocations and changes in the local environment (in particular, increasing urbanization) over time represent sources of inhomogeneity in the historical record which, if not accounted for, can introduce spurious trends.

Analyses of available instrumental land-based surface air temperature records have been conducted by several research groups (Jones et al., 1986a,b; Hansen and Lebedeff 1987, 1988; Vinnikov et al., 1987). Analyses differ in their treatment of potential sources of error and correction procedures for various biases. Hemispheric and global temperature trends derived by the Climatic Research Unit, University of East Anglia, UK (Jones et al., 1986a,b) have been presented in previous editions of this report (UNEP 1987, 1989) and are updated again here.

Variations in hemispheric and global surface air temperatures over land are given in Table 2.1 and plotted in Figure 2.2. The procedures employed for the computation

Northern Hemisphere

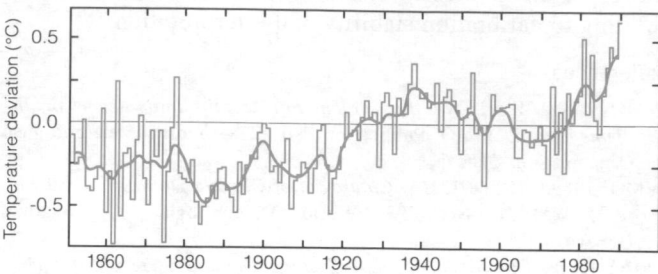

Southern Hemisphere

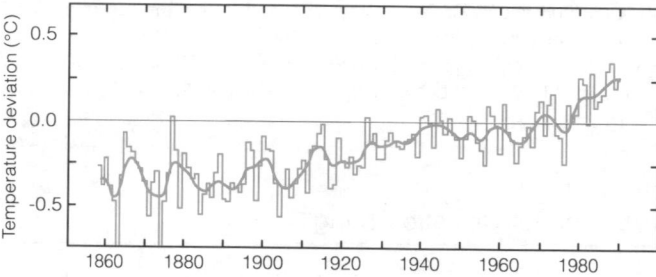

Global

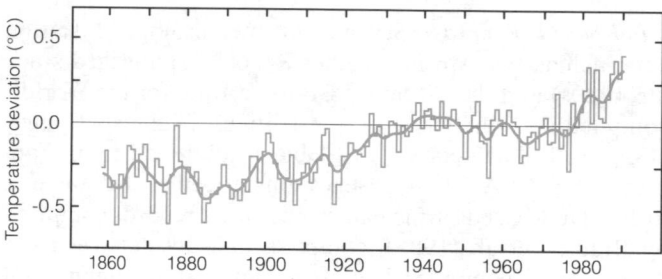

Figure 2.2 Trends in mean annual surface air temperatures derived from land-based measurements, 1851–1989 (expressed as deviations in °C from a reference period mean)
Source: figure provided by P. D. Jones, Climatic Research Unit, University of East Anglia, UK

of temperature trends are briefly outlined in the footnotes to the table; more comprehensive discussions are given by Jones and Wigley (1990a) and Jones et al. (1991). Results indicate that during the 1980s global temperatures have been higher than in any decade in the past 140 years. On average, global temperatures have increased by about 0.5°C since the beginning of the century. The pattern of temperature change differs markedly between hemispheres; in the Northern Hemisphere an irregular and abrupt warming of about 0.3°C occurred during the early 1920s, followed by a period of cooling between 1940–1960. Since the 1970s, temperatures have increased steadily. In the Southern Hemisphere, temperature increases during the 1920s and 1930s were followed by a period of relative stability, before rising again in the 1970s.

Increasing urbanization around fixed meteorological stations has been identified as the most serious potential

source of systematic error in the land-based temperature series. However, Jones et al. (1990) have estimated that the "urban heat-island effect" accounts for a maximum of 0.05°C of the 0.5°C warming observed during the past 100 years. Attempts have also been made to assess the likely influence of the large variations in the spatial coverage of temperature records; it is concluded that changes in station density since 1900 have relatively little impact on the estimates of hemispheric and global land temperature trends (Jones and Wigley, 1990a; Jones et al., 1991).

Land and Marine Records Further evidence of global warming has been obtained from analyses of sea-surface temperature (SST) records (WMO/UNEP, 1990). Approximately 80 million observations of SST made by commercial and weather ships and, more recently, by the increasing number of fixed and drifting buoys have been assembled to form the Comprehensive Ocean-Atmosphere Data Set (COADS) by Woodruff et al. (1987). A similar data set, comprising some 60 million observations, has been compiled by the UK Meteorological Office (Bottomley et al., 1990).

One of the principal sources of bias in SST records arises from changes in the method of sampling sea water for temperature measurement. Prior to 1940, measurements of SST were routinely made by hauling water onto the deck of a ship in a bucket and recording the temperature after a few minutes of standing. Since the early 1940s, SSTs have been more commonly recorded by thermometers inserted in engine cooling water intake pipes. Comparative studies have indicated that intake readings give results that are 0.3–0.7°C higher than bucket measurements. Moreover, different types of bucket, which differ in their insulating capacity, were used to collect samples. Corrections have thus been applied to the older bucket measurements of SST which take account of the evaporative cooling rates of different types of bucket (Jones and Wigley, 1990a; Jones et al., 1991).

Global and hemispheric temperature changes, derived from combined land and SST data sets are presented in Table 2.2 and Figure 2.3. From these data it is concluded that relative to the average for the period 1881–1900, global temperatures have increased by 0.45°C ± 0.15°C (WMO/UNEP, 1990). As with the land-based temperature series, inter-hemispheric differences are noted in the pattern of warming. A rapid increase in Northern Hemisphere temperatures during the 1920s and early 1930s contrasts with a more gradual increase in the Southern Hemisphere during this time. Between 1940 and 1970 temperatures remained relatively stable in the Southern Hemisphere; in the Northern Hemisphere, however, there is evidence of cooling. Since the mid-1970s temperatures have risen again although increases have been more pronounced in the Southern Hemisphere (WMO/UNEP, 1990).

Satellite Measurements Since 1979, measurements of thermal emissions of oxygen by satellite-based radiometers have provided globally-averaged estimates of the tempera-

Northern Hemisphere

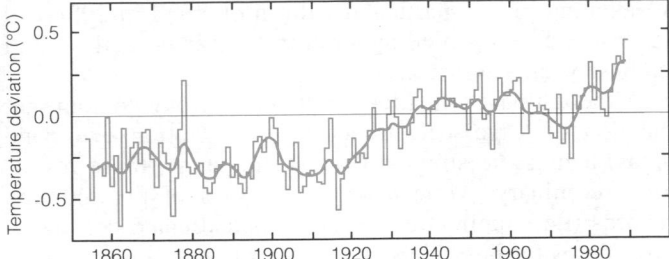

Southern Hemisphere

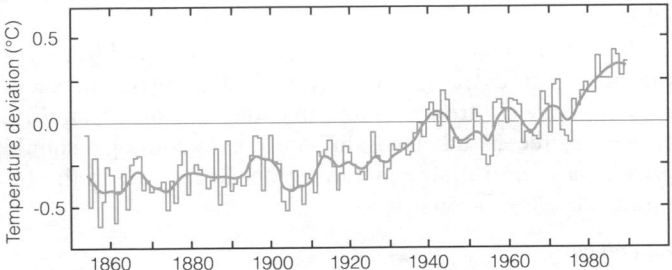

Global

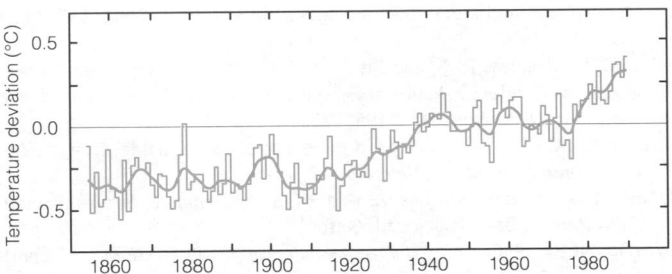

Figure 2.3 Variations in mean annual surface air temperatures derived from combined land and SST records, 1851–1989 (expressed as deviations in °C from a reference period mean)
Source: figure provided by P. D. Jones, Climatic Research Unit, University of East Anglia, UK

ture of the lower atmosphere. Results for the 10-year period, 1979–1988, show no statistically significant trends in global temperatures (Spencer and Christy, 1990). This finding is in broad agreement with traditional instrumental temperature measurements, particularly estimates of mid-tropospheric (850–300 mb) temperatures derived from a global network of 63 land-based radiosonde stations (Jones and Wigley, 1990b). Agreement between the two data sets adds further weight to the conclusion that incomplete spatial coverage and local urban warming effects may not represent major sources of bias in ground-based temperature series.

Trends in upper air temperatures, including the mid-troposphere, were reported in the previous edition of the 'UNEP Environmental Data Report' (UNEP, 1989) and will be updated in future editions. Examples of palaeoclimatic data sets, including temperature reconstructions from tree-rings and ice cores, are given in Part 1: Environ-

mental Pollution, Historical Monitoring. Proxy data sets of this type represent a useful means of reconstructing climatic characteristics prior to the advent of modern instrumental records.

References

Bottomley, M., Folland, C. K., Hsiung, J., Newell, R. E. and Parker, D. E. 1990 *Global Ocean Surface Temperature Atlas (GOSTA)*, Her Majesty's Stationery Office, London.

Bradley, R. S., Kelly, P. M., Jones, P. D., Diaz, H. F. and Goodess, C. 1985 *A Climate Data Bank for the Northern Hemisphere 1851–1980*, Technical Report Series TR017, US Department of Energy, Carbon Dioxide Research Division, Washington DC.

Hansen, J. and Lebedeff, S. 1987 Global trends of measured surface air temperature, *Journal of Geophysical Research* **92**, 13345–13372.

Hansen, J. and Lebedeff, S. 1988 Global surface temperatures: update through 1987, *Geophysical Research Letters* **15**, 323–326.

Jones, P. D., Raper, S. C. B., Bradley, R. S., Diaz, H. F., Kelly, P. M. and Wigley, T. M. L. 1986a Northern Hemisphere surface air temperature variations 1851–1984, *Journal of Climate and Applied Meteorology* **25**, 161–179.

Jones, P. D., Raper, S. C. B. and Wigley, T. M. L. 1986b Southern Hemisphere surface air temperature variations 1851–1984, *Journal of Climate and Applied Meteorology* **25**, 1213–1230.

Jones, P. D. and Wigley, T. M. L. 1990a Global warming trends, *Scientific American* **203**(2), 84–91.

Jones, P. D. and Wigley, T. M. L. 1990b Satellite data under scrutiny, *Nature* (London) **344**, 711.

Jones, P. D., Groisman, Ya. P., Coughlan, M., Plummer, N., Wang, W. C. and Karl, T. R. 1990 Assessment of urbanization effects in time series of surface air temperature over land, *Nature* (London) **347**, 169–172.

Jones, P. D., Wigley, T. M. L. and Farmer, G. 1991 Marine and land temperature data sets: a comparison and look at recent trends. In: *Greenhouse Gas Induced Climatic Change: A Critical Appraisal of Simulations and Observations*, M. E. Schlesinger (Ed.), Elsevier. In press.

Spencer, R. W. and Christy, J. R. 1990 Precise monitoring of global temperature trends from satellites, *Science* **247**, 1558–1562.

UNEP 1987 *United Nations Environment Programme Environmental Data Report*, Basil Blackwell, Oxford.

UNEP 1989 *United Nations Environment Programme Environmental Data Report*, Basil Blackwell, Oxford.

Vinnikov, K. Ya., Groisman, P. Ya., Lugina, K. M. and Golubev, A. A. 1987 Variations in Northern Hemisphere mean surface air temperatures over 1881–1985, *Meteorology and Hydrology* **1**, 45–53 (in Russian).

WMO/UNEP 1990 *Scientific Assessment of Climate Change*, Report prepared for the Intergovernmental Panel on Climate Change by Working Group 1, World Meteorological Organization, Geneva, and United Nations Environment Programme, Nairobi.

Woodruff, S. D., Slutz, R. J., Jenne, R. L. and Steurer, P. M. 1987 A comprehensive ocean-atmosphere data set, *Bulletin of the American Meteorological Society* **68**, 1239–1250.

Precipitation

Land-based Records Raw precipitation station data for use in large-area scale computations of long-term fluctuations are derived from the same sources as those for surface air temperatures over land. A number of such analyses have been attempted and have been reviewed recently by the IPCC (WMO/UNEP, 1990).

Analyses of precipitation records are generally more problematical than those for temperature. Precipitation has greater spatial and temporal variability than temperature and thus requires a higher density of station data in order to generate trend analyses of comparable accuracy. Furthermore, precipitation is subject to greater measurement difficulties; variations in the collection efficiency of rain gauges due to gauge design, siting and local climate represent major problems which are exacerbated by the lack of international standards for precipitation measurement. Monitoring of snowfall is especially prone to errors of this nature.

Estimates of long-term trends in precipitation over land areas of the Northern Hemisphere, according to Bradley et al. (1987), were reported in the 1989 edition of the 'UNEP Environmental Data Report' (UNEP, 1989). This work suggests, as does a more recent study by Diaz et al. (1989), that during the last few decades precipitation has tended to increase over land areas in the mid-latitudes of both hemispheres. Over tropical regions of the Northern Hemisphere, in contrast, precipitation has decreased. These large-scale features, which are broadly consistent with climate model predictions, do, however, contain considerable spatial variability (WMO/UNEP, 1990).

Of particular note is the prolonged period of dryer-than-average conditions in the sub-Saharan area of west Africa which have persisted since the early 1960s. Normalized fluctuations in April–October rainfall amount (expressed as a deviation from a long-term mean) for this region are shown in Figure 2.4. Summary data are presented in Table 2.3.

Atlantic (south of 10°N), lower SSTs in the Atlantic north of 10°N and higher SSTs in the tropical Indian Ocean has tended to coincide with drought in the sub-Saharan region. Weakening of this particular pattern of SSTs in 1988 and 1989 was accompanied by a return to near-normal rainfall in these years (Figure 2.4).

Although past climatic records have provided some indication of large-scale trends in precipitation over land areas, it must be stressed that, at this stage, these results are preliminary. More detailed analyses of precipitation records (i.e., application of more sophisticated correction procedures for possible sources of bias) and improved data coverage, in particular over oceans, are required before more concrete conclusions can be made (WMO/UNEP, 1990).

At the present time, monitoring of precipitation over the oceans is extremely patchy and of insufficient accuracy to assess trends with any degree of reliability. However, recent advances in satellite technology should provide a more reliable picture of ocean rainfall in the future.

References

Bradley, R. S., Diaz, H. F., Eischeid, J. K., Jones, P. D., Kelly, P. M. and Goodess, C. M. 1987 Precipitation fluctuations over the Northern Hemisphere land areas since the mid-19th century, *Science* **237**, 171–175.

Diaz, H. F., Bradley, R. S. and Eischeid, J. K. 1989 Precipitation fluctuations over global land areas since the late 1800s, *Journal of Geophysical Research* **94**, 1195–1210.

Druyan, L. M. 1989 Advances in the study of sub-Saharan drought, *International Journal of Climatology* **9**, 77–90.

UNEP 1989 *United Nations Environment Programme Environmental Data Report*, Basil Blackwell, Oxford.

WMO/UNEP 1990 *Scientific Assessment of Climate Change*, Report prepared for the Intergovernmental Panel on Climate Change by Working Group 1, World Meteorological Organization, Geneva, and United Nations Environment Programme, Nairobi.

Snow and Ice

The areal extents of snow and ice are key climatic variables in the earth's climatic system. Through the regulation of the exchange of heat, moisture and momentum between the ocean, the land and the atmosphere, snow and ice play a major role in determining the global heat balance. Furthermore, as the polar ice sheets store about 80 per cent of the world's fresh water, changes in their mass balance will influence global sea level.

Areas covered by snow and ice have a high albedo (reflectivity) and therefore have the capacity to affect the earth's radiation balance. It is widely assumed that a warmer world will have a smaller area of snow and ice, thus a lower capacity to reflect incoming solar radiation, which in turn will result in greater warming. This so-called "snow-ice albedo feedback" effect is believed to be the most probable cause of the polar amplification of warming in winter that is predicted by most climate models. As it is probable that global warming will be most pronounced in polar regions, the Arctic and Antarctic

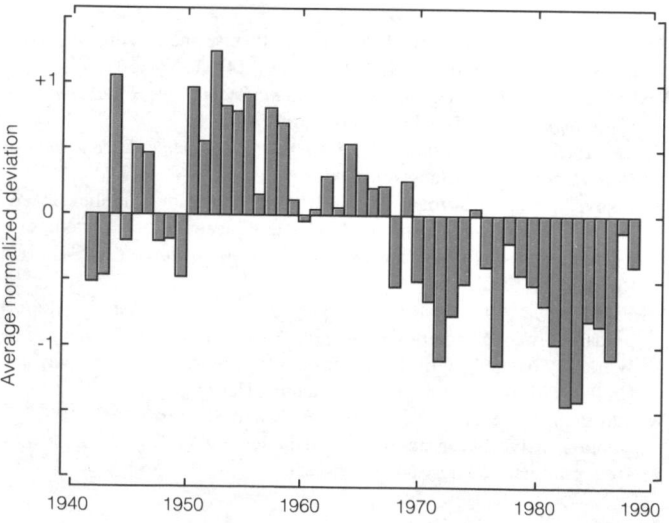

Figure 2.4 Variations in sub-Saharan rainfall, 1941–1990 (negative values indicate dryer-than-average conditions)
Source: data from Table 2.3

Occurrence of drought in the sub-Sahara is considered to be linked to anomalous patterns of SST in both the Atlantic and Indian oceans (Druyan, 1989; WMO/UNEP, 1990). The combination of anomalously high SSTs in the

environments may offer one of the best hopes for an early detection of climatic change.

Until the advent of satellite remote-sensing, relatively little routine monitoring of snow and ice had been conducted. However, satellite-derived estimates of snow and sea-ice area have been produced on a weekly basis for almost two decades. Satellite-based monitoring of continental snow cover is confined to the Northern Hemisphere where the large-scale variations in snow cover principally occur.

The preparation of a comprehensive inventory of the world's existing perennial ice and snow masses is an on-going task of the World Glacier Monitoring Service (WGMS). The original rationale for developing the World Glacier Inventory (WGI), initially proposed in the early 1970s, was to provide information about frozen freshwater resources as input to World Water Balance Studies. More recently, the WGI has gained increasing impetus and significance as a baseline data set for the detection of long-term climatic changes. The WGI work is supported by UNEP (through GEMS), the United Nations Educational, Scientific and Cultural Organization (UNESCO), the International Commission on Snow and Ice (ICSI) and the Swiss Federal Institute of Technology (ETH).

The WGI comprises detailed graphical and statistical information, describing the nature and extent of existing ice masses, that has been submitted to WGMS during the past 20 years by collaborating individuals and institutions. A review of the status of the WGI and of available data sets as of the end of 1988 has been published (Haeberli et al., 1989). Complete inventory data are stored in computerized format at both the WGMS in Zurich and at the World Data Center for Glaciology in Boulder, Colorado, USA.

Collection of systematic world-wide data on glaciated regions has proved to be a complex task; data compilation has been hampered by the remoteness of many of the areas under investigation, limitations of the existing techniques for measurement of glacier parameters and a lack of resources. Nevertheless, all the relevant regions of the world are now covered by some form of glacier inventory, although the level of completeness varies considerably between regions (Figure 2.5).

Based on the available WGI data, estimates of the extent of glaciated areas have been made (Table 2.4). The large ice sheets of Antarctica and Greenland together account for 96.6 per cent of the world's glaciated surface area. Of the remaining 3.4 per cent, approximately two-thirds (2.1 per cent) comprise smaller ice caps at high latitudes and around 1.3 per cent, the mountain glaciers (Haeberli et al., 1989). Although alpine glaciers account for a relatively minor proportion of the world's glaciated

Figure 2.5 World Glacier Inventory, status at the end of 1988 (filled and open circles indicate where the regional glacier catalogues are detailed or preliminary, respectively)
Source: Haeberli et al., 1989

regions, the most detailed inventories tend to exist for these ice bodies by virtue of their proximity to human settlements.

Snow Cover Snow cover in continental regions of the Northern Hemisphere has been assessed systematically since late 1966 with the aid of satellite-based instrumentation. Weekly Snow and Ice Cover Charts, compiled by the National Environmental Satellite, Data and Information Service (formerly the National Earth Satellite Service) of the National Oceanic and Atmospheric Administration (NOAA) in Washington DC, are derived from visible satellite imagery. Weekly charts have been converted into a digitized format using a 89 x 89 grid matrix from which snow cover area (in km^2) and time series of snow cover variations can be computed. The digitized data set is also archived at the World Data Center for Glaciology at the National Snow and Ice Data Center at Boulder, Colorado, USA.

Seasonal and annual average snow cover data spanning the 1966–1989 period are given in Table 2.5 for Eurasia, North America and the Northern Hemisphere as a whole. Data for the Northern Hemisphere are plotted in Figure 2.6. Improvements in the analysis of satellite data have increased the reliability of this data set after 1975; before 1973 the data set is generally considered to be suspect owing to the inconsistent representation of snow cover in the Himalayan region prior to this date.

Routine satellite monitoring over the past two decades has established the pronounced seasonal cycle in Northern Hemisphere snow cover. Snow cover reaches a maximum of around 47 x 10^6 km^2, or 9.1 per cent of the earth's total surface area during the Northern Hemisphere winter months, and shrinks to a minimum of 4 x 10^6 km^2 (0.8 per cent of the globe) in the summer months (Ropelewski, 1989).

Owing to the relatively short record of snow cover, inter-annual trends in snow cover are difficult to determine. There are, however, indications that Northern Hemisphere snow cover in the 1980s has decreased in areal extent relative to the 1970s. The changes are especially apparent in Eurasia where reductions in autumn and spring snow cover of 13 and 9 per cent respectively have been calculated (WMO/UNEP, 1990).

Information on snow cover and depth is also available from meteorological station records, some of which stretch back as far as the late 1800s. However, with the possible exception of low-lying areas in the mid-latitudes, consistent, high quality surface-based records of snow cover are generally lacking (WMO/UNEP, 1990).

Trends in the date of disappearance of snow cover in Arctic regions have been examined by Foster (1989). The analysis, which is based on records of varying length from 12 stations (located between 68°N and 74°N latitude), indicates that in much of the North American Arctic tundra the date of snow disappearance has been occurring earlier in the spring since the late 1960s. This trend is particularly evident at Barrow, Alaska (Figure 2.7).

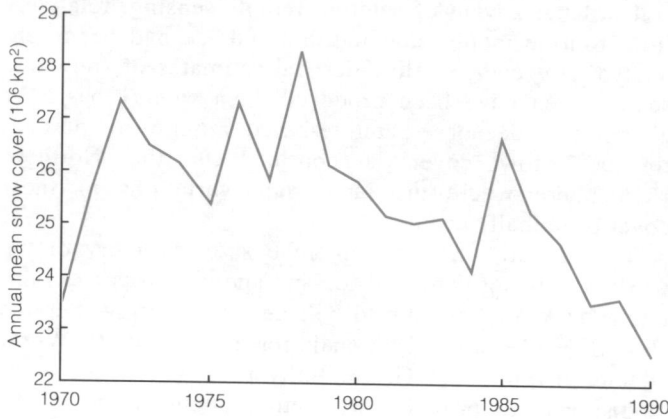

Figure 2.6 Variations in annual mean snow cover in the Northern Hemisphere, 1970–1990
Source: data from Table 2.5

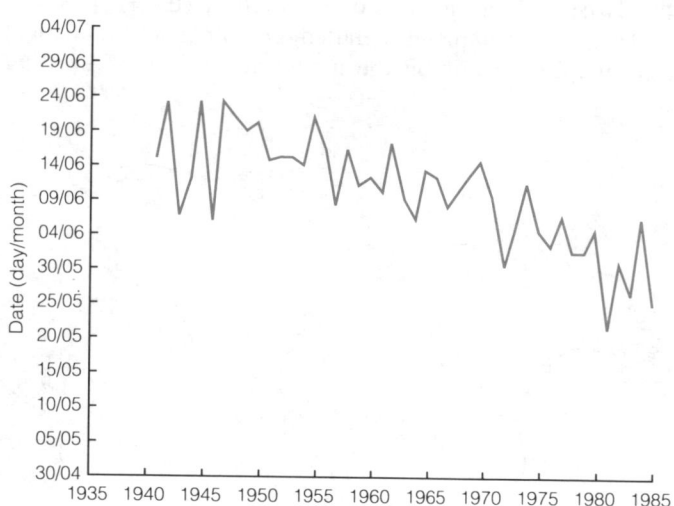

Figure 2.7 Annual date of snow disappearance at Barrow, Alaska, 1940–1985
Source: Foster, 1989

Sea-ice Extent and Thickness Although ship and harbour logs provide long historical records of the limits of sea ice and the dates of appearance and disappearance of harbour and coastal ice, such surface-based observations have found little application to studies of long-term climatic trends. Interpretation of such records is severely hampered by problems relating to observer bias and poor spatial coverage. Since the 1950s, ground-based observations of sea-ice extent are considered to be more reliable. Available records for areas of the Arctic have been compiled from a variety of sources and are described by Mysak and Manak (1989).

Satellite observations in the visible, infra-red and microwave bands have been used to map sea-ice extent in both the Arctic and Antarctic regions on a routine basis since 1973. Weekly charts are presently generated by the US Navy-NOAA Joint Ice Center (JIC). Ground truthing is provided by comparison against traditional ground-based and aircraft observations. Unlike the observation of snow cover (which relies on visible wave-lengths), satellite measurements of sea-ice extent (microwave radiation) are not impaired by cloud cover.

Satellite-derived charts are converted to digitized format by NOAA's Climate Analysis Center, Boulder, Colorado, from which spatial and temporal variations in sea-ice extent are computed. For the purposes of this analysis, sea-ice extent is defined as the area of ocean covered by at least 10–15 per cent of sea ice. Monthly and annual variations in sea-ice extent are presented in Tables 2.6 and 2.7. There is no evidence of significant trends in sea-ice extent during the period 1973–1989; throughout the available record sea-ice extent has fluctuated about a mean level in both hemispheres (WMO/UNEP, 1990).

It is likely that global warming will not only lead to a decrease in the areal extent of sea ice, but also to a reduction in thickness. In recent years, data on sea-ice thinning have been provided by upward-looking sonar measurements taken under ice by submarines. A significant decrease in mean sea-ice thickness over an area of 300,000 km^2 to the north of Greenland has been reported by Wadhams (1990). This result is based on a set of measurements initially made in October 1976 and later repeated in May 1987. However, without further data, it is not possible to determine whether this apparent change is representative of the whole Arctic basin (McLaren et al., 1990).

Land Ice (Mountain Glaciers) Alpine (i.e., mountain) glaciers represent only a small fraction of the total volume of ice on earth. Compared with the larger Greenland and Antarctic ice sheets, which respond only slowly to climatic change (on scales of centuries), smaller alpine glaciers and ice caps generally respond on annual to decadal time-scales. Variations in the properties of alpine glaciers, including frontal position, area, volume and mass balance are therefore potentially useful indicators of climatic change. Glacier mass balance, i.e., net change in glacier mass in a given year, is directly linked to climatic conditions and therefore is the most reliable indicator. Over time, changes in mass balance drive fluctuations in ice thickness, flow and volume and ultimately the positions of glacier fronts.

Standardized data on glacier mass balance, as well as data on positions of glacier fronts, area and volume, are routinely compiled by the WGMS. Data are compiled from information supplied by correspondents in individual countries world-wide and are available in published form as the report series, 'Fluctuations of Glaciers'. To date five volumes in this series have been published, spanning the periods 1959–1965 (Kasser, 1967), 1965–1970

(Kasser, 1973), 1970–1975 (Müller, 1977), 1975–1980 (Haeberli, 1985) and 1980–1985 (Haeberli and Müller, 1988). The next volume, containing data for the 1985–1990 period is scheduled for publication in 1992.

The greatest amount of glacier fluctuation data is available for variations in the position of glacier termini or fronts. Nevertheless, available WGMS records cover only a relatively small proportion of the number of glaciers world-wide (approximately 1 per cent) and are biased towards the European Alps and Iceland. Data on glacier mass balance are even more limited, and that for changes in glacier area and volume scarcer still. Assessment of long-term trends in alpine glaciers on a global scale is therefore difficult.

Data on mass balance for selected glaciers during the period 1960–1985 are given in earlier editions of this report (UNEP 1987, 1989). More recent information will be included in future editions of this report series as and when such data become available.

Analysis of existing data sets indicates that alpine glaciers have experienced a net retreat almost everywhere since the latter half of the 19th century (Haeberli, 1990; WMO/UNEP, 1990). The rate of recession appears to have been greatest during the middle of the present century, from 1920 to 1960. Between 1960 and 1980, however, there is evidence to suggest that the proportion of shrinking glaciers world-wide had declined; in the European Alps, for example, over 50 per cent of glaciers appear to have advanced during this period (Wood, 1988). Since 1980, mountain glacier trends have been more difficult to evaluate on a global scale, due to a lack of information for most world regions. In Europe, there are indications that glacier retreat is again the predominant trend (WMO/UNEP, 1990).

References

Foster, Y. L. 1989 The significance of the date of snow disappearance on the Arctic Tundra as a possible indicator of climate change, *Arctic and Alpine Research*, **21**(1), 60–70.

Haeberli, W. 1985 *Fluctuations of Glaciers 1975–1980, Volume IV*, International Association of Hydrological Sciences, Paris, and United Nations Educational, Scientific and Cultural Organization, Paris.

Haeberli, W. 1990 Glacier and permafrost signals of 20th century warming, *Annals of Glaciology* **14**, 99–101.

Haeberli, W. and Müller, P. 1988 *Fluctuations of Glaciers 1980–1985, Volume V*, International Association of Hydrological Sciences, Wallingford, United Nations Environment Programme, Nairobi, and United Nations Educational, Scientific and Cultural Organization, Paris.

Haeberli, W., Bösch, H., Scherler, K., Østrem, G. and Wallén C. C. (Eds) 1989 *World Glacier Inventory: Status 1988*, International Association of Hydrological Sciences, Wallingford, United Nations Environment Programme, Nairobi, and United Nations Educational, Scientific and Cultural Organization, Paris.

Kasser, P. 1967 *Fluctuations of Glaciers 1959–1965, Volume I*, International Association of Hydrological Sciences, Paris, and United Nations Educational, Scientific and Cultural Organization, Paris.

Kasser, P. 1973 *Fluctuations of Glaciers 1965–1970, Volume II*, International Association of Hydrological Sciences, Paris, and United Nations Educational, Scientific and Cultural Organization, Paris.

McLaren, A. S., Barry, R. G. and Bourke, R. H. 1990 Could Arctic ice be thinning, *Nature* (London) **345**, 762.

Müller, F. 1977 *Fluctuations of Glaciers 1970–1975, Volume III*, International Association of Hydrological Sciences, Paris, and United Nations Educational, Scientific and Cultural Organization, Paris.

Mysak, L. A. and Manak, D. K. 1989 Arctic sea-ice extent and anomalies 1953–1984, *Atmosphere-Ocean* **27**(2), 376–405.

Ropelewski, C. F. 1989 Monitoring large-scale cryosphere/atmosphere interactions, *Advances in Space Research* **9**(7), 213–218.

UNEP 1987 *United Nations Environment Programme Environmental Data Report*, Basil Blackwell, Oxford.

UNEP 1989 *United Nations Environment Programme Environmental Data Report*, Basil Blackwell, Oxford.

Wadhams, P. 1990 Evidence for thinning of Arctic ice cover north of Greenland, *Nature* (London) **345**, 795–797.

WMO/UNEP 1990 *Scientific Assessment of Climate Change*, Report prepared for the Intergovernmental Panel on Climatic Change by Working Group I, World Meteorological Organization, Geneva, and United Nations Environment Programme, Nairobi.

Wood, F. B. 1988 Global alpine glacier trends, 1960s to 1980s, *Arctic and Alpine Research* **20**(4), 404–413.

Sea Level

The prospect of a sea-level rise of up to 65 cm by the year 2100 represents a major threat to the well-being of 300 million people currently residing in low-lying areas world-wide. Most probable impacts include shoreline retreat, intrusion of salt water into estuaries and ground-water aquifers and increased frequency of storm surges. Countries most vulnerable to the impact of accelerated sea-level rise as a consequence of global warming include Bangladesh, Egypt, Indonesia, the Maldives, Mozambique, Pakistan, Thailand, the Gambia and Suriname.

Changes in sea level are monitored by a global network of around 1,300 tide gauges. Tide gauges record variations in relation to a fixed benchmark and thus measure "relative sea level". Available records, some of which extend back as far as the 1880s, are compiled and stored by the Permanent Service for Mean Sea Level (PSMSL) at the Bidston Observatory, Birkenhead, UK. Useful data sets are available for over 800 stations; however, many of these records are discontinuous and less than 20 years in length. Moreover, tidal records are biased towards Europe, North America and Japan; areas of Africa, Asia and the polar regions are poorly represented in the tidal records.

The PSMSL data set has been used to derive estimates of global mean sea-level changes during the last 100 years. Tide gauge measurements record sea-level variations caused by both "real" changes in the ocean level and vertical land movements (due to natural tectonic processes). In order to assess global changes in relative sea level, it is thus necessary to correct for the effect of land movements in the observational record.

A number of individual analyses of this type have been reported in recent years, some of which have been reported in earlier editions of this report (UNEP 1987, 1989). The analyses differ in their methodology, in particular with regard to station selection, geographical representation and correction procedures for land movements. The majority of studies indicate that global mean sea level has risen, on average, by 1–2 mm per year over the last 100 years (WMO/UNEP, 1990). Despite the appar-

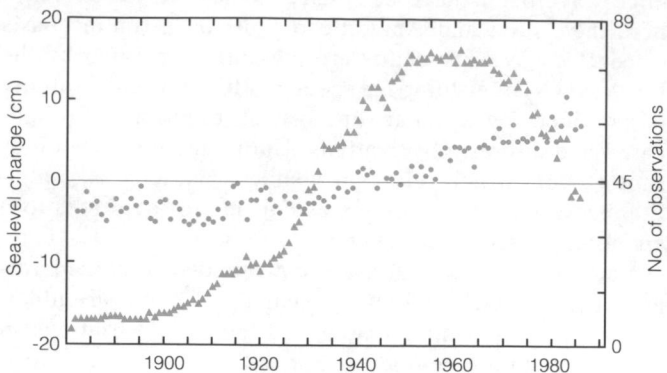

Figure 2.8 Trends in global mean sea level, 1880–1986 (the number of observations are shown as triangles)
Source: figure provided by T. P. Barnett, Scripps Institution of Oceanography, University of California, La Jolla, USA

ent coherence of analyses of this type, the possibility that all the studies are systematically biased cannot be ruled out. The most probable causes of the observed sea-level rise are the thermal expansion of sea water and the retreat of mountain glaciers (see previous section).

Estimates of global mean relative sea-level rise by Barnett (1984), reported in the first edition of this report (UNEP, 1987), are updated here in Figure 2.8. Based on the analysis of tide gauge records from 155 stations which span the period 1880–1986, an average rate of global mean sea-level rise of 1.15 mm a^{-1} is derived. A faster rate of sea-level rise, of 1.7 mm a^{-1}, is estimated for the period 1910–1980 (Barnett, 1988).

Using a different sub-selection of available tide gauge records and analysis procedure, Peltier and Tushingham (1989) have produced an estimate of 2.4 mm a^{-1} for the global rate of sea-level rise during 1920–1970. However, the authors note that their estimates vary according to the analysis procedures employed; if alternative tide gauge record sets are used, slower rates of RSL are calculated, which are in broad agreement with those of Barnett (1988) and others (WMO/UNEP, 1990).

References

Barnett, T. P. 1984 Estimation of "global" sea level change: a problem of uniqueness, *Journal of Geophysical Research* **89**, 7980–7988.

Barnett, T. P. 1988 Global sea level change. In: *Climate Variations over the Past Century and the Greenhouse Effect*, A report based on the First Climate Trends Workshop, 7–9 September 1988, Washington DC.

Peltier, W. R. and Tushingham, A. M. 1989 Global sea-level rise and the greenhouse effect: might they be connected, *Science* **244**, 806–810.

UNEP 1987 *United Nations Environment Programme Environmental Data Report*, Basil Blackwell, Oxford.

UNEP 1989 *United Nations Environment Programme Environmental Data Report*, Basil Blackwell, Oxford.

WMO/UNEP 1990 *Scientific Assessment of Climate Change*, Report prepared for the Intergovernmental Panel on Climate Change by Working Group I, World Meteorological Organization, Geneva, and United Nations Environment Programme, Nairobi.

Table 2.1 Trends in hemispheric and global mean annual surface air temperature derived from land-based records, 1851–1990 (deviations in °C from a reference period mean, 1951–1970)

Year	NH (ΔT°C)	SH (ΔT°C)	Global (ΔT°C)	Year	NH (ΔT°C)	SH (ΔT°C)	Global (ΔT°C)
1851	-0.08			1901	-0.03	-0.14	-0.09
1852	-0.26			1902	-0.29	-0.15	-0.22
1853	-0.22			1903	-0.26	-0.35	-0.31
1854	0.01			1904	-0.36	-0.56	-0.46
1855	-0.39			1905	-0.24	-0.38	-0.31
1856	-0.42			1906	-0.09	-0.26	-0.17
1857	-0.35			1907	-0.52	-0.44	-0.48
1858	-0.27	-0.25	-0.26	1908	-0.35	-0.35	-0.35
1859	0.08	-0.37	-0.15	1909	-0.31	-0.26	-0.28
1860	-0.55	-0.20	-0.38	1910	-0.24	-0.21	-0.22
1861	-0.30	-0.37	-0.34	1911	-0.27	-0.41	-0.34
1862	-0.74	-0.47	-0.61	1912	-0.42	-0.14	-0.28
1863	0.24	-0.84	-0.30	1913	-0.27	-0.12	-0.20
1864	-0.57	-0.31	-0.44	1914	-0.04	-0.04	-0.04
1865	-0.19	-0.04	-0.12	1915	-0.01	0.02	0.00
1866	-0.16	-0.13	-0.14	1916	-0.25	-0.20	-0.23
1867	-0.47	-0.16	-0.31	1917	-0.55	-0.38	-0.47
1868	-0.11	-0.23	-0.17	1918	-0.33	-0.36	-0.35
1869	0.04	-0.26	-0.11	1919	-0.27	-0.07	-0.17
1870	-0.34	-0.34	-0.34	1920	-0.14	-0.21	-0.17
1871	-0.50	-0.56	-0.53	1921	0.07	-0.25	-0.09
1872	-0.05	-0.35	-0.20	1922	-0.08	-0.18	-0.13
1873	-0.21	-0.28	-0.25	1923	-0.04	-0.29	-0.16
1874	-0.05	-0.75	-0.40	1924	-0.10	-0.24	-0.17
1875	-0.73	-0.47	-0.60	1925	0.04	-0.25	-0.11
1876	-0.30	-0.29	-0.30	1926	0.14	0.06	0.10
1877	-0.04	0.06	0.01	1927	0.03	-0.09	-0.03
1878	0.27	-0.15	-0.21	1928	0.07	-0.04	0.02
1879	-0.31	-0.51	-0.41	1929	-0.26	-0.20	-0.23
1880	-0.34	-0.17	-0.25	1930	0.13	-0.20	-0.04
1881	-0.36	-0.26	-0.31	1931	0.19	-0.08	0.05
1882	-0.23	-0.32	-0.28	1932	0.11	-0.03	0.04
1883	-0.48	-0.29	-0.38	1933	-0.18	-0.09	-0.14
1884	-0.62	-0.55	-0.59	1934	0.16	-0.12	0.02
1885	-0.51	-0.42	-0.47	1935	0.05	-0.13	-0.04
1886	-0.46	-0.35	-0.41	1936	0.06	-0.08	-0.01
1887	-0.38	-0.44	-0.41	1937	0.24	-0.07	0.09
1888	-0.46	-0.29	-0.38	1938	0.37	-0.04	0.17
1889	-0.28	-0.17	-0.23	1939	0.21	-0.18	0.01
1890	-0.27	-0.45	-0.36	1940	0.16	0.07	0.12
1891	-0.41	-0.47	-0.44	1941	0.18	0.08	0.13
1892	-0.45	-0.35	-0.40	1942	0.10	0.03	0.06
1893	-0.54	-0.38	-0.46	1943	0.12	-0.12	0.00
1894	-0.24	-0.41	-0.32	1944	0.25	0.11	0.18
1895	-0.44	-0.36	-0.40	1945	-0.04	0.05	0.01
1896	-0.26	-0.10	-0.18	1946	0.17	-0.04	0.07
1897	-0.20	-0.15	-0.18	1947	0.21	0.06	0.13
1898	-0.22	-0.46	-0.34	1948	0.15	-0.05	0.05
1899	-0.06	-0.24	-0.15	1949	0.09	-0.07	0.01
1900	0.00	-0.06	-0.03	1950	-0.18	-0.18	-0.18

Continued over

Table 2.1 Continued

Year	NH ($\Delta T^\circ C$)	SH ($\Delta T^\circ C$)	Global ($\Delta T^\circ C$)	Year	NH ($\Delta T^\circ C$)	SH ($\Delta T^\circ C$)	Global ($\Delta T^\circ C$)
1951	0.03	-0.07	-0.02	1971	-0.12	-0.04	-0.08
1952	0.10	0.08	0.09	1972	-0.29	0.15	-0.07
1953	0.31	0.05	0.18	1973	0.23	0.22	0.23
1954	-0.05	-0.09	-0.07	1974	-0.17	-0.04	-0.11
1955	-0.02	-0.14	-0.08	1975	0.08	-0.05	0.01
1956	-0.37	-0.23	-0.30	1976	-0.29	-0.22	-0.25
1957	-0.01	0.14	0.06	1977	0.19	0.15	0.17
1958	0.18	0.08	0.13	1978	0.01	0.05	0.03
1959	0.09	0.02	0.06	1979	0.14	0.09	0.12
1960	0.10	-0.16	-0.03	1980	0.18	0.32	0.25
1961	0.10	0.15	0.13	1981	0.52	0.28	0.40
1962	0.11	-0.02	0.05	1982	0.07	0.03	0.05
1963	0.13	-0.07	0.03	1983	0.42	0.35	0.38
1964	-0.20	-0.21	-0.20	1984	0.03	0.13	0.08
1965	-0.20	-0.11	-0.16	1985	-0.05	0.17	0.06
1966	-0.03	-0.05	-0.04	1986	0.18	0.21	0.20
1967	-0.04	-0.01	-0.01	1987	0.35	0.36	0.36
1968	-0.13	-0.11	-0.12	1988	0.47	0.41	0.44
1969	-0.08	0.11	0.02	1989	0.40	0.25	0.33
1970	-0.01	0.17	0.08	1990[a]	0.75	0.31	0.53

[a] Provisional data.

NH = Northern Hemisphere.
SH = Southern Hemisphere.

Mean annual hemispheric and global temperature changes are derived from raw land-based station observations according to the following procedure. Over 3,000 station records (2,666 from the Northern Hemisphere and 610 from the Southern Hemisphere) were tested for signs of inhomogeneity by comparing each station's record with that of stations situated within a range of a few hundred kilometres. Jumps or trends in the temperatures recorded at one station that were not observed at neighbouring stations, were taken to indicate inhomogeneity. Where possible, correction factors were applied to account for such biases, other records were rejected and subsequently excluded from the analysis.

At the remaining stations (1,584 in the Northern Hemisphere and 293 in the Southern Hemisphere), monthly and annual average temperatures were expressed as deviations from their average temperatures during a reference period (the period 1951–1970 was selected as the reference). Expressing temperatures as deviations from a mean overcomes some of the anomalies associated with changes in station numbers and locations throughout the historical record.

Finally, station data were processed to produce area-averages, initially on a 5° latitude by 10° longitude grid, subsequently to give hemispheric and global averages. Interpolating station data onto a grid in this way prevents areas with high station densities from unduly influencing the hemispheric averages.

Further details of the analysis procedures employed are given by:
Jones, P. D. and Wigley, T. M. L. 1990 Global warming trends, *Scientific American* **263**(2), 84–91.

Sources:
Jones, P. D., Raper, S. C. B., Bradley, R. S., Daiz, H. F., Kelly, P. M. and Wigley, T. M. L. 1986 Northern Hemisphere surface air temperature variations 1851–1984, *Journal of Climate and Applied Meteorology* **25**, 161–179.
Jones, P. D., Raper, S. C. B. and Wigley, T. M. L. 1986 Southern Hemisphere surface air temperature variations, 1851–1984, *Journal of Climate and Applied Meteorology* **25**, 1123–1230.
Jones, P. D. 1988 Hemispheric surface air temperature: recent trends and an update to 1987, *Journal of Climate* **1**(6), 654–660.
Jones, P. D. 1991 Personal communication, Climatic Research Unit, University of East Anglia, UK.

Table 2.2 Trends in hemispheric and global mean annual surface air temperature derived from both land- and marine-based records, 1854–1990 (deviations in °C from a reference period mean, 1950–1979)

Year	NH (ΔT°C)	SH (ΔT°C)	Global (ΔT°C)	Year	NH (ΔT°C)	SH (ΔT°C)	Global (ΔT°C)
1854	-0.15	-0.08	-0.12	1904	-0.46	-0.52	-0.49
1855	-0.51	-0.49	-0.50	1905	-0.29	-0.40	-0.34
1856	-0.33	-0.21	-0.27	1906	-0.18	-0.29	-0.23
1857	-0.32	-0.60	-0.46	1907	-0.47	-0.37	-0.42
1858	-0.37	-0.46	-0.42	1908	-0.44	-0.48	-0.46
1859	-0.02	-0.26	-0.14	1909	-0.36	-0.31	-0.34
1860	-0.43	-0.31	-0.37	1910	-0.35	-0.33	-0.34
1861	-0.25	-0.58	-0.41	1911	-0.38	-0.42	-0.40
1862	-0.67	-0.41	-0.54	1912	-0.42	-0.18	-0.30
1863	-0.09	-0.30	-0.20	1913	-0.43	-0.21	-0.32
1864	-0.47	-0.50	-0.49	1914	-0.22	-0.17	-0.20
1865	-0.20	-0.25	-0.23	1915	-0.04	-0.12	-0.08
1866	-0.17	-0.21	-0.19	1916	-0.32	-0.27	-0.30
1867	-0.30	-0.20	-0.25	1917	-0.59	-0.40	-0.50
1868	-0.11	-0.39	-0.25	1918	-0.40	-0.31	-0.36
1869	-0.10	-0.34	-0.22	1919	-0.33	-0.15	-0.24
1870	-0.27	-0.41	-0.34	1920	-0.29	-0.19	-0.24
1871	-0.44	-0.39	-0.41	1921	-0.16	-0.26	-0.21
1872	-0.17	-0.38	-0.28	1922	-0.30	-0.31	-0.31
1873	-0.24	-0.35	-0.29	1923	-0.25	-0.30	-0.28
1874	-0.30	-0.51	-0.41	1924	-0.28	-0.35	-0.31
1875	-0.61	-0.34	-0.48	1925	-0.12	-0.25	-0.19
1876	-0.39	-0.47	-0.43	1926	0.02	-0.07	-0.03
1877	-0.10	-0.25	-0.17	1927	-0.09	-0.21	-0.15
1878	0.19	-0.17	0.01	1928	-0.10	-0.24	-0.17
1879	-0.32	-0.42	-0.37	1929	-0.32	-0.34	-0.33
1880	-0.36	-0.30	-0.33	1930	-0.02	-0.28	-0.15
1881	-0.33	-0.25	-0.29	1931	0.06	-0.14	-0.04
1882	-0.30	-0.28	-0.29	1932	-0.04	-0.17	-0.11
1883	-0.44	-0.31	-0.38	1933	-0.22	-0.18	-0.20
1884	-0.48	-0.39	-0.44	1934	-0.10	-0.14	-0.12
1885	-0.41	-0.34	-0.38	1935	-0.14	-0.20	-0.17
1886	-0.33	-0.16	-0.25	1936	-0.07	-0.19	-0.13
1887	-0.31	-0.48	-0.40	1937	0.08	-0.08	0.00
1888	-0.29	-0.38	-0.34	1938	0.13	-0.02	0.05
1889	-0.20	-0.12	-0.16	1939	0.01	-0.10	-0.05
1890	-0.38	-0.40	-0.39	1940	-0.09	0.05	-0.02
1891	-0.31	-0.36	-0.34	1941	0.01	0.09	0.05
1892	-0.42	-0.32	-0.37	1942	0.05	0.02	0.04
1893	-0.48	-0.37	-0.43	1943	0.07	-0.04	0.02
1894	-0.35	-0.32	-0.34	1944	0.19	0.16	0.17
1895	-0.40	-0.20	-0.30	1945	0.02	0.11	0.06
1896	-0.17	-0.09	-0.13	1946	0.07	-0.17	-0.05
1897	-0.14	-0.10	-0.12	1947	0.02	-0.11	-0.05
1898	-0.23	-0.40	-0.31	1948	0.02	-0.14	-0.06
1899	-0.15	-0.22	-0.19	1949	0.03	-0.14	-0.05
1900	-0.03	-0.09	-0.06	1950	-0.12	-0.14	-0.13
1901	-0.09	-0.24	-0.17	1951	0.06	-0.12	-0.03
1902	-0.31	-0.25	-0.28	1952	0.12	0.05	0.09
1903	-0.35	-0.47	-0.41	1953	0.22	0.01	0.12

Continued over

Table 2.2 Continued

Year	NH ($\Delta T^{o}C$)	SH ($\Delta T^{o}C$)	Global ($\Delta T^{o}C$)	Year	NH ($\Delta T^{o}C$)	SH ($\Delta T^{o}C$)	Global ($\Delta T^{o}C$)
1954	-0.05	-0.21	-0.13	1973	0.09	0.22	0.16
1955	-0.02	-0.26	-0.14	1974	-0.20	-0.07	-0.14
1956	-0.23	-0.22	-0.23	1975	-0.11	-0.10	-0.11
1957	0.06	0.09	0.08	1976	-0.29	-0.14	-0.22
1958	0.19	0.11	0.15	1977	0.08	0.11	0.09
1959	0.08	0.06	0.07	1978	0.00	0.06	0.03
1960	0.08	-0.02	0.03	1979	0.09	0.16	0.13
1961	0.12	0.11	0.12	1980	0.12	0.20	0.16
1962	0.17	0.10	0.14	1981	0.28	0.14	0.21
1963	0.19	0.08	0.14	1982	0.06	0.14	0.10
1964	-0.14	-0.14	-0.14	1983	0.23	0.35	0.29
1965	-0.14	-0.08	-0.11	1984	0.00	0.23	0.12
1966	0.03	-0.09	-0.03	1985	-0.04	0.23	0.10
1967	0.02	-0.10	-0.04	1986	0.10	0.23	0.17
1968	-0.02	-0.12	-0.07	1987	0.27	0.39	0.33
1969	0.02	0.15	0.09	1988	0.32	0.36	0.34
1970	0.00	0.08	0.04	1989	0.27	0.24	0.25
1971	-0.14	-0.08	-0.11	1990[a]	0.48	0.30	0.39
1972	-0.16	0.19	0.02				

[a]   Provisional data.

NH = Northern Hemisphere.
SH = Southern Hemisphere.

Hemispheric and global mean annual temperature changes are derived from the Jones land-based data set (see Table 2.1), the Comprehensive Ocean-Atmosphere Data Set (COADS) and the UK Meteorological Office (UKMO) data sets for sea-surface temperature.
Further details of the analysis procedures employed are given by:
Jones, P. D. and Wigley, T. M. L. 1990 Global warming trends, *Scientific American* **263**(2), 84–91.

Jones, P. D., Wigley, T. M. L. and Farmer, G. 1991 Marine and land temperature data sets: a comparison and a look at recent trends. In: *Greenhouse-Gas-Induced Climatic Change: A Critical Appraisal of Simulations and Observations*, M. E. Schlesinger (Ed.), Elsevier. In press.

Sources:
Jones, P. D., Wigley, T. M. L. and Wright, P. B. 1986 Global temperature variations between 1861 and 1984, *Nature* (London) **322**, 430–434.
Jones, P. D. 1990 Personal communication, Climatic Research Unit, University of East Anglia, UK.

Table 2.3 Precipitation trends over sub-Saharan west Africa, 1941–1989

Year	Precipitation index	Year	Precipitation index	Year	Precipitation index	Year	Precipitation index
		1955	0.90	1970	-0.51	1985	-0.81
1941	-0.52	1956	0.14	1971	-0.70	1986	-0.87
1942	-0.46	1957	0.78	1972	-1.10	1987	-1.13
1943	1.02	1958	0.67	1973	-0.78	1988	-0.07
1944	-0.18	1959	0.09	1974	-0.53	1989	-0.39
1945	0.49	1960	-0.09	1975	0.05		
1946	0.44	1961	0.01	1976	-0.40		
1947	-0.20	1962	0.37	1977	-1.17		
1948	-0.19	1963	0.05	1978	-0.23		
1949	-0.46	1964	0.56	1979	-0.51		
1950	0.93	1965	0.28	1980	-0.55		
1951	0.54	1966	0.15	1981	-0.73		
1952	1.24	1967	0.19	1982	-1.02		
1953	0.81	1968	-0.54	1983	-1.49		
1954	0.77	1969	0.24	1984	-1.47		

Values of the sub-Saharan precipitation index are derived from April–October rainfall data from 20 stations located in the region of west Africa between 11-18°N and west of 9°E. The period April–October is selected for analysis as, on average, 97 per cent of the annual rainfall occurs during these months. Eighty per cent of the annual precipitation falls during the July–September rainy season.

The precipitation index cited above is based on a calculation of deviations in April–October rainfall amounts from a reference period mean, 1941–1982. Further details are given in the source documents.

Sources:
Lamb, P. J. 1983 Sub-Saharan rainfall update for 1982: continued drought, *Journal of Climatology* **3**, 419–422.
Lamb, P. J. 1985 Rainfall in sub-Saharan West Africa during 1941–83, *Zeitschrift für Gletscherkunde und Glazialgeologie* **21**, 131–139.
Lamb, P. J. 1991 Personal communication (data for 1984–1989), Illinois State Water Survey, Champaign, USA.

Table 2.4 Distribution of glacier ice, 1988 estimates

Region/location	Area (km²)	% distribution	Region/location	Area (km²)	% distribution
WORLD	15,861,766	100.00	ASIA	107,988	0.68
AFRICA	10	–	China	56,481	0.36
			Indonesia	7	–
NORTH AMERICA	2,002,500	12.60	Nepal/Bhutan	7,500	0.05
			Pakistan/India	40,000	0.25
Canada	200,806	1.27	Turkey/Iran/Afghanistan	4,000	0.03
Greenland	1,726,400	10.90			
Mexico	11	–	EUROPE	53,967	0.34
USA[a]	75,283	0.47			
			Alps	2,909	0.02
SOUTH AMERICA	25,908	0.16	Iceland	11,260	0.07
			Pyrenees/Mediterranean		
Argentina[b]	1,385	0.01	Mountains	12	–
Bolivia	566	–	Scandinavia[d]	3,174	0.02
Chile[c]	743	–	Svalbard	36,612	0.23
Colombia	111	–			
Ecuador	120	–	USSR	77,223	0.49
Peru	1,780	0.01	OCEANIA	13,594,170	85.70
Tierra del Fuego/					
Patagonian Icefields	21,200	0.13	Antarctica	13,586,310	85.65
Venezuela	3	–	Sub-Antarctic Islands	7,000	0.04
			New Zealand	860	–

[a] Includes Alaska.
[b] North of 47.5°S.
[c] North of 46.0°S.
[d] Includes Jan Mayen.

Source:
Haeberli, W., Bösch, H., Scherler, K., Østrem, G. and Wallén C. C. (Eds) 1989 *World Glacier Inventory: Status 1988*, International Association of Hydrological Sciences, Wallingford, United Nations Environment Programme, Nairobi, and United Nations Educational, Scientific and Cultural Organization, Paris.

Table 2.5 Seasonal and annual average snow cover in the Northern Hemisphere, 1967–1990 (10^6 km^2)

Year	Eurasia					North America					Northern Hemisphere				
	Winter	Spring	Summer	Autumn	Annual	Winter	Spring	Summer	Autumn	Annual	Winter	Spring	Summer	Autumn	Annual
1967	26.2	15.9	2.1	7.4	13.2	16.3	13.1	5.7	6.9	10.5	42.5	29.1	7.8	14.3	23.7
1968	30.1	16.6	1.7	7.6	13.9	15.8	11.5	4.3	7.0	9.8	46.0	28.1	6.0	14.6	23.6
1969	26.2	18.2	1.3	8.8	13.3	16.9	13.7	4.8	6.9	10.4	43.1	31.9	6.1	15.7	23.8
1970	24.5	16.1	2.1	8.5	13.0	15.9	13.0	4.5	8.0	10.5	40.4	29.2	6.6	16.5	23.5
1971	27.3	19.0	2.5	11.9	15.3	16.4	12.3	4.1	8.6	10.3	43.8	31.2	6.6	20.5	25.6
1972	30.6	18.2	2.2	14.0	16.3	16.4	12.8	4.7	9.8	11.0	47.0	31.0	6.9	23.8	27.4
1973	29.5	19.0	2.3	11.8	15.8	17.0	12.6	4.8	8.6	10.7	46.6	31.6	7.1	20.4	26.5
1974	28.9	19.0	3.7	10.8	15.2	16.6	14.1	4.3	8.9	11.0	45.6	33.2	8.0	19.7	26.2
1975	26.8	17.6	2.5	9.9	14.5	16.8	14.0	4.1	8.6	10.9	43.6	31.6	6.6	18.5	25.4
1976	28.3	20.2	3.7	15.4	16.7	16.5	12.6	5.1	8.6	10.6	44.8	32.8	8.7	23.9	27.3
1977	28.8	18.4	2.3	11.4	15.5	16.1	12.4	4.7	8.0	10.4	45.0	30.8	7.1	19.4	25.9
1978	31.6	18.9	3.7	12.0	16.4	17.7	13.9	5.8	9.6	11.9	49.3	32.7	9.5	21.5	28.3
1979	30.5	20.3	2.7	9.5	15.4	18.2	13.7	5.2	7.0	10.8	48.7	34.0	7.9	16.5	26.2
1980	27.4	20.8	3.3	9.8	15.3	16.7	12.9	4.7	7.9	10.5	44.0	33.7	8.0	17.7	25.8
1981	25.3	19.9	2.8	10.2	14.8	15.2	12.4	5.0	8.1	10.3	40.5	32.3	7.8	18.3	25.2
1982	27.8	16.4	1.6	11.2	14.2	17.4	13.4	3.7	8.7	10.8	45.2	29.8	5.4	19.9	25.0
1983	28.2	17.2	2.3	9.9	14.4	16.6	13.3	4.1	8.4	10.7	44.9	30.5	6.4	18.3	25.1
1984	27.0	17.1	1.3	9.8	13.8	17.5	12.5	3.3	8.3	10.3	44.5	29.6	4.6	18.1	24.1
1985	28.4	17.9	2.2	11.6	15.2	17.5	13.7	4.9	9.2	11.4	45.9	31.7	7.1	20.8	26.7
1986	28.4	17.4	1.7	10.2	14.5	17.3	12.7	4.6	9.3	10.8	45.7	30.1	6.3	19.5	25.3
1987	28.8	18.6	2.5	9.7	14.7	16.1	11.9	4.5	7.3	10.0	44.9	30.5	7.0	17.0	24.7
1988	27.3	16.7	1.1	8.4	13.4	16.9	12.0	3.6	8.2	10.1	44.2	28.7	4.7	16.6	23.5
1989	26.7	15.6	1.6	9.6	13.5	16.4	12.4	3.2	8.1	10.1	43.1	27.9	4.8	17.8	23.6
1990	27.1	14.6	0.8	8.4	12.8	16.7	11.9	3.4	7.7	9.9	43.9	26.4	4.1	16.1	22.6

Snow cover charts, compiled on a weekly basis from a manual analysis of satellite imagery (visible wavelengths), are drawn on a 1:50,000,000 polar stenographic projection of the Northern Hemisphere. Each map is subsequently digitized using a 89 x 89 square grid. Digitized snow charts are then used to compute monthly, seasonal and annual average snow coverages. Reliability of the data is constrained by a number of factors including the seasonal variation in illumination visible wavelengths in the polar region and the presence of persistent areas of cloud cover. Scattered mountain snows are often omitted as a result of the coarse grid resolution. Furthermore, Himalayan snow cover is inconsistently represented, particularly prior to 1975. Winter includes the months, December (of the previous calendar year), January and February; Spring the months March, April and May; Summer the months June, July and August and Autumn includes September, October and November. The annual average however, represents a mean value for the calendar year.

Source:
Stephens, G. 1991 Personal communication, National Oceanic and Atmospheric Administration, National Environmental Satellite, Data and Information Service, Washington DC, USA.

Table 2.6 Monthly and annual mean Arctic sea-ice extent[a], 1973–1990 (10^6 km²)

Year	Jan.	Feb.	Mar.	Apr.	May	Jun.	Jul.	Aug.	Sep.	Oct.	Nov.	Dec.	Annual
1973	15.2	15.8	15.6	14.5	12.8	10.8	9.4	7.7	7.5	9.5	11.3	13.7	12.0
1974	14.3	14.9	14.9	14.3	12.9	11.4	9.3	7.6	7.5	9.6	12.1	13.5	11.9
1975	14.8	15.6	15.4	14.4	12.6	10.8	9.3	7.7	7.5	9.6	11.8	13.8	11.9
1976	15.0	16.0	15.7	15.5	13.5	12.1	9.8	8.2	7.7	10.5	12.6	13.8	12.5
1977	15.4	16.0	16.2	15.0	13.7	11.7	8.7	7.4	7.1	9.8	11.8	13.9	12.2
1978	15.3	16.0	16.0	14.9	13.3	11.8	9.9	7.8	8.4	10.6	12.5	14.8	12.6
1979	15.6	16.7	16.3	15.0	12.9	11.6	9.4	7.7	7.2	9.8	11.6	13.8	12.3
1980	14.9	15.7	15.7	14.7	13.4	11.6	9.9	8.2	8.3	9.6	12.4	14.2	12.4
1981	15.4	15.5	15.3	14.5	12.9	11.5	9.9	7.6	7.4	9.7	12.0	14.2	12.2
1982	15.4	15.9	16.0	14.5	13.1	12.0	9.8	8.0	7.4	10.3	12.2	14.0	12.4
1983	15.5	16.1	15.9	14.3	12.8	11.8	10.1	8.3	7.9	10.3	11.9	13.8	12.4
1984	14.6	15.1	14.9	14.5	12.8	11.7	9.6	8.5	7.8	9.0	11.5	13.2	11.9
1985	14.9	15.5	15.9	14.7	13.4	11.9	9.5	7.1	7.5	9.0	11.9	13.8	12.1
1986	15.2	16.1	15.5	14.5	12.9	11.8	10.3	8.0	8.0	10.1	12.3	14.2	12.4
1987	15.6	16.4	15.4	14.8	12.8	11.9	9.9	8.0	7.9	9.6	12.5	14.1	12.4
1988	15.2	15.9	15.8	14.4	12.5	11.4	9.0	7.7	7.6	10.0	12.9	14.0	12.2
1989	15.4	15.6	15.3	13.7	12.5	11.7	10.0	7.7	7.7	10.1	12.3	14.1	12.2
1990	15.0	15.7	15.5	13.8	12.7								
Mean[b]	15.1	15.8	15.6	14.5	13.0	11.6	9.6	7.8	7.7	9.8	12.1	13.9	
Std dev.	0.4	0.4	0.4	0.4	0.3	0.4	0.4	0.3	0.3	0.4	0.4	0.3	

[a] Sea-ice extent is defined as that area of the ocean covered by at least 10–15 per cent of sea ice.
[b] Monthly mean values over the available record length.

Satellite observations in the visible, infra-red and microwave bands are used to map the extent of sea ice on a weekly basis in both the Arctic and Antarctic regions. Arctic charts are produced on a scale of 1:11,600,000; Antarctic charts on a scale of 1:16,000,000. Charts are plotted on an azimuthal equidistant projection. Weekly charts are digitized onto 1° latitude by 10° longitude segments; the digitized charts are then used to compute monthly and seasonal mean areas of sea ice.

Source:
Ropelewski, C. F. 1990 Personal communication, National Oceanic and Atmospheric Administration, Climate Analysis Center, US Department of Commerce, Washington DC, USA.

Table 2.7 Monthly and annual mean Antarctic sea-ice extent[a], 1973–1990 (10^6 km²)

Year	Jan.	Feb.	Mar.	Apr.	May	Jun.	Jul.	Aug.	Sep.	Oct.	Nov.	Dec.	Annual
1973	6.4	5.6	7.6	9.7	12.6	16.8	18.3	19.0	20.2	19.8	16.5	8.1	13.4
1974	4.2	3.7	6.5	9.0	13.0	16.6	18.3	20.5	20.0	19.2	14.3	9.1	12.9
1975	4.1	3.4	6.2	8.7	14.3	16.8	19.1	19.5	19.0	17.3	14.3	7.7	12.5
1976	4.2	4.2	5.8	7.8	11.6	15.0	17.2	17.9	17.6	15.7	11.9	7.5	11.4
1977	3.8	3.6	6.1	7.7	11.5	14.1	15.9	16.9	16.7	16.6	13.6	7.1	11.1
1978	5.0	4.0	5.1	8.2	10.6	14.1	15.8	16.7	17.3	16.7	12.8	6.6	13.3
1979	3.4	3.3	6.1	10.0	11.8	15.6	16.7	18.5	17.9	17.4	12.4	4.8	11.5
1980	3.0	2.7	4.8	6.5	10.3	13.4	16.0	18.2	17.6	17.4	13.9	8.3	11.0
1981	3.5	3.4	5.4	8.1	11.0	15.4	17.1	18.0	18.5	17.5	14.5	8.1	11.7
1982	4.6	3.1	6.0	9.4	12.6	15.1	17.4	18.7	19.4	17.3	14.2	8.1	12.2
1983	3.9	3.5	5.8	8.2	10.9	14.2	16.7	18.5	19.2	18.2	15.0	9.3	12.0
1984	4.3	3.7	5.8	8.4	11.4	14.7	17.4	18.5	18.6	17.8	15.8	9.5	12.2
1985	3.4	2.7	4.8	8.5	12.1	14.8	17.4	19.2	19.4	18.9	16.4	10.4	12.3
1986	4.6	3.4	5.1	8.2	11.7	14.6	17.4	18.4	18.6	17.6	14.3	8.8	11.9
1987	5.0	3.8	5.7	8.4	11.1	15.0	17.3	18.2	19.1	18.1	14.4	11.0	12.3
1988	4.7	3.5	5.3	7.7	11.6	14.2	16.8	17.8	18.7	18.1	14.7	9.7	11.9
1989	3.8	3.7	5.6	7.8	12.5	15.3	17.2	18.0	18.2	17.5	14.5	8.2	11.9
1990	4.0	3.4	6.5	9.0	11.2								
Mean[b]	4.2	3.6	5.8	8.4	11.8	15.0	17.2	18.4	18.6	17.7	14.4	8.4	
Std dev.	0.8	0.6	0.7	0.8	0.9	0.9	0.8	0.9	0.9	1.0	1.2	1.4	

Footnotes as Table 2.6.

Source:
Ropelewski, C. F. 1990 Personal communication, National Oceanic and Atmospheric Administration, Climate Analysis Center, US Department of Commerce, Washington DC, USA.

Part 3
Natural Resources

The continuing growth in human populations and industrial development places increasingly heavy demands on the world's finite natural resource base. Expanding populations and rising standards of living have created demands for land to grow crops and to raise livestock, for land to develop human settlements, for clean water, for energy and other minerals and for timber. Over-exploitation, poor management and degradation of the natural environment due to human activities have placed severe stresses on natural resources which, in some areas, have led to serious modification or depletion of the resource base.

With an ever-increasing population and a shrinking resource base, the need for monitoring changes in natural resources becomes vital. Data presented in this section of the 'UNEP Environmental Data Report' provide an overview of the status of, and recent trends in, a number of key natural resources, the utilization and degradation of which have major environmental consequences. These include, land resources, food production, forest resources and wood production, fresh-water resources and withdrawals, fisheries and biodiversity. Data on non-fuel mineral resources were included in the second edition of the 'UNEP Environmental Data Report', but have not been updated here. Future editions of this report will, however, again address this subject.

The Food and Agriculture Organization of the United Nations (FAO) is responsible for compiling much of the global information on agriculture, forestry and fisheries. Data are primarily collected by means of questionnaires circulated to national reporting agencies. The latest available data are presented here; data are, however, subject to constant revision as new information becomes available. The International Union for Conservation of Nature and Natural Resources (IUCN) is one of the major international organizations involved in the protection of wildlife resources and habitats, and in preserving biodiversity. UNEP works closely with the IUCN, as well as with FAO, the United Nations Educational, Scientific and Cultural Organization (UNESCO) and the World Wide Fund for Nature (WWF) on promoting public awareness, developing the scientific basis for land use strategies and natural resources management, formulating conservation treaties and maintaining biological diversity. Statistical information to support these activities are collated by the World Conservation Monitoring Centre (WCMC). Where there is no single data-gathering authority, information is collated from a variety of published sources.

Land Use and Availability

Human activities have radically reshaped the world's natural land cover. Vast areas of forests have become pasture and croplands, rangelands have been changed to croplands or to desert, and natural wetlands have been drained and filled in order to feed and house expanding populations.

The FAO's compilation of land use statistics, collected from decadal censuses of agriculture and annual reports of national authorities, documents some of the changes in land cover. The FAO classifies land area as either "cropland", "permanent meadows and pastures", "forest and woodland", or as "other land" (which includes cities, unmanaged rangeland, wetlands and land not otherwise classified). Data presented in Table 3.1 show that globally, forest area has declined from 33 per cent to 31 per cent of the total land area between 1966–1968 and 1986–1988. This decline is in spite of large increases in forest areas in a few large temperate countries, especially in Canada and the USSR. Rates of deforestation are discussed in more detail in a subsequent section (see Forests and Woodlands). While global totals have not changed, the data also show a significant expansion of agricultural land in many developing countries over the last 20 years. In Africa the countries with the most significant expansion were Burundi, Rwanda and Uganda (Table 3.1).

The expansion of cultivated and managed lands has predominantly occurred at the expense of wilderness. The amount of remaining wilderness has been estimated by the US Sierra Club (McCloskey and Spalding, 1989). In this analysis, areas of at least 4,000 km^2 showing no signs of human habitation or intervention were defined as wilderness areas. It is concluded that there is no wilderness remaining in Europe, with the exception of small areas in Iceland, Sweden, Norway and Finland (Table 3.2). Remaining wilderness areas are found in either arid regions (in Mauritania, for example, 69 per cent of the land area is classified as wilderness), at high altitudes (Chile retains 31 per cent of wilderness) or in equatorial moist forests of South America. Brazil (24 per cent) and Guyana (57 per cent), for example, contain significant areas of wilderness (Figure 3.1).

Recent advances in satellite remote-sensing techniques have provided a means of monitoring land use changes on national, regional and even global scales. However, in practice the use of such imagery is extremely limited. The principal barriers to a greater use of satellite monitoring

Figure 3.1 The global wilderness, status as of August 1988
Source: McCloskey and Spalding, 1989

are cost, manpower and legal restrictions. Satellite imagery alone cannot provide unambiguous information on the state of natural resources. It requires calibration from "ground truth" measurements, the traditional resource-intensive gathering of information through ground investigation. It also requires skilled, highly-trained personnel who understand its limitations, the resource topic under evaluation, and the area under investigation.

High resolution (30 m or better) satellite imagery is expensive, often limited due to cloud cover, and is generally more extensive over developed countries. Typically, existing high resolution satellite imagery does not consistently report data from the same place over time, and thus is not amenable to valid assessment of global or local land cover changes.

While low in resolution, AVHRR (Advanced Very High Resolution Radiometers) imagery is relatively inexpensive. For this reason it has taken on a work-horse role for the assessments of land cover changes. AVHRR data facilitate the calculation of the Normalized Difference Vegetation Index (NDVI) which provides a measure of the amount of photosynthetic activity on the ground. In recent years these data have found a variety of applications, including the study of the relationship between vegetation and carbon dioxide concentrations, land cover classifications, monitoring forest extent, monitoring biomass

burning, locating potential locust breeding areas, and developing warning systems of potential drought conditions.

The FAO, for example, have developed the ARTEMIS system (African Real Time Environmental Monitoring Using Imaging Satellites) for assessment of precipitation and vegetation conditions with a view to forecasting desert locust population development. The ARTEMIS system utilizes Meteosat data for estimating rainfall and AVHRR data for monitoring vegetation cover and changes (Hielkema, 1990). The Famine Early Warning System (FEWS) of the US Agency for International Development (USAID) also relies on NDVI images to monitor changes in photosynthetic activity. These images, when compared with those from the same time period in previous years can be used to target areas where crop production could be inadequate. Examples of other satellite-based monitoring activities are described in the appropriate sub-sections below.

References

Hielkema, J. U. 1990 Satellite environmental monitoring for migrant pest forecasting by FAO: the ARTEMIS system, *Philosophical Transactions of the Royal Society of London*, **B328**, 705–717.
McCloskey, J. M. and Spalding, H. 1989 A reconnaissance level inventory of the amount of wilderness remaining in the world, *Ambio* **18**(4), 221–227.

Agriculture

The quality and reliability of agricultural data vary widely around the globe. It is therefore difficult to make comparisons between countries, based on published data, that purport to illustrate with confidence the absolute differences in food supply or access. Over a period of several years, however, available data reflect some general trends, especially when recast into a self-referencing index of agricultural or food production.

Crop Production

The demand for crops and other food products is essentially linked to population growth; ignoring yearly fluctuations, the world's food supply has been increasing in parallel with rising populations. Food production may, however, be influenced by a wide range of other factors including world and local prices, the availability of water supplies, warfare, the availability of inputs, the adequacy of supportive infrastructure and government policies.

Data on crop production are published on an annual basis by the FAO in yearbooks on agriculture production and trade. These data are compiled from annual questionnaires returned to the FAO by the relevant statistical authority in individual countries. In cases where country reports are not returned estimates based on data from previous years or the experience of neighbouring countries or countries in a similar economic and climatic environment are made by the FAO.

Indices of agricultural and food production for the world, developed countries and developing countries, are given in Tables 3.3 and 3.4 respectively. The agricultural index includes all crop and livestock products; the food production index includes only edible agricultural products. Since the mid-1900s, overall trends in absolute and per capita indices for both agricultural and food production have been upwards. Since 1980, however, the rate of increase of agricultural production has tended to decrease in the developed countries, but has continued to increase dramatically in developing countries (Figures 3.2 and 3.3). The broad categories plotted in Figures 3.2 and 3.3 mask the stagnation of per capita food supplies in Latin America and the decline of per capita food supplies in Africa (WRI, 1990).

National data on cereal production and imports for two three-year periods, 1967–1969 and 1987–1989, are presented in Table 3.5. Over this 20-year period, most countries have increased their cereal production substantially. For example, in Côte d'Ivoire cereal production rose by 84 per cent, in Ghana by 76 per cent, and in Brazil by 112 per cent. Declines occurred in several countries; reductions in cereal production were in part caused by warfare in Angola, Mozambique and Uganda.

World trade in cereals also increased between the late 1960s and late 1970s, in both absolute and per capita terms. Per capita cereal imports more than doubled in Africa (rising from 22.3 kg a^{-1} to 45.9 kg a^{-1}), and in North America (10.8 kg a^{-1} to 28.4 kg a^{-1}). In South

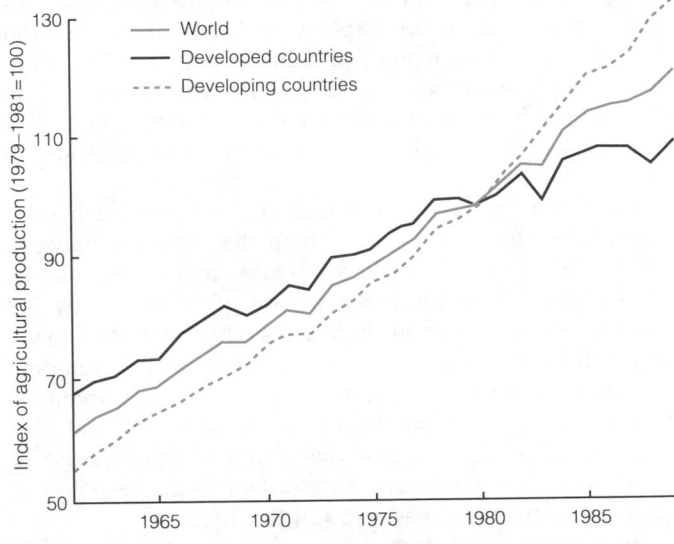

Figure 3.2 Trends in gross agricultural production, 1961–1989
Source: data from Table 3.4

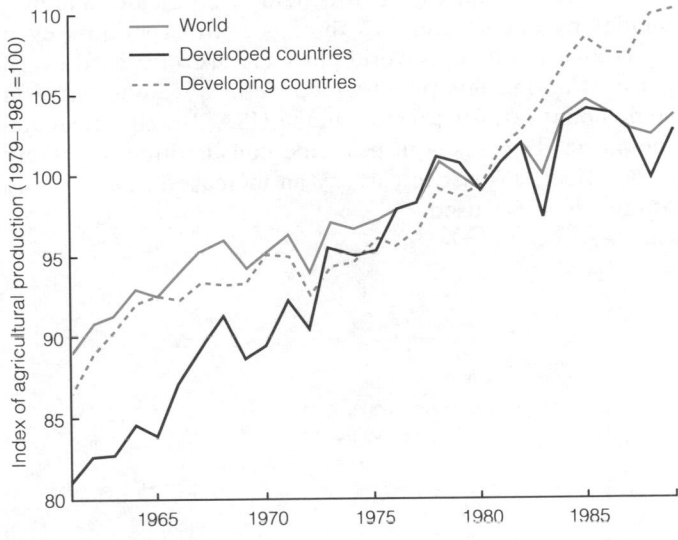

Figure 3.3 Trends in per capita agricultural production, 1961–1989
Source: data from Table 3.4

America (29.6 kg a^{-1} to 35.7 kg a^{-1}), Asia (20.4 kg a^{-1} to 29.8 kg a^{-1}) and Oceania (15.6 kg a^{-1} to 21.7 kg a^{-1}) increases were less pronounced. In Europe, per capita imports declined from 102.3 kg a^{-1} to 86.3 kg a^{-1} (Table 3.5).

Fertilizers and Pesticides

Much of the increase in global agricultural production over the last 30 years has come about through the adoption of high-input agricultural production systems. Indeed, the

"Green Revolution" comprised not only the development of new plant varieties but also the development of new varieties to fit within an implicit complex of agricultural behaviours, infrastructure and national policies. The adoption of high-input farming has been both a cause and an effect of the increase in agricultural production, and has led to an ever greater production of fertilizers and pesticides to fuel that increase.

Table 3.6 shows that fertilizer use world-wide has increased by almost 250 per cent in the 20 years between 1966–1968 and 1986–1988. While increasing almost everywhere, China increased its use of fertilizers by 7.7 times in the same period. Figure 3.4 illustrates the growth in fertilizer consumption for developed and developing countries. These trends can be compared with the trends in agricultural production shown in Figures 3.2 and 3.3. These relationships suggest that much of the increase in world food production can be ascribed to the response of crops to artificial increases in soil fertility.

In general, much less information on pesticide use is available than that for fertilizer use. A comprehensive set of estimates of pesticide use in 119 countries has been compiled by the UN Industrial Development Organization (UNIDO) for the period 1975–1984. Table 3.7 compares the average annual use of insecticides, fungicides and herbicides by country for two three-year time periods seven years apart. Although world pesticide use increased by 13 per cent during this time period, declines were reported in some countries, for example in the USA, Brazil, Japan and Indonesia. Decreases in pesticide consumption are likely to be offset, at least in part, by an increase in the potency of the pesticides used.

The use of pesticides has helped to reduce crop losses due to pest organisms. However, adverse environmental effects associated with pesticide use, such as food chain accumulation (see Part 1: Environmental Pollution, Biomonitoring), has led to the phasing out of several of the more toxic and persistent chemicals. Growing awareness of the adverse effects of pesticides has increased demand for more comprehensive data on pesticide use and their toxic effects. A number of key sources of information on pesticides, including toxicity assessments, environmental monitoring data, registration and regulatory information as well as production, consumption and trade statistics were described in the previous edition of this report (UNEP, 1989).

Pest Outbreaks

Agricultural pests clearly affect crop production adversely. In the second edition of this report, the impact of locusts on agricultural production was highlighted, with particular reference to Africa (UNEP, 1989). The Desert Locust Control Organization (DLCO) in Nairobi, Kenya, is responsible for taking active measures to limit locust damage in years of plague. DLCO also takes responsibility for monitoring and controlling two other important, but less well-known gregarious pests, the Quelea bird and the African armyworm.

The Red-billed Quelea (*Quelea quelea*), which are seed eaters, are accused of attacking most of the important grain crops of Africa. In Africa, they number between 10^9 and 10^{11} individuals, and have a range of over 500,000 km^2. Although these small (18 g) migratory weaverbirds consume only about 3 g of grass seed per day, each bird can destroy far more by knocking seed to the ground or by only partially eating grains. According to one estimate, Quelea can destroy up to 38 g of seed from cultivated crops per day. The total population of Quelea in Africa is estimated to consume 9×10^4 t to 9×10^6 t of grain per year. In the course of that consumption, up to 10 times as much grain is destroyed (Kranz et al., 1977; USAID, Undated)

Other than direct capture or poisoning, there appear to be no viable control measures for Quelea. As Quelea appear to prefer wild grains and grain fields near nesting sites, the concentration of control efforts on nesting groups, or on the protection of wild grasses, may therefore be a means by which to buffer their impact.

The African armyworm (i.e., the larvae of the moth *Spodoptera exempta*) is prevalent in Africa but also occurs in southern Asia and Australia. It feeds on almost any grass including the important cereal crops, but prefers young plants. Like locusts, armyworms generally occur in light densities and only occasionally congregate and move together as a swarm when conditions and numbers are favourable. In east Africa, armyworms move north in a predictable way depending on weather patterns. Control measures can therefore be put in place when needed during a year of high armyworm activity (Kranz et al., 1977).

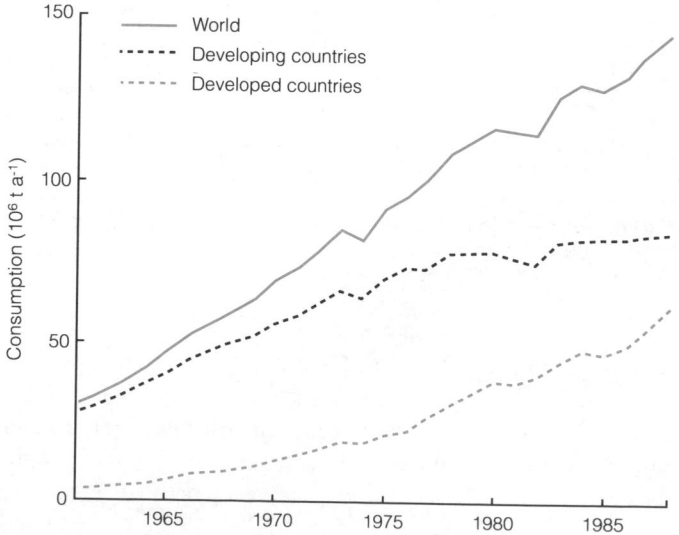

Figure 3.4 Fertilizer use in developed and developing countries, 1961–1989
Source: FAO, 1990 (Unpublished data)

Irrigation and Land Degradation

In arid and semi-arid zones, irrigation, whether from precise drip-irrigation or from flood techniques, can be an essential requirement for crop production of any kind. In wetter areas, irrigation in the form of pivot or other spray irrigators in high-input agricultural areas can supplement natural rainfall during drought, or optimize water availability during critical growth stages. Even in areas with a great deal of evenly spaced rainfall, irrigation or the micro-management of water using flooded fields is an essential part of wet-rice farming systems.

FAO routinely collects data on the extent of irrigated lands in each country. Table 3.8 shows the extent of irrigated lands for individual countries and regions of the world in two three-year periods 20 years apart. Globally, the land area under irrigation has increased by 45 per cent over the last 20 years and currently represents 15 per cent of all arable lands. Regional differences in the extent of irrigated lands are illustrated in Figure 3.5.

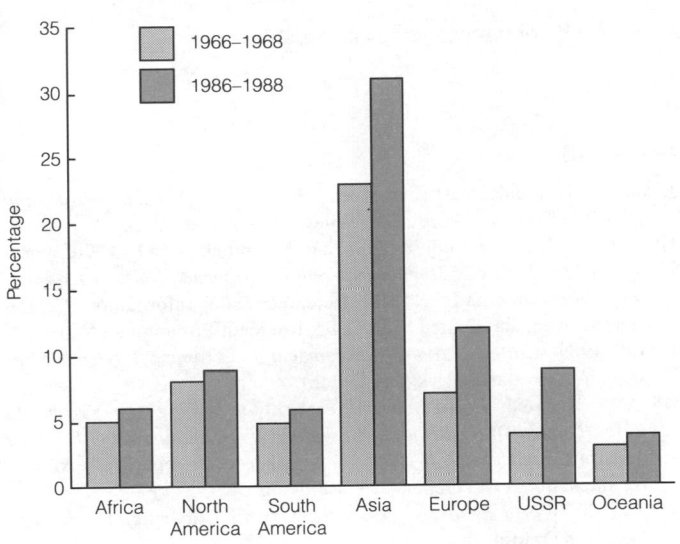

Figure 3.5 Percent of arable land under irrigation by world region, 1966–1968 and 1986–1988 (mean annual values)
Source: data from Table 3.8

The poor management of irrigation can lead to the destruction of otherwise arable soils in arid and semi-arid zones. Without adequate drainage, which would allow moderately saline water to move through the soil, salts can accumulate on the surface of the soil as irrigation water evaporates. Salinization is one of many forms of land degradation that can occur. Sodification, waterlogging, wind and water erosion, overgrazing and contamination are other forms of land degradation that collectively have in the past been called desertification.

In the past, comprehensive global information on the amount of land degraded through salinization and other forms of land degradation has been lacking. UNEP, working in co-operation with the International Soil Reference and Information Centre (ISRIC), have recently completed the first phase of the Global Assessment of Soil Degradation (GLASOD) project. Twelve distinct types of human-induced soil degradation have been identified and a series of world maps showing the extent and severity of soil degradation prepared (Oldeman et al., 1990).

The next phase of the GLASOD project will involve digitizing the world map; this will enable calculation, for any selected region, of the acreage of terrain affected by soil degradation type, degree and causative factor. A preliminary calculation for South America suggests that approximately 14 per cent of the land area is affected by some form of human-induced soil degradation. The percentage distribution of this land area, by type and degree of soil degradation, is summarized below:

Type	Degree (%)			
	Slight	Moderate	Severe	Total
Water erosion	14	29	4	47
Nutrient decline	12	17	5	34
Wind erosion	9	6		15
Waterlogging	3			3
Salinization	1			1
TOTAL	39	52	9	100

Source: Oldeman et al., 1990

Livestock Production

Livestock are maintained not only for food (meat, milk and eggs) but also for transportation, and for the production of wool, hair, feathers, leather and other raw materials. National data on numbers of the major categories of livestock species for the period 1987–1989 and the percent change from 1967–1969 are given in Table 3.9. The distribution of cattle populations world-wide is shown in Figure 3.6.

While livestock populations have risen substantially during the past 20 years, this increase has not matched the growth rate of human populations. Interestingly, India, with nearly 200×10^6 cattle, has only 12×10^6 ha under permanent pasture; Brazil with 69 per cent as many cattle has 14 times as much permanent pasture. The USA and the USSR also maintain cattle populations of over 100×10^6. Numbers of pigs have risen dramatically in Asia, from around 100×10^6 in 1960 to over 400×10^6 in 1989 (Figure 3.7). China now has 81 per cent of Asia's pig population and 40 per cent of the global total. This reflects not only cultural and gastronomic preferences but also the integration of the pig into Chinese farming systems. Intensive agriculture on farming land used beyond its capacity has been accompanied, in some areas, by soil

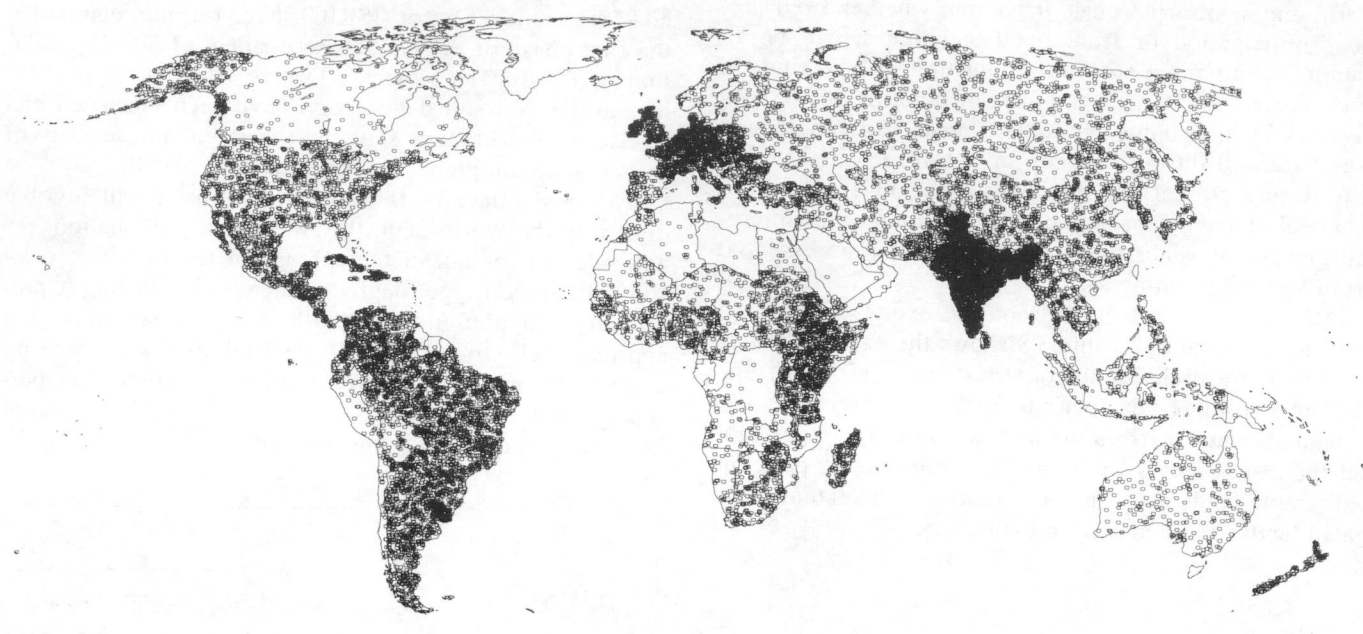

Figure 3.6 Distribution of cattle populations, 1987–1989 (mean annual values; each dot represents 10⁵ animals)
Source: data from Table 3.9

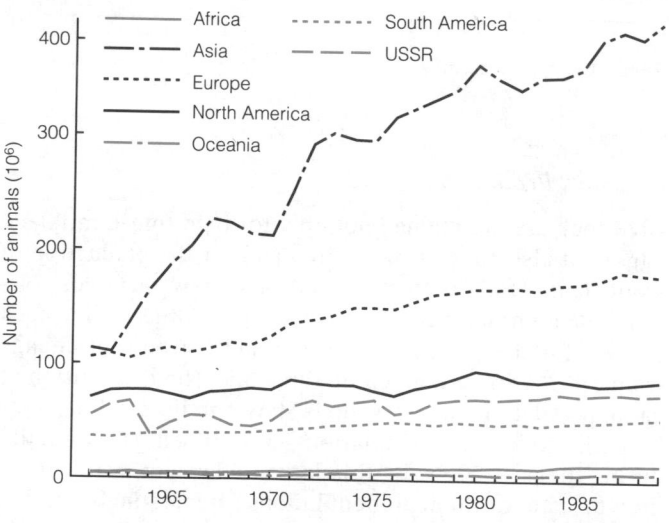

Figure 3.7 Trends in the number of pigs by world region, 1960–1989
Source: data from Table 3.9

degradation and leaching of essential nutrients. Excess nitrate and phosphate from animal wastes, as well as wastes themselves, have polluted water courses including ground water. Water quality and soil contamination are discussed in Part 1: Environmental Pollution.

References

Kranz, J., Schmuttere, H. and Koch, W. 1977 *Diseases, Pests and Weeds in Tropical Crops*, John Wiley & Sons, New York.

Oldeman, L. R., Hakkeling, R. T. A. and Sombroek, W. G. 1990 *World Map of the Status of Human Induced Soil Degradation: An Explanatory Note*, International Soil Reference and Information Centre, Wageningen, and United Nations Environment Programme, Nairobi.

UNEP 1989 *United Nations Environment Programme Environmental Data Report*, Basil Blackwell, Oxford.

US AID Undated *Preliminary Assessment of Damage by Vertebrate Pests (Quelea/Other Birds) to Cereal Crops in Sudan and Other East African Countries 1971–1979*, Unpublished draft report, US Agency for Intenational Development, Washington DC.

WRI 1990 *World Resources 1990–91*, Oxford University Press, New York and Oxford.

Forests and Woodlands

Forests represent a valuable resource not only for the timber and other products they contain, but also as reservoirs for the world's genetic diversity, for their role in the storage of carbon and for their aesthetic, cultural and scientific value. At the present time forests comprise only 31 per cent of the global land area (Table 3.1). Although pre-industrial estimates of forested land area are highly uncertain, it is clear that vast areas of temperate forest have since been eliminated in both North America and in Europe (to the Urals) in response to increasing demands for land for agriculture and for fuelwood. These same motivations drive forest destruction today in the tropical world.

According to FAO land use estimates, global forest area has declined by about 6 per cent over the past 20 years.

Forest Resources

Currently available national estimates of forest extent and recent rates of deforestation and reforestation for both closed and open forests are presented in Table 3.10. These data are based, for the most part, on the FAO/UNEP 1980 Assessment of Tropical Forests and subsequent update (FAO/UNEP, 1988).

The FAO, in conjunction with UNEP, is currently engaged in the preparation of a 1990 Forestry Assessment, the final results of which will be available by the end of 1992. Results of a preliminary study of recent (1981–1990) deforestation in the tropics have, however, been published recently (FAO, 1990). This current effort has lowered the previous estimate for forest extent in 1980, and reports a much higher rate of deforestation throughout the ensuing decade than was estimated in 1980. Preliminary estimates of forest area and annual average rates of deforestation (1981–1990) in tropical regions are summarized below:

	Forest area (10^3 ha)		Rate of deforestation	
Region	1980	1990	ha a^{-1}	% per year
Africa	289,700	241,800	4,800	-1.7
Latin America	825,900	753,000	7,300	-0.9
Asia	334,500	287,500	4,700	-1.4
TOTAL	1,450,100	1,282,300	16,800	-1.2

Source: FAO, 1990

Whereas the preliminary FAO 1990 Forest Assessment relied largely on published data and results of national surveys coupled with a model of forest exploitation, further assessment work will make use of available satellite data (AVHRR-based NDVI imagery). A separate assessment of forest change will be made by obtaining high resolution and cloud-free LANDSAT imagery from two time periods, about ten years apart, for randomly selected areas of the world's tropical forests. The comparison of the two images should show, unambiguously, the extent and rate of deforestation, as well as forest fragmentation. Results of the 1990 FAO assessment will be reported in greater detail in future editions of the 'UNEP Environmental Data Report' as and when data become available.

In recent years, satellite remote sensing techniques have been increasingly utilized for the monitoring and assessment of national forest resources. At the Brazilian Space Agency (INPE – Instituto de Pesquisas Espaciais), for example, several investigators have attempted to estimate the rate of change in the extent of closed forests in the Legal Amazon using a number of different techniques. Estimates of deforestation in 1987 and 1988 totalling 8×10^6 ha and 4.8×10^6 ha per year respectively, derived from AVHRR satellite imagery, have been reported by Setzer et al. (1988). An estimated 0.35×10^6 independent fires accounting for the 8×10^6 ha burned in 1987 have been reported (Setzer and Pereira, 1991). Over a longer period these authors reported that 20×10^6 ha of different vegetation types have been burned in the Amazon Basin.

High-resolution LANDSAT imagery has been used to estimate the rate of deforestation between 1988 and 1989 (Fearnside et al., 1990). The estimate obtained, 2.6×10^6 ha, represents a substantial decline from that recorded in previous years using AVHRR data. Although the apparent decrease in the rate of deforestation may, in part, be due to changes in measurement methodology, overall declines in the rate of deforestation were expected from 1987 to 1988 and from 1988 to 1989 due to changes in public policy and tax laws as well as to greater enforcement of forest protection laws.

Forest Production

The exploitation of forest resources, like the use of other natural resources, has increased significantly over the past 20 years. The FAO routinely compiles global data on the prices and production of trees and wood products. Production data for roundwood, industrial roundwood, fuelwood and charcoal for the top 20 producers of softwoods and hardwoods are shown in Tables 3.11 and 3.12 respectively, for the periods 1966–1968 and 1986–1988. Globally, softwood production has risen by about 28 per cent during this period. Hardwood production, however, has increased by 54 per cent during the same period.

In practice, sustainable forest management is not well implemented. Only about 20 per cent of the world's tropical forests are under any kind of harvesting control or silviculture. In a recent survey of 18 members of the International Tropical Timber Organization, only 1 per cent of the global tropical forest was found to be sustainably managed (WRI, 1990).

References

FAO/UNEP 1988 *An Interim Report on the State of Forest Resources in the Developing Countries,* Food and Agriculture Organization, Rome, and United Nations Environment Programme, Nairobi.

FAO 1990 *Interim Report on Forest Resources Assessment 1990 Project,* Tenth Session of the FAO Committee on Forestry, Rome, 24–28 September 1990, Food and Agriculture Organization, Rome.

Fearnside, P. M., Tardin, A. T., Filho, L. G. M. 1990 *Deforestation Rate in Brazilian Amazonia,* National Secretariat of Science and Technology, Brazil.

Setzer, A. W. and Pereira, M. C. 1991 Amazonia biomass burnings in 1987 and an estimate of their tropospheric emissions, *Ambio* **20**(1), 19–22.

Setzer, A. W., Pereira, M. C., Pereira Jr, A. C. and Almeida, S. A. O. 1988 *Relatório de atividades do projeto IBDF-INPE SEQE-ano de 1987,* Publication no. INPE-4534-RPE/565, The Brazilian Space Research Institute/Ministry of Science and Technolgy, INPE/MLT (in Portugese).

WRI 1990 *World Resources 1990–91*, Oxford University Press, New York and Oxford.

Fresh-water Resources

Adequate supplies of fresh water are essential not only to support human and other life, but also for many industrial and agricultural purposes. This section of the 'UNEP Environmental Data Report' presents data on the availability and use of water resources; aspects relating to water quality are discussed elsewhere (see Part 1: Environmental Pollution; Water Quality).

Information on the availability and use of fresh water is not widely reported; the reliability of what data are available is highly variable from country to country. The data presented in Table 3.13 on fresh-water resources and withdrawals represent the best attempt to date to estimate both supplies and uses by individual countries. A number of countries of the world withdraw large proportions of their renewable water resources, for example, Egypt, Israel, Afghanistan and Tunisia.

Data in Table 3.13 refer to renewable fresh-water resources, that is, water derived from precipitation and river flows from other countries. Non-renewable water resources, which include "fossil" ground water in sealed aquifers and desalinization plants, may also represent significant sources of fresh water in some countries. For example, non-renewable resources provide a high proportion of the water used in Libya and contribute to different extents to the water withdrawals in Qatar, Saudi Arabia, United Arab Emirates and Yemen.

Owing to the sparcity of data, trends in fresh-water withdrawals are difficult to assess for many world regions. However, data from OECD member countries, presented in the second edition of this report (UNEP, 1989), indicate that demands, and thus water withdrawals, have steadily increased since the 1960s.

Globally, and especially in Africa, Asia and South America, fresh water is primarily withdrawn for agricultural use (Figure 3.8). In Asia, 86 per cent of water withdrawals are utilized in agriculture, mainly for irrigation purposes. China, India, Japan and Pakistan, which together account for 74 per cent of the irrigated land area in Asia (Table 3.8), consume almost 1,000 km^3 per year, or nearly one-third of the world's total annual fresh-water withdrawal. In contrast, agricultural uses account for about 30 per cent of water withdrawals in Europe.

World-wide, withdrawal for industrial purposes is currently estimated to be about 760 km^3 per year, second to agricultural uses. In Europe, however, water withdrawals for industry exceed those taken for agricultural purposes. Globally, waste waters from industrial uses total some 660 km^3 per year (Belyaev, 1990). Most industrial waste waters, which may be heavily contaminated with chemicals and trace metals, are discharged into rivers and coastal waters.

Domestic and municipal demands for water are relatively modest, accounting for only 7 per cent of global water withdrawals. Withdrawals for domestic uses exceed 10 per cent of total withdrawals only in Europe, South America and Oceania. Although the need for water in the domestic sector may not be large in terms of quantity, water supplies of high quality are required. This may necessitate substantial treatment of water resources prior to supply for domestic drinking-water purposes.

References

Belyaev, A. V. 1990 Personal communication, Institute of Geography, USSR National Academy of Sciences, Moscow.

UNEP 1989 *United Nations Environment Programme Environmental Data Report*, Basil Blackwell, Oxford.

Fisheries

Three-quarters of the world's fish catch is used for direct human consumption and as such represents an important source of protein in the human diet. The FAO, in co-operation with regional fishery commissions, collects national data on the catch of fish (fresh-water and marine), molluscs and crustaceans. Average annual fish catch (which includes aquaculture production) in 1976–1978 and 1986–1988 are compared in Table 3.14 for the top 20 producing nations. Japan and the USSR are the largest producers, owing to a large contribution from marine production. China, the third largest producer, has a large fresh-water catch, most of which is derived from aquaculture (see below).

The global fish catch has increased steadily since the 1950s (Figure 3.9). Between 1976–1978 and 1986–1988 the average annual world catch of fish rose 37 per cent.

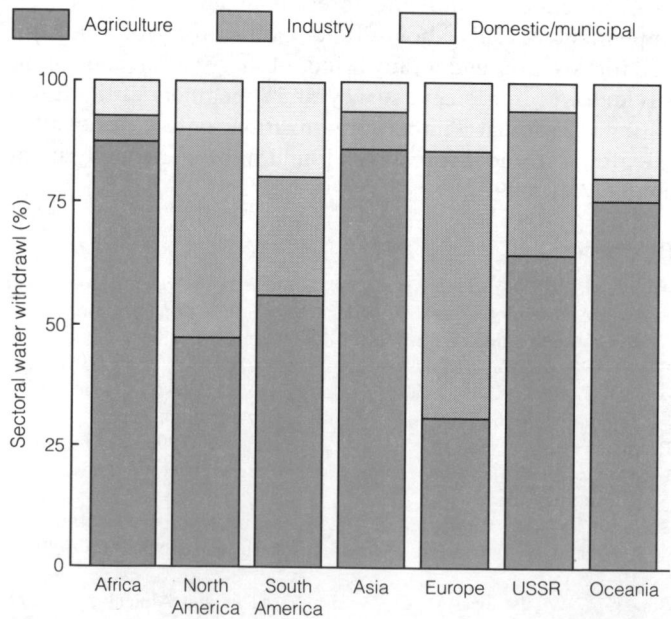

Figure 3.8 Sectoral fresh-water withdrawals in world regions, 1980s
Source: Belyaev, 1990

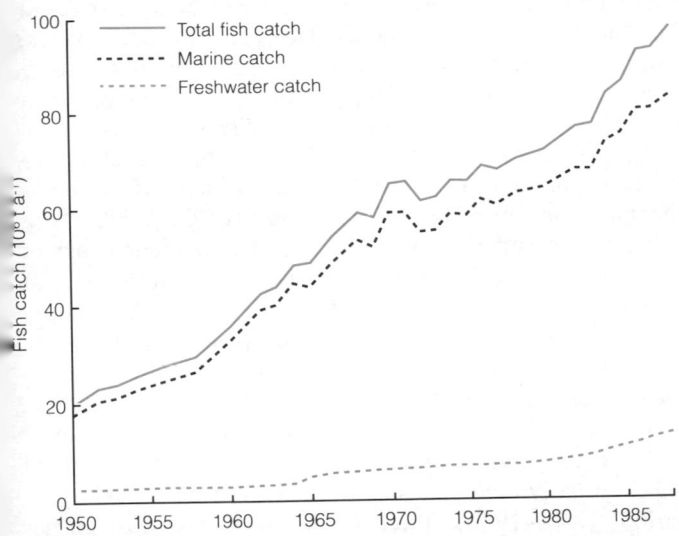

Figure 3.9 Global trends in marine, fresh-water and total marine fish catch, 1950–1988
Source: FAO, 1990 Unpublished data

The marine fish catch rose 32 per cent and the fresh-water catch rose 80 per cent during the same time span. The countries of Asia account for the majority of fish production, and their share continues to increase.

Increases in levels of production have severely stretched many fisheries, especially those in coastal areas. However, pelagic fisheries have also been affected. Table 3.15 shows the landings of selected species in specific ocean regions. The production of many of these species has declined over the 24 years documented in this table. Catches of Atlantic cod, haddock, Atlantic herring, capelin, Southern African pilchard, Pacific Ocean perch, King Crab and the Peruvian anchoveta have all declined. The landings of many other species have increased to compensate for these declines. Landings of the Japanese pilchard in the north-west Pacific, for example, have increased from 9×10^3 t in 1965 to 5.4×10^6 t in 1988.

Global catches of many marine mammal species have also declined, partly because populations have been reduced and partly because legal restrictions have been placed on the capture and killing of marine mammals. The International Whaling Commission (IWC) has collected detailed statistics on catches of selected whale species since 1930. These data, together with information on seal and dolphin species, have been discussed in more detail in the second edition of this report (UNEP, 1989).

Aquaculture, that is the farming of aquatic organisms, has increased substantially in recent decades in response to declines in catches of selected species of fish and crustaceans. The FAO has recently completed a global overview of aquaculture production; data for the top 20 producing nations, ranked in order of commercial value, are presented in Table 3.16 for the years 1984–1988. Although estimates of aquaculture production are included in the FAO fishery catch statistics, more detailed data on aquaculture production (such as those presented in Table 3.16) are available only for more recent years.

While diadromous (i.e., migratory) and marine fish production is important, the primary arena for fish aquaculture is in fresh water. Sixty-six per cent of the world's fresh-water fish production occurs in China. In 1988, the world production of all aquacultural products (fish, molluscs, crustaceans, seaweeds and other aquatic organisms) totalled 14.5×10^6 t, a 38 per cent increase from 1984 (Table 3.16).

Reference

UNEP 1989 *United Nations Environment Programme Environmental Data Report*, Basil Blackwell, Oxford.

Protected Areas and Wildlife

The development of effective conservation programmes relies on the gathering of basic data on wildlife species and natural habitats, particularly those under threat. The IUCN, together with the WWF, constitutes a world-wide network of governmental agencies and non-governmental organizations promoting the protection and sustainable use of wildlife resources. UNEP, FAO and UNESCO are also particularly active in this area.

Protected Areas

Recognizing the desirability of preserving certain natural areas, nations world-wide have designated numerous nature reserves and other protected areas. These can be classified

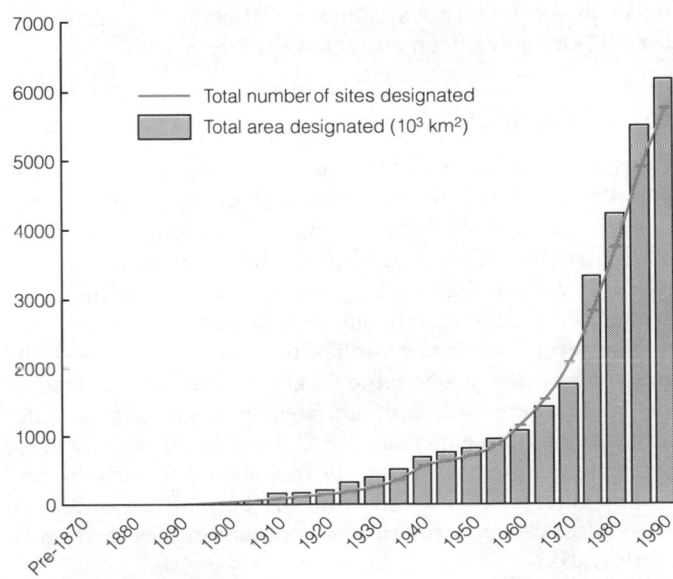

Figure 3.10 Growth in the number and coverage of nationally protected areas, pre-1870–1990 (cumulative total at the beginning of the year)
Source: WCMC, 1992

as either Nationally Protected areas, World Heritage Sites, Biosphere Reserves or Ramsar Wetlands (WCMC, 1992). World Heritage Sites are areas of "outstanding universal value" designated under the Convention Concerning the Protection of the World Cultural and National Heritage which was adopted in Paris in 1972. The establishment of Biosphere Reserves is not covered by a specific convention but is part of the UNESCO Man and the Biosphere Programme. Biosphere Reserves are not designated to protect unique areas but form a network of sites representing the world's ecosystems. The Convention on Wetlands of International Importance Especially as Waterfowl Habitat was signed in Ramsar (Iran) in 1971 and provides a framework for the conservation of wetland habitats. Ramsar criteria were adopted by the Conference of the Parties to the Convention in Regina in June 1987 (Scott, 1989).

Protected areas play a fundamental role in management and conservation of wild species and natural landscapes and habitats. The IUCN has developed a classification system for nationally protected areas, five of which can be regarded as being established for nature conservation purposes (IUCN, 1984). These five categories (I through V) are:

I Scientific Reserve/Strict Nature Reserve
II National Park
III Natural Monument/National Landmark
IV Managed Nature Reserve/Wildlife Sanctuary
V Protected Landscape or Seascape

The number and area of designated areas in IUCN Management Categories I–V, along with World Heritage Sites, Biosphere Reserves and Ramsar Wetlands, are listed in Table 3.17. Since the establishment of the first national parks in the late 1800s, some 5,750 areas, covering over 6×10^6 km^2 have been protected (Figure 3.10).

Loss of Natural Habitats

Destruction of natural habitats has proceeded along with population expansion and industrial development. Losses in one major habitat type – wetlands – are discussed in this edition of the 'UNEP Environmental Data Report'; other types of natural habitats, including coral reefs and mangroves, will be covered in subsequent editions.

The term "wetland" applies to a variety of low-lying areas where the water table is at, or near, the surface of the land, where soils are saturated or covered with water for parts of the year, and where there is an abundance of hydrophytic plants. Wetlands include tidal marshes and swamp forests and extend from the perma-frost underlain areas of extreme northern and southern climes to tropical rainforests.

Wetlands are among the most biologically productive ecosystems in the world, yet are often regarded as nuisances, wastelands, habitats for pests and threats to public health. In reality, wetlands help to regulate water flows, help to purify water and provide essential breeding habi-

tats for many species of flora and fauna. In general, there is a lack of global information on the status and changes in the extent of natural wetlands. However, in recent years, progress has been made in setting up data bases for some areas, for example the European flood plains (Wenger et al., 1990) and in the USA (Wilen and Frayer, 1990).

The US Fish and Wildlife Service has developed a series of inventories of the extent of natural wetlands spanning the period 1780s to 1980s (CEQ, 1989; Dahl, 1990; Wilen and Frayer, 1990). It was concluded that of the original 87×10^6 ha of wetlands existing at the time of settlement (i.e., the 1780s) in the conterminous USA, only 40×10^6 ha remained by the 1980s (Dahl, 1990). If the wetland areas in Alaska and Hawaii are added to the totals for the conterminous USA, the respective values become, in the 1780s, 158×10^6 ha and in the 1980s, 111×10^6 ha.

Table 3.18 and Figure 3.11 show estimated wetland losses in individual states of the USA during the 200-year period, 1780s–1980s. Twenty-two states have lost 50 per cent or more of their original wetlands. At the extremes, California has lost the greatest percentage (91 per cent) and Alaska the least (0.1 per cent). Florida has lost the greatest acreage – 3.76×10^6 ha. Overall, 66 per cent of the wetlands lost in the conterminous USA were forested with agricultural development being largely responsible for their destruction. Loss of natural wetland habitats are the cause, at least in part, of observed declines of selected North American breeding and wintering water fowl populations. Observed decreases in numbers of mallards and northern pintail are illustrated in Figure 3.12.

Assessments of wetland losses are not yet available in other countries and world regions. However, a number of surveys and inventories of existing wetlands have recently been compiled. In Canada, maps of wetland regions have been produced by the National Wetlands Working Group (Environment Canada, 1986). Directories of wetlands in Asia and in the western Palearctic have been published (Scott, 1989; Carp, 1980). Inventories of forested wetlands around the world have also recently been published (Jackson, 1990).

Wildlife

Biological diversity, or biodiversity as it is usually called, represents an important global resource. Increasing concern for the sustainability of wildlife resources and the threat of biodiversity loss as a result of human activities have made the conservation of biodiversity one of the key environmental challenges of the 1990s.

The WCMC, supported by the IUCN, WWF and UNEP, is responsible for the collection and dissemination of data on biological diversity. Data compiled by WCMC form the basis of IUCN's Red Data books on threatened species. A number of 'National Biodiversity Profiles', which provide an overview of wildlife resources at the country level have also been published by WCMC. WCMC are currently preparing a comprehensive work on wildlife resources which is designed to support the

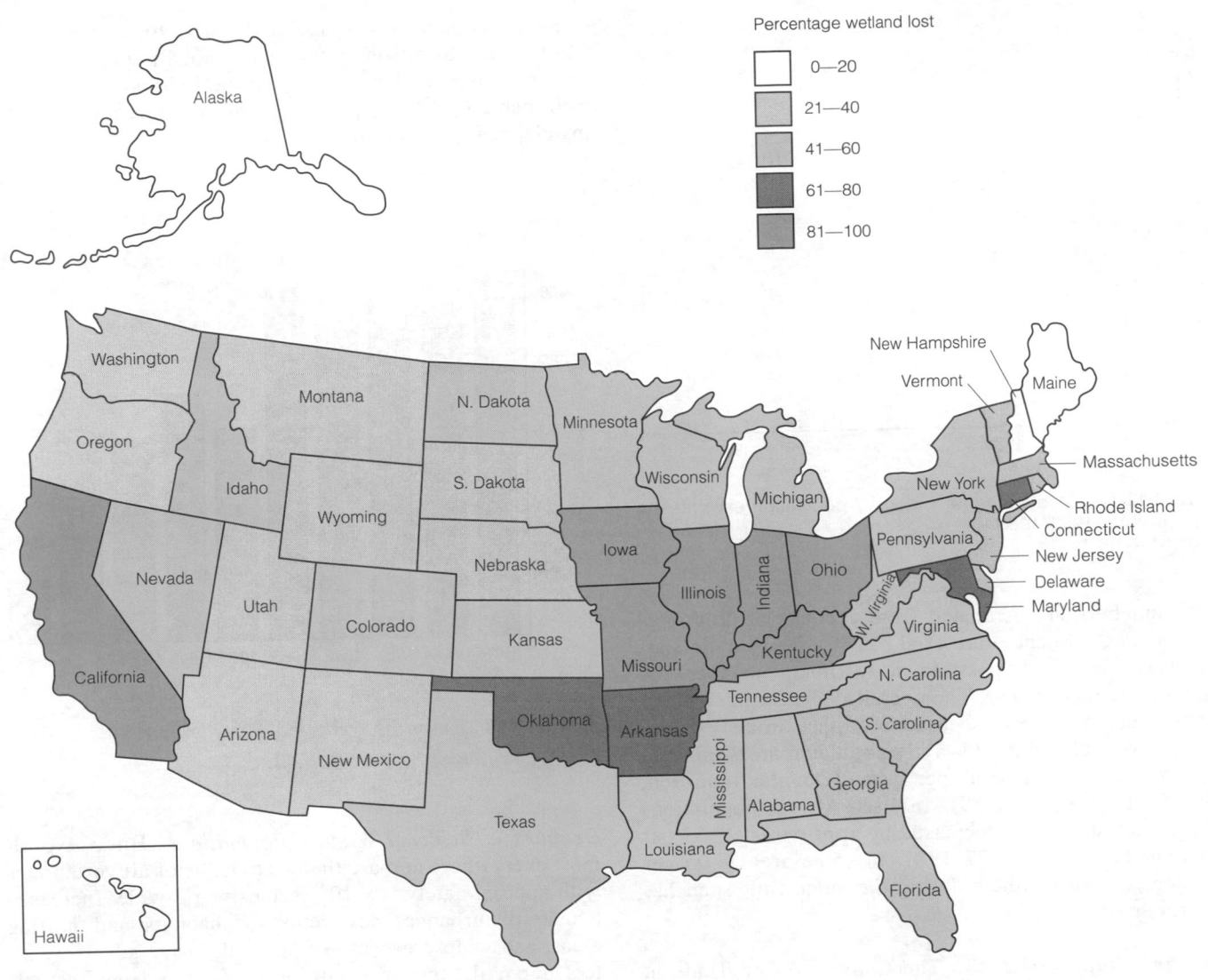

Figure 3.11 Percentage loss of wetlands in the USA, 1780s to 1980s (the state areas are not necessarily to the same scale)
Source: data from Table 3.18

WRI/IUCN/UNEP Biodiversity Conservation Strategy and Decade Action Plan (WCMC, 1992). Protection of freshwater and marine mamals, including cetaceans, (toothed whales and dolphins) is included within such strategies and is also addressed by aspects of the Regional Seas programmes of UNEP's Programme Activity Centre for Oceans and Coastal Areas.

Threatened Species A wide range of plant and animal species are threatened as a result of human activities including natural habitat destruction, exploitation and poaching. Natural processes, such as climatic change, may also pose threats to the survival of selected species. Estimates of population changes since 1940 of 29 species of mammals, reptiles and birds were presented in the second edition of this report (UNEP, 1989). Numbers of known and threatened species of mammals, reptiles, birds and amphibians are listed in Table 3.19 on a country basis. Similar

data on invertebrates are not readily available, except for the relatively well-documented swallowtail butterflies. For many individual species, insufficient data are available for conducting assessments of change in the status of populations. However, the monitoring of selected species such as the African elephant, the Black rhino and marine turtles is further advanced than for some other animals. Studies on continental elephant status began in 1976. These data were used to establish the African Elephant Database at UNEP/GRID in 1987. Using geographic information systems (GIS) computer technology this data base has developed into the most comprehensive of its kind for an endangered species (UNEP/GEMS, 1989).

Elephants once covered the whole of Africa in great numbers, but are now mainly confined to a central belt. The status of the African elephant in 1989 is shown, on a country basis, in Table 3.20. Data have not been easy to compile, especially in the Central African Rainforest

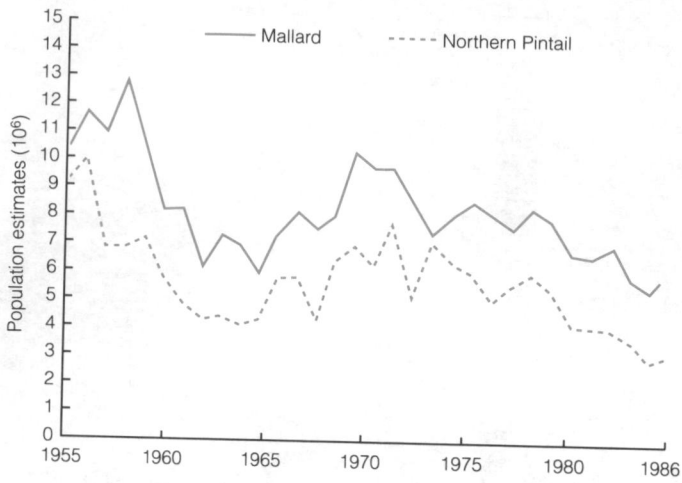

Figure 3.12 Selected waterfowl breeding population estimates in North America, 1955–1986
Source: CEQ, 1989

elephant populations transferred back to Appendix II (Barbier and Swanson, 1990). Since not all countries have agreed to the total ban in ivory trade, illegal trade may well increase, thereby posing a continued threat to remaining elephant populations.

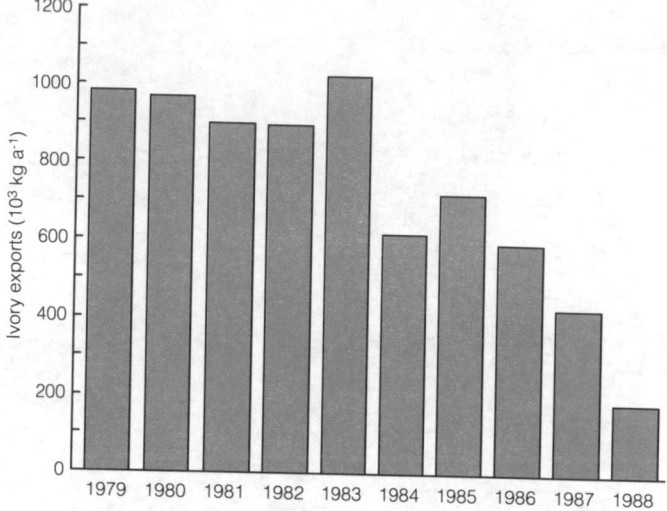

Figure 3.13 Decline in recorded ivory exports from Africa, 1979–1988
Source: WCMC, 1992

where numbers are estimated from a count of droppings (Barnes, 1989; Michelmore et al., 1989). Ivory trade statistics also make it possible to estimate numbers of elephant deaths per year. The overall decrease in elephant numbers has been estimated to be approximately 8 per cent per year, although in heavily populated areas this rate may exceed 17 per cent per year (Douglas-Hamilton, 1989; UNEP/GEMS, 1989). In East Africa, populations are considered to have decreased by approximately 57 per cent over the period 1977–1987. In some areas a 95 per cent decrease in numbers during the same time-span has been reported.

Trade in Wildlife Products The Convention on Trade in Endangered Species of Wild Fauna and Flora (CITES) is the most important control on international trade in currently endangered species. A detailed report on the function of CITES appeared in an earlier edition of the 'UNEP Environmental Data Report' (UNEP, 1989) along with data on trade in skins from the cat family (*Felidae*) and in parrots. In view of the current publicity associated with elephant declines, trade in ivory is highlighted in the present edition.

Exports of ivory from African countries during the period 1979–1988 are listed in Table 3.21 and presented graphically in summary form in Figure 3.13. Data reflect the considerable decline of recorded ivory exports in more recent years.

In 1985 a system of ivory export quotas, designed to control the international trade in African ivory, was proposed by the parties to CITES. This system came into force in 1986. At this juncture, elephants were listed in Appendix II, which permitted limited trade. In 1989 CITES voted to transfer elephants to Appendix I, a move which would ban all trade in ivory. At the same time, a number of countries banned imports of raw ivory. Some producer countries, however, have proposed to have their

Declines in Selected Wildlife Populations Birds live almost everywhere and are the most visible of all vertebrates with approximately 9×10^3 species world-wide. Increased human disturbance, destruction of habitats and nesting areas, and widespread use of pesticides have adversely affected populations of many species. Data from the UK Common Bird Census, started in 1962, suggest that many native bird species have declined over the past 20–30 years. The increased use of pesticides and changing agricultural practices are proposed as possible reasons for the reported declines (Merchant et al., 1990).

In the USA, a number of bird species have been closely monitored since 1970 (CEQ, 1989). Some seabirds are reported to be less abundant, whilst scavenging birds, such as seagulls and fulmers, are flourishing. The rise in numbers of scavenging birds is linked to the increased quantity of rubbish dumped on both land and in the sea. Terns, on the other hand, seem to be declining. Data collected during the International Shorebird Survey have also revealed declines in populations of a number of shorebird species between 1972 and 1983 (Howe et al., 1989).

Some songbird species are reported to be declining whilst others are expanding. Field birds have also exhibited species-specific population changes. Forest-dwelling birds have declined, probably as a result of habitat loss and fragmentation of forests (CEQ, 1989). The wood thrush, for example, is in dramatic decline, losing on average 5.1 per cent of the population annually. Numbers of blue jays are also dwindling, but at only 1.3 per cent per year. Overall, the health of most North American raptors (birds of prey) appears good, with some species increasing in numbers since DDT was banned in 1976.

North American breeding and wintering water fowl populations have also been monitored (CEQ, 1989). Duck breeding populations in North America have been declining continually since 1955, a trend which is attributed to wetland habitat destruction (see Loss of Natural Habitats). Since 1980, numbers of Canvasback ducks, in particular, have fallen dramatically. Population losses of Canvasback ducks are apparently related to a decline in the availability of submerged aquatic plants, their preferred food. Goose populations are, on the other hand, increasing in both Canada and eastern North America and invading new areas (CEQ, 1989).

References

Barbier, E. and Swanson, T. 1990 Ivory: the case against the ban, *New Scientist* **28**(1743), 52–54.

Barnes, R. 1989 *The Status of Elephants in the Forests of Central Africa: Results of a Reconnaisance Survey*, Report to the African Elephant Programme, EEC/WWF.

Carp, E. 1980 *Directory of Wetlands of International Importance in the Western Palearctic*, International Union for Conservation of Nature and Natural Resources, Gland.

CEQ 1989 *Environmental Trends*, Council on Environmental Quality, Executive Office of the President, Washington DC.

Dahl, T. E. 1990 *Wetland Losses in the United States, 1780s to 1980s*, US Department of the Interior, Fish and Wildlife Service, Washington DC.

Douglas-Hamilton, I. 1989 *Overview of Status and Trends of the African Elephant*, Report to the Ivory Trade Review Group, No. 1, EEC/WWF African Elephant Programme.

Environment Canada 1986 *Canada's Wetlands*, Department of Energy, Mines and Resources, Environment Canada, Ottawa.

Howe, M. A., Geissler, P. H. and Harrington, B. A. 1989 Population trends of North American shorebirds based on the International Shorebirds Survey, *Biological Conservation* **49**, 185–199.

IUCN 1984 Categories and criteria for protected areas. In: *Natural Parks, Conservational and Development: the Role of National Parks in Sustaining Society*, J. A. McNealy and K. R. Miller (Eds), Smithsonian Institute Press, Washington DC, 47–53.

Jackson, B. D. (Ed.) 1990 The international forested wetlands resources: identification and inventory. *Forest Ecology and Management* (special issue) **33/34**, 1–643.

Merchant, J., Hudson, R., Carter, S. and Whittington, P. 1990 *Population Trends in British Breeding Birds*, British Trust for Ornithology, Tring, and the Nature Conservancy Council, UK.

Michelmore, F., Beardsley, K., Barnes, R. and Douglas-Hamilton, I. 1989 *Elephant Population Estimates for the Central Africa Forests*, Report to the Ivory Trade Review Group, No. 2, African Elephant Programme, EEC/WWF.

Scott, D. A. (Ed.) 1989 *A Directory of Asian Wetlands*, International Union for Conservation of Nature and Natural Resources, Gland.

UNEP 1989 *United Nations Environment Programme Environmental Data Report*, Basil Blackwell, Oxford.

UNEP/GEMS 1989 *The African Elephant*, Environment Library Series Number 3, United Nations Environment Programme, Nairobi.

WCMC 1992 *Global Biodiversity 1992: Status of the Earth's Living Resources*, World Conservation Monitoring Centre, Cambridge. In press.

Wenger, E. L., Zinke, A. and Gutzweiler, K-A. 1990 Present situation of the European floodplain forests, *Forest Ecology and Management* **33/34**, 5–12.

Wilen, B. O. and Frayer, W. E. 1990 Status and trends of US wetlands and deep water habitats, *Forest Ecology and Management* **33/34**, 181–192.

Table 3.1   Land distribution in countries and changing usage, 1966–1968 and 1986–1988 (mean annual values)

Region/country	Total land area 1988 (10³ km²)	Cropland 1966–68	Cropland 1986–88	Permanent meadows and pastures 1966–68	Permanent meadows and pastures 1986–88	Forest and woodland 1966–68	Forest and woodland 1986–88	Other land 1966–68	Other land 1986–88	Major change Cropland	Major change Pastures	Major change Forest	Major change Other
WORLD	130,691	11	11	25	25	33	31	32	33				
AFRICA	29,640	6	6	27	27	25	23	42	44				
Algeria	2,382	3	3	16	13	1	2	80	82				
Angola	1,247	3	3	23	23	44	43	30	31				
Benin	111	14	17	4	4	43	33	39	47	3.1		-10.5	7.4
Botswana	567	2	2	74	78	2	2	22	18		3.2		-3.7
Br. Ind. Oc. Tr.	0.1	0	0	0	0	0	0	100	100				
Burkina Faso	274	8	12	37	37	29	25	26	27	3.9		-4.4	
Burundi	26	40	52	24	36	2	3	34	10	11.9	11.1		-23.6
Cameroon	465	13	15	19	18	58	53	10	14			-4.7	3.5
Cape Verde	4	10	10	6	6	–	–	84	84				
Cent. African Rep.	623	3	3	5	5	58	58	34	34				
Chad	1,259	2	3	36	36	12	10	50	51				
Comoros	2	40	44	7	7	16	16	38	33	4.5			-4.5
Congo	342	0	0	29	29	63	62	7	8				
Côte d'Ivoire	318	9	11	9	9	56	20	26	59			-36.0	33.1
Djibouti	23	0	0	9	9	–	–	91	91				
Egypt	995	3	3	0	0	–	–	97	97				
Equatorial Guinea	28	8	8	4	4	46	46	42	42				
Ethiopia	1,101	12	13	42	41	27	25	20	22				
Gabon	258	1	2	19	18	78	78	2	2				
Gambia	10	13	17	9	9	29	17	49	57	4.3		-11.8	7.5
Ghana	230	12	12	16	15	42	36	30	37			-6.1	6.6
Guinea	246	3	3	12	12	48	41	37	44			-7.3	7.1
Guinea-Bissau	28	10	12	38	38	39	38	13	12				
Kenya	570	3	4	7	7	7	6	82	83				
Lesotho	30	12	10	73	66	0	0	16	24		-6.6		8.2
Liberia	96	4	4	2	2	22	22	72	72				
Libya	1,760	1	1	6	8	–	–	93	91				
Madagascar	582	4	5	58	58	31	25	7	11			-5.2	3.9
Malawi	94	21	25	20	20	54	46	5	9	4.0		-8.3	4.3
Mali	1,220	1	2	25	25	8	7	66	67				

Continued below

Table 3.1 Continued

Region/country	Total land area 1988 (10³ km²)	Cropland 1966–68	Cropland 1986–88	Permanent meadows and pastures 1966–68	Permanent meadows and pastures 1986–88	Forest and woodland 1966–68	Forest and woodland 1986–88	Other land 1966–68	Other land 1986–88	Major change Cropland	Major change Pastures	Major change Forest	Major change Other
Mauritania	1,025	–	–	38	38	15	15	47	47				-3.6
Mauritius	2	53	58	4	4	32	31	11	7	4.7			-10.4
Morocco	446	17	19	39	47	12	12	32	22		7.4		
Mozambique	782	4	4	56	56	22	19	18	21				
Namibia	823	1	1	64	64	22	22	13	13				
Niger	1,267	2	3	8	7	3	2	87	88				3.1
Nigeria	911	32	34	21	23	22	16	24	27			-6.6	
Réunion	3	21	22	3	4	39	35	36	39			-4.0	
Rwanda	25	27	46	34	20	25	23	13	11	18.9	-14.2		
São Tomé & Príncipe	1	36	39	1	1	0	0	63	60				
Senegal	193	24	27	30	30	35	31	12	12	3.2		-3.7	-3.7
Seychelles	0.3	19	22	0	0	19	19	63	59	3.7			-3.9
Sierra Leone	72	20	25	31	31	30	29	19	15	4.8			
Somalia	627	1	2	46	46	16	14	37	38				
South Africa	1,221	11	11	69	67	3	4	17	19				
St Helena	0.3	6	6	6	6	3	6	84	81			3.2	-3.2
Sudan	2,376	5	5	24	24	24	20	48	51			-4.0	3.6
Swaziland	17	9	10	78	68	8	6	6	16		-10.0		10.7
Tanzania	886	5	6	40	40	51	48	5	7				
Togo	54	24	26	4	4	43	25	29	45			-18.4	16.1
Tunisia	155	28	31	16	20	3	4	53	46		3.2		-6.8
Uganda	200	25	34	25	25	32	29	19	13	9.0		-3.1	-6.0
Zaire	2,267	3	3	7	7	80	77	10	13				
Zambia	743	7	7	47	47	42	39	5	7				
Zimbabwe	387	6	7	13	13	52	52	30	29				
NORTH AMERICA	21,317	12	13	17	17	33	32	38	38			-3.8	
Antigua & Barbuda	0.4	17	18	7	9	15	11	61	61				
Bahamas	10	1	1	–	–	32	32	67	66				
Barbados	0.4	77	77	9	9	0	0	14	14				
Belize	23	2	2	2	2	46	44	50	51				
Bermuda	0.1	0	0	0	0	20	20	80	80				

Continued over

Table 3.1 Continued

Region/country	Total land area 1988 (10³ km²)	Distribution (percentage of total land area)								Major changes in distribution (3 percentage points change or more) 1966–68 to 1986–88			
		Cropland		Permanent meadows and pastures		Forest and woodland		Other land		Cropland	Pastures	Forest	Other
		1966–68	1986–88	1966–68	1986–88	1966–68	1986–88	1966–68	1986–88				
Br. Virgin Is.	0.2	20	27	33	33	7	7	40	33	6.7			-6.7
Canada	9,161	5	5	2	3	35	39	58	53			3.5	-5.1
Cayman Is.	0.3	0	0	8	8	23	23	69	69				
Costa Rica	51	10	10	23	45	55	32	13	12		22.1	-22.6	
Cuba	110	18	30	24	27	20	25	38	18	12.6		4.6	-19.6
Dominica	1	23	23	3	3	53	41	21	33			-12.0	12.0
Dominican Rep.	48	22	30	43	43	14	13	21	13	8.2			-7.4
El Salvador	21	31	35	29	29	9	5	32	30	4.9		-4.0	
Greenland	342	0	0	1	1	–	–	99	99				
Grenada	0.3	47	39	3	3	12	9	38	49	-7.8			10.8
Guadeloupe	2	26	19	10	17	35	42	29	22	-7.3	6.5	7.3	-6.5
Guatemala	108	14	17	11	13	48	37	27	33			-11.1	6.4
Haiti	28	28	33	22	18	3	2	47	47	5.1	-4.3		
Honduras	112	14	16	19	23	46	31	22	30		3.6	-14.5	8.6
Jamaica	11	24	25	22	18	19	17	35	40		-4.0		4.8
Martinique	1	23	19	12	19	42	36	24	27	-3.8	6.3	-5.7	3.1
Mexico	1,909	12	13	39	39	29	23	20	25			-5.9	5.2
Montserrat	0.1	20	20	10	10	10	40	60	30			30.0	-30.0
Neth. Antilles	1	7	8	0	0	0	0	93	92				
Nicaragua	119	10	11	35	44	50	31	4	14		8.8	-18.9	9.5
Panama	76	7	8	15	17	60	52	18	23			-7.9	5.0
Puerto Rico	9	29	14	36	38	14	20	21	28	-14.2		5.9	6.4
St Christopher & Nevis	0.4	44	39	11	3	19	17	25	42	-5.6	-8.3		16.7
St Lucia	1	26	29	5	5	20	13	49	53	3.3		-7.1	3.8
St Pierre & Miquelon	0.2	13	13	0	0	4	4	83	83				
St Vincent & Grenadines	0.3	46	44	3	5	36	36	15	15				
Trinidad & Tobago	5	19	23	2	2	47	43	32	31	4.4		-3.9	
Turks & Caicos Is.	0.4	2	2	0	0	0	0	98	98				
US Virgin Is.	0.3	19	21	26	26	6	6	49	47				
USA	9,167	20	21	28	26	32	29	20	24			-3.0	3.8

Continued below

Table 3.1 Continued

Region/country	Total land area 1988 (10³ km²)	Distribution (percentage of total land area)								Major changes in distribution (3 percentage points change or more) 1966–68 to 1986–88			
		Cropland		Permanent meadows and pastures		Forest and woodland		Other land		Cropland	Pastures	Forest	Other
		1966–68	1986–88	1966–68	1986–88	1966–68	1986–88	1966–68	1986–88				
SOUTH AMERICA	17,529	6	8	24	27	56	51	14	13			-4.3	
Argentina	2,737	11	13	53	52	22	22	13	13				
Bolivia	1,084	2	3	26	25	54	51	18	21				
Brazil	8,457	6	9	16	20	71	66	7	5		3.8	-4.7	
Chile	749	5	6	14	18	12	12	69	65		3.9		-4.5
Colombia	1,039	5	5	33	39	55	49	7	7		5.2	-5.8	
Ecuador	277	9	10	8	18	61	43	22	30		10.1	-18.3	7.8
Falkland Is.	12	0	–	99	99	0	0	1	1				
French Guiana	88	–	–	–	–	94	83	6	17			-11.3	11.3
Guyana	197	2	3	5	6	92	83	1	8			-9.3	7.5
Paraguay	397	2	6	36	50	53	39	8	5	3.2	14.6	-14.2	-3.5
Peru	1,280	2	3	21	21	58	54	19	22			-3.9	3.1
Suriname	156	–	–	–	–	96	95	4	4				
Uruguay	175	8	8	78	77	3	4	10	11				
Venezuela	882	4	4	18	20	42	35	36	41			-6.6	4.6
ASIA	26,787	16	17	26	25	22	20	35	38				
Afghanistan	652	12	12	46	46	3	3	39	39				
Bahrain	1	3	3	6	6	0	0	91	91				
Bangladesh	130	70	71	5	5	17	16	9	9				
Bhutan	47	2	3	5	6	51	55	41	36			3.7	-4.7
Brunei	5	3	1	1	1	93	48	3	49			-44.6	46.6
Cambodia	177	17	17	3	3	76	76	4	4				
China	9,326	11	10	34	34	16	14	39	42				3.1
Christmas Is.	0.1	0	0	0	0	0	0	100	100				
Cocos Is.	–	0	0	0	0	0	0	100	100				
Cyprus	9	17	17	1	1	13	13	69	69				
Gaza Strip	0.4	45	47	0	0	0	0	55	53				
Hong Kong	1	12	8	0	1	10	12	78	79	-4.3			
India	2,973	55	57	5	4	21	22	19	17				
Indonesia	1,812	10	12	7	7	68	63	15	19			-5.4	3.9
Iran	1,636	10	9	27	27	11	11	53	53				

Continued over

Table 3.1 Continued

Region/country	Total land area 1988 (10³ km²)	Distribution (percentage of total land area)								Major changes in distribution (3 percentage points change or more) 1966–68 to 1986–88			
		Cropland		Permanent meadows and pastures		Forest and woodland		Other land		Cropland	Pastures	Forest	Other
		1966–68	1986–88	1966–68	1986–88	1966–68	1986–88	1966–68	1986–88				
Iraq	437	11	12	9	9	4	4	75	74				-3.2
Israel	21	20	21	6	7	5	5	70	66				
Japan	377	15	13	–	2	67	67	17	19				
Jordan	89	3	4	9	9	1	1	87	86				
Korea	99	23	22	–	1	67	66	9	12				
Korea, Dem.	120	16	20	–	–	74	74	9	5	3.6			-3.6
Kuwait	18	–	–	8	8	–	–	92	92				
Laos	231	4	4	3	3	65	56	28	36				8.4
Lebanon	10	30	29	1	1	9	8	60	62			-8.7	
Macau	–	0	0	0	0	0	0	100	100				
Malaysia	329	13	15	–	–	74	60	13	26			-14.6	13.1
Maldives	0.3	10	10	3	3	3	3	83	83				
Mongolia	1,567	1	1	89	79	10	9	1	11		-10.4		10.5
Myanmar q.v. Burma	658	16	15	1	1	49	49	35	35				
Nepal	137	13	17	12	15	17	17	57	51	3.7			-5.3
Oman	212	–	–	5	5	0	0	95	95				
Pakistan	771	25	27	6	6	3	4	66	62				
Philippines	298	24	27	3	4	56	37	17	33	3.1		-19.6	15.3
Qatar	11	–	–	5	5	0	0	95	95	3.1			15.3
Saudi Arabia	2,150	–	1	40	40	1	1	59	59				
Singapore	1	21	5	0	0	6	5	73	90	-15.8			16.9
Sri Lanka	65	29	29	6	7	29	27	36	37				
Syria	184	33	30	41	45	3	3	24	22		4.1		
Thailand	511	26	39	1	1	48	28	26	31	13.6		-19.8	5.9
Turkey	770	34	36	14	11	26	26	25	27		-3.1		
United Arab Em.	84	–	–	2	2	0	–	97	97				
Viet Nam	327	18	20	1	1	43	30	38	49			-13.0	
Yemen	195	7	7	36	36	8	8	49	49				11.0
Yemen, Dem.	333	–	–	27	27	5	5	67	68				
EUROPE	4,721	31	30	19	18	31	33	18	19				
Albania	27	20	26	25	15	45	38	9	21	5.8	-10.5	-7.2	11.8
Andorra	0.5	2	2	56	56	22	22	20	20				

Continued below

Table 3.1 Continued

Region/country	Total land area 1988 (10³ km²)	Distribution (percentage of total land area)								Major changes in distribution (3 percentage points change or more) 1966–68 to 1986–88			
		Cropland		Permanent meadows and pastures		Forest and woodland		Other land					
		1966–68	1986–88	1966–68	1986–88	1966–68	1986–88	1966–68	1986–88	Cropland	Pastures	Forest	Other
Austria	83	20	18	27	24	39	39	14	19	-4.5	-3.3		5.5
Belgium	33	29	25	25	21	21	21	25	33		-3.5		7.6
Bulgaria	111	41	37	12	18	33	35	14	9	-3.8	6.7		-5.0
Czechoslovakia	125	43	41	14	13	36	37	8	9				
Denmark	42	64	61	8	5	11	12	18	22				4.7
Faeroe Is.	1	2	2	0	0	0	0	98	98				
Finland	305	8	8	–	–	72	76	19	15		-3.4	4.0	-3.6
France	550	36	35	25	22	24	27	15	17				
German Dem. Rep.	105	47	47	14	12	28	28	12	13				
Germany, Fed. Rep.	244	31	31	22	18	30	30	17	21		-3.8		4.2
Gibraltar	–	0	0	0	0	0	0	100	100				
Greece	131	30	30	40	40	20	20	10	10				
Hungary	92	61	57	14	13	16	18	9	11	-3.7			
Iceland	100	–	–	23	23	1	1	76	76				
Ireland	69	21	14	61	68	3	5	15	13	-6.3	6.5		
Italy	294	52	41	18	17	21	23	10	19	-10.5			9.1
Liechtenstein	0.2	25	25	31	38	19	19	25	19		6.3		-6.3
Malta	0.3	44	41	0	0		0	56	59	-3.1			3.1
Netherlands	34	27	27	39	32	9	9	24	32		-6.8		7.7
Norway	307	3	3	1	–	24	27	72	70				
Poland	304	51	49	14	13	27	29	8	9				
Portugal	92	44	41	8	8	32	32	16	18				
Romania	230	46	46	19	19	28	28	8	7				
San Marino	0.1	17	17	0	0	0	0	83	83				
Spain	499	41	41	24	20	27	31	8	7		-3.4	3.9	
Sweden	403	8	7	2	1	69	70	22	22				
Switzerland	40	10	10	45	40	25	26	21	23		-4.3		
UK	242	31	29	50	48	8	10	12	13				
Yugoslavia	255	32	30	25	25	35	37	8	8				
USSR	22,272	10	10	17	17	41	42	32	30				

Continued over

Table 3.1 Continued

Region/country	Total land area 1988 (10³ km²)	Distribution (percentage of total land area)								Major changes in distribution (3 percentage points change or more) 1966–68 to 1986–88			
		Cropland		Permanent meadows and pastures		Forest and woodland		Other land		Cropland	Pastures	Forest	Other
		1966–68	1986–88	1966–68	1986–88	1966–68	1986–88	1966–68	1986–88				
OCEANIA	8,427	5	6	53	52	22	19	19	24			-3.8	4.3
American Samoa	0.2	20	20	0	0	70	70	10	10				
Australia	7,618	5	6	57	56	18	14	20	24			-4.2	4.7
Canton Is.	0.1	0	0	0	0	0	0	100	100				
Cook Is.	0.2	26	26	0	0	0	0	74	74				
Fiji	18	11	13	4	3	65	65	20	19				
French Polynesia	4	18	20	5	5	31	31	45	43				
Kiribati	1	53	52	0	0	3	3	44	45				
Nauru	–	0	0	0	0	0	0	100	100				
New Caledonia	18	1	1	14	15	39	39	47	45				
New Zealand	268	2	2	48	52	27	27	23	19		3.7		-3.5
Niue	0.3	77	65	25	4	19	19	4	12	-11.5	3.8		7.7
Norfolk Is.	–	0	0	25	25	0	0	75	75				
Pacific Is. Tr. Tr.	2	30	33	10	13	22	22	38	31	3.4	3.4		-6.7
Papua New Guinea	453	1	1	1	–	85	84	14	14				
Solomon Is.	28	2	2	1	1	91	91	5	5				
Tokelau	–	0	0	0	0	0	0	100	100				
Tonga	1	56	67	3	6	15	11	26	17	11.1		-4.2	-9.7
Tuvalu	0.2	0	0	0	0	0	0	100	100				
Vanuatu	12	7	12	2	2	1	1	89	85	4.7			-4.7
Wallis Is.	0.2	20	25	0	0	0	0	80	75	5.0			-5.0

Total land area excludes area under major inland water bodies. Land use definitions vary considerably between countries; however, in general, "Cropland" refers to arable land and land under temporary or permanent cultivation; "Permanent meadows and pasture" includes pastures and lands used for five years or more for natural or cultivated forage crops respectively; "Forests and woodlands" refers to natural or planted stands of trees, and includes cleared forest land that is to be reforested; "Other land" includes barren or waste land, parks, built-on areas and roads. Continental aggregates may include countries not listed. For more detailed notes on definitions and countries, refer to the most recent edition of the 'FAO Production Yearbook'.

Source:
FAO 1990 Unpublished data, Food and Agriculture Organization, Rome.

Table 3.2 Wilderness areas in selected countries, mid-1980s

Region/country	Wilderness area (10^3 ha)	Percentage of total land area	Number of areas
WORLD	4,806,995	32	1,038
AFRICA	823,238	28	434
Algeria	140,424	59	42
Angola	27,049	22	29
Benin	1,209	11	2
Botswana	31,255	54	23
Burkina Faso	750	3	1
Cameroon	1,320	3	1
Cent. African Rep.	20,917	34	14
Chad	61,254	48	24
Congo	11,837	35	5
Côte d'Ivoire	4,268	13	4
Egypt	42,540	43	17
Ethiopia	19,716	19	19
Gabon	7,333	27	5
Kenya	11,221	19	14
Lesotho	2,133	70	2
Liberia	1,420	13	1
Libya	65,497	37	32
Madagascar	691	1	1
Malawi	781	8	1
Mali	58,814	47	17
Mauritania	71,370	69	17
Mozambique	6,130	8	5
Namibia	22,239	27	16
Niger	65,633	55	15
Nigeria	1,526	2	2
Senegal	1,586	8	2
Somalia	10,460	17	14
Sudan	79,377	32	73
Tanzania	7,053	8	5
Tunisia	1,901	12	2
Uganda	530	2	1
Western Sahara	18,166	68	8
Zaire	11,763	5	9
Zambia	15,075	20	11
NORTH AMERICA	907,742	38	85
Canada	640,587	65	59
Greenland	217,400	100	1
Honduras	1,126	10	2
Mexico	3,050	2	3
Nicaragua	1,521	10	2
USA	44,058	5	18

Region/country	Wilderness area (10^3 ha)	Percentage of total land area	Number of areas
SOUTH AMERICA	374,597	21	90
Argentina	14,976	5	14
Bolivia	17,810	16	16
Brazil	202,061	24	23
Chile	23,086	31	2
Colombia	15,156	13	4
French Guiana	4,095	45	2
Guyana	12,204	57	3
Paraguay	7,726	19	7
Peru	36,660	29	9
Suriname	11,080	68	3
Venezuela	29,742	33	7
ASIA	377,586	14	144
Afghanistan	8,740	14	9
Bhutan	1,179	25	1
China	210,776	22	47
India	1,161		2
Indonesia	11,761	6	12
Iran	15,685	10	5
Iraq	6,477	15	6
Laos	437	2	1
Malaysia	2,844	9	3
Mongolia	24,131	15	22
Myanmar q.v. Burma	2,547	4	3
Oman	4,769	18	2
Pakistan	2,737	3	3
Saudi Arabia	67,889	28	17
Thailand	2,809	6	3
United Arab Em.	1,938	26	2
Yemen	2,067	11	2
Yemen, Dem.	9,639	34	4
EUROPE	13,855	3	11
Finland	2,939	9	3
Iceland	2,975	29	2
Norway	5,627	17	4
Sweden	2,315	5	2
USSR	752,022	34	182
OCEANIA	237,057	20	91
Australia	229,431	30	83
New Zealand	3,723	14	5
Papua New Guinea	3,903	8	3
ANTARCTICA	1,320,898	100	1

Estimates of wilderness areas are based on an analysis of 65 detailed navigation maps compiled by the US Defense Mapping Agency in the early and mid-1980s. Areas showing no evidence of development, such as settlements, roads, buildings, airports, railroads, pipelines, powerlines and reservoirs are indentified as wilderness areas. Only large blocks of wilderness over 40 x 10^4 ha are identified. Totals may differ due to rounding.

Source:
McCloskey, J. M. and Spalding, H. 1989 A reconnaissance-level inventory of the amount of wilderness remaining in the world, *Ambio* **18**(4), 221–227.

Table 3.3 Indices of agricultural production, 1965–1989 (relative to a base period, 1979–1981 output = 100)

Year	Total			Per capita		
	World	Developed countries	Developing countries	World	Developed countries	Developing countries
1965	69.4	73.6	65.2	92.6	83.9	92.7
1970	79.2	82.4	76.1	95.4	89.6	95.2
1971	81.8	85.7	77.9	96.5	92.3	95.1
1972	81.3	84.8	77.8	93.9	90.5	92.6
1973	85.8	90.4	81.2	97.2	95.5	94.5
1974	87.0	90.7	83.3	96.7	95.1	94.7
1975	89.1	91.7	86.6	97.3	95.3	96.2
1976	91.4	94.9	88.0	98.0	97.9	95.7
1977	93.4	96.1	90.8	98.4	98.3	96.6
1978	97.5	99.9	95.2	101.0	101.4	99.3
1979	98.3	100.0	96.7	100.1	100.8	98.7
1980	99.1	98.7	99.4	99.1	98.7	99.5
1981	102.6	101.3	103.9	100.8	100.5	101.8
1982	105.8	104.3	107.3	102.2	102.7	102.9
1983	105.5	99.5	111.4	100.1	97.4	104.6
1984	111.4	106.4	116.3	103.9	103.5	107.0
1985	114.3	108.0	120.7	104.9	104.3	108.8
1986	115.4	108.8	122.1	104.1	104.3	107.7
1987	116.3	108.0	124.5	103.0	102.9	107.7
1988	117.8	105.6	130.0	102.6	99.9	110.1
1989	121.4	109.5	133.2	103.8	102.9	110.4

The index of agricultural production represents the disposable output (net of feed and seed use) of a region's agriculture sector relative to the base period 1979–1981. The index numbers include all crop and livestock products.

Source:
FAO 1990 Unpublished data, Food and Agriculture Organization, Rome.

Table 3.4 Indices of food production, 1965–1989 (relative to a base period, 1979–1981 output = 100)

Year	Total			Per capita		
	World	Developed countries	Developing countries	World	Developed countries	Developing countries
1965	68.1	72.3	63.7	90.8	82.5	90.4
1970	78.7	81.7	75.6	94.7	88.9	94.5
1971	81.3	85.3	77.0	95.8	91.9	94.0
1972	80.5	84.1	76.7	93.0	89.7	91.4
1973	85.3	90.0	80.4	96.6	95.2	93.5
1974	86.4	90.5	82.2	96.1	94.9	93.4
1975	89.0	91.6	86.3	97.1	95.2	95.9
1976	91.7	94.8	88.4	98.2	97.8	96.1
1977	93.2	95.8	90.6	98.2	98.0	96.4
1978	97.6	100.0	95.1	101.0	101.6	99.1
1979	98.4	100.1	96.7	100.1	100.8	98.7
1980	99.2	98.9	99.6	99.3	98.9	99.7
1981	102.4	101.1	103.7	100.6	100.3	101.6
1982	105.8	104.4	107.3	102.2	102.9	102.8
1983	105.6	99.9	111.5	100.2	97.8	104.7
1984	111.1	106.8	115.7	103.7	103.8	106.4
1985	114.0	108.1	120.2	104.6	104.4	108.3
1986	116.0	109.4	122.9	104.6	104.9	108.5
1987	116.3	108.3	124.6	103.0	103.1	107.7
1988	117.7	105.6	130.2	102.4	99.9	110.3
1989	121.5	110.0	133.4	103.9	103.4	110.6

The index of food production represents the disposable output (net of feed and seed use) of a region's agriculture sector relative to the base period 1979–1981. The index numbers include all edible agricultural products that contain nutrients.

Source:
FAO 1990 Unpublished data, Food and Agriculture Organization, Rome.

Table 3.5 Area under cereal production, cereal production and cereal imports, 1966–1968 and 1986–1988 (mean annual values)

Region/country	Major cereal crops[a]	Total cereal area harvested (10³ ha a⁻¹)		Cereal production (10³ t a⁻¹)			Cereal imports (10³ t a⁻¹)		Cereal imports per capita (kg a⁻¹)	
		1966–68	1986–88	1966–68	1986–88	% change	1966–68	1986–88	1966–68	1986–88
WORLD		679,317	707,433	1,129,895	1,802,239	60			22.3	45.9
AFRICA		61,780	73,904	55,954	83,554	49	7,628	27,310		
Algeria	w,b	2,513	2,746	1,515	2,082	37	783	4,868	62.1	210.7
Angola	m,w,s	631	968	514	364	-29	54	251	10.3	27.3
Benin	m,s	515	608	289	486	68	17	90	6.7	20.8
Botswana	s,m	129	159	42	49	16	52	135	91.4	118.8
Burkina Faso	s,m	2,013	2,714	1,040	1,876	80	22	115	4.1	13.8
Burundi	s,m	273	341	272	431	58	8	14	2.4	2.8
Cameroon	s,m	851	831	667	906	36	49	254	8.1	23.4
Cape Verde	m	15	26	8	16	108	9	59	35.1	170.3
Cent. African Rep.	m,s	114	134	89	125	40	11	38	6.4	14.0
Chad	s,r	1,077	1,161	717	733	2	6	51	1.7	9.8
Comoros	r,m	12	21	15	23	48	11	29	44.3	67.2
Congo	m,r	11	15	13	10	-22	21	99	18.9	48.7
Côte d'Ivoire	m,r,s	678	1,265	590	1,084	84	131	611	26.9	54.9
Djibouti			—				12	46	91.0	123.3
Egypt	m,w,r,s	1,922	1,813	6,890	9,041	31	2,583	8,745	83.5	174.4
Equatorial Guinea							6	8	20.5	21.3
Ethiopia	m,s,b,w	5,126	4,946	4,140	5,894	42	39	913	1.5	20.4
Gabon	m	6	7	9	11	30	11	56	22.2	52.9
Gambia	s,r,m	82	89	80	105	31	12	88	27.3	110.2
Ghana	m,s,b	614	1,084	585	1,027	76	120	194	14.8	14.3
Guinea	r,m	562	763	478	638	33	48	192	11.2	29.7
Guinea-Bissau	r,s,m	85	239	71	222	213	11	46	22.1	49.4
Kenya	m,s,w,b	1,728	1,813	2,368	3,164	34	69	174	6.7	7.9
Lesotho	m,s,w	299	245	217	161	-26	30	114	29.6	70.1
Liberia		136	237	145	295	104	48	117	38.5	50.5
Libya	b,w	576	427	162	282	74	218	1,549	123.9	378.3
Madagascar	r,m	1,125	1,344	1,847	2,409	30	32	201	5.1	18.5
Malawi	m,s	1,092	1,269	1,178	1,370	16	14	40	3.4	5.1
Mali	s,r,m	1,400	1,957	1,074	1,959	82	13	125	2.6	16.1
Mauritania	s,m	258	230	97	131	34	57	194	50.3	104.1
Mauritius	m	—	1	—	5		116	176	146.8	169.4
Morocco	b,w,m	4,720	5,233	4,003	6,736	68	740	1,830	52.4	78.5

Continued over

Table 3.5 Continued

Region/country	Major cereal crops[a]	Total cereal area harvested ($10^3\ ha\ a^{-1}$) 1966–68	Total cereal area harvested ($10^3\ ha\ a^{-1}$) 1986–88	Cereal production ($10^3\ t\ a^{-1}$) 1966–68	Cereal production ($10^3\ t\ a^{-1}$) 1986–88	% change	Cereal imports ($10^3\ t\ a^{-1}$) 1966–68	Cereal imports ($10^3\ t\ a^{-1}$) 1986–88	Cereal imports per capita ($kg\ a^{-1}$) 1966–68	Cereal imports per capita ($kg\ a^{-1}$) 1986–88
Mozambique	m,s,r	789	871	745	512	-31	67	383	7.6	26.3
Namibia	m,s	161	201	68	99	44				
Niger	s	2,418	4,514	1,172	1,898	62	8	92	2.0	13.5
Nigeria	s,m,r	10,592	10,191	6,974	10,878	56	188	766	3.1	7.2
Réunion	m	3	3	13	13	0	76	144	184.1	254.9
Rwanda	s,m	182	256	188	285	51	4	17	1.2	2.6
São Tomé & Príncipe	m	–	–	–	1	63	6	7	83.5	63.3
Senegal	s,m,r	1,210	1,215	663	950	43	252	465	61.3	66.9
Seychelles							5	10	105.5	145.4
Sierra Leone	r	357	375	470	523	11	56	130	22.3	33.9
Somalia	s,m	447	760	226	573	154	35	276	10.7	48.4
South Africa	w,m	6,963	6,811	8,313	11,230	35	565	403	27.1	12.2
St Helena							0	1	95.5	88.5
Sudan	s	2,168	6,402	1,623	3,522	117	195	697	15.2	30.2
Swaziland	m	103	71	58	106	83	12	39	30.0	54.1
Tanzania	m,s,r	1,706	3,174	1,164	3,779	225	70	174	5.7	7.3
Togo	m,s	537	524	265	412	55	11	86	6.3	26.3
Tunisia		1,145	1,081	770	962	25	334	1,532	69.2	201.1
Uganda	s,m	1,192	832	1,149	1,041	-9	41	22	4.6	1.4
Zaire	m,r	784	1,353	562	1,151	105	173	433	9.5	13.3
Zambia	m	1,131	745	966	1,517	57	63	149	16.5	20.6
Zimbabwe	m,s	1,328	1,839	1,446	2,466	71	114	65	24.2	7.2
NORTH AMERICA		95,673	94,837	250,783	343,316	37	3,303	11,647	10.8	28.4
Antigua & Barbuda		–	–	–	–		5	6	82.4	66.7
Bahamas	m	–	1	–	1	275	14	17	95.6	70.1
Barbados	m	–	1	1	2	82	28	66	120.1	259.0
Belize	m,r	8	15	8	26	83	12	12	105.6	65.7
Bermuda						250	4	4	71.3	71.0
Br. Virgin Is.		–	–	–	–		1	0	69.8	37.4
Canada	w,b,m	19,748	21,332	34,386	48,156	40	764	621	37.4	24.0
Cayman Is.		–	–	–	–		0	1	0.0	43.4
Costa Rica	r,m	125	134	188	296	57	79	216	50.1	83.0
Cuba	r,m	153	233	181	605	234	1,063	2,334	130.7	226.8

Continued below

Table 3.5 Continued

Region/country	Major cereal crops[a]	Total cereal area harvested (10³ ha a⁻¹)		Cereal production (10³ t a⁻¹)			Cereal imports (10³ t a⁻¹)		Cereal imports per capita (kg a⁻¹)	
		1966–68	1986–88	1966–68	1986–88	% change	1966–68	1986–88	1966–68	1986–88
Dominica	m	—	—	—	—	68	5	8	72.5	101.2
Dominican Rep.	r,m	110	155	225	587	162	102	607	25.1	90.4
El Salvador	m,s	333	407	429	685	60	98	203	30.1	41.0
Greenland		—	—	—	—	—	2	3	40.8	53.9
Grenada	m	—	—	—	—	17	9	9	92.9	90.1
Guadeloupe	m	—	—	1	—	-81	40	84	128.7	249.2
Guatemala	m,w	773	843	718	1,400	95	83	232	17.1	27.5
Haiti	m,s,r	464	364	498	410	-18	48	194	11.3	31.5
Honduras	m,s,r	324	381	392	559	43	48	140	19.9	30.0
Jamaica	m	5	4	5	6	18	233	395	129.7	164.5
Martinique							42	55	132.5	166.5
Mexico	m,s,w	9,778	9,856	13,327	22,366	68	55	4,385	1.1	53.6
Montserrat		—	—	—	—	116	1	1	91.6	88.5
Neth. Antilles							22	32	107.5	173.2
Nicaragua	m,s,r	303	297	323	537	66	63	166	33.5	47.4
Panama	r,m	237	182	237	295	25	44	80	31.0	35.3
Puerto Rico	r	7	—	11	3	-72	5	4		100.0
St Christopher & Nevis		—	—	—	—	77	7	17	74.1	119.3
St Lucia	m	—	—	—	—		1	1	131.7	83.9
St Pierre & Miquelon		—	—	—	—					
St Vincent & Grenadines	m	—	—	—	1	53	7	27	85.1	228.3
Trinidad & Tobago	r,m	5	4	12	9	-26	146	255	159.1	208.8
US Virgin Is.							8		145.9	
USA	w,m,s	63,299	60,626	198,394	267,372	35	266	1,471	1.3	6.0
SOUTH AMERICA		32,233	39,540	45,374	80,611	78	5,252	9,919	29.6	35.7
Argentina	w,m,s	11,905	9,523	17,730	23,561	33	59	8	2.6	0.2
Bolivia	m,w,r,b	422	604	448	809	80	184	337	45.7	50.0
Brazil	m,r	14,379	22,955	19,536	41,438	112	2,587	3,835	29.1	27.1
Chile	w,m,b,r	995	822	1,923	2,764	44	487	284	54.4	22.6
Colombia	m,r,s	1,306	1,330	1,846	3,296	78	263	861	13.4	29.2
Ecuador	m,r,b,w	628	838	570	1,325	132	82	417	14.9	42.1
French Guiana	r,m	—	3	—	12		5	10	111.9	115.0
Guyana	r	124	93	227	232	2	49	47	78.0	59.5
Paraguay	m,w,r	199	750	233	1,275	447	83	11	38.3	2.9
Peru	m,r,b,w	780	878	1,240	2,180	76	618	1,675	50.9	82.8

Continued over

Table 3.5 Continued

Region/country	Major cereal crops[a]	Total cereal area harvested (10³ ha a⁻¹)		Cereal production (10³ t a⁻¹)			Cereal imports (10³ t a⁻¹)		Cereal imports per capita (kg a⁻¹)	
		1966–68	1986–88	1966–68	1986–88	% change	1966–68	1986–88	1966–68	1986–88
Suriname	r	33	72	112	279	150	26	52	74.6	123.4
Uruguay	w,m,r,s	769	493	653	1,063	63	79	131	28.9	44.1
Venezuela	m,s,r	692	1,179	855	2,376	178	730	2,250	76.1	123.1
ASIA		285,869	305,079	420,672	781,217	86	39,198	86,618	20.4	29.8
Afghanistan	w,m,r	3,204	3,277	3,744	4,350	16	112	206	9.6	10.8
Bahrain							32	68	157.5	225.3
Bangladesh	r,w	9,726	10,569	16,167	24,175	50	1,033	2,095	16.8	19.7
Bhutan	m,r,w,s	81	121	116	193	66	22	29	23.8	21.5
Brunei	m	3	1	5	1	-69	13	36	118.2	151.5
Cambodia	r	2,282	1,717	2,841	2,149	-24	18	103	2.7	13.5
China	r,w,m	91,490	89,384	175,458	351,810	101	5,249	13,039	7.0	12.2
Cyprus	w,b	142	54	137	117	-15	67	438	112.3	644.7
Hong Kong		9	—	16	—	-100	668	791	174.3	141.1
India	r,s,w,m	95,872	101,717	92,678	167,355	81	8,993	1,074	17.6	1.3
Indonesia	r,m	10,924	13,081	17,762	46,406	161	655	1,818	6.0	10.6
Iran	w,b,r	7,222	9,446	6,288	12,351	96	305	4,610	11.8	98.0
Iraq	w,b	2,426	2,392	2,270	2,200	-3	151	4,006	17.8	234.8
Israel	w,b	143	118	222	269	22	920	1,835	337.4	419.6
Japan	r	4,102	2,590	20,312	14,733	-27	11,889	27,644	118.3	226.6
Jordan	w,b	321	116	287	109	-62	184	847	87.6	223.3
Korea	r,b	2,266	1,493	6,920	8,746	26	907	8,512	30.3	202.3
Korea, Dem.	r,s,m,b	1,570	2,521	4,562	11,528	153	369	533	28.8	25.0
Kuwait	b	—	1	—	3		126	410	217.8	220.4
Laos	r,m	862	600	801	1,263	58	78	72	30.6	18.9
Lebanon	w,b	87	13	84	24	-72	412	519	181.3	195.0
Macau							25	36	107.6	83.8
Malaysia	r	618	649	1,301	1,733	33	838	2,167	83.5	131.2
Maldives	s	—	—	—	1	-52	5	21	46.5	108.1
Mongolia		405	628	271	790	192	22	52	19.1	25.7
Myanmar q.v. Burma	r,m,w,s	5,087	5,130	7,663	14,401	88				
Nepal		1,842	2,810	3,195	4,688	47	1	43	0.0	2.5
Oman		3	1	4	1	-59	25	284	41.6	211.0
Pakistan	w,r,m	9,079	11,253	8,747	19,344	121	1,188	963	21.4	9.4
Philippines	m,r	5,465	7,034	5,980	13,217	121	717	1,108	21.1	19.0

Continued below

Table 3.5 Continued

Region/country	Major cereal crops[a]	Total cereal area harvested (10³ ha a⁻¹) 1966–68	1986–88	Cereal production (10³ t a⁻¹) 1966–68	1986–88	% change	Cereal imports (10³ t a⁻¹) 1966–68	1986–88	Cereal imports per capita (kg a⁻¹) 1966–68	1986–88
Qatar	r,w		1		3		19	101	219.4	305.0
Saudi Arabia	w,s	334	700	438	2,907	563	327	7,308	63.7	552.3
Singapore	r						743	898	376.0	343.6
Sri Lanka		592	822	1,196	2,444	104	958	804	81.8	49.2
Syria	b,w	1,565	2,839	1,216	3,493	187	306	1,120	53.9	99.5
Thailand	r,m	7,592	11,403	13,675	23,380	71	59	249	1.8	4.6
Turkey	w,b	13,040	13,724	16,479	29,842	81	87	690	2.6	13.1
United Arab Em.	w		1		5		40	506	239.2	348.3
Viet Nam	r,m	5,036	6,132	8,930	16,425	84	1,446	547	38.8	8.4
Yemen	s,w,b	1,092	830	825	713	-14	36	729	7.3	86.0
Yemen, Dem.	s,w,m	59	70	82	47	-42	155	306	110.1	134.7
EUROPE		73,745	70,390	185,454	293,580	58	46,060	42,682	102.3	86.3
Albania	w,b,m	328	348	474	1,016	114	84	19	42.5	6.2
Austria	w,b,m	905	1,008	2,877	5,144	79	602	107	82.1	14.1
Belgium	w,b	538	373	1,955	2,211	13	2,886	4,471	302.2	453.3
Bulgaria	w,b,m	2,236	2,060	6,214	7,864	27	305	1,271	36.7	141.4
Czechoslovakia	w,b,m	2,586	2,496	6,668	11,481	72	1,794	482	125.5	30.9
Denmark	w,b	1,643	1,558	6,299	7,752	23	702	304	145.2	59.3
Faeroe Is.							3	5	78.5	98.7
Finland	w,b	1,168	1,183	2,283	2,843	25	133	151	28.8	30.7
France	w,b,m	9,269	9,365	30,774	53,222	73	1,304	1,047	26.3	18.8
German Dem. Rep.	w,b	2,309	2,460	7,033	10,900	55	1,887	2,097	110.5	126.0
Germany, Fed. Rep.	w,b,m	4,999	4,752	17,307	25,529	48	6,595	4,604	111.2	75.3
Greece	w,b,m	1,705	1,464	3,009	5,114	70	270	980	31.1	98.0
Hungary	w,b,m	3,213	2,871	8,003	14,478	81	400	336	39.1	31.6
Iceland							24	24	120.0	98.2
Ireland	w,b	352	360	1,276	2,086	64	528	474	182.0	133.3
Italy	w,b,r,m	5,905	4,711	14,863	18,174	22	7,550	7,397	143.4	129.0
Malta	w,b	3	3	4	9	104	83	142	257.9	412.3
Netherlands	w,b	440	181	1,706	1,198	-30	3,859	5,127	306.4	349.7
Norway	w,b	231	338	649	1,171	80	727	466	192.1	111.4
Poland	w,b	8,416	8,353	16,669	25,200	51	2,121	2,760	66.2	73.3
Portugal	w,b,r,m	1,672	993	1,693	1,595	-6	705	1,593	77.4	156.8
Romania	w,b,m	6,694	6,213	13,394	31,525	135	30	603	1.6	26.3
Spain	w,b,m	7,182	7,774	10,496	20,290	93	3,058	2,868	93.4	73.9

Continued over

Table 3.5 Continued

Region/country	Major cereal crops[a]	Total cereal area harvested (10³ ha a⁻¹)		Cereal production (10³ t a⁻¹)			Cereal imports (10³ t a⁻¹)		Cereal imports per capita (kg a⁻¹)	
		1966–68	1986–88	1966–68	1986–88	% change	1966–68	1986–88	1966–68	1986–88
Sweden	w,b	1,406	1,376	4,320	5,241	21	175	198	22.3	23.7
Switzerland	w,b,m	170	183	631	1,004	59	1,200	875	200.2	134.0
UK	w,b	3,810	3,954	13,744	22,371	63	8,384	3,734	152.7	65.6
Yugoslavia	w,m	5,238	4,172	13,113	16,163	23	649	547	32.7	23.3
USSR	w,b,m	117,337	109,008	155,939	196,604	26	4,525	31,580	19.2	111.6
OCEANIA		12,679	14,676	15,720	23,356	49	280	547	15.6	21.7
American Samoa							2	5	67.6	135.8
Australia	w,b,s	12,504	14,437	15,115	22,335	48	3	27	0.3	1.6
Cook Is.							1	3	68.3	145.8
Fiji	r,m	10	13	18	29	56	50	86	102.1	119.3
French Polynesia							17	34	167.9	192.4
Kiribati							4	7	76.1	111.5
Nauru							1		246.1	
New Caledonia	w,s	1	1	1	2	96	13	29	128.9	190.1
New Zealand	w,b	163	221	582	985	69	105	99	38.8	29.8
Niue							0	0	68.5	34.7
Pacific Is. Tr. Tr.							8	8	95.3	51.3
Papua New Guinea	s,m	–	–	–	–	103	59	212	26.2	57.2
Solomon Is.	m	1	2	2	4	86	7	18	45.6	60.3
Tonga		–	1	1	1	11	4	7	54.7	72.7
Vanuatu	m	1	1	–	1	92	5	11	61.4	74.0
Wallis Is.							0	1	45.5	55.6

a Major cereal crops are defined as those occupying more than 5 per cent of the total land under cereal production; b = barley, m = maize, r = rice, s = sorghum and millet, w = wheat.

Annual average cereal yields (in t ha⁻¹) may be calculated by dividing annual average cereal production by the annual average cereal area harvested.
For more detailed notes on definitions and countries, refer to the most recent edition of the 'FAO Production Yearbook'.

Sources:
FAO July 1990 Unpublished data, Food and Agriculture Organization, Rome.
Winrock International 1987 Agricultural Development Indicators, Winrock International, Institute for Agricultural Development, Morrilton.

Table 3.6 Consumption of fertilizers in selected countries, 1966–1968 and 1986–1988 (mean annual values)

Region/country	Total consumption of fertilizers (10^3 t a^{-1})		Consumption per cropping area (kg ha^{-1} a^{-1})		Consumption of nitrogen fertilizers (10^3 t a^{-1})		Consumption of phosphate fertilizers (10^3 t a^{-1})		Consumption of potash fertilizers (10^3 t a^{-1})	
	1966–68	1986–88	1966–68	1986–88	1966–68	1986–88	1966–68	1986–88	1966–68	1986–88
WORLD	56,159	139,174	40.6	94.4	24,212	75,549	18,197	36,494	13,730	27,130
AFRICA	1,263	3,586	8.2	19.3	608	1,974	460	1,157	195	454
Algeria	57	228	8.4	30.2	17	90	25	92	15	46
Angola	7	11	1.9	3.0	5	4	1	3	1	3
Benin	2	9	1.4	4.7	1	3	–	4	1	2
Botswana	2	1	2.0	0.6	2	–	–	0	0	0
Burkina Faso	–	16	0.1	5.0	0	7	–	5	0	4
Burundi	–	3	0.1	2.1	–	1	0	1	0	–
Cameroon	4	46	2.4	6.5	9	22	1	11	4	12
Cape Verde	0	–	0.0	2.2	0	–	0	–	0	–
Cent. African Rep.	1	1	0.7	0.3	1	1	–	–	–	–
Chad	1	5	0.3	1.7	1	2	–	2	–	1
Congo	3	2	20.5	9.8	1	–	–	–	2	1
Côte d'Ivoire	13	34	4.7	9.4	4	7	2	7	6	21
Djibouti	0	–	0.0	–	0	–	0	–	0	0
Egypt	297	933	106.1	364.7	256	711	39	190	1	32
Equatorial Guinea	1	0	5.0	0.0	1	0	–	0	–	0
Ethiopia	4	61	0.3	4.3	1	24	2	37	0	0
Gabon	0	2	0.0	3.9	0	1	0	–	0	1
Gambia	–	3	3.4	19.3	–	2	–	1	–	1
Ghana	1	10	0.5	3.6	–	5	1	2	–	2
Guinea	3	1	4.7	1.0	1	0	1	0	2	0
Guinea-Bissau	0	0	0.0	0.0	0	0	0	0	0	0
Kenya	32	116	16.6	48.4	12	59	18	49	2	9
Lesotho	1	4	1.6	13.2	–	1	1	4	–	–
Liberia	1	3	3.8	7.7	1	1	0	–	0	1
Libya	9	83	4.3	38.8	3	27	5	54	1	1
Madagascar	7	9	3.0	3.0	3	5	2	2	2	2
Malawi	6	46	3.0	19.2	4	27	1	12	1	7
Mali	2	20	1.1	9.6	1	11	1	5	0	4
Mauritania	–	2	0.4	8.9	0	1	–	–	0	–
Mauritius	21	29	213.1	269.7	9	11	4	4	8	14
Morocco	78	318	10.6	36.6	29	142	33	120	16	56
Mozambique	5	5	2.0	1.5	4	2	–	2	1	1

Continued over

Table 3.6 Continued

Region/country	Total consumption of fertilizers (10^3 t a^{-1})		Consumption per cropping area (kg ha^{-1} a^{-1})		Consumption of nitrogen fertilizers (10^3 t a^{-1})		Consumption of phosphate fertilizers (10^3 t a^{-1})		Consumption of potash fertilizers (10^3 t a^{-1})	
	1966–68	1986–88	1966–68	1986–88	1966–68	1986–88	1966–68	1986–88	1966–68	1986–88
Niger	–	2	0.1	0.6	–	1	–	–	–	–
Nigeria	8	289	0.3	9.2	4	149	3	96	1	44
Réunion	15	14	272.6	260.8	5	5	3	4	8	6
Rwanda	–	1	0.1	1.1	–	1	–	–	0	–
Senegal	19	23	4.2	4.3	5	8	9	9	5	7
Seychelles	0	0	0.0	0.0	0	0	0	0	0	0
Sierra Leone	1	2	0.6	0.9	–	1	1	1	0	–
Somalia	2	3	1.9	2.5	2	2	–	–	–	–
South Africa	469	786	35.8	59.7	124	357	256	307	89	122
Sudan	37	60	3.3	4.8	37	59	1	1	0	0
Swaziland	6	9	36.9	52.5	3	4	1	2	1	2
Tanzania	9	45	2.0	8.6	4	30	2	12	3	3
Togo	–	11	0.1	7.4	0	4	–	3	0	3
Tunisia	25	104	5.9	21.7	7	48	15	52	3	4
Uganda	5	1	0.9	0.1	2	–	2	–	1	–
Zaire	3	4	0.4	0.5	2	2	–	1	1	1
Zambia	15	86	3.1	16.4	8	57	5	20	2	8
Zimbabwe	81	150	36.3	53.9	39	79	23	41	19	30
NORTH AMERICA	15,333	22,830	60.2	83.4	6,877	12,629	4,680	4,947	3,776	5,254
Bahamas	1	1	88.9	50.0	–	–	–	–	–	–
Barbados	6	3	193.3	101.0	3	1	–	1	3	1
Belize	2	4	38.1	74.3	–	2	1	1	–	1
Bermuda	0	–			–	–	–	–	–	–
Canada	807	2,173	19.3	47.2	280	1,164	361	625	165	384
Costa Rica	36	94	73.6	177.8	20	55	6	13	10	25
Cuba	361	639	185.5	191.8	162	313	98	82	101	244
Dominica	0	3	0.0	174.5	0	1	0	1	0	1
Dominican Rep.	17	74	15.5	50.2	14	40	1	18	2	15
El Salvador	52	80	82.0	109.4	33	57	14	20	6	3
Guadeloupe	10	9	220.5	283.1	2	3	2	3	5	3
Guatemala	33	124	21.4	67.0	19	82	11	28	3	14
Haiti	–	2	0.2	2.4	–	1	–	1	0	–
Honduras	15	32	9.7	18.0	9	16	2	6	4	11
Jamaica	21	24	81.9	88.2	9	12	3	4	9	8

Continued below

Table 3.6 Continued

Region/country	Total consumption of fertilizers (10³ t a⁻¹)		Consumption per cropping area (kg ha⁻¹ a⁻¹)		Consumption of nitrogen fertilizers (10³ t a⁻¹)		Consumption of phosphate fertilizers (10³ t a⁻¹)		Consumption of potash fertilizers (10³ t a⁻¹)	
	1966–68	1986–88	1966–63	1986–88	1966–68	1986–88	1966–68	1986–88	1966–68	1986–88
Martinique	16	21	671.0	1,039.4	6	6	3	4	7	11
Mexico	442	1,814	18.9	73.4	309	1,313	106	413	27	88
Nicaragua	25	65	20.7	51.2	15	51	8	11	2	3
Panama	12	37	21.1	64.8	10	21	1	6	1	10
St Christopher & Nevis	1	3	87.5	211.9	–	1	–	1	1	2
St Lucia	2	2	106.4	96.2	1	2	–	–	1	1
St Vincent & Grenadines	2	4	96.3	219.2	1	3	–	1	1	1
Trinidad & Tobago	8	4	78.6	35.4	5	2	1	1	2	1
US Virgin Is.	–	1	72.1	185.7	0	1	–	–	–	0
USA	13,465	17,617	75.3	92.8	5,979	9,481	4,061	3,708	3,425	4,428
SOUTH AMERICA	972	5,687	9.2	40.4	336	1,837	409	2,165	227	1,685
Argentina	53	161	2.0	4.5	31	96	25	51	7	14
Bolivia	2	7	1.1	2.0	1	4	1	2	–	1
Brazil	442	3,757	8.4	48.4	107	864	196	1,565	138	1,328
Chile	103	296	26.1	68.0	34	149	57	126	12	21
Colombia	141	483	28.0	90.7	48	240	53	111	40	131
Ecuador	44	62	17.2	23.4	23	26	15	19	5	18
French Guiana	0	1	0.0	158.7	0	1	0	–	0	0
Guyana	9	16	24.2	33.1	6	10	1	4	2	2
Paraguay	2	12	2.2	5.4	–	3	2	6	–	4
Peru	70	206	26.5	55.4	53	145	11	37	6	24
Suriname	2	10	44.6	146.3	1	6	–	2	–	2
Uruguay	52	61	36.6	46.1	9	18	38	41	4	3
Venezuela	44	615	12.5	159.6	21	277	10	201	13	137
ASIA	8,769	46,139	20.1	102.1	5,321	31,325	2,326	10,753	1,122	4,061
Afghanistan	9	66	1.1	8.2	8	48	1	17	0	0
Bahrain	0	1	0.0	553.3	0	1	0	–	0	–
Bangladesh	93	713	10.3	77.3	68	483	20	175	6	55
Bhutan	0	–	0.0	0.8	0	–	0	0	0	0
Brunei	0	1	0.0	98.1	0	–	0	–	0	–
Cambodia	3	–	1.1	0.1	2	0	1	0	–	–
China	2,777	21,321	27.0	221.4	2,094	16,005	668	4,158	15	1,157
Cyprus	22	21	135.4	132.9	10	12	9	8	3	1
India	1,467	9,519	9.0	56.2	994	6,229	322	2,359	151	931

Continued over

Table 3.6 Continued

Region/country	Total consumption of fertilizers (10³ t a⁻¹) 1966–68	Total consumption of fertilizers (10³ t a⁻¹) 1986–88	Consumption per cropping area (kg ha⁻¹ a⁻¹) 1966–68	Consumption per cropping area (kg ha⁻¹ a⁻¹) 1986–88	Consumption of nitrogen fertilizers (10³ t a⁻¹) 1966–68	Consumption of nitrogen fertilizers (10³ t a⁻¹) 1986–88	Consumption of phosphate fertilizers (10³ t a⁻¹) 1966–68	Consumption of phosphate fertilizers (10³ t a⁻¹) 1986–88	Consumption of potash fertilizers (10³ t a⁻¹) 1966–68	Consumption of potash fertilizers (10³ t a⁻¹) 1986–88
Indonesia	181	2,246	10.2	105.8	138	1,438	38	579	6	229
Iran	67	972	4.3	65.6	42	528	23	437	2	6
Iraq	9	218	1.8	39.9	6	150	2	65	–	3
Israel	44	98	107.6	224.9	27	52	12	18	6	28
Japan	2,078	2,011	360.8	427.2	766	667	663	748	649	595
Jordan	4	18	12.1	49.6	2	11	1	5	2	2
Korea	463	842	200.5	393.2	268	430	126	193	69	219
Korea, Dem.	215	771	109.2	321.9	128	614	64	141	23	17
Kuwait	0	1	0.0	125.8	0	1	0	0	0	0
Laos	1	–	1.4	0.3	1	–	1	–	–	–
Lebanon	22	20	72.7	66.6	12	11	7	6	3	4
Malaysia	118	713	27.6	146.2	43	261	45	151	30	302
Mongolia	0	21	0.0	16.0	0	13	0	3	0	5
Myanmar q.v. Burma	20	137	1.9	13.6	11	98	7	31	2	8
Nepal	3	52	1.7	22.2	2	37	1	14	–	1
Oman	0	3	0.0	55.4	0	1	0	1	0	1
Pakistan	182	1,748	9.4	83.9	163	1,313	18	398	1	37
Philippines	124	460	17.7	57.9	65	347	32	63	28	50
Qatar	0	1	0.0	149.2	0	1	0	0	0	0
Saudi Arabia	4	465	5.5	393.4	2	219	2	199	0	47
Singapore	3	5	210.5	1,811.1	1	2	1	1	1	3
Sri Lanka	112	203	59.7	107.3	48	104	26	41	38	58
Syria	24	255	3.9	45.5	17	140	6	106	1	9
Thailand	89	632	6.8	31.6	46	367	33	162	10	102
Turkey	283	1,637	10.7	59.3	140	1,058	135	532	8	47
United Arab Em.	0	5	0.0	125.6	0	3	0	1	0	1
Viet Nam	92	492	15.3	74.5	54	372	27	73	11	46
Yemen	–	14	–	10.0	–	12	0	1	0	–
Yemen, Dem.	0	1	0.0	7.6	0	1	0	–	0	0
EUROPE	20,625	32,145	139.2	228.3	7,873	15,740	6,571	7,884	6,181	8,521
Albania	21	96	37.2	134.4	10	70	9	23	2	3
Austria	332	323	198.3	214.1	100	141	129	78	103	104
Belgium	503	419	520.9	513.0	170	198	153	88	179	133
Bulgaria	642	819	140.8	198.0	332	469	282	241	28	109
Czechoslovakia	997	1,617	186.0	315.1	306	626	267	481	424	511

Continued below

Table 3.6 Continued

Region/country	Total consumption of fertilizers (10³ t a⁻¹)		Consumption per cropping area (kg ha⁻¹ a⁻¹)		Consumption of nitrogen fertilizers (10³ t a⁻¹)		Consumption of phosphate fertilizers (10³ t a⁻¹)		Consumption of potash fertilizers (10³ t a⁻¹)	
	1966–68	1986–88	1966–68	1986–88	1966–68	1986–88	1966–68	1986–88	1966–68	1986–88
Denmark	534	621	197.5	239.9	232	375	124	98	178	147
Finland	378	508	149.1	210.4	109	211	153	152	116	145
France	3,740	5,896	189.1	308.1	1,122	2,576	1,485	1,430	1,132	1,890
German Dem. Rep.	1,396	1,704	284.3	345.0	446	785	348	342	602	577
Germany, Fed. Rep.	2,798	3,137	366.0	420.0	924	1,573	794	669	1,081	895
Greece	294	644	73.3	163.5	161	408	108	176	15	59
Hungary	510	1,406	90.6	265.9	242	619	151	345	117	442
Iceland	22	23	3,589.1	2,919.4	11	12	6	6	4	5
Ireland	327	684	230.4	694.1	55	344	148	147	123	193
Italy	1,131	2,152	74.3	177.3	490	994	465	723	177	436
Malta	–	1	29.7	44.5	–	–	–	–	–	–
Netherlands	574	646	619.5	701.8	340	466	106	81	128	99
Norway	176	227	207.7	264.7	67	111	51	46	58	70
Poland	1,851	3,495	118.9	236.0	606	1,415	461	914	783	1,166
Portugal	154	282	40.9	74.8	91	153	54	84	19	45
Romania	421	1,377	39.9	129.0	275	719	129	427	17	232
Spain	950	1,956	47.2	95.9	507	1,110	351	520	103	326
Sweden	425	391	137.9	133.3	179	235	129	75	117	80
Switzerland	134	176	339.0	427.3	32	72	45	40	58	65
UK	1,732	2,522	240.5	360.2	841	1,553	461	438	480	531
Yugoslavia	523	1,023	63.3	131.7	225	504	161	261	137	258
USSR	7,654	27,032	33.3	116.2	3,066	11,616	2,517	8,491	2,071	6,924
OCEANIA	1,522	1,756	35.8	36.0	130	428	1,234	1,097	157	231
Australia	1,120	1,353	27.4	28.8	119	376	929	831	73	146
Fiji	6	23	27.6	95.0	4	11	1	9	–	4
French Polynesia	0	1	0.0	12.0	0	–	0	–	0	–
New Caledonia	0	1	0.0	50.0	0	–	0	–	0	–
New Zealand	335	365	769.8	717.8	7	34	304	255	84	76
Papua New Guinea	1	14	2.2	35.2	–	7	–	2	–	4
Tonga	0	0	0.0	0.0	0	0	0	0	0	0

The mean annual consumption of fertilizers represents the quantity of nutrients applied to cropland in the form of nitrogen (N), phosphate (P₂O₅) and potash (K₂O).

The fertilizer year is from July 1 to June 30; thus data refer to the year beginning in July. For further information relating to these data, please refer to the most recent edition of the 'FAO Fertilizer Yearbook'.

Source: FAO 1990 Unpublished data, Food and Agriculture Organization, Rome.

Table 3.7 Consumption of pesticides in selected countries, 1975–1977 and 1982–1984 (mean annual values)

Region/country	All pesticides (t a^{-1} active ingredient)		Insecticides (t a^{-1} active ingredient)		Fungicides (t a^{-1} active ingredient)		Herbicides (t a^{-1} active ingredient)	
	1975–77	1982–84	1975–77	1982–84	1975–77	1982–84	1975–77	1982–84
WORLD	1,908,059	2,153,718	467,451	448,008	789,239	858,713	632,526	832,336
AFRICA	68,181	66,608	25,570	30,362	34,758	34,632	350	1,614
Algeria	16,457	21,400	2,540	4,200	13,567	16,100	350	1,100
Burundi	22	59	20	59	3			
Egypt	26,970	19,567	14,876	11,967	12,093	7,600		
Ethiopia	200	993	200	867		127		
Gambia		67		67				
Kenya	623	1,307	623	1,307				
Liberia	1,223	310	1,200	237	23	73		
Libya	870	2,017	237	583	633	1,433		
Madagascar		1,630		1,630				
Mali		683		633		50		
Mauritania	7		7					
Morocco	1,483	3,350	417	1,183	1,067	2,167		
Niger	451	106	413	106	34			
Nigeria		2,667		2,667				
South Africa	19,292	11,053	4,755	4,003	7,037	6,567		483
Swaziland	5		5					
Tunisia		1,330		827		503		
Zimbabwe	577	69	277	27	300	12		30
NORTH AMERICA	529,194	484,052	144,986	113,519	143,753	145,408	238,616	224,764
Canada	26,928	54,767	5,160	5,700	2,322	6,000	18,875	43,067
Costa Rica	3,027	3,667	2,433	3,000	317	410	277	257
Cuba	7,817	9,567	4,200	5,133	1,600	2,667	751	1,767
Dominican Rep.	1,961	3,297	1,250	1,733	513	1,130	197	433
Guatemala	4,627	5,117	1,419	1,737	2,625	2,833	582	547
Honduras	940	859	552	393	257	290	131	23
Jamaica	861	1,420	416	883	433	537	12	
Mexico	19,148	27,630	11,307	15,916	6,147	7,671	1,694	3,834
Nicaragua	2,943	2,003	798	600	1,823	1,050	322	353
Panama	1,542	2,393	1,050	1,757	383	487	109	150
USA	459,400	373,333	116,400	76,667	127,333	122,333	215,667	174,333
SOUTH AMERICA	108,324	99,350	48,325	31,945	29,525	29,159	27,721	38,199
Argentina	7,448	14,313	2,747	3,545	1,567	4,189	3,135	6,548
Bolivia	612	833	293	410	143	207	175	217
Brazil	59,292	46,698	27,682	13,192	17,155	14,589	14,455	18,918
Chile	1,838	1,800	441	483	978	843	419	473
Colombia	19,344	16,100	10,969	7,067	4,558	4,300	3,817	4,733
Ecuador	5,445	3,110	654	617	797	843	1,241	1,650
Guyana	705	658	152	147	481	433	71	78
Paraguay	2,957	3,423	1,483	1,893	1,250	1,217	224	313
Peru	2,370	2,753	903	1,210	350	527	1,117	1,017
Uruguay	1,390	1,517	300	331	822	351	267	819
Venezuela	6,923	8,143	2,700	3,050	1,423	1,660	2,800	3,433
ASIA	284,476	315,910	126,429	140,229	123,087	128,306	31,530	39,663
Bangladesh		234		181				53
Cambodia	1,593	833	560	660	833	173	200	

Continued opposite

Table 3.7   Continued

Region/country	All pesticides (t a^{-1} active ingredient)		Insecticides (t a^{-1} active ingredient)		Fungicides (t a^{-1} active ingredient)		Herbicides (t a^{-1} active ingredient)	
	1975–77	1982–84	1975–77	1982–84	1975–77	1982–84	1975–77	1982–84
China	150,467	159,267	48,067	52,600	89,700	92,967	12,700	13,700
India	52,506	53,087	41,429	40,221	6,752	9,959	1,066	2,842
Indonesia	18,687	16,344	16,487	15,597	2,200	747		
Israel	600	847	93	147	423	537	83	163
Japan	33,960	32,000	3,133	8,267	18,367	10,533	12,460	13,200
Korea, Dem.	1,333		433		733		167	
Korea	4,675	12,273	1,107	1,403	1,441	1,279	2,127	2,358
Myanmar q.v. Burma	3,721	15,300	3,658	7,467	5	7,833		
Pakistan	2,120	1,856	2,015	1,546	50	210	55	55
Sri Lanka		697		338		16		343
Thailand	13,120	22,289	8,569	11,337	1,767	3,636	2,672	6,949
Viet Nam	1,693	883	877	467	817	417		
EUROPE	506,830	585,405	53,154	57,806	258,795	277,178	191,562	243,878
Albania	4,510	5,183	400	333	2,733	2,900	1,377	1,950
Austria	3,449	4,548	345	389	1,526	1,722	1,550	2,352
Belgium	8,847	13,263	780	1,160	3,567	5,337	4,500	6,767
Bulgaria	28,287	32,400	2,100	2,967	22,453	23,367	3,733	6,067
Czechoslovakia	13,967	14,970	1,126	1,400	2,240	2,271	8,852	10,630
Denmark	4,998	7,729	452	473	570	2,058	3,975	5,061
Finland	1,768	2,639	107	192	81	101	1,525	2,347
France	83,017	98,733	10,017	10,833	33,933	46,700	39,067	41,200
German Dem. Rep.	11,900	14,133	1,133	1,283	2,000	2,233	8,767	10,617
Germany, Fed. Rep.	23,693	29,836	1,593	2,051	5,433	7,504	16,667	18,587
Greece	30,570	29,240	2,469	2,140	27,106	22,400	996	4,700
Hungary	26,267	27,595	2,700	2,633	11,367	10,967	12,200	12,133
Ireland	1,721	2,250	78	107	300	497	1,343	1,647
Italy	83,724	98,496	10,700	10,467	56,233	60,633	15,667	25,467
Netherlands	6,593	9,670	1,413	1,887	1,797	2,150	3,383	5,633
Norway	1,494	1,508	34	28	95	93	1,331	1,364
Poland	11,360	15,277	2,656	2,925	1,850	4,768	6,526	7,487
Portugal	24,375	16,016	648	579	22,846	12,502	881	2,900
Romania	29,397	17,237	4,367	970	12,067	8,067	12,963	8,200
Spain	55,267	71,533	5,167	9,633	33,567	36,533	16,533	25,367
Sweden	5,454	5,736	427	293	1,540	755	3,487	4,678
Switzerland	1,945	1,699	138	150	1,041	722	767	827
UK	25,137	34,147	703	913	4,700	9,167	19,733	24,067
Yugoslavia	19,091	31,567	3,600	4,000	9,751	13,733	5,739	13,833
USSR	348,767	535,400	65,500	69,333	186,333	230,067	90,933	236,000
OCEANIA	62,289	66,993	3,487	4,813	12,988	13,963	45,814	48,217
Australia	60,638	65,200	3,338	4,667	12,367	13,200	44,933	47,333
New Zealand	1,651	1,793	149	147	621	763	881	883

Active ingredients are those chemicals having pesticidal properties. In a formulated pesticide, active ingredients are often mixed with inert ingredients which aid or dilute delivery of the active ingredients.
Totals may not tally due to rounding or may include tonnage of active ingredients that are not otherwise identified. Regional and world totals include only the listed countries.
The pesticide data presented in the above table were compiled by UNIDO. Available FAO statistics on national pesticide use for the period 1975–1984 were supplemented with UNIDO estimates based on extrapolation and, in some cases, on an econometric need model. Further details of the calculation method are given in the source document.

Sources:
UNIDO 1988 *Global Overview of the Pesticide Industry Sub-sector*, Sectoral Working Paper prepared by the Industrial Statistics and Sectoral Surveys Branch, Policy and Perspectives Division, United Nations Industrial Development Organization, Vienna.
UNIDO 1988 Unpublished data, United Nations Industrial Development Organization, Vienna.

Table 3.8 Irrigated land area, 1966–1968 and 1986–1988 (mean annual values)

Region/country	Area of irrigated land (10³ ha)		Irrigated land as % of arable land		Region/country	Area of irrigated land (10³ ha)		Irrigated land as % of arable land	
	1966–68	1986–88	1966–68	1986–88		1966–68	1986–88	1966–68	1986–88
WORLD	156,738	226,626	11	15	Costa Rica	26	113	5	22
					Cuba	378	865	19	26
AFRICA	8,502	11,033	5	6	Dominican Rep.	120	225	11	15
					El Salvador	20	116	3	16
Algeria	235	357	3	5	Guadeloupe	2	3	5	9
Benin	2	6	–	–					
Botswana	1	2	–	–	Guatemala	49	77	3	4
Burkina Faso	3	15	–	–	Haiti	46	70	6	8
Burundi	18	69	2	5	Honduras	66	87	4	5
					Jamaica	24	34	9	13
Cameroon	5	24	–	–	Martinique	1	6	4	30
Cape Verde	2	2	5	5					
Chad	5	10	–	–	Mexico	3,317	5,120	14	21
Congo	0	4	0	2	Nicaragua	24	84	2	7
Côte d'Ivoire	12	58	–	2	Panama	18	30	3	5
					Puerto Rico	39	39	15	30
Egypt	2,794	2,556	100	100	St Lucia	1	1	6	6
Ethiopia	153	162	1	1					
Gambia	6	12	5	7	St Vincent & Grenadines	1	1	6	6
Ghana	2	8	–	–	Trinidad & Tobago	12	22	13	18
Guinea	5	20	1	3	USA	15,500	18,102	9	10
Kenya	20	46	1	2	SOUTH AMERICA	5,206	8,525	5	6
Liberia	0	2	0	1					
Libya	158	238	8	11	Argentina	1,177	1,720	4	5
Madagascar	330	877	14	29	Bolivia	78	162	4	5
Malawi	3	18	–	1	Brazil	677	2,500	1	3
					Chile	1,123	1,258	28	29
Mali	67	200	4	10	Colombia	242	492	5	9
Mauritania	8	12	3	6					
Mauritius	14	17	15	16	Ecuador	463	545	18	21
Morocco	905	1,255	12	14	Guyana	111	129	30	26
Mozambique	20	105	1	3	Paraguay	40	66	4	3
					Peru	1,073	1,230	41	33
Namibia	4	4	1	1	Suriname	20	57	55	86
Niger	16	31	1	1					
Nigeria	800	855	3	3	Uruguay	42	104	3	8
Réunion	5	5	9	9	Venezuela	161	263	5	7
Rwanda	4	4	1	–					
					ASIA	101,327	141,610	23	31
Senegal	97	175	2	3					
Sierra Leone	3	31	–	2	Afghanistan	2,280	2,660	29	33
Somalia	95	112	10	11	Bahrain	1	1	50	50
South Africa	923	1,128	7	9	Bangladesh	841	2,172	9	24
Sudan	1,580	1,870	14	15	Bhutan	14	33	14	25
					Brunei	0	1	0	14
Swaziland	42	62	27	38					
Tanzania	32	147	1	3	Cambodia	100	91	3	3
Togo	3	7	–	–	China	34,887	44,335	34	46
Tunisia	80	270	2	6	Cyprus	30	32	19	20
Uganda	4	9	–	–	Hong Kong	8	3	62	35
					India	26,917	41,773	16	25
Zaire	0	9	0	–					
Zambia	4	30	–	1	Indonesia	4,202	7,387	24	35
Zimbabwe	42	208	2	7	Iran	5,000	5,743	32	39
					Iraq	1,403	2,013	28	37
NORTH AMERICA	20,039	25,797	8	9	Israel	158	214	39	49
					Japan	3,415	2,910	59	62
Belize	0	2	0	4					
Canada	395	798	1	2					

Continued opposite

Table 3.8   Continued

Region/country	Area of irrigated land (10^3 ha)		Irrigated land as % of arable land		Region/country	Area of irrigated land (10^3 ha)		Irrigated land as % of arable land	
	1966–68	1986–88	1966–68	1986–88		1966–68	1986–88	1966–68	1986–88
Jordan	33	57	11	16	Bulgaria	959	1,247	21	30
Korea	1,177	1,346	51	63	Czechoslovakia	120	265	2	5
Korea, Dem.	500	1,173	25	49	Denmark	75	420	3	16
Kuwait	0	2	0	50	Finland	9	62	–	3
Laos	16	120	2	13	France	720	1,327	4	7
Lebanon	67	86	22	29	German Dem. Rep.	132	150	3	3
Malaysia	233	338	5	7	Germany, Fed. Rep.	273	325	4	4
Mongolia	5	46	1	3	Greece	635	1,154	16	29
Myanmar q.v. Burma	790	1,045	8	10	Hungary	244	161	4	3
Nepal	107	657	6	28	Italy	2,500	3,050	16	25
Oman	25	41	89	86	Malta	1	1	7	8
Pakistan	12,528	15,927	65	76	Netherlands	350	540	38	59
Philippines	760	1,477	11	19	Norway	29	93	3	11
Saudi Arabia	358	425	44	36	Poland	265	100	2	1
Sri Lanka	403	562	21	30	Portugal	621	633	15	17
Syria	507	652	8	12	Romania	432	3,306	4	31
Thailand	1,785	3,986	14	20	Spain	2,340	3,299	12	16
Turkey	1,550	2,187	6	8	Sweden	24	108	1	4
United Arab Em.	4	5	40	13	Switzerland	24	25	6	6
Viet Nam	980	1,803	16	27	UK	100	155	1	2
					Yugoslavia	118	161	1	2
Yemen	195	250	15	18					
Yemen, Dem.	49	58	48	49	USSR	10,020	20,578	4	9
EUROPE	10,206	16,995	7	12	OCEANIA	1,438	2,089	3	4
Albania	230	410	41	57	Australia	1,352	1,819	3	4
Austria	4	4	–	–	Fiji	1	1	–	–
Belgium	1	1	–	–	New Zealand	85	269	17	53

Irrigated land refers to areas purposefully provided with water, either several times or only once during the year. Irrigated land includes areas flooded by river water for crop production or pasture improvement.
Regional aggregates include listed countries only.

Source:
FAO 1990 Unpublished data, Food and Agriculture Organization, Rome.

Table 3.9 Livestock populations, 1967–1969 and 1987–1989 (mean annual values)

Region/country	Cattle[a] No. of animals (10³) 1987–89	Cattle[a] % change since 1967–69	Sheep and goats No. of animals (10³) 1987–89	Sheep and goats % change since 1967–69	Pigs No. of animals (10³) 1987–89	Pigs % change since 1967–69	Equines[b] No. of animals (10³) 1987–89	Equines[b] % change since 1967–69	Buffaloes and camels No. of animals (10³) 1987–89	Buffaloes and camels % change since 1967–69
WORLD	1,271,390	20	1,681,889	14	841,089	55	117,584	8	157,507	29
AFRICA	179,525	24	367,568	24	12,936	94	18,663	14	16,726	27
Algeria	1,484	77	17,522	77	5	94	675	6	133	-24
Angola	3,400	57	1,240	47	480	52	6	33	0	
Benin	914	69	1,821	64	648	99	6	73	0	
Botswana	2,305	62	1,720	77	11	22	174	277	0	
Burkina Faso	2,804	15	8,167	113	500	275	404	43	5	0
Burundi	388	-37	1,097	70	80	456	0		0	
Cameroon	4,471	129	5,821	67	1,238	280	63	-54	0	
Cape Verde	12	-13	82	59	70	232	8	-43	0	
Cent. African Rep.	2,306	289	1,287	123	383	364	0	-100	0	
Chad	4,059	-11	4,487	7	12	149	387	-14	509	41
Comoros	85	35	105	19	0		4	42	0	
Congo	70	136	250	175	48	97	0		0	
Côte d'Ivoire	959	161	3,000	91	450	192	2	0	0	
Djibouti	71	266	914	23	0		8	97	57	182
Egypt	1,923	–	2,788	-7	15	23	1,947	48	2,671	33
Equatorial Guinea	5	51	43	26	5	18	0		0	
Ethiopia	27,633	6	42,000	-1	19	47	7,900	21	1,060	9
Gabon	9	141	147	45	154	57	0		0	
Gambia	300	36	398	94	13	84	27		0	
Ghana	1,299	53	4,067	57	523	145	15	-35	0	
Guinea	1,800	35	920	33	50	108	2	-30	0	
Guinea-Bissau	340	48	415	80	290	74	4	2	0	
Kenya	13,051	68	13,227	47	97	61	2	0	790	63
Lesotho	529	23	2,470	10	72	10	246	82	0	
Liberia	42	62	475	70	140	80	0		0	
Libya	215	90	6,715	118	0		107	-28	185	-20
Madagascar	10,234	20	1,768	44	1,455	191	–	-91	0	
Malawi	1,013	118	1,160	60	210	33	1	115	0	
Mali	4,736	-5	10,943	1	59	105	517	-24	222	-1
Mauritania	1,237	-46	7,317	4	0		166	-24	807	17
Mauritius	31	-34	102	37	11	179	–	–	–	14
Morocco	3,293	-4	21,367	-7	9	-51	1,547	-8	54	-76
Mozambique	1,360	15	494	-14	160	20	20	17	0	
Namibia	2,047	-15	8,924	65	48	93	123	32	0	
Niger	3,500	-19	11,040	22	37	75	807	58	418	18
Nigeria	12,200	9	39,200	17	1,300	63	950	-22	18	2
Réunion	19	-33	46	190	90	20	–	-89	0	
Rwanda	604	-9	1,419	135	101	157	0		0	
Senegal	2,275	-8	4,953	103	470	434	497	40	8	-54
Sierra Leone	330	15	510	91	50	90	0		0	
Somalia	4,990	37	33,500	47	10	74	49	10	6,660	47
South Africa	11,823	10	35,633	-21	1,462	9	454	-22	0	
Sudan	22,500	92	32,667	65	0		681	10	2,917	15
Swaziland	650	25	354	29	19	68	16	-8	0	
Tanzania										

Continued opposite

Table 3.9 Continued

Region/country	Cattle[a] No. of animals (10³) 1987–89	% change since 1967–69	Sheep and goats No. of animals (10³) 1987–89	% change since 1967–69	Pigs No. of animals (10³) 1987–89	% change since 1967–69	Equines[b] No. of animals (10³) 1987–89	% change since 1967–69	Buffaloes and camels No. of animals (10³) 1987–89	% change since 1967–69
Togo	238	36	2,144	82	244	6	4	57	0	
Tunisia	606	-5	6,107	3	4	-26	353	10	184	-26
Uganda	3,909	4	4,468	68	453	1,061	17	1	0	
Zaire	1,410	68	3,912	55	795	40	0	-100	0	
Zambia	2,768	89	499	64	193	104	2	50	0	
Zimbabwe	6,075	42	2,836	64	231	37	125	37	0	
NORTH AMERICA	165,427	2	33,735	-27	88,743	9	21,361	20	9	46
Antigua & Barbuda	18	144	25	87	4	21	2	-27	0	
Bahamas	5	39	59	54	20	72	–	-100	0	
Barbados	18	4	89	47	49	75	5	0	0	
Belize	50	50	5	75	25	85	9	38	0	
Canada	12,002	-4	735	-15	10,673	81	344	-6	0	
Costa Rica	1,925	41	16	354	228	28	126	7	0	
Cuba	4,973	-27	493	45	2,467	57	744	5	0	
Dominican Rep.	2,155	98	635	91	409	-43	596	42	0	
El Salvador	1,131	-7	19	2	437	6	118	16	0	
Greenland			22	-36	0		0		0	
Grenada	5	-28	26	67	11	-8	1	-63	0	
Guadeloupe	75	-1	36	17	43	107	1	-56	0	
Guatemala	2,144	60	736	13	873	32	158	-24	0	
Haiti	1,523	81	1,294	11	867	-40	732	32	0	
Honduras	2,740	78	34	14	589	-25	260	-7	0	
Jamaica	290	19	443	-1	249	55	37	-32	0	
Martinique	39	-9	136	279	48	55	2	-48	0	
Mexico	31,642	48	16,476	3	16,574	70	12,472	13	0	
Nicaragua	1,733	-20	9	11	738	33	310	24	0	
Panama	1,471	33	7	46	236	32	176	6	0	
Puerto Rico	584	17	21	-7	196	5	26	15	0	
St Lucia	12	19	27	100	12	-29	3	0	0	
St Vincent & Grenadines	7	-9	20	116	9	100	1	-6	0	
Trinidad & Tobago	78	32	62	61	84	81	5	-11	9	46
USA	100,336	-8	12,330	-53	53,680	-9	5,255	63	0	
SOUTH AMERICA	260,684	51	133,314	-3	54,976	28	21,141	12	1,138	1,065
Argentina	50,788	1	32,254	-38	4,133	8	3,188	-21	0	
Bolivia	5,443	151	11,950	38	1,747	125	1,017	6	0	
Brazil	135,558	92	31,051	38	32,793	11	9,136	15	1,111	1,037
Chile	3,446	16	7,100	-5	1,353	32	528	-1	0	
Colombia	24,316	29	3,604	46	2,566	68	3,243	77	0	
Ecuador	3,968	69	2,075	4	4,160	131	773	54	0	
Falkland Is.	7	-39	696	12	0		2	-56	0	
Guyana	210	-28	197	51	185	141	4	-48	0	
Paraguay	7,742	80	568	25	2,074	192	372	-15	0	
Peru	3,897	4	14,907	-19	2,400	33	1,367	6	0	
Suriname	75	68	12	17	20	110	–	-31	0	
Uruguay	10,109	16	25,687	18	217	-46	434	-3	0	
Venezuela	12,727	62	1,825	32	3,051	100	1,007	4	0	

Continued over

Table 3.9 Continued

Region/country	Cattle[a]		Sheep and goats		Pigs		Equines[b]		Buffaloes and camels	
	No. of animals (10³) 1987–89	% change since 1967–69	No. of animals (10³) 1987–89	% change since 1967–69	No. of animals (10³) 1987–89	% change since 1967–69	No. of animals (10³) 1987–89	% change since 1967–69	No. of animals (10³) 1987–89	% change since 1967–69
ASIA	388,319	15	615,687	29	412,110	77	43,889	25	138,683	28
Afghanistan	3,633	1	20,533	-16	0		1,740	7	277	-8
Bahrain	6	60	23	55	0		0		1	36
Bangladesh	22,785	-7	11,889	31	0		45	9	1,950	160
Bhutan	410	82	59	141	63	24	43	35	7	91
Brunei	3	21	1	-42	23	201	0		10	-33
Cambodia	1,929	-14	2	-58	1,495	36	15	106	706	-17
China	74,019	30	175,638	24	335,641	79	26,863	53	21,667	42
Cyprus	45	21	540	-23	256	245	8	-82	0	
Hong Kong	2	-85	–	29	353	12	1	100	–	-92
India	195,933	11	158,717	48	10,267	84	2,431	11	74,690	34
Indonesia	9,796	48	15,277	42	6,407	118	725	15	3,284	15
Iran	8,357	68	48,130	8	0	-100	2,199	-15	257	-41
Iraq	1,610	-3	10,717	-28	0		490	-29	198	-59
Israel	337	52	441	29	130	155	11	-30	10	-3
Japan	4,681	46	70	-79	11,648	100	22	-90	0	
Jordan	29	-33	1,683	36	0		25	-63	15	14
Korea	2,456	96	187	37	4,160	210	3	-85	0	
Korea, Dem.	1,243	77	658	98	3,098	142	48	66	0	
Kuwait	26	445	315	116	0		3		8	-26
Laos	757	96	89	178	1,329	35	42	68	1,041	25
Lebanon	52	-42	612	5	22	81	17	-52	–	-91
Macau	–	-40	0		6	-16	0		0	
Malaysia	633	97	446	15	2,253	121	5	4	218	-31
Mongolia	2,516	24	17,656	4	123	782	2,042	-11	546	-16
Myanmar q.v. Burma	9,971	53	1,409	64	2,996	140	147	157	2,203	54
Nepal	6,350	4	6,034	29	502	60	0		2,940	-14
Oman	136	104	948	466	0		25	3	82	717
Pakistan	17,186	19	60,520	145	0		3,542	84	14,943	55
Philippines	1,716	6	2,142	222	7,464	25	300	10	2,885	-31
Qatar	8	60	199	182	0		1		21	185
Saudi Arabia	265	96	11,069	348	0		119	37	417	288
Singapore	–	-94	2	12	367	-62	0		–	-95
Sri Lanka	1,819	11	536	-10	100	-17	1	-32	1,053	37
Syria	728	48	14,351	114	1	82	252	-31	6	-52
Thailand	5,023	17	179	163	4,246	-6	19	-89	5,999	8
Turkey	12,050	-13	52,550	-7	10	-31	2,030	-41	543	-58
United Arab Em.	50	397	1,277	360	0		–	33	119	14
Viet Nam	2,908	59	454	129	11,834	36	137	37	2,794	19
Yemen	1,049	5	4,363	26	0		523	-10	62	13
Yemen, Dem.	96	18	2,333	22	0		170	79	81	-53
EUROPE	126,826	3	163,624	14	188,690	54	5,830	-50	0	
Albania	674	59	2,434	-1	220	80	116	-4	2	-50
Austria	2,589	5	289	33	3,874	32	44	-33	0	
Belgium	2,961	6	191	91	5,864	138	24	-73	0	
Bulgaria	1,647	22	9,454	-8	4,068	81	481	-12	25	-75
Czechoslovakia	5,064	16	1,137	-5	7,151	34	38	-77	0	

Continued opposite

Table 3.9   Continued

Region/country	Cattle[a] No. of animals (10³) 1987–89	% change since 1967–69	Sheep and goats No. of animals (10³) 1987–89	% change since 1967–69	Pigs No. of animals (10³) 1987–89	% change since 1967–69	Equines[b] No. of animals (10³) 1987–89	% change since 1967–69	Buffaloes and camels No. of animals (10³) 1987–89	% change since 1967–69
Denmark	2,346	-25	76	-29	9,192	13	29	-30	0	
Faeroe Is.	2	-20	73	6	0		0		0	
Finland	1,433	-29	66	-60	1,309	78	37	-70	0	
France	21,894	2	11,478	10	12,492	24	324	-67	0	
German Dem. Rep.	5,745	15	2,666	28	12,602	35	104	-52	0	
Germany, Fed. Rep.	14,950	7	1,456	61	23,622	28	365	28	1	-96
Greece	759	-29	14,321	21	1,192	149	316	-64	0	
Hungary	1,693	-17	2,311	-31	8,407	41	91	-67	0	
Iceland	72	36	770	-7	14	274	57	64	0	
Ireland	5,614	10	4,330	44	967	-3	76	-61	0	
Italy	8,796	-9	12,574	35	9,387	50	389	-55	104	132
Malta	14	53	10	-67	95	265	2	-61	0	
Netherlands	4,530	15	1,152	104	14,092	208	64	-44	0	
Norway	936	-6	2,327	13	760	23	17	-65	0	
Poland	10,398	-5	4,407	26	19,250	36	1,066	-60	0	
Portugal	1,357	19	5,968	1	2,857	65	289	-1	0	
Romania	7,123	42	19,928	33	15,112	167	733	-1	209	9
Spain	5,102	27	25,397	18	16,837	193	492	-65	0	
Sweden	1,660	-20	396	27	2,276	10	58	-18	0	
Switzerland	1,848	–	435	25	1,909	9	51	-15	0	
UK	12,078	-2	27,671	-1	7,832	6	185	25	26	-49
Yugoslavia	4,890	-12	7,736	-24	8,059	47	400	-66		
USSR	120,499	25	147,295	2	78,201	49	6,193	-29	583	-19
OCEANIA	30,608	9	220,666	-4	5,298	34	507	-16	–	-68
Australia	21,981	13	155,343	-8	2,674	31	351	-25	0	
Fiji	159	14	60	-6	29	27	42	77	0	
French Polynesia	10	-7	4	-66	54	381	2	-39	0	
Kiribati			0		10	0	0		0	
New Caledonia	135	15	24	33	38	93	10	12	0	
New Zealand	8,087	-1	65,834	9	432	-27	101	29	0	
Pacific Is. Tr. Tr.	12	35	4	-21	29	37	0		0	
Papua New Guinea	102	74	15	109	1,713	66	1	3	0	
Tonga	9	337	14	253	81	153	11	38	0	
Vanuatu	123	80	13	45	79	40	3	157	0	
Wallis Is.	–	-81	8	49	30	233	–	-50	0	

[a]   Cattle include both dairy and beef cattle.
[b]   Equines include horses, mules and asses.

Livestock numbers include all animals within a country, irrespective of place or purpose of their breeding.

Only countries having at least 20,000 cattle, sheep, goats, pigs, equines or buffaloes and camels are listed. Regional and world totals, however, include livestock populations in countries not listed here.

Source:
FAO 1990 Unpublished data, Food and Agriculture Organization, Rome.

Table 3.10 Forest resources and estimates of mean annual rates of deforestation and reforestation, 1980s

Region/country	Extent of forest and woodlands (10³ ha)			Deforestation						Reforestation
	Closed forests	Open forests	All forests	Closed forests		Open forests		All forests		
				10³ ha a⁻¹	% per year	10³ ha a⁻¹	% per year	10³ ha a⁻¹	% per year	10³ ha a⁻¹
WORLD	2,838,770	1,242,768	4,081,538	11,057	0.4	3,777	0.3	15,517	0.4	14,713
AFRICA	219,811	464,591	684,402	1,577	0.7	2,406	0.5	4,040	0.6	297
Algeria	1,518	249	1,767					40	2.3	52
Angola	2,900	50,700	53,600	44	1.5	50	0.1	94	0.2	3
Benin	47	3,820	3,867	1	2.6	66	1.7	67	1.7	–
Botswana		32,560	32,560			20	0.1	20	0.1	
Burkina Faso	271	4,464	4,735	3	1.1	77	1.7	80	1.7	2
Burundi	27	14	41	1	2.6	–	2.9	1	2.7	
Cameroon	16,500ᵃ	6,800ᵃ	23,300ᵃ	100ᵇ	0.6	90ᵇ	1.3	190ᵇ	0.8	3
Cape Verde										1
Cent. African Rep.	3,590	32,300	35,890	5	0.1	50	0.2	55	0.2	1
Chad	500	13,000	13,500			80	0.6	80	0.6	
Comoros	16		16	1	3.1			1	3.1	
Congo	21,340		21,340	22	0.1			22	0.1	–
Côte d'Ivoire	4,458	5,376	9,834	290	6.5	220	4.1	510	5.2	6
Djibouti										
Egypt	2	68	70							2
Equatorial Guinea	1,295		1,295	3	0.2			3	0.2	
Ethiopia	4,350	22,800	27,150	8	0.2	80	0.4	88	0.3	10
Gabon	20,500	75	20,575	15	0.1			15	0.1	1
Gambia	65	150	215	2	3.4	3	2.0	5	2.4	–
Ghana	1,718	6,975	8,693	22	1.3	50	0.7	72	0.8	2
Guinea	2,050	8,600	10,650	36	1.8	50	0.6	86	0.8	–
Guinea-Bissau	660	1,445	2,105	17	2.6	40	2.8	57	2.7	–
Kenya	1,105	1,255	2,360	19	1.7	20	1.6	39	1.7	10
Lesotho		40	40							1
Liberia	2,000		2,040	46	2.3			46	2.3	2
Libya	134	56	190							
Madagascar	10,300	2,900	13,200	150	1.5	6	0.2	156	1.2	31
Malawi	186	4,085	4,271			150	3.7	150	3.5	12
Mali	500	6,750	7,250			36	0.5	36	0.5	1
Mauritania	29	525	554	1	2.4	13	2.4	13	2.4	1
Mauritius	3		3	–	3.3			–		–
Morocco	1,533	1,703	3,236					13	0.4	13

Continued below

Table 3.10 Continued

| Region/country | Extent of forest and woodlands (10³ ha) | | | Deforestation | | | | | | Reforestation |
	Closed forests	Open forests	All forests	Closed forests 10³ ha a⁻¹	Closed forests % per year	Open forests 10³ ha a⁻¹	Open forests % per year	All forests 10³ ha a⁻¹	All forests % per year	10³ ha a⁻¹
Mozambique	935	14,500	15,435	10	1.1	110	0.8	120	0.8	4
Niger	100	2,450	2,550	3	2.5	65	2.6	67	2.6	2
Nigeria	5,950	8,800	14,750	300	5.0	100	1.1	400	2.7	26
Rwanda	120	110	230	3	2.6	2	1.8	5	2.3	3
Senegal	220	10,825	11,045			50	0.5	50	0.5	3
Sierra Leone	740	1,315	2,055	6	0.8			6	0.3	0
Somalia	1,540	7,510	9,050	4	0.2	10	0.1	14	0.1	1
South Africa	300		300							63
Sudan	650	47,000	47,650	4	0.6	500	1.1	504	1.1	13
Swaziland	4	70	74							5
Tanzania	1,440	40,600	42,040	10	0.7	120	0.3	130	0.3	9
Togo	304	1,380	1,684	2	0.7	10	0.7	12	0.7	0
Tunisia	186	111	297					5	1.7	3
Uganda	765	5,250	6,015	10	1.3	40	0.8	50	0.8	2
Zaire	105,750	71,840	177,590	400ᶜ	0.4	188	0.3	588	0.3	0
Zambia	3,010	26,500	29,510	40	1.3	30	0.1	70	0.2	2
Zimbabwe	200	19,620	19,820			80	0.4	80	0.4	4
NORTH AMERICA	541,009	261,276	802,285	1,003	0.2	20	–	1,182	0.1	2,541
Canada	264,100	172,300	436,400							720
Costa Rica	1,638	160	1,798	55ᵈ	3.4			55ᵈ	3.1	0
Cuba	1,455		1,455	2	0.2			2	0.1	11
Dominican Rep.	629		629	4	0.6			4	0.6	1
El Salvador	141		141	5	3.2			5	3.2	0
Guatemala	4,442	100	4,542	90	2.0			90	2.0	8
Haiti	48		48	2	3.8			2	3.8	0
Honduras	3,797	200	3,997	90	2.3			90	2.3	
Jamaica	67		67	2	3.0			2	3.0	1
Mexico	46,250	2,100	48,350	595	1.3	20	1.0	615	1.3	22
Nicaragua	4,496		4,496	121	2.7			121	2.7	1
Panama	4,165		4,165	36	0.9			36	0.9	0
Trinidad & Tobago	208		208	1	0.4			1	0.4	1
USA	209,573ᵉ	86,416ᵉ	295,989ᵉ					159ᶠ	0.1	1,775

Continued over

Table 3.10 Continued

Region/country	Extent of forest and woodlands (10³ ha)			Deforestation						Reforestation
	Closed forests	Open forests	All forests	Closed forests		Open forests		All forests		
				10³ ha a⁻¹	% per year	10³ ha a⁻¹	% per year	10³ ha a⁻¹	% per year	10³ ha a⁻¹
SOUTH AMERICA	653,605	204,520	858,125	4,467	0.7	1,293	0.6	5,810	0.7	608
Argentina	44,500		44,500							40
Bolivia	44,010	22,750	66,760	87	0.2	30	0.1	117	0.2	1
Brazil	357,480	157,000	514,480	2,600[g]	0.7	1,050	0.7	3,650	0.7	449
Chile	7,550		7,550					50	0.7	74
Colombia	46,400	5,300	51,700	820	1.8	70	1.3	890	1.7	8
Ecuador	14,250	480	14,730	340	2.4	0	0.2	340	2.3	4
Guyana	18,475	220	18,695	2	–	1		3	–	–
Paraguay	4,070	15,640	19,710	190	4.7	22	0.1	212	1.1	1
Peru	69,680	960	70,640	300[c]	0.4	0		300[c]	0.4	6
Suriname	14,830	170	15,000	3	–	0	–	3	–	–
Uruguay	490		490							5
Venezuela	31,870	2,000	33,870	125	0.4	120	6.0	245	0.7	19
ASIA	409,418	82,147	491,565	3,986	1.0	57	0.1	4,460	0.9	5,582
Afghanistan	810	400	1,210							
Bangladesh	927		927							17
Bhutan	2,100	40	2,140	8	0.9			8	0.9	
Cambodia	7,548	5,100	12,648	1	0.1			1	0.1	1
China	97,847	17,200	115,047	25	0.3	5	0.1	30	0.2	–
Cyprus	153	24	177							
India	36,540[h]	27,660[h]	64,200[h]	1,500[j]	4.1			1,500	2.3	4,552
Indonesia	113,895	3,000	116,895	900[j]	0.8	20	0.7	920	0.8	138
Iran	2,750	1,000	3,750					20	0.5	131
Iraq	70	1,160	1,230							
Israel	80	20	100							2
Japan	23,890	1,390	25,280							240
Jordan	50	50	50							3
Korea	4,887		4,887							67
Korea, Dem.	4,800		4,800							200
Laos	8,410	5,215	13,625	100	1.2	30	0.6	130	1.0	1
Lebanon	20	20	20							
Malaysia	20,996		20,996	310[c]	1.5			310[c]	1.5	
Mongolia	9,528		9,528							20
Myanmar q.v. Burma	31,941		31,941	677[k]	2.1			677[k]	2.1	0

Continued below

Table 3.10 Continued

Region/country	Extent of forest and woodlands (10³ ha)			Deforestation						Reforestation
				Closed forests		Open forests		All forests		
	Closed forests	Open forests	All forests	10³ ha a⁻¹	% per year	10³ ha a⁻¹	% per year	10³ ha a⁻¹	% per year	10³ ha a⁻¹
Nepal	1,941	180	2,121	84	4.3			84	4.0	4
Pakistan	2,185	295	2,480	7	0.3			9	0.4	7
Philippines	9,510		9,510	143[l]	1.5	2	0.7	143[l]	1.5	50
Saudi Arabia	30	170	200							
Sri Lanka	1,659		1,659	58	3.5			58	3.5	13
Syria	60	90	150					397[m]	2.5	24
Thailand	9,235	6,440	15,675							82
Turkey	8,856	11,343	20,199							
Viet Nam	8,770	1,340	10,110	173[n]	2.0			173[n]	1.7	29
Yemen		10	10							
EUROPE	137,005	21,887	158,892							1,031
Albania	1,280		1,280							21
Austria	3,754		3,754							19
Belgium	682	80	762							50
Bulgaria	3,328	400	3,728							37
Czechoslovakia	4,435	145	4,580							
Denmark	466	18	484							158
Finland	19,885	3,340	23,225							51
France	13,875	1,200	15,075							
German Dem. Rep.	2,700	285	2,985							
Germany, Fed. Rep.	6,989	218	7,207							62
Greece	2,512	3,242	5,754							19
Hungary	1,612	25	1,637							
Iceland		100	100							9
Ireland	347	33	380							15
Italy	6,363	1,700	8,063							
Netherlands	294	61	355							2
Norway	7,635	1,066	8,701							79
Poland	8,588	138	8,726							106
Portugal	2,627	349	2,976							4
Romania	6,265	410	6,675							
Spain	6,906	3,905	10,811							92
Sweden	24,400	3,442	27,842							207
Switzerland	935	189	1,124							7

Continued over

Table 3.10 Continued

Region/country	Extent of forest and woodlands (10^3 ha)			Deforestation						Reforestation
	Closed forests	Open forests	All forests	Closed forests		Open forests		All forests		
				10^3 ha a^{-1}	% per year	10^3 ha a^{-1}	% per year	10^3 ha a^{-1}	% per year	10^3 ha a^{-1}
UK	2,027	151	2,178							40
Yugoslavia	9,100	1,390	10,490							53
USSR	791,600	137,000	928,600							4,540
OCEANIA	86,322	71,347	157,669	25	–	1	–	26	–	115
Australia	41,658	65,085	106,743							
Fiji	811		811	2	–			2	–	62
New Zealand	7,200	2,300	9,500	2	0.2			2	0.2	7
Papua New Guinea	34,230	3,945	38,175	22	0.1	1	–	23	0.1	43
Solomon Islands	2,423	17	2,440	1	–			1	–	2

a   Stocks for 1986.
b   Mean annual rate of deforestation during 1976–1986.
c   Deforestation in 1989.
d   Deforestation in 1986.
e   Stocks for 1987.
f   Mean annual rate of deforestation during 1977–1987.
g   Mean annual rate of deforestation during 1988–1989.
h   Stocks for 1982.
i   Mean annual rate of deforestation during 1975–1982.
j   Mean annual rate of deforestation during 1979–1984.
k   Mean annual rate of deforestation during 1975–1981.
l   Mean annual rate of deforestation during 1981–1988.
m   Mean annual rate of deforestation during 1978–1985.
n   Mean annual rate of deforestation during 1976–1981.

The term deforestation used here refers to the permanent clearing of forest lands for shifting cultivation, permanent agriculture or settlements; it does not include other alterations such as selective logging. Deforestation rates for total forest areas may not tally for some countries because of missing information in some forest classes.

The term reforestation used here refers to the establishment of plantations for industrial and non-industrial uses; it does not, in general, include regeneration of old tree crops although some countries may report regeneration as reforestation.

Regional and world totals include listed countries only.

Data on forest resources and estimates of rates of deforestation presented in the above table are largely derived from FAO compilations. However, data from other sources have been used in place of FAO deforestation estimates for closed forests in the case of Brazil, Costa Rica, India, Indonesia, Malaysia, Myanmar, Peru, the Philippines, Viet Nam and Zaire, and for total forests in the case of Thailand and Cameroon.

Sources:
DENR 1988 *1987 Philippine Forestry Statistics*, Philippines Forest Management Bureau, Department of Environment and Natural Resources, Philippines.
FAO 1985 *Forest Resources, 1980*, Food and Agriculture Organization, Rome.
FAO 1988 *An Interim Report on the State of the Forest Resources in Developing Countries*, Forest Resources Division, Food and Agriculture Organization, Rome.
FAO/UN-ECE 1985 *The Forest Resources of the ECE Region*, Food and Agriculture Organization, Rome and the United Nations Economic Commission for Europe, Geneva.
Fearnside, P. M., Tardin, A. T. and Meira Filho, L. G. 1990 *Deforestation Rate in Brazilian Amazonia*, National Secretariat of Science and Technology, Brazil.
Joint Interagency 1988 *Cameroon Tropical Forestry Action Plan*, Joint Interagency Planning and Review Mission for the Forestry Sector, Rome.
Kyaw, U. S. 1987 National Report: Burma. In: *Proceedings of the Ad Hoc FAO/ECE/FINNIDA Meeting of Experts on Forest Resource Assessment*, Kotka, Finland, 26–30 October 1987, Finnish International Development Agency, Helsinki.
Library of Congress 1979 *Draft Environmental Report on Jordan*, Science and Technology Division, Library of Congress, Washington DC.
Myers, N. 1989 *Deforestation Rates in Tropical Forests and Their Climatic Implications*, Friends of the Earth, London.
National Remote Sensing Agency 1983 *Mapping of Forest Cover in India from Satellite Imagery 1972–75 and 1980–82*, Government of India, Hyderabad.
Quy, V. 1988 Vietnam's ecological situation today, *ESCAP Environment News* **6**(4), 5.

Royal Forestry Department of Thailand 1986 *Forestry Statistics of Thailand 1986*, Centre for Agricultural Statistics, Office of Agricultural Economics, Ministry of Agriculture and Co-operatives, Bangkok.
Saavedra, C. and de Freitas, G. S. 1989 *Manu - Two Decades Later*, World Wide Fund for Nature, Gland.
Sader, S. A. and Joyce, A. T. 1988 Deforestation rates and trends in Costa Rica 1940 to 1984. *Biotropica* **20**(1). 14.
Savenzi Zavod Za Statistiku 1986 *Statisticki Godisnjak Jugoslavija 1985* (and earlier editions), Socijalisticka Federativna Republika Jugoslavija Savenzi Zavod Za Statistiku, Belgrade.
State Statistical Bureau 1985 *China: A Statistics Survey in 1985*, New World Press, Beijing.
Thang, H. C. 1987 *Forest Resource Assessment in Malaysia*, Forest Management Unit, Department of the Environment, Kuala Lumpur.
USDA 1989 Unpublished data, Forest Service, US Department of Agriculture, Washington DC.
Vohra, B. B. 1987 Confusion on the forestry front. Unpublished paper.
Waddel, K. L., Oswald, D. D. and Powell, D. W. 1987 *Forest Statistics of the United States 1989*, Forest Service, US Department of Agriculture, Portland.
World Bank 1988 *Indonesia: Forests, Land and Water, Issues in Sustainable Development*, World Bank Asia Regional Office.
World Bank/UNDP 1990 *Costa Rica Forest Utilization Study*, Volume 1, World Bank, Washington DC, and United Nations Development Programme, New York.

Table 3.11 Softwood production in selected countries, 1966–1968 and 1986–1988 (mean annual values)

Country	Total roundwood (10³ m³)			Industrial roundwood (10³ m³)			Fuelwood (10³ m³)		
	1966–68	1986–88	% change	1966–68	1986–88	% change	1966–68	1986–88	% change
USA	237,558	337,213	42	232,838	314,361	35	4,720	22,852	384
USSR	312,688	323,900	4	250,235	267,500	7	62,453	56,400	-10
Canada	100,195	162,715	62	97,529	160,958	65	2,667	1,757	-34
Sweden	44,538	44,409	–	43,005	42,737	-1	1,533	1,672	9
Brazil	17,534	41,480	137	8,623	27,278	216	8,911	14,202	59
Finland	28,065	35,479	26	26,388	34,510	31	1,676	969	-42
Germany, Fed. Rep.	18,645	23,052	24	17,879	21,707	21	767	1,345	75
France	16,675	20,869	25	12,675	16,869	33	4,000	4,000	0
Japan	32,864	19,986	-39	32,809	19,982	-39	55	4	-93
Poland	14,489	18,586	28	13,605	16,334	20	883	2,252	155
Czechoslovakia	10,951	14,647	34	9,798	13,644	39	1,153	1,003	-13
Austria	9,772	11,469	17	9,199	10,920	19	573	549	-4
Mexico	6,279	10,689	70	3,962	6,546	65	2,317	4,143	79
Turkey	8,602	10,182	18	3,192	5,457	71	5,411	4,725	-13
Chile	3,522	10,001	184	2,920	9,154	213	602	847	41
Spain	4,956	9,728	96	2	9,434	150	1,599	294	-82
India	5,460	9,505	74	1,106	2,763		4,354	6,742	55
Norway	7,098	9,386	32	6,777	9,125	35	321	261	-19
New Zealand	6,680	9,305	39	6,227	9,280	49	453	25	-94
German Dem. Rep.	5,392	8,453	57	4,650	7,743	66	742	710	-4
TOTAL, 20 COUNTRIES	891,963	1,131,053	27	786,773	1,006,301	28	105,190	124,752	19
TOTAL, WORLD	951,734	1,214,840	28	825,075	1,064,151	29	126,660	150,689	19

Total roundwood production refers to the volume of all rough wood felled or otherwise harvested from forests for either industria or fuelwood purposes. Industrial roundwood production refers to all roundwood products, other than fuelwood, and includes sawlcgs, veneer logs, sleepers, pitprops and pulpwood. Fuelwood production comprises all rough wood used for cooking, heating and power generating purposes.

The 20 countries listed above are ranked in descending order of total roundwood production (softwoods) during the period 1986–1988 (mean annual values) and account for 93 per cent of the global production of softwoods.

Source:
FAO 1990 Unpublished data, Food and Agriculture Organization, Rome.

Table 3.12 Charcoal and hardwood production in selected countries, 1966–1968 and 1986–1988 (mean annual values)

Country	Total roundwood (10³ m³)			Industrial roundwood (10³ m³)			Fuelwood (10³ m³)			Charcoal (10³ t)		
	1966–68	1986–88	% change	1966–68	1986–88	% change	1966–68	1986–88	% change	1966–68	1986–88	% change
India	150,439	238,822	59	10,022	21,370	113	140,416	217,452	55	1,192	1,846	55
USA	87,886	184,628	110	68,251	93,230	37	19,635	91,398	365		500	
Indonesia	91,967	167,059	82	6,605	35,954	444	85,362	131,105	54	78	120	54
Brazil	91,058	166,850	83	10,876	39,058	259	80,181	127,792	59	3,497	5,573	59
Nigeria	46,409	93,210	101	2,914	7,868	170	43,495	85,342	96	716	1,406	96
USSR	65,917	64,233	-3	32,270	33,833	5	33,647	30,400	-10			
Malaysia	18,327	40,309	120	14,779	34,595	134	3,548	5,715	61	224	362	61
Philippines	30,128	37,114	23	11,696	6,046	-48	18,432	31,068	69		29	
Ethiopia	22,142	34,341	55	965	1,725	79	21,177	32,616	54	139	214	54
Thailand	22,914	34,132	49	4,502	4,566	1	18,412	29,566	61	368	592	61
Zaire	18,830	33,194	76	1,744	2,642	51	17,086	30,552	79			
Tanzania	12,244	29,485	141	879	1,461	66	11,365	28,024	147	72	144	100
Bangladesh	17,002	28,613	68	993	856	-14	16,009	27,757	73			
Viet Nam	16,301	25,830	58	2	3,090		14,500	22,740	57			
Pakistan	11,496	21,742	89	271	1,116	312	11,226	20,626	84			
Kenya	9,497	20,860	120	407	978	140	9,090	19,883	119	932	2,039	119
Myanmar q.v. Burma	13,256	20,181	52	2,459	3,483	42	10,797	16,699	55			
France	20,422	19,711	-3	10,655	13,911	31	9,767	5,800	-41	94	105	12
Nepal	10,339	16,702	62	540	540	0	9,800	16,162	65	16	26	68
Canada	11,673	15,335	31	7,082	10,258	45	4,591	5,077	11			
TOTAL, 20 COUNTRIES	768,245	1,292,351	68	189,712	316,579	67	578,534	975,772	69	7,327	12,956	77
TOTAL, WORLD	1,144,652	1,757,088	54	317,048	470,724	48	827,603	1,286,364	55	12,236	20,800	70

Total roundwood production refers to the volume of all rough wood felled or otherwise harvested from forests for either industrial or fuelwood purposes. Industrial roundwood production refers to all roundwood products, other than fuelwood, and includes sawlogs, veneer logs, sleepers, pitprops and pulpwood. Fuelwood and charcoal production comprises all rough wood used for cooking, heating and power generating purposes.

The 20 countries listed above are ranked in descending order of total roundwood production (hardwoods) during the period 1986–1988 (mean annual values) and account for 74 per cent of the global production of hardwoods.

Source:
FAO 1990 Unpublished data, Food and Agriculture Organization, Rome.

Table 3.13 Fresh-water resources and withdrawals (annual values)

Region/country	Renewable water resources, 1990		Withdrawal (from renewable and non-renewable resources)				Sectoral withdrawal (%)		
	Total (km³ a⁻¹)	Per capita (10³ m³ a⁻¹)	Year of data	Total (km³ a⁻¹)	Per capita (m³ a⁻¹)	% of renewable water resources	Domestic purposes	Industrial purposes	Agricultural purposes
WORLD	40,673[a]	7.69	1987	3,296[a]	660	8	8	23	69
AFRICA	4,184[a]	6.46	1987	144[a]	244	3	7	5	88
Algeria	19.1[b]	0.75	1980	3.00	161	16	22	4	74
Angola	158[a]	15.77	1987	0.48[a]	43	–	14	10	76
Benin	26	5.48	1987	0.11[a]	26	–	28	14	58
Botswana	18[b]	0.78	1980	0.09	98	1	5	10	85
Burkina Faso	28[a]	3.11	1987	0.15[a]	20	1	28	5	67
Burundi	3.6[a]	0.66	1987	0.10[a]	20	3	36	0	64
Cameroon	208	18.50	1987	0.40[a]	30	–	46	19	35
Cape Verde	0.2	0.53	1972	0.04	148	20	9	2	89
Cent. African Rep.	141[a]	48.40	1987	0.07[a]	27	–	21	5	74
Chad	38.4[a]	6.76	1987	0.18[a]	35	–	16	2	82
Comoros	1[a]	1.97	1987	0.01[a]	15	1	48	5	47
Congo	802[a,b]	90.77	1987	0.04[a]	20	–	62	27	11
Côte d'Ivoire	74	5.87	1987	0.71[a]	68	1	22	11	67
Djibouti	0.3	0.74	1973	0.01	28	2	28	21	51
Egypt	58.3[b]	0.03	1985	56.40	1,202	97	7[c]	5[c]	88[c]
Equatorial Guinea	30[a]	68.18	1987	0.01[a]	11	–	81	13	6
Ethiopia	110	2.35	1987	2.21[a]	48	2	11	3	86
Gabon	164[a]	140.05	1987	0.06[a]	51	–	72	22	6
Gambia	22[b]	3.50	1982	0.02	33	–	7	2	91
Ghana	53	3.53	1970	0.30	35	1	35	13	52
Guinea	226[a]	32.87	1987	0.74[a]	115	–	10	3	87
Guinea-Bissau	31[a]	31.41	1987	0.01[a]	18	–	31	6	63
Kenya	14.8	0.59	1987	1.09[a]	48	7	27	11	62
Lesotho	4[a]	2.25	1987	0.05[a]	34	1	22	22	56
Liberia	232[a]	90.84	1987	0.13[a]	54	–	27	13	60
Libya	0.7	0.15	1985	2.62	262	374	15	10	75
Madagascar	40	3.34	1984	16.30	1,675	41	1	0	99
Malawi	9[a]	1.07	1987	0.16[a]	22	2	34	17	49
Mali	62[a]	6.62	1987	1.36[a]	159	2	2	1	97
Mauritania	7.4[b]	0.20	1978	0.73	473	10	12	4	84
Mauritius	2.2	1.99	1974	0.36	415	16	16	7	77
Morocco	30	1.19	1985	11.00	501	37	6[c]	3[c]	91[c]

Continued over

Table 3.13 Continued

Region/country	Renewable water resources, 1990 Total (km³ a⁻¹)	Per capita (10³ m³ a⁻¹)	Withdrawal (from renewable and non-renewable resources) Year of data	Total (km³ a⁻¹)	Per capita (m³ a⁻¹)	% of renewable water resources	Sectoral withdrawal (%) Domestic purposes	Industrial purposes	Agricultural purposes
Mozambique	58[a]	3.70	1987	0.76[a]	53	1	24	10	66
Namibia	9[a]	4.80	1987	0.14[a]	73	2	6	12	82
Niger	44[a,b]	1.97	1987	0.29[a]	44	1	21	5	74
Nigeria	308[a,b]	2.31	1987	3.63[a]	44	1	31	15	54
Réunion			1987	0.04[a]	72		33	14	53
Rwanda	6.3[a]	0.87	1987	0.15[a]	23	2	24	8	68
São Tomé & Príncipe			1987	–[a]	10		78	9	13
Senegal	35.2[a,b]	3.15	1987	1.36[a]	201	4	5	3	92
Seychelles			1987	–[a]	15		58	7	35
Sierra Leone	160[a]	38.54	1987	0.37[a]	99	–	7	4	89
Somalia	11.5	1.52	1987	0.81[a]	167	7	3	0	97
South Africa	50	1.42	1970	9.20	404	18	16	17	67
Sudan	130[b]	1.19	1977	18.60	1,089	14	1	0	99
Swaziland	7[a]	8.82	1987	0.29[a]	414	4	5	2	93
Tanzania	76[a]	2.78	1970	0.48	36	1	21	5	74
Togo	11.5	3.33	1987	0.09[a]	40	1	62	13	25
Tunisia	4.4[b]	0.46	1985	2.30	325	53	13	7	80
Uganda	66[a]	3.58	1970	0.20	20		32	8	60
Western Sahara	1.1	6.18	1987	0.01[a]	29	–	22	3	75
Zaire	1,019[a]	28.31	1987	0.70[a]	22	–	58	25	17
Zambia	96[a]	11.35	1970	0.36	86	–	63	11	26
Zimbabwe	23[a]	2.37	1987	1.22[a]	129	5	14	7	79
NORTH AMERICA	6,945[a]	16.26	1987	697[a]	1,692	10	9	42	49
Barbados	0.1	0.20	1962	0.03	117	51	52	41	7
Belize	16	87.91	1987	0.02[a]	104		10	0	90
Canada	2,901	109.37	1980	36.15	1,501	1	18	70	12
Costa Rica	95	31.51	1970	1.35	779	1	4	7	89
Cuba	34.5	3.34	1975	8.10	868	23	9	2	89
Dominica			1987	–[a]	14		73	0	27
Dominican Rep.	20	2.79	1987	2.97[a]	453	15	5	6	89
El Salvador	19	3.61	1975	1	241	5	7	4	89
Greenland			1987	–[a]	11		91	0	9
Grenada			1987	–[a]	16		73	0	27

Continued below

Table 3.13 Continued

Region/country	Renewable water resources, 1990 — Total $(\mathrm{km}^3\,\mathrm{a}^{-1})$	Per capita $(10^3\,\mathrm{m}^3\,\mathrm{a}^{-1})$	Withdrawal (from renewable and non-renewable resources) — Year of data	Total $(\mathrm{km}^3\,\mathrm{a}^{-1})$	Per capita $(\mathrm{m}^3\,\mathrm{a}^{-1})$	% of renewable water resources	Sectoral withdrawal (%) — Domestic purposes	Industrial purposes	Agricultural purposes
Guadeloupe			1987	0.03[a]	78	1	14	0	84
Guatemala	116	12.61	1970	0.73	139	–	9	17	74
Haiti	11	1.69	1987	0.04[a]	46	1	24	8	68
Honduras	102	19.85	1970	1.34	508	1	4	5	91
Jamaica	8.3	3.29	1975	0.32	157	4	7	7	86
Martinique			1987	0.07[a]	199		5	0	95
Mexico	357.4	4.03	1975	54.20	901	15	6	8	86
Montserrat			1987	0[a]	10		100	0	0
Nicaragua	175	45.21	1975	0.89	370	1	25	21	54
Panama	144	59.55	1975	1.30	744	1	12	11	77
St Lucia			1987	0.01[a]	89		11	0	89
St Vincent & Grenadines			1987	0.01[a]	108		13	0	87
Trinidad & Tobago	5.1[a]	3.98	1975	0.15	149	3	27	38[c]	35[c]
USA	2,478	9.94	1985	467	2,162	19	12[c]	46[c]	42[c]
SOUTH AMERICA	10,376[a]	34.96	1987	133[a]	476	1	18	23	59
Argentina	994[b]	21.47	1976	27.60	1,059	3	9	18	73
Bolivia	300[a]	41.02	1987	1.24[a]	184	–	10	5	85
Brazil	6,950[b]	34.52	1987	35.04[a]	212	1	43	17	40
Chile	468[a]	35.53	1975	16.80	1,625	4	6	5	89
Colombia	1,070	33.63	1987	5.34[a]	179	–	41	16	43
Ecuador	314	29.12	1987	5.56[a]	561	2	7	3	90
French Guiana	120	1,304.35	1987	0.01[a]	79	–	74	18	8
Guyana	241[a]	231.73	1971	5.40	7,616	2	1	0	99
Paraguay	94[a,b]	21.98	1987	0.43[a]	111	–	15	7	78
Peru	40	1.79	1987	6.10[a]	294	15	19	9	72
Suriname	200[a]	496.28	1987	0.46[a]	1,181	–	6	5	89
Uruguay	59[a,b]	18.86	1965	0.65	241	1	6	3	91
Venezuela	1,317[b]	43.37	1970	4.10	387	–	43	11	46
ASIA	10,485	3.37	1987	1,531[a]	526	15	6	8	86
Afghanistan	50	3.02	1987	26.11[a]	1,436	52	1	0	99
Bahrain	0	0.00	1975	0.20	735		60	36	4
Bangladesh	2,357[b]	11.74	1987	22.50[a]	211	1	3	1	96
Bhutan	95[a]	62.66	1987	0.02[a]	15	0	36	10	54
Brunei	8.3	36.68	1987	–[a]	13	–	53	26	21

Continued over

Table 3.13 Continued

Region/country	Renewable water resources, 1990		Withdrawal (from renewable and non-renewable resources)				Sectoral withdrawal (%)		
	Total (km³ a⁻¹)	Per capita (10³ m³ a⁻¹)	Year of data	Total (km³ a⁻¹)	Per capita (m³ a⁻¹)	% of renewable water resources	Domestic purposes	Industrial purposes	Agricultural purposes
Cambodia	498.1	10.68	1987	0.52ª	69	—	5	1	94
China	2,800	2.47	1980	460	462	16	6	7	87
Cyprus	0.9	1.28	1985	0.54	807	60	7ᶜ	2ᶜ	91ᶜ
India	2,085ᵇ	2.17	1975	380	612	18	3	4	93
Indonesia	2,530	14.02	1987	16.59ª	96	1	13	11	76
Iran	117.5	2.08	1975	45.40	1,362	39	4	9	87
Iraq	100ᵇ	1.80	1970	42.80	4,575	43	3	5	92
Israel	2.2ᵇ	0.37	1986	1.90	447	88	16ᶜ	5ᶜ	79ᶜ
Japan	547	4.43	1980	107.80	923	20	17	33	50
Jordan	1.1	0.16	1975	0.45	173	41	29	6	65
Korea	63	1.45	1976	10.70	298	17	11	14	75
Korea, Dem.	67ª	2.92	1987	14.16ª	1,649	21	11	16	73
Kuwait	0	0.00	1974	0.01	10		64	32	4
Laos	270	66.32	1987	0.99ª	228		8	10	82
Lebanon	4.8	1.62	1975	0.75	271	16	11	4	85
Maldives			1987	—ª			47	37	16
Malaysia	456	26.30	1975	9.42	765	2	23	30	47
Mongolia	24.6	11.05	1987	0.55ª	272	2	11	27	62
Myanmar q.v. Burma	1,082	25.96	1987	3.96ª	103	—	7	3	90
Nepal	170	8.88	1987	2.68ª	155	2	4	1	95
Oman	2	1.36	1975	0.43	561	22	3	3	94
Pakistan	468ᵇ	2.43	1975	153.40	2,053	33	1	1	98
Philippines	323	5.18	1975	29.50	693	9	18	21	61
Qatar	0	0.06	1975	0.04	234	174	36	26	38
Saudi Arabia	2.2	0.16	1975	2.33	321	106	45	8	47
Singapore	0.6	0.22	1975	0.19	84	32	45	51	4
Sri Lanka	43.2	2.51	1970	6.30	503	15	2	2	96
Syria	35.5ᵇ	0.61	1976	3.34	449	9	7	10	83
Thailand	179ᵇ	1.97	1987	31.90ª	599	18	4	10	90
Turkey	203ᵇ	3.52	1985	15.60	317	8	24ᶜ	6	57ᶜ
United Arab Em.	0.3	0.19	1980	0.42	429	140	11	9	80
Viet Nam	376ª	5.60	1987	5.07ª	81	1	13	9	78
Yemen	1	0.12	1987	1.47ª	183	147	4	2	94
Yemen, Dem.	1.5	0.60	1975	1.93	1,167	129	5	2	93

Continued below

Table 3.13 Continued

Region/country	Renewable water resources, 1990		Withdrawal (from renewable and non-renewable resources)				Sectoral withdrawal (%)		
	Total (km³ a⁻¹)	Per capita (10³ m³ a⁻¹)	Year of data	Total (km³ a⁻¹)	Per capita (m³ a⁻¹)	% of renewable water resources	Domestic purposes	Industrial purposes	Agricultural purposes
EUROPE	2,321ᵃ	4.66	1987	359ᵃ	726	15	13	54	33
Andorra	0.4	7.87	1987	—ᵃ	79	1	86	0	14
Albania	21.3ᵇ	3.08	1970	0.20	94	1	6	18	76
Austria	90.3ᵇ	7.51	1980	3.13	417	3	19	73	8
Belgium	12.5ᵇ	0.85	1980	9.03	917	72	11	85	4
Bulgaria	205ᵇ	2.00	1980	14.18	1,600	7	7	38	55
Czechoslovakia	90.6ᵇ	1.79	1980	5.80	379	6	23	68	9
Denmark	13ᵇ	2.15	1977	1.40	277	11	30	27	43
Finland	113ᵇ	22.11	1980	3.70	774	3	12	85	3
France	185ᵇ	3.03	1984	33.30	606	18	16	69	15
German Dem. Rep.	34ᵇ	1.02	1980	9.13	545	27	14	68	18
Germany, Fed. Rep.	161ᵇ	1.30	1981	41.40	671	26	10	70	20
Gibraltar	0	0.00	1987	0ᵃ			100	0	0
Greece	58.7ᵇ	4.49	1980	7.00	726	12	8	29	63
Hungary	115ᵇ	0.57	1980	5.38	502	5	9	55	36
Iceland	170	671.94	1987	0.09ᵃ	349	–	31	63	6
Ireland	50	13.44	1972	0.40	135	1	16	74	10
Italy	187ᵇ	3.13	1981	46.35	811	25	14	27	59
Liechtenstein	0.2ᵇ	5.71	1987	0ᵃ					
Luxembourg	5ᵇ	2.72	1976	0.06	166	1	42	45	13
Malta	—	0.07	1978	0.02	68	92	76	8	16
Monaco	0		1987	—ᵃ			100	0	0
Netherlands	90ᵇ	0.68	1980	14.20	1,004	16	5	61	34
Norway	413ᵇ	96.15	1980	2.00	489	–	20	72	8
Poland	56.2ᵇ	1.29	1980	16.80	472	30	16	60	24
Portugal	65.6ᵇ	3.31	1980	10.50	1,062	16	15	37	48
Romania	208ᵇ	1.59	1980	25.40	1,144	12	8	33	59
San Marino			1987	—ᵃ			94	0	6
Spain	111.3ᵇ	2.80	1985	26.30	682	24	12	26	62
Sweden	180ᵇ	21.11	1980	3.98	479	2	36	55	9
Switzerland	50ᵇ	6.52	1985	3.20	502	6	23	73	4
UK	120ᵇ	2.11	1980	28.35	507	24	20	77	3
Yugoslavia	265ᵇ	6.29	1980	8.77	393	3	16	72	12
USSR	4,684ᵇ	15.22	1980	353	1,330	8	6	29	65

Continued over

Table 3.13   Continued

Region/country	Renewable water resources, 1990		Withdrawal (from renewable and non-renewable resources)				Sectoral withdrawal (%)		
	Total (km³ a⁻¹)	Per capita (10³ m³ a⁻¹)	Year of data	Total (km³ a⁻¹)	Per capita (m³ a⁻¹)	% of renewable water resources	Domestic purposes	Industrial purposes	Agricultural purposes
OCEANIA	2,011[a]	75.96	1987	23.00[a]	907	1	64	2	34
Australia	343	20.48	1975	17.80	1,306	5	65	2	33
Fiji	28.6[a]	38.12	1987	0.03[a]	37	0	20	20	60
Kiribati			1987	–[a]	10		65	0	35
Nauru			1987	–[a]	191		54	0	46
New Caledonia			1987	–[a]	10		67	0	33
New Zealand	397	117.49	1980	1.20	379	–	46	10	44
Niue			1987	–[a]	13		67	0	33
Norfolk			1987	–[a]	10		67	0	33
Papua New Guinea	801[a]	199.70	1987	0.10[a]	25	0	29	22	49
Solomon Is.	44.7[a]	149.00	1987	0[a]	18	0	40	20	40
Tokelau			1987	–[a]	10		67	0	33
Tonga			1987	–[a]	22		27	0	73
Tuvalu			1987	–[a]	29		28	0	72

a   Estimated by the Institute of Geography, Moscow.
b   Includes a contribution from river flows from other countries.
c   Sectoral percentages date from an alternative year than that specified for the other withdrawal data.

Renewable water resources may include the average annual flow of rivers and aquifers generated from endogenous precipitation and river flows from other countries. National estimates of renewable water resources and water withdrawal are not directly comparable as data are based on a variety of sources. Where available, data are taken from published sources; other values are derived from models based on estimates of cropland under irrigation, livestock numbers, precipitation amount and other factors.

Per capita annual renewable water resources are based on population estimates for 1990. Per capita annual withdrawals are based on population data for the year of the withdrawal data.

Sectoral withdrawal is broadly classified into three categories: domestic (includes drinking-water supplies and water supplied to homes, commercial establishments and to public and municipal services); industrial (includes use of water for cooling thermoelectric power plants) and agricultural (for livestock and irrigation).

Sources:
J. Margat 1988   Personal communication, Bureau of Geological and Mining Research, National Geological Survey, Orleans.
Solley, W. B., Merk, C. F. and Pierce, R. R. 1988   *Estimated Use of Water in the United States in 1985*, US Geological Survey Circular, No. 1004, US Geological Survey, Reston.
Belyaev, A. V. 1990   Personal communication, Institute of Geography, USSR National Academy of Sciences, Moscow.

Table 3.14 Nominal[a] catch of marine and fresh-water fish, crustaceans and molluscs in selected countries, 1976–1978 and 1986–1988 (mean annual values)

Country	Marine catch (10³ t a⁻¹)			Fresh-water catch (10³ t a⁻¹)			Total catch (10³ t a⁻¹)		
	1976–78	1986–88	% change	1976–78	1986–88	% change	1976–78	1986–88	% change
Japan	9,892	11,700	18	212	207	-2	10,103	11,907	18
USSR	8,733	10,280	18	757	970	28	9,491	11,251	19
China	3,329	5,200	56	1,064	4,035	279	4,392	9,235	110
USA	3,074	5,396	76	76	310	307	3,150	5,706	81
Peru	3,444	5,575	62	11	36	230	3,455	5,612	62
Chile	1,542	5,198	237		1		1,542	5,199	237
India	1,438	1,733	21	826	1,259	52	2,264	2,992	32
Korea	2,074	2,852	38	25	50	104	2,098	2,902	38
Indonesia	1,151	1,924	67	412	658	60	1,563	2,582	65
Thailand	1,845	2,185	18	137	177	29	1,982	2,362	19
Philippines	1,185	1,433	21	281	549	96	1,466	1,982	35
Norway	3,121	1,896	-39	–	–	-6	3,121	1,897	-39
Denmark	1,807	1,820	1	15	23	49	1,822	1,842	1
Korea, Dem.	1,131	1,600	41	59	100	70	1,190	1,700	43
Iceland	1,309	1,683	29	–	1	41	1,309	1,684	29
Canada	1,190	1,508	27	45	49	9	1,235	1,556	26
Spain	1,391	1,391	–	19	28	50	1,410	1,419	1
Mexico	589	1,205	105	4	157	4,090	592	1,362	130
South Africa	583	1,180	102	–	1	700	583	1,181	102
France	764	836	10	–	40		764	876	15
TOTAL, 20 COUNTRIES	49,591	66,595	34	3,943	8,653	119	53,534	75,248	41
TOTAL, WORLD	62,174	82,029	32	7,010	12,641	80	69,184	94,671	37

[a] The nominal catch is the live weight equivalent of the landed quantities, i.e., landings of each species adjusted for on-board processing such as gutting, filleting and drying.

Countries listed are those reporting the greatest annual average nominal fish catch during the 1986–1988 period; these countries collectively account for about 80 per cent of the total global catch.

Data include all fish, crustaceans, molluscs and other aquatic animal products but exclude aquatic mammals and plants. Country totals include production from aquaculture and quantities caught by vessels flying the national flag but landed at foreign ports.

Sources:
FAO 1980 *1978 Fishery Statistics Yearbook – Catches and Landings*, Food and Agriculture Organization, Rome.
FAO 1990 *1988 Fishery Statistics Yearbook – Catches and Landings*, Food and Agriculture Organization, Rome.

Table 3.15 Trends in the nominal[a] annual catch of selected fish species, 1965–1988 (10^3 t a^{-1})

Ocean region	Species	1965	1966	1967	1968	1969	1970	1971	1972
ATLANTIC, NORTH-EAST	Atlantic herring	3,735	3,665	3,302	2,381	1,422	1,471	1,403	1,362
	Capelin	274	514	506	616	850	1,506	1,575	1,870
	Sandeels	141							365
ATLANTIC, EASTERN-CENTRAL	Yellowfin tuna	55	56	52	86	80	71	68	91
	Chub mackerel	67	43	94	138	206	268	240	222
	Round sardinella								
ATLANTIC, SOUTH-EAST	Southern African pilchard	985	940	1,049	1,492	1,227	607	393	551
	Southern African anchovy	178	160	298	331	397	404	395	372
	Cape hakes	361	506	550	745	676	762	798	1,122
	Cape horse mackerel	180	115	77	64	74	62	240	84
ATLANTIC, NORTH-WEST	Atlantic cod	1,426	1,475	1,684	1,879	1,509	1,199	1,077	1,057
	Haddock	249	204	117	97	73	48	47	29
	Capelin	7	6	8	4	4	7	6	74
	Atlantic herring	266	423	595	947	972	851	740	554
INDIAN, WESTERN	Indian oil sardine	268	260	267	309	184	229	213	220
	Skipjack tuna	13	16	18	17	19	20	29	30
	Yellowfin tuna	17	26	26	52	37	25	27	38
PACIFIC, NORTH-EAST	Pacific halibut	39	39	35	30	36	34	30	27
	Pacific Ocean perch	455	335	256	182	122	121	125	131
	King crab	62	89	72	53	40	36	40	44
PACIFIC, EASTERN-CENTRAL	Yellowfin tuna	97	83	87	101	130	151	121	181
	Central Pacific anchoveta	42	67	61	69	13	34	55	35
	Californian pilchard	21	19	30	27	30	36	51	54
PACIFIC, SOUTH-EAST	Peruvian anchoveta	7,681	9,621	10,530	11,282	9,711	13,060	11,238	4,815
	Chilean jack mackerel								111
	South American pilchard	50	64	125	99	121	69	181	138
PACIFIC, WESTERN-CENTRAL	Scads	201	196	207	161	219	332	319	
	Skipjack tuna		36	35	43	42	54	85	
	Stolephorus anchovies								
PACIFIC, NORTH-WEST	Alaska pollack	826	965	1,162	1,493	1,698	1,959	2,645	2,783
	Japanese pilchard	9	14	17	24	21	17	58	58
	Chub mackerel	694	641	707	1,062	1,093	1,401	1,400	1,411

[a] The nominal catch is the live weight equivalent of the landed quantities, i.e., landings of each species adjusted for on-board processing such as gutting, filleting and drying.

Sources:
FAO 1972 *1970 Yearbook of Fishery Statistics, Catches and Landings,* Food and Agriculture Organization, Rome.

1973	1974	1975	1976	1977	1978	1979	1980	1981	1982	1983	1984	1985	1986	1987	1988
1,494	1,132	1,078	855	708	644	633	677	737	803	989	1,038	1,305	1,318	1,305	1,394
1,777	1,610	1,878	2,996	3,774	3,062	2,894	2,563	2,761	1,802	2,509	2,494	2,132	1,292	1,022	1,032
307	532	445	517	803	812	639	769	653	660	592	739	657	973	857	1,042
102	106	113	131	110	107	107	115	130	128	122	76	110	103	106	87
157	149	177	154	174	87	109	135	115	200	180	212	156	215	118	332
				85	97	86	91	78	75	74	40	103	133	175	181
500	623	665	640	326	149	96	62	99	89	112	89	90	88	107	105
547	599	410	307	368	564	570	506	491	390	424	286	323	315	969	682
906	738	656	804	598	520	454	318	342	439	456	493	542	541	444	476
280	197	316	548	688	552	465	569	624	665						
809	793	639	530	469	483	574	598	617	704	701	651	640	657	610	643
26	23	29	26	40	61	54	80	83	67	56	49	50	54	35	36
273	291	367	361	229	93	33	27	39	42	41	62	54	84	66	110
487	433	448	323	282	297	253	260	225	180	166	166	219	223	287	284
166	233	225	301	209	282	250	218	327	263	210	252	240	227	198	238
31	37	32	32	26	25	27	36	36	36	48	91	125	136	149	182
30	27	34	41	40	32	24	23	29	38	48	85	89	106	116	170
21	13	17	16	13	13	13	13	15	17	23	27	34	41	42	43
83	88	69	65	38	20	13	31	29	23	24	24	22	32	34	33
35	44	44	48	45	59	70	84	40	17	12	8	7	12	13	10
175	184	203	216	173	161	188	152	167	138	127	157	247	296	308	308
60	16	45	122	170	79	121	172	110	77	160	116	245	110	191	60
65	84	122	142	123	156	186	328	344	433	381	278	372	471	477	446
1,705	3,793	3,319	4,297	811	1,416	1,413	823	1,550	1,826	126	94	987	4,945	2,101	3,613
164	323	299	396	848	1,026	1,306	1,280	1,740	2,205	1,654	2,314	2,148	1,961	2,682	3,246
320	464	295	530	1,492	1,991	3,346	3,253	2,804	3,290	3,996	5,361	5,814	4,333	4,686	4,998
				248	211	228	196	215	264	253	255	284	321	310	319
				275	364	298	303	304	311	463	500	371	541	525	619
				133	188	189	196	199	199	181	191	203	193	208	226
3,927	3,755	3,906	3,959	3,617	3,203	3,135	3,193	3,131	3,484	3,667	4,614	4,733	5,154	5,009	5,107
301	352	530	1,077	1,471	1,934	2,156	2,595	3,613	3,966	4,465	5,156	4,723	5,191	5,321	5,429
1,411	1,658	1,559	1,302	1,759	2,239	2,016	1,679	1,358	1,177	1,224	1,331	1,217	1,479	1,133	1,138

FAO 1978 *1976 Yearbook of Fishery Statistics, Catches and Landings,* Food and Agriculture Organization, Rome.
FAO 1984 *1982 Yearbook of Fishery Statistics, Catches and Landings,* Food and Agriculture Organization, Rome.

FAO 1990 *1988 Yearbook of Fishery Statistics, Catches and Landings,* Food and Agriculture Organization, Rome.

Table 3.16 Aquaculture production in selected countries, 1984–1988

FRESH-WATER FISH (10^3 t a^{-1})

Country	1984	1985	1986	1987	1988
China	1,775	2,379	2,932	3,484	3,898
Japan	26	25	24	26	25
Philippines	32	50	62	84	81
USA	135	134	165	181	171
USSR	230	282	312	336	351
Norway					
Ecuador				–	–
Korea	1	1	3	5	7
Indonesia	149	168	182	205	209
Korea, Dem.					
France	2	8	8	7	8
Viet Nam	223	110	110	115	115
India	732	400	400	410	418
Spain		–	–	–	–
Thailand	49	73	85	78	78
Bangladesh	109	113	119	135	138
Italy	2	2	2	2	2
UK	–	–	–	–	–
Romania	37	39	38	38	38
Finland					
TOTAL					
20 COUNTRIES	3,503	3,785	4,442	5,107	5,540
WORLD	3,811	4,132	4,789	5,463	5,925

DIADROMOUS FISH (10^3 t a^{-1})

Country	1984	1985	1986	1987	1988
China					
Japan	75	77	76	82	89
Philippines	239	194	180	198	188
USA	39	61	57	82	73
USSR	22	8	8	9	8
Norway	26	35	50	56	89
Ecuador				–	–
Korea	1	1	1	3	1
Indonesia	85	87	104	107	119
Korea, Dem.					
France	25	25	27	31	32
Viet Nam					
India					
Spain		12	14	12	16
Thailand	1	1	1	1	1
Bangladesh					
Italy	25	27	28	39	35
UK	16	19	22	26	33
Romania					
Finland	9	10	11	13	16
TOTAL					
20 COUNTRIES	562	556	579	659	702
WORLD	708	694	722	822	908

MARINE FISH (10^3 t a^{-1})

Country	1984	1985	1986	1987	1988
China	9	14	19	29	33
Japan	185	189	189	208	225
Philippines					
USA					
USSR	–	–	–	–	–
Norway				–	
Ecuador					
Korea	–	1	3	2	1
Indonesia	4	4	4	5	5
Korea, Dem.					
France	–	–	–	–	–
Viet Nam					
India					
Spain		–	1	–	–
Thailand	1	1	1	1	1
Bangladesh					
Italy	4	4	6	4	4
UK					
Romania					
Finland					
TOTAL					
20 COUNTRIES	204	213	223	250	269
WORLD	210	221	233	261	281

CRUSTACEANS (10^3 t a^{-1})

Country	1984	1985	1986	1987	1988
China	22	43	85	156	202
Japan	2	2	2	3	3
Philippines	30	31	32	37	46
USA	27	30	45	44	31
USSR					
Norway					
Ecuador	34	30	31	74	75
Korea	–	–	–	–	–
Indonesia	32	37	43	60	71
Korea, Dem.	11	11	11	11	11
France	–	–	–	–	–
Viet Nam	13	18	24	29	30
India	12	13	14	15	17
Spain			–	3	3
Thailand	16	18	23	36	36
Bangladesh	8	11	15	15	17
Italy					
UK				–	–
Romania	–	–	–	–	
Finland					
TOTAL					
20 COUNTRIES	208	244	325	482	542
WORLD	230	277	389	589	608

Continued opposite

Table 3.16 Continued

Country	Annual production 1984	1985	1986	1987	1988
MOLLUSCS (10^3 t a^{-1})					
China	343	386	523	711	945
Japan	332	360	392	412	454
Philippines	35	38	29	22	28
USA	143	130	138	131	124
USSR	–	–	–	–	–
Norway			–	–	–
Ecuador				–	–
Korea	283	370	441	449	425
Indonesia					
Korea, Dem.	88	88	88	88	200
France	166	176	196	187	181
Viet Nam					
India	2	2	2	2	3
Spain		249	251	249	250
Thailand	45	42	19	36	77
Bangladesh					
Italy	44	49	49	49	49
UK	–	–	1	2	4
Romania					
Finland					
TOTAL					
20 COUNTRIES	1,481	1,891	2,129	2,339	2,741
WORLD	2,043	2,230	2,441	2,668	3,077
OTHER[a] (10^3 t a^{-1})					
China	1,641	1,683	1,489	1,325	1,581
Japan	587	531	608	502	629
Philippines	142	183	169	221	256
USA					
USSR	4	4	4	3	5
Norway					
Ecuador					
Korea	395	417	545	417	464
Indonesia	60	58	77	77	77
Korea, Dem.	620	620	620	620	620
France		–	–		
Viet Nam	1	2	2	2	2
India					
Spain					
Thailand	–	–	–	–	–
Bangladesh					
Italy					
UK					
Romania					
Finland					
TOTAL					
20 COUNTRIES	3,450	3,496	3,514	3,167	3,635
WORLD	3,467	3,512	3,530	3,183	3,666

Country	Annual production 1984	1985	1986	1987	1988
TOTAL PRODUCTION (10^3 t a^{-1})					
China	3,790	4,505	5,048	5,705	6,659
Japan	1,207	1,184	1,291	1,233	1,325
Philippines	478	496	472	562	599
USA	344	355	405	438	399
USSR	256	294	324	348	364
Norway	26	35	50	56	89
Ecuador	34	30	31	74	75
Korea	680	790	993	876	898
Indonesia	330	354	410	454	481
Korea, Dem.	719	719	719	719	831
France	193	209	231	225	221
Viet Nam	237	130	136	146	147
India	746	415	416	427	438
Spain		261	266	264	269
Thailand	112	135	129	152	193
Bangladesh	117	124	134	150	155
Italy	75	82	85	94	90
UK	16	19	23	28	37
Romania	37	39	38	38	38
Finland	9	10	11	13	16
TOTAL					
20 COUNTRIES	9,406	10,186	11,212	12,002	13,324
WORLD	10,468	11,066	12,105	12,988	14,466
TOTAL PRODUCTION (10^6 US$ a^{-1})					
China	4,059	4,953	5,870	6,361	7,951
Japan	2,264	2,279	3,439	3,902	4,572
Philippines	447	468	511	560	720
USA	500	429	484	564	609
USSR	357	331	438	519	606
Norway	133	178	233	314	589
Ecuador	235	211	215	542	581
Korea	253	266	331	440	551
Indonesia	265	340	382	481	551
Korea, Dem.	399	421	421	421	486
France	226	244	428	477	471
Viet Nam	327	255	301	344	356
India		278	324	336	353
Spain	209	218	231	253	289
Thailand	106	115	147	238	262
Bangladesh	109	175	171	210	210
Italy	140	134	166	217	192
UK	63	80	104	128	160
Romania	93	98	95	95	95
Finland	43	46	49	67	86
TOTAL					
20 COUNTRIES	10,229	11,520	14,342	16,470	19,687
WORLD	11,684	13,097	16,197	18,829	22,453

[a] "Other" includes frogs, turtles and aquatic plants.

Aquaculture, that is, the farming of aquatic organisms, is defined here as the active intervention during the rearing of aquatic organisms. Such intervention may comprise regular stocking, feeding and protection from predators. Only aquatic organisms that are wholly owned (i.e., throughout their rearing period) and harvested by individuals or corporate bodies are included.

The 20 countries listed are those reporting the greatest volume of aquaculture production in 1988 and are ranked in descending order of commercial value.

Source:
FAO 1990 Unpublished data, Food and Agriculture Organization, Rome.

Table 3.17 Nationally and internationally designated protected areas, current status

Region/country	Nationally protected areas			World Heritage Sites	Biosphere Reserves		Ramsar Wetlands	
	Number	Area (ha)	% of total land area	Number	Number	Area (ha)	Number	Area (ha)
WORLD	6,940	651,487,597	3.2	86	283	152,520,161	503	30,216,861
AFRICA	601	117,087,952	3.9	26	40	20,055,905	33	3,189,702
Algeria	19	11,897,687	5.0	1	1	7,200,000	2	4,900
Angola	6	2,692,170	2.2					
Benin	2	843,500	7.5	0	1	880,000		
Botswana	9	10,025,000	17.4					
Burkina Faso	7	738,900	2.7	0	1	16,300	3	
Burundi	1	37,870	1.4	0				
Cameroon	13	2,099,705	4.4	1	3	850,000		
Cape Verde	0	0	0.0	0				
Cent. African Rep.	7	3,904,000	6.2	1	2	1,640,200		
Chad	1	114,000	0.1				1	195,000
Comoros	0	0	0.0					
Congo	10	1,333,100	3.9	0	2	172,000		
Côte d'Ivoire	12	2,019,850	6.3	3	2	1,480,000		
Djibouti	1	10,000	0.4					
Egypt	9	685,300	0.7	0	1	1,000	2	105,700
Equatorial Guinea	0	0	0.0					
Ethiopia	24	6,222,600	6.1	1				
Gabon	5	1,790,000	6.7	0	1	15,000	3	1,080,000
Gambia	2	12,000	1.1	0				
Ghana	8	1,074,637	4.5	0	1	7,700	1	7,260
Guinea	2	129,170	0.5	1	2	133,300		
Guinea-Bissau	0	0	0.0				1	39,098
Kenya	36	3,347,447	5.7		4	851,359	1	18,800
Lesotho	1	6,805	0.2					
Liberia	1	130,747	1.2					
Libya	3	155,000	0.1	0				
Madagascar	36	1,077,732	1.8	0	1	140,000		
Malawi	9	1,066,900	11.3	1				
Mali	7	889,100	0.7	0	1	771,000		
Mauritania	3	1,733,000	1.7	1			1	1,173,000
Mauritius	3	4,023	2.2					
Mayotte	0	0	0.0	0			0	0
Morocco	11	368,359	0.8	0			4	10,580
Mozambique	1	2,000	0.0	0				
Namibia	9	10,346,302	12.6					
Niger	4	1,654,240	1.4	0			1	220,000
Nigeria	15	1,546,591	1.7	0	1	460		
Réunion	2	5,369	2.1	0			0	0
Rwanda	2	327,000	12.4		1	15,065		
St Helena	2	17,600	42.8	0			0	0
São Tomé & Príncipe	0	0	0.0					
Senegal	10	2,180,709	11.1	2	3	1,093,756	4	99,720
Seychelles	4	38,568	95.5	2				
Sierra Leone	3	100,700	1.4					
Somalia	0	0	0.0					

Continued opposite

Table 3.17 Continued

Region/country	Nationally protected areas			World Heritage Sites	Biosphere Reserves		Ramsar Wetlands	
	Number	Area (ha)	% of total land area	Number	Number	Area (ha)	Number	Area (ha)
South Africa	178	6,309,779	5.3				7	208,044
Sudan	13	7,731,500	3.1	0	2	1,900,970		
Swaziland	3	39,545	2.3					
Tanzania	20	11,913,075	12.7	4	2	2,337,600		
Togo	11	646,906	11.4					
Tunisia	7	45,230	0.3	1	4	32,425	1	12,600
Uganda	19	1,755,629	7.4	0	1	220,000	1	15,000
Western Sahara	0	0	0.0					
Zaire	9	8,827,000	3.8	4	3	297,700		
Zambia	20	6,360,900	8.5	1				
Zimbabwe	21	2,830,707	7.3	2				
NORTH AMERICA	1,640	232,688,637	9.6	21	67	93,617,617	58	15,147,389
Anguilla	0	0	0.0	0			0	0
Antigua & Barbuda	0	0	0.0	0				
Aruba	0	0	0.0	0			1	70
Bahamas	5	123,390	8.9					
Barbados	0	0	0.0					
Belize	8	74,314	3.2					
Bermuda	2	12,200	3.7	0			0	0
Br. Virgin Is.	0	0	0.0	0			0	0
Canada	426	49,452,283	5.0	6	6	1,049,978	30	12,937,549
Cayman Is.	2	5,041	19.5	0			0	0
Costa Rica	28	606,000	11.9	1	2	728,955		
Cuba	29	714,224	6.2	0	4	323,600		
Dominica	1	6,840	9.1					
Dominican Rep.	14	551,509	11.4	0				
El Salvador	9	26,152	1.2					
Greenland	2	71,050,000	32.7		1	70,000,000	11	1,044,500
Grenada	0	0	0.0					
Guadeloupe	2	21,200	11.9	0			0	0
Guatemala	9	88,272	0.8	1			1	
Haiti	2	7,700	0.3	0				
Honduras	34	709,369	6.3	1	1	500,000		
Jamaica	0	0	0.0	0				
Martinique	1	70,150	65.0	0			0	0
Mexico	61	9,419,669	4.8	1	6	1,288,454	1	47,480
Montserrat	0	0	0.0					
Neth. Antilles	4	14,796	18.5	0			5	2,010
Nicaragua	6	43,300	0.3	0				
Panama	16	1,326,140	16.9	1	1	597,000		
Puerto Rico	0	0	0.0		2	15,346		
St Christopher & Nevis	0	0	0.0	0				
St Lucia	0	0	0.0					
St Vincent & Grenadines	0	0	0.0					
Trinidad & Tobago	6	15,278	3.0					
Turks & Caicos Is.	3	1,634	3.8	0			1	
USA	968	98,341,751	10.5	10	43	19,108,157	8	1,115,780
US Virgin Is.	2	7,425	21.5	0	1	6,127	0	0

Continued over

Table 3.17 Continued

Region/country	Nationally protected areas			World Heritage Sites	Biosphere Reserves		Ramsar Wetlands	
	Number	Area (ha)	% of total land area	Number	Number	Area (ha)	Number	Area (ha)
SOUTH AMERICA	552	101,350,573	5.6	8	24	11,918,971	5	232,085
Argentina	113	12,638,733	4.5	2	5	2,409,980		
Bolivia	23	6,774,165	6.2	0	3	435,000	1	5,240
Brazil	162	20,525,324	2.4	1				
Chile	65	13,649,718	18.2	0	7	2,406,633	1	4,877
Colombia	42	9,301,690	8.2	0	3	2,514,375		
Ecuador	14	10,685,664	5.8	2	2	1,446,244		
French Guiana	0	0	0.0	0			0	0
Guyana	1	11,655	0.1	0				
Paraguay	12	1,185,731	2.9	0				
Peru	24	5,517,835	4.3	3	3	2,506,739		
Suriname	14	762,970	4.7				1	12,000
Uruguay	8	31,726	0.2	0	1	200,000	1	200,000
Venezuela	74	20,265,362	22.2				1	9,968
ASIA	1,392	90,607,198	3.3	9	36	7,438,042	40	1,354,493
Afghanistan	4	142,438	0.2	0				
Bahrain	0	0	0.0					
Bangladesh	8	96,790	0.7					
Bhutan	7	924,314	19.8					
Br. Ind. Oc. Tr.	0	0	0.0	0			0	0
Brunei	4	122,367	21.2					
Cambodia	0	0	0.0					
China	394	22,235,681	10.3		7	1,819,305		
Cyprus	0	0	0.0	0				
Hong Kong	12	37,811	35.6	0			0	0
India	359	13,481,148	4.3	5			6	192,973
Indonesia	169	17,799,787	9.3	0	6	1,482,400		
Iran	60	7,528,976	4.6	0	9	2,609,731	18	1,087,550
Iraq	0	0	0.0	0				
Israel	18	225,886	10.9					
Japan	65	2,402,418	6.5		4	116,000	3	9,892
Jordan	7	92,900	1.0	0			1	7,372
Korea, Dem.	2	57,890	0.5		1	132,000		
Korea	17	577,766	5.9	0	1	37,430		
Kuwait	0	0	0.0					
Laos	0	0	0.0	0				
Lebanon	1	3,500	0.3	0				
Malaysia	45	1,162,204	3.5	0				
Maldives	0	0	0.0	0				
Mongolia	14	5,617,840	3.6	0				
Myanmar, q.v. Burma	2	173,271	0.3					
Nepal	11	958,500	6.8	2			1	17,500
Oman	2	54,000	0.2	0				
Pakistan	53	3,654,969	4.5	0	1	31,355	9	20,990
Philippines	28	583,999	1.9	0	2	1,174,345		
Qatar	0	0	0.0	0				
Saudi Arabia	7	5,619,400	2.3	0				

Continued opposite

Table 3.17 Continued

Region/country	Nationally protected areas			World Heritage Sites	Biosphere Reserves		Ramsar Wetlands	
	Number	Area (ha)	% of total land area	Number	Number	Area (ha)	Number	Area (ha)
Singapore	1	2,715	4.4	1	2	9,376	1	6,216
Sri Lanka	43	783,708	11.9	0				
Syria	0	0	0.0	0	3	26,100		
Thailand	83	5,105,746	9.9	0				
Turkey	18	269,176	0.3	1				
United Arab Em.	0	0	0.0				1	12,000
Viet Nam	58	891,998	2.7	0				
Yemen	0	0	0.0	0				
Yemen, Dem.	0	0	0.0	0				
EUROPE	1,658	36,813,333	7.6	11	83	3,853,037	311	2,790,047
Albania	13	54,500	1.9	0				
Andorra	0	0	0.0					
Austria	129	1,593,894	19.0		4	27,600	5	102,369
Belgium	2	71,829	2.4				6	9,607
Bulgaria	39	129,125	1.2	2	17	25,201	4	2,097
Czechoslovakia	61	1,963,689	15.4		6	364,170	8	16,958
Denmark	65	422,518	9.8	0			27	734,468
Faeroe Is.	0	0	0.0	0			0	0
Finland	35	807,250	2.4	0			11	101,343
France	81	4,779,473	8.8	1	5	502,627	1	85,000
German Dem. Rep.	225	1,998,168	18.5	0	2	24,960	8	46,127
Germany, Fed. Rep.	54	2,955,880	11.9	0	1	13,100	21	314,767
Greece	20	103,703	0.8	0	2	8,840	11	107,400
Holy See	0	0	0.0	0				
Hungary	46	511,149	5.5	0	5	128,884	13	110,389
Iceland	22	915,924	8.9				2	57,500
Ireland	6	26,810	0.4		2	8,808	21	12,562
Italy	108	1,300,565	4.3	0	3	3,798	45	54,458
Liechtenstein	0	0	0.0					
Luxembourg	0	0	0.0	0				
Malta	0	0	0.0	0			1	11
Monaco	0	0	0.0	0				
Netherlands	68	355,031	8.6				11	306,278
Norway	68	4,767,438	14.7	0	1	1,555,000	14	16,256
Poland	78	2,230,100	7.1	1	4	25,836	5	7,090
Portugal	21	453,642	5.0	0	1	395	2	30,563
Romania	36	561,574	2.4	0	3	41,213		
San Marino	0	0	0.0					
Spain	161	3,511,091	7.0	1	10	614,977	17	98,887
Sweden	99	1,758,408	3.9	0	1	96,500	30	382,750
Switzerland	15	111,159	2.7	0	1	16,870	2	1,816
UK	138	4,639,164	19.0	3	13	44,258	44	173,257
Yugoslavia	68	791,249	3.1	3	2	350,000	2	18,094
USSR	176	24,073,717	1.1	0	20	10,891,366	12	2,987,185

Continued over

Table 3.17 Continued

Region/country	Nationally protected areas			World Heritage Sites	Biosphere Reserves		Ramsar Wetlands	
	Number	Area (ha)	% of total land area	Number	Number	Area (ha)	Number	Area (ha)
OCEANIA	911	48,631,938	5.7	11	13	4,745,223	44	4,515,960
American Samoa	0	0	0.0	0			0	0
Australia	728	45,654,429	5.9	8	12	4,743,223	39	4,477,861
Cook Is.	1	160	0.7	0			0	0
Fiji	2	5,342	0.3					
French Polynesia	4	10,547	2.7		1	2,000		
Guam	0	0	0.0	0			0	0
Kiribati	3	26,630	38.9					
Marshall Is.	0	0	0.0					
Micronesia	0	0	0.0					
Nauru	0	0	0.0					
New Caledonia	12	64,352	3.4	0			0	0
New Zealand	152	2,839,133	10.7	2			5	38,099
Niue	0	0	0.0	0			0	0
Northern Marianas Is.	3	1,129	2.4					
Palau	1	1,200	3.3					
Papua New Guinea	5	29,016	0.1					
Pitcairn Is.	0	0	0.0	1			0	0
Solomon Is.	0	0	0.0					
Tokelau	0	0	0.0	0			0	0
Tonga	0	0	0.0					
Tuvalu	0	0	0.0					
Vanuatu	0	0	0.0					
Wallis Is.	0	0	0.0	0			0	0
Samoa	0	0	0.0				0	0
ANTARCTICA	10	234,249	0.0	0	0	0	0	0
Antarctica	9	197,549	0.0					
Falkland Is. (Malvinas)	0	0	0.0	0			0	0
French Southern Territories	1	36,700	5.1	0			0	0

A nationally protected area is defined as an area over 10^3 ha that falls within IUCN Management Categories I to V, inclusive. Areas within these categories include Scientific Reserves (strict nature reserves), National Parks, Natural Monuments (natural landmarks), Managed Nature Reserves (wildlife sanctuaries) and Protected Landscapes and Seascapes.

Source:
WCMC 1992 *Global Biodiversity 1992: Status of the Earth's Living Resources*, World Conservation Monitoring Centre, Cambridge. In press.

Table 3.18 Distribution of wetlands in the USA, 1780s and 1980s

State	Wetland status, 1780s		Wetland status, 1980s		Wetland losses, 1780s–1980s	
	Area (ha)	% of total land area	Area (ha)	% of total land area	Area (ha)	% of wetland area lost
TOTAL	158,386,321	16.9	111,054,231	11.9	47,332,089	30
Alabama	3,062,442	22.9	1,531,221	11.5	1,531,221	50
Alaska	68,876,209	45.3	68,795,273	45.3	80,936	–
Arizona	376,755	1.3	242,807	0.8	133,948	36
Arkansas	3,985,513	29.0	1,118,368	8.1	2,867,144	72
California	2,023,390	4.9	183,724	0.4	1,839,667	91
Colorado	809,356	3.0	404,678	0.2	404,678	50
Connecticut	271,134	20.9	69,807	5.4	201,327	74
Delaware	194,158	36.4	90,243	16.9	103,915	54
Florida	8,225,087	54.2	4,466,958	29.5	3,758,129	46
Georgia	2,769,293	18.2	2,144,065	14.1	625,228	23
Hawaii	23,795	1.4	20,962	1.3	2,833	12
Idaho	354,903	1.6	156,084	0.7	198,818	56
Illinois	3,323,216	22.8	507,669	3.5	2,815,548	85
Indiana	2,266,197	24.1	303,765	3.2	1,962,433	87
Iowa	1,618,712	11.1	170,734	1.2	1,447,979	89
Kansas	340,334	1.6	176,197	0.8	164,137	48
Kentucky	633,726	6.1	121,403	1.2	512,322	81
Louisiana	6,553,559	52.1	3,554,773	28.3	2,998,786	46
Maine	2,614,220	30.4	2,104,002	24.5	510,218	20
Maryland	667,719	24.4	178,058	6.5	489,660	73
Massachusetts	331,027	15.5	238,147	11.1	92,879	28
Michigan	4,532,394	30.1	2,259,480	15.0	2,272,915	50
Minnesota	6,098,499	28.0	3,520,699	16.2	2,577,799	42
Mississippi	3,994,982	32.3	1,645,826	13.3	2,349,156	59
Missouri	1,960,261	10.9	260,208	1.4	1,700,053	87
Montana	464,166	1.2	340,051	0.9	124,115	27
Nebraska	1,177,816	5.9	771,114	3.9	406,701	35
Nevada	197,220	0.7	95,646	0.3	101,574	52
New Hampshire	89,029	3.7	80,936	3.4	8,094	9
New Jersey	607,017	29.9	370,669	18.3	236,348	39
New Mexico	291,368	0.9	195,014	0.6	96,354	33
New York	1,036,785	8.1	414,795	3.2	621,990	60
North Carolina	4,487,678	33.0	2,302,416	16.9	2,185,262	49
North Dakota	1,994,051	10.9	1,007,648	5.5	986,403	49
Ohio	2,023,390	19.0	195,379	1.8	1,828,012	90
Oklahoma	1,150,338	6.4	384,323	2.1	766,015	67
Oregon	915,382	3.6	564,081	2.2	351,301	38
Pennsylvania	456,072	3.9	201,940	1.7	254,132	56
Rhode Island	41,556	13.2	26,366	8.4	15,190	37
South Carolina	2,595,605	32.3	1,885,395	23.4	710,210	27
South Dakota	1,106,835	5.5	720,327	3.6	386,508	35
Tennessee	783,861	7.2	318,482	2.9	465,380	59
Texas	6,474,728	9.4	3,080,576	4.4	3,394,152	52
Utah	324,552	1.5	225,810	1.0	98,741	30
Vermont	137,995	5.5	89,029	3.6	48,966	35
Virginia	748,250	7.1	434,872	4.1	313,377	42
Washington	546,315	3.1	379,588	2.1	166,727	31
West Virginia	54,227	0.9	41,277	0.7	12,950	24
Wisconsin	3,965,845	27.3	2,157,497	14.8	1,808,348	46
Wyoming	809,356	3.2	505,848	2.0	303,509	38

Totals may not tally due to rounding.
Data were originally reported in acres and have been converted to hectatres using the conversion factor: 1 hectare = 2.4711 acres.
The total land area of the USA is assumed to be 936,270,160 hectares.

Source:
Dahl, T. E. 1990 *Wetland Losses in the United States, 1780s to 1980s*, US Department of the Interior, Fish and Wildlife Service, Washington DC.

Table 3.19 Diversity and current status of animal species

Region/country	Mammals		Birds		Reptiles		Amphibians		Swallowtail butterflies	
	No. of species known	No. at risk	No. of species known	No. at risk	No. of species known	No. at risk	No. of species known	No. at risk	No. of species known	No. at risk
AFRICA										
Algeria	97	15		4		2			3	0
Angola	275	13		12		7			27	1
Benin	187	7				5			21	1
Botswana	162	8	1,044	3		1			6	0
Burkina Faso	147	6							4	0
Burundi	103	6		4		1			15–20	1
Cameroon	297	18	848	16		5		1	39	2
Cape Verde	9	3		4	12	3	0		5	0
Cent. African Rep.	208	8		1		3			24–29	1
Chad	131	11		1		3			7–8	0
Comoros				9		1			3–4	2
Congo	198	12		3		7			37–38	1
Côte d'Ivoire	232	23	756	6		6		1	23	1
Djibouti	22	6		1					6–7	0
Egypt	105	12		2	83	4	6		0–1	0
Equatorial Guinea	182	13		3		4		1	13–21	1
Ethiopia	242	11	847	10	6	3			15–16	0
Gabon	190	9		5		7			25–31	1
Gambia	108	5				5			6	0
Ghana	222	10	721	7		7			25	1
Guinea	188	13		4		4			15	1
Guinea-Bissau	109	11		2		7		1	6	0
Kenya	307	12	860	12	106	5	97	4	30	1
Lesotho	33	2		4					4	0
Liberia	193	14		9		6		1	22	1
Libya	76	9		1		3			0–1	0
Madagascar				29	252	11	144		13	3
Malawi	192	5	624	9		1			22	0
Mali	136	11		2		2			5	0
Mauritania	61	10		2		5			5	0
Mauritius		2		8		6			2	1
Morocco	108	13		3		4			2	0
Mozambique	183	6		16		5			16	0
Namibia	161	12		6		2			6	0
Niger	131	9		1		1			5	0
Nigeria	274	57	831	8	114	9	19	3	30	1
Réunion				2		3			2	1
Rwanda	147	9		6		2			18–21	2
Senegal	166	13		3		8			10	0
Seychelles				10		2		3	0	0
Sierra Leone	178	11		7		6			20	1
Somalia	173	14	639	6		4			12	0
South Africa	279	20		10					12	0
Sudan	266	19		5		3			20	0
Swaziland	46	3		4		1			5	0
Tanzania	310	15	1,016	27		7			34	1
Togo	196	6		0		6			23	1
Tunisia	77	14		2		2			3	0

Continued opposite

Table 3.19 Continued

Region/country	Mammals		Birds		Reptiles		Amphibians		Swallowtail butterflies	
	No. of species known	No. at risk	No. of species known	No. at risk	No. of species known	No. at risk	No. of species known	No. at risk	No. of species known	No. at risk
Uganda	311	10	989	14		2			31–32	2
Western Sahara	15	7		3		2			–	–
Zaire	409	24	1,086	27		6			48	3
Zambia	228	6	728	8		2			23	0
Zimbabwe	194	7	635	7		1			14	0
NORTH AMERICA										
Bahamas	17	2	218	8	39	18	6	0	5	0
Belize	121	9	504	1	107	8	26	0	31	0
Bermuda		1		1					1	0
Canada	210	7	426	14	42	1	41	0	18	0
Cayman Is.				3		5			3	0
Costa Rica	203	10	796	5	218	8	151	1	41	0
Cuba	39	9	286	14	100	10	40	0	13	1
El Salvador	129	7	432	3	92	7	38	0	25	0
Greenland	26	7		2					0	0
Guatemala	174	9	666	8	204	10	99	0	41	0
Honduras	179	8	672	5	161	9	57	0	34	0
Jamaica	29	2	223	5	38	4	20	0	7	2
Mexico	439	32	961	123	717	35	284	4	52	2
Neth. Antilles	9	0	171	0	22	3	2	0	1	0
Nicaragua	177	9	610	4	162	9	59	0	31	0
Panama	217	13	920	6	212	10	155	2	38	0
Puerto Rico	17	1	220	11	46	15	26	1	2–3	0
Trinidad & Tobago	114	2	504	6	115	8	23	0	13–14	0
USA	466	49	1,090	79	368	26	222	8	30–31	1
SOUTH AMERICA										
Argentina	255	26	927	18	204	7	124	1	36–37	1
Bolivia	267	24	1,177	5	180	10	96	0	43–44	2
Brazil	394	42	1,567	35	467	19	487	1	74	8
Chile	90	10	393	6	82	3	38	0	2–3	0
Colombia	358	25	1,665	28	383	24	375	0	59	0
Ecuador[a]	280	21	1,447	17	345	36	350	0	64	0
French Guiana	142	11	628	3	136	14	89	0	29–31	3
Guyana	198	12	728	3	137	14	105	0	30–31	1
Paraguay	157	14	630	8	110	8	69	0	26–32	0
Peru	359	30	1,642	10	297	15	235	0	58–59	2
Suriname	200	11	670	3	131	12	99	0	30–31	1
Uruguay	77	7	367	3	66	9	37	1	7–8	0
Venezuela	305	18	1,295	8	246	20	183	0	35–39	1
ASIA										
Afghanistan		10		2	103	2	6		19	1
Bangladesh		5		4	108	8	19		10–15	0
Bhutan		12		3		1			22–30	2
Brunei		6				3			35–37	1
China		30		7	358		218		136	7
China,Taiwan					78		30		32	1
Cyprus					23		4		1	0

Continued over

Table 3.19 Continued

Region/country	Mammals No. of species known	Mammals No. at risk	Birds No. of species known	Birds No. at risk	Reptiles No. of species known	Reptiles No. at risk	Amphibians No. of species known	Amphibians No. at risk	Swallowtail butterflies No. of species known	Swallowtail butterflies No. at risk
India	341	29	1,178	135	400	12	181		82	2
Indonesia		22		14		11			121	14
Iran		9		3	164	6	11		7–9	0
Iraq		8		3		1			6–7	0
Japan	186	4	632	35	85	3	58	1	22	1
Korea, Dem.		8		10	19		13		14	0
Korea		8		9	18		13		14–15	0
Malaysia		8		7		7			56	3
Mongolia		6		4					11	1
Myanmar q.v. Burma	300	14	1,000	3	360	8			68	1
Nepal		17		2		4			37–38	1
Pakistan		13		6	143	9	17		14	0
Philippines	96	7	541	2	192	1	66		49	9
Sri Lanka		7		2		34		4	15	1
Turkey	124	2	217	36	102		18	1	10	2
Viet Nam	273		774		180		80		46	1
EUROPE										
Albania					31		13		7	1
Austria	83	38	201	121	14		20		6	1
Belgium					8		17		2	0
Bulgaria					33		17		7	1
Czechoslovakia			390		12		19		6	1
Denmark	49	14	190	41	5	0	14	3	3	0
Faeroe Is.					0	0	0	0	0	0
Finland	62	7	232	14	5	1	5	1	2	1
France	113	59	342	136	32	14	32	18	9	2
German Dem. Rep.					8		19		4	1
Germany, Fed. Rep.	94	44	305	98	12	9	20	11	5	1
Greece					51		15		8	1
Hungary					15		17		4	1
Iceland					0	0	0	0	0	0
Ireland	31	5	139	33	1	0	3	1	0	0
Italy	97	13	419	60	40	24	34	13	8	2
Liechtenstein					7		10		4	1
Luxembourg	60		140	54	7	7	14	11	2	0
Malta					8		1		1	0
Monaco					6		3		1	0
Netherlands	60	39	257	85	7	6	16	10	3	1
Norway	54	4	220	23	5	1	5	2	2	1
Poland					9		18		4	1
Portugal	56	25	288	113	29		17		2	0
Romania					25		19		7	1
Spain	135	17	357	22	53	1	25	1	5	1
Sweden	65	10	250	17	6	0	13	5	3	1
Switzerland	86		190	74	14		18		5	1
UK	77	24	233	35	8	5	7	2	1	0
Yugoslavia					41		23		7	1
USSR	357	78	765	80	144	37	34	9	36	2

Continued opposite

Table 3.19 Continued

Region/country	Mammals		Birds		Reptiles		Amphibians		Swallowtail butterflies	
	No. of species known	No. at risk	No. of species known	No. at risk	No. of species known	No. at risk	No. of species known	No. at risk	No. of species known	No. at risk
OCEANIA										
Australia	320	43	700	23	550	9	150	6	19	0
Fiji				5	25	5	2		1	0
Guam					10		0	0	2	0
Marshall Is.					7		0	0	0	0
New Caledonia		1		4	32		0		3–4	0
New Zealand	69	14	282	16	39	7	5		0	0
Northern Marianas Is.					10		0	0	0	0
Papua New Guinea		10		1		7			37	9
Solomon Is.		1		3	57	5	15		15	3
Tonga					6		0	0	0	0
Vanuatu		1		1	22	2	0	0	4	0
Western Samoa				1	8	1	0	0	1	0

a   Includes the Galapogos Islands.

Reptile data generally exclude marine species.

Source:
WCMC 1992 *Global Biodiversity 1992: Status of the Earth's Living Resources*, World Conservation Monitoring Centre, Cambridge. In press.

Table 3.20 African elephant populations, status in 1989

Region/country	No. of elephants	Density (No. per km^2)
AFRICA	609,000	0.11
CENTRAL AFRICA	277,000	0.10
Cameroon	22,000	0.09
Cent. African Rep.	23,000	0.07
Chad	2,100	0.01
Congo	42,000	0.20
Equatorial Guinea	500	0.02
Gabon	74,000	0.30
Zaire	112,000	0.08
EASTERN AFRICA	110,000	0.07
Ethiopia	8,000	0.05
Kenya	16,000	0.04
Rwanda	50	0.02
Somalia	2,000	0.04
Sudan	22,000	0.06
Tanzania	61,000	0.12
Uganda	1,600	0.10
SOUTHERN AFRICA	204,000	0.16
Angola	18,000	0.04
Botswana	68,000	0.74

Region/country	No. of elephants	Density (No. per km^2)
Malawi	2,800	0.15
Mozambique	17,000	0.07
Namibia	5,700	0.04
South Africa	7,800	0.35
Zambia	32,000	0.15
Zimbabwe	52,000	0.46
WESTERN AFRICA	19,000	0.07
Benin	2,100	0.10
Burkina Faso	4,500	0.12
Ghana	2,800	0.13
Guinea	560	0.07
Guinea-Bissau	40	0.13
Côte d'Ivoire	3,600	0.07
Liberia	1,300	0.06
Mali	840	0.02
Mauritania	100	0.02
Niger	440	0.09
Nigeria	1,300	0.04
Senegal	140	0.01
Sierra Leone	380	0.13
Togo	380	0.06

Numbers above 5,000 are rounded to the nearest thousand, numbers between 1,000–5,000 are rounded to the nearest hundred and numbers below 1,000 are rounded to the nearest 10.

Source:
Douglas-Hamilton, I. 1989 *Overview of Status and Trends of the African Elephant*, Report to the Ivory Trade Review Group, No. 1, EEC/WWF African Elephant Programme.

Table 3.21 Export of ivory from African countries, 1979–1988 (kg a^{-1})

Country	1979	1980	1981	1982	1983	1984	1985	1986	1987	1988	Total
TOTAL	979,492	966,615	895,300	890,877	1,017,807	610,996	711,534	587,014	426,481	182,212	7,268,328
Angola	0	0	5	0	50	10	0	0	0	0	65
Benin	0	0	0	195	0	0	10	0	0	0	205
Botswana	12,699	5,529	5,716	4,019	5,580	2,333	16,487	360	388	755	53,866
Burkina Faso	0	0	35	26	0	0	20	0	0	0	81
Burundi	138,880	147,333	61,399	46,488	132,124	183,984	215,218	247,000	92,000	8,339	1,272,765
Cameroon	13,036	7,870	2,195	2,794	869	1,896	1,591	805	3,132	2,900	37,088
Cent. African Rep.	197,204	167,274	105,764	205,796	197,981	88,608	116,624	16,928	1,308	413	1,097,900
Chad	31,321	3,203	10,551	29,325	33,750	4,383	30	0	1,606	0	114,169
Congo	109,876	175,499	234,013	117,232	46,425	86,875	67,860	13,383	84,297	19,287	954,747
Djibouti	0	0	3	0	0	0	0	0	0	10,901	10,904
Ethiopia	0	0	0	0	0	172	6,193	4,600	1,764	2,160	14,889
Gabon	3,746	1,482	1,107	239	1,121	223	372	415	4,244	14,238	27,187
Ghana	500	28	80	112	15	30	0	70	75	0	910
Guinea	0	10	0	0	15	0	5	0	0	0	30
Kenya	46,461	30,198	5,642	12,399	4,012	12,883	18,733	383	21,882	6,293	158,886
Liberia	90	105	0	10	17	4	25	21	26	0	298
Malawi	560	2	735	263	1,191	329	830	79	958	762	5,709
Mali	0	0	0	0	0	0	0	5	3	0	8
Mozambique	5,949	714	10	870	16	960	860	2,597	6,336	7,802	26,114
Namibia	22,005	1,754	152	5,683	1,642	3,040	1,840	988	1	0	37,105
Niger	0	0	0	0	0	0	0	0	18	0	18
Nigeria	210	640	522	420	273	162	232	92	18	6,000	8,569
Rwanda	0	170	80	0	0	0	35	3,224	0	0	3,509
South Africa	37,900	35,198	33,540	28,372	45,175	34,929	39,696	40,460	17,668	9,554	322,492
Senegal	0	273	89	0	1	6	55	0	30	0	454
Sierra Leone	0	48	29	10	5	0	10	0	0	0	102
Somalia	0	108	18,240	7,468	852	7,247	4,508	64,413	158	22,638	125,632
Sudan	124,438	205,626	272,588	272,778	327,836	52,270	18,705	74,130	63,934	0	1,412,305
Swaziland	0	0	0	0	0	0	276	0	0	0	276
Tanzania	33,110	43,755	23,068	17,639	14,601	43,955	54,676	59,575	86,135	41,702	418,216
Togo	0	200	20	0	50	160	170	90	135	0	825
Uganda	25,147	19,292	45,125	10,403	12,702	227	89,925	3,081	4	281	206,187
Zaire	157,779	96,202	45,256	79,837	159,121	66,395	21,144	35,851	27,507	19,314	708,406
Zambia	15,551	22,452	28,033	34,352	18,308	1,659	12,645	10,983	4,925	1,671	150,579
Zimbabwe	3,030	1,650	1,303	14,147	14,075	18,256	22,759	7,481	7,929	7,202	97,832

The data represent minimum estimates of net quantities of raw ivory declared to have originated in each African producing country.

Source:
WCMC 1992 *Global Biodiversity 1992: Status of the Earth's Living Resources.* The World Conservation Monitoring Centre, Cambridge. In press.

Part 4
Population/Settlements

Population growth and distribution are crucial environmental issues of this century, and will continue to be so into the next. The world population coupled with levels of development have a major impact on the environment. Demands for agricultural land, energy and water resources, and for waste management expand with the population. Forests are already being depleted at a rapid rate, topsoil loss is contributing to desertification, waterways and ground water are being polluted, and airborne pollution spreads throughout industrialized nations and across borders. Increasing pressure from the growing global population will exacerbate these problems.

Information on population size and growth, the extent of poverty and availability of resources, are of fundamental importance for evaluations of environmental change. Tables in Part 4 present data on population increase, fertility, age and sex structure, birth and death rates, family planning, settlements (in particular urbanization) and access to drinking water and sanitation services. Also included in this part is information on refugees. Increasing attention is being given to the range of environmental problems associated with large numbers of refugees. The main concerns are twofold. Firstly, environmental problems can ensue when large numbers of people move to a new region and place demands for food, fuel and water on their new home. Secondly, environmental degradation of their homeland often causes people to become refugees.

Population data are collected on a systematic basis by the United Nations Statistical Office (UNSO), the United Nations Fund for Population Activities (UNFPA) and the United Nations Department of International Economic and Social Affairs (UNDIESA), and are published regularly in various reports. The UN 'Demographic Yearbooks', for example, contain world-wide statistical data on population and demography compiled from census material of the originating country. The UNDIESA maintains a data base of population projections containing historical and forecasting data for 165 countries.

Information on settlements is published by the United Nations Centre for Human Settlements (Habitat). It has been estimated in the mid-late 1980s that approximately one billion people world-wide were poorly housed and at least 100 million completely without shelter (UNEP, 1988). Habitat, in association with the World Health Organization (WHO), the United Nations Educational, Scientific and Cultural Organization (UNESCO) and other UN organizations, have adopted the principles of the 'New

Agenda for Human Settlements' developed by the United Nations Commission on Human Settlements and are working towards achieving the goal of 'Shelter for All'.

Reference

UNEP 1988 *The United Nations System-wide Medium-term Environment Programme 1990–1995*, United Nations Environment Programme, Nairobi.

Population

Population Growth

It is estimated that the world's population is currently increasing at the rate of three people every second (Sadik, 1990). In 1984 UN projections estimated that the "most likely" course for world population was one of medium growth towards an eventual total stabilizing at around 10 billion by the year 2100. However, growth rates have not been reduced as quickly as was anticipated. More recent UN estimates point to a world population stabilizing at about 11 billion towards the year 2100 (Sadik, 1990).

In the developed countries the average annual rate of population increase has slowed considerably, from 1.19 per cent in 1960–1965 to a projected 0.48 per cent in 1990–1995. In the developing world, however, average annual growth rates rose from 2.35 per cent in 1960–1965 to 2.38 per cent in 1970–1975 before dropping to 2.1 per cent in 1980–1985. Average annual population growth rates in developing countries are expected to decrease slightly during the period 1990–1995 to a projected 2.06 per cent (Table 4.1). Despite these declining growth rates, the global population is still rising and is estimated to rise by a billion people over the next decade from the 1989 population of 5.3 billion. Figure 4.1 illustrates the increase in world population since 1960.

Recent estimates of both birth rates and death rates are presented in Table 4.2 and Figure 4.2. Annual average birth and death rates for the periods 1955–1960 and 1980–1985 were compared in the 1989 edition of the 'UNEP Environmental Data Report' (UNEP, 1989). The global crude birth rate has decreased from an average value of 37 per thousand during 1950–1955 to 27 per thousand for the period 1980–1985 (UN, 1989a). The crude birth rate is influenced by the changing age and sex structure of the

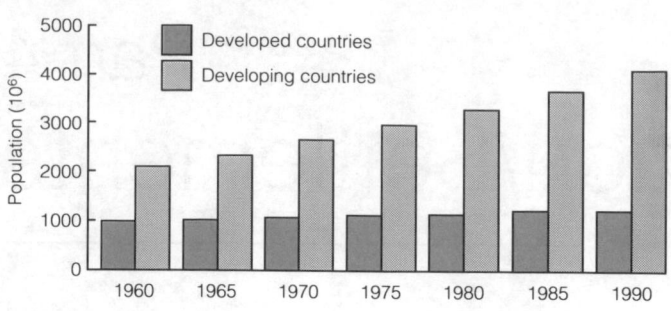

Figure 4.1 Population growth in developed and developing world regions, 1960–1990
Source: data from Table 4.1

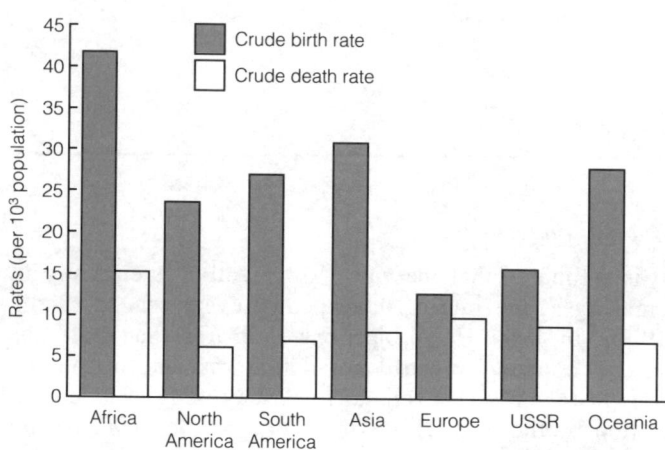

Figure 4.2 Crude birth rates (number of live births per 10^3 population) and crude death rates (number of deaths per 10^3 population) by world region, 1990
Source: data from Table 4.2

population, and in particular by the number of women in the population of childbearing age.

The total fertility rate is defined as the average number of live births that would typically be borne by a woman of childbearing age. In 1960–1965 the global average number of children born per woman was almost five (UN, 1989a) which compares with an average value of 3.3 in 1990 (Table 4.2). In the more developed regions the fertility rate has declined steadily and is now expected to remain fairly stable for the next few decades. The current fertility rate in developed regions averages 1.9 (Table 4.2). In developing regions, the fertility rate differs considerably between countries. In Africa the total fertility rate has scarcely declined since the 1950s when it was around 6.6 children per woman. In 1985 it was at 6.4 children per woman but has since fallen slightly to 6.0 in 1990 (Table 4.2). In Latin America and south-eastern Asia fertility rates have declined considerably since the 1970s to around 3.3 and 3.2 respectively (UN, 1989a).

Fertility rates are influenced by levels of contraceptive use and availability of family planning services. Information on the level of use of family planning services is given in Table 4.2. National data on the use of different methods of contraception were listed in the 1989 edition of this report (UNEP, 1989). Data on contraceptive use are based on the results of national surveys and are not necessarily strictly comparable. A recent UN study on contraceptive use in 1988 indicated that in developed countries around 70 per cent of couples, where the woman was of reproductive age, were using some form of contraceptive. In the developing countries this level was estimated to be around 45 per cent (UN, 1989b).

The countries for which contraceptive prevalence has been assessed for the 1988 UN study contain over 80 per cent of the total world population. Increasingly, governments are supporting national surveys to report levels of contraceptive use. The UN report notes that monitoring of contraceptive use in the developing countries has been so effective that this is one of the few demographic topics where more data are available for developing regions as a whole than for developed countries (UN, 1989b).

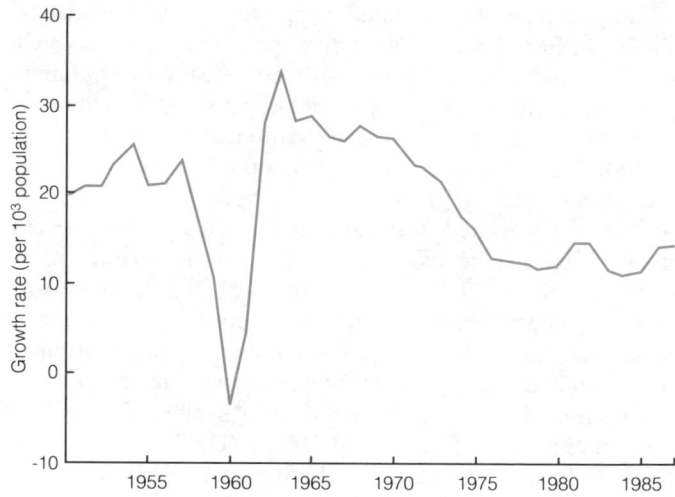

Figure 4.3 Trends in population growth rates in China, 1955–1987
Source: State Statistical Bureau of the People's Republic of China, 1988

The UN study also revealed marked variations in the level of contraceptive use between world regions. In Africa, an estimated 14 per cent of couples use contraceptives, whereas the level of use is around 50 per cent in Asia and about 56 per cent in Latin America.

China has one of the highest rates of contraceptive use of all developing countries. When China is excluded from the overall total for developing countries the rate drops to around 30 per cent (UN, 1989b). In the 1950s and 1960s the total fertility rate in China was six children per woman (UN, 1989a). During the 1970s family planning services were routinely offered by the government, and in 1979 incentives were offered to couples who agreed to limit themselves to one child (Stein, 1990). In 1990 an estimated 75 per cent of the population used birth control, and the fertility rate had dropped to 2.2 (Sadik, 1990). However, the 1990 census showed a slight increase in birth rate in China over that shown in the previous census. The birth rate between mid-1989 and mid-1990 was 20.98 per thousand, compared with 20.91 in 1981, as shown in the 1982 census (Anon., 1990). Figure 4.3 shows the trends in natural population growth in China from 1955–1987. The major decrease in 1960 is related to natural disasters (see Part 9: Natural Disasters, Table 9.7).

Government-supported family planning programmes have been implemented in an increasing number of countries during the last two decades. In 1976 only 97 governments provided direct support for family planning, compared with 125 in 1988. In contrast, the number of governments limiting access to family planning fell from 15 in 1976, to seven in 1988. However, there are still 31 countries in the developing world where couples have virtually no access to modern family planning methods (UN, 1989b).

Age Structure

The data presented in Table 4.3 illustrate differences in the age composition of the population in different world regions. In the developing regions, the number of children aged under 15 years accounts for about 37 per cent of the total population in those regions, and represents 84 per cent of the world population of children (UN, 1989a). In contrast, only 22 per cent of the total population are under 15 years in developed regions. There is also a marked difference between developed and developing regions in the proportion of the population aged over 65 years. In 1985 6 per cent of the total world population was aged over 65. The over-65 age group accounted for 11 per cent of the total population in developed regions in 1985, whereas in the developing world this age group represented only 4 per cent of the population (Table 4.3).

The median age of the population in developed countries is higher than that of developing countries; 32.5 years compared with 21 years in 1985 (UN, 1988). Figure 4.4 illustrates significant regional differences in median age. Europe has the highest median age of all world regions, at 33.9 years in 1985. The median age of the population in developed regions is expected to continue to increase over the next few decades due to consistently low fertility rates and declining mortality rates (UN, 1989a).

Africa is the only world region in which the median age has decreased significantly since 1970. In 1985 Africa had the lowest median age of all regions, at 17.3 years, due to high fertility rates and decreasing child mortality. Little change in Africa's median age is expected until after 1995. In other developing regions, the combined effects of declines in fertility rates and in mortality are expected to increase the median age in the future (UN, 1989a).

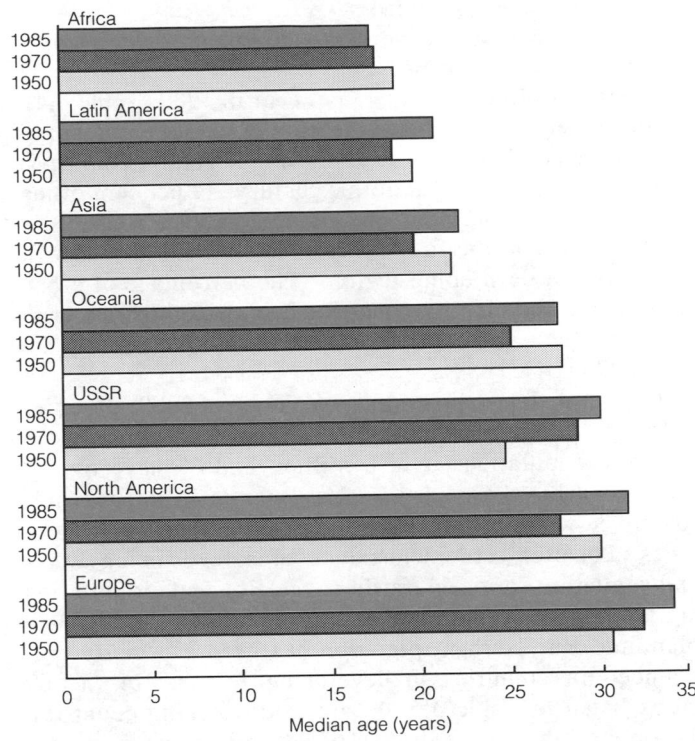

Figure 4.4 Median age of populations in major world regions, 1950–1985
Source: UN, 1988

References

Anon. 1990 The 1990 Census, *Beijing Review* 33(46), 17–19.
Sadik, N. 1990 *The State of the World Population*, United Nations Population Fund, New York.
State Statistical Bureau of the People's Republic of China 1988 *China Statistical Yearbook 1988*, International Centre for the Advancement of Science and Technology, China Statistical Information and Consultancy Service Centre, Beijing.
Stein, D. 1990 Family planning with Chinese characteristics, *China Now* **133**, 15.
UN 1988 *World Population Trends and Policies: 1987 Monitoring Report*, United Nations, New York.
UN 1989a *World Population Prospects 1988*, Population Studies No. 106, United Nations Department of International Economic and Social Affairs, New York.
UN 1989b *Levels and Trends of Contraceptive Use As Assessed in 1988*, Population Studies No. 110, United Nations Department of International Economic and Social Affairs, New York.
UN 1990 *Demographic Yearbook 1988*, United Nations Department of International Economic and Social Affairs, New York.
UNEP 1989 *United Nations Environment Programme Environmental Data Report*, Basil Blackwell, Oxford.

Settlements

Urbanization

Estimates of the size and growth of urban populations in 1970 and 1990 are compared in Table 4.4 for individual countries and major world regions. Information on population density is also provided.

During the past two decades, the share of the world's population living in urban areas has risen steadily from 37 per cent in 1970 to around 43 per cent in 1990 (Table 4.4). In recent years a slowing of the growth rate of urban populations has been observed in several countries. Nevertheless, by the end of this century, 47 per cent of the population is expected to be living in urban areas. It is predicted that in the future the greatest urban growth will take place in developing regions. The percentage of urban residents in developing countries is expected to rise from the 1989 value of 33 per cent to nearly 40 per cent by the year 2000 (UN, 1989).

UN estimates indicate that by the year 2000, 25 cities will have populations of over 9 million. Currently, 29 cities have populations over 6 million and 69 have over 3 million (Table 4.5). Large cities generate major demands for food, water, shelter, transport and other public services. Squatter settlements, lack of safe drinking water and sanitation services, traffic congestion and air pollution are the legacies of rapid urban expansion without adequate planning. Rural-urban migration has been especially pronounced in countries in developing regions; of the 69 cities listed in Table 4.5, 45 are in developing countries. In some cases a concentration of government development efforts in the cities rather than in rural areas may inadvertently have promoted rural-urban migration.

Water Supply and Sanitation

In 1980 the International Drinking Water Supply and Sanitation Decade (1981–1990) was launched at the UN General Assembly with the aim of "... providing water and sanitation for all" (Deck, 1986). The WHO has been responsible for monitoring progress during the decade and has compiled data on water supply and on sanitation services throughout the period. Information is provided to the WHO on standard forms, generally by the relevant government departments or public agencies. Few developing countries have regular reporting systems so estimates are used. In some regions data may represent only 50 per cent or less of the population and estimates, particularly for rural areas, have required extrapolations. In general, availability of data on water supplies is better than on sanitation services.

Table 4.6 shows the status of access to drinking-water and sanitation services in developing countries in 1988. Data for 1970–1985 were reported in Table 4.6 of the 1989 edition of the 'UNEP Environmental Data Report' (UNEP, 1989). From the inception of the International Water Supply and Sanitation Decade there has been a sub-

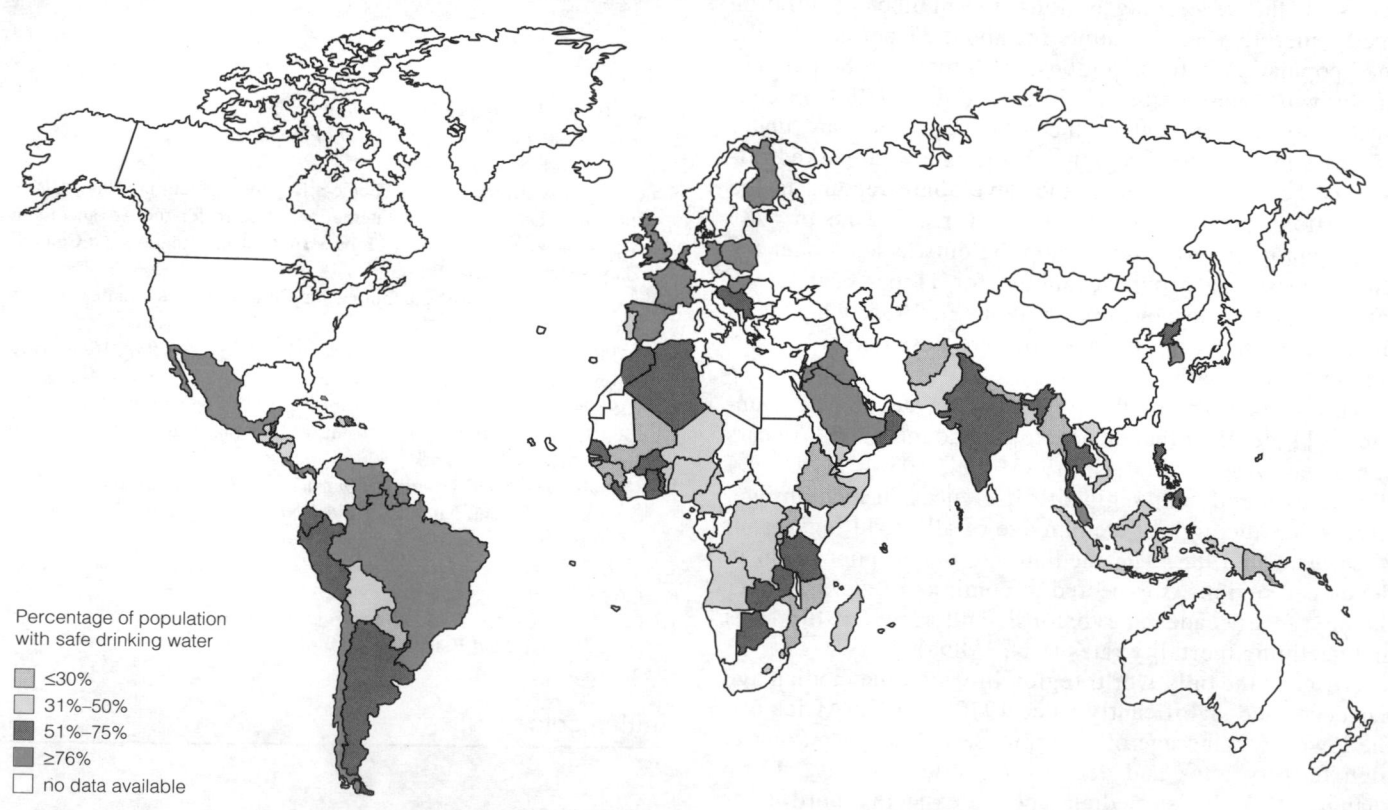

Percentage of population
with safe drinking water

⬛ ≤30%
⬛ 31%–50%
⬛ 51%–75%
⬛ ≥76%
⬜ no data available

Figure 4.5 Percentage of the population with access to safe drinking water, 1988
Source: Sadik, 1990

stantial increase in the number of people in developing countries who are served by drinking-water and sanitation services, although advances in the percentage of the population served have not been as great due to population growth.

From 1980 to 1988 the provision of water supplies in urban areas in developing countries has risen from 76 per cent to 78 per cent. In rural areas access to safe drinking water increased between 1980 and 1988 from 31 per cent to 46 per cent. Figure 4.5 shows the extent of access to safe drinking water in 1988.

The availability of sanitation services is not as extensive as safe drinking-water supply, especially in rural areas. Some progress has, however, been made; in 1988, 66 per cent of urban residents and 17 per cent of rural residents had access to sanitation facilities compared with 56 per cent and 14 per cent respectively in 1980.

Refugees

Each year thousands of people are displaced from their homes as a result of war, famine, natural disasters, political persecution, or a combination of these factors. Increasingly, people are leaving their homelands because of environmental degradation caused in part by human activities such as overgrazing and deforestation.

The United Nations 1951 Convention Relating to the Status of Refugees, as amended by the 1967 Protocol Relating to the Status of Refugees, defines as a refugee a person who "owing to well-found fear of being persecuted for reasons of race, religion, nationality, membership of a particular social group or political opinion, is outside the country of his nationality and is unable or, owing to such fear, is unwilling to avail himself of the protection of that country" (El-Hinnawi, 1985).

Refugee statistics are generally of uncertain reliability, with some reported estimates varying significantly between different sources. Differences in the definition of the term "refugee" between reporting agencies and countries present a major obstacle. Political pressures may also affect refugee numbers; it may be in the political interest of an asylum country government to understate its refugee problem, or to overstate reported numbers (USCR, 1990). Furthermore, constantly changing circumstances of refugee populations add to the difficulties in collecting accurate statistics.

The United Nations High Commissioner for Refugees (UNHCR) publishes a series of fact sheets detailing the refugee situation in individual countries. These outline the number and location of refugees in a country, their legal status, assistance measures being provided and financial requirements (UNHCR, 1990).

Global statistics on numbers of refugees and asylum seekers are compiled by the US Committee for Refugees (USCR) from a wide range of different sources which include official government reports, UN agencies – in particular the UNHCR – international aid organizations and media reports. Available estimates for 1989, summa-

rized in Table 4.7, indicate that there are over 15 million displaced persons world-wide (USCR, 1990).

In 1989 Afghanistan, Mozambique and Ethiopia alone accounted for over 50 per cent of the total estimated refugee population (Table 4.8). Table 4.7 shows that it is often the poorest developing countries which are host to the highest numbers of refugees. The USCR has estimated that nine of the 10 countries with the highest ratio of refugees to general population have low per capita annual incomes (under US$ 1,000) (USCR, 1990). Refugees have immediate basic needs for food, water, medicines and shelter which host countries may be unable to provide. Sanitation may be inadequate, leading to the spread of disease (see Part 5: Human Health). Often, the natural resources of the host country can be seriously over-exploited in an attempt to find food and fuel for the influx of refugees, placing heavy reliance on international aid programmes.

The 1951 Convention's definition of "refugee" does not recognize those persons who are displaced within their own country, though the UNHCR has been authorized to help these people (El-Hinnawi, 1985). Table 4.9 shows the number of people who have been displaced within their own borders. The number of people who are displaced from their homeland due to environmental degradation or disaster is not precisely known. The UN does not accord refugee status to those who are displaced due to economic hardships, unless these are a result of war, or to those displaced by natural hazards (El-Hinnawi, 1985). Environmental refugees can be divided into three categories: those displaced temporarily due to natural disasters such as floods or earthquakes; those displaced because environmental degradation has undermined their livelihood or poses major health risks; and those who resettle due to permanent changes to their homeland, such as desertification (Jacobson, 1988). Natural disasters with far-reaching and severe socio-economic, health and physical consequences are discussed further in Part 9 of the 'UNEP Environmental Data Report'.

References

Deck, F. L. O. 1986 Community water supply and sanitization in developing countries, 1970–1990, *World Health Statistics Quarterly* **39**, 2–31.

El-Hinnawi, E. 1985 *Environmental Refugees*, United Nations Environment Programme, Nairobi.

Jacobson, J.L. 1988 *Environmental Refugees: A Yardstick of Habitability*, Worldwatch Paper 86, Worldwatch Institute, Washington DC.

Sadik 1990 *Safeguarding the Future*, United Nations Population Fund, New York.

UN 1989 *Prospects of World Urbanization 1988*, Population Studies No. 112, United Nations Department of International Economic and Social Affairs, New York.

UN 1990 *Demographic Yearbook 1988*, United Nations Department of International Economic and Social Affairs, New York.

UNEP 1989 *United Nations Environment Programme Environmental Data Report*, Basil Blackwell, Oxford.

UNHCR 1990 *Fact Sheets: May*, Vol. 4(1), United Nations High Commissioner for Refugees Public Information Service, Geneva.

USCR 1990 *World Refugee Survey: 1989 in Review*, US Committee for Refugees, American Council for Nationalities Service, Washington DC.

Table 4.1   Trends in world population size and rate of increase, 1960–1990

Region	Population (10⁶)					Rate of increase[a] (%)			
	1960	1970	1980	1985	1990	1960–65	1970–75	1980–85	1990–95
WORLD	3,019	3,698	4,450	4,854	5,292	1.99	1.96	1.74	1.71
Developed regions[b]	945	1,049	1,136	1,174	1,205	1.19	0.86	0.65	0.48
Developing regions[c]	2,075	2,649	3,314	3,680	4,087	2.35	2.38	2.10	2.06
Africa	281	363	481	557	648	2.48	2.69	2.95	3.01
Latin America	218	285	362	404	448	2.80	2.48	2.19	1.94
Northern America	199	226	252	265	276	1.49	1.06	1.00	0.71
Asia	1,667	2,101	2,583	2,834	3,108	2.19	2.27	1.86	1.82
Europe	425	460	484	492	498	0.91	0.58	0.32	0.22
USSR	214	243	266	277	288	1.49	0.96	0.84	0.68
Oceania	16	19	23	25	26	2.09	1.78	1.55	1.34

a   Estimated average annual rate of increase.
b   North America, Europe, Australia, Japan, New Zealand and the USSR.
c   Africa, Latin America, East and South Asia and Oceania (excluding Australia, Japan and New Zealand).

Totals in this table may differ from those in Table 4.4 due to different regional classifications. See source document for further details of regional classifications.

Source:
UN 1989 *World Population Prospects 1988*, Population Studies Report No. 106, United Nations Department of International Economic and Social Affairs, New York.

Table 4.2 Birth rates, death rates, fertility rates, availability and use of family planning services, 1990

Region/country	Birth rate[a]	Death rate[b]	Family planning services Users (%)	Family planning services Government support	Total fertility rate[c]
WORLD	26	9	44		3.3
Developed countries	13	9	55		1.9
Developing countries	29	9	33[d]		3.7
AFRICA	42	15			6.0
Algeria	36	7		Y	5.2
Angola	46	18		Y	6.3
Benin	49	17	9	Y	6.9
Botswana	44	9	27	Y	5.9
Burkina Faso	46	17		Y	6.4
Burundi	44	15	8	Y	6.1
Cameroon	41	14	2	Y	5.7
Cape Verde	34[e]	8[e]		Y	
Cent. African Rep.	43	18		Y	5.8
Chad	43	17		Y	5.8
Comoros	46	46			5.8
Congo	43	15		Y	5.8
Côte d'Ivoire	50	12	2	Y	7.3
Djibouti	47[f]	47			
Egypt	30	8	29	Y	4.2
Equatorial Guinea	42[f]	42			
Ethiopia	46	21		Y	6.3
Gabon	39	15		N	5.3
Gambia	47[f]	21			
Ghana	42	11	9	Y	6.2
Guinea	45	20		Y	6.1
Guinea-Bissau	41[f]	20[f]			
Kenya	50	9	17	Y	7.6
Lesotho	39	10	5	Y	5.6
Liberia	44	12	6	Y	6.4
Libya	43	8		N	6.7
Madagascar	44	12		Y	6.5
Malawi	51	18	6	Y	6.9
Mali	48	19	4	Y	6.6
Mauritania	45	17	0	Y	6.4
Mauritius	17	5	75	Y	1.9
Morocco	31	8	35	Y	4.2
Mozambique	43	16		Y	6.2
Namibia	41	10			5.7
Niger	50	18		Y	7.0
Nigeria	48	14	4	Y	6.8
Réunion	22[f]	6			
Rwanda	49	15	10	Y	8.0
São Tomé & Príncipe	36[e]	9[e]			
Senegal	44	17	11	Y	6.2
Seychelles	25[f]	8			
Sierra Leone	47	21		Y	6.4
Somalia	46	18			6.5
South Africa	29	8	48	Y	4.2
Sudan	43	14	4	Y	6.3

Continued over

Table 4.2 Continued

Region/country	Birth rate[a]	Death rate[b]	Family planning services		Total fertility rate[c]
			Users (%)	Government support	
Swaziland	47[f]	13[f]			
Tanzania	49	12		Y	7.0
Togo	43	12		Y	6.0
Tunisia	26	6	41	Y	3.4
Uganda	49	13		Y	6.8
Zaire	44	12		Y	6.0
Zambia	49	12		Y	7.0
Zimbabwe	39	8	38	Y	5.3
NORTH AMERICA	24	6			3.0
Antigua	13[f]	4[f]			
Bahamas	18[f]	6[f]			
Belize	36[g]	4[g]			
Bermuda	16[g]	7[g]			
Br. Virgin Is.	18[g]	7[g]			
Canada	12	7	73	Y	1.7
Costa Rica	25	4	69	Y	3.0
Cuba	15	7		Y	1.7
Dominica	21[h]	5[g]			
Dominican Rep.	28	6	50	Y	3.3
El Salvador	36	6	47	Y	4.5
Greenland	22[i]	8[f]			
Guadeloupe	20[f]	7[f]			
Guatemala	38	7	23	Y	5.4
Haiti	33	11	6	Y	4.4
Honduras	37	7	34	Y	4.9
Jamaica	22	5	51	Y	2.4
Martinique	19[i]	6[f]			
Mexico	26	5	53	Y	3.1
Nicaragua	38	6	27	Y	5.0
Panama	24	5	58	Y	2.9
Puerto Rico	19	6	70		2.3
Trinidad & Tobago	21	6	52	Y	2.5
USA	14	8	68	Y	1.9
SOUTH AMERICA	27	7			4.0
Argentina	20	8		Y	2.8
Bolivia	41	12	26	N	5.8
Brazil	26	7	65	Y	3.2
Chile	22	6		Y	2.7
Colombia	26	7	64	Y	3.3
Ecuador	33	7	44	Y	4.3
Guyana	21	5	31	Y	2.4
Paraguay	33	6	44	Y	4.3
Peru	31	7	45	Y	4.0
Uruguay	18	10		Y	2.5
Venezuela	28	5	49	Y	3.5
ASIA	31	8			4.0
Afghanistan	52	21		Y	6.8
Bahrain	28	4[f]		Y	

Continued opposite

Table 4.2   Continued

Region/country	Birth rate[a]	Death rate[b]	Family planning services		Total fertility rate[c]
			Users (%)	Government support	
Bangladesh	40	13	25	Y	5.1
Bhutan	38	15		Y	5.5
Brunei	30[g]	3[f]			
Cambodia	36	14		N	4.4
China	21	6	74	Y	2.2
Cyprus	19	8[f]		Y	
East Timor	44[f]	22[f]			
Hong Kong	13	6	72		1.6
India	31	10	34	Y	4.1
Indonesia	25	10	47	Y	2.9
Iran	39	6		Y	5.4
Iraq	40	6		N	5.9
Israel	20	6		Y	2.7
Japan	12	7	64	Y	1.8
Jordan	45	5	26	Y	6.9
Korea	16	6		Y	1.8
Korea, Dem.	26	4		Y	3.2
Kuwait	28	2			4.3
Laos	38	14		N	5.3
Lebanon	30[f]	8[f]		Y	3.1
Malaysia	25	5	51	Y	3.1
Mongolia	37	7		N	5.2
Myanmar q.v. Burma	29	8		Y	3.7
Nepal	36	12	13	Y	5.5
Oman	44	10		N	7.1
Pakistan	41	10	7	Y	5.9
Philippines	33[f]	8[f]			
Qatar	31[f]	4[f]		N	
Saudi Arabia	41	6		N	7.1
Singapore	15	5	74	Y	1.7
Sri Lanka	20	5	62	Y	2.5
Syria	41	5	19	Y	6.3
Thailand	20	6	67	Y	2.2
Turkey	26	7	51	Y	3.2
United Arab Em.	20	3		N	4.3
Viet Nam	30	8		Y	3.7
Yemen	47	13	1	Y	6.8
Yemen, Dem.	46	14		Y	6.5
EUROPE	13	10			2.0
Albania	21	5		N	2.7
Austria	11	11	71	Y	1.5
Belgium	11	11	81	Y	1.6
Bulgaria	12	11	76	Y	1.8
Czechoslovakia	13	11	95	Y	2.0
Denmark	11	11	63	Y	1.5
Finland	11	10	80	Y	1.7
France	13	9	78	Y	1.8
German Dem. Rep.	11	11		Y	1.7
Germany, Fed. Rep.	10	11	77	Y	1.4

Continued over

Table 4.2 Continued

Region/country	Birth rate[a]	Death rate[b]	Family planning services		Total fertility rate[c]
			Users (%)	Government support	
Greece	11	10		Y	1.7
Hungary	11	12	73	Y	1.8
Iceland	17[f]	7[i]		Y	
Ireland	17	8		N	2.4
Italy	11	10	78	Y	1.5
Liechtenstein	13[g]	7[g]			
Luxembourg	12[i]	10[i]		N	
Malta	16	8[f]		Y	
Netherlands	11	8	72	Y	1.5
Norway	12	10	71	N	1.7
Poland	14	9	75	Y	2.1
Portugal	13	10	66	Y	1.7
Romania	15	10	58	N	2.0
San Marino	10[f]	7[f]			
Spain	12	9	59	Y	1.7
Sweden	11	12	78	Y	1.7
Switzerland	11	10	71	N	1.6
UK	13	11	83	Y	1.8
Yugoslavia	13	8	55	Y	1.9
USSR	16	9		Y	2.3
OCEANIA	28	7			3.0
American Samoa	43[e]	4[e]			
Australia	14	7		Y	1.8
New Zealand	15	8	69	Y	1.8
Papua New Guinea	36	10		Y	5.3
Tonga	30[e]	4[e]			

[a] Number of live births per 10^3 population.
[b] Number of deaths per 10^3 population.
[c] Average number of live births typically born to a woman of childbearing age.
[d] Estimate only; where reported data are missing for selected countries, UN estimates have been used. This estimate excludes China.
[e] 1985.
[f] 1987.
[g] 1986.
[h] 1984.
[i] 1988.

Data are estimates and are for 1990 unless otherwise indicated. Where a year other than 1990 is stated, the source of the data is the UN 'Demographic Yearbook 1988'.

Developed countries comprise the USA, Canada, Japan, all countries of Europe, Australia, New Zealand and the USSR.
Developing countries comprise all countries of Africa, Latin America and Asia, excluding Japan, Melanesia, Micronesia and Polynesia.

Sources:
Anon. 1990 The 1990 Census, *Beijing Review* **33**(46), 17–19 (birth and death rates for China).
UN 1990 *Demographic Yearbook 1988*, United Nations Department of International Economic and Social Affairs, New York.
Sadik, N. 1990 *The State of World Population*, United Nations Population Fund, New York.

Table 4.3 Estimates[a] of population distribution by age and sex, 1985

Region	Both sexes Population (10⁶) All ages	Percentage distribution <15	15–64	>65	Males Population (10⁶) All ages	Percentage distribution <15	15–64	>65	Females Population (10⁶) All ages	Percentage distribution <15	15–64	>65
WORLD	4,854	34	60	6	2,441	34	61	5	2,413	33	60	7
AFRICA	557	45	52	3	277	46	51	3	280	45	52	3
Eastern Africa	167	47	50	3	83	47	51	2	84	46	50	4
Middle Africa	60	45	52	3	30	47	50	3	30	43	53	3
Northern Africa	124	43	54	3	63	43	54	3	62	42	55	3
Southern Africa	36	39	58	3	18	39	56	5	18	39	56	5
Western Africa	169	47	50	2	84	48	50	2	86	47	50	2
NORTH AMERICA	265	22	66	12	129	22	67	10	135	21	66	14
LATIN AMERICA	404	38	58	4	202	38	58	4	202	37	58	5
Caribbean	31	32	61	6	16	31	63	6	16	31	63	6
Central America	105	42	54	4	52	42	54	4	52	40	56	4
South America	268	36	59	5	134	37	59	4	134	36	59	5
ASIA	2,834	35	60	5	1,451	35	61	4	1,383	35	60	5
Eastern Asia	1,249	29	65	6	640	29	66	5	610	29	65	7
Southern Asia	1,070	39	57	4	553	39	57	4	517	39	57	4
South Eastern Asia	401	39	57	4	199	40	57	3	201	38	58	4
Western Asia	114	41	55	4	59	41	56	3	55	42	55	4
EUROPE	492	21	67	13	240	22	68	10	252	20	65	15
Eastern Europe	112	23	66	11	54	24	67	9	57	23	65	12
Northern Europe	83	19	65	16	41	20	66	15	42	19	64	17
Southern Europe	142	22	66	12	70	23	67	10	73	21	66	13
Western Europe	155	18	68	13	75	19	70	10	80	18	66	16
USSR	277	25	66	10	130	28	67	5	147	23	64	13
OCEANIA	25	28	65	8	12	28	64	7	12	27	63	10
Australia and New Zealand	19	24	66	10	9.5	24	67	9	9.5	23	65	12
Melanesia	4.8	41	56	3	2.5	41	56	3	2.3	41	56	3
Micronesia	0.3	41	55	4	0.2	40	57	4	0.2	42	54	4
Polynesia	0.5	44	52	4	0.3	44	52	3	0.3	44	52	4

[a] All figures are estimates and are subject to ε substantial margin of error. See source document for definition of regions used.

Source:
UN 1990 *Demographic Yearbook 1988*, United Nations Department of International Economic and Social Affairs, New York.

Table 4.4 Demographic data for countries and major world regions, 1970 and 1990

Region/country	Population (10³)		Density[a]		Urban population (%)		Average annual urban growth rate (%)	
	1970	1990	1970	1988	1970	1990	1970	1990[b]
WORLD	3,685,973	5,300,027	88	115	37	43	2.7	2.6
Developed countries[c]	1,046,958	1,205,192	68	77	67	72	1.5	0.8
Developing countries[d]	2,638,372	4,086,985	231	302	26	33	3.8	3.6
AFRICA	356,925	647,518	31	53	23	34	4.8	4.9
Algeria	13,746	25,363	6	10	40	44	3.5	4.1
Angola	5,588	10,020		8	15	28	6.6	5.4
Benin	2,708	4,740		39	16	41	8.2	5.9
Botswana	623	1,285	1	2	9	23	9.8	7.0
Burkina Faso	5,076	9,006	20	31	6	9	3.9	5.9
Burundi	3,456	5,451	129	185	2	7	1.6	7.7
Cameroon	6,745	11,245	12	22	20	49	7.8	5.0
Cape Verde	271	379	61	89	6	63	0.0	2.5
Cent. African Rep.	1,875	2,912	2	4	30	46	4.3	4.2
Chad	3,652	5,678	3	4	11	33	8.1	5.8
Comoros	271	518	125	218	11	64	10.6	3.5
Congo	1,201	1,994	3	6	35	42	3.1	4.3
Côte d'Ivoire	5,553	12,595	13	36	27	46	6.9	5.6
Egypt	33,053	54,059		52	44	48	2.5	3.4
Equatorial Guinea	291	440	10	15	39	30	5.1	4.6
Ethiopia	30,623	46,743	20	39	9	12	4.3	5.2
Gabon	950	1,170	2	4	26	45	4.5	5.1
Gambia	469	858	32	72	15	48	4.1	1.7
Ghana	8,614	15,020	38	59	29	33	3.5	4.3
Guinea	4,388	6,875	16	21	14	25	5.3	5.2
Guinea-Bissau	526	987	15	26	18	47	7.0	2.7
Kenya	11,290	25,129	19	41	10	23	8.4	7.3
Lesotho	1,064	1,773	34	55	318	20	1.5	6.2
Liberia	1,365	2,553	11	22	26	44	6.1	5.1
Libya	1,986	4,544		2	36	70	8.6	4.7
Madagascar	6,716	11,979	11	19	14	25	5.5	5.9
Malawi	4,518	8,427	38	65	6	14	7.5	7.0
Mali	5,685	9,361	4	7	14	19	4.0	4.7
Mauritania	1,247	2,024	1	2	14	42	9.3	5.7
Mauritius	848	1,103	409	528	42	42	1.4	1.7
Morocco	15,310	25,138	35	54	35	48	4.1	3.8
Mozambique	8,140	15,663		19	6	26	12.3	7.6
Namibia	1,042	1,875	1	2	33	56	5.6	4.8
Niger	4,146	7,109	3	5	9	19	6.9	6.5
Nigeria	57,221	113,016	60	114	16	35	5.6	5.7
Réunion	441	594	177	229	44	44	3.7	2.6
Rwanda	3,718	7,231	136	256	3	7	7.7	7.4
Senegal	4,008	7,369	20	36	33	38	3.9	4.1
Sierra Leone	2,835	4,150		55	18	32	4.6	5.0
Somalia	2,634	7,554	4	11	23	36	6.9	4.4
South Africa	22,760	35,248	16	28	48	58	3.3	3.1
Sudan	13,859	25,195	6	9	16	22	4.9	4.6
Swaziland	425	789	24	42	10	37	9.9	2.6
Tanzania	13,513	27,328	14	25	7	32	12.0	7.9
Togo	2,020	3,454	33	57	13	25	6.0	5.9

Continued opposite

Table 4.4 Continued

Region/country	Population (10³)		Density[a]		Urban population (%)		Average annual urban growth rate (%)	
	1970	1990	1970	1988	1970	1990	1970	1990[b]
Tunisia	5,127	8,168	31	48	43	54	4.1	2.7
Uganda	9,806	18,441	41	73	8	10	4.1	6.1
Zaire	19,481	35,990	7	14	30	39	4.0	4.8
Zambia	4,189	8,455	6	10	30	55	6.4	5.5
Zimbabwe	5,308	9,720	13	23	17	27	5.9	5.4
NORTH AMERICA	318,309	425,682	135	164	58	71	3.0	2.1
Barbados	239	261	595	590	37	80	1.2	3.5
Canada	21,406	26,525	2	3	76	76	1.2	1.0
Costa Rica	1,732	3,014		56	40	53	4.2	3.6
Cuba	8,572	10,324	73	94	60	74	2.5	1.6
Dominican Rep.	4,289	7,169	89	141	40	60	4.9	3.3
El Salvador	3,582	5,251	165	243	39	44	2.9	3.5
Guadeloupe	320	340	184	199	41	74	0.9	1.1
Guatemala	5,246	9,196	47	80	36	41	3.5	4.0
Haiti	4,605	6,504	175	199	20	30	4.5	4.0
Honduras	2,639	5,138	23	43	29	43	5.6	4.7
Jamaica	1,869	2,520	182	223	42	52	3.3	2.5
Martinique	326	331	307	300	54	89	2.1	3.6
Mexico	51,176	88,597	26	42	59	72	4.2	2.7
Nicaragua	2,053	3,870	15	28	47	59	4.3	4.2
Panama	1,531	2,417	19	30	48	54	3.0	2.9
Puerto Rico	2,718	3,708	319	405	58	73	3.0	2.0
Trinidad & Tobago	955	1,282	184	242	39	69	5.2	2.6
USA	205,051	249,235	22	26	74	74	1.1	0.8
SOUTH AMERICA	190,420	296,687	11	16	60	76	3.8	2.6
Argentina	23,962	32,321	9	12	78	86	2.2	1.5
Bolivia	4,325	7,313	4	6	41	51	3.4	4.2
Brazil	95,847	150,367	11	17	56	76	4.3	2.7
Chile	9,456	13,173	13	17	75	85	2.4	1.9
Colombia	20,803	31,819	19	27	57	70	3.3	2.6
Ecuador	6,051	10,781	21	36	40	56	4.8	4.1
Guyana	709	1,039	4	5	29	34	2.4	3.2
Paraguay	2,290	4,276	6	10	37	47	4.4	4.0
Peru	13,193	22,332	11	17	57	70	3.9	3.1
Suriname	372	403	2	2	46	50	-0.7	3.0
Uruguay	2,808	3,128	16	17	82	85	0.6	1.0
Venezuela	10,604	19,735	11	21	76	90	4.4	2.8
ASIA	2,101,207	3,108,475	270	380	24	29	3.4	3.3
Afghanistan	13,623	16,556	26	24	5	21	5.1	9.7
Bahrain	220	515	360	710	78	27	4.9	5.1
Bangladesh	66,671	115,593		726	8	13	5.9	5.6
Bhutan	1,045	1,516	18	31	3	5	4.4	5.9
Cambodia	6,938	8,245	38	43	12	11	-2.1	4.2
China	830,675	1,135,495	79	115	20	21	2.0	2.7
Cyprus	615	700	68	74	41	33	1.5	6.9
East Timor	604	736	40	48	10	22	0.2	5.1
Hong Kong	3,942	5,840	3,955	5,437	90	93	2.7	1.2
India	554,911	853,372	168	242	20	28	3.9	4.1

Continued over

Table 4.4 Continued

Region/country	Population (10³)		Densityª		Urban population (%)		Average annual urban growth rate (%)	
	1970	1990	1970	1988	1970	1990	1970	1990ᵇ
Indonesia	120,280	180,513	81	92	17	28	4.9	4.0
Iran	28,397	56,585	17	32	41	54	4.9	3.7
Iraq	9,356	18,919	22	40	56	74	5.2	4.1
Israel	2,974	4,580	140	214	84	91	3.2	1.7
Japan	104,331	123,456	280	325	71	76	1.8	0.6
Jordan	2,299	4,269	24	40	51	68	4.1	4.9
Korea	31,923	66,519	323	424	41	72	5.1	2.3
Korea, Dem.	13,892	22,936	115	182	50	67	4.4	3.0
Kuwait	744	2,090	44	110	78	95	7.6	3.3
Laos	3,019	4,070	13	16	10	18	5.3	5.5
Lebanon	2,469	2,965	268	272	59	83	3.1	2.5
Malaysia	10,863	17,339	24	51	27	42	4.8	3.9
Mongolia	1,248	2,226	1	1	45	51	4.1	3.6
Myanmar q.v. Burma	27,102	41,675	41	59	23	24	2.6	3.2
Nepal	11,488	19,143	81	130	4	9	6.9	6.5
Oman	654	1,468	3	6	5	10	7.8	6.9
Pakistan	65,706	122,666	121	132	25	31	3.9	4.5
Philippines	37,540	58,721ᵉ	196	33	42ᵉ	4	7.7	0.5
Qatar	111	367		31	80	84	7.7	0.5
Saudi Arabia	5,745	14,131	4	7	49	77	7.9	4.6
Singapore	2,075	2,701	3,528	4,283	100	99	1.5	1.0
Sri Lanka	12,514	17,209	191	253	22	21	1.6	2.2
Syria	6,258	12,500	33	61	43	51	4.3	4.5
Thailand	36,370	55,701	70	106	13	22	5.1	4.0
Turkey	35,321	55,616	45	67	38	48	3.6	3.0
United Arab Em.	223	1,588	33	18	42	77	21.3	2.2
Viet Nam	42,729	67,170	120	194	18	21	2.9	4.2
Yemen	4,835	8,016	29	39	8	24	9.2	6.6
Yemen, Dem.	1,497	2,490	4	8	32	43	3.6	4.9
EUROPE	459,098	497,740	149	160	67	73	1.2	0.6
Albania	2,138	3,245	75	109	34	35	2.4	2.7
Austria	7,447	7,492	89	91	52	57	0.6	0.5
Belgium	9,638	9,938	317	325	94	96	0.3	0.2
Bulgaria	8,514	9,010	77	81	52	70	2.2	0.9
Czechoslovakia	14,362	15,667	113	122	55	68	1.9	1.1
Denmark	4,929	5,120	114	119	80	86	1.0	0.3
Finland	4,606	4,974	14	15	50	67	2.1	1.2
France	50,670	56,173	93	101	71	74	0.9	0.6
German Dem. Rep.	17,066	16,649	150	154	74	77	0.1	0.3
Germany, Fed. Rep.	60,700	60,539	240	246	81	86	0.5	0.1
Greece	8,793	10,047	67	76	53	62	1.9	1.0
Hungary	10,353	10,551	111	114	46	60	1.9	1.0
Iceland	204	253	2	2	85	13	1.5	4.8
Ireland	2,954	3,719	42	50	52	59	2.1	1.7
Italy	53,565	57,321	178	191	64	68	0.0	0.5
Luxembourg	339	367	131	145	68	82	2.1	3.4
Malta	326	352	1,030	1,101	77	52	2.0	2.2
Netherlands	13,032	14,751	319	361	86	88	1.1	0.4
Norway	3,877	4,211	12	13	65	74	1.4	0.7
Poland	32,657	38,423	105	121	52	63	1.9	1.1

Continued opposite

Table 4.4 Continued

Region/country	Population (10^3)		Density[a]		Urban population (%)		Average annual urban growth rate (%)	
	1970	1990	1970	1988	1970	1990	1970	1990[b]
Portugal	8,628	10,284	105	113	26	33	2.5	1.8
Romania	20,360	23,271	85	97	42	50	2.3	1.0
Spain	33,779	39,332	66	77	66	78	2.0	0.9
Sweden	8,043	8,339	18	19	81	83	0.6	0.1
Switzerland	6,267	6,520	152	158	54	59	0.6	0.5
UK	55,480	56,926	228	234	88	92	0.3	0.3
Yugoslavia	20,371	23,848	80	92	35	50	2.9	2.0
USSR	241,700	287,990	11	13	57	67	2.1	1.2
OCEANIA	18,314	26,476	11	16	70	70	2.1	1.3
Australia	12,552	16,745	2	2	85	85	1.7	1.1
Fiji	520	748	28	40	35	44	3.0	2.1
New Zealand	2,820	3,378	10	12	81	84	1.4	0.9
Papua New Guinea	2,422	4,011	3	8	10	15	5.3	4.9

[a] Population per square kilometre. Figures are the quotients of population divided by area and are not intended to reflect density in the urban sense or to indicate the supporting power of a territory's land and resources.
[b] Projected average annual rate of growth for 1990–1995.
[c] Developed countries comprise the USA, Canada, Japan, all countries of Europe, Australia, New Zealand and the USSR.
[d] Developing countries comprise all countries of Africa, South America, North America (excluding the USA and Canada), Asia (excluding Japan), and Oceania (excluding Australia and New Zealand).
[e] 1988.

Population figures are estimates, derived by using direct and indirect demographic estimation techniques, and are continually being revised. Consequently the figures may differ from those found in other UN publications.
Regional totals include data for small countries not listed here (usually less than 300,000 population).
The precise definition of an urban area varies between countries. Most countries define an urban area as a locality containing a minimum population of between 2,000 and 5,000. Some countries use different criteria, such as the number of dwelling units, population density, or types of economic activity and living facilities. Definitions of urban areas are specified in the source document.

Sources:
Sadik, N. 1990 *The State of World Population*, United Nations Population Fund, New York.
UN 1971 *Demographic Yearbook 1970,* United Nations Department of International Economic and Social Affairs, New York.
UN 1989 *Prospects of World Urbanization 1988*, Population Studies Report No. 112, United Nations Department of International Economic and Social Affairs, New York.
UN 1990 *Demographic Yearbook 1988*, United Nations Department of International Economic and Social Affairs, New York.
UN Centre for Human Settlements (Habitat) 1987 *Global Report on Human Settlements*, Oxford University Press, Oxford.

Table 4.5 Cities/metropolitan regions of the world of 3 million population or more, 1970 and 1990

Country	City	Population (10⁶) 1970	Population (10⁶) 1990	Country	City	Population (10⁶) 1970	Population (10⁶) 1990
Japan	Tokyo/Yokohama	14.91	20.52	Spain	Madrid	3.37	5.06
Mexico	Mexico City	9.12	19.37	India	Bangalore	1.66	4.86
Brazil	São Paulo	8.22	18.42	Korea	Pusan	1.85	4.75
USA	New York	16.29	15.65	Chile	Santiago	3.01	4.70
China	Shanghai	11.41	12.55	China	Shenyang	3.14	4.46
India	Calcutta	7.12	11.83	Italy	Naples	3.59	4.33
Argentina	Buenos Aires	8.55	11.58	USA	Philadelphia	4.05	4.23
Korea	Seoul	5.42	11.33	Pakistan	Lahore	1.97	4.08
India	Greater Bombay	5.98	11.13	Venezuela	Caracas	2.12	3.96
Brazil	Rio de Janeiro	7.17	11.12	USA	Detroit	3.99	3.86
UK	London	10.59	10.57	Brazil	Belo Horizonte	1.62	3.81
Japan	Osaka/Kobe	7.61	10.49	Australia	Sydney	2.68	3.79
USA	Los Angeles	8.43	10.47	Italy	Rome	3.07	3.72
China	Beijing	8.29	9.74	China	Wuhan	2.73	3.66
Indonesia	Jakarta	4.48	9.42	China	Guangzhou	2.50	3.62
USSR	Moscow	7.07	9.39	Turkey	Ankara	1.67	3.62
Iran	Tehran	3.29	9.21	Poland	Katowice	2.77	3.56
Egypt	Cairo/Giza	5.69	9.08	India	Ahmedabad	1.74	3.55
France	Paris	8.34	8.75	India	Hyderabad	1.80	3.49
India	New Delhi	3.64	8.62	Algeria	Alger	1.20	3.43
Philippines	Manila/Quezon	3.60	8.40	USA	San Francisco	3.01	3.39
China	Tianjin	6.87	8.38	Canada	Toronto	2.55	3.32
Italy	Milan	5.52	7.90	Spain	Barcelona	2.66	3.31
Pakistan	Karachi	3.14	7.67	Egypt	Alexandria	1.99	3.28
Nigeria	Lagos	1.44	7.60	Morocco	Casablanca	1.51	3.26
Thailand	Bangkok	3.27	7.16	USA	Houston	1.69	3.19
USA	Chicago	6.76	6.89	Myanmar q.v. Burma	Yangon	1.43	3.18
Peru	Lima-Callo	2.92	6.50	Viet Nam	Ho Chi Minh Village	2.00	3.17
Bangladesh	Dhaka	1.54	6.40	Brazil	Porto Alegre	1.52	3.11
India	Madras	3.12	5.69	Australia	Melbourne	2.34	3.10
Colombia	Bogota	2.37	5.59	China	Chengdu	1.58	3.06
Hong Kong	Hong Kong	3.53	5.44	Mexico	Guadalajara	1.51	3.06
USSR	Leningrad	3.96	5.39	USA	Washington DC	2.49	3.03
Iraq	Baghdad	2.10	5.35	Indonesia	Medan	0.61	3.00

Cities are ranked in descending order of size in 1990.

Source:
UN 1989 *Prospects of World Urbanization 1988*, Population Studies Report No. 112, United Nations Department of International Economic and Social Affairs, New York.

Table 4.6 Access to safe drinking water and sanitation services in developing countries, 1988

Region/country	Access to safe drinking water (% of population)			Access to sanitation services (% of population)		
	Urban	Rural	Total	Urban	Rural	Total
AFRICA						
Angola	75	19	47	25	20	22
Benin	66	46	56	42	31	36
Botswana	70			98	20	59
Burkina Faso	44	72	58	35	5	20
Burundi	100	34	67	80	5	42
Cameroon	100	96	98			
Cape Verde	87	65	76	35		
Cent. African Rep.	13	11	12		11	
Congo	92	2	47		2	
Côte d'Ivoire	100	75	87	69	20	44
Egypt	96	82	89	100	34	67
Ethiopia	70	11	40	97	7	52
Gabon	90	50	70			
Gambia	92	73	82			
Ghana	93	39	66	64	15	39
Guinea	55	24	39	65		
Guinea-Bissau	18	27	22	30	18	24
Lesotho	59	45	52	14	23	18
Liberia	93	22	57		8	
Libya	100	80	90	100	85	92
Madagascar	62	10	36			
Mali	100	36	68	94	5	49
Mauritania	67	65	66	34		
Mauritius	100	92	96	92	96	94
Morocco	100	25	62	100	19	59
Mozambique	44	17	30	61	11	36
Niger	100	52	76	39	3	21
Nigeria	100	20	60			
Rwanda	46	64	55	45	62	53
São Tomé & Príncipe	33	32	32	8	13	10
Seychelles	100	98	99	19	97	58
Somalia	50	29	39	41	5	23
Tanzania	75	46	60	76	77	76
Togo	100	61	80	42	16	29
Tunisia	100	31	65	71	15	43
Zaire	59	17	38	14	14	14
Zambia	76	43	59	77	34	55
Zimbabwe	31	80	55	95	22	58
NORTH AMERICA						
Belize	94	44	69	94	28	61
Costa Rica	100	84	92	100	93	96
Dominican Rep.	86	28	57	77	36	56
El Salvador	76	10	43	86	39	62
Guatemala	91	41	66	72	48	60
Haiti	55	36	45		15	
Honduras	89	60	74	88	44	66
Jamaica	95	46	70			
Mexico	79	49	64	100	12	56
Nicaragua	78	19	48			

Continued over

Table 4.6 Continued

Region/country	Access to safe drinking water (% of population)			Access to sanitation services (% of population)		
	Urban	Rural	Total	Urban	Rural	Total
Panama	100	66	83	100	68	84
Trinidad & Tobago	100	87	93	100	97	98
SOUTH AMERICA						
Argentina	73	17	45	100	29	64
Bolivia	77	15	46	55	13	34
Brazil	100	86	93	89	41	65
Chile	100	21	60	100	6	53
Colombia	88	87	87	85	18	51
Ecuador	75	37	56	75	34	54
Guyana	94	74	84	85	86	85
Paraguay	65	7	36	55	60	57
Peru	78	22	50	71	17	44
Suriname	82	56	69	64	36	50
Uruguay	85	5	45	60	65	62
Venezuela	89	89	89	97	70	83
ASIA						
Afghanistan	39	17	28	20		
Bahrain	100	57	78	100	94	97
Bangladesh	37	89	63	37	4	20
Brunei	100	95	97	100	98	99
China	87	66	76	100	95	97
Cyprus	100	100	100	100	100	100
Hong Kong	100	71	85	100	50	75
India	79	73	76	38	4	21
Indonesia	60	40	50	40	45	42
Iran	100	75	87	100	35	67
Iraq	100	72	86	92	18	55
Jordan	100	98	99	100	100	100
Korea	91	49	70	99	100	99
Kuwait	100			98		
Laos	61	17	39		6	
Malaysia	92	68	80		75	
Mongolia	78	50	64	100	43	71
Myanmar q.v. Burma	38	28	33	35	27	31
Nepal	66	33	49			
Oman	87	42	64	100	34	67
Pakistan	99	35	67	40	8	24
Philippines	100	75	87	98	85	91
Qatar	100	48	74	100	85	92
Saudi Arabia	100	74	87	100	30	65
Singapore	100			97		
Sri Lanka	87	40	63	74	44	59
Thailand	67	76	71	84		
Viet Nam	48	45	46	48	55	51
Yemen	100	48	74	66		
OCEANIA						
Cook Is.	99	94	96	100	99	99
Fiji		68		90	65	77

Continued opposite

Table 4.6 Continued

Region/country	Access to safe drinking water (% of population)			Access to sanitation services (% of population)		
	Urban	Rural	Total	Urban	Rural	Total
Guam	100	100	100	100	90	95
Kiribati	98	44	71	82	44	63
Papua New Guinea	93	23	58	54	56	55
Samoa	83	70	76	95	91	93
Solomon Is.	82	68	75	56	5	30
Tonga	100	88	94	95	70	82
Tuvalu	99	100	99	79	77	78
Vanuatu	100	64	82	82	33	57

Safe drinking water includes treated surface water and untreated water from protected springs, boreholes and wells. The WHO defines access to safe drinking water in urban areas as piped water to housing units or to public stand pipes (within 200 metres). In rural areas reasonable access implies that fetching water does not take up a disproportionate part of the day.
Urban and rural populations with access to sanitation services were defined as those served by connections to public sewers or household disposal systems such as pit privies, pour flush latrines, septic tanks, communal toilets, etc.

Source:
WHO 1990 Information from the Community Water Supply and Sanitation Data Base, World Health Organization, Geneva.

Table 4.7 Refugees and asylum seekers, as assessed in 1989

Region/country of asylum	Total no. of refugees	Source country(ies)	No. of refugees	Region/country of asylum	Total no. of refugees	Source country(ies)	No. of refugees
AFRICA	4,524,800			Liberia	200		
Algeria	170,000	Western Sahara	165,000[a]	Malawi	812,000	Mozambique	812,000
		Others	5,000	Mauritania	22,000	Senegal	22,000
Angola	26,500	South Africa	10,000	Morocco	800		
		Zaire	9,500	Mozambique	400	South Africa	200
		Namibia	7,000			Chile	100
Benin	900	Chad	900			Others	100
Botswana	800	South Africa	300	Namibia	25,000	Angola	25,000
		Angola	200	Nigeria	5,100	Chad	4,000
		Others	300			Others	1,100
Burkina Faso	300	Chad	300	Rwanda	20,500[a]	Burundi	20,500[a]
Burundi	90,200	Rwanda	80,000[a]	Senegal	48,000	Mauritania	43,000
		Zaire	9,600			Guinea-Bissau	4,800
		Uganda	400			Others	200
		Others	200	Sierra Leone	100		
Cameroon	4,200	Chad	4,000	Somalia	350,000	Ethiopia	350,000[a]
		Others	200	South Africa	201,000[a]	Mozambique	65,000[a]
Cent. African Rep.	2,800	Chad	2,600			Lesotho	4,000
		Sudan	100	Sudan	694,300[a]	Ethiopia	663,200[a]
		Others	100			Chad	241,000
Congo	2,100	Chad	1,500			Zaire	5,000
		Zaire	300			Uganda	200
		Others	300	Swaziland	71,700[a]	Mozambique	65,000[a]
Côte d'Ivoire	55,800	Liberia	55,000			South Africa	6,700[a]
		South East Asia	300	Tanzania	266,200	Burundi	156,000
		Others	500			Mozambique	72,000
Djibouti	46,500	Somalia	30,000			Rwanda	21,000
		Ethiopia	16,500			Zaire	16,000
Egypt	7,500	Palestinians	5,800			Others	1,200
		Ethiopia	700	Togo	500	Ghana	400
		Somalia	600			Others	100
		Angola	200	Tunisia	200		
		Others	200	Uganda	170,500[a]	Rwanda	118,000[a]
Ethiopia	740,000	Sudan	385,000			Sudan	50,000
		Somalia	355,000			Zaire	1,000
Gabon	100					Others	1,500
Ghana	100			Zaire	338,800	Angola	311,500
Guinea	13,000	Liberia	13,000			Rwanda	12,000
Kenya	15,500[a]	Uganda	6,400			Burundi	10,000
		Somalia	3,000[a]			Uganda	4,000
		Ethiopia	2,800			Others	1,300
		Rwanda	2,000	Zambia	131,700	Angola	97,000
		Others	1,300			Mozambique	20,000
Lesotho	4,000[a]	South Africa	4,000[a]				

Continued opposite

Table 4.7 Continued

Region/country of asylum	Total no. of refugees	Source country(ies)	No. of refugees	Region/country of asylum	Total no. of refugees	Source country(ies)	No. of refugees
		Zaire	9,000	Iran	2,825,000[a]	Afghanistan	2,350,000
		South Africa	3,200			Iraq	475,000[a]
		Others	2,500	Iraq	60,000[a]	Iran	60,000[a]
Zimbabwe	185,500[a]	Mozambique	185,000[a]	Jordan	899,800	Palestinians	899,800
		South Africa	500	Lebanon	298,700	Palestinians	294,300
NORTH AMERICA	123,400					Others	4,400
Canada	21,700[a]			Nepal	12,000	China (Tibet)[b]	12,000
USA	101,700	Nicaragua	35,400	Pakistan	3,588,000[a]	Afghanistan	3,579,000
		El Salvador	29,700			Iran	9,000[a]
		Guatemala	15,500	Syria	272,800	Palestinians	272,800
		Others	21,100	West Bank	398,400	Palestinians	398,400
ASIA	574,100			Yemen	56,700[a]	Yemen, Dem.	55,000[a]
Hong Kong	55,400	Viet Nam	55,400			Ethiopia	1,700
Indonesia	8,000	Viet Nam	8,000	EUROPE	577,200		
Japan	2,000	Viet Nam	2,000	Austria	22,800		
Korea	200	Viet Nam	200	Belgium	8,000		
Macau	400	Viet Nam	400	Cyprus	1,000		
Malaysia	19,900	Viet Nam	19,900	Denmark	4,600		
Papua New Guinea	8,100	Irian Jaya	8,100	France	60,000		
Philippines	26,300	Viet Nam	25,800	Germany, Fed. Rep.[c]	121,000a		
		Laos	300				
		Cambodia	240	Hungary	27,000		
Singapore	300	Viet Nam	300	Netherlands	14,000		
Taiwan	200	Viet Nam	200	Norway	4,400		
Thailand	436,600	Laos	68,740	Sweden	32,000		
		Myanmar q.v. Burma	38,000	Switzerland	24,400[a]		
		Cambodia	317,200	Turkey	233,000[a]	Iran	200,000[a]
		Viet Nam	12,650			Iraq	33,000
Viet Nam	16,700	Cambodia	16,700	UK	10,000		
MIDDLE EAST & SOUTH ASIA	9,141,600			Yugoslavia	8,000		
Gaza Strip	469,400	Palestinians	469,400	Other European (Greece, Italy, Portugal, Spain)	7,000		
India	260,800[a]	Sri Lanka	103,000				
		China (Tibet)[b]	100,000				
		Bangladesh	50,000[a]				
		Afghanistan	5,500				
		Myanmar q.v. Burma	800				
		Others	1,500				

Continued over

Table 4.7 Continued

Region/country of asylum	Total no. of refugees	Source country(ies)	No. of refugees	Region/country of asylum	Total no. of refugees	Source country(ies)	No. of refugees
LATIN AMERICA & THE CARIBBEAN	152,800			French Guiana	10,000	Suriname	10,000
Argentina	2,100[a]	Chile	1,400[a]	Guatemala	4,400	Nicaragua	3,300[a]
		South East Asia	400			El Salvador	1,100
		Europe	200	Honduras	34,900[a]	Nicaragua	23,600[a]
		Others	100			El Salvador	10,900[a]
Belize	5,100[a]	El Salvador	4,000			Guatemala	400[a]
		Guatemala	1,100	Mexico	46,300[a]	El Salvador	3,700[a]
Bolivia	200					Guatemala	41,300[a]
						Others	1,300
Brazil	200	Europe	100	Nicaragua	7,400	El Salvador	7,000
		Chile	100			Guatemala	400
Chile	100	Europe	100	Panama	1,200	El Salvador	700
Colombia	700	Chile	600			Guatemala	400
		Others	100			Others	100
Costa Rica	33,400[a]	Nicaragua	26,500[a]	Peru	700	Cuba	400
		El Salvador	4,000[a]			Europe	200
		Cuba	2,500			Chile	100
		Others	400	Uruguay	100		
Cuba	3,000			Venezuela	200		
Dominican Rep.	1,600[a]			OCEANIA			
Ecuador	700	Chile	400	Australia[d]	11,100	Viet Nam	3,750
		Others	300			El Salvador	1,000
El Salvador	500	Nicaragua	500			Other	6,350

[a] Sources vary significantly in number reported.
[b] Tibet Autonomous Region, China.
[c] Excludes 720,000 ethnic Germans who entered as immigrants in 1989.
[d] Data are provided by the Refugee Council of Australia and refer to 1987–1988.

Asylum seekers are those persons who applied for asylum during the past year. Reports of refugee numbers often vary greatly depending on the source of the information, partly due to rapidly changing political and environmental situations and partly due to differing definitions of refugee status.

Source:
USCR 1990 *World Refugee Survey: 1989 in Review*, US Committee for Refugees, American Council for Nationalities Service, Washington DC.

Table 4.8 Principal sources of the world's refugees, as assessed in 1989

Country	No. of refugees	Country	No. of refugees
Afghanistan	5,934,500	Western Sahara	165,000[a]
Palestinians	2,340,500	Viet Nam	124,779
Mozambique	1,354,000[a]	China (Tibet)[b]	112,000
Ethiopia	1,035,900	Sri Lanka	103,000
Iraq	508,000[a]	Nicaragua	89,700
Angola	438,000[a]	Laos	69,044
Sudan	435,100	Liberia	68,000
Somalia	388,600[a]	El Salvador	61,100[a]
Cambodia	334,166	Guatemala	58,700[a]
Iran	270,100[a]	Yemen, Dem.	55,000[a]
Rwanda	233,000[a]	Zaire	50,400
Burundi	186,500[a]	Bangladesh	50,000[a]

[a] Sources vary significantly in number reported.
[b] Tibet Autonomous Region, China.

The above values may be an underestimate of the total number of refugees originating from a given country as asylum nations do not always specify countries of refugees' origin.

Source:
USCR 1990 *World Refugee Survey: 1989 in Review*, US Committee for Refugees, American Council for Nationalities Service, Washington DC.

Table 4.9 Internally displaced refugees, as assessed in 1989

Region/country	No. of displaced refugees	Region/country	No. of displaced refugees
AFRICA		**SOUTH AMERICA**	
Angola	638,000–1,178,000	Peru	80,000
Chad	150,000–300,000		
Ethiopia	700,000–1,500,000[a]	**ASIA**	
Somalia	70,000–400,000		
South Africa	3,570,000[a]	Afghanistan	2,000,000
		Cyprus	265,000
Sudan	2,000,000–3,200,000	India	65,000[b]
Uganda	300,000	Iran	500,000[b]
		Iraq	500,000–1,000,000[a]
NORTH AMERICA			
		Lebanon	500,000–1,000,000
El Salvador	147,000–397,000	Myanmar q.v. Burma	100,000–200,000[a]
Guatamala	100,000–500,000[a]	Philippines	450,000
Honduras	22,000	Sri Lanka	500,000[b]
Nicaragua	390,000		
		USSR	500,000

[a] Includes persons forcibly relocated in government resettlement programmes as a result of their race, religion, ethnicity, social group or imputed political opinion.
[b] Different data sources vary significantly in the number of refugees reported.

Because information on internal displacement is fragmentary, this table presents only reported estimates or ranges.

Source:
USCR 1990 *World Refugee Survey: 1989 in Review*, US Committee for Refugees, American Council for Nationalities Service, Washington DC.

Provision of fresh air, clean water, wholesome food and adequate shelter are essential environmental components or determinants necessary for the health and well-being of all people. If the quality of any one of these components is inadequate, human health can be adversely affected both directly and indirectly. Water- and food-borne diseases, which are especially widespread in developing countries, as well as the chronic effects of chemical contaminants in foods, may have significant impacts on the health, social and economic well-being of many millions of people. Inadequate and insufficient food, as well as the occurrence of so-called natural disasters, transport-related accidents and uncontrolled industrialization, urbanization and development, are additional environmental health hazards. Indeed, to a large degree the type and severity of environmental hazards which may affect human health are determined by the level of economic development.

In the past, the hazards of environmental pollution have been associated largely with urban air and drinking-water quality but, more recently, the range of concerns has widened. Indoor air pollution, improper disposal of hazardous wastes, exposure to ionizing radiation and noise pollution represent potential hazards to human health which have received increased attention in recent years.

Trends in a number of the above factors are detailed in other parts of this report. More specifically, human exposure to a range of environmental pollutants is discussed in Part 1: Environmental Pollution; population growth and urbanization in Part 4: Population/Settlements; hazardous waste generation and disposal in Part 8: Wastes; and disasters in Part 9: Natural Disasters.

In the earlier editions of the 'UNEP Environmental Data Report' (UNEP 1987, 1989) data which illustrate the type and extent of information available were presented for a range of health indicators. Comments were also made on the inadequate, unreliable and incomplete nature of some of the environmental health data and for the need to strengthen the basic institutional capacity of some countries both to tackle and to report on their own situations.

It has been estimated that about 1,000 million people, or 29 per cent of the world's population, live in poverty and the correlation with ill-health is high (Backett, 1989). The greatest health problems are reported to be in sub-Saharan Africa where 160 million, or 30 per cent of the population, are undernourished and ill (WHO, 1989). In southern and eastern Asia, South and Central America, North Africa and the Middle East a similar percentage of

the population suffer from disease and malnutrition. Every year in the developing world, 14 million children die before reaching the age of five. Millions more suffer from ill-health, disabilities or poor growth (UNICEF, 1990). The effects of environmental quality on children have been specifically addressed in a recently published report (UNEP/UNICEF, 1990).

The maintenance and improvement of human health in the face of increasing population growth, urbanization and industrialization represent a major challenge. The World Health Organization (WHO), the United Nations Children's Fund (UNICEF) and the International Agency for Research on Cancer (IARC) are major organizations involved in the collection of data, research and assessment to meet this challenge. Health-related data are routinely submitted to these organizations via questionnaires or reports from national health or statistical offices of the member states. Most of the data included in Part 5: Human Health are extracted from WHO published reports and data bases.

Assessments of the health effects of priority chemicals are conducted by the International Programme on Chemical Safety (IPCS), a joint effort of UNEP, WHO and the International Labour Organization (ILO), and by UNEP's International Register of Potentially Toxic Chemicals (IRPTC). Data collected by the GEMS health-related monitoring programmes, which are implemented by the WHO, form the basis of regular assessments of the health implications of urban air quality, fresh-water quality and food contamination (see Part 1: Environmental Pollution). The potential health hazards created by new and emerging technologies within the industrial, agricultural and transportation sectors are addressed by WHO, FAO, ILO and UNEP. Other international organizations with work programmes aimed at improving human health care include the International Red Cross and Red Crescent Societies and the Save the Children Fund.

Environmental health issues are becoming an increasingly important component of development programmes, both at a national and at a local community level. The current status of programmes on the control of such issues and their integration is extremely variable between world regions, between countries and, in some cases, even within national borders. Data presented in this part on Human Health clearly illustrate these conclusions. Comparisons between the health status of countries and geographical areas are an important method of assessing the role of different environmental factors in the aetiology of disease. Conversely, the health of a population is a useful indicator of the state of that population's environment.

References

Backett, M. 1989 The first forty years: a personal view, *World Health Forum* **10**, 48–57.

UNEP 1987 *United Nations Environment Programme Environmental Data Report*, Basil Blackwell, Oxford.

UNEP 1989 *United Nations Environment Programme Environmental Data Report*, Basil Blackwell, Oxford.

UNEP/UNICEF 1990 *Children and the Environment: The State of the Environment 1990*, United Nations Environment Programme, Nairobi, and United Nations Children's Fund, New York.

UNICEF 1990 *All for Health: A Resource Book for Facts for Life*, United Nations Children's Fund, New York.

WHO 1989 Report on world health, *WHO Features*, World Health Organization, Geneva.

General Health Status Indicators

Causes of Death

Approximately 50 million deaths occur each year, 78 per cent of them in developing countries (WHO, 1989). In developing countries, deaths of people under 65 years of age account for almost 60 per cent of total deaths whereas in developed countries only 30–35 per cent of the deaths are in this age group (Tables 5.1 and 5.2).

Mortality statistics are published annually by the WHO and cover approximately 30 per cent of all the deaths which occur each year. In countries with small populations, an average annual number of deaths has been calculated in order to reduce the effect of random variation. Many of the data come from the developed world as reliable data are not readily available from a large number of the developing countries. One reason for the paucity of data in developing countries is a shortage of health personnel to record and to classify deaths by cause (see Health Care below). Furthermore, the developing countries which do regularly submit data to WHO are those with low to medium mortality rates (see Table 4.2 in Part 4: Population/Settlements) and none has a life expectancy of less than 63 years. As a result, these data may not represent an accurate reflection of the mortality situation in the developing world as a whole.

Data on the proportions of deaths due to the five leading causes of death by sex and age group are presented in Tables 5.1 and 5.2. Table 5.1 provides national data for selected countries, compiled from the mortality statistics published in WHO's annual statistical reports. Table 5.2 is a regional summary of the data from Table 5.1 but also contains mortality data for countries not listed in Table 5.1.

Deaths due to infectious and parasitic diseases are six times more frequent in developing countries than in developed countries and people in developing countries have a 50 per cent higher risk of dying of respiratory diseases. Circulatory diseases cause half the deaths in developed countries and approximately 27 per cent of the deaths in developing countries. Malignant neoplasms are also more common in developed countries; 11 per cent of the deaths in developing countries were due to malignant neoplasms compared with 21 per cent in developed countries (see Figure 5.1).

Reference

WHO 1989 Introduction. In: *World Health Statistics Annual 1989*, World Health Organization, Geneva, vi–xxiv.

Child Mortality and Life Expectancy

Children, particularly infants, are highly vulnerable to adverse environmental conditions. It is this sector of the population whose health, good or poor, reflects the state of the environment. The infant mortality rate (IMR, defined as the death rate of infants less than one year of age per 1,000 live births) and the child mortality rate (CMR, defined as the death rate of children between one year and five years of age per 1,000 one-year-old children) are often used as

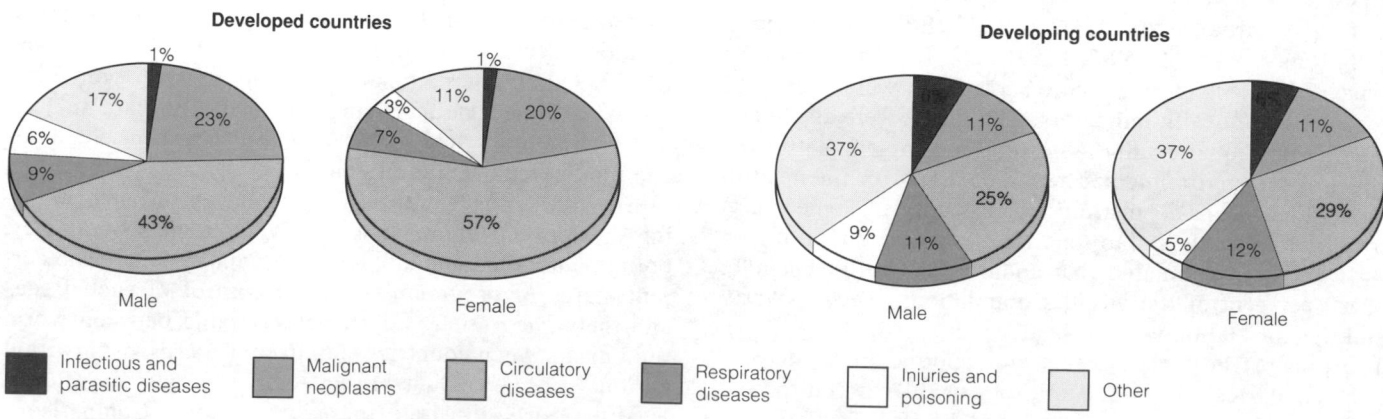

Figure 5.1 Proportional mortality by sex and level of development, 1980s
Source: data from Table 5.2

indicators of environmental conditions. Factors which influence the death rates of children under five years of age include maternal health, drinking water quality and sanitation facilities, nutritional status and housing conditions. Estimates of IMR (in 1990) and CMR (annual average for the period 1985–1990) by country are presented in Table 5.3. Data on infant mortality by cause appeared in the 1989 edition of the 'UNEP Environmental Data Report' (UNEP, 1989).

The IMRs and CMRs of developed countries were computed using the civil registration data submitted by each country to the United Nations Statistical Office (UNSO). As few developing countries have satisfactory civil registration data, their rates have been derived from censuses or from other types of surveys (such as those carried out by the World Fertility Survey). Eighteen countries still have no reliable data at the national level and for 11 others the latest available data are from 1970 or earlier. Latin American data are generally better than data from other developing regions (UN, 1988; Sadik, 1990).

Globally, the IMR and CMR have both declined since 1950. However, there are marked variations in the magnitude of decreases in IMR and CMR between world regions and countries. The world average IMR has decreased by slightly more than half from an annual average of 156 in 1950–1955 to an annual average of 78 in 1980–1985. In the same time period, the global average CMR dropped from 100 to 43. In developed regions there has been a convergence to a low average IMR and CMR of 12 and 3 respectively; however, the rates are still highly variable amongst developing countries. An average IMR of 71 and CMR of 44 were reported for developing countries (Table 5.3).

The world average life expectancy at birth has increased from an annual average of 50 years in 1960–1965 to 63 years in 1990. The greatest increase has occurred in developing countries, with an increase from 46 in 1960–1965 to 61 in 1990. An increase of four years over the same period has brought the life expectancy of people born in developed countries to 74 years. As can be seen from Table 5.3, the countries with the lowest life expectancy are also those with the highest IMRs and CMRs. Most of these countries are in Africa, whereas the areas with highest life expectancy and lowest IMRs and CMRs are in North America and northern and western Europe.

References

Sadik, N. 1990 *The State of World Population*, United Nations Population Fund, New York.

UN 1988 *Mortality of Children Under Age 5: World Estimates and Projections 1950–2025*, United Nations, New York.

UNEP 1989 *United Nations Environment Programme Environmental Data Report*, Basil Blackwell, Oxford.

Maternal Mortality

Maternal mortality has been described as a "neglected tragedy" because of the number of young lives lost (Rosenfield and Maine, 1985). Each year half a million women die as a result of pregnancy and related causes; 99 per cent of these deaths occur in developing countries. Royston and Armstrong (1989) argue that the maternal mortality rate (MMR, defined as the number of deaths during pregnancy and childbirth per 10^4 live births) is a better health indicator than others, including the IMR, because it shows a greater disparity between rich and poor countries than any other public health indicator and therefore may be a more sensitive measure of inequality.

In developing countries, haemorrhage is the greatest cause of maternal deaths (Table 5.4) and this is directly related to the inadequacy of prenatal and delivery care (Figure 5.2). In developed countries, toxaemia accounts for 23–25 per cent of maternal deaths with indirect causes a close second. Due to the social stigma attached to abortion in many countries, the true extent of abortion's contribution to maternal deaths is difficult to assess. In Romania, where abortion laws are reported to be very restrictive (Royston and Armstrong, 1989), 86 per cent of maternal deaths are due to abortion. In many developing countries reports have cited abortion as one of the major underlying causes of maternal mortality.

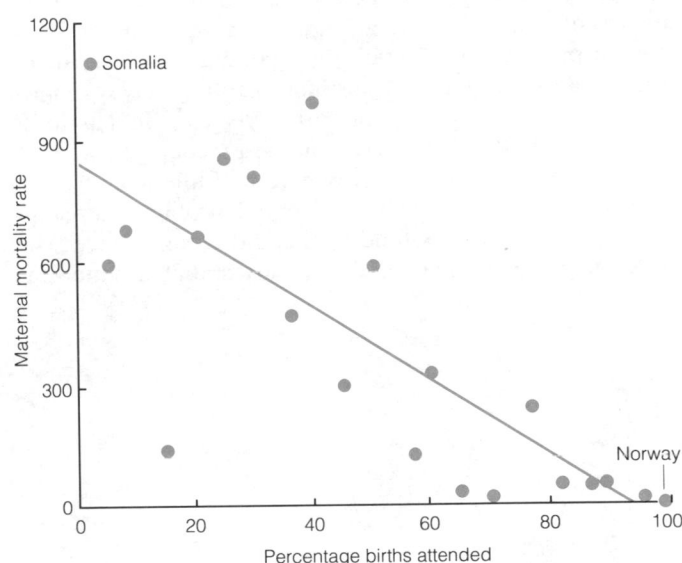

Figure 5.2 Maternal mortality and percentage of births attended by trained personnel in selected countries
Source: Grant, 1990

There are few data on maternal morbidity but it is estimated that for every maternal death, there are approximately 16 women who suffer damage to their health which may affect the rest of their lives. Many of these injuries can also be related to the lack of health care facilities and personnel for pregnant women in developing countries (Royston and Armstrong, 1989).

Table 5.4 was compiled from the WHO's annual statistical volumes and is therefore subject to the same qualifications about the reliability of its data as outlined in the Cause of Death section above.

References

Grant, J. P. 1990 *The State of the World's Children 1990*, Oxford University Press, Oxford.
Rosenfield, A. and Maine, D. 1985 Maternal mortality – a neglected tragedy, *Lancet*, 83–85.
Royston, E. and Armstrong, S. 1989 *Preventing Maternal Deaths*, World Health Organization, Geneva.

Nutritional Status

Nutritional status is a key index in assessing the health of a population. Malnutrition, under- and over-nutrition cause a large number of diseases and are often underlying causes of death. In developing countries, 40 million children suffer from Vitamin A deficiency and more than 500,000 children lose their sight each year as a result. Anaemia, caused by iron deficiency, affects 800–900 million people. Iodine deficiency causes goitre in 211 million people, cretinism in 5.7 million and some form of intellectual deficit and/or motor defect in 20 million more (WHO, 1990). In a Latin American study, malnutrition was reported to be the underlying cause of death in two-thirds of the deaths of children (WHO, 1980).

Table 5.5 shows the percentages of children by country who are underweight, stunted in growth and who show evidence of muscle wasting. Malnourishment in pregnant women prevents the foetus from gaining weight in utero. Infants born weighing less than 2,500 g have a much higher chance of dying in their first year of life than heavier babies (WHO, 1986). Data on the percentage of infants born underweight are also presented in Table 5.5.

In developed countries, nutritional problems are typically related to excess food intake and an unbalanced diet which may lead to obesity, dental caries, diabetes mellitus, hypertension and other cardiovascular diseases. Figure 5.3 shows the proportion of children who are obese in selected countries. Obesity is defined as two standard deviations above the median weight for height.

Breast milk provides all the nutrients an infant needs and can protect it from diarrhoea and other common infections. As shown in Table 5.6, the prevalence of breast-feeding is highest in Africa and lowest in Europe and the Americas. Due to public education campaigns, an increasing number of educated and economically advantaged women in developed countries are choosing to breast-feed while in the developing countries the incidence of breast-feeding has been declining over the last 30 years. In developing countries, an increase in both urbanization and the numbers of women entering the labour force is believed to be responsible for the decrease in the number of women breast-feeding. A similar trend was observed in earlier years in developed countries.

Data on the level of exposure of infants to contaminants in breast milk is addressed in the Human Exposure section of Part 1: Environmental Pollution.

References

WHO 1980 *Sixth Report on the World Health Situation 1973–1977, Part 1: Global Analysis*, World Health Organization, Geneva.
WHO 1986 Infant mortality and birth weight. In: *World Health Statistics Annual 1986*, World Health Organization, Geneva, 13.
WHO 1989 *Global Nutritional Status: Anthropometric Indicators, Update 1989*, WHO Publication NUT/ANTREF/1/89, World Health Organization, Geneva.
WHO 1990 *Global Estimates for Health Situation Assessment and Projections 1990*, World Health Organization, Geneva.

Health Care

The number of people in the health care professions has been increasing since the 1960s. In most countries the growth of the health care sector has been faster than that of the population. However, problems with access to health professionals still exist, as health workers and health facilities are still heavily concentrated in urban areas leaving millions of people without reasonable access to health care. Table 5.7 shows the proportion of people with access to local health care. A health care centre is defined as "local" if it is within one hour's walk or travel (WHO, 1988).

In healthy women, childbirth rarely requires much medical intervention. However, in developing countries, where women may be suffering from malnutrition, the effects of overwork and of high parity, skilled intervention saves lives. Figure 5.2 illustrates the relationship between maternal mortality and health care during pregnancy and childbirth.

Table 5.8 shows the number of health care professionals per 10,000 population in selected countries. While many countries provide data on the numbers of doctors and nurses, the availability of data on other health professionals varies considerably between regions. It is therefore more appropriate to make comparisons between countries within a given world region. The required number of

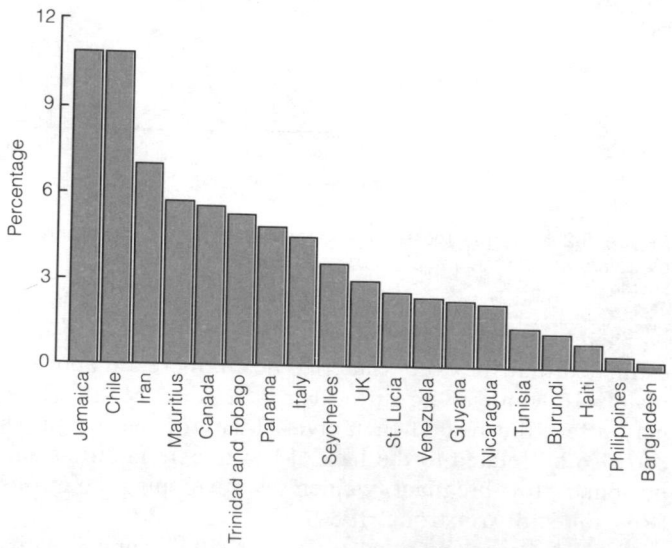

Figure 5.3 Percentage of obese children under age five years in selected countries world-wide
Source: WHO, 1989

trained health care personnel varies with a population's age distribution, sanitation conditions, housing and nutritional status. For example, Southwick (1985) estimates that in most countries, 10 physicians per 10,000 population are required to provide adequate coverage.

References

Southwick, C. H. 1985 The human condition, economics and health. In: *Global Ecology*, C. H. Southwick (Ed.), Sinauer Associates Inc., Sunderland, Massachussetts, 243–252.
WHO 1988 The health professions in the 1980s: a statistical update. In: *World Health Statistics Annual 1988*, Section B, World Health Organization, Geneva, 43–70.

Immunizational Status

An essential part of health care is the immunization of children against the six common vaccine preventable childhood diseases: measles, diphtheria, pertussis (whooping cough), tuberculosis, poliomyelitis and tetanus. Approximately 46 million infants are not fully immunized against these diseases, resulting in the deaths of 2.8 million children each year while at least another 3 million are disabled. The Expanded Programme on Immunization (EPI), established by WHO in 1974, is the international effort working to expand immunization coverage world-wide. At current coverage levels, it is estimated that 2.2 million deaths in children per year due to measles, neonatal tetanus and whooping cough (pertussis) have been prevented by immunization as well as over 200,000 cases of poliomyelitis (Figure 5.4). Immunization coverage also provides an indicator of the number of people with access to health care services. It is likely that if it is possible for someone to access health facilities for the vaccination of their children, they can also utilize the health facilities for other primary health services (WHO, 1990).

Figure 5.5 illustrates the relationship between CMR and immunization coverage. Some countries have achieved a low rate of child mortality without high levels of immunization. Conversely, Tanzania, with 81 per cent its children immunized, has a CMR of 179. This suggests that the combination of water quality, sanitation and other improvements for health must occur in conjunction with immunization in order to reduce child mortality rates to the lowest possible levels.

In 1974, the EPI estimated that only 5 per cent of infants world-wide had received a vaccine against poliomyelitis. However, by 1989, 67 per cent of all infants had received the full course of the vaccine (the poliomyelitis vaccine is administered in three doses) against the disease, thus working towards the commitment of WHO to the global eradication of poliomyelitis by the year 2000 (WHO, 1988).

With the exception of immunization against tetanus, the other diseases in the programme have shown similar improvements in their coverage levels. Table 5.9 presents the data on immunization coverage for 1988 and 1989 and Table 5.10 shows the incidence of diseases covered by the EPI. Data on immunization coverage between 1980–1987

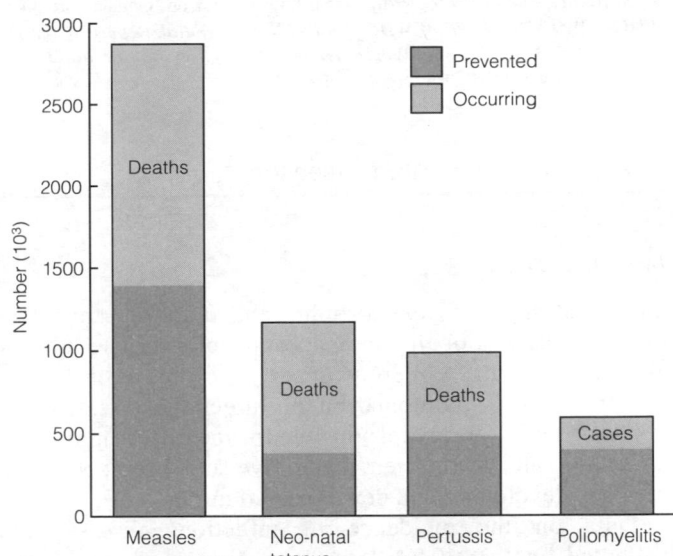

Figure 5.4 Vaccine preventable diseases: number of deaths or cases, prevented and still occurring, 1988
Source: WHO, 1990

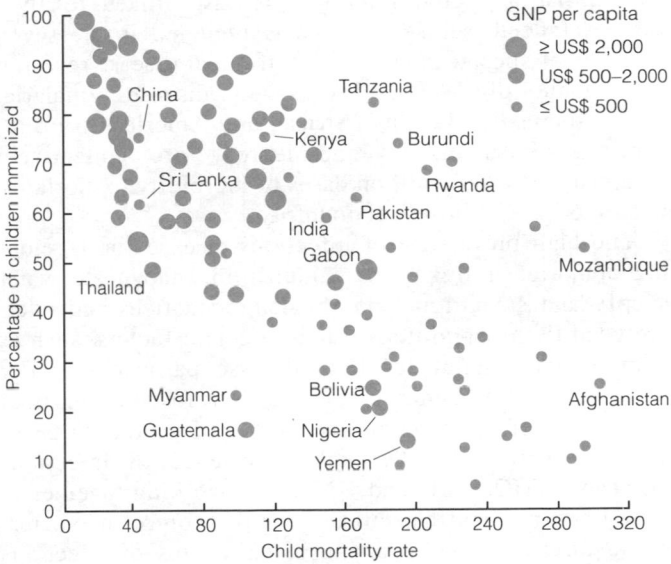

Figure 5.5 The relationship between immunization and child mortality, 1987
Source: Barke, 1990

appeared in the second edition of this report (UNEP, 1989).

References

Barke, M. 1990 Workers of the world, *Geographical* **62**(6), Geographical Analysis Supplement, 1–4.
UNEP 1989 *United Nations Environment Programme Environmental Data Report*, Basil Blackwell, Oxford.

WHO 1988 Development of immunization services. In: *World Health Statistics Annual 1988*, World Health Organization, Geneva, 30–34.

WHO 1990 *The Work of WHO 1988–1989: Biennial Report of the Director-General to the World Health Assembly and to the United Nations*, World Health Organization, Geneva.

Environmentally-related Diseases

Infectious Diseases

The greatest causes of morbidity and mortality are infectious diseases. Globally, they account for over one-third of all deaths, with children under five being the most susceptible. The combination of infectious diseases and malnutrition is largely responsible for the differential in the mortality rate of children under five and life expectancy between developing and developed countries.

Data on the incidence of infectious diseases are collected by the WHO. Infectious diseases mainly comprise acute infections caused by metazoan, protozoan, bacterial and viral parasites (see Table 5.11); however, chronic infections are a growing concern. Acquired Immune Deficiency Syndrome (AIDS) and liver cancer induced by hepatitis B are two examples of diseases caused by chronic infection. The metazoan disease, schistosomiasis, an acute infection, is also linked to liver cancer. Indeed, schistosomiasis is included in the seven diseases of special interest to the tropical disease research programme of WHO. The seven diseases, malaria, schistosomiasis, filariasis, African and American trypanosomiasis, leishmaniasis and leprosy are collectively responsible for 607 million cases of morbidity or mortality in tropical and subtropical countries.

The high prevalence of infectious diseases in developing countries is linked to malnutrition, inadequate water supply and sanitation, poor hygienic practices and overcrowded living conditions. Environmental factors, such as climate and habitat for both disease pathogens and/or vectors, can also enhance transmission. In addition, poor immunization coverage and resistance of vectors to pesticides contribute to the high prevalence of infectious diseases. WHO, FAO and UNEP are working together to strengthen national capabilities for the control of vector-borne diseases. The reporting of epidemics of infectious diseases in Table 5.12 is far from complete, but the data do reflect the high number of epidemics in developing countries compared with developed countries.

The most widespread of the infectious diseases are those transmitted by infected human faeces. The most common manifestation of these infections are diarrhoeal diseases which are estimated to cause up to 10 per cent of all deaths in developing countries and 28 per cent of deaths in children world-wide. Figure 5.6 shows the proportional causes of deaths in children under the age of five years. For the purposes of the figure, one cause has been allocated for each child death. However, in practice, children die from multiple causes and malnutrition is a contributory cause in approximately one-third of all child deaths. Infectious diseases account for at least 71 per cent of all child deaths.

Data on the incidence of infectious diseases are incomplete for most developing countries in which the bulk of these diseases occur. Some specific diseases are discussed in the following sections, but data should be interpreted with caution as an increase in notifications may actually be an artefact of increased reporting of the disease. Data on acute respiratory infections, malaria, onchocerciasis (river blindness) and AIDS appeared in the 1989 edition of this report (UNEP, 1989) and data on cholera and schistosomiasis were presented in the 1987 edition (UNEP, 1987).

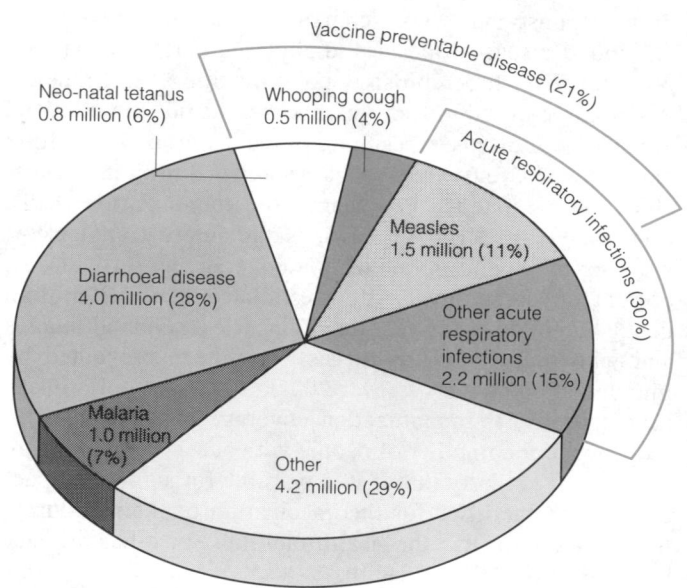

Figure 5.6 Leading causes of child deaths world-wide
Source: Grant, 1990

Diarrhoea and ORT   Diarrhoea is the greatest single cause of morbidity and mortality in children in developing countries (Figure 5.6). According to estimates produced by the WHO Control of Diarrhoeal Diseases Program (CDD), diarrhoea caused 1,362 million episodes of illness in children in 1988 (Table 5.13) resulting in 4 million deaths. Diarrhoea also causes many episodes of illness (though rarely death) in older children and adults.

Factors such as malnutrition, inadequate access to safe water and sanitation facilities, and poor hygienic practices increase the occurrence and severity of diarrhoeal episodes. There are limited data which illustrate the role of food in the transmission of pathogens causing diarrhoea; however, undercooked food, food stored at ambient temperatures, and inadequately reheated foods may account for 15–70 per cent of all diarrhoea episodes (Huttly, 1990).

Most of the deaths due to diarrhoea in children are caused by acute dehydration and may be prevented by oral rehydration therapy (ORT). In 1988, one-third of all diarrhoeal episodes in children under five were treated with ORT (Table 5.13). An estimated 1 million lives were saved as a result (Grant, 1990).

Yellow Fever A vaccine against yellow fever has been available since 1937, but yellow fever remains a major public health threat in Africa and South America. Yellow fever is an acute haemorrhagic disease transmitted by *Aedes aegypti* mosquitoes. Transmission by the peridomestic species of the mosquito results in dengue fever and transmission by wild species results in jungle fever. The liver of an infected individual may fail after a short, violent fever, causing jaundice. The heart and kidney are also involved in the resultant pathology.

In 1988, 2,058 cases and 1,709 deaths were reported to WHO, giving yellow fever the high case-fatality ratio of 83 per cent. As can be seen in Table 5.14 and Figure 5.7, the three-year period 1986–1988 has been the most active period of yellow fever since reporting began in 1947.

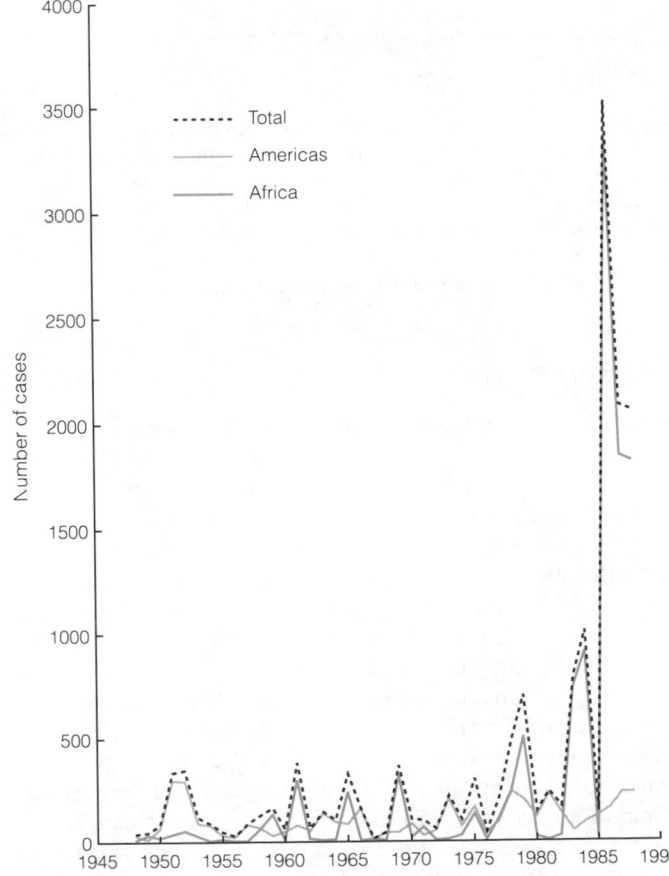

Figure 5.7 The incidence of yellow fever in selected continents, 1948–1988
Source: data from Table 5.14

According to WHO, yellow fever is seriously underreported, especially in Africa. Village-based serological tests have shown that yellow fever is under-reported by 10 to 500 times. Based on the maximum estimate of under-reporting, in the three-year period 1986–1988, Nigeria alone probably had 440,000 cases of yellow fever and 250,000 deaths (WHO, 1990).

Human Plague Human plague is caused by an infection due to *Yersinia pestis*, an enterobacteria which causes an acute regional lymphatic disease, commonly called bubonic plague. However, other clinical forms include septicemic, pneumonic and meningeal plagues. *Y. pestis* is transmitted by the fleas of rats and other rodents. Plague is primarily a disease of rodents but spreads to humans when rats and people are in close contact, such as in slums where sanitation is poor.

Outbreaks of human plague tend to occur when natural disasters or wars disrupt sanitary services. Four epidemics of plague were reported to WHO in 1990 (Table 5.12). Table 5.15 presents data on the incidence of plague by country. In 1989, close to 50 per cent of all plague cases were reported from Viet Nam and 25 per cent from Madagascar. This bacterial disease is responsible for devastating pandemics because of its high mortality rates and is also seriously under-reported to the WHO. The world is presently experiencing the fourth pandemic (Hart, 1991).

References

Grant, J. P. 1990 *The State of the World's Children 1990*, Oxford University Press, Oxford.
Hart, D. 1991 Personal communication, King's College London, University of London, UK.
Huttly, S. R. A. 1990 The impact of inadequate sanitary conditions on health in developing countries, *World Health Statistics Quarterly* **43**(3), 118–126.
UNEP 1987 *United Nations Environment Programme Environmental Data Report*, Basil Blackwell, Oxford.
UNEP 1989 *United Nations Environment Programme Environmental Data Report*, Basil Blackwell, Oxford.
WHO 1990 Yellow fever in 1988, *Weekly Epidemiological Record*, **65**(28), 213–219.

Cardiovascular Diseases

Cardiovascular diseases (CVD) are a leading cause of preventable morbidity and mortality. In developed countries, CVDs account for 40–50 per cent of all deaths and in developing countries they are the second leading cause of death, after infectious and parasitic diseases.

Mortality from ischaemic heart disease (IHD) started to decline in the USA in the 1960s and has now declined by 50 per cent. Mortality rates have also declined in Australia, Belgium, Canada, Finland, Japan, the Netherlands and New Zealand, whereas rates are increasing in the developing countries and in some eastern European countries (WHO, 1989a). In addition, in countries where IHD is increasing, a disturbing trend towards increased incidence in younger men has been observed (WHO, 1990).

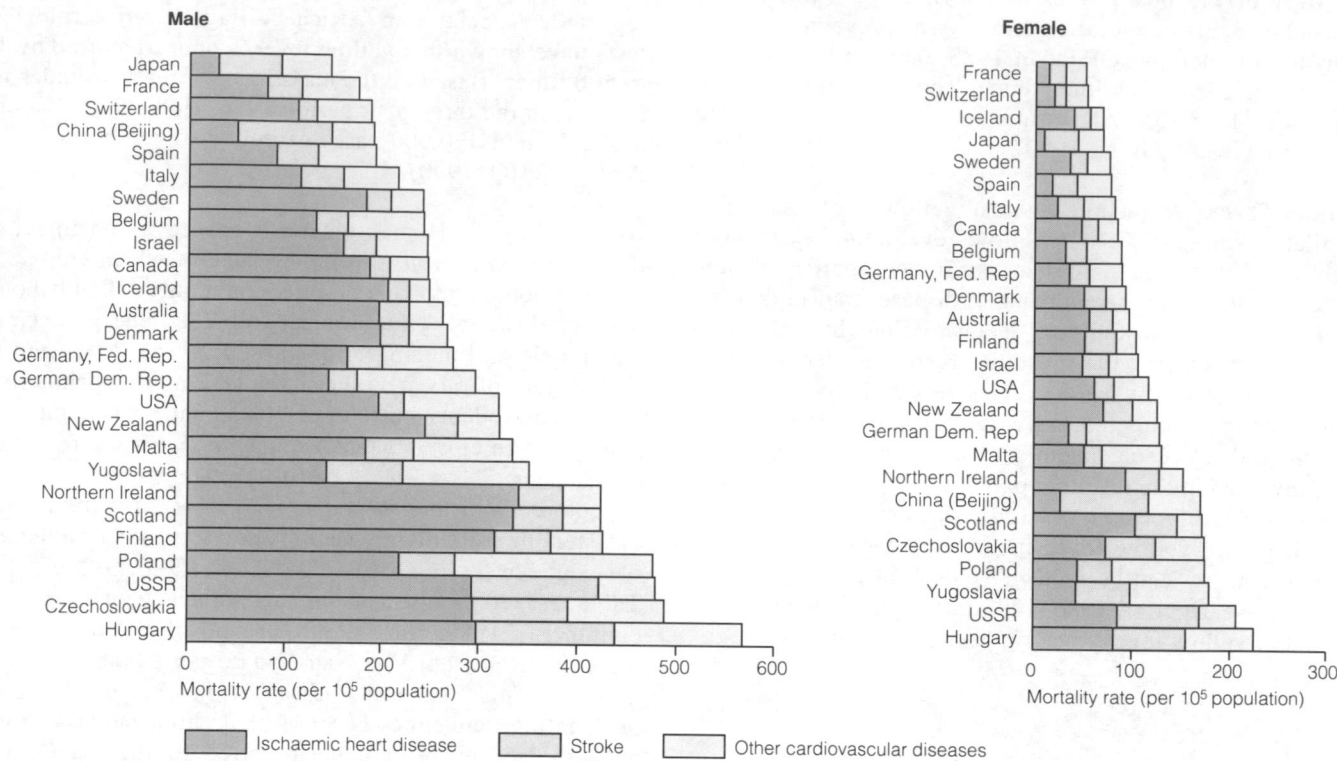

Figure 5.8 Age-standardized CVD rates for males and females in the age group 35–64 years (national data), mid-1980s
Source: data from Table 5.16

In order to monitor the role of environmental factors in cardiovascular disease, the WHO has established the MONICA project (Multilateral Monitoring of Trends and Determinants in Cardiovascular Disease). Trends in fatal and non-fatal coronary heart disease (IHD) and stroke, as well as trends in risk factors (smoking, obesity, high cholesterol levels and high blood pressure), are to be monitored over the 10-year period 1984–1993 using a standard methodology to facilitate comparisons between countries. Approximately 15 million men and women in the age group 35–64 are to be studied through MONICA's 39 collaborating centres in 26 countries. Figure 5.8 shows the age-standardized rates by sex for all CVD, IHD and stroke from the MONICA study.

Data on the prevalence of risk factors appeared in the second edition of this report (UNEP, 1989). According to the most recent published analysis of MONICA data, there are very few countries with low levels of risk factors (WHO, 1989b). Table 5.16 shows the considerable variation between countries in the age-standardized mortality rates for all CVD, IHD and stroke. Also presented are the percentages of the total deaths caused by all CVD, IHD and stroke, for individual countries and MONICA centres. Only in France (national and MONICA data) was the proportion of total deaths due to CVD under 25 per cent.

References

UNEP 1989 *United Nations Environment Programme Environmental Data Report*, Basil Blackwell, Oxford.

WHO 1989a Causes of death in developed countries. In: *World Health Statistics Annual 1989*, World Health Organization, Geneva, 17–19.
WHO 1989b The WHO MONICA project: A world-wide monitoring system for cardiovascular disease. In: *World Health Statistics Annual 1989*, Section B, World Health Organization, Geneva, 27–149.
WHO 1990 *Global Estimates for Health Situation Assessment and Projections 1990*, World Health Organization, Geneva.

Neoplastic Diseases

In 1980, the estimated global incidence of neoplastic diseases (cancer) was 6,350,000 resulting in 4.2 million deaths. There is a considerable amount of evidence to suggest that a significant proportion of all cancers are either directly or indirectly caused by environmental factors (Tomatis, 1990). Thus many of these cases and deaths were potentially avoidable. After cardiovascular disease, cancer is the second leading cause of preventable mortality and morbidity in many parts of the world.

IARC, within the framework of the WHO, is involved in the global surveillance of cancer incidence. Descriptive epidemiology is used to examine and compare the incidence of cancer in different geographical areas and population groups in order to assess the role of cancer risk factors (Figure 5.9). Environmental risk factors include exposure to ionizing radiation and carcinogenic chemicals in air, food and water or through smoking, alcohol and drugs. The human papilloma virus (HPV), hepatitis B and schistosomiasis parasites are examples of biotic agents of carcinogenesis. Table 5.17 compares the areas of the world having the highest and the lowest incidence rates of cancer by site; the ratio between the rates gives an idea of the potential scope for prevention of these cancers. Using information on the prevalence of the major risk factors for cancer in different parts of the world, Table 5.18 indicates the potential reduction in incidence (or in deaths) which could be achieved through different preventive measures.

Public apprehension over the capacity of ionizing radiation to induce cancer in humans is one of the major environmental concerns. Exposure to ionizing radiation was linked to cancer in 1902 when skin carcinomas on the hands of radiologists were reported, only seven years after the discovery of X-rays. Ionizing radiation can induce cancer in any organ in which cancer naturally occurs (Tomatis, 1990).

Several studies of underground miners indicate that exposure to radon and its decay products causes lung cancer, and work in the last few years suggests that this may also be true for domestic exposures (IARC, 1988). In a recent study, estimated national average exposure to radon was found to correlate with incidence rates of myeloid

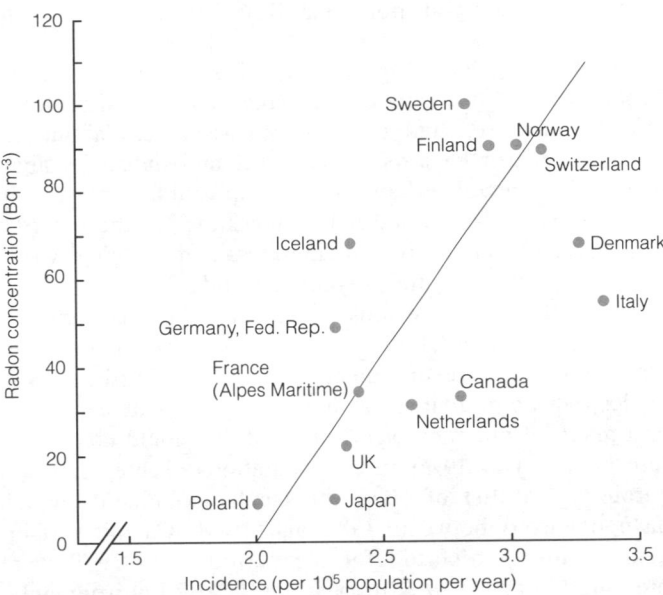

Figure 5.10 Radon concentration versus international incidence of myeloid leukaemia
Source: Henshaw et al., 1990

leukaemia (Figure 5.10) and also cancer of the kidney, melanoma and certain other cancers, raising the possibility of other causal relationships (Henshaw et al., 1990).

Data showing a correlation between the global incidence of malignant melanomas and latitude appeared in the 1989 edition of the 'UNEP Environmental Data Report' (UNEP, 1989). Data on human exposure to terrestrial radiation and radon are presented in the Human Exposure section of Part 1: Environmental Pollution.

References

Henshaw, D. L., Eatough, J. P. and Richardson, R. B. 1990 Radon as a causative factor in induction of myeloid leukaemia and other cancers, *Lancet* **335**, 1008–1012.

IARC 1988 *Man-made Mineral Fibes and Radon*, IARC Monographs on the Evaluation of Carcinogenic Risks to Humans, Volume 43, International Agency for Research on Cancer, Lyon.

Parkin, D. M., Läärä, E. and Muir, C. S. 1988 Estimates of the worldwide frequency of sixteen major cancers in 1980, *International Journal of Cancer* **41**, 184–197.

Tomatis, L. (Ed.) 1990 *Cancer. Causes, Occurrence and Control*, IARC Scientific Publications No. 100, International Agency for Research on Cancer, Lyon.

UNEP 1989 *United Nations Environment Programme Environmental Data Report*, Basil Blackwell, Oxford.

Environmentally-related Accidents

In most countries, accidents are one of the top five causes of death. The importance of accidents as a cause of death is increasing each year. In developed countries, road traffic accidents are the most common cause of accidental death for both men and women. The highest proportion of deaths

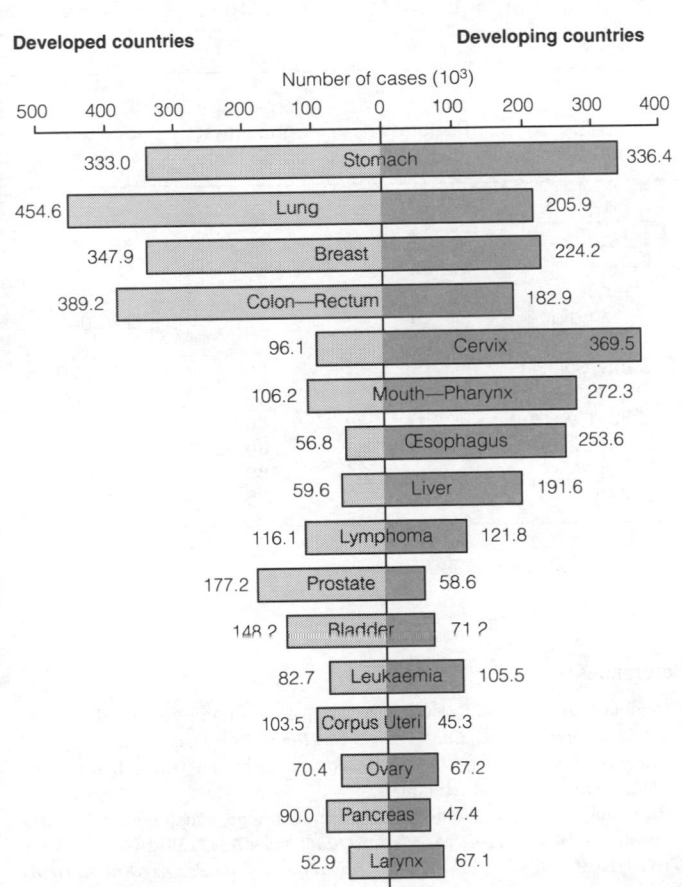

Figure 5.9 Number of new cancer cases by site and level of development, 1980
Source: Parkin et al., 1988

due to road traffic accidents occur in the 15–44 age group (see Part 7: Transport, Tourism, Table 7.2). For each accidental death, several more disabilities of varying severity occur.

Major and widely reported chemical and nuclear accidents, such as those in Bhopal (India) and in Chernobyl (USSR) have resulted in increased awareness about the potential health hazards of chemical and industrial accidents. The result is an increase in public interest in environmental issues and public resistance to the location of nuclear power stations, incinerators and chemical waste processing plants in their neighbourhoods.

More than 200 serious chemical accidents/incidents occur each year in OECD (Organisation for Economic Co-Operation and Development) countries (UNEP, 1989). Widespread contamination of the environment can occur as a result of chemical accidents and this could lead to future health risks to exposed populations. Table 5.19 is a chronological list of chemical accidents/incidents which have occurred between 1980 and 1988. Chemical accidents/incidents reported for the period 1950–1979 were presented in the 1989 edition of the 'UNEP Environmental Data Report' (UNEP, 1989).

Reference

UNEP 1989 *United Nations Environment Programme Environmental Data Report*, Basil Blackwell, Oxford.

Acute Pesticide Poisonings

Pesticides are chemicals used in agriculture for pest, weed and plant disease control. They are also important in the control of the vectors of vector-borne infectious diseases. Approximately 3 million tons of pesticides were used world-wide in 1985. Pesticide usage is expected to double between 1985 and 1995, particularly in the developing world where damage by pests may cause crop losses of up to 75 per cent (WHO/UNEP, 1989).

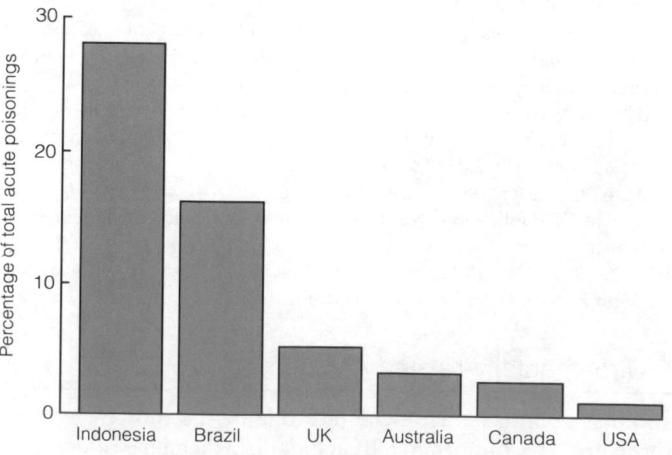

Figure 5.11 Proportion of acute poisonings due to pesticides in selected countries, 1980s
Source: Jeyaratnam, 1990

The quantity of the product in use and its inherent toxicity to living organisms make misuse of pesticides particularly hazardous to humans. In developed countries, the main health risks are those associated with chronic exposure to low levels of pesticides from environmental contamination and residues in food. In developing countries, acute pesticide poisonings are a major public health problem. Figure 5.11 shows that very few acute poisonings in developed countries are due to pesticides whereas in Indonesia, for example, pesticide poisonings constitute almost a third of all acute poisonings.

The majority of acute pesticide poisonings are suicides rather than accidents (Jeyaratnam, 1990). A study in Malaysia found that 73.4 per cent of poisonings involving the herbicide, paraquat, were due to suicides, 13.8 per cent were accidents and 1.07 per cent were occupational accidents (Jeyaratnam, 1990).

The WHO estimates that each year over one million unintentional acute pesticide poisonings with severe manifestations and more than 220,000 deaths occur worldwide. Other data suggest that 11 million acute pesticide poisonings, including those with only minor effects, occur annually in Africa (Choudbury, 1989). The table below shows the number of poisonings in selected countries in Africa. Rates per 100,000 agricultural workers vary from 2,286 in Mozambique to 213 in Mauritius.

Country	Population (10^6)	Percentage agricultural labour force	Number of cases (a^{-1})
Sudan	24	80	384,000
Tanzania	23	85	368,000
Kenya	22	80	350,000
Uganda	17	80	272,000
Mozambique	15	70	240,000
Cameroon	11	80	175,000
Zimbabwe	10	80	160,000
Côte d'Ivoire	10	80	160,000
Malawi	8	85	128,000
Senegal	7	80	112,000
Mauritius	2	75	3,200

Source: Jeyaratnam, 1990

References

Choudbury, A. W. 1989 Health hazards of pesticide use in Africa. In: *Proceedings of the East Africa Regional Symposium on Chemical Accidents and Occupational Health*, S. Lehtinen (Ed.), Institute of Occupational Health, Helsinki.

Jeyaratnam, J. 1990 Acute pesticide poisoning: a major global health problem, *World Health Statistics Quarterly* **43**(3), 139–144.

WHO/UNEP 1989 *Public Health Impact of Pesticides used in Agriculture*, Report of a WHO/UNEP Working Group, World Health Organization, Geneva, and the United Nations Environment Programme, Nairobi.

Table 5.1 Mortality in selected countries by cause, age group and sex

Region/country	Year	Age group (years)	Total no. of deaths		Proportional mortality[a]									
					Infectious and parasitic diseases		Malignant neoplasms		Diseases of the circulatory system		Respiratory diseases		Injuries and poisonings	
			Male	Female	Male	Female	Male	Female	Male	Female	Male	Female	Male	Female
AFRICA														
Cape Verde	1980	All ages	1,087	1,194	21.3	18.8	5.7	6.7	16.3	18.8	9.7	9.1	6.3	1.8
		0–14	540	486	35.0	38.7	0.2	0.8	2.8	2.9	16.1	17.3	2.2	1.9
		15–44	75	97	17.3	14.4	8.0	12.4	13.3	21.6	5.3	3.1	36.0	5.2
		45–64	129	131	10.1	6.9	14.0	16.8	37.2	45.0	3.9	3.8	10.1	2.3
		65+	343	480	4.7	2.7	10.8	8.8	30.3	27.3	2.6	3.5	4.7	0.8
Mauritius	1986	All ages	3,721	2,901	3.2	2.2	7.3	8.9	43.6	45.6	9.5	9.5	4.9	3.7
		0–14	382	292	11.0	8.6	2.4	4.1	2.4	2.1	10.2	11.6	5.2	6.5
		15–44	560	360	3.0	3.1	5.5	12.2	28.8	23.9	5.2	6.7	15.4	16.7
		45–64	1,301	612	2.2	2.0	7.4	15.8	52.0	46.1	7.1	6.2	3.4	1.8
		65+	1,478	1,637	2.1	1.0	9.3	6.4	52.5	58.0	13.2	10.9	2.2	1.0
AMERICAS														
Argentina	1985	All ages	133,388	105,793	3.1	3.1	17.8	17.5	43.8	49.0	6.1	5.5	5.1	2.8
		0–14	12,408	9,485	7.8	9.1	2.4	2.3	4.1	4.3	8.1	9.0	8.6	6.9
		15–44	12,008	7,121	4.2	6.1	11.6	22.1	22.0	24.7	4.0	4.9	22.8	8.7
		45–64	36,195	18,671	3.0	3.3	24.4	33.2	44.0	37.6	4.5	4.0	4.4	2.7
		65+	70,276	68,956	2.2	1.9	18.4	15.0	55.2	61.2	7.0	5.4	1.8	1.7
Bahamas	1984–85	All ages	679	544	2.9	3.5	19.1	17.6	25.6	30.7	11.0	11.9	5.2	4.4
		0–14	94	83	6.4	3.6	3.2	1.2	7.4	6.0	18.1	19.3	5.3	8.4
		15–44	158	84	2.5	7.1	10.8	20.2	13.9	17.9	7.0	14.3	13.3	11.9
		45–64	190	109	5.3	3.7	27.9	34.9	28.9	27.5	10.5	7.3	3.2	2.8
		65+	234	265	0.9	2.3	25.6	15.1	39.3	43.8	11.5	10.9	1.7	1.5
Brazil	1986	All ages	477,138	333,388	6.3	6.5	8.3	9.9	24.4	29.9	8.1	8.5	9.0	3.7
		0–14	97,764	75,090	16.3	16.8	1.2	1.2	1.0	1.2	11.3	11.8	6.0	4.2
		15–44	101,799	41,685	4.5	6.1	4.1	11.9	12.1	21.1	4.0	6.0	25.0	11.9
		45–64	115,175	65,673	4.4	4.1	13.8	19.3	34.8	37.6	6.3	6.2	6.7	2.8
		65+	157,925	148,672	2.5	2.3	11.6	9.6	39.7	43.6	10.1	8.6	2.2	1.5
Canada	1987	All ages	101,252	83,701	0.5	0.7	26.4	26.1	40.5	44.0	8.5	7.0	6.3	3.8
		0–14	2,462	1,716	1.3	1.6	6.0	4.5	1.8	1.9	2.7	3.8	18.0	15.7
		15–44	9,188	3,953	0.5	1.3	11.8	32.4	11.0	10.1	1.6	2.5	35.9	21.1
		45–64	22,388	12,761	0.5	0.7	34.8	51.8	38.5	24.1	4.3	3.9	5.3	3.8
		65+	67,188	65,257	0.5	0.6	26.4	21.3	46.6	51.0	11.0	7.9	2.1	2.4

Continued over

Table 5.1 Continued

Region/country	Year	Age group (years)	Total no. of deaths		Proportional mortality[a]									
					Infectious and parasitic diseases		Malignant neoplasms		Diseases of the circulatory system		Respiratory diseases		Injuries and poisonings	
			Male	Female	Male	Female	Male	Female	Male	Female	Male	Female	Male	Female
Cuba[b]	1987	All ages	36,620	28,459	1.5	1.4	19.7	17.9	42.4	44.9	9.2	9.9	13.8	8.9
		0–14	2,155	1,492	9.3	9.9	4.0	4.4	2.8	2.5	6.9	8.5	17.9	13.7
		15–44	4,542	3,159	1.3	1.6	8.4	15.5	14.9	15.7	2.8	5.1	58.9	40.6
		45–64	7,173	5,319	1.1	1.0	24.8	30.6	43.7	38.6	5.0	6.1	13.7	6.4
		65+	22,713	18,480	0.9	0.8	21.9	15.7	51.2	55.2	12.0	12.0	4.5	3.9
Ecuador	1987	All ages	28,235	23,332	12.0	12.1	7.8	10.8	14.5	17.3	11.4	12.0	12.9	4.8
		0–14	8,926	7,502	23.2	25.0	1.2	1.3	1.1	1.3	20.1	21.8	8.2	5.8
		15–44	5,315	3,088	9.3	12.1	4.7	11.8	7.8	12.0	3.6	4.5	33.1	10.1
		45–64	4,624	3,225	7.6	6.1	13.9	24.6	19.8	23.1	5.4	4.6	14.4	4.8
		65+	9,180	9,180	5.0	3.8	13.1	13.7	28.5	30.3	10.6	9.5	4.7	2.3
Guatemala	1984	All ages	35,848	30,412	23.6	26.1	2.6	4.5	6.4	7.0	16.4	17.8	3.1	1.0
		0–14	18,836	17,168	29.7	32.6	0.2	0.2	0.0	0.1	19.1	20.7	0.9	0.5
		15–44	5,932	3,888	17.8	22.7	2.6	6.8	5.0	8.2	10.5	13.8	10.7	3.7
		45–64	4,552	3,352	20.7	18.3	6.6	14.3	13.5	13.8	12.7	13.6	3.7	1.0
		65+	6,420	5,924	13.1	14.0	7.0	9.8	21.4	22.3	16.9	14.2	1.7	0.7
Mexico	1986	All ages	224,138	172,423	10.3	11.9	7.3	11.3	15.9	21.8	10.1	11.1	15.2	5.5
		0–14	49,940	40,041	26.0	29.2	1.7	1.6	2.5	2.5	17.8	18.8	10.5	7.1
		15–44	51,221	21,177	5.0	10.8	3.7	13.9	5.9	13.0	2.6	4.6	36.8	14.7
		45–64	44,703	30,598	6.3	6.5	10.6	22.7	18.5	20.8	5.1	5.4	13.0	4.3
		65+	75,112	78,411	6.2	5.6	11.9	11.3	30.4	34.8	13.2	11.2	4.9	2.7
Peru	1983	All ages	48,676	44,614	20.0	20.6	5.4	6.8	10.9	13.1	21.9	22.7	7.1	2.4
		0–14	20,786	18,763	27.8	30.5	0.5	0.4	1.0	0.9	28.7	29.0	2.8	1.8
		15–44	6,462	5,333	18.9	19.7	4.2	9.0	7.4	10.5	9.9	11.4	27.7	7.2
		45–64	6,576	4,872	15.0	13.7	11.2	21.3	15.8	17.2	14.1	12.8	9.4	3.1
		65+	12,807	13,748	10.1	9.4	11.4	10.0	27.0	29.8	20.3	21.6	2.8	1.0
Uruguay	1986	All ages	15,639	13,133	2.2	2.2	24.7	21.4	36.4	44.6	7.4	5.1	5.9	3.2
		0–14	1,055	821	10.0	9.9	2.7	1.8	1.7	2.9	6.9	8.6	12.1	8.0
		15–44	1,045	659	2.4	2.1	13.1	31.0	15.6	14.6	5.1	4.9	35.1	14.1
		45–64	4,018	2,017	1.5	2.1	32.6	38.4	32.9	30.6	5.0	4.6	5.1	3.9
		65+	9,410	9,581	1.6	1.5	25.1	18.9	44.1	53.2	8.8	5.0	2.3	1.9

Continued below

Table 5.1 Continued

Region/country	Year	Age group (years)	Total no. of deaths Male	Female	Proportional mortality[a] Infectious and parasitic diseases Male	Female	Malignant neoplasms Male	Female	Diseases of the circulatory system Male	Female	Respiratory diseases Male	Female	Injuries and poisonings Male	Female
USA	1987	All ages	1,107,958	1,015,365	1.3	1.5	23.0	21.9	42.6	48.8	8.5	7.7	5.9	3.0
		0–14	31,638	22,986	2.0	2.3	3.2	3.3	3.5	3.7	3.3	3.8	16.5	12.3
		15–44	119,313	49,874	1.5	2.2	8.7	23.8	12.6	13.5	2.3	3.6	30.0	20.9
		45–64	241,259	147,985	1.2	1.4	30.6	42.4	41.2	31.2	5.3	5.9	4.4	2.9
		65+	715,339	794,347	1.3	1.4	23.7	18.5	49.9	55.7	10.9	8.5	1.8	1.6
SOUTH EAST ASIA														
Sri Lanka	1983	All ages	56,368	38,806	7.8	7.7	3.8	5.5	15.4	11.1	6.2	7.2	6.8	3.3
		0–14	10,540	8,873	15.9	15.9	1.1	1.0	3.0	2.5	13.8	15.0	5.6	4.4
		15–44	10,451	6,129	6.2	8.9	3.1	7.0	10.9	9.8	3.0	5.6	18.3	8.4
		45–64	12,837	6,317	8.0	7.2	7.8	16.1	27.3	22.2	6.1	7.1	6.7	2.8
		65+	22,470	17,433	4.6	3.3	3.2	3.3	16.4	11.9	4.1	3.7	2.1	1.0
EUROPE														
Austria	1988	All ages	38,491	44,772	0.5	0.3	24.5	21.4	47.9	57.5	5.2	3.8	6.0	3.7
		0–14	582	431	2.4	1.9	4.3	3.9	2.9	1.6	3.3	1.6	13.1	11.6
		15–44	2,905	1,119	0.9	0.5	12.5	29.0	12.7	13.7	2.6	3.2	34.3	20.1
		45–64	8,633	4,494	0.8	0.4	31.3	48.3	37.7	27.0	3.4	2.5	6.5	3.2
		65+	26,371	38,728	0.4	0.3	24.0	18.2	56.1	63.0	6.1	4.0	2.5	3.2
Czechoslovakia[b]	1988	All ages	92,645	85,523	0.3	0.3	23.6	19.0	49.9	59.0	6.5	5.1	5.1	4.5
		0–14	2,135	1,503	0.6	0.8	5.8	5.9	1.2	1.7	7.0	5.9	15.8	10.8
		15–44	6,931	2,679	0.5	0.7	16.7	37.1	20.1	15.8	3.4	5.6	24.8	11.0
		45–64	26,088	12,374	0.4	0.4	31.8	39.2	43.6	38.2	4.4	3.0	4.6	2.5
		65+	56,590	66,755	0.3	0.3	21.5	15.2	58.0	65.5	7.7	5.4	2.6	4.4
Finland	1987	All ages	24,289	23,696	0.8	0.8	20.5	19.3	48.7	54.3	7.3	6.0	7.2	3.4
		0–14	335	238	0.6	0.8	7.2	5.9	1.5	2.1	3.3	0.4	13.1	9.7
		15–44	2,389	776	0.4	1.3	8.3	25.6	15.2	14.2	2.3	1.9	29.5	16.2
		45–64	6,231	2,689	0.8	1.1	23.3	38.6	48.3	35.9	4.2	3.7	8.9	5.2
		65+	15,334	19,993	0.8	0.7	21.5	16.6	55.1	59.0	9.4	6.5	2.9	2.6
France	1987	All ages	275,360	251,716	1.2	1.3	29.9	21.0	31.4	39.8	6.5	5.7	6.4	5.7
		0–14	5,287	3,653	2.1	2.3	5.0	5.6	2.4	3.1	2.3	2.8	15.3	13.5
		15–44	22,555	8,630	0.9	1.2	14.1	27.4	10.2	8.9	1.9	2.4	30.3	20.5
		45–64	63,331	25,873	1.0	1.2	42.3	46.5	22.8	17.7	3.5	2.9	5.8	5.0
		65+	184,187	213,560	1.3	1.3	28.3	17.9	37.7	44.4	8.3	6.3	3.5	5.0

Continued over

Table 5.1 Continued

Region/country	Year	Age group (years)	Total no. of deaths		Proportional mortality[a]									
					Infectious and parasitic diseases		Malignant neoplasms		Diseases of the circulatory system		Respiratory diseases		Injuries and poisonings	
			Male	Female	Male	Female	Male	Female	Male	Female	Male	Female	Male	Female
Germany, Fed. Rep.	1988	All ages	322,939	364,577	0.7	0.7	26.2	23.2	45.6	53.2	6.8	4.5	3.4	2.4
		0–14	4,332	2,980	1.9	2.8	4.6	4.6	1.7	1.4	2.5	3.3	12.7	10.8
		15–44	18,623	8,660	1.0	1.1	15.3	33.5	13.6	12.1	1.6	2.6	25.4	13.0
		45–64	75,642	38,702	0.8	0.7	34.0	48.0	36.0	25.1	3.8	2.9	3.3	2.2
		65+	224,342	314,234	0.6	0.6	24.9	20.0	52.4	58.3	8.3	4.8	1.5	2.1
Hungary	1988	All ages	73,339	66,703	0.9	0.6	22.8	19.7	48.5	58.2	5.2	3.3	6.0	4.8
		0–14	1,512	1,105	1.3	1.2	4.9	4.5	1.4	1.0	6.2	5.3	9.9	5.6
		15–44	6,527	2,746	0.9	0.9	14.0	28.2	22.3	20.4	2.3	2.7	21.1	9.7
		45–64	22,620	11,342	1.1	0.8	27.9	33.3	42.0	38.7	3.9	2.7	5.6	3.6
		65+	42,680	51,510	0.8	0.5	22.1	16.6	57.6	65.8	6.3	3.5	3.8	4.8
Italy	1986	All ages	284,788	259,701	0.5	0.4	28.0	21.4	40.6	50.0	8.2	5.9	4.8	3.4
		0–14	4,661	3,385	1.6	1.8	6.8	7.1	2.2	3.0	4.8	5.6	11.8	7.7
		15–44	14,901	6,848	0.9	0.9	18.8	39.4	15.5	13.4	2.2	3.4	34.1	16.7
		45–64	67,669	32,923	0.6	0.7	40.5	47.1	31.2	26.3	4.1	3.0	5.0	3.2
		65+	197,557	216,545	0.4	0.3	24.9	17.2	46.7	55.5	10.2	6.4	2.4	2.9
Netherlands	1987	All ages	64,956	57,243	0.5	0.6	31.0	26.1	40.4	43.0	8.3	5.6	3.1	2.8
		0–14	1,194	876	2.3	3.3	4.9	5.3	0.5	2.2	3.3	4.0	12.0	9.8
		15–44	3,585	2,027	0.7	0.6	19.6	37.0	17.4	12.9	0.9	1.9	20.8	11.0
		45–64	13,074	6,937	0.4	0.5	39.1	51.9	39.4	23.6	3.2	3.0	2.4	2.1
		65+	47,103	47,403	0.4	0.6	30.3	22.2	43.5	47.9	10.3	6.2	1.7	2.4
Poland	1988	All ages	198,064	172,757	1.1	0.7	20.5	17.6	47.9	57.0	5.3	3.3	6.6	2.9
		0–14	7,499	5,205	5.8	6.0	3.9	4.3	1.5	2.3	5.4	5.3	12.6	9.0
		15–44	20,645	7,045	1.1	1.6	10.9	32.4	22.8	20.4	1.6	3.3	30.9	12.4
		45–64	62,396	29,419	1.2	0.9	29.4	37.1	43.1	39.3	4.0	2.8	5.6	2.6
		65+	107,524	131,088	0.7	0.3	18.4	12.9	58.7	65.1	6.6	3.3	2.1	2.3
Portugal	1988	All ages	51,527	46,709	1.1	0.6	18.4	16.5	39.8	49.4	7.8	5.8	6.6	2.6
		0–14	1,572	1,128	3.6	5.3	5.3	5.3	2.5	2.2	6.4	6.6	15.8	11.9
		15–44	4,681	1,703	1.7	1.7	10.0	28.8	9.7	12.4	3.5	3.6	34.8	15.1
		45–64	11,428	5,944	1.7	1.1	26.1	37.6	30.2	29.1	5.9	3.8	7.4	3.7
		65+	33,846	37,934	0.7	0.4	17.6	12.9	49.0	55.6	9.2	6.2	2.1	1.6

Continued below

Table 5.1 Continued

| | | | Total no. of deaths | | Proportional mortality[a] | | | | | | | | | |
| | | | | | Infectious and parasitic diseases | | Malignant neoplasms | | Diseases of the circulatory system | | Respiratory diseases | | Injuries and poisonings | |
Region/country	Year	Age group (years)	Male	Female	Male	Female	Male	Female	Male	Female	Male	Female	Male	Female
Romania	1984	All ages	123,170	110,529	1.1	0.5	13.2	11.5	52.5	65.1	12.0	10.2	9.0	3.5
		0–14	7,406	5,553	5.8	5.5	3.0	3.6	0.9	0.9	29.9	35.4	18.5	14.6
		15–44	10,879	5,290	2.8	2.0	11.6	24.1	19.0	17.3	7.1	6.5	42.4	20.5
		45–64	35,769	20,422	1.3	0.4	22.3	27.7	42.4	46.3	8.9	5.9	10.4	5.2
		65+	69,104	79,255	0.2	0.1	9.9	7.1	68.5	77.6	12.5	9.8	2.1	1.1
Sweden	1987	All ages	49,342	43,973	0.5	0.6	20.9	21.2	53.2	54.1	7.4	7.1	3.7	2.5
		0–14	518	396	0.6	1.0	6.9	5.8	2.3	2.8	3.3	3.8	10.2	9.6
		15–44	2,334	1,122	0.4	1.0	11.2	34.0	12.6	9.4	2.9	2.9	24.1	11.7
		45–64	7,583	4,114	0.4	0.7	26.6	50.1	45.2	24.9	4.0	4.7	4.9	1.9
		65+	38,907	38,341	0.5	0.6	20.6	17.9	57.9	59.1	8.4	7.5	2.1	2.2
Turkey[b,c,d]	1987	All ages	75,744	58,281	4.9	4.7	10.9	7.7	46.0	49.3	7.7	7.5	4.8	2.2
		0–14	15,679	12,525	15.4	16.5	1.0	1.2	10.1	10.1	14.9	17.0	4.6	3.1
		15–44	9,314	4,744	4.3	4.8	10.2	15.6	36.4	37.9	4.9	6.4	19.4	9.7
		45–64	22,091	11,022	2.3	1.9	18.0	16.7	56.3	57.5	6.0	4.9	3.3	2.2
		65+	28,398	29,818	1.4	0.9	11.2	5.8	61.1	64.5	6.1	4.7	1.2	0.6
UK	1988	All ages	319,119	330,059	0.5	0.4	26.2	23.9	46.4	47.9	11.2	10.4	2.6	1.7
		0–14	5,683	4,018	2.4	2.6	4.2	5.0	1.6	2.0	6.1	6.2	10.2	7.1
		15–44	14,528	7,887	1.2	1.3	16.3	41.3	17.5	12.5	3.4	4.3	25.3	10.6
		45–64	62,017	38,041	0.5	0.5	32.8	48.6	48.2	30.3	5.6	6.3	2.4	1.7
		65+	236,891	280,113	0.4	0.3	25.7	19.6	48.8	52.0	13.2	11.1	1.0	1.4
USSR	1987	All ages	1,326,462	1,478,323	2.9	1.5	18.4	13.7	45.4	65.8	9.3	6.7	9.9	3.1
		0–14	123,057	91,196	14.4	15.5	2.4	2.4	0.6	0.8	29.3	32.8	12.8	10.3
		15–44	166,625	60,832	3.9	4.6	9.4	23.7	17.0	15.8	2.7	4.0	39.8	17.9
		45–64	473,833	264,502	2.2	1.0	28.6	31.0	41.6	45.1	6.7	4.2	8.6	4.9
		65+	562,432	1,061,395	0.6	0.2	16.0	9.9	66.8	79.4	9.1	5.2	1.5	1.2
EASTERN MEDITERRANEAN														
Egypt	1980	All ages	223,395	197,832	3.0	1.8	2.2	1.4	20.0	18.5	15.6	16.4	2.7	1.2
		0–14	95,263	92,418	4.1	2.3	0.3	0.2	4.1	3.7	27.7	29.2	1.7	0.9
		15–44	25,215	16,897	5.3	5.3	5.7	5.1	25.6	31.7	6.3	6.9	12.6	6.6
		45–64	44,179	24,837	2.5	1.9	5.3	5.1	38.5	41.7	8.4	7.3	2.1	1.3
		65+	58,738	63,680	0.5	0.2	1.5	0.9	29.6	27.5	5.5	3.8	0.5	0.2

Continued over

Table 5.1 Continued

| Region/country | Year | Age group (years) | Total no. of deaths | | Proportional mortality[a] | | | | | | | | | |
| | | | Male | Female | Infectious and parasitic diseases | | Malignant neoplasms | | Diseases of the circulatory system | | Respiratory diseases | | Injuries and poisonings | |
					Male	Female	Male	Female	Male	Female	Male	Female	Male	Female
Kuwait	1987	All ages	2,711	1,576	2.5	3.6	10.7	11.8	33.4	30.0	7.0	7.5	16.5	5.6
		0–14	670	500	2.4	4.8	3.0	3.0	1.2	2.2	7.0	8.8	14.9	7.6
		15–44	542	170	2.8	2.4	10.9	25.3	24.0	27.1	4.8	6.5	43.7	13.5
		45–64	772	300	1.7	2.3	16.3	24.0	55.3	46.3	6.1	5.0	9.5	5.3
		65+	668	567	3.6	3.5	12.3	9.0	47.5	46.0	9.6	8.3	3.9	1.4
WESTERN PACIFIC														
Australia	1987	All ages	63,611	53,710	0.5	0.6	25.3	22.7	44.1	51.4	8.4	5.9	5.8	3.2
		0–14	1,816	1,228	1.3	1.9	3.9	4.9	1.0	0.9	3.4	2.3	17.8	12.6
		15–44	5,586	2,464	1.1	0.9	11.9	32.5	11.3	10.3	2.4	4.8	37.1	20.5
		45–64	14,154	7,348	0.5	0.5	34.4	47.3	41.8	28.3	5.4	6.2	4.0	3.0
		65+	42,038	42,664	0.4	0.5	25.0	18.4	51.2	59.2	10.4	6.0	1.7	1.9
China[b,c]	1987	All ages	315,171	264,390	4.8	3.6	21.2	15.4	32.0	36.7	17.5	19.6	9.8	8.5
		0–14	25,463	19,712	5.9	6.8	2.4	2.1	0.6	0.7	19.2	22.3	21.3	17.4
		15–44	35,227	25,773	8.1	7.6	19.8	17.6	9.5	12.8	3.9	4.6	39.6	36.3
		45–64	86,246	56,317	5.8	4.4	33.7	28.3	29.7	34.6	12.1	13.3	7.1	6.6
		65+	168,163	162,553	3.4	2.3	18.0	12.3	42.7	45.6	22.8	23.9	3.3	3.7
Japan	1988	All ages	428,094	364,920	1.6	1.2	28.5	22.9	34.5	43.0	11.9	9.7	5.0	2.4
		0–14	6,646	5,010	3.4	3.2	6.8	7.4	5.3	5.2	6.2	6.0	21.1	14.2
		15–44	29,136	14,824	1.4	1.7	18.0	37.5	19.5	16.1	2.9	3.6	25.1	9.1
		45–64	107,268	52,936	1.6	1.5	39.4	45.5	27.2	26.3	4.5	4.0	5.9	3.2
		65+	284,621	292,094	1.6	1.1	26.0	18.3	39.5	48.1	15.7	11.1	2.2	1.7
New Zealand	1986	All ages	14,533	12,519	0.6	0.6	23.1	22.8	44.9	47.8	10.7	10.3	7.0	4.0
		0–14	518	379	3.1	2.6	5.8	4.5	1.2	1.8	7.5	5.0	15.3	14.8
		15–44	1,360	615	1.0	0.5	12.1	32.8	12.1	13.2	3.2	5.7	44.8	20.8
		45–64	3,199	1,878	0.7	0.9	30.1	44.8	48.5	31.5	5.9	8.5	4.6	2.9
		65+	9,456	9,647	0.4	0.4	23.3	18.6	50.9	54.9	13.6	11.1	1.9	2.7

a Percentage contribution to all deaths.
b Deaths caused by violence and suicide are included in the "Injuries and poisoning" category.
c Deaths are classified according to the 8th revision of the International Classification of Diseases.
d Data are from reporting areas within the country only.

All deaths are classified according to the 9th revision of the International Classification of Diseases unless otherwise indicated. The category "Injuries and poisonings" does not include death by violence or suicide unless otherwise indicated. Data are for the five leading causes of death only; therefore percentages do not add up to 100.

Source:
WHO 1989 *World Health Statistics Annual 1989* (and earlier editions), World Health Organization, Geneva.

Table 5.2 Mortality by world region, cause, age group and sex (summary to Table 5.1)

| Region | No. of countries | Age group (years) | Total no. of deaths | | Proportional mortality[a] | | | | | | | | | |
| | | | Male | Female | Infectious and parasitic diseases | | Malignant neoplasms | | Diseases of the circulatory system | | Respiratory diseases | | Injuries and poisonings[b] | |
					Male	Female	Male	Female	Male	Female	Male	Female	Male	Female
AFRICA	4	All ages	5,658	4,880	9.7	9.5	7.0	8.0	34.1	34.5	10.1	10.0	5.4	3.1
		0–14	1,270	1,109	29.4	32.1	0.8	1.5	2.1	2.0	14.7	16.0	3.8	3.5
		15–44	722	526	5.8	7.0	6.5	12.4	25.1	22.2	5.3	6.7	19.0	13.9
		45–64	1,579	838	4.1	3.7	9.0	16.9	48.4	43.9	7.0	6.2	4.2	2.0
		65+	2,087	2,404	3.2	1.7	9.8	6.9	45.9	48.9	11.2	9.3	2.6	1.0
AMERICAS	16	All ages	2,282,292	1,909,913	4.3	4.4	17.1	17.8	34.1	40.4	8.9	8.7	7.6	3.4
		0–14	254,870	201,988	17.8	19.8	1.6	1.5	1.7	1.8	13.7	14.9	8.1	5.7
		15–44	327,985	145,197	3.9	6.2	6.4	17.6	11.3	15.8	3.3	5.1	29.2	15.6
		45–64	503,051	304,884	3.0	3.1	23.8	33.9	36.6	31.1	5.7	5.9	6.1	3.1
		65+	1,182,808	1,248,967	2.0	2.0	20.7	16.7	46.5	51.9	10.9	8.8	2.2	1.7
SOUTH EAST ASIA	1	All ages	56,368	38,806	7.8	7.7	3.8	5.5	15.4	11.1	6.2	7.2	6.8	3.3
		0–14	10,540	8,873	15.9	15.9	1.1	1.0	3.0	2.5	13.8	15.0	5.6	4.4
		15–44	10,451	6,129	6.2	8.9	3.1	7.0	10.9	9.8	3.0	5.6	18.3	8.4
		45–64	12,837	6,317	8.0	7.2	7.8	16.1	27.3	22.2	6.1	7.1	6.7	2.8
		65+	22,470	17,433	4.6	3.3	3.2	3.3	16.4	11.9	4.1	3.7	2.1	1.0
EUROPE	16	All ages	3,915,472	3,692,182	1.6	1.1	22.0	18.9	44.7	61.3	8.4	6.9	6.6	3.3
		0–14	197,776	146,432	11.3	12.3	2.9	3.0	1.9	2.2	22.1	24.9	12.2	9.5
		15–44	348,661	139,749	2.6	2.9	11.7	28.1	17.1	15.9	2.7	3.8	34.4	16.1
		45–64	1,103,790	584,501	1.5	0.9	30.7	36.6	39.7	37.9	5.6	4.0	6.5	3.9
		65+	2,263,489	3,088,653	0.6	0.4	21.0	14.2	55.1	65.2	9.5	6.1	1.9	2.0
EASTERN MEDITERRANEAN	3	All ages	227,026	200,057	3.0	1.8	2.3	1.5	20.2	18.6	15.5	16.3	2.8	1.3
		0–14	96,117	93,078	4.0	2.3	0.3	0.2	4.1	3.7	27.5	29.7	1.8	1.0
		15–44	25,899	17,120	5.3	5.3	5.8	5.3	25.6	31.6	6.2	6.9	13.3	6.7
		45–64	45,201	25,279	2.5	1.9	5.5	5.4	38.8	41.8	8.3	7.3	2.2	1.4
		65+	59,750	54,541	0.5	0.3	1.7	1.0	29.8	27.7	5.5	3.8	0.5	0.2
WESTERN PACIFIC	7	All ages	958,546	792,485	2.9	2.1	24.1	19.2	33.6	40.4	12.6	12.3	7.7	5.0
		0–14	40,499	31,299	5.1	5.8	3.6	3.5	3.1	3.7	15.0	17.3	23.0	18.0
		15–44	98,732	55,484	4.7	5.5	16.5	24.3	15.0	15.6	3.0	4.1	34.1	2.4
		45–64	259,577	140,841	3.5	2.8	34.5	35.7	29.6	31.7	7.0	7.7	6.6	5.0
		65+	559,143	554,748	2.1	1.4	22.2	15.5	40.9	47.1	16.7	14.0	2.5	2.3

a Percentage contribution to all deaths.
b With the exception of data from China, Cuba, Czechoslovakia, Switzerland and Turkey, deaths due to violence and suicide are not included.

Regional summary statistics include countries not listed in Table 5.1.

Source:
WHO 1989 *World Health Statistics Annual 1989* (and earlier editions), World Health Organization, Geneva.

Table 5.3   Life expectancy, infant mortality and mortality of children under age five

Region/country	Life expectancy at birth 1990 (years)	Infant mortality rate[a] 1990	Child mortality rate[b]	Region/country	Life expectancy at birth 1990 (years)	Infant mortality rate[a] 1990	Child mortality rate[b]
WORLD	63	64	38	AMERICAS			
				Argentina	71	29	6
More developed regions[c]	74	12	3	Barbados	74	10	3
Less developed regions[d]	61	71	44	Brazil	66	57	24
				Canada	77	6	1
AFRICA				Chile	71	19	4
Algeria	64	60	33	Colombia	65	42	23
Angola	46	127	110	Costa Rica	75	17	4
Benin	48	101	82	Cuba	74	13	3
Botswana	60	58	27	Dominican Rep.	67	57	19
Burkina Faso	49	126	111	Ecuador	66	57	26
Burundi	51	102	87	El Salvador	66	48	26
Cameroon	52	86	65	Guatemala	64	48	43
Cape Verde	63	56	24	Guyana	70	25	7
Cent. African Rep.	47	122	105	Haiti	56	106	61
Chad	47	122	105	Honduras	65	57	40
Comoros	54	71	51	Jamaica	74	16	5
Congo	50	65	45	Martinique	75	11	6
Côte d'Ivoire	54	87	53	Mexico	70	41	22
Equatorial Guinea	48	117	100	Nicaragua	66	50	34
Ethiopia	43	142	121	Panama	72	21	10
Gabon	53	94	74	Paraguay	67	39	20
Gambia	45	131	139	Peru	64	76	37
Ghana	56	81	61	Puerto Rico	75	13	2
Guinea	44	136	119	Suriname	70	25	7
Guinea-Bissau	47	121	105	Trinidad & Tobago	71	18	3
Kenya	60	64	44	Uruguay	71	25	3
Lesotho	58	89	39	USA	76	7	2
Liberia	56	79	95	Venezuela	70	33	8
Madagascar	55	110	33				
Malawi	48	138	132	SOUTH EAST ASIA			
Mali	46	159	147	Bangladesh	52	107	78
Mauritania	48	116	100	Bhutan	49	118	78
Mauritius	70	19	6	East Timor	45	149	99
Mozambique	48	130	115	India	60	87	55
Namibia	58	97	78	Indonesia	58	74	46
Niger	46	124	107	Korea, Dem.	70	20	7
Nigeria	52	96	76	Mongolia	65	39	13
Réunion	72	12	3	Myanmar q.v. Burma	62	59	24
Rwanda	50	111	95	Nepal	53	118	78
Senegal	47	117	104	Sri Lanka	71	28	10
Sierra Leone	43	142	147	Thailand	67	32	10
South Africa	62	62	25				
Swaziland	57	107	62	EUROPE			
Tanzania	53	96	77	Albania	72	32	9
Togo	55	85	64	Austria	75	9	2
Uganda	53	93	74	Belgium	75	8	2
Zaire	54	90	69	Bulgaria	73	14	3
Zambia	55	71	51	Czechoslovakia	72	13	2
Zimbabwe	60	64	44				

Continued opposite

Table 5.3 Continued

Region/country	Life expectancy at birth 1990 (years)	Infant mortality rate[a] 1990	Child mortality rate[b]
Finland	75	5	1
France	76	6	2
German Dem. Rep.	74	8	2
Germany, Fed. Rep.	75	8	2
Greece	76	13	2
Hungary	71	16	2
Iceland	78	5	1
Israel	76	9	2
Italy	76	9	1
Luxembourg	75	8	2
Netherlands	77	7	2
Norway	77	6	2
Poland	71	16	2
Portugal	74	12	3
Romania	71	19	5
Spain	77		2
Sweden	77	5	1
Switzerland	77	6	2
Turkey	66	62	17
UK	76	7	2
USSR	70	20	5
Yugoslavia	73	20	3

EASTERN MEDITERRANEAN

Region/country	Life expectancy at birth 1990 (years)	Infant mortality rate[a] 1990	Child mortality rate[b]
Afghanistan	43	162	166
Bahrain	71	22	5
Cyprus	76	9	1
Egypt	63	70	42
Iran	67	53	54
Iraq	66	56	27
Jordan	67	36	13

Region/country	Life expectancy at birth 1990 (years)	Infant mortality rate[a] 1990	Child mortality rate[b]
Kuwait	73	16	3
Lebanon	68	34	10
Libya	63	68	39
Morocco	63	68	39
Oman	58	84	63
Pakistan	59	98	63
Qatar	70	25	7
Saudi Arabia	65	58	29
Somalia	46	121	121
Sudan	51	99	77
Syria	67	39	15
Tunisia	67	47	29
United Arab Em.	71	22	7
Yemen	53	102	86
Yemen, Dem.	53	106	86

WESTERN PACIFIC

Region/country	Life expectancy at birth 1990 (years)	Infant mortality rate[a] 1990	Child mortality rate[b]
Australia	76	6	2
Cambodia	50	115	72
China	70	26	12
Fiji	71	23	5
Hong Kong	76	6	2
Japan	78	5	2
Korea	70	20	7
Laos	50	97	56
Malaysia	70	20	9
New Zealand	75	9	2
Papua New Guinea	56	52	23
Singapore	73	7	2
Viet Nam	63	53	26

[a] Number of deaths of infants less than one year of age per 10^3 live births.
[b] Probability (per 10^3 one-year-old children) of dying between age one and age five, annual average for the period, 1985–1990.
[c] More developed regions include Canada, USA, Japan, Europe, Australia, New Zealand and the USSR.
[d] Less developed regions include Africa, Americas (except Canada and the USA) South East Asia and Western Pacific (except Australia and New Zealand).

Sources:
Sadik, N. 1990 *The State of World Population,* United Nations Population Fund, United Nations, New York.
UN 1988 *Mortality of Children Under Age 5: World Estimates and Projections, 1950–2025,* United Nations, New York.

Table 5.4 Total number of maternal mortalities and distribution by cause for selected countries

| | | Maternal deaths, all causes | | Maternal mortality by cause | | | |
| | | | | Abortion | | Haemorrhage during pregnancy and childbirth | |
	Year	Deaths	Rate[a]	Deaths	% of total	Deaths	% of total
AFRICA							
Mauritius	1987	19	9.9	9	47.4	1	5.3
São Tomé & Príncipe	1984–85	8	20.4	1	12.5	2	25.0
Seychelles	1985–87	0	0.0				
AMERICAS							
Argentina	1985	386	5.6	136	35.2	60	15.5
Bahamas	1984–85	2	3.8	1	50.0	0	0.0
Barbados	1984	3	6.9	0	0.0	1	33.3
Belize	1982–84	2	3.3	0	0.0	0	0.0
Brazil[b]	1986	1,814	4.6	241	13.3	291	16.0
Canada	1987	15	0.4	4	26.7	1	6.7
Chile	1987	135	4.8	47	34.8	11	8.2
Costa Rica	1988	15	1.8	1	6.7	4	26.7
Cuba	1987	88	4.9	16	18.2	5	5.7
Dominica	1980–84	1	5.8	0	0.0	1	100.0
Dominican Rep.	1982	124	6.4	15	12.1	25	20.2
Ecuador	1987	355	17.4	27	7.6	80	22.5
El Salvador	1984	99	7.0	7	7.1	7	7.1
Guatemala	1984	236	7.9	40	17.0	4	1.7
Guyana	1984	17	11.2	5	29.4	7	41.2
Honduras	1981	28	1.7	1	3.6	2	7.1
Jamaica[c]	1981–83	184	10.2	9	4.9	38	20.7
Martinique	1985	0	0.0				
Mexico	1986	1,681	6.6	149	8.9	416	24.8
Panama	1987	22	3.8	5	22.7	1	4.6
Paraguay[b]	1986	140	26.1	19	13.6	43	30.7
Peru	1983	611	8.9	68	11.1	202	33.1
Puerto Rico	1986	10	1.6	2	20.0	1	10.0
St Lucia	1980	0	0.0				
St Vincent & Grenadines	1982–85	1	3.2	0	0.0	0	0.0
Suriname	1985	7	6.0	1	14.3	5	71.4
Trinidad & Tobago	1983	18	5.4	8	44.4	1	5.6
Uruguay	1986	14	2.6	5	35.7	1	7.1
USA	1987	251	0.7	44	17.5	33	13.2
Venezuela	1983	303	5.9	60	19.8	48	15.8
EUROPE							
Austria	1988	5	0.6	0	0.0	3	60.0
Belgium	1986	4	0.3	1	25.0	0	0.0
Bulgaria	1987	23	2.0	9	39.1	2	8.7
Czechoslovakia	1988	28	1.3	6	21.4	6	21.4
Denmark[d]	1987	5	0.9				
Finland	1987	3	0.5	0	0.0	1	33.3
France	1987	74	1.0	10	13.5	10	13.5
German Dem. Rep.[e]	1988	20	0.9	5	25.0	3	15.0
Germany, Fed. Rep.	1988	60	0.9	12	20.0	5	8.3
Greece	1986	9	0.8	1	11.1	3	33.3

Continued opposite

Toxaemia during pregnancy		Complications of the puerperium		Other direct obstetric causes		All indirect obstetric causes	
Deaths	% of total	Deaths	% of total	Deaths	% of total	Deaths	% of total
3	15.8	0	0.0	6	31.6	0	0.0
2	25.0	1	12.5	2	25.0	0	0.0
61	15.8	51	13.2	70	18.1	8	2.1
0	0.0	0	0.0	1	50.0	0	0.0
0	0.0	1	33.3	1	33.3	0	0.0
1	50.0	1	50.0	0	0.0	0	0.0
521	28.7	292	16.1	335	18.5	134	7.4
1	6.7	8	53.3	0	0.0	1	6.7
16	11.9	33	24.4	21	15.6	7	5.2
4	26.7	2	13.3	4	26.7	0	0.0
2	2.3	10	11.4	28	31.8	27	30.7
0	0.0	0	0.0	0	0.0	0	0.0
25	20.2	16	12.9	39	31.5	4	3.3
94	26.5	39	11.0	108	30.4	7	2.0
5	5.1	8	8.1	71	71.7	1	1.0
24	10.2	36	15.3	124	52.5	8	3.4
3	17.7	1	5.9	0	0.0	1	5.8
0	0.0	2	7.1	23	82.1	0	0.0
				115	62.5	22	12.0
331	19.7	150	8.9	608	36.2	27	1.6
4	18.2	0	0.0	11	50.0	1	4.6
25	17.9	24	17.1	23	16.4	6	4.3
51	8.4	88	14.4	197	32.2	5	0.8
4	40.0	2	20.0	1	10.0	0	0.0
1	100.0	0	0.0	0	0.0	0	0.0
1	14.3	0	0.0	0	0.0	0	0.0
3	16.7	2	11.1	4	22.2	0	0.0
1	7.1	2	14.3	5	35.7	0	0.0
34	13.6	84	33.5	41	16.3	15	6.0
62	20.5	57	18.8	55	18.2	21	6.9
1	20.0	0	0.0	1	20.0	0	0.0
1	25.0	1	25.0	1	25.0	0	0.0
5	21.7	4	17.4	3	13.0	0	0.0
0	0.0	5	17.9	10	35.7	1	3.6
0	0.0	1	33.3	0	0.0	1	33.3
5	6.8	19	25.7	27	36.5	3	4.1
				12	60.0		
16	26.7	15	25.0	10	16.7	2	3.3
1	11.1	2	22.2	2	22.2	0	0.0

Continued over

Table 5.4 Continued

| | | Maternal deaths, all causes | | Maternal mortality by cause | | | |
| | | | | Abortion | | Haemorrhage during pregnancy and childbirth | |
	Year	Deaths	Rate[a]	Deaths	% of total	Deaths	% of total
Hungary	1988	21	1.7	7	33.3	4	19.1
Iceland	1988	0	0.0				
Ireland	1987	2	0.3	0	0.0	0	0.0
Israel	1986	2	0.2	0	0.0	0	0.0
Italy	1986	31	0.6	9	29.0	4	12.9
Luxembourg	1988	0	0.0				
Malta	1988	0	0.0				
Netherlands	1987	14	0.8	0	0.0	3	21.4
Norway	1987	3	0.6	0	0.0	0	0.0
Poland	1988	68	1.2	11	16.2	19	27.9
Portugal	1988	8	0.6	1	12.5	2	25.0
Romania	1984	522	14.8	449	86.0	17	3.3
Spain	1985	20	0.4	9	45.0	3	15.0
Sweden[d]	1987	5	0.5	0	0.0	0	0.0
Switzerland[d]	1988	8	1.0				
Turkey[b,d]	1987	58	0.4				
UK	1988	50	0.6	9	18.0	5	10.0
USSR[e]	1987	2,596	4.6	715	27.5	372	14.3
Yugoslavia	1987	19	0.5	8	42.1	5	26.3
EASTERN MEDITERRANEAN							
Bahrain	1987	1	0.8	0	0.0	0	0.0
Egypt	1980	1,461	9.3	156	10.7	791	54.1
Kuwait	1987	1	0.2	0	0.0	1	100.0
SOUTH EASTERN PACIFIC							
Sri Lanka	1983	236	5.9	31	13.1	98	41.5
WESTERN PACIFIC							
Australia	1987	6	0.3	2	33.3	1	16.7
China[b,d,e]	1987	474	2.9	31	6.5	309	65.2
Hong Kong	1987	3	0.4	0	0.0	1	33.3
Japan	1988	126	1.0	8	6.4	31	24.6
Korea	1987	63	0.9	3	4.8	12	19.1
New Zealand	1986	10	1.9	1	10.0	0	0.0
Singapore	1987	3	0.7	1	33.3	0	0.0

[a] Number of maternal deaths per 10^4 live births.
[b] Data from reporting areas in the country only.
[c] Source: Walker, G. J. A., Ashley, D. E. C., McCaw, A. M. and Bernard, A. W. 1986 Maternal mortality in Jamaica, *Lancet* **1**(8479), 486–488.

[d] Deaths are classified according to the 8th revision of the International Classification of Diseases.
[e] Deaths caused by complications of the puerperium and deaths due to other direct obstetric causes are not separated.

Toxaemia during pregnancy		Complications of the puerperium		Other direct obstetric causes		All indirect obstetric causes	
Deaths	% of total	Deaths	% of total	Deaths	% of total	Deaths	% of total
0	0.0	4	19.1	5	23.8	1	4.8
1	50.0	0	0.0	1	50.0	0	0.0
	0.0	1	50.0		0.0	1	50.0
6	19.4	2	6.5	10	32.3	0	0.0
5	35.7	4	28.6	2	14.3	0	0.0
0	0.0	0	0.0	3	100.0	0	0.0
5	7.4	15	22.1	16	23.5	2	2.9
1	12.5	4	50.0	0	0.0	0	0.0
11	2.1	30	5.8	15	2.9	0	0.0
3	15.0	2	10.0	3	15.0	0	0.0
1	20.0	2	40.0	2	40.0	0	0.0
5	10.0	16	32.0	5	10.0	10	20.0
243	9.4			1,266	48.7		
		6	31.6			0	0.0
1	100.0	0	0.0	0	0.0	0	0.0
8	0.6	251	17.2	106	7.3	149	10.2
0	0.0	0	0.0	0	0.0	0	0.0
49	20.8	6	2.5	46	19.5	6	2.5
		2	33.3			1	16.7
68	14.4			66	13.9		
0	0.0	2	66.7	0	0.0	0	0.0
18	14.3	35	27.8	15	11.9	19	15.1
18	28.6	18	28.6	11	17.5	1	1.6
0	0.0	5	50.0	1	10.0	3	30.0
1	33.3	1	33.3	0	0.0	0	0.0

All deaths are classified according to the 9th revision of the International Classification of Diseases unless otherwise indicated.

Source:
WHO 1989 World Health Statistics Annual 1989 (and earlier editions), World Health Organization, Geneva.

Table 5.5 Nutritional status of children under five years of age in selected countries, 1980s

| Region/country | Infants with low birthweight[a] 1982–1988 (%) | Prevalence of nutritional disorders in children (1980–1987) | | |
		Percentage underweight[b] (0–4 years)	Percentage suffering from wasting[c] (12–23 months)	Percentage suffering from stunting[d] (24–59 months)
AFRICA				
Benin	8	34	14	
Botswana	8	15	19[e]	51[e]
Burundi	9[f,g]	38	10	60[h]
Cameroon	13[f,g]	17[f,i]	2[f]	43[f]
Congo	12	24	13	33
Côte d'Ivoire	14[f,g]	40	4[j]	10[k]
Ethiopia		38	19	43
Ghana	17	37	28	31
Kenya	15		10	42
Lesotho	11	16[g]	7	23
Liberia		35	7	38
Madagascar	10	33[j]	18	41[l]
Malawi	20	22	8	61
Mali	17	31[m]	16	34[h]
Mauritius	9	24	16[n]	22[n]
Niger	15[f]	49	23[n]	38[n]
Rwanda	17[f]	37	23	45
Senegal	11[f,g]	22[o]	8	28[h]
Sierra Leone	17	23	26	46
Tanzania	14	48	17	
Zaire	13	20	11	40
Zambia	14[g]	28	12	41
Zimbabwe	15[f,g]	12[p]	1[p]	29[p]
AMERICAS				
Bolivia	12	15[q]	1	46
Brazil	8	13	2	31
Chile	7	3[r]	1	10[s]
Colombia	15	12[m]	1	27[h]
Costa Rica	10	6	3	8
Dominican Rep.	16	12[o]	3	26[h]
El Salvador	15	55		54[g]
Guatemala	10[f]	34[m]	3	68[h]
Guyana	11	24	9	21
Haiti	17	27[t]	17	51
Honduras	20	21	2[n]	34[n]
Jamaica	8	9[f]	5[u]	9[k]
Nicaragua	15	11		22
Panama	8	16	7	24
Peru	9	13[r]	3	43
Trinidad & Tobago		7[m]	5	4[h]
Uruguay	8[f]	7[r]		16[r]
Venezuela	9	10	3	7
SOUTH EAST ASIA				
Bangladesh	28	60	17[u]	59[k]
Indonesia	14	51[u]	17	

Continued opposite

Table 5.5 Continued

| | | Prevalence of nutritional disorders in children (1980–1987) | | |
Region/country	Infants with low birthweight[a] 1982–1988 (%)	Percentage underweight[b] (0–4 years)	Percentage suffering from wasting[c] (12–23 months)	Percentage suffering from stunting[d] (24–59 months)
Myanmar q.v. Burma	16	38[m]	17	75[h]
Sri Lanka	28[f]	38[m]	19	34[h]
Thailand	12	26[m]	10	28[h]
EASTERN MEDITERRANEAN				
Egypt	5[g]	11[t,r]	3[f]	34
Iran	5	43	23	55
Kuwait	7	6	2	14
Morocco		16[m]	6	34[h]
Pakistan	25	39[t]	17[l,u]	42[k,v]
Tunisia	7		3	45
Yemen		61[q]	17	69
Yemen, Dem.	13[e]	26[w]	8	36[x]
WESTERN PACIFIC				
Laos	39	37	20	44
Malaysia	10		12	33
Papua New Guinea	25[f]	35		58
Philippines	18	33[r]	7	42
Viet Nam	18	52	12	60[n]

[a] 2,500 g or less.	[o] 6–36 months.
[b] Below -2 standard deviations from median weight for age of reference population.	[p] 3–60 months.
[c] Below -2 standard deviations from median weight for height of reference population.	[q] 6–59 months.
	[r] 0–71 months.
	[s] 24–71 months.
[d] Below -2 standard deviations from median height for age of reference population.	[t] Below 75 per cent of median weight for age of reference population.
[e] Hospital or clinic data.	[u] Below 80 per cent of median of reference population.
[f] Data for one year only between 1971 and 1981.	[v] 25–60 months.
[g] Reporting areas only.	[w] 0–65 months.
[h] 24–86 months.	[x] 0–53 months.
[i] 3–47 months.	
[j] 0–23 months.	Values represent annual average values for the time-span stated, unless otherwise indicated.
[k] Below 90 per cent of median of reference population.	
[l] 12–23 months.	*Source:*
[m] 3–36 months.	Grant, J. P. 1990 *The State of the World's Children 1990,* Oxford University Press, Oxford.
[n] 0–59 months.	

Table 5.6 Prevalence and duration of breast-feeding by world region, 1980–1989

	Africa	Americas	South East Asia	Europe	Eastern Mediterranean	Western Pacific
Number of countries	44	34	11	34	23	20
Percentage of countries reporting data	52	68	55	65	70	85
Percentage of infants breast-fed[a]						
At any age	92–98	81–93	73–94	67–86	84–97	63–89
At 3 months	79–98	56–70	73–93	35–61	27–93	72–89
At 6 months	59–97	42–59	56–83	9–37	29–83	46–80
At 12 months	53–86	16–46	35–76	12–24	31–66	52–66
Duration of breast-feeding[b] (months)						
Average	14–24	1–19	3–25	2–9	6–19	10–14
Median	5–21	3–14	4–24	2–6	2–20	1–18
Urban population as percentage of total	29	71	24	68	41	29

[a] Range of unweighted average values obtained from breast-feeding data for each region and population group (i.e., urban versus rural groups and socio-economic groups).

[b] Range of figures reported by countries irrespective of the population group.

Source:
WHO 1989 The prevalence and duration of breast-feeding: updated information, 1980–1989, *Weekly Epidemiological Record* **64**(42), 321–324.

Table 5.7 Local health care coverage within WHO regions[a], 1985

Coverage level	Number of countries							Population	
	Africa	Americas	South East Asia	Europe	Eastern Mediterranean	Western Pacific	Total	Total (10^6)[b]	Percentage of total
Less than 40.0%	6	0	0	0	3	0	9	66	1.4
40.0%–59.9%	7	2	3	0	1	1	14	330	6.8
60.0%–79.9%	7	0	1	0	4	2	14	1,065	22.1
80.0% or more	5	13	4	28	13	12	75	1,197	24.8
SUB-TOTAL	25	15	8	28	21	15	112	2,658	55.1
No information	19	19	3	7	1	5	54	2,168	44.9
TOTAL	44	34	11	35	22	20	166	4,826	100.0

a   WHO Member States only.
b   1985 estimate of the total population of WHO Member States.

Source:
WHO 1986 Global Overview, *World Health Statistics Annual 1988*, Section A, World Health Organization, Geneva, 11–29.

Table 5.8   Personnel in major health professions in selected countries (number per 10^4 population)[a]

Region/country	Year	Physicians	Dentists	Nurses	Assistant/ auxilliary nurses	Midwives	Pharmacists	Health assistants	Other[b]
AFRICA									
Algeria	1984	4.3	1.2			0.2	0.6	4.7	25.5
Burkina Faso	1983	0.2		2.5		2.0[c]	0.1	0.2	14.5
Burundi	1984	0.5		2.5	0.7	0.1			0.4
Congo	1982	1.3		15.5				1.4	1.1
Ethiopia	1984	0.1		0.4		1.5		1.4	
Guinea-Bissau	1985	1.4		2.5	5.0	1.2			1.5
Kenya	1982	1.2	0.1	4.2			0.0		7.6
Liberia	1983	1.1		4.4		1.2			1.7
Malawi	1984	0.4		0.6				0.5	1.4
Mali	1983	0.4	0.0	2.7	2.1	2.1[c]	0.0		0.3
Mauritania	1984	0.8		3.8	2.3	0.6			0.8
Niger	1984	0.3				12.2[c]			11.1
Nigeria	1982	1.3		4.3		4.3	0.4		1.9
São Tomé & Príncipe	1983	5.4	0.1	26.7	11.7		0.1	0.1	0.3
Senegal	1984	0.5		1.4		0.8	0.2	2.2	0.8
Sierra Leone	1984	0.7	0.1	3.7[d]		3.5[c]	0.0	1.5	0.4
Swaziland	1983	0.5	0.0	6.2	1.6		0.1	1.7	2.6
Togo	1984	0.8	0.0	3.8	0.6	2.4[c]	0.2	0.4	2.7
Zambia	1983	1.4		1.8	5.5	1.8[c]		0.9	3.6
AMERICAS									
Argentina	1984	27.0	2.2	4.7	5.6		0.2		0.2
Bahamas	1984	9.8	1.4	42.8	7.5				
Barbados	1984	9.4	1.0	31.1	16.3				0.4
Belize	1984	2.8		17.1	3.6				0.1
Bermuda	1984	7.0	5.0	93.7			0.7		
Bolivia	1984	7.2	0.6	1.9					0.1
Brazil	1984	9.3	1.3	2.0	6.4				0.1
Br. Virgin Is.	1984	6.9	3.4	45.4			0.4		
Canada	1984	19.6	4.9		45.4		6.2		
Cayman Is.	1984	21.5	3.0	41.0	34.3				1.7
Chile	1984	8.0	2.6	2.8	23.8		2.8		0.8
Colombia	1984	8.4	3.6	3.5	12.4				
Costa Rica	1984	10.1	3.1	5.2	16.3		0.7		
Cuba	1984	19.1		26.5	9.0		2.0		
Dominica	1984	3.3		26.9					0.3

Continued below

Table 5.8 Continued

Region/country	Year	Physicians	Dentists	Nurses	Assistant/ auxilliary nurses	Midwives	Pharmacists	Health assistants	Other[b]
Dominican Rep.	1984	6.2	0.4	0.9	8.2		0.1		0.1
Ecuador	1984	11.5	4.5	3.1	12.3		1.2		0.1
El Salvador	1984	3.4	1.2	3.4	6.9		1.8		0.0
Grenada	1984	4.0		14.7					0.1
Guadeloupe	1984	14.0	3.1	30.4			3.5		
Guatemala	1984	14.0	3.1	30.4	7.7		3.5		0.0
Guyana	1984	1.6	0.1	3.7	9.0		0.3		
French Guiana	1984	15.9	3.4	98.6	3.1		3.3		
Haiti	1984	1.6	0.2	1.9					
Honduras	1984	6.6	1.4	2.6	12.3				
Jamaica	1984	4.9	0.5	15.8	4.8		0.4		0.1
Martinique	1984	14.2	3.4	33.2			4.4		
Mexico	1984	6.9	0.4	4.6	6.5				
Nicaragua	1984		0.8	4.6	15.0				
Panama	1984	10.4	2.0	10.4	15.8				
Paraguay	1984	7.3	0.6	2.2	8.5		2.2		0.3
Peru	1984	9.5	2.2	7.8					0.2
Suriname	1984	8.7	0.6	27.0	12.8				0.2
Trinidad & Tobago	1984	10.6	0.9	29.2	10.3		1.0		3.0
USA	1984	21.4	5.9	83.0	54.2		6.7		
Uruguay	1984	19.3	7.7	5.0	5.0				
Venzuela	1984	14.3	2.6	5.3	3.7				
SOUTH EAST ASIA									
Bangladesh	1985	0.7		0.5	0.8[d]	0.5			
Bhutan	1982	0.4		0.4				1.0	0.8
India	1984	3.9	0.1	2.2	1.2	2.2	0.2	0.2	
Indonesia	1983	1.0	0.1	1.2[d]	6.5	0.1	1.6		1.9
Mongolia	1981	22.7	0.4		41.5	5.8[c]		75.7	12.4
Myanmar q.v. Burma	1985	2.7		3.7[d]	7.5[d]	0.7	0.0	1.1	0.0
Nepal	1984	0.3		0.3		2.0		0.6	0.6
Sri Lanka	1985	1.2	0.2	5.1			0.7		1.8
Thailand	1984	1.6	0.3	10.7		1.7			
EUROPE									
Albania	1977	10.5	2.5	11.4	21.6[d]	20.4	2.1		7.8
Austria	1985	26.1	4.1	35.7		1.4			25.7
Belgium	1985	30.2	6.3				10.9		

Continued over

Table 5.8 Continued

Region/country	Year	Physicians	Dentists	Nurses	Assistant/ auxilliary nurses	Midwives	Pharmacists	Health assistants	Other[b]
Bulgaria	1984	27.6	6.3	55.4		8.8	4.7	8.5	112.1
Czechoslovakia	1985	35.6[e]		68.0			4.6		
Denmark	1984	25.1	8.8	131.7[d]	31.1	1.6	4.1		6.1
Finland	1985	22.3	9.3	87.0	126.2	39.4			
France	1986	31.9	7.2				9.3		18.8
German Dem. Rep.	1985	22.5	7.0	69.1		1.0[c]	2.2		
Germany, Fed. Rep.	1984	25.6	5.7						8.7
Greece	1984	28.5	8.5	20.2		1.9			
Hungary	1985	31.9[e]		54.1		2.4	4.2		
Iceland	1983	23.0	8.1	61.4[d]	45.7	7.8			4.3
Ireland	1984	14.7	3.2	71.5					
Israel	1983	29.0	7.1	65.5[d]					28.2
Luxembourg	1985	18.5	4.7				7.1		
Malta	1982	11.2	1.5	41.9[d]	44.3	2.8	10.0		
Monaco	1982	21.9	11.9	77.0		2.2	20.7		
Netherlands	1985	22.4	4.9			0.7	1.3		
Norway	1984	22.2	8.9	85.9	89.1				8.9
Poland	1985	19.5	4.6	45.6	2.1	5.3	4.3		
Portugal	1985	24.2	0.4				4.7	0.9	6.9
Spain	1984	31.3	1.2	36.8		1.5	7.4		0.8
Sweden	1985	26.4	11.0	84.6			2.3		42.4
Turkey	1985	7.1	1.6	6.0					2.1
USSR	1985	42.1[e]				3.5	3.3	11.4	6.5
UK	1981	16.4	3.1	32.5	30.5		3.1		
Yugoslavia	1986	18.3	4.3	5.2		3.7	2.7		15.5
EASTERN MEDITERRANEAN									
Afghanistan	1987	2.0	0.2	1.5					
Bahrain	1985	12.4	0.5	30.2[d]					
Cyprus	1986	13.5	4.9	32.0			1.4		
Djibouti	1984	1.8	0.1	8.3[d]		4.1[c]	0.2		4.5
Iran	1987	3.3	0.5	8.4				0.1	3.3
Iraq	1987	5.5	0.9	5.8					
Jordan	1984	11.4	2.4	9.9[d]					
Kuwait	1986	15.1	1.8	47.5					
Libya	1983	13.8	1.1	7.8[d]	7.5[d]				
Morocco	1987	2.1	0.2	9.5			1.7		

Continued below

Table 5.8 Continued

Region/country	Year	Physicians	Dentists	Nurses	Assistant/ auxilliary nurses	Midwives	Pharmacists	Health assistants	Other[b]
Pakistan	1987	3.1	0.1	1.8					
Qatar	1987	19.8	2.9	51.3					
Saudi Arabia	1986	14.0	1.0	30.0					
Somalia	1984	0.6	0.0	6.3					
Sudan	1984	1.0	0.1	6.2[d]				1.9	
Syria	1987	7.7	2.2	11.2					
Tunisia	1986	4.6		12.5			1.2		14.7
United Arab Em.	1984	10.1	0.8	26.3[d]					
Yemen, Dem.	1985	2.2	0.0	8.9[d]			0.1		
Yemen	1985	1.7	0.1	4.1[d]			0.1		
WESTERN PACIFIC									
Australia	1986	22.9		93.4[d]					
China	1986	9.1		7.2[d]				16.9	
Fiji	1982	4.9		20.4[d]					
French Polynesia	1985	12.2		22.4[d]					
Guam	1986	12.0		48.7[d]					
Hong Kong	1986	9.3		41.5[d]					
Japan	1984	15.1		54.1[d]					
Malaysia (peninsular)	1986	3.7		9.6[d]				1.6	
New Zealand	1986	17.4		123.8[d]					
Papua New Guinea	1985	0.8		11.8[d]				0.9	
Philippines	1984	1.5		3.7[d]					
Korea	1986	8.6		16.9[d]					
Singapore	1986	4.2		19.2[d]				3.4	
Viet Nam	1986	3.1		13.0		2.8		6.9	

a Data for latest available year.
b "Other" refers to nutritionists in the Americas. In other regions, this category may include one or any combination of the following: paramedics, village health care workers, X-ray technicians, orthopaedists, laboratory technicians, biophysicists, administrators, sanitarians, biologists, first-aid workers, public health personnel, acupuncturists, dispensers and malaria workers.
c Includes assistant midwives and/or traditional birth attendants.
d Includes midwives.
e Includes dentists.

Source:
WHO 1988 The health professions in the 1980s: a statistical update. In: World Health Statistics Annual 1988, Section B, Geneva, 43–70.

Table 5.9 Immunization status of EPI vaccines in selected countries, 1988 and 1989

Region/country	BCG 1988	BCG 1989	DPT 3 1988	DPT 3 1989	Polio 3 1988	Polio 3 1989	Measles 1988	Measles 1989	Tetanus[a] 1988	Tetanus[a] 1989
WORLD	71	81	66	72	67	74	61	68	25	27
Developing countries	73	81	67	71	67	73	59	66	29	31
Developed countries	59	85	65	86	68	88	76	82		
AFRICA										
Cameroon	26		20		19		14		15	
Cape Verde	100		88		85		78		86	
Cent. African Rep.	43		42		42		55		39	
Côte d'Ivoire			25	33						
Ethiopia	27	44	16	26	16	26	15	23	10	24
Ghana	94		45		44		67		28	
Madagascar	54		35		34		28		32	
Mali		67		21		21		98		30
Mauritius	91		90		90		75		74	
Mozambique	49		38		38		44		19	
Niger						16				19
Nigeria	53	76	42	47		47		31		
São Tomé & Príncipe	88		77		72		69		50	
Senegal		93		71		81		68		
Seychelles	94		97		97		89			98
Togo		73	66	45	62	44		42	76	33
Uganda	77	100	40	60	41	60	49	60	14	20
Zaire									29	
AMERICAS										
Anguilla	90		100		100		98			
Antigua & Barbuda			98		100		95			
Argentina	74	90	61	72	70	79	68	77		
Bahamas			85		84		78			
Barbados	75		76		73		84			
Belize	97		73		73		70			
Bermuda			83		85		86			
Bolivia	27	70	39	40	40	50	44	70		20
Brazil	67	66	54	51	89	96	60	56		
Br. Virgin Is.	48		84		76		62			
Canada							85[b]			
Cayman Is.	86		93		95		99			
Chile	98	99	96	94	96	94	95	89		
Colombia	99	90	74	75	94	93	74	73		40
Costa Rica	87		87	89	86	91	97	88		90
Cuba	98	99	94	97	94	97	85	99		
Dominica	98		96		97		90			
Dominican Rep.	38	41	39	47	64	75[c]	26	46		24
Ecuador	86	84	54	50	57	58	52	52		5
El Salvador	65	57	61	59	62	66	63	67		19
Grenada			65		64		58			
Guatemala	38	41	47	52	55	58	54	53		18
Guyana	64		64		69		55			
Haiti	45		54		54		63		23	
Honduras	85	75	74	78	70	83	76	86		16

Continued opposite

Table 5.9 Continued

Region/country	BCG 1988	BCG 1989	DPT 3 1988	DPT 3 1989	Polio 3 1988	Polio 3 1989	Measles 1988	Measles 1989	Tetanus[a] 1988	Tetanus[a] 1989
Jamaica	96		82		83		68			
Mexico	72	80	60	65	95	96	70	85		
Montserrat	86		91		91		86			
Nicaragua	89	90	51	64	83	83	55	62		25
Panama	91	90	75	71	73	72	75	76		27
Paraguay	56	58	57	68	82	72	63	59		
Peru	73	61	66	57	67	58	57	51		12
St Christopher & Nevis	75		94		93		77			
St Lucia	85		78		87		83			
St Vincent & Grenadines	95		98		97		97			
Suriname			64		64		83			
Trinidad & Tobago			82		83		72			
Turks & Caicos Is.	94		94		92		92			
Uruguay	98	97	82	82	82	82	72	76		13
USA			97		97		98			
Venezuela	78		51	50	68	60	49	44		
SOUTH EAST ASIA										
Bangladesh	26	98	16	54	16	53	13	58	12	37
Bhutan	37	56	28	46	28	46	22	36	11	24
India	79	80	80	79	75	74	55	56	65	67
Indonesia	74	81	61	71	62	74	55	65	29	41
Korea, Dem.	99		94		96		97			
Maldives	90	98	81	91	81	91	79	88	62	83
Mongolia	78	92		84	69	85		86		
Myanmar q.v. Burma	37	66	28	50	22	45	25	50	22	42
Nepal	89	88	68	71	67	71	52	58	30	24
Sri Lanka	66	89	68	87	69	88	55	77	42	43
Thailand	55	98	47	84	47	84	36	66	35	70
EUROPE										
Albania	92	94	96	94	96	96	96	96		
Austria	90		90		90		60			
Belgium			80		95	95	75			
Bulgaria	99		99		99		99			
Czechoslovakia	99	99	99	99	99	99	98	91		
Denmark			88[d]		100	100	72	80		
Finland	94	91	91	90	88	90	95	95		
France	79	80	79	95	81	95	52	60		
German Dem. Rep.	99	99	95	95	98	97	99	98		
Germany, Fed. Rep.	79		93[d]	94[d]	94		47			
Greece			83		90		82			
Hungary	99		99	99	99	99	99	99		
Iceland			99		99	99	99	99		
Ireland			43		72		68	68		
Israel			87		93		86			
Italy	30		85[d]	85[d]	85	85	10	50		
Luxembourg	50		90[d]		90		71			
Malta	67	79	87[d]	85[d]	79	85	41	86		
Monaco	100	100	100	100	100	100	100	100		
Netherlands			97	94	97	94	93	93		

Continued over

Table 5.9 Continued

Region/country	BCG		DPT 3		Polio 3		Measles		Tetanus[a]	
	1988	1989	1988	1989	1988	1989	1988	1989	1988	1989
Norway			83	87	84	84	87	84		
Poland	95		98		99		96			
Portugal	86		81	91	81	92	84	100		
Romania			96	96	92	95	78	79		
Spain			73	73	73		84			
Sweden	14						94			
Switzerland			90	90	95	98	70	90		
Turkey	16	16	68	74	68	74	59	67		
UK	75	75	73	75	87	87	76	80		
Yugoslavia	89		91		92		93			
EASTERN MEDITERRANEAN										
Afghanistan	40	38	35	33	35	33	34	22	9[e]	20
Bahrain			97	97	97	97	78	85	22	34
Cyprus			88		90		74			
Djibouti	87	80	65	77	65	77	68	61		48
Egypt	80	83	87	90	89	90	84	93	49	26
Iran	89	90	90	89	90	89	88	89	56	50
Iraq	87	94	86	83	86	83	78	82		27
Jordan			98	94	98	94	87	84	54	23
Kuwait			92	94	92	94	85	98	25	24
Lebanon			33		33		15			
Libya	94	90	76	84	76	84	72	70	9	6
Morocco	82	91	78	80	78	80	76	82		64
Oman	95	95	88	96	88	96	86	94	37	41
Pakistan	77	78	64	71	64	71	55	63	28	32
Qatar	72	79	69	81	69	81	57	73		
Saudi Arabia	94	96	89	91	89	91	81	83		62
Somalia	39	31	26	18	26	18	33	30	37	5
Sudan	54	51	41	41	41	41	35	34	17	25
Syria	87	91	59	87	59	87	52	80	7[e]	19
Tunisia	85	82	91	93	91	93	83	82	46	32
United Arab Em.	94	93	73	81	73	81	65	66		
Yemen	45	71	31	53	31	53	30	46	3	7
WESTERN PACIFIC										
American Samoa			45				46			
Brunei	86		91		93		100		33	
China[f]	85	98	75	95	78	95	77	95		
Cook Is.	90		94		94		92			
Fiji	100		98		100		69			
French Polynesia	96		89		89		81			
Hong Kong	99	94	82	88	92	96	33			
Kiribati	98	100	62	79	62	86	54	63	2	
Korea	57		58		59		70			
Laos	27	29	17	21	17	22	19	20	5	4
Macau	100		93		93		91			
Malaysia	99		73		73		75		59	
Marshall Is.			92		37		25			
Nauru	95		68		68					
Papua New Guinea	80	82	48	53	48	52	46	52	62	100

Continued opposite

Table 5.9 Continued

Region/country	BCG 1988	BCG 1989	DPT 3 1988	DPT 3 1989	Polio 3 1988	Polio 3 1989	Measles 1988	Measles 1989	Tetanus[a] 1988	Tetanus[a] 1989
Philippines	95	89	79	79	78	78	77	83	37	43
Samoa	97		90		90		75		54	
Singapore	98		90		90		87			
Solomon Is.	79	82	69	67	68	66	59	92	52	47
Tokelau	86		43		43					
Tonga	95		92		92		81		58	
Vanuatu	73	80	58	61	58	63	46	46	21	
Viet Nam	76	94	70	88	70	89	66	89	5	18

[a] Includes boosters.
[b] Measles immunization given at, or later than, age 12 months and up to age 60 months.
[c] Two doses only.
[d] DT only (i.e., diphtheria and tetanus).
[e] Data applicable to women in the age group 15–45 years.
[f] Data are based on cluster sampling surveys in infants aged between 12–23 months in 30 provinces and municipalities. Results of the surveys have been weighted in proportion to the size of the surveyed population.

EPI = Expanded Programme on Immunization, established by the World Health Organization.
BCG = Vaccine for tuberculosis.

DPT 3 = Vaccine for diphtheria, pertussis and tetanus. Vaccine is administered in three doses.
Polio 3 = Vaccine for poliomyelitis. Vaccine is administered in three doses.

Data in the table are the percentage of children immunized by 12 months of age and the percentage of pregnant women immunized against tetanus, unless otherwise stated.
Data were extracted from the Expanded Programme on Immunization Database during July 1990. The Database is updated twice a year.

Source:
Kim-Farley, R. J. 1990 Personal communication, World Health Organization, Geneva, Switzerland.

Table 5.10 Incidence of diseases covered by the EPI in selected countries, 1975–1989

Region/country	Diphtheria				Measles			
	1975	1980	1985	1989	1975	1980	1985	1989
AFRICA								
Algeria	350	116	66	4	8,899	15,527	20,114	4,169
Botswana	9	2	1		8,832	4,091	1,684	
Burkina Faso	21	725	51		33,683	13,713	17,461	
Burundi	33	6	14	2	30,949	49,227	36,740	28,014
Cameroon	0		41				47,178	
Comoros						1,801		
Congo	2	2	0		16,611	11,892	7,600	436
Ethiopia		142	99	3	5,157	10,690	66,544	
Gambia	3	0			2,580	284	1,628	
Ghana	120	40	1		140,821	82,684	64,517	405
Kenya	7	6,395			33,868	28,473		
Lesotho	41	13	26		5,806	7,935	7,362	
Mali	71	143	259		34,481	10,007	29,732	
Mauritania	42	0	129	20	9,501	11,441	15,113	2,117
Mauritius	1	0	1			35	2	
Mozambique	2	11	1		10,414	30,070	16,507	
Nigeria	32	165	1,996	59	134,976	162,106	161,768	17,217
Rwanda	1	3	15		44,721	80,402	16,760	
Togo	0	0	0		24,304	29,454	25,729	3,489
Zaire	46	43			51,040	32,596	19,414	7,571
Zambia	49	12	35		91,461	98,659	51,000	
AMERICAS								
Argentina	148	86	45	11	23,108	16,102	9,240	3,730
Bahamas	0	0	0		14	484	25	
Barbados	2	11			382	27	2	
Belize	1	0	0	0	429	607	7	11
Bolivia	229	30	31		2,244	4,181	217	
Brazil	4,004	4,646	2,304	836	19,764	99,263	75,993	18,783
Canada	103	55	9		13,143	13,864	2,816	11,236
Chile	428	253	224	36	8,413	3,844	16,790	11,904
Colombia	260	263	32	35	10,706	9,222	5,572	10,235
Costa Rica	6	0	0	0	743	1,000	1	33
Cuba	1	0	0		10,585	3,806	3,874	
Dominican Rep.	299	187	100	25	4,224	9,123	4,392	1,185
Ecuador	40	16	44		241	2,722	1,183	
El Salvador	4	2	4	0	511	2,315	1,413	15,917
Guatemala	7	7			3,007	2,703		2,415
Jamaica	27	11	5		705	36	67	
Mexico	37	3	4	6	1,530	10,546	23,410	20,076
Nicaragua	0	5	2	0	1,934	3,784	956	130
Paraguay	13	14	27	8	140	745	419	220
Peru	161	185	112		6,749	19,246	7,725	
Trinidad & Tobago	25	0	0		244	394	3,549	
Uruguay	1	0	0	0	5,754	141	160	18
USA	307	3	3	2	24,374	13,506	2,822	

Continued opposite

Pertussis				Polio				Tuberculosis			
1975	1980	1985	1989	1975	1980	1985	1989	1975	1980	1985	1989
1,379	710	520	32	317	116	66	18		2,702	13,832	
989	110	29		3	1	3		3,534	2,662	2,706	
4,369	3,888	5,078		162	145	113			879	387	
10,289	9,613	4,516	895	23	43	25	22	1,062	789	1,282	
1,099	290	11,126			255	230			2,434	3,080	
					3						
4,971	11,198	772		139	136	6	0	1,026	742	2,648	
8,445	23,429	5,148	692	701	234	182	111	30,454	18,041	40,949	58,035
529	157	56		8	1	2		343	239		
22,009	13,216	8,698		275	145	185	28	6,355	5,207	3,211	
15,011	13,281			351	455			5,086	6,941		
1,643	2,020	186		6	36	29		2,795	4,082	2,927	
7,980	2,811	4,165		695	234	271			839	752	
4,207	7,576	5,958	631	39	159	141	8	5,320	3,058	4,406	
	0	0		0	0	0		222	132	111	
		1,201		11	65	26		2,142	7,457	5,645	
34,362	48,996	92,266		569	816	959	151	18,498	9,877	14,937	
20,813	16,189	1,384		9	24	7			1,495	1,327	
9,304	3,901	2,440	576	24	178	69	7	305	208	227	
29,687	15,335	1,590	492	881	263	98	17		5,122		
30,174	21,232	1,303		353	276	128		13,418	16,869	8,789	
10,917	27,208	4,654	2,936	5	26	1		14,850	16,406	12,484	
5	15	0		0	0	0		60	74	67	
0	0	13		0	0	0		26	64	12	
128	11	36	1	0	3	0		29	21	25	
3,078	2,596	964		213	40	0	2	9,914	10,627	7,013	
18,772	45,752	22,119	10,741	3,596	1,290	461	41	53,419	70,596	84,310	
3,387	2,872	2,376		2	0	1	0	3,089	2,875	1,984	
2,550	2,795	633	206	2	0	0	0	8,190	8,523		
17,353	7,664	1,629	1,668	487	129	36	14	22,923	22,228	15,963	
1,165	960	133	85	0	0	0	0	588	352	315	
326	131	195		0	0	0	0	1,327	1,130	680	
5,023	412	174	299	121	147	0	0	1,537	2,174	2,624	
2,382	836	741		101	11	1	3	2,790	3,950	4,798	
1,675	1,005	464	34	31	55	10	2	2,875	2,255	1,461	
724	1,513			43	76	29	3	6,335	7,153		
215	13	5		0	0	0		347	166	130	
3,450	3,040	2,201	1,400	931	602	140	25	11,417	11,165	10,662	
1,414	2,469	150	324	40	21	0	0	1,160	649	1,650	
557	652	272	371	182	7	3	0	1,031	1,354	1,368	
12,794	12,134	6,215		109	182	67	16	16,688	16,011	17,653	
30	10	9		0	0	0		85	86	112	
37	192	399	40	0	0	0	1	1,900	1,874	1,055	
1,738	1,730	3,589	3,745	8	9	7	0	33,989	27,749	22,201	21,520

Continued over

Table 5.10 Continued

Region/country	Diphtheria				Measles			
	1975	1980	1985	1989	1975	1980	1985	1989
SOUTH EAST ASIA								
Bangladesh	706	1,559	204		3,030	11,077	11,699	
India	34,269	34,241	11,936		133,561	124,031	151,322	
Indonesia	939	3,674	1,161		205	28,935	9,458	
Myanmar q.v. Burma	384	830	268		4,326	21,457	16,386	
Sri Lanka	310	37	7		4,997	5,032	8,797	1,930
Thailand	1,934	1,918	762		3,392	16,795	32,156	
EUROPE								
Austria	1	0	1					
Bulgaria	0	2	0		20,162	10,763	972	
Denmark	0	0	1		14,167	28,249	13,187	
Finland	0	0	0		3,384	2,147	614	
France	19	3	3		1,813	1,244	399	
German Dem. Rep.	0	0	0		1,493	28,745	568	
Germany, Fed. Rep.	46	19	4					
Greece	5	0	0		8,931	13,464	1,484	
Hungary	6	6	1		638	1,198	20	
Iceland	0	0	0		11	13	374	
Ireland	0	0	0		2,957	1,106	9,903	
Israel	1	0	0		4,795	215	3,005	
Italy	256	35	5		52,033	27,459	73,190	35,568
Luxembourg	0	0	0		288	63	62	
Malta	0	0	0		23	14	175	
Netherlands	0	0	0			178	24	
Poland	0	0	0		146,664	24,882	35,750	
Romania	8	12	1		110,703	10,476	5,007	
Spain	23	7	0		179,638	145,322	80,663	
Sweden	0	4	11		7,841	1786	326	
Turkey	265	86	145		24,317	8,618	14,695	
UK	12	5	4		158,619	147,962	104,774	
USSR	199	345	1,511	852	363,784	355,654	272,807	51,955
EASTERN MEDITERRANEAN								
Afghanistan	22	1,939	3,179	286	466	32,455	14,457	1,170
Egypt	584	333	663	110	3,492	839	5,554	4,057
Iran	1,556	139	143	223	33,640	31,130	20,582	5,895
Iraq	1,281	1, 122	1,348	238	55,889	26,542	22,186	11,617
Pakistan	3,138	14,328	1,450	167	6,892	28,573	26,686	2,240
Sudan	431	587	342	108	58,028	50,168	67,589	439
WESTERN PACIFIC								
Australia	22	1	17		632	170		
China	38,246	9,767	1,423	343	2,553,084	1,122,285	418,159	85,049
Hong Kong	0	2	0	0	138	1,669	280	139
Japan	139	66	10		15,217	13,219	2,810	3,109
Malaysia	218	131	39		1,377	8,727	5,163	
Papua New Guinea	11	0	0	0	4,172	12,125	5,680	8,303
Philippines	450	1,920	1,669		4,086	26,765	5,680	
Viet Nam	738	1,730	2,361		63,896	86,901	82,231	

EPI = Expanded Programme on Immunization, established by the World Health Organization.

Data were extracted from the Expanded Programme on Immunization Database during July 1990. The Database is updated twice a year.

Pertussis				Polio				Tuberculosis			
1975	1980	1985	1989	1975	1980	1985	1989	1975	1980	1985	1989
	12,436	23,897		162	65	810		11,549	36,512	36,772	
345,527	320,110	184,368		13,401	16,685	18,458		675,508	657,469	903,917	
58	32,999	1045		106	182	88		17,402	25,235	17,681	
11,451	26,878	10,238		37	244	109	40	10,585	12,744	10,506	
1,341	542	506		190	264	11		7,324	6,212	5,889	
3,281	4,820	2,533		440	300	65			14,980	22,907	
388	186	301		0	1	0		2,366	2,623	1,442	
486	154	40		0	15	0	1	4,273	3,280	1,884	
1,457	4,970	1,832		0	0	0				359	312
188	187	308		0	0	1		3,497	2,247	1,376	
372	100	83		18	10	2	2	2,843	17,199	11,290	
360	258	306		0	0	0		6,163	4,067	3,101	
				24	6	5	2	34,070	25,924	16,973	
6,398	3,083	1,020		0	0	1		7,955	5,412	1,556	
59	22	21		2	1	1		6,333	5,412	4,582	
138	41	16		0	0	0				24	13
355	547	3,689		0	1	0		1,154	1,152		
101	19	24		13	11	2	0	416	249	368	
10,397	16,643	15,425	6,777	4	1	0	0	4,189		6,079	
20	46	17		0	0	0		104	90	51	
36	2	140		0	0	0		53	31	28	
	30	1,522		0	0	0		2,230	1,701	1,346	
1,056	232	308		11	3	3	0	62,410	25,807	21,650	
13,646	11,441	1,810		31	125	11	10	21,036	12,093	10,418	
		60,564		261	17	8	2	3,131	4,859	10,752	
2,172	5,221	10,839		0	0	0	1	1,478	926	712	
3,036	1,520	2,678		368	182	83	9	20,314	36,716	30,960	
9,946	22,924	24,244		3	3	4	2	12,620	10,488	6,647	
14,885	13,908	53,871	37,541	133	165	138	89				113,590
1	15,748	8,531	1,494	116	880	1,981	55	1,788	71,685	10,742	3,398
141	49	18	9	2,175	2006	416	394	1,076	1,637	1,308	1,391
31,660	20,395	11,519	2,699	1,111	80	53	13	11,919	42,717	8,728	6,606
11,755	16,687	2,768	368	1,046	997	198	10	20,273	11,809	6,485	7,012
10,028	42,947	55,659	1,324	5,052	2,980	747	816	92,687	316,340	111,419	3,297
37,135	28,631	10,314	28	2,864	4151	84	51	208,688	32,971	1,509	701
	124	587		1	0	0		1,508	1,549	1,088	
1,814,134	613,688	147,298	26,985	7,815	7442	1,537	4,628				6,704
0	12	21	4	0	2	1	0	8,192	8,065	7,545	
1,084	5,033	938		4	2	1		110,118	73,230	58,567	
205	97	150		25	5	4		10,483	7,025	8,904	
1,243	2,693	1,757	1,697	29	22	9	26	1,856	2,841	3,453	
3,637	19,844	19,628		793	790	551		19,438	112,307	151,028	
39,025	96,557	44,011		176	1,741	1,600		19,514	43,062	62,794	

Source:
Kim-Farley, R. J. 1990 Personal communication, World Health Organization, Geneva, Switzerland.

Table 5.11 Global estimates of the prevalence of common parasitic diseases, 1989

Disease	Common name	No. at risk (10^6)	No. infected (10^6)	Prevalence range[a]	Preventive measures
Dracunculiasis	Guinea worm	140	10	10%–60%	Safe water supply, drinking-water filters
Intestinal parasitoses:					
Amoebiasis	Amoebic dysentery	4,000	400		Sanitary disposal, safe water supply and clean vegetables
Ancylostomiasis	Hookworm	4,000	900	30%–90%	Wearing of shoes
Ascariasis	Roundworm	4,000	1,000	20%–95%	Sanitary disposal, personal hygiene
Giardiasis		World-wide	200		Safe water supply
Strongyloidiasis	Threadworm	World-wide	30		Sanitary disposal, personal hygiene
Trichuriasis	Whipworm	World-wide	500	Up to 95%	Sanitary disposal, personal hygiene
Leishmaniasis (visceral and cutaneous)	Kala azar, Oriental sore Espundia, Chiclero ulcer	370	12	Up to 70%	Sandfly control, rodent and other animal reservoir control environmental management
Lymphatic filariasis	Elephantiasis	900	90	15%	Mosquito control
Onchocerciasis	River blindness	80	18	10%–40%	Blackfly control
Schistosomiasis	Bilharziasis	600	200	22%–50%	Sanitary disposal, systematic chemotherapy campaigns snail control and safe water supply
Trypanosomiasis, African	Sleeping sickness	50	0.04	1%–5%	Systematic case detection and chemotherapy, tsetse control
Trypanosomiasis, American	Chagas disease	100	13–15	10%–70%	Triatomine bug control, housing improvement

[a] Estimate of the proportion of the population of an affected area infected by the parasite.

Source:
WHO 1990 *The Work of WHO 1988–1989: Biennial Report of the Director-General to the World Health Assembly and to the United Nations,* World Health Organization, Geneva.

Table 5.12 Epidemics of infectious diseases, 1987–1990

Year	Month	Country	Location	Type of epidemic	No. of deaths	No. affected	Notes
1987	Jan.	India	State of Kashmir	Measles	90		Deaths as reported January 1987; number affected as reported February 1987
	Feb.	Guinea	Salambande	Meningitis	18	30	Deaths as reported for November 1986
	Apr.	Nigeria	Cross River State and Benue State	Yellow fever	309		
	May	Nigeria	State of Bauchi	Measles, meningitis	89		
	Jun.	Angola	Luanda region	Cholera	59	673	
	Jun.	Nigeria	Oyo, Lagos, Ibadan and surrounding area	Yellow fever	10,000		
	Aug.	Turkey	Southern Turkey	Cholera	11	150	
	Sep.	Bangladesh	Northern areas	Diarrhoea	550	600,000	Dysentry after floods
	Oct.	Guinea-Bissau	Bissau, Mansoa, Samif and Orango	Cholera			Several dead, several hundred affected
	Oct.	Mali	Kita and Kati regions	Yellow fever	37		Population at risk 4.75 million
	Oct.	Zaire	Along Zaire River	Cholera	450		Over a 4-week period
	Nov.	Mauritania	Seven regions	Yellow fever	22	160	
	Nov.	Nigeria	South-eastern Cross River State	Measles	100	120	Several hundred affected
	Dec.	Bangladesh	Chittagong and Cox's Bazar	High fever and renal failure	100		Epidemic occurred over a 2-week period, location given
	Dec.	Bangladesh	Dhamrai near Dhaka	Diarrhoea	100	1000	was the most severely affected
	Dec.	Sri Lanka		Encephalitis	53		
1988	Mar.	Bangladesh	Pirojpur and Barguna districts	Cholera	700	2,000	
	Mar.	Brazil	Rio de Janerio	Leptospirosis	300	588	Due to floods
	Mar.	China	Xinjiang province	Hepatitis A	600	122,000	Over a 18-month period
	Mar.	China	Shanghai and eastern China	Hepatitis A	11	500,000	
	Apr.	Angola	Northern province Zaire, Luanda and Benguela	Cholera	2,000	24,730	
	Apr.	Bangladesh	Northern area	Diarrhoea	205		
	Apr.	Chad	N'Damena and surrounding areas	Meningitis	230	24,730	
	May	Sudan	Central region, Khartoum, Darfur and Kordofan	Meningitis	1,200	18,700	
1989	May	China	Xinjiang Autonomous Region	Cholera	17	1,186	
	Jul.	Fiji	Central and Western Divisions	Dengue fever		57	Some cases were dengue haemorrhagic fever
	Oct.	Malawi		Meningitis	35		
	Nov.	Angola	Luanda and Uige provinces	Cholera		444	Rates: Luanda 45 cases per day; Uige 1 case per day; Epidemic started in September
	Dec.	Venezuela	Poruguesa, Maracay City and surrounding areas	Dengue haemorrhagic fever	25	165	
	Dec.	Venezuela	Feceral district	Dengue haemorrhagic fever	27	845	Largest number of cases reported in the Aragua (355) and Falcon (136) provinces
1990	Jan.	Nigeria	Kaduna	Yellow fever	375		
	Jan.	Nigeria	Bauchi	Yellow fever	150		

Continued over

Table 5.12 Continued

Year	Month	Country	Location	Type of epidemic	No. of deaths	No. affected	Notes
	Jan.	Nigeria	Kano State	Yellow fever		1,067	
	Jan.	USA	Louisiana	Legionnaires disease	2	34	Due to contamination in a reservoir of a supermarket refrigerator for fruit and vegetables
	Jan.	Venezuela	Nation-wide, especially Caracas	Dengue fever	51	5,416	1,500 cases were dengue haemorrhagic fever
	Feb.	Trinidad & Tobago		Dengue fever	0	1,211	
	Feb.	Uganda		Meningitis			Types A & C
	Mar.	Guyana		Malaria		35,470	Epidemic of 1988; in 1989 down to 19,094 cases
	Mar.	Madagascar	Fianarantsoa II district	Bubonic plague	0	10	400 km from Antananarivo
	Mar.	Madagascar	Ambositra	Bubonic plague	12	227	250 km from Antananarivo
	Mar.	Madagascar	Antananarivo	Bubonic plague	8	54	One affected case was pneumonic plague
	Mar.	Malawi		Cholera	489		
	Apr.	Angola	Luanda province	Cholera		10,350	Started in November 1989 Down from 50 cases per day in February to 20 cases per day
	Apr.	Fiji		Dengue fever			
	Apr.	Vanuatu		Dengue fever	29	591	Started in January 1990
	Jun.	Bangladesh	Northern region	Kalazar	120	15,000	Over a 4-month period
	Jul.	Romania	Tulcea and Galati	Cholera	0	15	
	Aug.	Guatemala		Measles			
	Aug.	Honduras		Measles			
	Aug.	Morocco	Meknes, Fez and Taza	Cholera	30		
	Aug.	Nicaragua	Nation-wide, particularly southern region	Measles		2,436	In the southern region there were 1,300 cases and 60 deaths
	Aug.	USA	Dallas, Houston, Chicago, Milwaukee and Los Angeles	Measles		7,600	Epidemic affecting the entire country; locations listed were those most severely affected
	Aug.	USSR	Stavropol	Cholera	3	45	
	Sep.	Kenya	Nairobi, low income neighbourhood	Bubonic plague		23	
	Sep.	Nepal	Kathmandu Valley	Cholera	466	24,712	
	Sep.	Romania	Districts: Tulcea (63), Galati (12) and Braila (10)	Cholera	0	85	Due to consumption of water from the Danube River
	Oct.	Botswana	Boteti district	Bubonic plague	12	162	Between October 1989 and April 1990

The year and month refer to the date the epidemic was reported. Sources of information are mainly scientific journals and media reports.

Sources:
UNDRO 1987 *Disaster Briefs – Summary UNINET Data Base* (and earlier editions), United Nations Disaster Relief Organization, Geneva.
UNEP 1988 Environmental Events Record, supplements in *UNEP News* (and earlier editions), United Nations Environment Programme, Nairobi.
WHO 1990 *Weekly Epidemiological Record* (and earlier editions), **65**(40), 310.

Table 5.13 Incidence of diarrhoea and use of oral rehydration salts (ORS) and oral rehydration therapy (ORT) in children aged under five years, 1988

Region/country	Population aged <5 years (10³)	Average no. of episodes of diarrhoea per child (a⁻¹)	Total number of episodes	Total ORS available (10³ l)	Availability of ORS per 100 episodes[a] (l)	Percentage of population with access to ORS[b]	ORS use[c] (%)	ORT use[d] (%)
WORLD[e]	396,603.0	3.4	1,362,642.9	332,835.9	24.4	61	19	32
AFRICA	87,350.1	4.4	382,669.4	27,309.5	7.1	52	16	28
Algeria	4,050.2	2.5[f]	10,125.5	2,000.0	19.8	48[f]	15[f]	16[f]
Angola	1,737.1	2.0[f]	3,474.3	1,358.0	39.1	50[g]	12[f]	12
Benin	877.0	5.5[f]	4,823.6	349.3	7.2	60[g]	11[g]	26[g]
Botswana	238.0	2.3[f]	547.4	212.5	38.8	85[g]	45[g]	64[g,h]
Burkina Faso	1,530.9	4.6[g]	7,042.0	239.0	3.4	79[f]	15[f]	16[g]
Burundi	943.5	4.2[f]	3,962.5	522.5	13.2	60[f]	30[l]	30[l]
Cameroon	1,818.5	2.4[j]	4,364.3	633.6	14.5	36[k]	16[f]	24[j,l]
Cape Verde	59.4	4.8[m]	285.2	90.0	31.6	81[g]	9[f]	9
Cent. African Rep.	483.3	6.1[f]	2,947.9	15.3	0.5	41[g]	6[g]	15[g]
Chad	939.5	8.0[f]	7,515.9	674.0	9.0	22[k]	2[n]	2
Comoros	90.6	5.2[j]	471.0	124.3	26.4	70[g]	13[j]	83[h,j]
Congo	336.0	6.6[f]	2,217.7	189.2	8.5	40[g]	6[g]	6
Côte d'Ivoire	2,404.0	3.9[f]	9,375.6	431.0	4.6	12[k]	4[f]	16[l]
Equatorial Guinea	70.9	7.2[f]	510.7	84.0	16.4	70[g]	17[g]	21[f]
Ethiopia	7,489.1	4.8[g]	35,947.7	350.1	1.0	50[g]	38[g]	38
Gabon	149.5	3.3[f]	493.4	70.5	14.3	70[g]	4[j]	10[g]
Gambia	145.9	4.3[g]	627.2	104.0	16.6	60[g]	15[g]	39[g]
Ghana	2,583.1	6.8[f]	17,564.9	310.7	1.8	38[g]	7[g]	21[g]
Guinea	1,167.5	4.3[f]	5,020.5	751.6	15.0	37[k]	20[l]	1
Guinea-Bissau	152.6	8.9[j]	1,358.3	0.2	0.0	19[g]	1[f]	1
Kenya	5,080.4	4.0[f]	20,321.7	6,045.5	29.7	74[k]	22[j,o]	54[j,o]
Lesotho	287.3	8.8[f]	2,527.8	250.0	9.9	50[l]	27[f]	68[f]
Liberia	445.8	4.8[m]	2,139.9	82.7	3.9	22[g]	6[l]	9[l]
Madagascar	2,044.1	4.8[m]	9,811.6	387.2	3.9	51[g]	10[g]	80[g]
Malawi	1,538.3	6.0[g]	9,229.9	126.6	1.4	56[g]	14[g]	14[g]
Mali	1,701.4	2.7[g]	4,593.8	24.4	0.5	46[g]	2[f]	3[f]
Mauritania	343.2	9.8[f]	3,412.0	256.8	7.5	30[g]	13[g,p]	23
Mauritius	92.9	4.8[m]	445.7	115.0	25.8	65[k]	7[n]	7
Mozambique	2,633.4	4.7[f]	12,400.3	707.5	5.7	40[f]	14[f]	14
Niger	1,313.8	6.9[g]	9,065.0	510.0	5.6	44[g]	21[g]	38[g,h]
Nigeria	21,037.5	4.0[f]	84,149.9	699.8	0.8	60[g]	16[g]	35[j,l,o]
Rwanda	1,360.4	2.8[f]	3,809.1	1,205.4	31.6	79[k]	8[n]	24[f]
São Tomé & Príncipe	23.0	2.8[f]	64.4	10.0	15.5	100[f]	46[f]	46

Continued over

Table 5.13 Continued

Region/country	Population aged <5 years (10³)	Average no. of episodes of diarrhoea per child (a⁻¹)	Total number of episodes	Total ORS available (10³ l)	Availability of ORS per 100 episodes[a] (l)	Percentage of population with access to ORS[b]	ORS use[c] (%)	ORT use[d] (%)
Senegal	1,253.3	6.5^g	8,146.7	764.5	9.4	16^g	5^j	27^{h,j,o}
Seychelles	14.2	4.8^m	68.1	0.0	0.0		5^j	
Sierra Leone	720.7	3.2^f	2,306.1	2.4	0.1	60^f	11^f	31^f
Swaziland	1,423.6	4.8^m	6,833.4	300.0	4.4		15^j	
Togo	598.4	7.0^f	4,188.6	0.7	0.0	56^f	20^j	21^{j,l}
Uganda	3,456.4	6.3^j	21,775.4	4,182.6	19.2	48^k	14^j	14^{j,l}
Tanzania	5,192.8	5.0^f	25,964.1	378.7	1.5	61^f	11^f	14^f
Zaire	6,275.6	2.3^f	14,433.9	896.8	6.2	48^g	10^f	18^g
Zambia	1,628.2	6.5^f	10,583.1	1,727.0	16.3	74^f	32^f	59^f
Zimbabwe	1,609.0	4.8^m	7,723.3	126.6	1.6	70^g	1^f	26^f
AMERICAS	55,034.5	4.6	252,645.1	87,004.2	34.4	65	25	41
Antigua & Barbuda	7.2	3.0^m	21.5	6.0	27.9	70^f		
Argentina	3,150.7	3.0^m	9,452.0	1,340.0	14.2	52^g	13^g	13
Barbados	23.1	3.0^m	69.2	50.0	72.2	100^k	10^n	10
Belize	38.0	1.5^f	57.0	50.0	87.8	100^k	65^f	65
Bolivia	1,195.4	3.0^g	3,586.2	2,215.0	61.8	40^g	22^{j,o}	26^l
Brazil	18,214.3	3.9^j	71,035.8	40,094.5	56.4	68^f	26^j	39^{j,l}
Chile	1,428.2	1.5^g	2,142.3	103.8	4.8	12^k	1^n	1
Colombia	3,991.5	4.8^f	19,159.1	4,711.7	24.6	62^k	6^n	12^f
Costa Rica	374.2	4.6^f	1,721.4	890.0	51.7	90^g	73^f	78^f
Cuba	774.6	3.0^f	2,323.8	537.6	23.1	100^g	75^g	75
Dominica	9.0	3.0^m	27.0	6.0	22.2	70^f	30^g	51^g
Dominican Rep.	942.0	7.0^g	6,593.7	428.6	6.5	50^f	24^f	24
Ecuador	1,565.2	4.1^g	6,417.2	1,138.9	17.7	55^g	45^g	45
El Salvador	803.7	4.0^g	3,214.8	2,491.3	77.5	79^g		70^g
Grenada	12.3	3.0^f	37.0	6.0	16.2	100^g		
Guatemala	1,517.6	5.2^f	7,891.6	4,603.6	58.3	60^g	17^f	17
Guyana	115.3	3.0^f	346.0	50.0	14.5	36^k	10^f	10
Haiti	908.5	7.0^f	6,359.5	531.4	8.4	21^k	25^j	35^q
Honduras	821.9	3.0^g	2,465.7	2,708.6	109.9	60^g	40^p	66^g
Jamaica	299.0	1.0^f	299.0	173.6	58.1	76^g	10^g	15^g
Mexico	11,102.5	5.9^j	65,504.5	16,665.5	25.4	86^g	34^j	72^f
Nicaragua	645.7	2.0^g	1,291.4	3,000.0	232.3	75^g	38^g	38
Panama	286.7	3.0^g	860.2	775.5	90.2	49^g	41^{g,p}	41
Paraguay	620.6	2.1^f	1,303.2	159.0	12.2	57^f	32^f	36^f
Peru	3,083.4	8.6^j	26,517.5	2,769.6	10.4	23^g	10^j	10

Continued below

Table 5.13 Continued

Region/country	Population aged <5 years (10³)	Average no. of episodes of diarrhoea per child (a⁻¹)	Total number of episodes	Total ORS available (10³ l)	Availability of ORS per 100 episodes[a] (l)	Percentage of population with access to ORS[b]	ORS use[c] (%)	ORT use[d] (%)
St Christopher & Nevis	5.1	3.0^m	15.2	3.0	19.8	100^f	2^f	2
St Lucia	17.9	3.0^m	53.8	5.0	9.3	85^f	57^f	75^f
St Vincent & Grenadines	16.4	3.0^m	49.1	20.0	40.7	100^g	98^g	98
Suriname	47.1	0.8^f	37.7	59.2	157.1	65^f	47^{g,p}	47^f
Trinidad & Tobago	139.6	3.0^m	418.8	33.0	7.9	100^f	53^f	60^f
Uruguay	274.5	1.3^q	356.8	264.0	74.0	56^f	40^j	40
Venezuela	2,603.4	5.0^g	13,017.2	1,113.8	8.6	80^g	30^g	30
SOUTH EAST ASIA	166,991.9	2.9	476,098.5	107,299.0	22.5	63	15	28
Bangladesh	18,028.4	5.2^f	93,747.6	24,191.6	25.8	60^g	17^g	32^g
Bhutan	22.1	4.1^f	90.8	400.0	440.6	54^f	40^f	40
India	109,771.1	2.7^g	296,382.0	64,784.0	21.9	57^k	12^g	23^g
Indonesia	20,322.2	1.9^g	38,612.3	8,045.8	20.8	90^f	25^g	56^g
Korea, Dem.	2,912.9	0.7^g	2,039.0	685.0	33.6	82^g	52^g	52
Maldives	33.1	2.7^f	89.3	21.0	23.5	59^k	8^f	12^f
Mongolia	354.4	3.4^f	1,205.0	184.0	15.3	50^f	41^f	59^f
Myanmar q.v. Burma	5,345.2	2.7^f	14,432.0	2,010.1	13.9	35^k	21^f	21
Nepal	2,934.5	5.4^f	15,846.9	2,500.0	15.8	80^g	28^g	28
Sri Lanka	1,764.0	1.5^f	2,645.9	877.5	33.2	95^g	43^g	77^g
Thailand	5,503.8	2.0^f	11,007.6	3,600.0	32.7	81^g	19^g	30^g
EAST MEDITERRANEAN	64,470.9	3.0	193,909.2	93,397.8	48.2	68	29	43
Afghanistan	2,700.7	2.5^m	6,751.7	4,533.7	67.1	16^f	11^f	11
Bahrain	60.5	2.4^f	145.2	42.0	28.9	73^k	53^f	53
Cyprus	61.7	2.5^m	154.2	12.2	7.9	20^k	2^n	2
Djibouti	71.4	2.8^j	200.0	203.3	101.7	76^f	46^j	51^j
Egypt	7,808.1	3.4^f	26,547.7	4,530.0	17.1	98^f	29^j	83^f
Iran	9,540.0	2.7^g	25,758.1	15,312.9	59.4	70^g	35^j	38^j
Iraq	3,183.3	2.1^j	6,684.9	5,015.3	75.0	81^f	44^j	51^f
Jordan	783.8	2.0^j	1,567.7	436.5	27.8	70^k	37^f	53^g
Kuwait	284.9	2.5^m	712.3	100.0	14.0	33^k	4^g	4
Lebanon	371.4	2.5^m	928.5	323.7	34.9	21^f	3^g	10^f
Libya	772.1	1.7^g	1,312.6	1,000.0	76.2	100^k	60^g	60^g
Morocco	3,577.5	7.5^f	26,831.0	6,564.0	24.5	38^f	6^j	45^{i,l}
Oman	255.8	2.5^m	639.6	1,000.0	156.4	100^k	19^f	19
Pakistan	21,616.7	2.5^g	54,041.8	33,170.2	61.4	74^g	42^f	42^f
Qatar	47.7	2.7^f	128.8	0.0	0.0	100^f	15^f	15

Continued over

Table 5.13 Continued

Region/country	Population aged <5 years (10³)	Average no. of episodes of diarrhoea per child (a⁻¹)	Total number of episodes	Total ORS available (10³ l)	Availability of ORS per 100 episodes[a] (l)	Percentage of population with access to ORS[b]	ORS use[c] (%)	ORT use[d] (%)
Saudi Arabia	2,366.3	2.0[f]	4,732.7	2,470.0	52.2	96[f]	29[j]	32[j,l]
Somalia	1,394.9	2.5[m]	3,487.1	1,400.0	40.1	31[f]	12[f]	12
Sudan	4,275.6	4.4[f]	18,812.8	12,022.9	63.9	39[f]	23[f]	25[f]
Syria	2,217.3	2.5[f]	5,543.3	1,341.0	24.2	61[k]	28[f]	31[f]
Tunisia	1,045.6	3.9[j]	4,077.8	70.0	1.7	100[f]	33[j]	48[j,l]
United Arab Em.	160.0	2.1[f]	336.1	2,500.0	743.9	78[f]	13[f]	13
Yemen	1,442.7	2.5[m]	3,606.8	1,000.0	27.7	34[f]	6[n]	6
Yemen, Dem.	432.7	2.1[f]	908.7	350.0	38.5	27[f]	10[f]	10
WESTERN PACIFIC[e]	22,755.7	2.5	57,320.7	17,825.5	31.1	57	12	36
Brunei	32.6	0.2[f]	7.8	0.0	0.0			
Cambodia	1,297.6	4.5[f]	5,839.3	145.0	2.5	6[k]	6[f]	6
China	105,394.8	3.2[j]	333,047.5	1,030.0	0.8	5[j]	1[j]	30[j]
Cook Is.	2.3	1.2[f]	2.8	2.4	0.8	58[f]	8[f]	8
Fiji	91.5	2.5[f]	228.8	273.0	119.3	100[k]	16[f]	16
Kiribati	7.8	2.5[f]	19.6	24.0	122.7	100[k]	19[f]	19
Laos	637.3	3.4[f]	2,166.8	408.0	18.8	65[g]	12[g]	30[g]
Malaysia	2,182.2	1.3[j]	2,836.9	600.0	7.0	95[g]	15[g]	20[g]
Papua New Guinea	649.5	2.5[j]	1,623.7	300.0	18.5	57[g]	15[g]	46[g]
Philippines	8,745.9	2.8[f]	24,488.6	11,458.1	46.8	60[g]	10[f]	14[f]
Samoa	23.6	1.1[f]	26.0	24.0	92.5	70[f]	7[f]	7
Solomon Is.	58.2	2.8[f]	162.8	100.0	61.4	100[k]	28[f]	75
Tonga	16.1	4.1[g]	66.0	25.0	37.9	100[k]	30[g]	30[g]
Vanuatu	25.0	3.3[f]	82.4	27.0	32.8	82[k]	31[f]	31
Viet Nam	8,986.1	2.2[g]	19,769.4	4,438.9	22.5	51[g]	17[g]	74[j]

a Total ORS available/total number of diarrhoea episodes x 100 expressed as litres.

b Proportion of the population <5 years of age with reasonable access to a provider of ORS who is trained in its use and receives adequate supplies.

c Percentage of diarrhoea episodes in children <5 years of age treated with ORS.

d Percentage of diarrhoea episodes in children <5 years of age treated with ORS or a physiologically appropriate household solution.

e Excluding China.

f Estimate for 1987 used in the absence of new or more reliable data.

g National Diarrhoeal Diseases Control Programme (CDD) estimate.

h Includes estimate for use of recommended home fluid other than sugar-salt solution.

i Best estimate from available data.

j Based on household sample surveys.

k Based on total ORS reported as produced or imported in 1988. Assumes that of 100 episodes of diarrhoea, 10 will need ORS, and that 40 litres of ORS are required to treat 10 episodes (see n). Thus 40 litres of ORS are assumed to provide access for 100 episodes of diarrhoea.

l Estimates for both ORS and sugar-salt solution (or recommended home fluid) use rates available. The midpoint between the sum and the greater of the two values is used as the ORT use rate.

m Regional median based on available country estimates.

n Based on total ORS reported as produced or imported in 1988 assuming that 50 per cent of available ORS is used for cases <5 years at a rate of 2 litres per episode.

o Data available for 1989 and 1986 or 1987. The 1988 estimate is interpolated.

p Reported use rate assumed to apply only to cases with access. Figure shown is access rate x use rate/100.

q From report survey or evaluation from various sources/agencies.

Source:
WHO 1990 Programme for Control of Diarrhoeal Diseases: Seventh Programme Report 1988–1989. World Health Organization, Geneva.

Table 5.14   Trends in the incidence[a] of yellow fever, 1948–1988

Year	Africa	Americas	Total	Year	Africa	Americas	Total
1948	7	31	38	1968	0	47	47
1949	34	12	46	1969	322	48	370
1950	17	64	81	1970	23	86	109
1951	39	297	336	1971	70	28	98
1952	55	292	347	1972	6	55	61
1953	29	89	118	1973	9	207	216
1954	6	83	89	1974	27	76	103
1955	14	34	48	1975	134	168	302
1956	4	26	30	1976	3	44	47
1957	5	81	86	1977	110	102	212
1958	60	71	131	1978	249	240	489
1959	133	30	163	1979	508	205	713
1960	7	50	57	1980	24	120	144
1961	300	82	382	1981	7	231	238
1962	10	52	62	1982	31	140	171
1963	3	141	144	1983	743	50	793
1964	7	98	105	1984	917	95	1,012
1965	243	87	330	1985	13	125	138
1966	0	159	159	1986	3,361	159	3,520
1967	5	12	17	1987	1,847	235	2,082
				1988	1,823	235	2,058

[a]   Number of cases reported to the World Health Organization.

Sources:
WHO 1988 *World Health Statistics Annual 1988*, World Health Organization, Geneva.

WHO 1990 Yellow fever in 1988, *Weekly Epidemiological Record* **65**(28), 213–220.
WHO 1990 *Global Estimates for Health Situation Assessment and Projections 1990*, World Health Organization, Geneva.

Table 5.15 Trends in the incidence[a] of human plague, 1975–1989

Region/country	1975	1976	1977	1978	1979	1980	1981	1982	1983	1984	1985	1986	1987	1988	1989
WORLD	1,581	1,609	1,556	819	694	569	231	801	1,159	1,453	544	1,118	1,270	1,516	874
AFRICA															
Angola	49	0	0	0	0	25	6	0	0	0	0	0	0	0	0
Botswana	0	0	0	0	0	0	0	0	0	0	0	0	0	0	0
Kenya	0	0	0	175	228	7	0	0	0	0	0	0	0	0	112
Lesotho	16	0	0	0	0	0	0	0	0	0	0	0	0	0	0
Libya	0	25	17	0	0	0	0	0	0	8	0	0	0	0	0
Madagascar[b]	76	60	74	31	36	16	57	57	34	57	103	35	27	112	222
Mozambique	0	21	111	12	0	0	0	0	0	0	0	0	0	0	0
South Africa	0	0	0	0	0	0	0	20	0	0	0	0	0	0	0
Tanzania	0	0	4	0	0	60	15	94	618	644	151	417	390	680	35
Uganda	0	0	0	0	0	0	0	156	0	0	0	367	0	0	0
Zaire[b]	1	22	7	0	2	0	0	1	0	0	0	0	634	455	1
Zimbabwe	46	0	0	0	0	0	0	5	1	0	2	0	0	0	0
AMERICAS															
Bolivia	2	29	38	70	10	28	22	1	25	14	0	109	3	2	0
Brazil	501	97	1	11	0	98	59	152	82	39	66	62	43	25	26
Ecuador	0	9	0	0	0	0	8	0	65	8	5	0	0	0	0
Peru	3	1	0	7	0	0	34	11	19	444	47	0	37	15	0
USA	24	19	20	14	15	23	17	22	46	37	19	10	14	15	4
ASIA															
China					14	50	1	0	40	0	8	11	9	10	16
Mongolia															8
Myanmar q.v. Burma[b]	295	728	617	177	75	77	1	166	99	0	0	0	0	0	36
Viet Nam[b]	568	598	667	322	314	185	11	116	130	202	143	107	113	202	411
EUROPE															
USSR[c]															3

a Number of cases, including deaths, reported to the World Health Organization.
b Includes suspected cases.
c Kazakh Republic.

Source:
WHO 1990. Human plague in 1989, *Weekly Epidemiological Record* **42**, 321–323.

Table 5.16 The WHO 'MONICA' project: cardiovascular disease mortality[a], mid-1980s

Region/country	Area	Percentage contribution to total mortality (all causes)						Age-standardized mortality rates per 10^5 population					
		Males			Females			Males			Females		
		CVD	IHD	Stroke	CVD	IHD	Stroke	CVD	IHD	Stroke	CVD	IHD	Stroke
AMERICAS													
Canada	National	38.5	28.9	3.4	24.6	13.7	5.0	249	187	22	84	47	17
	Halifax County	43.7	34.4	2.5	24.8	11.4	6.1	282	222	16	89	41	22
USA	National	40.4	25.3	3.5	29.9	14.5	5.2	315	197	27	126	61	22
	Stanford	37.6	25.7	2.4	25.1	12.9	4.3	266	182	17	93	48	16
EUROPE													
Belgium	National	32.9	17.8	4.5	23.9	8.3	5.9	243	131	33	89	31	22
	Ghent	28.5	13.3	4.0	22.0	7.7	3.7	216	101	30	94	33	16
	Charleroi	27.3	15.3	4.0	28.3	8.7	7.3	296	166	43	127	39	33
	Luxembourg Province[b]	34.3	19.5	4.1	24.1	7.5	7.7	316	180	38	97	30	31
Czechoslovakia	National	42.3	25.5	8.4	36.4	15.2	10.8	489	295	97	175	73	52
	Czechoslovakia-MONICA	44.7	23.2	7.7	36.6	11.8	9.1	424	220	73	149	48	37
Denmark	National	35.9	26.7	4.0	19.7	10.7	4.9	268	199	30	92	50	23
	Glostrup	36.8	25.2	3.9	19.9	9.2	3.6	285	195	30	95	44	17
Finland	National	47.8	35.5	6.4	32.8	16.2	10.2	427	317	57	103	51	32
	North Karelia	54.0	41.0	7.4	38.5	20.3	11.0	600	456	82	140	74	40
	Kuopio Province	49.5	37.1	6.1	37.0	14.5	14.5	476	357	59	120	47	47
	Turku/Loimaa	44.0	33.0	6.4	29.9	16.1	8.7	394	296	57	89	48	26
France	National	22.3	10.1	4.6	16.7	4.3	5.6	174	79	36	51	13	17
	Bas-Rhin	24.4	11.5	4.5	20.1	6.6	6.0	216	102	40	64	21	19
	Haute-Garonne	24.3	13.6	4.3	15.3	4.3	5.1	140	78	25	39	11	13
	Lille	21.5	10.1	4.1	17.5	4.9	5.4	224	105	43	72	20	22
German Dem. Rep.	National	36.5	16.9	3.5	29.3	7.9	4.3	313	145	30	129	35	19
	Berlin-Lichtenberg	42.6	22.9	3.5	30.1	11.8	4.3	307	165	25	125	49	18
	Cottbus County	36.1	15.1	3.7	30.4	7.0	4.2	324	136	33	130	30	18
	Halle County	36.1	18.3	5.3	29.8	9.0	6.1	322	163	47	132	40	27
	Karl-Marx Stadt County	34.5	17.0	3.8	28.6	8.0	4.8	298	147	33	126	35	21
	Rest of DDR-MONICA	37.6	17.4	4.1	30.2	9.8	3.1	314	145	34	136	44	14
Germany, Fed. Rep.	National	37.2	22.3	5.0	25.3	9.9	6.0	274	164	37	89	35	21
	Bremen	36.4	20.8	4.3	21.6	7.0	5.7	308	176	36	80	26	21
	Rhein-Neckar Region	36.5	22.4	5.2	25.8	10.2	5.9	246	151	35	83	33	19

Continued over

Table 5.16 Continued

| Region/country | Area | Percentage contribution to total mortality (all causes) | | | | | | Age-standardized mortality rates per 10^5 population | | | | | |
| | | Males | | | Females | | | Males | | | Females | | |
		CVD	IHD	Stroke	CVD	IHD	Stroke	CVD	IHD	Stroke	CVD	IHD	Stroke
	Augsburg (urban)	35.3	21.2	4.5	22.7	9.9	5.7	283	170	36	80	35	20
	Augsburg (rural)	37.4	21.7	5.1	21.4	8.4	5.5	263	153	36	66	26	17
Hungary	National	40.6	21.3	10.0	37.6	13.6	12.3	569	299	140	226	82	74
	Budapest	42.1	22.3	8.2	35.5	13.5	8.6	555	294	108	227	86	55
	Pecs	36.9	17.8	8.6	36.8	12.6	10.3	488	235	113	208	71	58
Iceland	National	46.7	38.5	4.3	25.4	14.3	6.3	250	206	23	69	39	17
	Iceland-MONICA	46.8	38.6	4.3	25.4	14.3	6.3	250	206	23	69	39	17
Israel	National	40.7	26.2	5.8	29.3	13.3	7.3	247	159	35	108	49	27
	Tel-Aviv	44.7	29.5	5.8	28.4	13.1	7.4	256	169	33	100	46	26
Italy	National[c]	31.5	16.6	6.5	25.8	7.4	8.7	218	115	45	80	23	27
	Area Latina	34.4	15.8	8.1	29.2	7.6	10.6	200	92	47	77	20	28
	Area Brianza[d]	30.5	17.5	6.2	24.7	8.1	8.1	212	122	43	73	24	24
Malta	National	47.7	26.2	7.1	35.2	13.7	5.1	335	184	50	131	51	19
Poland	National	40.3	18.4	5.1	36.6	9.4	7.5	479	219	60	176	45	36
	Tarnobrzeg Voivodship	40.1	17.3	4.4	40.4	7.5	8.5	399	172	44	166	31	35
	Warsaw	32.0	13.9	5.7	29.8	9.2	7.8	416	180	74	165	51	43
Spain	National[b]	30.4	14.0	6.8	27.8	6.1	9.0	193	89	43	77	17	25
	Catalonia	25.7	12.7	6.0	20.7	4.6	7.6	138	68	32	49	11	18
Sweden	National	42.1	31.8	4.5	23.1	11.7	6.0	242	183	26	69	35	18
	Gothenburg	34.9	25.8	3.7	21.0	11.7	4.7	247	183	26	72	40	16
	Northern Sweden	50.7	39.8	5.9	28.8	13.6	9.9	302	237	35	87	41	30
Switzerland	National	32.6	19.2	3.3	19.4	6.8	4.3	190	112	19	54	19	12
	Vaud/Fribourg	29.6	16.5	3.0	18.8	6.1	4.3	185	103	19	52	17	12
	Ticino	35.6	20.1	4.6	19.0	6.1	6.5	202	114	26	47	15	16
USSR	National[e]	39.1	23.9	10.5	41.1	16.9	16.7	480	294	129	207	85	84
	Kaunas	27.3	19.6	3.0	20.8	9.0	5.0	334	240	37	92	40	22
	Moscow (intervention)	46.6	27.9	10.3	36.6	16.1	12.0	465	278	103	159	70	52
	Moscow (control)	44.8	29.0	7.7	38.4	17.1	11.7	503	326	86	180	80	55
	Novosibirsk (intervention)[c]	41.5	30.9	9.1	44.7	22.9	15.7	545	405	119	248	127	87
	Novosibirsk (control)[c]	41.1	28.8	8.7	46.3	21.3	19.3	597	418	127	272	125	113

Continued below

Table 5.16 Continued

Region/country	Area	Percentage contribution to total mortality (all causes)						Age-standardized mortality rates per 10^5 population					
		Males			Females			Males			Females		
		CVD	IHD	Stroke	CVD	IHD	Stroke	CVD	IHD	Stroke	CVD	IHD	Stroke
UK (Northern Ireland)	National	51.3	41.2	5.6	34.9	21.2	8.0	425	341	46	153	93	35
	Belfast	47.7	37.3	5.5	32.8	19.0	8.0	445	348	51	152	88	37
UK (Scotland)	National	48.6	38.4	5.8	33.7	20.3	8.5	425	336	51	171	103	43
	Glasgow	42.5	32.2	5.3	33.0	19.4	7.8	501	380	62	225	132	53
Yugoslavia	National[c]	36.6	14.9	8.3	38.6	9.3	11.9	352	143	80	179	43	55
	Novi Sad[c]	42.4	23.6	7.3	33.7	12.2	11.7	554	308	96	193	70	67
WESTERN PACIFIC													
Australia	National	41.7	31.1	5.1	28.8	16.6	7.1	264	197	32	97	56	24
	Perth	37.7	28.4	4.3	23.7	13.0	5.7	211	159	24	71	39	17
	Newcastle	44.1	33.0	5.9	34.5	20.6	9.4	309	231	41	136	81	37
China	Beijing	40.6	10.4	20.8	45.8	7.3	24.3	191	49	98	170	27	90
Japan	National	27.7	5.5	12.3	26.8	3.7	13.4	146	29	65	69	9	35
	Part of Japan	28.1	6.4	12.9	25.6	3.7	13.4	144	33	66	63	9	33
New Zealand	National	45.8	34.7	4.8	30.3	16.7	7.4	324	246	34	127	70	31
	Auckland	45.2	32.9	5.6	29.2	15.1	7.5	317	231	39	124	64	32

CVD = All cardiovascular diseases.
IHD = Ischaemic heart disease.

"National" data are the official statistics of the country. Data for populations monitored by the 'MONICA' programme are listed below the national data. 'MONICA' data refer either to selected areas within a country or to the country as whole.

Source:
WHO 1989 The WHO MONICA project: a world-wide monitoring system for cardiovascular diseases. In: *World Health Statistics Annual 1989*, Section B. World Health Organization, Geneva, 27–149.

a   Data are for the period 1984–1986 unless otherwise indicated and refer to the age group 34–65 years.
b   Age standardized mortality rates are for 1984 only.
c   Age standardized mortality rates are for 1984–1985.
d   Age standardized mortality rates are for 1985–1986.
e   Age standardized mortality rates are for 1985 only.

MONICA = Multilateral Monitoring of Trends and Determinants in Cardiovascular Disease.

Table 5.17 World-wide variations in the incidence[a] of cancers at various sites, around 1980

Site	Males			Females		
	Highest	Lowest	Ratio	Highest	Lowest	Ratio
Lip	15.1 (Canada, Newfoundland)	0.1 (Japan, Osaka)	151.0	1.6 (Australia, South)	0.1 (UK, England and Wales)	16.0
Oral cavity	13.5 (France, Bas-Rhin)	0.5 (Japan, Miyagi)	27.0	15.7 (India, Bangalore)	0.2 (Japan, Miyagi)	78.5
Nasopharynx	30.0 (Hong Kong)	0.3 (UK, south-western)	100.0	12.9 (Hong Kong)	0.1 (USA, Iowa)	129.0
Oesophagus	29.9 (France, Calvados)	1.2 (Romania, Ciuj County)	24.9	12.4 (India, Poona)	0.3 (Czechoslovackia, Slovakia)	41.3
Stomach	82.0 (Japan, Nagasaki)	3.7 (Kuwait)[b]	22.2	36.1 (Japan, Nagasaki)	3.0 (USA, Iowa)	12.0
Colon	34.1 (USA, Connecticut)[c]	1.8 (India, Madras)	18.9	29.0 (USA, Detroit)[d]	1.8 (India, Nagpur)	16.1
Rectum	21.5 (Germany, Fed. Rep., Saarland)	3.0 (Kuwait)[b]	7.2	13.2 (Germany, Fed. Rep., Saarland)	1.3 (India, Madras)	10.2
Liver	34.4 (China, Shanghai)	0.7 (Canada, Nova Scotia)	49.1	11.6 (China, Shanghai)	0.4 (Australia, New South Wales)	29.0
Pancreas	16.4 (USA, Los Angeles)[e]	0.9 (India, Madras)	18.2	9.4 (USA, Alameda)[d]	1.3 (India, Bombay)	7.2
Larynx	17.8 (Brazil, Sao Paulo)	2.2 (Japan, Miyagi)	8.1	2.7 (USA, Connecticut)[d]	0.2 (Japan, Miyagi)	13.5
Lung	111.0 (USA, New Orleans)[d]	5.8 (India, Madras)	19.0	68.1 (New Zealand)[f]	1.2 (India, Madras)	56.8
Melanoma	30.9 (Australia, Queensland)	0.2 (Japan, Osaka)	154.5	28.5 (Australia, Queensland)	0.2 (India, Bombay)	142.5
Other skin	167.2 (Australia, Tasmania)	0.9 (India, Madras)	185.8	89.3 (Australia, Tasmania)	0.6 (Switzerland, Zurich)	148.8
Breast	3.4 (Brazil, Recife)	0.2 (Finland)	17.0	93.9 (USA, Hawaii)[g]	14.0 (Israel)[h]	6.7
Cervix uteri				24.6 (German Dem. Rep.)	5.5 (Finland)	4.5
Corpus uteri				25.7 (USA, San Francisco Bay Area)[c]	4.4 (Romania, Ciuj County)	5.8
Ovary				15.3 (Norway)	5.4 (Spain, Zaragoza)	2.8
Prostate	70.2 (USA, Utah)	9.8 (Romania, Ciuj Country)	7.2			
Testis	8.3 (Switzerland, Basel)	1.1 (Spain, Tarragona)	7.5			
Penis	1.7 (USA, New Mexico)[i]	0.5 (Finland)	3.4			
Bladder	27.8 (Switzerland, Basel)	7.7 (Hungary, Vas)	3.6	7.4 (USA, Connecticut)[c]	1.2 (Hungary, Vas)	6.2
Kidney	12.2 (Iceland)	1.7 (Romania, Ciuj County)	8.8	7.6 (Iceland)	1.3 (Romania, Ciuj County)	5.8
Brain	9.2 (USA, Los Angeles)[c]	2.4 (Hungary, Szaboics)	3.8	10.0 (Iceland)	1.3 (Hungary, Szaboics)	7.7
Thyroid	5.6 (Iceland)	0.4 (Poland, Warsaw)	14.0	13.3 (Iceland)	1.3 (Poland, Warsaw City)	10.0
Hodgkin's disease	4.8 (Canada, Quebec)	1.0 (Hungary, Szaboics)	4.8	3.9 (Switzerland, Neuchâtel)	0.6 (Canada, Newfoundland)	6.5
Non-Hodgkin's lymphoma	11.5 (Switerland, Vaud)	2.4 (Hungary, Szaboics)	4.8	8.7 (USA, San Francisco Bay Area)[c]	1.0 (Hungary, Szaboics)	8.7
Multiple myeloma	5.7 (Australian Capital Territory)	1.1 (Poland, Warsaw City)	5.2	3.2 (Switzerland, Neuchâtel)	0.7 (Ireland, southern)	4.6
Leukaemia	11.6 (Canada, Ontario)	3.0 (Hungary, Szaboics)	3.9	8.0 (Italy, Varese)	2.7 (Hungary, Szaboics)	3.0

a Number of cases per 10^5 population.
b Kuwaitis.
c Whites.
d Blacks.
e Koreans.
f Maoris.
g Hawaiians.
h Non-Jews.
i Hispanics.

Source:
Tomatis L. (Ed.) 1990 *Cancer: Causes, Occurrence and Control,* IARC Scientific Publications No. 100, International Agency for Research on Cancer, Lyon.

Table 5.18 Theoretical preventability and estimated reduction in risk for cancers at selected sites

Site	Estimated no. of cases world-wide (1980)	Difference between highest and lowest recorded incidences (%) Male/Female	Preventative measures	Regions or countries to which data apply	Potential reduction in incidence or mortality
Oral cavity & pharynx	378,500	85/88	Elimination of tobacco smoking and chewing Elimination of tobacco smoking and reduction in alcohol consumption Avoidance of salted fish (for nasopharynx)	Asia Europe, Americas Southern Chinese populations	60–80% 60–80% 10–90%
Oesophagus	310,400	96/94	Elimination of tobacco smoking and reduction in alcohol consumption General improvement in nutrition	USA, Caribbean, southern Europe India Central Asia, China	75% 35% Uncertain
Stomach	669,400	36/85	High consumption of fresh vegetables and fruit Screening by photofluorography	World-wide Japan	Up to 50%[a] Up to 50%[a,b]
Colon/rectum	572,100	80/80	Low fat and animal protein consumption; high vegetable consumption Screening by proctosigmoidoscopy or for occult blood in faeces	Western countries Western countries	Up to 35%[a] Uncertain[b]
Liver	251,200	93/90	Vaccination against hepatitis B virus Reduction of aflatoxin contamination Reduction of alcohol consumption	Sub-Sahara Africa, south-east Asia Sub-Sahara Africa, south-east Asia Western countries	70%[a] 40%[a] 15%[a]
Pancreas	137,400	70/73	Elimination of tobacco smoking	World-wide	30%
Larynx	120,000	84/87	Elimination of tobacco smoking and reduction in alcohol consumption	World-wide	85%
Lung	660,500	75/92	Elimination of tobacco smoking Elimination of certain occupational exposures Reduction of air pollution	World-wide Industrialized countries Industrialized countries and large urban areas	80–90% males 60–80% females[c] 10% Uncertain
Skin (melanoma)	70,000	96/95	Reduction in recreational sun exposure Use of sun-screens Surveillance of high-risk groups	Europe, North America Australia/New Zealand Europe, North America Australia/New Zealand	>40% Uncertain[b]
Skin (non-melanoma)	Unknown	97/99	Reduction in sun exposure	Europe, North America Australia/New Zealand	Uncertain, but high

Continued over

Table 5.18 Continued

Site	Estimated no. of cases world-wide (1980)	Difference between highest and lowest recorded incidences (%) Male/Female	Preventative measures	Regions or countries to which data apply	Potential reduction in incidence or mortality
Breast	572,100	NA/79	Low fat and animal protein consumption Weight reduction for the obese Screening by mammography every two years at 50 or more years of age	Western countries World-wide Western countries	Uncertain 10%[d] 35–40%[b,d]
Cervix	465,600	NA/78	Elimination of tobacco smoking Reduction in high parity Use of barrier contraceptives Reduction in infection of sexually transmitted diseases Cytological screening: 3 yearly at ages 35–64 10 yearly at ages 35–64	Western countries Developing countries World-wide World-wide	Uncertain 30%[a] Uncertain 50% 80% 55%
Endometrium	148,800	NA/83	Weight reduction for the obese Elimination of post-menopausal oestrogens	World-wide USA, Europe	25% 40%[e]
Ovary	137,600	NA/65	Uncertain		f
Prostrate	235,800	86/NA	Uncertain		
Bladder	219,400	72/84	Elimination of tobacco smoking Elimination of certain occupational exposures Elimination of schistosomal infection	World-wide Industrialized countries Africa, eastern Mediterranean	30–70% 10–20% 50%
Kidney	100,000	86/83	Elimination of tobacco smoking	Western countries	30–40%
Lymphoma	237,900	79/87	Control of malaria	Sub-Saharan Africa	25%[a]
Leukaemia	188,200	74/66	Avoidance of unnecessary exposure to radiation and of exposure to benzene	World-wide	Uncertain

a   Estimates very approximate.
b   Refers to reduction in mortality only (no change in incidence).
c   Uncertain (but less) for women in China.
d   Women over 50 years of age.
e   Reduction in relation to a situation of the 1960s and 1970s.
f   Evidence of a reduced risk following use of combined oral contraceptives.

NA = Not applicable.

The difference between the highest and lowest recorded incidence is the difference between the incidences expressed as a percentage of the highest incidence. See also Table 5.17. Western countries are those in Western Europe, Canada, USA, Australia and New Zealand.

Source:
Tomatis, L. (Ed.) 1990 Cancer: Causes, Occurrence and Control, IARC Scientific Publications No. 100, International Agency for Research on Cancer, Lyon.

Table 5.19   Major chemical accidents/incidents, 1980–1988

Year	Country	Location	Type of accident/incident	Chemical(s) involved	Deaths	Injuries[a]	Evacuated[b]
1980	Canada	Ocean Ranger	Turnover of platform	Petrol	84	0	0
	France	Lyon	Waste treatment		2	170	
	India	Mandir Asod	Plant explosion	Explosives	50		
		Raipur	Explosion	Fireworks	>40	>11	
			Plant explosion	Explosives	40		
	Iran	DehBos Org	Fire, explosion	Dynamite	80	43	
	Japan	Shizuoka	Explosion	Propane	14	199	0
	Malaysia	Port Kelang	Explosion/fire	Ammonia, oxyacetylene	3	200	>3,000
	Norway	Alexander Kjelland	Turnover of platform	Petrol	123	0	0
	Spain	Ortuella	Explosion	Explosives	51		
	Thailand	Bangkok	Armament explosion	Explosives	54		
	Turkey	Danacuiobasi		Butane	107	0	0
	UK	Barking	Plant fire	Sodium cyanide		12	3,500
	USA	Alaska	Platform fire	Petrol	51	0	0
		Garland	Derailment	Styrene		5	8,600
		Muldraugh	Derailment	Vinyl chloride		4	6,500
		New York City	Road accident	Propane	0	0	5,000
		Newark	Rail accident (fire)	Ethylene oxide			4,000
		Sommerville	Rail accident	Phosphorus trichloride		343	23,000
		Texas	Rail accident	Styrene monomer		5	8,600
1981	Brazil	San Juan	Leakage	Chlorine	0	2,000	0
	Mexico	Montana	Derailment	Chlorine	29	1,000	5,000
	Puerto Rico	San Juan	Rupture in factory	Chlorine		200	2,000
	Spain	Madrid[c]	Food contamination (oil)	Unknown	340	20,000[d]	
	USA	Castaic	Plant	Propylene		100	
		Fraser	Transport accident	Chlorine	0	0	6,000
		Gelsmar	Plant	Chlorine		140	
		San Francisco	Road accident	Silicon tetrachloride	0	0	7,000
			Road accident (leakage)	Nitric acid	0	0	15,000
	Venezuela	Tacoa	Explosion	Oil	145	1,000[d]	
	Viet Nam	Saigon	Contaminated product (talcum powder)	Warfarin	177[e]	564[e]	
1982	Australia	Melbourne	Transport accident	Butadiene	0	>1,000	0
	Canada		Rail accident	Hydrofluoric acid	0	0	1,200
	Italy	Todi	Application		34	140	
	Japan	Sakai	Explosion	Acrylonitrile	4	80	5,000
	USA	Gulfport	Fire	Petrol, inorganic acids	3	80	5,000
		Livingston	Rail accident	Various chemicals			3,000

Continued over

Table 5.19 Continued

Year	Country	Location	Type of accident/incident	Chemical(s) involved	Deaths	Injuries[a]	Evacuated[b]
		Taft	Explosion	Acrolein			17,000
		Vernon	Plant	Methyl acrylate		355	
			Rail accident (leakage)	Chlorosulphonic acid	0	0	5,000
			Process failure	Chlorine	0	126	0
	Venezuela	Caracas	Tank explosion	Explosives	101	1,000	
		Tacoa	Tank explosion	Hydrocarbons	145	1,000	40,000
1983	Brazil	Pojuca	Fire, explosion	Petrol	42		>1,000
	Egypt	Nile River	Explosion	Natural gas	317	44	0
	India	Dhurabari	Fire	Oil	76	>60	0
	Nicaragua	Corinto	Tank explosion	Oil			23,000
	Turkey	Armutcuk	Mine explosion		98	86	
		Istanbul	Application		42	50	
	USA	Denver	Rail accident	Nitric acid		43	2,000
1984	Brazil	Cubatao	Pipeline explosion	Petrol	89		2,500
		Sao Paulo	Pipeline explosion	Petrol	508	3	
		Southern region	Explosion in coal mine		934		0
	Canada	Ontario	Release	Chlorine	0	0	9,000
	India	Bhopal	Leakage	Methyl isocyanate	2,988	100,000	200,000
	Indonesia	Jakarta	Fire	Ammunition	>14	>200	10
	Mexico	Matamoras	Fertilizer factory	Ammonia		200	3,000
		St J. Ixhuatepec	Tank explosion	Natural gas	452	4,248	31,000
	Pakistan	Garhi Dhoda	Gaspipe explosion	Natural gas	60		
	Peru	Callao	Pipeline explosion				3,000
	Romania			Various chemicals	100	100	
	USA	Binghamton	Rail accident	Butane	0	0	5,000
		Linden	Plant	Malathion		161	
		Middleport	Plant	Methyl isocyanate		110	
		Sauget	Plant	Phosphorus oxychloride		125	
			Leakage (storage)	Nitric acid	0	0	10,000
	USSR	Severomorsk	Explosion	Ammunition	200		
		Tbilisi	Explosion	Natural gas	100		0
1985	Brazil	Cubatao	Leakage	Ammonia	0	0	5,000
	China	Chungking	Explosion in sewer pipe		24	92	
	France	Forbach	Explosion in mine		22	103	0
	India	Cochin	Leakage	Hexacyclopentadiene	0	200	0
		Karnataka	Tanker crash, explosion	Petrol	39	80	
		New Delhi	Leakage	Sulphuric acid	1	340	10
		Padaval	Fire	Petrol	>43	82	
		Tamil Nadu	Transport accident	Petrol	60	0	0
	Italy	Napoli	Storage fire	Petrol	4	200	0
		Priolo	Leakage	Propylene	0	0	>20,000

Continued opposite

Table 5.19   Continued

Year	Country	Location	Type of accident/incident	Chemical(s) involved	Deaths	Injuries[a]	Evacuated[b]
	Mexico	Guadalajara	Rail accident (leakage)	Sulphuric acid	0	49	5,000
	Spain	Algeciras	Trans-shipment		33	34	
	USA	Anaheim	Fire	Pesticides	0	12	10,000
		Coachella	Fire	Pesticides	0	236	2,000
		Institute	Leakage	Aldicarboxime		140	
		Peabody	Plant	Benzene	1	125	
1986	Canada	Hinton	Rail accident		40	90	
		Ontario	Transport accident	Petrol	0	0	5,000
	Italy	Naples		Petrol	5	150	2,000
	Mexico	Cardenas	Pipeline leakage	Natural gas	0	2	>20,000
	Switzerland	Basel	Warehouse fire	Various chemicals			
	UK	Hemel Hempstead	Road accident	Lead oxide	0	150	0
	USA	Lynchburg	Transport accident	Phosphorus oxychloride		125	
		Miamisburg	Fire (rail accident)	Phosphoric acid	0	140	40,000
		St Petersburg	Fire	Chlorine	0	90	7,000
			Leakage	Ammonia	0	52	8,000
	USSR	Chernobyl[f]	Reactor explosion	Radionuclides	29	300	135,000
1987	Brazil	Goiana	Abandoned cancer-treatment device	Radionuclides	2	241	0
	China	Guangxi provice		Methyl alcohol	55	3,600	
		Shanzi	Drinking water contamination	Ammonium bicarbonate	0	15,400	
	Egypt	Alexandria	Explosion	Smoke bombs	6	460	1,000
	France	Nantes	Fire	Fertilizers	0	24	25,000
	Guatemala	Puerto Camperiico	Clam contamination	Toxic waste	22		
	India	Bhopal	Industry, panic	Ammonia	0	0	200,000
	Mexico	Minatitlan	Process failure	Acrylonitrile		>200	10,000s
	USA	Miamisburg	Rail accident	Red phosphorus		569	30,000
		Minot	Fire	Parathion	0	20	10,000
		Nantichoke	Fire	Sulphuric acid	0	0	18,000
		Salt Lake City	Industry	Ammonia	1	0	30,000
		Texas City	Process failure	Hydrofluoric acid	0	540	3,000
		Wilcon country	Rail accident	Sulphuric acid	0	0	3,000
	USSR	Annau	Rail accident	Chlorine	0	200	
1988	Canada	Quebec	Plant fire	Toxic smoke (PCBs)			3,500
	China	Liu Pan Shui	Explosion	Coal gas	45	5	
		Shanghai	Explosion, refinery	Petrochemicals	25		
			Explosion	Natural gas	45	23	
	France	St Avold	Explosion	Various chemicals			
		Tours	Leakage	Various chemicals	0	3	200,000
	India	Bombay	Fire at refinery	Oil	32		

Continued over

Table 5.19 Continued

Year	Country	Location	Type of accident/incident	Chemical(s) involved	Deaths	Injuries[a]	Evacuated[b]
	Mexico	Chihuahua	Explosion (storage)	Petrol	0	7	150,000
		Guadalupe	Explosion (storage)	Crude oil	20		200,000
		Mexico City	Explosion	Fireworks	62	87	
	Pakistan	Islamabad	Explosion (storage)	Explosives	>100	3,000	
	Singapore		Food contamination	Pesticides	0	105	0
	UK	North Sea	Explosion, fire (platform)	Oil, gas	167		
	USA	California	Chemical plant (leakage)	Chlorine gas			20,000
		Henderson	Explosion, fire	Perchlorinated ammonia	2	250	640
		Los Angeles	Process failure	Chlorine		37	20,000
		Springfield	Leakage, fire	Chlorine	0	275	20,000
	USSR	Arzamas	Explosion, rail accident	Explosives	73	720	90,000
		Shakhunya	Rail car fire	Herbicides			20,000
		Sverdlovsk	Explosion, rail accident	Explosives	4	500	
	Yugoslavia	Sibanik	Process failure, fire	Fertilizer	0	0	60,000

[a] Or affected in cases of poisonings.
[b] Majority of data are approximations.
[c] Deaths and injuries continued into 1982.
[d] Approximation.
[e] Infants.
[f] Accompanied by widespread contamination of livestock and crops.

Accidents/incidents listed are those which have caused at least 50 deaths or injuries and/or 1,000 evacuated.
Accidents/incidents associated with the *use* of pesticides or drugs are not included.
Figures for number of injuries do not include numbers of deaths.
Incidents need not be of accidental origin and commonly result from ignorance or malpractice (e.g., uncontrolled chemical waste disposal or misuse of chemicals).

Sources:
Buffler, P. A., Crane, M. and Key, M. M. 1985 Possibilities of detecting health effects by studies of populations exposed to chemicals from waste disposal sites, *Environmental Health Perspectives* **62**, 423–456.

Guha-Sapir, D. 1990 Personal communication, (data from The Centre for Research on the Epidemiology of Disasters (CRED) Database), CRED, Brussels, Belgium.
Krishna Murti, C. R. 1988 A systems approach to the control of chemical disasters. In: *Risk Assessment of Chemicals in the Environment*, M. L. Richardson (Ed.), Royal Society of Chemistry, UK.
OECD 1987 *OECD Environmental Data Compendium 1987* (and subsequent edition), Organisation for Economic Co-operation and Development, Paris.
UNEP 1989 *United Nations Environment Programme Environmental Data Report*, Basil Blackwell, Oxford.
UNEP 1989 *UNEP NEWS* (and earlier editions), United Nations Environment Programme, Nairobi.
WHO 1987 *Environmental Epidemiology Bibliography on Health Effects of Environmental Hazards in Developing Countries*, World Health Organization, Geneva.

Part 6
Energy

Energy is a requirement of life. Fuel for cooking, lighting and heating, and energy for transport and industry are the corner-stones upon which national economies and living standards are built. However, the production, transportation, conversion and consumption of energy are the root cause of some of the world's most serious environmental problems.

The environmental impacts of fossil fuel combustion are of major concern; the long-range transport of waste gas emissions have extended the range of impacts from local to regional (acidic deposition) and even to global (climatic change) scales. Combustion of fossil fuels contributes a large proportion of global anthropogenic emissions of carbon dioxide (55–80 per cent), sulphur dioxide (90 per cent) and nitrogen oxides (85 per cent)

(IEA, 1990). Fossil fuel combustion is also a significant source of atmospheric emissions of some trace metals. More detailed data on anthropogenic emissions of these pollutants are given in Part 1: Environmental Pollution, Atmosphere.

As in previous editions, this section of the 'UNEP Environmental Data Report' includes data tables on reserves, production and consumption of commercial energy. Tables on the production and capacity of selected renewable forms of energy, including hydraulic, tidal, solar, wind and geothermal energy and on alcohol fuels, are also presented.

Although there is no single focal point for energy concerns within the United Nations (UN) system, a number of UN bodies undertake programme activities in this field.

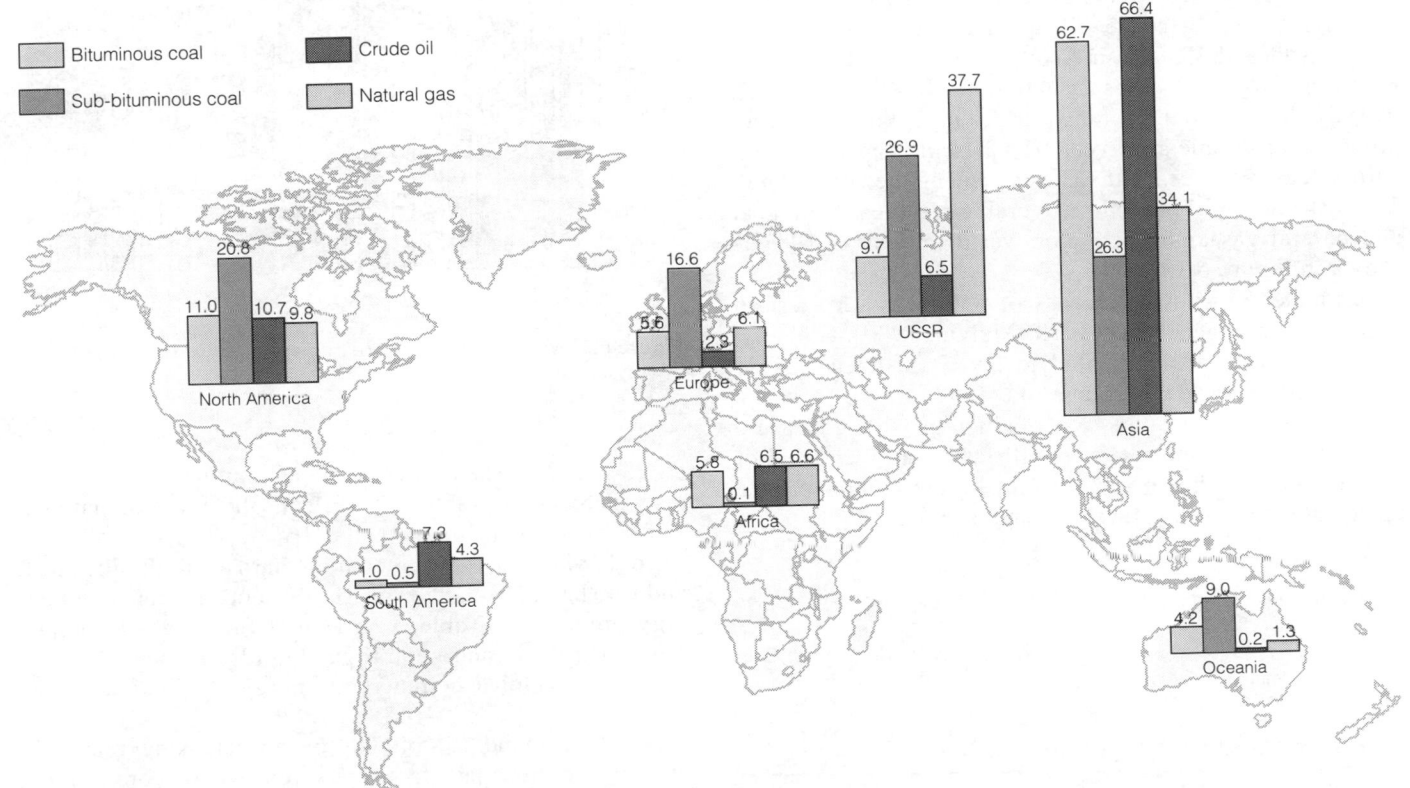

Figure 6.1 Distribution of proved recoverable reserves of commercial energy resources among major world regions, 1987 (expressed as a percentage of global reserves)
Source: data from Table 6.1

These include, for example, the United Nations Development Programme (UNDP), the United Nations Statistical Office (UNSO) and the International Atomic Energy Agency (IAEA). The UNEP Collaborating Centre on Energy and the Environment is based at the Risø National Laboratory in Denmark. Other international organizations involved in the collection and dissemination of information relating to energy include the World Energy Council (WEC), formerly the World Energy Conference, and the International Energy Agency (IEA).

References

IEA 1990 *Energy and the Environment: Policy Overview*, Organisation for Economic Co-operation and Development, Paris.

Energy Resources

National estimates of proved recoverable energy resources as assessed in 1987 are given in Table 6.1 for bituminous coal/anthracite, sub-bituminous coal/lignite, crude oil and natural gas liquids (NGL), natural gas and uranium. Data on energy resources are compiled and published on a regular basis by the WEC from questionnaires to member countries, supplemented with data from earlier WEC surveys and from other expert sources (WEC, 1989).

In terms of tonnage, coal accounts for the largest proportion of non-renewable energy reserves. China has the largest reserves, with nearly 731×10^9 t, followed by the USSR with 241×10^9 t, and the USA with 215×10^9 t. The largest reserves of crude oil and natural gas liquids are found in the USSR and in Asia, especially in the Middle East. The largest reserves of natural gas are in the USSR; in 1987 these accounted for 38 per cent of the total world proved recoverable reserves. Iran has the second largest natural gas reserves, with 13 per cent of the world total. The distribution of proved recoverable reserves of oil, coal and natural gas amongst major world regions in 1987 is shown in Figure 6.1.

Estimates of known reserves of natural gas have risen regularly every year since 1970 (Melvin, 1989). Globally, proved reserves are estimated to be of sufficient size to allow production to continue at the 1987 rate for 55 years. Reserve/production ratios (R/P), which provide a measure of the length of time reserves will last at a given level of production, are shown for 1987 in Figure 6.2 for proved reserves of coal, oil, natural gas and uranium.

References

Melvin, A. 1989 Gas taps its natural flare, *New Scientist* **124**(1685), 59–61.
WEC 1989 *1989 Survey of Energy Resources*, World Energy Conference, London.

Production and Consumption

National data on production and consumption of commercial energy according to fuel type for 1987 are presented in Table 6.2. Such data are compiled by the UNSO and are published regularly as the 'Energy Statistics Yearbook'

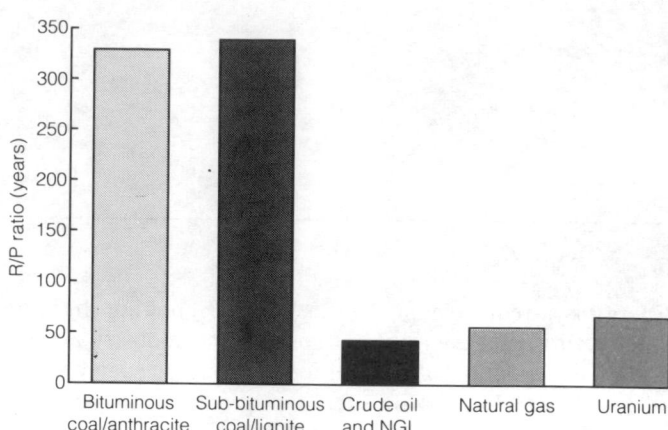

Figure 6.2 World reserve/production (R/P) ratios, 1987
Source: data from Tables 6.1 and 6.2

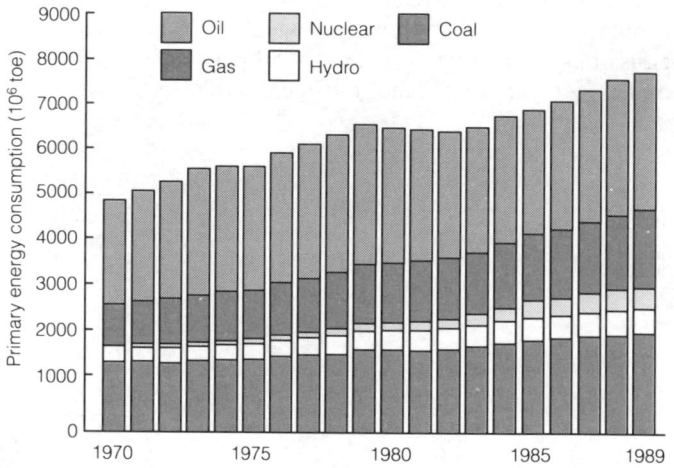

Figure 6.3 World consumption of primary energy, 1970–1989
Source: BP, 1990

(UNSO, 1989). The production/consumption ratio, which is also included in Table 6.2, reflects the level of national self-sufficiency in commercial energy.

In 1987 solid fuels, including hard coal, lignite, peat and oil shale, accounted for 31 per cent of total world energy production (Table 6.2). Liquid fuels, which include crude petroleum and natural gas liquids, accounted for 41 per cent of global commercial energy production (Table 6.2).

World demand for oil has been increasing relatively slowly over the past five years relative to consumption patterns for other energy sources (Figure 6.3). Oil is being displaced in electricity production and the industrial sector by nuclear energy, coal and natural gas, and for household and tertiary uses by natural gas, electricity and coal

(WEC, 1989). However, oil remains the major energy source for transportation.

Production and utilization of natural gas is expected to increase in coming decades as a result of mounting concern about global warming (for the same thermal energy production coal combustion releases approximately 75 per cent more CO_2 than that of natural gas) and continued discoveries of reserves. Global production levels of 1.65 giga tonnes of oil equivalent (Gtoe) in 1987 are expected to rise to 2.1 Gtoe by the year 2000 (WEC, 1989). Since the 1970s networks for trading in natural gas have expanded, especially through the building of pipelines (Melvin, 1989; WEC, 1989). The increasing importance of natural gas as a proportion of world consumption of primary energy since 1970 is evident from Figure 6.3.

Coal is one of the most widely used fuels for electricity production, supplying 44 per cent of the world's electricity requirements (WEC, 1989). Pollution from coal combustion is a major environmental concern. Increasingly, coal-fired power plants are being fitted with flue gas desulphurization (FGD) equipment in order to cut emissions of SO_2. The number of operational units has risen from seven in 1972 to 501 in 1989 (Soud, 1990). However, FGD installations are limited to 12 countries (mainly in North America, Japan and Western Europe) and account for only a small proportion of total electricity generation (Soud, 1990).

Figure 6.4 shows differences in regional per capita energy consumption in toe in 1969, 1979 and in 1989. Many countries are becoming aware of the need to reduce per capita energy consumption, particularly through increasing energy efficiency. Energy efficiency benefits not only the environment but can also have cost-saving effects. In Brazil, a study of the electrical sector found that for a total investment of US$ 10 billion in more energy-efficient technologies it would be feasible to defer construction of 22,000 MW of electrical capacity, resulting in net capital savings of US$ 34 billion in the period 1986–2000 (Goldemberg and Marcovitch, 1989).

Per capita energy consumption is a crude indicator of energy efficiency. An alternative indicator is energy intensity; i.e., the total primary energy requirement divided by gross domestic product (GDP) or toe per US$ 1,000 of gross national product (GNP) at constant 1980 prices. Energy intensity data for selected countries were discussed in more detail in the 1989 edition of this report (UNEP, 1989).

References

BP 1990 *Statistical Review of World Energy*, British Petroleum Company, London.

Goldemberg, J. and Marcovitch, J. 1989 Energy policy in Brazil and the Latin American countries, *Interciencia* **14**(5), 258–263.

Melvin, A. 1989 Gas taps its natural flare, *New Scientist* **124**(1685), 59–61.

Soud, H. 1990 Personal communication, International Energy Agency Coal Research, London, UK.

UNEP 1989 *United Nations Environment Programme Environmental Data Report*, Basil Blackwell, Oxford.

UNSO 1989 *1987 Energy Statistics Yearbook*, United Nations, New York.

WEC 1989 *1989 Survey of Energy Resources*, World Energy Conference, London.

Nuclear Power Reactors

Table 6.3 illustrates the status of nuclear power generation in 1989. Globally, there are a total of 426 operational reactors. In 1988, these reactors generated nearly 17 per cent of the world's total electricity (IAEA, 1989). Figure 6.5 shows the increase in nuclear electricity generation in terawatt hours and as a percentage of total electricity generation over the 1960–1988 period. Between 1970–1980 nuclear electricity generation experienced an average annual growth of 24 per cent, and between 1980–1985 an

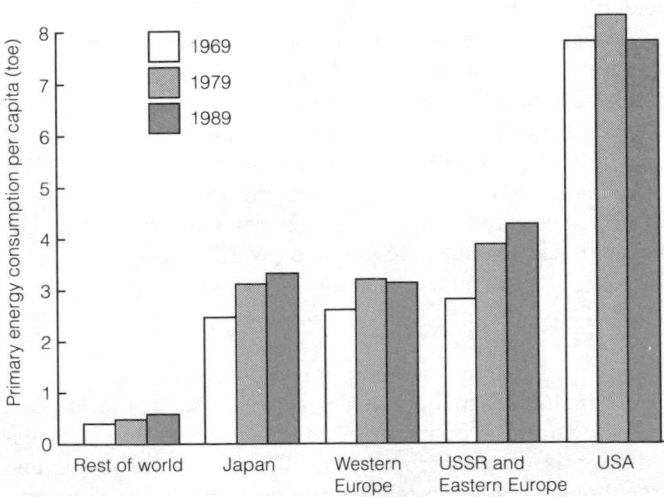

Figure 6.4 Energy consumption per capita, 1969, 1979 and 1989
Source: BP, 1990

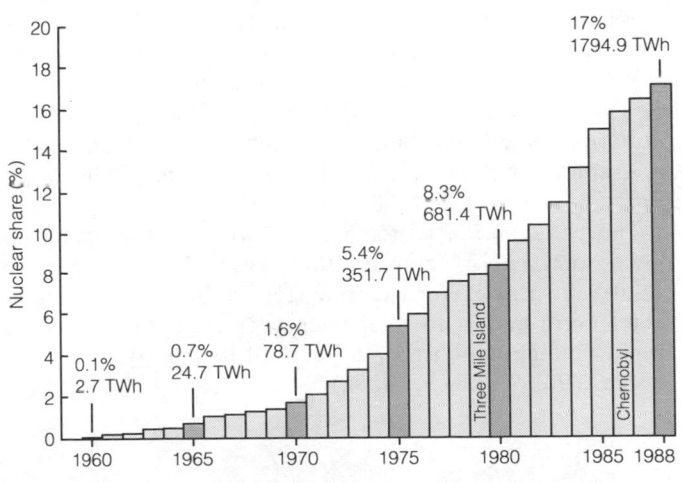

Figure 6.5 Nuclear electricity generation, 1960–1988
Source: IAEA, 1989

average annual growth of 16.4 per cent (IAEA, 1989). The period between 1985 and 1988 saw a further fall in the average annual growth, to 7.2 per cent, reflecting the decrease in the number of new reactors built since the early 1980s (IAEA, 1989).

The nuclear fuel cycle gives rise to several environmental concerns. Mining and milling of uranium releases radon, and the tailings from the mining process can leak into ground water. The effects on human health of exposure to radiation from the nuclear power generation cycle is an issue of considerable public concern, particularly since accidents occurred at Three Mile Island in 1979 and Chernobyl in 1986. However, the probability of such occurrences is relatively low. Disposal of nuclear waste can also have long-term adverse environmental effects (see Part 8: Wastes).

References

IAEA 1989 *Nuclear Power and Fuel Cycle: Status and Trends 1989*, International Atomic Energy Agency, Vienna.

IAEA 1990 *Energy, Electricity and Nuclear Power Estimates for the Period up to 2005*, International Atomic Energy Agency, Vienna.

Renewable Energy

Public and political concerns about the contribution of commercial energy sources to environmental problems have encouraged countries to focus increasingly on renewable forms of energy. In terms of pollution and use of finite resources, renewable energy sources generally impact on the environment to a lesser extent and are thus widely viewed as important alternatives to commercial sources insofar as environmental protection is concerned. Nevertheless, different forms of renewable energy have their own specific environmental impacts associated with their use.

Data on most forms of renewable energy are routinely compiled by the WEC. Tables 6.4–6.11 summarize available data on capacity and production of a range of renewable forms of energy, including hydraulic, tidal, solar, wind and geothermal. Data on biomass fuels were provided in the 1989 edition of this report (UNEP, 1989). Statistical data on these resources are generally limited and difficult to compile due to various reporting methods used by individual countries. More detailed data on exploitation methods and research and development programmes within individual countries are given in the source document (WEC, 1989).

The contribution of renewable forms of energy to national total energy consumption varies from country to country. In Brazil, for example, renewables make a significant contribution to total energy consumption; in 1986 Brazil obtained almost 60 per cent of its energy from such sources (Pollock Shea, 1988a).

Hydraulic Energy

The WEC defines hydraulic energy as energy which is produced as the result of the natural accumulation of water in streams or reservoirs being channelled through water wheels or water turbines (WEC, 1989). Table 6.4 provides data on the capacity and production of existing and planned hydraulic energy schemes with a capacity of over 1 megawatt (MW). Hydroelectricity supplied about 21 per cent of total electricity produced world-wide in 1989 (Brown et al., 1989).

One of the main attractions of hydraulic power is its low operational cost once the project has been built, although initial costs can be high (WEC, 1989). Hydraulic energy can be of benefit in developing countries as small hydroelectric projects can supply electricity to local communities, reducing the need for connections to national grids. Large developments can, however, potentially provide a substantial proportion of a nation's total energy needs. Despite having considerable hydroelectric resources, the lack of investment capital often inhibits development of hydraulic power schemes in many developing countries.

Hydroelectric power is not without adverse environmental effects. Land use conflicts can result from the construction of new dams: farmland and forest can be submerged, communities displaced, flora and fauna habitats destroyed, and the deviation of water courses can change both upstream and downstream environments (Pollock Shea, 1988a). However, small hydroelectric plants generally do not face the same environmental problems as large ones, and may even contribute to local water management efforts (Christensen, 1991).

Tidal Energy

The global applications of tidal energy are limited. Tidal power plants can only be situated where there are large tidal movements and where physical features allow construction of tidal basins at relatively low costs. Capital costs tend to be high and construction times are typically long (WEC, 1989). Table 6.5 shows the number of existing or planned tidal power plants, and their installed or expected capacity.

Research is being carried out to gain a better understanding of the environmental impacts of large tidal power plants. Potential impacts include reduced tidal range and reduced tidal flow (Pollock Shea, 1988b). Construction of tidal power plants may cause damage to coastlines. Concerns have been raised about fish mortality in the Bay of Fundy in Canada, and in the Severn Estuary in the UK where major schemes are planned (WEC, 1989).

Solar Energy

There are several methods for collecting solar energy. These include dispersed active systems, such as flat plate and vacuum tube collectors, and solar ponds. Passive solar radiation is used in crop drying, heating of buildings, and greenhouses. Photovoltaic energy systems are used to produce electricity from solar radiation using photovoltaic cells. Photovoltaic cells consist of materials which absorb light and convert it directly to electricity. Table 6.6 presents data on the installed capacity and production of solar energy using photovoltaic and thermo-electrical methods in selected countries.

Solar energy is particularly suitable for electricity generation in many developing countries. However, cost is an inhibiting factor. Electricity generated by solar energy is still more expensive than that produced by conventional means, although significant developments and cost reductions are foreseen in the next couple of decades (Christensen, 1991).

Geothermal Energy

Tables 6.7 and 6.8 show the capacity and production of geothermal energy in selected countries in 1989. Electricity can be generated from geothermal sources in two ways – by harnessing hot water and steam from areas which are volcanically active, or by drilling through to igneous rock and pouring water onto the hot rock, thus producing steam. Geothermal electricity production is therefore practicable only in areas prone to volcanic or tectonic activity.

Electricity generation from geothermal sources tends to be less efficient than that from other sources of energy. Energy losses of up to 90 per cent may occur unless the heat is used directly in buildings or greenhouses (Foley, 1987). Pollution from elements released in the process of converting geothermal energy to electricity is potentially damaging to natural watercourses. Damage can be avoided by reinjecting water into the zone from which it has been taken, a process which adds to the cost of operations (Foley, 1987).

For various reasons, direct use of geothermal energy is difficult to quantify. Complicating factors include the small size of some projects, the fact that some countries have numerous projects which are often managed by different organizations, discrepancies between design data and operating data, and different methods of reporting (WEC, 1989).

Wind Energy

Over 100,000 wind machines (with a total capacity in excess of 2,500 MW) have been constructed during the 15 years up to 1989. Of this capacity, 1500 MW represent electrical capacity, with the remaining 1000 MW utilized directly by water pumping machines, corn grinding and other mechanical applications (WEC, 1989). Table 6.9 provides data on the number of wind turbines constructed world-wide from 1981 to 1986. Table 6.10 presents national data on wind power capacity in 1989.

Although suitable wind regions are available in most parts of the world, their value as a resource depends on wind variation (hour, day, season) and reliability. In order to assess their potential, detailed studies of the specific sites and of local meteorological data need to be conducted. Good wind positions are usually found along coastlines, mountain passes and in "open" areas. In some

areas, however, land use conflicts may be of potential concern, especially for large-scale applications. Other environmental concerns include noise emissions and visual impact, and safety hazards due to mechanical failure (Pasztor et al., 1988).

Alcohol Fuels

Alcohol fuels, for example methanol and ethanol, are increasing in popularity, especially in developing countries (Rosillo Calle, 1990). Ethanol fuels are made by fermentation and at present, sugar cane (in Brazil and other developing countries) and corn (in the USA) are the two main sources. Ethanol fuels have a number of applications including electricity generation and as a petroleum substitute in the transport sector especially when blended with diesel, and as an octane enhancer/booster. Brazil has pioneered the application of ethanol fuels to power vehicle transport. Methanol fuels can be produced by either the distillation of wood or by a synthetic distillation processes. Methanol is also used as a substitute for, or as an additive to, transportation fuels, although it is generally less popular than ethanol.

Table 6.11 provides data on world-wide production and capacity of ethanol fuels in 1984. It is estimated that global fermentation ethanol capacity has increased eightfold since 1977 (Rosillo Calle, 1990).

Although alcohol fuels offer a number of environmental benefits (for example, combustion of ethanol fuels produces less carbon monoxide and hydrocarbons per unit energy produced than, say, oil), a number of detrimental impacts are recognized. These include the possibility of soil damage due to long-term agricultural production, adverse effects on ecosystems, local air and water pollution problems, and possible occupational hazards (Rosillo Calle, 1990).

References

Brown, L., Flavin, C. and Postel, S. 1989 Outlining a global action plan. In: *State of the World 1989*, L. Starke (Ed.), Worldwatch Institute, Washington DC, 174–194.

Christensen, J. 1991 Personal communication, UNEP Collaborating Centre on Energy and the Environment, Roskilde, Denmark.

Foley, G. 1987 *The Energy Question*, Penguin, London.

Pasztor, J., Christensen, J., Ndegwa, W. and Hancock, J. 1988 Environmental impacts of renewable sources of energy. Paper presented at the PAP/RAC Training Course on Renewable Energy use in the Mediterranean Region, 21 November–2 December 1988, Unpublished paper.

Pollock Shea, C. 1988a Shifting to renewable energy. In: *State of the World 1988*, L. Starke (Ed.), Worldwatch Institute, Washington DC, 62–82.

Pollock Shea, C. 1988b *Renewable Energy: Today's Contribution, Tomorrow's Promise*, Worldwatch Paper 81, Worldwatch Institute, Washington DC.

Rosillo Calle, F. 1990 Liquid fuels. In: *Bioenergy and the Environment*, J. Pasztor and L. Kristoferson (Eds), Westview Press, Oxford, 113–161.

UNEP 1989 *United Nations Environment Programme Environmental Data Report*, Basil Blackwell, Oxford.

WEC 1989 *1989 Survey of Energy Resources*, World Energy Conference, London.

Table 6.1 Commercial energy resources, 1987

Region/country	Bituminous coal/anthracite (10^6 t)	Sub-bituminous coal/lignite (10^6 t)	Crude oil and NGL (10^6 t)	Natural gas (10^9 m^3)	Uranium (10^3 t)
WORLD	1,030,283	464,454	122,876	108,612	2,356
AFRICA	62,631	279	8,033	7,225	778
Algeria	43		1,593[a]	3,000	26
Angola			156	50	
Botswana	3,500				
Cameroon			71	110	
Cent. African Rep.		4			16
Congo			98	70	
Côte d'Ivoire			16	100	
Egypt	13	40	600	290	
Ethiopia		11		24	
Gabon			130	17	19
Ghana			3		
Libya			2,865	728	
Malawi	12				
Morocco	45		<1	2	
Mozambique	240			65	
Namibia				28	110
Niger	70				173
Nigeria	21	169	2,200	2,380	
Rwanda				40	
Somalia				6	7
South Africa	55,333			28	426
Sudan			41	85	
Swaziland	1,820				
Tanzania	200			116	
Tunisia			245	85	
Zaire	600		15[a]	<1	2
Zambia		55			
Zimbabwe	734				
NORTH AMERICA	118,055	106,038	13,131	10,708	638
Barbados			<1		
Canada	3,831	3,135	960[a]	2,730	243
Guatemala			6		
Mexico	1,252	634	7,703[a]	2,119	8
Trinidad & Tobago			77	294	
USA	112,972	102,269	4,385[a]	5,565	387
SOUTH AMERICA	11,074	2,518	8,973	4,658	176
Argentina		130	308	670	12
Bolivia			22	143	
Brazil		1,245	361	105	163
Chile	31	1,150	40	120	<1
Colombia	9,666		216	110	
Ecuador		23	157	12	
Peru	960	100	75[a]	18	2
Venezuela	417		7,794	3,480	

Continued opposite

Table 6.1 Continued

Region/country	Bituminous coal/ anthracite (10^6 t)	Sub-bituminous coal/lignite (10^6 t)	Crude oil and NGL (10^6 t)	Natural gas (10^9 m³)	Uranium (10^3 t)
ASIA	674,352	134,130	81,645	36,847	56
Afghanistan	66			64	
Bahrain			45	195	
Bangladesh			<1	360	
Brunei			220		
China	610,700	120,000	2,450	870	
China, Taiwan	100	100	1	25	
India	60,648	1,900	657[a]	500	46
Indonesia	1,000	2,000	1,142	2,068	
Iran	193		13,048	13,864	
Iraq			13,600	745	
Israel			<1	<1	
Japan	856	17	6	29	7
Jordan			1	<1	
Korea	158				
Korea, Dem.	300	300			
Kuwait			12,700	1,050	
Malaysia	4		434[a]	1,462	
Myanmar q.v. Burma	2	3,700	8	268	
Oman			550	270	
Pakistan		102	13	635	
Philippines		82	2		
Qatar			430	4,440	
Saudi Arabia			22,712	3,963	
Syria			235	144	
Thailand			13[a]	105	
Turkey	175	5,929	37	25	4
United Arab Em.			13,340	5,765	
Viet Nam	150				
EUROPE	59,992	84,443	2,795	6,656	181
Albania			27	7	
Austria			11	12	
Belgium	410				
Bulgaria	30	3,700	2	5	
Czechoslovakia	1,870	3,500	4[a]	13	
Denmark			62[a]	125	
Finland					2
France	213	45	30[a]	34	62
German Dem. Rep.		21,000	<1	190	
Germany, Fed. Rep.	23,919	35,150	36	179	5
Greece		3,000	3	4	<1
Greenland					27
Hungary	596	3,865	39	125	
Ireland	5	9		26	
Italy		39	91[a]	300	5
Netherlands	497		26	1,770	
Norway		10	1,543[a]	2,773	
Poland	28,700	11,700	2[a]	130	
Portugal	3	33			9
Romania			175	235	

Continued over

Table 6.1 Continued

Region/country	Bituminous coal/ anthracite (10^6 t)	Sub-bituminous coal/lignite (10^6 t)	Crude oil and NGL (10^6 t)	Natural gas (10^9 m^3)	Uranium (10^3 t)
Spain	379	391	5[a]	14	34
Sweden		1			39
UK	3,300	500	710	630	
Yugoslavia	70	1,500	30	84	
USSR	104,000	137,000	8,000	41,080	
OCEANIA	179	47	301	1,439	526
Australia	179	45	279[a]	1,281	526
New Zealand	<1	2	22	130	
Papua New Guinea				28	

[a] Includes natural gas liquids.

NGL = Natural gas liquids.

Data for coal, crude oil, NGL and natural gas refer to proved recoverable resources, i.e., the tonnage (or volume) that can be recovered under present and expected local economic conditions with existing available technology.
Data for uranium are proved reserves, i.e., recoverable uranium that occurs in known mineral deposits of such size, grade and configuration that it could be recovered within the stated production cost ranges with currently proven mining and processing technology at a cost of less than US$ 130 per kg. Costs are expressed in terms of the US$ at 1 January 1988.
Regional and world totals do not take account of the reserves in countries for which data are not reported or are unavailable.
Totals may not equal those reported in the source document due to rounding.

Source:
WEC 1989 *1989 Survey of World Energy Resources*, World Energy Conference, London.

Table 6.2 Production and consumption of commercial energy, 1987

Region/country	Primary energy production (10^{15} J)					Energy consumption (10^{15} J and 10^9 J per capita)						P/C ratio[a]
	Total	Solids	Liquids	Gas	Electricity	Total	Solids	Liquids	Gas	Electricity	Per capita	
WORLD	292,279	91,049	123,170	66,651	13,409	281,414	91,228	109,973	66,723	13,447	87	1.05
AFRICA	16,988	4,124	10,860	1,832	172	7,347	2,979	3,031	1,166	171	10	2.31
Algeria	3,627	0	2,313	1,313	1	976	33	274	668	1	42	3.72
Angola	744		733	6	5	24	0	13	6	5	3	31.00
Benin	15		15			6		5		1	1	2.50
Burkina Faso	0	0				6		6			1	
Burundi	0	0				2		2			1	
Cameroon	368	0	360		8	85		77		8	8	4.33
Cent. African Rep.	0				0	4		4			1	
Chad	0					3		3			1	
Comoros	0				0	1		1			2	
Congo	265		264	0	1	22		21		1	12	12.05
Côte d'Ivoire	42		37		5	70		65		5	6	0.60
Djibouti						4		4			11	
Egypt	2,132		1,941	169	22	991	32	768	169	22	20	2.15
Equatorial Guinea	0				0	1		1		0	2	
Ethiopia	2				2	34	0	34		2	1	0.06
Gabon	335		326	7	2	36		27	7	2	34	9.31
Gambia	0					3		3			4	
Ghana	17		0		17	55	0	39		16	4	0.31
Guinea	1				1	14		13		1	2	0.07
Guinea-Bissau	0					2		2			2	
Kenya	8				8	67	3	55		9	3	0.12
Liberia	1				1	10	0	9		1	4	0.10
Libya	2,180		2,007	173		339	0	200	139		83	6.43
Madagascar	1				1	12		11		1	1	0.08
Malawi	2				2	8	1	5		2	1	0.25
Mali	1				1	6		5		1	1	0.17
Mauritania	0				0	42	0	42		0	23	0.06
Mauritius	1				1	17	2	14		1	16	0.12
Morocco	28	22	1	3	2	229	47	177	3	2	10	0.07
Mozambique	1	1			0	14	2	11		1	1	
Niger	2	2				10	2	8		0	2	0.20
Nigeria	2,756	4	2,600	144	8	495	3	340	144	8	5	5.57
Réunion	2				2	12		10		2	21	0.17
Rwanda	1			0	1	6		5	0	1	1	0.17

Continued over

Table 6.2 Continued

Region/country	Primary energy production (10¹⁵ J)					Energy consumption (10¹⁵ J and 10⁹ J per capita)						
	Total	Solids	Liquids	Gas	Electricity	Total	Solids	Liquids	Gas	Electricity	Per capita	P/C ratio[a]
Senegal	0					28		28			4	
Sierra Leone	0					8		8			2	
Somalia	0					12		12			2	
South Africa	3,956	3,939			17	3,154	2,686	452		16	83	1.25
Sudan	2				2	44	0	42		2	2	0.05
Tanzania	2				2	27	0	25		2	1	
Togo	0	0			0	5		4		1	2	0.07
Tunisia	226		209			146	3	113	30	0	19	1.55
Uganda	2			17	2	12		10		2	1	0.17
Zaire	76	3	54		19	61	9	34		18	2	1.25
Zambia	41	11			30	55	11	19		25	7	0.75
Zimbabwe	151	142			9	189	145	30		14	21	0.80
NORTH AMERICA	75,878	20,885	29,932	20,919	4,142	81,019	18,676	37,347	20,865	4,131	62	0.94
Barbados	4		3			11	0	10	1		43	0.36
Canada	9,739	1,394	3,699	3,229	1,417	7,518	1,055	3,027	2,177	1,259	291	1.30
Costa Rica	10				10	41		30		11	15	0.24
Cuba	38		37		0	426	5	420			42	0.09
Dominican Rep.	3			1	3	82	0	79	1	3	12	0.04
El Salvador	6				6	27		21		6	5	0.22
Guadeloupe	0					10		10			30	
Guatemala	10		8			41		39			5	0.24
Haiti	1				2	9	0	8		2	1	0.11
Honduras	3				3	26	0	22		4	6	0.12
Jamaica	0				0	74	0	74		0	31	
Martinique	0					10		10			30	
Mexico	7,316	233	5,990	1,011	82	4,129	228	2,813	1,013	75	50	1.77
Nicaragua	2				2	31		28		3	9	0.06
Panama	7				7	38	0	31	0	7	17	0.18
Puerto Rico	1				1	260	6	253		1	73	–
Trinidad & Tobago	496		338	158		207	0	49	158		169	2.40
USA	58,242	19,258	19,857	16,519	2,608	68,079	17,382	30,423	17,515	2,759	280	0.86
SOUTH AMERICA	11,704	596	8,021	2,003	1,084	8,305	652	4,495	2,012	1,146	28	1.41
Argentina	1,735	9	967	657	102	1,745	42	854	746	103	56	0.99
Bolivia	138		43	91	4	61	0	45	12	4	9	2.26
Brazil	2,151	138	1,228	114	671	3,178	408	1,924	114	732	22	0.68

Continued below

Table 6.2 Continued

Region/country	Primary energy production (10¹⁵ J)					Energy consumption (10¹⁵ J and 10⁹ J per capita)						P/C ratio[a]
	Total	Solids	Liquids	Gas	Electricity	Total	Solids	Liquids	Gas	Electricity	Per capita	
Chile	198	46	74	34	44	345	54	214	33	44	28	0.57
Colombia	1,480	397	820	171	92	717	137	317	171	92	24	2.06
Ecuador	392		373	3	16	182		163	3	16	18	2.15
Guyana	0				0	14		14		0	14	
Paraguay	10				10	32		22		10	8	0.31
Peru	437	4	368		40	342	6	271	25	40	17	1.28
Suriname	10		7		3	14	0	11		3	36	0.71
Uruguay	15				15	59	0	44		15	19	0.25
Venezuela	5,138	2	4,141	908	87	1,616	5	616	908	87	88	3.18
ASIA	73,584	27,093	37,792	6,579	2,120	61,896	30,458	22,678	6,640	2,120	89	1.19
Afghanistan	121	5		113	3	60	5	28	24	3	4	2.02
Bahrain	268		100	168		200	0	32	168		430	1.34
Bangladesh	144		5	137	2	201	1	61	137	2	2	0.72
Bhutan	0				0	0	0	0		0	1	
Brunei	680		309	371		71	0	29	42		293	9.58
Cambodia	0				0	6		6		0	1	
China	25,930	19,407	5,616	547	360	23,469	19,163	3,399	547	360	22	1.10
Cyprus	0					48	4	44			72	
Hong Kong	0					311	179	137		-5	55	
India	6,115	4,379	1,273	235	228	6,462	4,339	1,660	235	228	8	0.95
Indonesia	3,864	51	2,706	1,080	27	1,381	86	1,015	253	27	8	2.80
Iran	5,464	36	4,783	622	23	1,931	42	1,244	622	23	38	2.83
Iraq	4,423		4,275	146	2	367	0	326	39	2	22	12.05
Israel	3		1		2	359	100	258		-1	82	0.01
Japan	1,440	336	26	86	992	13,367	3,008	7,649	1,718	992	110	0.11
Jordan	1		1			117		118		-1	31	0.01
Korea	628	467			161	2,173	922	1,002	88	161	52	0.29
Korea, Dem.	1,482	1,377			105	1,698	1,457	136		105	79	0.87
Kuwait	2,919		2,719	200		501		194	307		269	5.83
Laos	4				4	4		3		1	1	1.00
Lebanon	2				2	108	0	106		2	39	0.02
Malaysia	1,525		1,030	477	18	609	14	402	175	18	38	2.50
Mongolia	88	88			0	106	72	34		0	53	0.83
Myanmar q.v. Burma	92	2	42	44	4	77	3	26	44	4	2	1.19
Nepal	2	2			2	12	2	8		2	1	0.17

Continued over

Table 6.2 Continued

Region/country	Primary energy production (10^{15} J) Total	Solids	Liquids	Gas	Electricity	Energy consumption (10^{15} J and 10^9 J per capita) Total	Solids	Liquids	Gas	Electricity	Per capita	P/C ratio[a]
Oman	1,512		1,427	85		327		242	85		245	4.62
Pakistan	543	48	85	353	57	814	71	333	353	57	7	0.67
Philippines	70	23	12		35	450	50	365		35	8	0.16
Qatar	808		624	184		209		25	184		642	3.87
Saudi Arabia	9,697		8,790	907		2,328		1,421	907		185	4.17
Singapore	0					366	0	366		0	140	
Sri Lanka	8				8	61	0	53		8	4	0.13
Syria	521		509	7	5	337	0	325	7	5	30	1.55
Thailand	343	75	89	164	15	771	83	508	164	16	14	0.44
Turkey	823	635	110	11	67	1,535	707	748	11	69	29	0.54
United Arab Em.	3,862		3,222	640		803		275	528		552	4.81
Viet Nam	164	164				217	150	60		7	3	0.76
Yemen	38		38			40		40			5	0.95
EUROPE	41,672	18,893	9,187	9,296	4,296	64,357	22,006	25,153	12,789	4,409	137	0.65
Albania	187	34	126	15	12	117	41	51	15	10	38	1.60
Austria	246	31	45	42	128	883	156	425	194	108	118	0.28
Belgium	271	117		1	153	1,616	357	807	307	145	163	0.17
Bulgaria	613	542	12	5	54	1,557	723	546	218	70	173	0.39
Czechoslovakia	1,991	1,861	6	26	98	2,879	1,848	537	384	110	185	0.69
Denmark	293		193	99	1	802	342	391	60	9	157	0.37
Finland	142	22			120	825	190	433	61	141	167	0.17
France[b]	1,966	526	154	137	1,149	6,064	865	3,106	1,051	1,042	109	0.32
German Dem. Rep.	2,812	2,671	2	92	47	3,849	2,857	614	318	60	231	0.73
Germany, Fed. Rep.	4,438	3,178	159	558	543	10,023	3,166	4,386	1,914	557	165	0.44
Greece	316	250	51	5	10	718	284	417	5	12	72	0.44
Hungary	645	253	116	236	40	1,187	351	360	398	78	112	0.54
Iceland	15				15	38	2	21		15	157	0.39
Ireland	116	49		63	4	367	153	147	63	4	101	0.32
Italy[c]	887	12	165	556	154	5,991	603	3,768	1,383	237	105	0.15
Luxembourg	0				0	120	41	50	16	13	326	
Malta	0					18	5	13			52	
Netherlands	2,820		196	2,611	13	3,107	291	1,225	1,565	26	213	0.91
Norway	3,657	11	2,087	1,187	372	831	34	363	63	371	199	4.40
Poland	5,288	5,108	7	158	15	5,321	4,345	546	409	21	141	0.99
Portugal	40	7			33	399	75	280		44	39	0.10
Romania	2,676	630	450	1,551	45	3,108	822	598	1,632	56	136	0.86

Continued below

Table 6.2 Continued

Region/country	Primary energy production (10^{15} J)					Energy consumption (10^{15} J and 10^9 J per capita)						
	Total	Solids	Liquids	Gas	Electricity	Total	Solids	Liquids	Gas	Electricity	Per capita	P/C ratio[a]
Spain	769	424	69	27	249	2,402	696	1,344	118	244	62	0.32
Sweden	504	1			503	1,224	118	606	11	489	147	0.41
Switzerland[d]	202				202	727	18	476	65	168	111	0.28
UK	9,732	2,500	5,182	1,837	213	8,521	2,861	3,104	2,301	255	150	1.14
Yugoslavia	1,046	666	167	90	123	1,663	762	539	238	124	71	0.63
USSR	68,457	15,522	26,175	25,295	1,465	54,725	15,000	15,861	22,524	1,340	194	1.25
OCEANIA	5,996	3,936	1,203	727	130	3,765	1,457	1,408	727	130	90	1.59
American Samoa						20		7			189	
Australia	5,670	3,883	1,147	589	51	3,242	1,406	1,196	589	51	201	1.75
Cook Is.						20		9			429	
Fiji	1				1	8	0	7		1	11	0.13
French Polynesia						20		8			47	
Guam						20		17			144	
Nauru						20		2			222	
New Caledonia	1				1	20	5	15		1	126	0.05
New Zealand	322	53	56	138	75	373	46	114	138	75	113	0.86
Pacific Is. Tr. Tr.						2		2			12	
Papua New Guinea	2				2	34	0	32		2	9	0.06
Samoa						2		2		0	12	
Solomon Is.						2		2			7	
Tonga						1		1			9	
Vanuatu						1		1			7	

a   Production/consumption ratio.
b   Including Monaco.
c   Including San Marino.
d   Including Liechtenstein.

Zero equals less than 0.5 of the unit specified or nil. Solids include hard coal, lignite, peat and oil shale; liquids comprise crude petroleum and natural gas liquids; gas comprises natural gas; and electricity includes primary electricity generation from hydro, nuclear and geothermal sources.

Data on production refer to the first stage of production; for hard coal this is mine production, for crude petroleum and natural gas it is production at oil and gas wells, and for natural gas liquids it is production at wells and processing plants. Data on consumption refer to "apparent consumption" which is defined as production plus imports minus exports minus bunkers and takes into account changes in stocks. Regional and global totals represent totals for countries listed here and may differ from those given in the source document.

Source:
UN Statistical Office   1989   1987 Energy Statistics Yearbook, United Nations, New York.

Table 6.3 Nuclear power reactors in operation and under construction, 1989

Region/country	Reactors in operation		Reactors under construction		Nuclear electricity supply	
	No. of units	Capacity (MWe)	No. of units	Capacity (MWe)	(TWe.h)	% of total
WORLD	426	318,271	96	78,907	1,854.5	
AFRICA						
South Africa	2	1,842			11.1	7.4
NORTH AMERICA						
Canada	18	12,185	4	3,524	75.4	15.6
Cuba			2	816		
Mexico	1	654	1	654		
USA	110	98,331	4	4,284	529.4	19.1
SOUTH AMERICA						
Argentina	2	935	1	692	4.6	11.4
Brazil	1	626	1	1,245	1.7	0.7
ASIA						
China			3	2,148		
China, Taiwan	6	4,924			27.1	35.2
India	7	1,374	7	1,540	3.4	1.6
Iran			2	2,392		
Japan	39	29,300	12	10,629	185.8	27.8
Korea, Dem.	9	7,220	2	1,900	45.0	50.2
Pakistan	1	125			0.1	0.2
EUROPE						
Belgium	7	5,500			38.8	60.8
Bulgaria	5	2,585	2	1,906	14.6	32.9
Czechoslovakia	8	3,264	8	5,120	22.9	27.6
Finland	4	2,310			18.0	35.4
France	55	52,588	9	12,245	289.0	74.6
German Dem. Rep	6	2,102	5	3,024	11.1	10.9
Germany, Fed. Rep.	24	22,716	1	295	141.2	34.3
Hungary	4	1,645			13.0	49.8
Italy	2	1,120				
Netherlands	2	508			3.8	5.4
Romania			5	3,125		
Spain	10	7,544			53.7	38.4
Sweden	12	9,817			62.8	45.1
Switzerland	5	2,952			21.5	41.6
UK	39	11,242	1	1,188	63.4	21.7
Yugoslavia	1	632			4.5	5.9
USSR	46	34,230	26	22,180	212.6	12.3

MWe = Megawatts (10^{12}) (electrical).
TWe.h = Terawatt (10^{12}) hours (electrical).

Source:
IAEA 1990 *Nuclear Power Reactors in the World*, Reference Data Series No. 2, International Atomic Energy Agency, Vienna.

Table 6.4 Capacity and production of hydraulic energy in selected countries, 1987 (schemes >1MW)

Region/country	In operation			Under construction		Planned		Other capacity (MW)
	Capacity (MW)	Probable production (GWh a⁻¹)	Actual production (GWh a⁻¹)	Capacity (MW)	Probable production (GWh a⁻¹)	Capacity (MW)	Probable production (GWh a⁻¹)	
WORLD	537,647	1,119,821	1,993,535	128,506	568,665	387,312	1,297,376	1,442,725
AFRICA	16,799	10,559	41,182	3,181	2,296	20,493	19,150	10,904
Algeria	285	—	300	—	—	100	150	—
Angola	400	—	1,335	520	—	300	3,400	—
Cameroon	528	2,900	2,325	120	790	284	1,850	—
Cent. African Rep.	22	—	74	—	—	—	—	—
Congo	120	—	233	—	—	—	—	—
Côte d'Ivoire	885	—	1,290	—	—	1,598	—	—
Egypt	2,700	—	6,000	—	—	450	—	7,235
Ethiopia	248	—	631	450	—	150	1,000	—
Gabon	125	715	675	256	1,285	1,302	5,871	—
Ghana	1,072	4,834	4,676	—	—	—	—	3,669
Malawi	146	—	564	40	—	300	—	—
Morocco	619	—	620	90	—	1,750	—	—
Mozambique	1,523	—	60	1,625	—	1,000	—	—
Nigeria	1,900	—	2,210	—	—	3,600	—	—
Rwanda	56	—	170	—	—	53	—	—
South Africa	540	1,240	1,617	—	—	—	—	—
Sudan	225	—	516	—	—	1,610	6,879	—
Tanzania	259	870	610	80	221	—	—	—
Tunisia	64	—	113	—	—	2,000	—	—
Zaire	2,486	—	5,156	—	—	—	—	—
Zambia	1,963	—	9,512	—	—	3,729	—	—
Zimbabwe	633	—	2,495	—	—	2,267	—	—
NORTH AMERICA	153,895	34,160	590,637	7,986	16,399	21,755	102,365	405,387
Canada	57,711	—	313,159	4,324	15,172	12,237	68,714	195,937
Costa Rica	714	4,564	2,994	—	—	2,276	9,702	42,794
Cuba	49	—	44	—	—	—	—	—
Dominican Rep.	165	—	950	143	526	673	2,255	—
El Salvador	233	—	1,030	180	—	120	—	—
Greenland	—	—	—	—	—	130	580	—
Haiti	70	—	320	—	—	—	—	—
Honduras	130	—	880	—	—	—	—	—

Continued over

Table 6.4 Continued

Region/country	In operation Capacity (MW)	In operation Probable production (GWh a⁻¹)	In operation Actual production (GWh a⁻¹)	Under construction Capacity (MW)	Under construction Probable production (GWh a⁻¹)	Planned Capacity (MW)	Planned Probable production (GWh a⁻¹)	Other capacity (MW)
Guatemala	445	–	680	–	–	600	2,470	27,155
Jamaica	25	–	125	3	63	30	146	177
Mexico	7,704	26,278	18,200	350	638	2,867	5,792	139,324
Nicaragua	103	470	268	–	–	2,091	8,684	–
Panama	551	2,848	2,032	–	–	731	4,022	–
Puerto Rico	85	–	260	2,986	–	–	–	–
USA	85,910	–	249,695		–	–	–	–
SOUTH AMERICA	70,371	332,723	328,556	32,080	173,662	200,474	873,261	768,617
Argentina	6,591	–	21,909	4,370	24,000	27,800	100,400	39,500
Bolivia	295	–	1,129	7	21	200	1,300	–
Brazil	39,497	231,260	198,782	17,456	94,760	114,647	636,193	181,332
Chile	2,254	11,506	12,102	766	4,306	8,852	52,084	68,410
Colombia	4,675	–	25,558	3,000	–	19,512	–	
Ecuador	1,088	7,700	4,532	656	5,700	1,715	15,000	2,525
Guyana	2	10	5	–	–	2,200	–	–
Paraguay	2,990	19,320	18,440	5,525	43,600	3,116	24,600	–
Peru	2,150	–	11,050	–	–	13,557	–	390,000
Uruguay	1,039	7,577	4,210	–	–	282	1,230	–
Venezuela	9,790	55,350	30,839	300	1,275	8,593	42,454	86,850
ASIA	95,889	188,813	329,201	47,102	117,595	115,752	237,568	146,219
Afghanistan	281	–	764	260	–	338	–	–
Bangladesh	197	–	530	50	390	100	780	–
China	26,500	4,952	93,700	13,908	53,750	52,000	167,000	–
China, Taiwan	1,507	4,952	5,121	13	41	346	1,458	11,878
India	17,263	53,000	47,396	13,953	53,000	–	–	–
Indonesia	1,600	–	7,290	1,400	–	1,518	–	–
Iran	1,850	7,500	8,400	1,100	4,200	6,500	11,200	–
Iraq	100	–	610	1,760	–	25,000	–	–
Israel	2	–	8	–	–	4	–	–
Japan	25,900	89,800	80,800	1,400	2,900	19,400	41,600	–
Jordan	7	19	19	–	–	–	–	–
Korea	1,232	3,184	3,963	263	–	296	–	–
Korea, Dem.	4,600	–	29,100	–	–	–	–	184
Malaysia	1,403	5,284	4,560	69	374	1,010	1,666	52,260

Continued below

Table 6.4 Continued

Region/country	In operation		Actual production (GWh a^{-1})	Under construction		Planned		Other capacity (MW)
	Capacity (MW)	Probable production (GWh a^{-1})		Capacity (MW)	Probable production (GWh a^{-1})	Capacity (MW)	Probable production (GWh a^{-1})	
Myanmar q.v. Burma	–	258	–	1,121	2,534	–	706	2,600
Pakistan	2,901	15,251	15,531	1,064	406	3,148	10,758	–
Philippines	2,153	7,565	5,220	80	–	820	2,400	17,925
Syria	827	2,000	1,500	50	–	–	–	2,000
Thailand	2,254	–	4,071	2,485	–	–	–	–
Turkey	4,992	–	18,618	8,126	–	5,272	–	59,372
Viet Nam	320	–	2,000	–	–	–	–	–
EUROPE	126,249	317,016	442,390	28,198	13,713	25,634	62,182	82,290
Albania	680	–	3,350	–	–	7,694	20,913	18,200
Austria	10,575	31,608	35,580	–	–	5	17	–
Belgium	140	–	425	5	–	–	–	–
Bulgaria	1,975	–	2,538	–	–	291	1,280	–
Czechoslovakia	1,630	3,580	3,529	439	1,929	–	–	–
Denmark	10	–	29	41	–	66	192	–
Finland	2,645	12,000	13,658	<1	108	133	503	<1
France	21,274	–	70,264	289	–	–	–	–
German Dem. Rep.	–	50	250	–	–	–	–	–
Germany, Fed. Rep.	–	4,113	16,000	18,283	60	–	–	–
Greece	–	2,137	–	2,779	700	1,283	327	783
Hungary	46	720	169	440	2,055	70	230	–
Ireland	220	–	688	–	–	–	–	–
Italy	15,803	46,788	40,495	580	910	1,630	4,840	11,100
Netherlands	3	4	1	35	150	–	–	–
Norway	25,250	105,110	103,750	1,860	3,720	3,700	14,160	26,500
Poland	675	2,000	1,526	90	300	1,000	2,500	–
Portugal	2,839	10,106	9,060	1,435	1,897	3,033	4,080	4,837
Romania	4,640	–	12,590	852	1,284	4,800	6,500	20,000
Spain	13,430	32,000	27,210	–	–	–	–	–
Sweden	16,000	62,500	70,990	225	600	350	1,500	870
UK	1,409	4,300	4,035	–	–	9	30	–
Yugoslavia	7,000	–	26,253	845	–	1,570	5,110	–
USSR	62,580	215,100	219,800	9,300	245,000	–	–	–

Continued over

Table 6.4 Continued

Region/country	In operation			Under construction		Planned		Other capacity (MW)
	Capacity (MW)	Probable production (GWh a⁻¹)	Actual production (GWh a⁻¹)	Capacity (MW)	Probable production (GWh a⁻¹)	Capacity (MW)	Probable production (GWh a⁻¹)	
OCEANIA	11,864	21,450	41,769	659	–	3,204	2,850	29,308
Australia	7,144	–	13,939	227	–	1,060	2,850	29,308
New Zealand	4,580	21,450	27,392	432	–	300	–	–
Papua New Guinea	140	–	438	–	–	1,844	–	–

MW = Megawatts (10^6).
GWh = Gigawatt (10^9) hours.

In the above table a dash denotes "data unknown" or a zero value. Probable production is the probable annual generation of energy (expressed in GWh) at the sites based on historical average flows reaching them (modified flows), with the net heads and plant capacities reported and making allowance for plant and system availability.

"Actual production" is the generation of hydroelectricity in 1987. "Other capacity" refers to all other sites with sufficient gradient, flow and physical conditions that development is expected to be feasible based on present and expected local economic conditions with existing available technology.

Source:
WEC 1989 *1989 Survey of World Energy Resources,* World Energy Conference, London.

Table 6.5 Existing or studied tidal power plants, status in 1989

Region/country	Location	Mean tidal range (m)	Basin area (km²)	Installed capacity (MW)	Design output (GWh)	In service (date) or status
NORTH AMERICA						
Canada	Annapolis, Bay of Fundy	6.4	6	17.8	50	1984
	A8, Bay of Fundy	9.2	90	1,400	3,420	Study 1984
	B9, Bay of Fundy	11	240	4,864	14,004	Study 1981
ASIA						
China	Jiangxia	7.1	2	3.2	11	1980[a]
Korea	Garolim	5.1	85	400	800	Under study
India	Kutch	5	170	600	1,600	Under study
EUROPE						
France	Rance	8	17	240	540	1966
UK	Severn	8.3	520	8,000	14,400	Under study
USSR	Kislaya Guba	2.4	2	0.4		1968

MW = Megawatts (10^6).
GWh = Gigawatt (10^9) hours.

[a] First unit.

Source:
WEC 1989 *1989 Survey of World Energy Resources,* World Energy Conference, London.

Table 6.6 Installed capacity and production of solar energy in selected countries, 1987

Region/country	Photovoltaic Installed capacity (kW)	Photovoltaic Production (MWh a^{-1})	Thermo-electric Installed capacity (kW)	Thermo-electric Production (MWh a^{-1})	Direct output (TJ a^{-1})
AFRICA					
Burundi	58	68	–	–	0.7
Ethiopia	55	330	–	–	–
Ghana	5,982	39	–	–	–
South Africa	1,220	–	–	–	
NORTH AMERICA					
Canada	500	500	–	–	450
Costa Rica	–	–		–	360
Mexico	360	710	20	–	
USA	15,000	30,000	134,000	389,000	–
SOUTH AMERICA					
Argentina	a	–	–	–	a
Uruguay	b	–	–	–	–
Venezuela	1	9	–	–	–
ASIA					
China, Taiwan	13		–	–	140
Hong Kong	c	–	–	–	c
Israel	100	175	–	–	6,000
Japan	1,644	–	–	–	–
Jordan	40	73	–	–	–
Korea	371	349	–	–	112
Malaysia	16	23	–	–	–
Pakistan	266	326	–	–	–
EUROPE					
Belgium	15	–	–	–	–
France	1,000	1,000	–	–	360
Germany, Fed. Rep.	334	300	–	–	240
Italy	690	–	–	–	–
Netherlands	–	–	–	–	6
Norway	1,600	1,280	–	–	0.7
Portugal	–	–	–	–	32
Spain	1,000	2,000	–	–	636
Sweden	–	–	–	–	720
UK	32		–	–	140
USSR	100	20	5,000	15	1,500
OCEANIA					
Australia	2,000	–	25	–	2,900
New Zealand	100	–	–	–	–

a Isolated photovoltaic applications exist, whose power at the end of 1984 did not exceed 15 kW.

b Planned project for the utilization of photovoltaics in rural areas.

c A negligible amount of solar energy is used for heating purposes. A small amount of electricity produced by photovoltaic means is used for navigational warning lights.

kW = Kilowatts (10^3).

MWh = Megawatt (10^6) hours.
TJ = Terajoules (10^{12}).

In the above table, a dash denotes "data unknown" or a zero value.

Source:
WEC 1989 *1989 Survey of World Energy Resources*, World Energy Conference, London.

Table 6.7 Electricity generation from geothermal systems in selected countries, 1989

Region/country	Installed capacity (MWe)	Electricity generation (GWh a^{-1})
AFRICA		
Kenya	45	–
Zambia	0.2	–
NORTH AMERICA		
El Salvador	<0.1	–
Guadeloupe	4	–
Mexico	650	4,418
Nicaragua	35	–
USA	2,022	10,775
SOUTH AMERICA		
Argentina	0.6	–
ASIA		
China	17	80
China, Taiwan	3	4.1

Region/country	Installed capacity (MWe)	Electricity generation (GWh a^{-1})
Indonesia	88	–
Japan	215	1,100
Philippines	894	–
Turkey	15	58
EUROPE		
German Dem. Rep.	3	–
Greece (Milos)	2	–
Iceland	39	181
Italy	506	2,986
Portugal (Azores)	3	–
USSR	11	25
OCEANIA		
Australia	<0.1	–
New Zealand	165	1,224

MWe = Megawatts (10^6) (electrical).
GWh = Gigawatt (10^9) hours.

In the above table, a dash denotes "data unknown" or a zero value.

Source:
WEC 1989 *1989 Survey of World Energy Resources*, World Energy Conference, London.

Table 6.8 Direct use of geothermal energy in selected countries, 1989

Region/country	Annual output (GWh a^{-1})	(TJ a^{-1})
WORLD	28,570	102,852
NORTH AMERICA		
USA	390	1,400
ASIA		
China	1,945	7,000
Japan	6,805	24,500
Turkey	423	1,520
EUROPE		
France	2,330	8,390
Hungary	2,615	9,410

Region/country	Annual output (GWh a^{-1})	(TJ a^{-1})
Iceland	5,517	19,860
Italy	970	3,490
Romania	987	3,550
Spain	12	43
Sweden	327	1,180
USSR	4,167	15,000
OCEANIA		
Australia	<0.1	<0.1
New Zealand	1,500	5,400

GWh = Gigawatt (10^9) hours.
TJ = Terajoules (10^{12}).

Source:
WEC 1989 *1989 Survey of World Energy Resources*, World Energy Conference, London.

Table 6.9 Number of new wind turbines erected world-wide, 1981–1986

Wind turbine size (kW)	1981	1982	1983	1984	1985	1986
<5	3,500	4,900	6,200	10,600	12,200	15,000
6–25	600	700	1,000	1,000	1,100	200
26–100	300	1,500	2,100	3,800	5,300	2,500
101–300	0	17	150	400	310	550
301–700	0	1	2	8	5	9
>700	3	3	2	0	17	2
TOTAL	4,403	7,121	9,454	15,808	18,932	18,261

Source:
WEC 1989 *1989 Survey of World Energy Resources*, World Energy Conference, London.

Table 6.10 Electrical wind energy capacity and target capacity, 1989

Region/country	Current capacity (MW)	No. of turbines (>5 MW)	Target capacity and date (MW)
AFRICA			
Egypt[a]	2		1,250 by 2000
ASIA			
China	8		100–200 by 2000
India	6		250–300 by 1991
			5,000 by 2000
Israel			200 by 2000
NORTH AMERICA			
Canada	5	1	
USA	1,300	6	
EUROPE			
Belgium	5		
Denmark[b]	140	3	100 by 1990
			4,000 by 1995
Germany, Fed. Rep.[c]	2	3	100
Greece			20 by 1992
Italy		1	300–500 by 2000
Netherlands	25	1	100–150 by 1991
Spain		1	1,000 by 2000
Sweden	5	3	
UK	6	3	

[a] Target covers all renewables.
[b] Target applies to Danish utilities.
[c] Target under discussion.

MW = Megawatts (10^6).

Source:
WEC 1989 *1989 Survey of World Energy Resources*, World Energy Conference, London.

Table 6.11 Global production of alcohol fuels, 1984

Region/country	Installed capacity (10^6 l a^{-1})	Under construction (10^6 l a^{-1})	Planned (10^6 l a^{-1})
AFRICA			
Ethiopia			34
Kenya	38		
Malawi	18[a]		
Mali	11[a]		
Sudan			39
Zambia			1.5
Zimbabwe	42		
NORTH AMERICA			
Canada	6.8	7.6	200[b]
Costa Rica	31		0.6
Dominican Rep.			56.8
El Salvador	15.1		159
Guatemala	0.2	18	
Honduras			21.6
Jamaica	15[c]		
USA	4.5[c]	360	2.3[c]
SOUTH AMERICA			
Argentina	380		
Brazil	16,200[d]		3,800[d]
Colombia	38		
Ecuador		5.4	
Paraguay	26.1		
ASIA			
Thailand	203	162	
EUROPE			
Sweden	6		
OCEANIA			
New Zealand	15		
Papua New Guinea		5.4	

[a] 1988.
[b] Estimate.
[c] 1990.
[d] Installed capacity in 1987.

l = litres.

This table shows ethanol fermentation capacity excluding non-fuel purposes.

Sources:
Rosillo Calle, F. 1990 Liquid fuels. In: *Bioenergy and the Environment*, J. Pasztor and L. Kristoferson (Eds), Westview Press, Oxford.
Rosillo Calle, F. 1991 Personal communication, King's College London, London, UK.

Transport/Tourism

Transport statistics are collected by several international trade and commercial user federations and by specialized UN organizations. Statistics on roads and road traffic, for example, are issued annually by the International Road Federation (IRF). Data on railways and rail traffic are compiled by the Union Internationale des Chemins de Fer (UIC), and information on air transport by the International Civil Aviation Organization (ICAO) and the International Air Transport Association (IATA). The International Maritime Organization (IMO) has specific mandates dealing with, amongst other issues, maritime transport and arrangements for combating pollution from ships and fixed or floating platforms in the sea.

Despite the number of international organizations collecting transport statistics there are gaps and inconsistencies in the existing data base; data for roads, rail and inland waterways are often incomplete (especially for some developing countries). Comparisons between countries are difficult because of different criteria for the collection of statistics.

This chapter incorporates information on tourism, as did the 1987 edition of the 'UNEP Environmental Data Report' (UNEP, 1987). Tourism is of growing concern as a source of environmental problems. Demand for tourist accommodation, services and resources can place stress on local environments and can interfere with the cultures and lifestyles of indigenous peoples. Increasing research on the impact of tourism on the environment reflects growing awareness of these issues.

Data from a survey conducted by the World Wildlife Fund (WWF) are included in this section and serve to illustrate the growing number of tourists to areas of natural beauty, including protected areas. However, this kind of tourism, whilst reflecting a growing appreciation of the natural environment, brings large numbers of people to areas which may be environmentally sensitive.

Reference

UNEP 1987 *United Nations Environment Programme Environmental Data Report*, Basil Blackwell, Oxford.

Transport

Roads, Vehicles and Traffic

Road transport is the most popular mode of transport for both passengers and freight in the developed nations and is becoming increasingly important in developing countries. Motor vehicles are fast and convenient, and provide a degree of personal freedom and flexibility unavailable in other modes of transport. However, the adverse effects of road transport, which include air and noise pollution, traffic accidents and depletion of natural resources (fossil fuels and land for roads), make road transport costly in economic, human and environmental terms. The contributions of transport sources to national emissions of road traffic-related air pollutants, such as carbon monoxide (CO), nitrogen oxides (NO_x) and lead (Pb), are discussed for selected countries in Part 1: Environmental Pollution, Atmosphere, of this volume.

Table 7.1 illustrates the extent and density of road networks world-wide. During the 10-year period covered by the data table, the majority of countries in all world regions reported an increase in the length of road networks. Of the 77 countries for which comparable sets of data on total road length are available, 58 countries reported an increase in road length, five reported no change and 14 reported a decrease in road length.

Data on vehicle ownership and vehicle-km travelled are presented in Table 7.2. Statistics on deaths due to road traffic accidents are also included. It is difficult to compare data between countries due to differences in the definition of "death due to road accident". Definitions can vary from deaths which occur within 24 hours of an accident to deaths which occur up to 30 days after an accident. Despite such discrepancies, some general conclusions may be drawn regarding trends in road traffic-related deaths over the last 10 to 15 years. In the 48 countries for which two years of data, 1978 and 1988, are available for comparison, deaths due to road accidents have, on average, declined by 4 per cent. This overall trend masks differences between countries; 29 countries have reported increases and 19 have reported decreases in road deaths. More detailed data on road accidents, which include estimates of the number of injuries in addition to fatalities, were presented in the 1989 edition of this report (Tables 5.16 and 5.17) (UNEP, 1989).

In 1988 there were an estimated 500 million vehicles in use in the world. The World Bank reports that developing countries account for only 10 per cent of the global automobile population, 20 per cent of buses, and just over 20 per cent of the global transport energy consumption. In comparison, the USA alone consumes about 35 per cent of the world's transport energy (Faiz et al., 1990).

The number of motor vehicles world-wide is expected to double in the next 20 to 30 years. Developing countries will account for much of the growth as vehicle ownership in developed countries stabilizes. Between 1984 and 1988, the average annual growth rate in the number of motor vehicles reached 26 per cent in Kenya, 14 per cent in China, 11 per cent in Brazil, and 9 per cent in Pakistan and Thailand, compared with about 2 per cent in the USA and 3 per cent in the UK (Faiz et al., 1990). Rapid urban expansion will affect the demand for different forms of transport. Past experience indicates that urbanization increases reliance on private motor vehicles (Faiz et al., 1990). Vehicle ownership is also linked to population size and to GNP (gross national product). Figure 7.1 illustrates the comparative growth rates of population and vehicle numbers since 1950.

Despite increasing reliance on motor vehicles in recent years, developing countries are still heavily dependent on traditional forms of transport. In Kenya, for example, more than 90 per cent of rural trips are made on foot; less than 3 per cent are made by car or bus (Repogle, 1989).

Tri-shaws, cycle-rickshaws, pedal carts, becaks and other similar forms of transport account for a large share of road transport use in developing countries. Data on the number of these in use are, however, not readily available. Many of these vehicles are pedal-operated, but a growing number are motorized. Emissions from motorized tri-shaws and similar vehicles may result in increasing air pollution as urban populations and vehicle numbers continue to grow.

In some countries, bicycles represent an important mode of transport. In 1989 China and India together had an estimated 600 million bicycles, but only 1 per cent of the world's automobiles (Repogle, 1989). Table 7.3 shows the ratio of bicycles to automobiles in selected countries.

Bicycle usage cannot be assessed accurately by listing the number of bicycles sold or owned. In the USA bicycle ownership is high, with one bicycle for every two people, yet the share of trips by bicycle is low. Table 7.4 gives the share of trips made by bicycle in various cities. Not surprisingly, many inhabitants of Chinese cities rely heavily on the bicycle. However, in some developed countries bicycles are increasingly being recognized as an important mode of transport, especially for short trips. Bicycling lanes and routes are becoming more common in cities in both Europe and North America where some employers are encouraging their workers to use bicycles rather than cars.

Increased use of non-motorized forms of transport will assist efforts to reduce the transport sector's total energy consumption in the future. Already advances in technology have improved vehicle fuel efficiency; consumption of motor fuel (in tonnes per annum per car) for selected countries in 1971 and 1985 are compared below:

Country	1971	1985	% change
Belgium	1.05	0.76	-28
Denmark	1.36	1.05	-23
France	1.00	0.70	-30
Germany, Fed. Rep.	1.12	0.98	-12
Ireland	1.66	1.24	-25
Italy	0.90	0.54	-41
Netherlands	1.16	1.11	-4
UK	1.22	1.08	-11
USA	2.78	2.26	-19

Source: Open University, 1989

Though detailed data for the developing countries are not readily available vehicles are, on average, less fuel efficient. The lack of access to new technologies, older vehicle fleets and badly maintained roads are contributory factors leading to poor fuel efficiency (Faiz et al., 1990).

In some countries, the use of alternative fuels in vehicles is increasing. Biofuels, in particular, are utilized in several countries, most notably Brazil and the USA (see Part 6: Energy).

Rail and Inland Waterways

The environmental effects of rail transport include noise and vibration along railway lines and land taken for lines and terminals. Railway lines can partition or destroy neighbourhoods, farmland and wildlife habitats (OECD, 1988). Rail transport also contributes to atmospheric pollution, though to a lesser degree than road transport. In the UK in 1988, for example, rail transport was responsible for

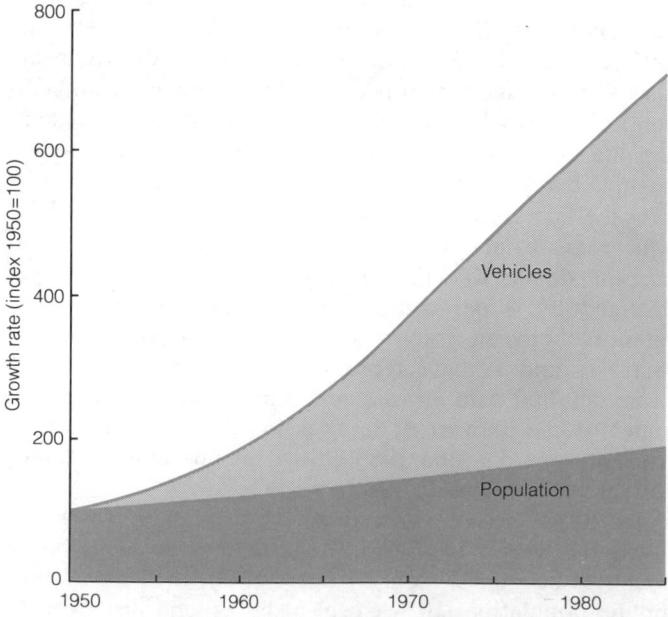

Figure 7.1 Rate of increase of the human population and vehicle numbers, 1950–1985
Source: Sadik, 1990

emitting 0.68 t of NO$_x$ per passenger-km, compared with 1.07 t per passenger-km emitted via road transport (Howard, 1990).

Inland waterway transport may affect the environment in several ways. It requires modification of water systems during canal cutting and dredging, occupies land for infrastructure and causes disposal problems when vessels are withdrawn from service. Transport of fuels and hazardous substances can increase the risk of environmental damage in the case of accidental spillage (OECD, 1988). Accidental releases of chemical substances, a considerable proportion of which result from transportation accidents, are documented in Part 5: Human Health, of this report.

Information on rail networks and inland waterways is generally more limited than that which is available on road or air transport. What data are available indicate that rail transport, in contrast to road and air, has not expanded significantly over the past 15 years. Although the majority of reporting countries have experienced either stationary or declining trends in the length of rail networks, approximately half showed an increase in train-km implying a more intensive use of existing line and stock. Between 1970 and 1985, the length of rail networks had declined by 4.1 per cent in Europe and by 1.8 per cent in Japan (European Conference of Ministers of Transport, 1990). Information on the length of national rail networks and inland waterways (the latter relates mainly to Europe) can be found in the 1989 edition of the 'UNEP Environmental Data Report' (UNEP, 1989).

The relative importance of different modes of transport for freight and passengers varies significantly between countries (Table 7.5). In the case of freight, variations depend on several factors, including the degree of government regulation of the freight industry, the types of goods transported, and the distances involved. The percentage of freight transported by inland waterways in Europe has declined slightly since 1980, from 7.0 per cent to 5.8 per cent (UN-ECE, 1990).

Air

The environmental effects of air transport include noise around airports, use of land for airport construction and infrastructure and air pollution (OECD, 1988). It is estimated that the world's aircraft fleet consumed 15×10^6 t of aviation fuel in 1987, which produced 2.75×10^6 t of nitrogen oxides (Egli, 1990). Emissions of NO$_x$ to the upper atmosphere can lead to an increase in concentrations of tropospheric ozone (see Part 1: Environmental Pollution, Atmosphere).

Relative to other modes of transport, especially rail and waterways, civil air transport is generally well documented. National statistics on scheduled air traffic, including numbers of departures and aircraft-km flown for 1977 and 1987, were presented in the previous edition of this report (UNEP, 1989).

Tables 7.6 and 7.7 summarize available data on aircraft numbers and volume of traffic in different world regions

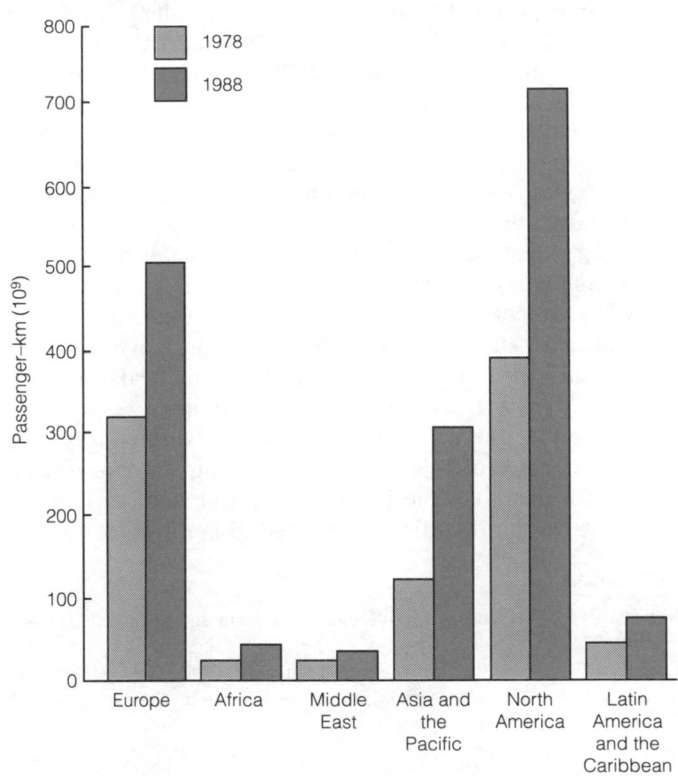

Figure 7.2 Passenger-km flown by commercial aircraft, 1978 and 1988
Source: data from Table 7.7

for 1978 and 1988. Table 7.6 compares the number of commercial aeroplanes in service world-wide according to engine type. Fixed-wing (i.e., excluding helicopters) aircraft numbers have increased by 26 per cent in the decade between 1978 and 1988.

Table 7.7 presents data on the number of tonne-km and passenger-km flown, categorized by world region. All regions have experienced increases in scheduled commercial aircraft tonne-km and passenger-km flown between 1978 and 1988 (see Figure 7.2). The Asian and Pacific regions have experienced the greatest increases, with 172 per cent more tonne-km and 145 per cent more passenger-km in 1988 than in 1978. Africa also shows high increases, with 133 per cent more tonne-km and 90 per cent more passenger-km in 1988 than in 1978 (Table 7.7).

Sea

Maritime transport can cause several environmental problems. Port construction can require modification of coastal areas, and land is taken for infrastructures. The risk of environmental damage due to accidents is increased when fuels and hazardous substances are transported (OECD, 1988).

Movement of all goods by sea was reported, by country of origin, in the second edition of this report (UNEP,

1989) (Table 7.4). Data indicate that the total tonnage of goods transported by sea and the average length of haul have both declined since the mid-1970s (UNEP, 1989).

In 1990 there were over 3,000 tankers and combined carriers in service world-wide (Table 7.8). Although the world's tanker fleet has decreased in number since 1970, the carrying capacity has increased by around 80 per cent. The carrying capacity of combined carriers has also increased over the same period. This is a consequence of the doubling of the size of individual tankers during the late 1970s and early 1980s. In recent years this trend towards larger vessels has reversed and has now stabilized.

Figure 7.3 shows the main inter-area oil movements by sea in 1987 (in million barrels daily). In the wake of such disasters as the Exxon Valdez oil spill there is growing concern about the safety of tankers. Not surprisingly, the greatest density of oil spills occurs along the busiest sea routes, for example, the Persian Gulf and south-east Asia. Information on oil spills is presented in Part 8: Wastes.

References

Egli, R. A. 1990 Nitrogen oxide emissions from air traffic, *Chimia* **44**, 369–371.

European Conference of Ministers of Transport 1990 *Transport Policy and the Environment*, Organisation for Economic Co-operation and Development, Paris.

Faiz, A., Sinha, K., Walsh, M. and Varma, A. 1990 *Automotive Air Pollution: Issues and Options for Developing Countries*, The World Bank, Washington DC.

Howard, D. 1990 *Energy, Transport and the Environment*, Transnet, London.

OECD 1988 *Transport and the Environment*, Organisation for Economic Co-operation and Development, Paris.

Open University 1989 Evidence prepared for the House of Commons Energy Select Committee Enquiry into the Greenhouse Effect, February 1989, Open University Energy and Environment Research Unit, Open University, Milton Keynes.

Repogle, M. 1989 Let them drive cars, *New Internationalist* **195**, 18–19.

Sadik, N. 1990 *The State of the World Population 1990*, United Nations Population Fund, New York.

SBS 1989 *International Oil Movements*, Shell Briefing Service, No. 1, Shell International Petroleum Company, London.

UN-ECE 1990 *Annual Bulletin of Transport Statistics for Europe*, United Nations Economic Commission for Europe, Geneva.

UNEP 1989 *United Nations Environment Programme Environmental Data Report*, Basil Blackwell, Oxford.

Tourism

Tourism is currently one of the fastest growing industries in the world. Since the late 1970s, tourism has become the second most important item in world trade, surpassed only by oil (Genot, 1991). It can bring great benefits to areas that attract tourists, and is frequently sought for its

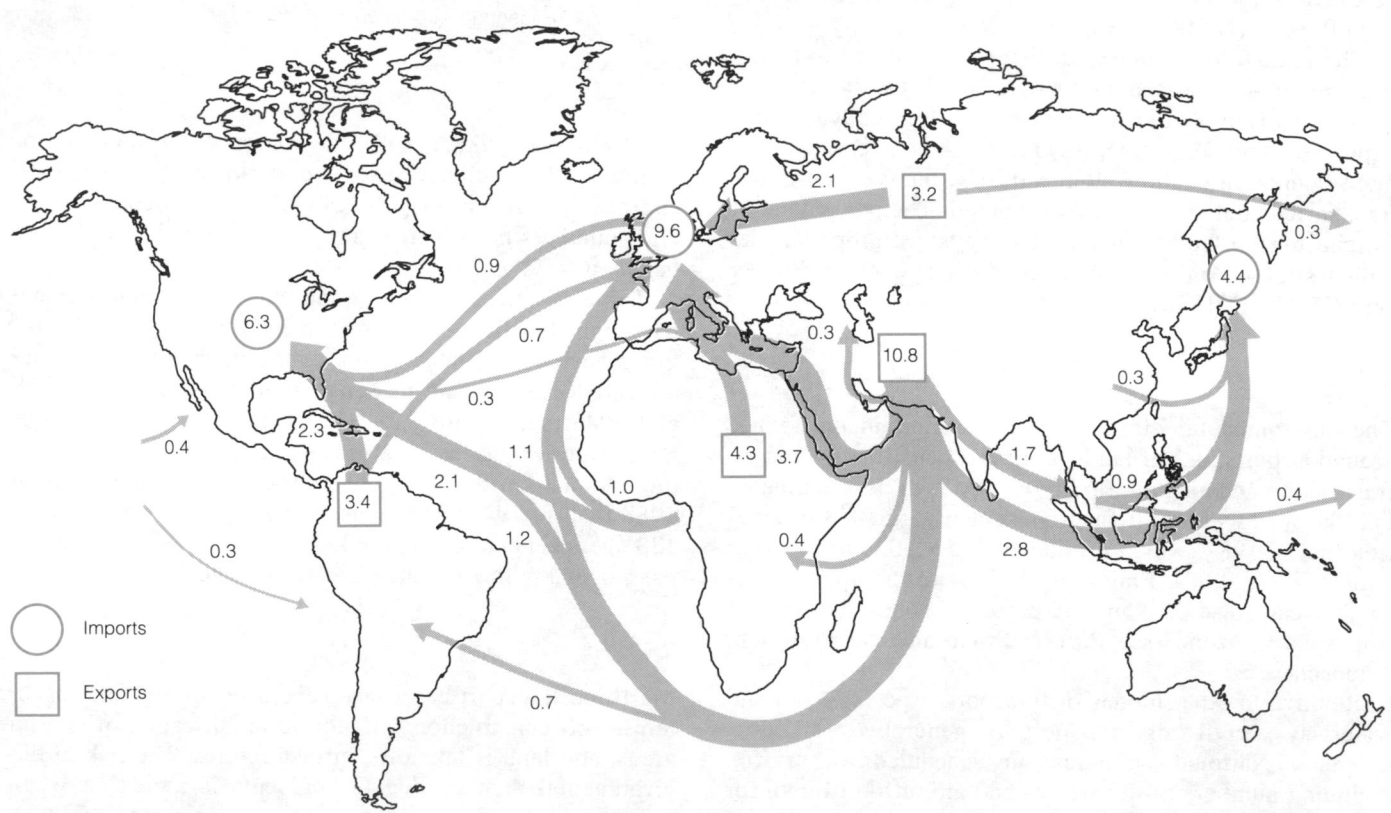

Figure 7.3 Movement of oil by sea, 1987 (the map shows movements of oil in excess of 0.2 x 10^6 barrels per day; regional totals for imports and exports therefore do not necessarily equal the sum of individual movements between regions)
Source: SBS, 1989

contribution to the economy. In 1988 international tourism, measured in terms of the number of arrivals, totalled some 390×10^6; expenditures and receipts amounted to US\$ 195×10^9. This represents a doubling of arrivals and an eightfold increase in receipts since 1972 (Genot, 1991). International tourist arrivals in major world regions in 1972 and 1988 are compared below:

| | Arrivals (10^6) | |
Region	1978	1988
Europe	184.4	250.3
North America	32.6	49.4
Latin America and Caribbean	17.0	24.9
Africa	5.1	12.7
East Asia - Pacific	12.7	47.3
South Asia	2.1	3.1
Middle East	4.2	7.4

Sources: WTO 1980, 1990; Beekhuis, 1989

In 1982 a joint declaration by the World Tourism Organization (WTO) and UNEP said: "The satisfaction of tourism requirements must not be prejudicial to the social and economic interests of the population in the tourist areas, to the environment, or above all to natural resources which are fundamental attractions of tourism." There is increasing recognition among national governments and international bodies of the need for careful tourism management in order to minimize impacts on the environment.

Table 7.9 lists, in descending order of number of visitors, the major tourist destinations as assessed in 1985. It is evident that the greatest volume of travel occurs in the developed world, especially to Europe. However, tourism to developing countries has increased significantly in recent years. Tourist numbers to Mauritius, for example, have increased from 1,800 visitors in 1968 to 180,000 in 1988 (O'Grady, 1990).

In particular, nature tourism, i.e., tourism to natural areas such as national parks or to areas of great natural beauty or ecological interest, has become increasingly popular in recent years. However, without careful planning and management, tourism can frequently have adverse impacts on the environment and on indigenous peoples and cultural values. For example, Kakadu National Park, a World Heritage Site in northern Australia, is a popular tourist destination and during the 1980s visitor numbers rose dramatically. The very success of tourism in this area has, however, had detrimental effects. Vandalism of sacred Aboriginal rock art and soil erosion due to trampling are two of the most serious concerns facing park managers.

A recent study by the World Wildlife Fund (WWF) has examined the effects of tourism in several Central American countries (Boo, 1990). The following table illustrates the high proportion of visitors to protected areas in the countries studied:

Country	No. of visitors surveyed	No. of visitors to protected areas (%)
Belize	99	64
Costa Rica	104	54
Dominica	83	41
Ecuador	79	75
Mexico	71	55

Source: Boo, 1990

Table 7.10 reflects the increase in tourist numbers to Ecuador's natural areas. Until the late 1960s, there was little tourist industry in Ecuador. Between 1973 and 1980 tourist arrivals increased by over 200 per cent, with the Galapagos Islands as the primary attraction. Tourism is now the second largest earner of foreign exchange in Ecuador. Tourist revenues mean that the GNP of the Galapagos Islands province is the highest in Ecuador. However, tourism has caused environmental problems, including changes in the habits of native animals, path erosion and littering (Boo, 1990).

References

Beekhuis, J. 1989 *Travel and Leisure: World Travel Overview 1988–89*, American Express Publishing Corporation, New York.

Boo, E. 1990 *Ecotourism: The Potentials and Pitfalls*, World Wildlife Fund, Washington DC.

Genot, H. 1991 Personal communication, United Nations Environment Programme Industry and Environment Office, Paris, France.

O'Grady, A. 1990 *The Challenge of Tourism: Learning Resources for Study and Action*, Ecumenical Coalition on Third World Tourism, Bangkok.

WTO 1980 *Yearbook of Tourism Statistics*, World Tourist Organization, Madrid.

WTO 1990 *Yearbook of Tourism Statistics*, World Tourist Organization, Madrid.

Table 7.1 Road networks, 1978 and 1988

Region/country	Total length[a] (10^3 km)		Percentage paved		Density (km km^{-2})	
	1978	1988	1978	1988	1978	1988
AFRICA						
Algeria	72.1		54			
Benin		7.4[b]		11[b]		0.07[b]
Botswana	10.5	13.5[c]	6	15[c]	0.02	0.02[c]
Burkina Faso	16.7	11.2[c]	4	12[c]	0.06	0.04[c]
Burundi	10.5[d]		5[d]		0.01[d]	
Cameroon		52.2[e]		6[e]		0.11[e]
Cent. African Rep.	22.0	20.3[c]	2	2[c]	0.03[d]	0.03[c]
Congo	8.2		7		0.02	
Côte d'Ivoire	45.2		5		0.14	
Djibouti		2.9[c]		17[c]		0.13[c]
Egypt	28.9	32.8	53	53	0.03	0.03
Ethiopia	36.8	39.5	8	20	0.03	0.03
Gabon	6.9		7		0.03	
Gambia		2.4[b]		21[b]		0.21[b]
Ghana	32.2		25		0.14	
Kenya	50.6		9		0.09	
Lesotho	4.0	4.3[b]	6	12[b]	0.13	0.14[b]
Liberia	5.4	8.1[e]	5	9[e]	0.05	0.08[e]
Madagascar	50.6	49.6	9	11	0.09	0.08
Malawi	10.6[f]	12.2[b]	17[f]	21[b]	0.09[f]	0.10[b]
Mali	14.7		11[g]		0.01[g]	
Mauritania		7.3[b]		22[b]		0.01[b]
Mauritius	1.8	1.8	92	92[c]	1.54	1.57
Morocco	56.3[f,h]	59.2[c]	49[f]	47[c]	0.09[f]	0.08[c]
Mozambique		26.1[c]		20[c]		0.03[c]
Niger	7.6[h]	19.0[e]	25	18[e]	0.006	0.01[e]
Nigeria	106.1		24		0.12	
Rwanda	6.6	12.1[e]	4	7[e]	0.25	0.40[e]
Senegal	13.9	15.0[c]	22	30[c]	0.07	0.07[c]
Sierra Leone	7.4		16		0.10	
South Africa	185.5	183.0[e]	24	29[e]	0.16	0.16[e]
Sudan		6.6[b]		59[b]		
Swaziland	2.5[d]		15[d]		0.14[d]	
Tanzania	45.0	81.8[i]	8	4[i]	0.05	
Togo	7.5	7.5[e]	54	22[e]	0.13	0.13[h]
Tunisia	23.6	27.8	52	59	0.14	0.17
Uganda	25.6	28.3[b]	9	22[b]	0.11	0.14[b]
Zaire	145.0	145.0[b]	2	2[b]	0.06	0.06[b]
Zambia	36.4	37.4	13	17	0.05	0.05
Zimbabwe	85.8[j]	77.9[b]	14[j]	17[b]		0.20[b]
NORTH AMERICA						
Canada	493.8[g]	844.4[e,k]	33[g]	29[e,k]	0.03[g]	0.09[e,k]
Costa Rica	28.5		9			
Dominican Rep.	16.6[f]		80[f]		0.34[f]	
El Salvador	12.3[j]	12.2[e]	14[j]	14[e]		0.58[l]
Guadeloupe		2.1[c]		80[c]		1.17[c,l]
Guatemala	17.3		16		0.13	
Honduras		14.2[c]				0.13[c,l]
Mexico	207.2	225.7[c]	30	45[c]	0.10[d]	0.11[c]

Continued opposite

Table 7.1 Continued

Region/country	Total length[a] (10³ km)		Percentage paved		Density (km km⁻²)	
	1978	1988	1978	1988	1978	1988
Nicaragua	6.7[j]	15.0[c]	10[j]	11[c]	0.05	0.12[c,l]
Panama	8.3		32		0.11	
Puerto Rico		9.4[c]		87[c]		1.05[c,l]
Trinidad & Tobago		5.2[b]				1.01[c,l]
USA	6,251.7	6,233.3[e]	82	56[e,k]	0.67	0.67[e]
SOUTH AMERICA						
Argentina	207.6	211.4[c]	22	27[c]	0.07	0.08[c]
Brazil	1,544.7	1,673.7	5	8	0.18	0.20
Chile	75.4	79.2[e]	12	13[e]	0.10	0.10[e]
Colombia	63.1	106.2[c]	15[d]	10[c]	0.05	0.09[c]
Ecuador	33.0[j]	37.6	13[j]	17	0.12	0.13[c]
French Guiana	0.1[j]	1.1	75[j]	40	0.007	0.01
Suriname		9.1[c]		26[c]		0.06[c]
Uruguay	25.0[d]		39[d]		0.14[d]	
Venezuela	61.8[j]	100.6[c]	37[j]	33[c]	0.07[j]	0.11[c]
ASIA						
Afghanistan	18.8		15		0.03	
China	17.5		69		0.49	
Cyprus	9.8	11.7[e]	49	48[e]	1.06	1.26[e]
Hong Kong	1.1	1.4	100	100	1.07	1.34
India	1,545.9		40		0.47	
Indonesia		219.0[c]		62[c]		0.11[c]
Iraq	9.7[m]	44.5	53[m]	81	0.02[m]	0.10
Israel	4.5		100		0.22	
Japan	1,097.2	1,104.3	40	67	2.91	2.92
Jordan	4.8	5.6[e]	70	100[e]	0.05	0.06[e]
Korea	45.7	55.8	27	61	0.46	0.56
Kuwait	2.4	4.1	100		0.15	0.22[e]
Malaysia	21.5	40.1	76	81	0.16	0.22
Nepal	4.6		41		0.03	
Pakistan	86.3	111.2	68	53	0.10	0.14
Philippines	152.4	157.4	13	14	0.50	0.52
Saudi Arabia	38.2	91.3[c]	51	37[c]	0.02	0.04[c]
Singapore	2.5[j]	2.6[b]	88[j]	95[b]	4.00	4.55[b,l]
Sri Lanka	24.9	20.7[b]	70	41[b,k]	0.48	0.32[b,k]
Syria		28.9		79		0.16
Thailand	62.0	77.6	32	46	0.12	0.15
Turkey	231.8	320.6	74[j]	14	0.30	0.41
Yemen		37.5		0		0.19
EUROPE						
Austria	106.6	107.1	100	100	1.27	1.30
Belgium	125.0	128.3[e]	94	96[e]	4.10	4.20[e]
Bulgaria	36.3	36.9	76[g]	95	0.33	0.33
Czechoslovakia	73.8[j]	73.0	98[j]	100	0.57	0.57
Denmark	67.5	70.7	100	100	1.56	1.64
Finland	74.4	76.5	45	59	0.22	0.22
France	801.9	805.1	92	95	1.45	1.46
German Dem. Rep.	48.0[d,h]	47.0[e,h]			0.44[d,h]	0.44[e,h]
Germany, Fed. Rep.	479.7	492.5[c]	97	99[c]	1.93	1.98[c]

Continued over

Table 7.1 Continued

Region/country	Total length[a] (10^3 km)		Percentage paved		Density (km km^{-2})	
	1978	1988	1978	1988	1978	1988
Greece	36.8	34.5[b]	5	83[b]	0.28	0.26[b]
Hungary	91.0	90.7[e]	44[d]	56[e]	0.98	0.97[e]
Iceland	11.6	11.4	2	17	0.11	0.11
Ireland	92.3[d]	92.3	99[d]	94	1.34[d]	1.30
Italy	293.3	301.6[c]		100[c]	0.97	1.00[c]
Luxembourg	5.1	5.1	99	99	1.96	1.97
Monaco	46.0[j]	50.0	100[j]	100	23.00	25.00
Netherlands	90.6	115.3	100	88	2.20	2.78
Norway	79.8	87.6	53	67	0.25	0.27
Poland	299.5	360.6	59	61	0.96	1.15
Portugal	50.8	52.0[b,h]	66		0.57	0.59[b,h]
Romania	73.4	72.9[e]	43	49[e]	0.31[j]	0.31[e]
Spain	227.5	318.0	65	56	0.45	0.63
Sweden	129.0	131.0	56	71	0.31	0.32
Switzerland	62.7	71.0			1.50	1.70
UK	349.3	352.3	96	100	1.52	1.53
Yugoslavia	112.4	119.6	45	58[c]	0.44	0.47c
USSR	1,403.0[h,m]	1,609.9[c]		74[c]	0.06[h,m]	0.07[c]
OCEANIA						
Australia	816.8	853.0[b]	29	50[b]	0.11	0.11[b]
New Zealand	92.8	93.1[e]	51	55[e]	0.35	0.35[e]
Papua New Guinea		19.7[c]		6[c]		0.04[c,l]

a Definitions of roads included vary from country to country.
b 1985.
c 1986.
d 1977.
e 1987.
f 1979.
g 1976.
h Excludes certain minor roads.
i 1984.
j 1981.
k Change in classification: not comparable with earlier data.
l Data obtained from alternative source(s), including the UN Statistical Yearbook.
m 1975.

Density refers to the total road network in km per km^2. It may be affected by reported changes in country area.

Sources:
IRF 1982 *World Road Statistics 1977–1981*, International Road Federation, Geneva and Washington DC.
IRF 1989 *World Road Statistics 1984–1988*, International Road Federation, Geneva and Washington DC.

Table 7.2 Vehicles in use and road accidents, 1978 and 1988

Region/country	Vehicles[a] Per 10³ persons 1978	1988	Per km of road 1978	1988	Vehicle-km (10⁹) 1978	1988	Deaths due to road accidents[b] Number killed 1978	1988	Rate[c] 1978	1988
AFRICA										
Botswana	25	36[c]	1.8	5.1[d]			92	191[e]		0.4
Cameroon		11.3[d]		2.3[d]				1,034[e]		
Cent. African Rep.		0.6[d]		0.1[d]		2[d]				
Congo	12		2.1				120[f]		36[f]	
Côte d'Ivoire		23.2[g]		0.4[g]						
Egypt	2	1	1.2	40.7	1[h]		4,786			
Ethiopia	9	1[g]	3	3.8	3		847	910	0.6	
Kenya	8[d]			4[g]			1,588		69[f]	
Lesotho		6[e]	2.3[f]	2[e]			129[f]	80[e]	0.1	
Liberia	3		1	1[e]			109			
Madagascar		1[e]	3[i]							
Malawi	4[i]	45[d]		25[d]			132	109[d]		
Mauritius	43		22				2,570			
Morocco	30	36[d]	10.0	12.3[d]			172	148[e]		
Niger	5		3.1							
Nigeria	3		2.3		22		9,252		33	
Rwanda	2	3	1.5	1.4			273	264[d]		
Senegal	18		7.1				156	450		
Sierra Leone	10		4.5				156		23.6	
South Africa	132	150	17	24	45	80	6,550	10,691	14.3	12
Swaziland	30[f]		6[f]				140[f]			
Tanzania	3[j]	1.2[e]	1.1[j]	0.6[e]			264	200[e]		
Togo	1.2		0.5				839			
Tunisia	34	59	8.6	17.0		20		1,081		
Uganda	2	3[k]	1.1	1.3[k]				365		
Zaire		3[g]		0.8[g]						7
NORTH AMERICA										
Canada	530				194	143[e,l]	185[f]	4,285[e]	0.2[f]	
Dominican Rep.	25						198			
Panama	61.7		13						2.0	1.5
USA	665	732	23.8	28.7	2,455	3,080[e]	51,153	46,385[e]		

Continued over

Table 7.2 Continued

Region/country	Vehicles[a] Per 10^3 persons 1978	1988	Per km of road 1978	1988	Vehicle-km (10^9) 1978	1988	Deaths due to road accidents[b] Number killed 1978	1988	Rate[c] 1978	1988
SOUTH AMERICA										
Argentina	77	172[d]				50[d]				
Brazil	48	115	5.6	9.9			3,933	5,683		
Chile	26	75[d]	7	12			1,207	1,200[e]	10[f]	9.2[e]
Colombia					7	15[e]	2,355	819[d]	16.9	
Ecuador					7	21[d]		907[e]		
Venezuela	126		29			2	4,895	2,438[d]	4.6	
ASIA										
Afghanistan	4		3.6							
China	24		23.2				100		10	
Cyprus	20	36[e]	10	17[e]						
Hong Kong	46	57	190	226	4	7	437	301	11.4	4.0
India	2		0.9							
Indonesia										
Iraq	117		98		9			9,714		0.6
Israel	296	427	31.1	47.5		29	619	4,959	6.2	11.7
Japan	40		14.2		361	549[e]	8,783[m]	10,344	2.5	1.9
Jordan					3	8[e]	415	396[e]	12.7	29.0
Korea	63	48	32.6	140.1		26	5,114	11,563		
Kuwait	2	290	5.3			14	457[i]	312		2.2
Malaysia	2		4				2,568[n]	3,335		
Nepal										
Pakistan		4		4						
Philippines	90	15	17.8	5.7			3,725	5,281		
Saudi Arabia	11		6.4				2,033	922		
Sri Lanka	17		10.9				891	2,703[d]		
Thailand	23	35	16.2	25.0	15[i]	31	3,952	2,015		7[e]
Turkey	21	36	10.8	6.6	19	22	5,753[m]	7,007	16	29
Yemen		32		8.4		7	508	866		12.2
EUROPE										
Austria	294	398	20.7	28.3	34	48[d]	1,886[o]	1,446	4.5	
Belgium	329	336[d]	26	26[d]	43	11[q]	2,589	1,951[d]	6.0	4.1[d]
Bulgaria		132[p]					1,153	1,153		10.4
Czechoslovakia	143		29.5				1,933	1,464		

Continued below

Table 7.2 Continued

Region/country	Vehicles[a] Per 10³ persons 1978	1988	Per km of road 1978	1988	Vehicle-km (10⁹) 1978	1988	Deaths due to road accidents[b] Number killed 1978	1988	Rate[c] 1978	1988
Denmark	329	370	25.0	26.9	28	35	849	713	3.1	2.0
Finland	267	408	17.1	26.4	25	37	610	653	2.0	1.8
France	375	481	25.0	33.5	289	399	12,137[f]	10,548[f]	4.7	2.6
Germany, Fed. Rep.	377	499	48	62[e]	305	417	14,662	8,205	4.6	2.0[e]
Greece	115	193[k]	30	54[k]	20	37[k]	1,694	1,829[k]	7.8	4.9[k]
Hungary	89	176[e]	10.4	19.6[e]	19		2,018	1,573[e]	9	
Iceland	375	567	7.2	12.5	1		27	29	2.3	
Ireland	212	247	7.6	9.5	17	22[e]	628	462[e]	3.5	2.1[e]
Italy	322	467[a]	59	85.7[d]	213	279[e]	7,965	6,784[s]	3.3	2.2
Luxembourg	421	481	30	35		3	88	84		2.8
Netherlands	319	412	49	50	63	88	2,294	1,366	3.5	1.5
Norway	321	465	17	22	14[p]	55	434	375	3.1	7
Poland	70	146	8.2	15.3	41			4,851		
Portugal	105	244[d]	20	84.9	65		2,170[t]	2,303[e,t]	7.9	6.8
Spain	209	328	53.8		65	693	5,359	6,296[m]		
Sweden	367	445	24	29		59	1,034	682		1.1
Switzerland	352	453	35.4	42.2			1,268	945		
UK	302	382	48	60	274	327	6,831	5,050	2.5	1.8
Yugoslavia	96	137[d]	20	27[d]		35[d]	5,349	4,414[d]		
USSR		51				50[u]		47,197		
OCEANIA										
Australia	480	575[k]	16.0	10.6[k]			3,705	2,937[k]	4.2	
New Zealand	471	608[e]		21.3[e]	17[p]	18[k,p]	654	797[e]		

a Includes cars, buses, coaches and goods vehicles; excludes tractors and two-wheeled vehicles.
b The number of persons killed refers to the number dying within 30 days of the accident except where stated.
c The number of mortalities per unit distance travelled by road vehicles, i.e., number of deaths per 10⁹ vehicle-kilometres.
d 1986.
e 1987.
f 1977.
g 1984.
h Urban traffic not included.
i 1979.
j 1980.
k 1985.
l Excludes buses.
m Deaths within 24 hours of accident.
n No time limit for deaths due to accidents.
o Deaths within three days of accident.
p Cars only.
q Excludes goods vehicles.
r Deaths within six days of accident.
s Deaths within seven days of accident.
t Deaths on the spot or on route to hospital.

Totals may not tally due to rounding.

Sources:
IRF 1982 *World Road Statistics 1977–1981*, International Road Federation, Geneva and Washington DC.
IRF 1989 *World Road Statistics 1984–1988*, International Road Federation, Geneva and Washington DC.

Table 7.3 Number of bicycles and automobiles in selected countries, mid-1980s

Country	Bicycles (10^6)	Automobiles (10^6)	Bicycle/auto ratio
China	300.0	1.2	250.0
India	45.0	1.5	30.0
Korea	6.0	0.3	20.0
Egypt	1.5	0.5	3.0
Mexico	12.0	4.8	2.5
Netherlands	11.0	4.9	2.2

Country	Bicycles (10^6)	Automobiles (10^6)	Bicycle/auto ratio
Japan	60.0	30.7	2.0
Germany, Fed. Rep.	45.0	26.0	1.7
Argentina	4.5	3.4	1.3
Tanzania	0.5	0.5	1.0
Australia	6.8	7.1	1.0
USA	103.0	139.0	0.7

Countries are listed in order of decreasing magnitude of the bicycles : automobiles ratio.

Source:
Lowe, M. D. 1990 Cycling into the future. In: *State of the World 1990*, L. Starke (Ed.), W. W. Norton and Company, New York, 119–134.

Table 7.4 Cycling as share of daily passenger trips in selected cities, 1990

City/country	Share of daily trips (%)
Tianjin, China	77[a]
Shenyang, China	65
Groningen, Netherlands	50
Beijing, China	48
Delft, Netherlands	43
Dacca, Bangladesh	40[b]
Erlangen, Germany, Fed. Rep.	26
Odense, Denmark	25
Tokyo, Japan	25[c]
Moscow, USSR	24[c]

City/country	Share of daily trips (%)
New Delhi, India	22
Copenhagen, Denmark	20
Basel, Switzerland	20
Hannover, Germany, Fed. Rep.	14
Manhattan, USA	8[d]
Perth, Australia	6
Toronto, Canada	3[d]
London, UK	2
Sydney, Australia	1

[a] Share of non-walking trips.
[b] Trips by cycle rickshaw only.
[c] Share of cycling or walking to work.
[d] Vehicle-trips (versus passenger-trips).

Source:
Lowe, M. D. 1990 Cycling into the future. In: *State of the World 1990*, L. Starke (Ed.), W. W. Norton and Company, New York, 119–134.

Table 7.5 Inland surface goods and passenger transport in selected countries, latest available year

| Region/country | Year | Inland surface goods transport | | | | | | Inland surface passenger transport | | |
| | | By road | | By inland waterways | | By rail | | By road (10⁶ passenger-km) | | By rail (10⁶ passenger-km) |
		(10^6 t)	(10^6 t-km)	(10^6 t)	(10^6 t-km)	(10^6 t)	(10^6 t-km)	Public	Private	
AFRICA										
Cameroon	1986	11[a]				2	884			412
Egypt	1988	186	30,137	4	2,333	14	6,315	23,364	9,321	12,750
Madagascar	1988	1[b]	326[b]	1		1	204			221
South Africa	1987	317		94		174	93,158			
Tunisia	1988		975[c]	15		12	2,190	2,010[c]		1,014
NORTH AMERICA										
USA	1987		1,081,024		713,232		1,589,024	37,000	3,494,000	19,630[d]
SOUTH AMERICA										
Brazil	1986		238,862[b]	61	79,303[b]	221	111,263		499,200[b]	14,758
Chile	1987			14		14	2,105	340[b]		1,158
Colombia	1986	24	10,007	4[e]	2,849	1	807	67,223	41,394	230
Ecuador	1988	29	264			55	8,311	1	1	63
ASIA										
Hong Kong	1988	7		11		2	71	20,487	5,655	7,280
Japan	1987	5,287	230,048[f]	470	204,608	83	21,106	102,895	456,030	334,728
Korea	1988	188	8,783	49	16,883	62	14,005	85,325	22,498	25,978
Turkey	1988		63,480					123,237		
EUROPE										
Austria	1988			9	1,626	56	11,392	520		160
Belgium	1985	353	19,430	96	5,144	73	8,386	32,249		7,746
Bulgaria	1988	933	14,961	1	114	71	15,484	39,109		19,408
Czechoslovakia	1988	344	13,288	15	5,489	300	76,499	9,000		4,500
Denmark	1988	209[c,g]	10,262[c,h]			3	1,016		50,500	
Finland	1988	427	23,876	13	4,166	34	7,940	8,600	43,900	3,201
France	1988	1,514	139,802	62	7,417	141	51,511	43,000[j]	554,000[j]	73,000
Germany, Fed. Rep.	1988	2,657	155,956	237	53,746	307	60,960	61,300[k]	510,300[k]	

Continued over

Table 7.5 Continued

| Region/country | Year | Inland surface goods transport | | | | | | Inland surface passenger transport | | |
| | | By road | | By inland waterways | | By rail | | By road (10⁶ passenger-km) | | By rail (10⁶ passenger-km) |
		(10⁶ t)	(10⁶ t-km)	(10⁶ t)	(10⁶ t-km)	(10⁶ t)	(10⁶ t-km)	Public	Private	
Hungary	1987	565	12,969	11	10,868	118	22,079	28,159		11,324
Italy	1986		153,058		164		18,566	39,441	467,002	43,849
Luxembourg	1987	14^k	243^k	2		3	602			296
Netherlands	1988	370^c	20,549^c	91	7,564	5	1,075	12,100	147,400^l	9,664
Norway	1986	250	7,182	76	12,428	9	1,862	3,816	38,342	2,584
Poland	1988	1,440	39,417	16	1,416	435	124,159	57,073		52,134
Portugal	1987					6	1,640			5,907
Spain	1988		126,229			37	14,697	35,362	133,028	15,779
Sweden	1988	342^c	25,400			54	18,456			5,961
UK	1987	1,567	115,113	145	55,067	143	17,577	41,000	451,000	38,000
Yugoslavia	1986	176	22,697	20	4,623	91	28,014	31,393	37,000	12,398
USSR	1987	28,034	499,826	684	256,743	4,132	3,885,895	470,588		402,200
OCEANIA										
New Zealand	1985			10^m		11	3,241			

a 1984.
b 1985.
c 1987.
d Not including urban mass transit.
e Including coastal trade.
f Excluding vehicle-km by light motor vehicles (less than 550 cc).
g Domestic trucks over 6 tonnes total weight.

h Trucks over 2 tonnes total weight.
i Public and private bus transport.
j Private cars and taxis.
k 1986.
l Including bicycles.
m Coastal shipping.

Source:
IRF 1990 World Road Statistics 1984–88, International Road Federation, Geneva and Washington DC.

Table 7.6 Number of commercial aeroplanes in service world-wide by category, 1978 and 1988

Aircraft category	1978			1988		
	Scheduled	Non-scheduled	Total	Scheduled	Non-scheduled	Total
TURBO-JET	5,250	440	5,690	7,310	790	8,100
4-engines	1,510	170	1,680	1,120	170	1,290
3-engines	1,860	60	1,920	2,210	160	2,370
2-engines	1,880	210	2,090	3,980	460	4,440
TURBO-PROPELLER	1,180	240	1,420	1,530	380	1,910
4-engines	300	110	410	230	100	330
3-engines	–	–	–	–	–	–
2-engines	880	130	1,010	1,300	280	1,580
PISTON-PROPELLER	720	550	1,270	360	230	590
4-engines	200	90	290	80	30	110
3-engines	–	–	–	–	–	–
2-engines	520	460	980	280	200	480
TOTAL	7,150	1,230	8,380	9,200	1,400	10,600

Data refer to aeroplanes of 9,000 kg maximum take-off weight (MTOW) and over; aeroplane numbers from the USSR and China are not included.

In the above table, a dash signifies "not applicable".

Sources:
ICAO 1988 *Statistical Yearbook: Civil Aviation Statistics of the World 1987*, International Civil Aviation Organization, Montreal.
ICAO 1989 *Statistical Yearbook: Civil Aviation Statistics of the World 1988*, International Civil Aviation Organization, Montreal.

Table 7.7 Scheduled traffic of commercial air carriers, 1978 and 1988

Region[a]	Tonne-km (10^6)		Passenger-km (10^6)		Region[a]	Tonne-km (10^6)		Passenger-km (10^6)	
	1978	1988	1978	1988		1978	1988	1978	1988
WORLD	113,540	211,295			ASIA AND PACIFIC	15,350	41,775		
Passengers	84,335	153,035	936,360	1,698,730	Passengers	11,050	26,895	125,640	308,090
Freight	25,940	53,450			Freight	4,065	14,300		
Mail	3,265	4,810			Mail	230	580		
EUROPE	39,715	65,475			NORTH AMERICA	46,525	83,165		
Passengers	28,960	46,185	321,270	508,580	Passengers	35,675	65,420	393,170	720,890
Freight	9,660	17,995			Freight	9,015	15,000		
Mail	1,090	1,295			Mail	1,830	2,745		
AFRICA	2,855	6,660			LATIN AMERICA AND CARIBBEAN	5,635	9,550		
Passengers	2,180	4,165	24,050	45,600	Passengers	4,140	7,010	46,590	78,670
Freight	635	2,440			Freight	1,445	2,455		
Mail	40	55			Mail	50	85		
MIDDLE EAST	3,465	4,680							
Passengers	2,320	3,360	25,640	36,910					
Freight	1,115	1,265							
Mail	25	50							

[a] Regions are ICAO regions of carrier registration. Refer to source document for further details of member countries.

Passenger weight is generally converted to tonne-km at a rate calculated to be 90 kg per passenger, which allows for both free and excess baggage. However, in reporting, the conversion from passenger weight to tonne-km is left to the discretion of the operator, and conversion factors other than 90 kg may be used.

Sources:
ICAO 1988 *Statistical Yearbook: Civil Aviation Statistics of the World 1987*, International Civil Aviation Organization, Montreal.
ICAO 1989 *Statistical Yearbook: Civil Aviation Statistics of the World 1988*, International Civil Aviation Organization, Montreal.

Table 7.8 World tanker and combined carrier fleets, 1970–1990

Year	Tankers[a]			Combined carriers[b]		
	Number	Total capacity[c] (10^7 dwt)	Average capacity[d] (dwt)	Number	Total capacity[c] (10^7 dwt)	Average capacity[d] (dwt)
1970	3,235	152	46,897	212	15	70,733
1971	3,331	171	51,446	246	20	82,493
1972	3,359	190	56,485	299	29	95,355
1973	3,458	216	62,346	351	37	104,852
1974	3,638	256	70,305	381	41	108,248
1975	3,674	291	79,323	394	44	110,728
1976	3,636	321	88,209	410	46	111,413
1977	3,564	332	93,287	421	48	113,259
1978	3,370	328	97,472	417	48	114,821
1979	3,320	328	98,760	409	47	115,084
1980	3,338	325	97,302	406	47	115,291
1981	3,351	320	95,564	390	45	115,205
1982	3,264	304	93,049	366	42	115,671
1983	3,115	283	90,921	344	40	114,920
1984	3,012	270	89,537	329	38	115,119
1985	2,874	247	85,840	307	35	113,244
1986	2,874	241	83,846	291	33	114,064
1987	2,886	239	82,940	293	34	114,972
1988	2,923	243	83,295	294	34	115,656
1989	2,978	250	84,097	291	34	115,197
1990	3,015	255	84,474	290	33	115,333

[a] Commercial tankers include oil company owned or other privately owned vessels, and those owned by governments. Vessels which are owned or are under long-term charter to governments for military use, or tankers which were originally built or have been subsequently converted or classed primarily for non-transportation service are not included.
[b] Vessels retaining the ability to carry both wet and dry cargoes.

[c] Total fleet carrying capacity in deadweight tons (dwt).
[d] Average carrying capacity per vessel in deadweight tons (dwt).

Source:
John I. Jacobs PLC 1990 *World Tanker Fleet Review*, January–June 1990, John I. Jacobs PLC, London.

Table 7.9 Numbers of international visitors[a] to selected tourist destinations, 1985

Rank	Country	No. of visitors (10³)
1	Spain	43,235[b]
2	France	36,748
3	Italy	25,047
4	USA	21,018
5	Austria	15,168[c]
6	UK	14,483
7	Canada	13,245
8	Germany, Fed. Rep.	12,686[c]
9	Hungary	9,724
10	Switzerland	9,528[c]
11	Yugoslavia	8,436[c]
12	USSR	7,756[d]
13	Bulgaria	7,295
14	Belgium	7,078[d]
15	Greece	6,574
16	Andorra	6,000[e,f]
17	Portugal	4,989
18	Czechoslovakia	4,869
19	Romania	4,772[e]
20	Mexico	4,207
21	Macau	4,182
22	Denmark	3,573[c,d]
23	Netherlands	3,387[g]
24	Malaysia	2,906
25	San Marino	2,812
26	Poland	2,749[d]
27	Singapore	2,738
28	Hong Kong	2,426
29	Ireland	2,423
30	Thailand	2,397[d]
31	Japan	2,327
32	Turkey	2,230
33	Morocco	2,180
34	Iraq	2,153
35	Tunisia	2,003
36	Finland	1,933[g]
36	Norway	1,933[g]
38	Jordan	1,890
39	Argentina	1,800[d]
40	Brazil	1,736
41	Puerto Rico	1,532
42	Egypt	1,518
43	German Dem. Rep.	1,500[c,d]
44	China, Taiwan	1,452
45	Korea	1,426
46	China	1,370[h]
47	Bahamas	1,368
48	Saudi Arabia	1,268[i]
49	India	1,259
50	Israel	1,243
51	Australia	1,143
52	Jersey	1,100
53	Uruguay	1,031
54	Syria	986
55	Sweden	853[c,d]
56	Cyprus	814[j]
57	Colombia	784
58	Philippines	755
59	Indonesia	749
60	South Africa	728
61	Dominican Rep.	723[d]
62	Algeria	714
63	Luxembourg	689[c]
64	New Zealand	670
65	Jamaica	572
66	Neth. Antilles	570[d]
67	Kenya	541
68	Malta	518
69	Panama	454
70	Pakistan	441
71	US Virgin Is.	411
72	Bermuda	406
73	Brunei	398
74	Chile	394
75	Guam	365
76	Barbados	359
77	Cayman Is.	352[k]
78	Botswana	327
79	Zimbabwe	320
79	Guernsey	320[d]
81	Isle of Man	315[d]
82	Peru	300
83	Paraguay	263
84	Costa Rica	262
85	Sri Lanka	257
86	Guatemala	252
87	Fiji	246
88	Monaco	242
89	Senegal	241
90	Cuba	240
91	Venezuela	239[d]
92	Ecuador	238
93	Côte d'Ivoire	210[d]
94	Bahrain	207[d]
95	Aruba	206
96	Swaziland	200[c]
97	Martinique	193
98	Trinidad & Tobago	191[d]
99	Nepal	181
100	Lesotho	177
101	Br. Virgin Is.	168
102	Mauritius	161
103	Guadeloupe	151[g]
104	Bangladesh	145

Continued opposite

Table 7.9 Continued

Rank	Country	No. of visitors (10³)	Rank	Country	No. of visitors (10³)
105	Zambia	144[d]	138	Malawi	44[d]
105	Haiti	144[d]	140	St Vincent	42
107	Antigua & Barbuda	140	141	Myanmar q.v. Burma	41
108	El Salvador	133	142	Yemen	40
109	Cameroon	130[d]	143	Somalia	39[d]
110	Bolivia	127	144	Gambia	38[d]
111	Libya	126[d]	145	Suriname	36[d]
111	Honduras	126	146	Zaire	35
113	French Polynesia	122	147	Congo	34[b]
114	Maldives	115	148	Papua New Guinea	30
115	Togo	113[c]	149	Samoa	30[d]
116	Nigeria	103[d]	150	Niger	29[d]
117	Qatar	98[g]	150	Turks & Caicos Is.	29
118	Kuwait	97	150	Laos	29[d]
118	Iceland	97	150	Cook Is.	29
120	St Lucia	95	154	Gabon	28
121	Belize	93	154	Mali	28[g]
122	Iran	89	156	Montserrat	25
123	Gibraltar	86	156	Vanuatu	25
123	Liechtenstein	86	158	Norfolk Is.	24
125	American Samoa	85	159	Sudan	22
126	Réunion	79[d,g,k]	160	Dominica	21
127	Seychelles	73	160	Cambodia	21[d]
128	Ethiopia	61	162	Pacific Is. Tr. Tr.	20[f]
129	Tanzania	59	163	Madagascar	15[d]
130	Burundi	54	164	Uganda	14[d]
131	Sierra Leone	53[d]	164	Tonga	14
132	Grenada	52	166	St Pierre & Miquelon	11[f]
133	New Caledonia	51	166	Solomon Is.	11[f]
134	Ghana	50[d]	168	Afghanistan	9[d]
135	Benin	48[d]	169	Cent. African Rep.	7[d]
136	Anguilla	47	170	Comoros	5
136	St Christopher & Nevis	47	171	Bhutan	2[d]
138	Burkina Faso	44			

[a] Arrivals at frontiers; excluding excursionists and cruise passengers.
[b] Arrivals at main hotels.
[c] Arrivals at all forms of accommodation.
[d] Estimate.
[e] Including excursionists.
[f] Latest data available.
[g] Arrivals at hotels.
[h] Excluding ethnic Chinese arriving from Hong Kong, Macau and Taiwan (11,670 x 10³ in 1984) but including excursionists.
[i] 1986.
[j] South only.
[k] 1984.

A tourist is defined as any person travelling from his or her country of residence to any other country for a period of at least one night and not exceeding one year and for any reason other than exercising a remunerated activity or an activity remunerated from within the country visited.

Sources:
The Economist Publications 1987 *The World in Figures*, The Economist Publications, London.
WTO 1990 Personal communication, World Tourist Organization, Madrid, Spain (data for Saudi Arabia).

Table 7.10 Visitors to Ecuador's natural areas, 1980–1987

Natural area (date of creation)	1980	1981	1982	1983	1984	1985	1986	1987
Cotopaxi National Park (Aug. 1975)	44,661	49,743	51,158	46,248	43,453	47,279	41,316	33,196
Galapagos National Park (May 1936)	17,539	16,323	17,124	17,766	18,859	17,850	26,023	33,196
Machalilla National Park (Jul. 1979)	517	820	1,420	2,530	2,250	8,897		2,983
Podocarpus National Park (Dec. 1982)				52	80	150	133	175
Sangay National Park (Jun. 1975)		483	776	945	1,796	652		1,438
Limoncocha Biological Reserve (Sep. 1985)						3,127	2,974	2,676
Cayambe-Coca Ecological Reserve (Nov. 1970)	1,512	3,520	10,112	9,715	6,398	2,450		9,056
Cotacachi-Cayapas Ecological Reserve (Aug. 1968)		5,235	17,629	29,116	53,185	84,398		95,077
Pululahua Geobotanical Reserve (Jan. 1966)			1,188	2,773	4,036	5,325	3,245	3,380
Cuyabeno Wildlife Protection Reserve (Jul. 1979)			40	12	141	155	365	185
Boliche Recreation Area (Jul. 1979)	35,063	43,416	43,904	43,416	40,181	34,869		40,932
Cajas Recreation Area (Jun. 1977)	17,000	19,200	22,400	25,100	32,000	40,240	48,000	53,800

Boo, E. 1990 *Ecotourism: The Potentials and Pitfalls*, World Wildlife Fund, Washington DC.

Part 8
Wastes

Population growth, increasing urbanization and industrialization, and rising standards of living have all contributed to an increase in both the amount and variety of waste generated in most countries. Furthermore, many countries are now faced with dealing not only with greater volumes of, but also more dangerous, waste materials. This section of the 'UNEP Environmental Data Report' is concerned principally with the generation and disposal of solid waste arisings and liquid effluents. Potential environmental and human health effects resulting from waste generation and disposal are briefly discussed. Gaseous wastes emitted to the atmosphere are dealt with in Part 1: Environmental Pollution, Atmosphere, and international agreements relating to the transboundary movement of hazardous waste, in particular the Basel Convention, are considered in Part 10: International Co-operation.

The quality of statistics on solid waste arisings and disposal continues to be very variable. The data presented in this report are taken selectively from statistical reports produced by government agencies, international organizations and trade associations, and from research papers published in the scientific literature.

Within UNEP, issues relating to the generation and disposal of wastes, in particular hazardous wastes, are addressed by the International Register of Potentially Toxic Chemicals (IRPTC), Geneva. The UNEP Industry and Environment Office (IEO), Paris, established in 1975 to facilitate the adoption of environmentally sound decisions regarding industrial development by governments,

provides access to practical information and guidance relating to the safe disposal of industrial wastes and to waste minimization technologies. Furthermore, UNEP in co-operation with partner organizations such as the World Health Organization (WHO), the International Atomic Energy Agency (IAEA), the International Maritime Organization (IMO) and the Organisation for Economic Co-operation and Development (OECD), supports a number of programme activities relating to specific waste management problems.

Waste Generation

Wastes, which arise from virtually all man's activities, can be classified conveniently with respect to their source. Major categories include household and consumer wastes (i.e., municipal wastes), industrial wastes, agricultural wastes, extraction wastes, energy production wastes and sewage sludges. Wastes can also be classified by hazard and by composition. Information on waste arisings, particularly on industrial and hazardous wastes, is often difficult to assemble. Inefficient data collection methods, infrequency of surveys, reluctance of industry to supply information, and confusion over definitions of hazardous wastes are all contributory factors.

Table 8.1 shows waste arisings in five source categories: municipal, industrial, agricultural, mining (and quarrying) and sewage sludges. These data provide an incomplete picture of the total amount of wastes with which

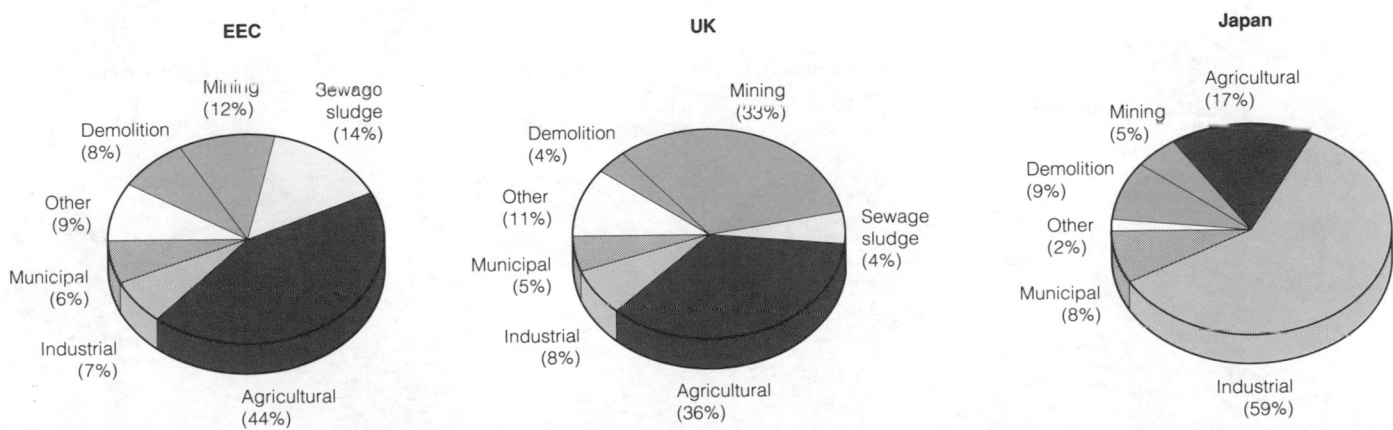

Figure 8.1 Waste arisings in EEC member countries (late 1980s), the UK (late 1980s) and Japan (1985) by source category
Sources: EUROSTAT, 1989; Haines, 1989

any of the listed countries may have to deal. Generally speaking, municipal wastes (in terms of mass) are a relatively small part of total waste arisings when compared with waste arisings from industry, agriculture and mining. However, the relative importance of the source categories for wastes largely depends on the economic base. Figure 8.1 illustrates the differences in the sources of waste arisings in selected countries.

Municipal Wastes

The term "municipal wastes" applies to those wastes generated by households and to wastes of similar character derived from shops, offices and other commercial units. Figure 8.2 shows that levels of municipal waste production are related to levels of industrialization and levels of income. Per capita waste generation varies between 2.75 and 4.0 kg per day in high-income countries, but is as low as 0.5 kg per day in those countries with lowest incomes (Cointreau, 1982).

Table 8.2 reflects recent changes in the composition of municipal wastes in selected countries. Data are given on the percentage contribution of paper (and cardboard), glass, plastics, metals, organic matter and petruscible matter to the total mass of municipal wastes in 1975, 1980 and 1985. It is generally very difficult to discern any trends in these figures, although in most developed countries it is generally accepted that the proportion of plastics in municipal wastes is growing (OECD, 1991). Packaging materials are becoming an increasingly important component of municipal wastes in developed countries. Recent estimates suggest that packaging materials account for about 30 per cent of municipal wastes in the USA (US EPA, 1990). Municipal wastes in developing countries tend to have a higher organic and ash/grit content, and also a higher moisture content (Figure 8.3).

Data reflecting the availability of municipal waste services in selected countries are presented in Table 8.3. It is evident that in OECD member countries more than 75 per cent of the total population, and certainly all urban populations, have access to municipal waste services. In

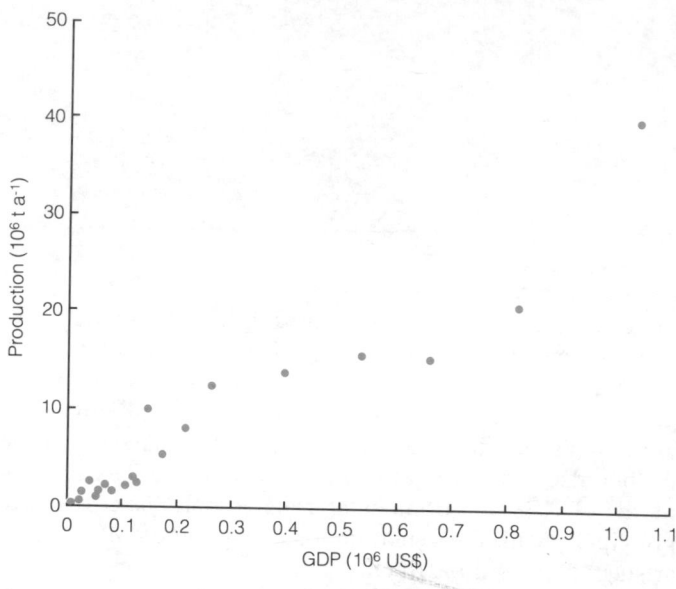

Figure 8.2 Municipal waste production as a function of GDP in OECD countries, 1980
Source: OECD, 1985

contrast, in many developing countries only a small proportion of the population in many urban areas has access to municipal waste services (WHO, 1990). Collection tends to be concentrated in commercial areas, markets and city centres. In other parts of the cities, waste collection and disposal is left to individuals or local communities or waste may be left to accumulate in the streets. For example, in small cities in Indonesia and in Vientiane, the capital city of Laos, only about 30 per cent of solid waste generated is collected (WHO, 1990).

Many small businesses, commercial units and hospitals, especially those in developing countries, rely on municipal waste services. Consequently, the municipal stream may often contain some hazardous wastes, such as hospital wastes, paints, solvents and batteries. Careless handling and disposal of municipal wastes may thus pose a threat to

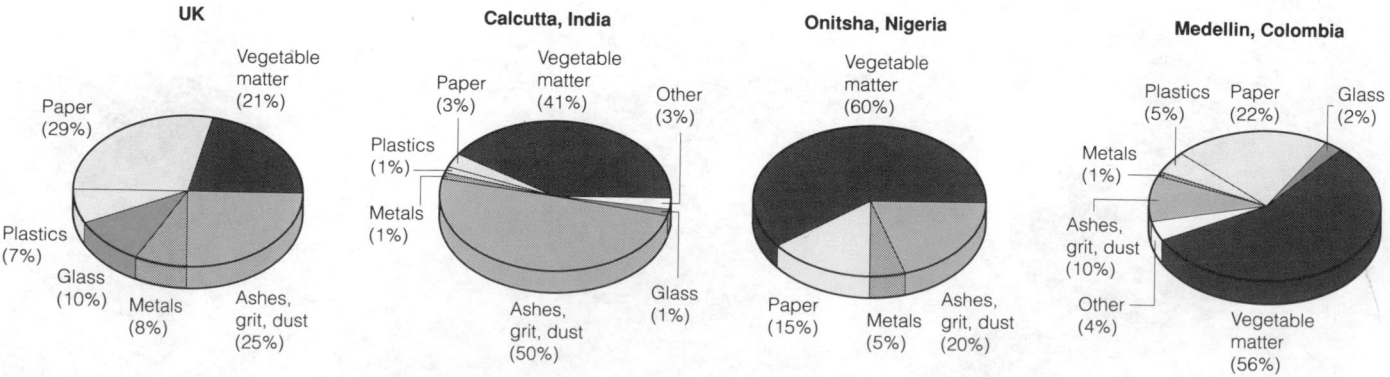

Figure 8.3 Composition of municipal wastes in the UK (1985), Calcutta (late 1970s), Onitsha (late 1970s) and Medellin (late 1970s)
Sources: Cook and Kalbermatten, 1982; OECD, 1989

human health in many developing countries. The practice of scavenging from municipal waste dump sites is also a matter of grave concern in some countries.

Agricultural Wastes and Sewage Sludges

Wastes produced by agricultural activities comprise animal slurries, silage effluents, end of spray residues and tank washings following pesticide use, and empty plastic packaging. Sewage sludges are produced as a result of the treatment of industrial and domestic wastes.

Animal manures and silage effluents are the main components of agricultural wastes. Like sewage sludges, these comprise a slurry of fine-grained, organic-rich particles. Sewage sludges may be contaminated with heavy metals, water-soluble organic chemicals, greases and oils depending on the source of effluent and efficiency of treatment. Data on typical trace metal concentrations found in sewage sludges are presented elsewhere in this report (see Part 1: Environmental Pollution, Soils and Sediments).

Industrial Wastes and Mining Wastes

Industrial process wastes encompass a very wide range of materials and may include general factory rubbish, packaging materials, organic wastes, acids, alkalis and metalliferous sludges. Mining wastes arise as by-products of the extraction process and may include topsoil, rock and dirt, and may be contaminated with small quantities of such materials as metals and coal. The most important feature of industrial and mining wastes is that a significant proportion is regarded as hazardous and as such requires special treatment and disposal.

Hazardous Wastes

It is generally accepted that the bulk of hazardous and toxic wastes are generated by process industries, the main sources being the chemical sector, mineral and metal processing industries and the engineering industry. Estimates of hazardous waste arisings are uncertain because of difficulties in providing a concise definition of hazardous waste. For example, estimates of the amounts of hazardous waste arisings in the European Economic Community (EEC) vary from 17 per cent to 50 per cent of all industrial waste arisings depending on the interpretation of the EEC definition (Haines, 1989).

Hazardous wastes arise not only as the by-products of industrial processes, but also when consumers discard empty chemical packaging and other items at the end of their useful life. Many countries are concerned about the increasing quantities of hazardous materials in, for example, aerosol cans, "empty" chemical packages and batteries, that find their way into the municipal waste stream. In addition, many "white goods" (i.e., washing machines, refrigerators, etc.) contain small quantities of chemicals such as polychlorinated biphenyls (PCBs) and chlorofluorocarbons (CFCs).

Available estimates of the quantities of hazardous and special wastes generated in selected countries are summarized in Table 8.4. Caution should be exercised when making comparisons between countries as "hazardous" wastes are inconsistently defined. The data presented in Table 8.4 also illustrate the fact that some hazardous waste is moved between countries. Where export of wastes allows more environmentally-sound disposal, this is considered a valid practice. However, as environmental and safety laws in Europe and North America have become more stringent and the cost of hazardous waste disposal has mounted, an increase in exports to developing countries which often have neither the resources nor the knowledge for safe disposal has been reported (Vir, 1989; Wilson and Balkau, 1990).

Accurate information on the amounts and types of wastes exported, their origin and their destination is not widely available. However, it has been estimated that about 20 per cent of exported hazardous wastes are currently shipped from industrialized to developing nations (Brady, 1989). The table below lists countries that have reported receiving hazardous wastes from developed countries between 1986–1988:

Region/country	Date of shipment(s)	Amount (t)
AFRICA		
Guinea	February 1988	15,240
Morocco	1988	487,680
Nigeria	1987–1988	4,064[a]
Sierra Leone	September 1987	635
South Africa	1986–1988	49.4
Zimbabwe	1986	0.3
NORTH AMERICA		
Haiti	February 1988	4,572[a]
Mexico	1987–1988	49,814
SOUTH AMERICA		
Brazil	1987–1988	29,758
Chile	1988	0.2
ASIA		
Lebanon	May 1988	2,450
Syria	December 1987	2,205
Turkey	1987	1,524
EUROPE		
German Dem. Rep.	1986–1988	3,048,000[a]
Hungary	1986	767[b]
Romania	1986	4,064[a]

[a] Estimate only.
[b] Wagons.

Source: Vallette, 1988

Although proposals had been made to ship almost 18×10^6 t of waste per year from North America and Europe to less developed nations (more than 1×10^6 t per year were to be sent to Antigua, Barbuda, Benin, Guinea-Bissau, Panama, Peru, Suriname and Morocco alone), over 44 developing countries have since rejected these proposals. Furthermore, 33 countries have officially banned imports of foreign wastes (Vallette, 1988). The Basel Convention, which is scheduled to come into force 90 days after 20 countries have ratified it, uses the rule of prior written consent and notification to control the trade in hazardous wastes, and its implementation should curb illegal dumping in developing countries in the future (see Part 10: International Co-operation).

Radioactive Wastes

Radioactive wastes arise primarily from nuclear power generation (see Part 6: Energy); smaller quantities are derived from military sources and a variety of uses in medical, industrial and university establishments. There are many types of radioactive wastes which can be classified either according to their radioactive properties or according to the sources from which they originated. Low-level radioactive wastes generally consist of contaminated laboratory debris, biological materials, building materials and uranium mine tailings. Spent fuels from nuclear power reactors, together with liquid and solid residues from reprocessing of spent fuels are classified as high-level radioactive waste.

Table 8.5 presents data on the level of radioactivity in effluents discharged by nuclear electricity generating plants. In most countries the radioactivity of effluents has decreased in 1985 compared with 1980. The total activity fell by more than 50 per cent in the UK; however, the activity of effluents from UK reactors remains higher than that reported from reactors in other countries. Data on the activity of effluents from nuclear fuel reprocessing plants in France and the UK have been summarized in previous editions of this report (UNEP 1987, 1989).

References

Brady, D. 1989 New curbs on the commerce in poison, *Our Planet* **1**(2/3), 18–20.

Cointreau, S. J. 1982 *Environmental Management of Urban Solid Wastes*, The World Bank, Washington DC.

Cook, D. B. and Kalbermatten, J. M. 1982 Prospects for resource recovery from urban solid wastes in developing countries. In: *Reuse of Solid Waste*, Proceedings of a Conference on the Practical Implications of the Reuse of Solid Waste, 11–12 November 1981, Thomas Telford, London.

EUROSTAT 1989 *Environmental Statistics*, Statistical Office of the European Communities, Luxembourg.

Haines, R. C. 1989 *A Study of the Safety Aspects Relating to the Handling and Monitoring of Hazardous Wastes*. Report prepared for the European Foundation for the Improvement of Living and Working Conditions, European Foundation, Luxembourg.

OECD 1985 *OECD Environmental Data Compendium 1985*, Organisation for Economic Co-operation and Development, Paris.

OECD 1989 *OECD Environmental Data Compendium 1989*, Organisation for Economic Co-operation and Development, Paris.

OECD 1991 *The State of the Environment*, Organisation for Economic Co-operation and Development, Paris.

UNEP 1987 *United Nations Environment Programme Environmental Data Report*, Basil Blackwell, Oxford.

UNEP 1989 *United Nations Environment Programme Environmental Data Report*, Basil Blackwell, Oxford.

US EPA 1990 *Characterization of Municipal Solid Waste in the United States: 1990 Update*, US Environmental Protection Agency, Research Triangle Park, North Carolina.

Vallette, J. 1988 *The International Trade in Wastes: A Greenpeace Inventory*, 3rd edition, Report prepared for the Ad Hoc Working Group of Legal and Technical Experts with a Mandate to Prepare a Global Convention on the Control of Transboundary Movements of Hazardous Wastes, Geneva, 7–16 November 1988, Greenpeace, London.

Vir, A. 1989 Toxic trade with Africa, *Environmental Science and Technology* **23**(1), 23–25.

WHO 1990 *Report of a Regional Workshop on Municipal Solid Waste Management*, Kuala Lumpur, 26 February–2 March 1990, World Health Organization, Geneva.

Wilson, D. C. and Balkau, F. 1990 Adapting hazardous waste management to the needs of developing countries – an overview and guide to action, *Waste Management and Research* **8**(2), 87–97.

Waste Disposal

Municipal Wastes

Table 8.6 shows estimates of the quantities of municipal wastes disposed of by various routes in selected countries. In most countries, especially where there is no shortage of land with suitable geological formations, landfill remains the predominant form of disposal. Disposal to landfill accounts for over 70 per cent of municipal wastes in Canada, the USA and most western European countries. In some countries, for example the UK, over 90 per cent of municipal wastes are landfilled. Data reflecting trends in the disposal of total and per capita quantities of municipal wastes in individual countries during 1970–1985 were given in an earlier edition of this report (UNEP, 1989).

Household wastes in landfill sites generate methane (a greenhouse gas) as a result of biological decomposition of organic matter under anaerobic conditions. On a global scale it is estimated that 7 per cent of methane emissions come from landfill sites (see Part 1: Environmental Pollution, Atmosphere). In some countries methane emissions from landfill sites are used as a fuel source. In addition, leachates are produced as the result of chemical breakdown of both industrial and household wastes in landfill. If the leachate enters surface or ground water before dilution has occurred, serious pollution by trace metals and other contaminants can result.

Incineration is the other main disposal option for municipal wastes; some industrial wastes, hazardous wastes and sewage sludge are also incinerated. The main advantage of incineration for the disposal of municipal wastes over landfill is the large reduction in the volume of material requiring final disposal. The heat energy generated by combustion may also be recovered. However, against this are the high construction and operational costs of incineration plant. Incinerators represent a source of air pollution; flue gases contain dust, acidic gases, vaporized metals and metal salts. A much publicized problem is the small amount of dioxins that arise as a result of the combustion process, especially at low temperatures (Suess, 1985). The environmental impact of dioxins has been the subject of much controversy (WHO, 1989).

Hazardous Wastes

Estimates of the quantities of hazardous wastes disposed of by various countries, according to treatment method and disposal option, are presented in Table 8.7. Landfill continues to remain the dominant method of disposal in many countries; about 70 per cent of hazardous wastes in the USA and 50 per cent in the EEC member countries are disposed of in this way. In developing countries the proportion of hazardous wastes disposed of to landfill is generally high because of the lack of treatment and/or recycling activities. However, until a consistent classification for hazardous wastes is devised it will remain difficult to tabulate comparable data for the international community.

Increased public concern about the danger posed by hazardous waste has prompted both governments and industries to seek methods of minimizing the amount of waste generated and to find ways of recycling wastes. In recent years, the amount of hazardous waste recycled has grown (Biswas, 1989).

Disposal at Sea

The dumping of wastes at sea is generally well documented for some regions as many coastal countries are signatories to international conventions such as the Oslo Convention and London Dumping Convention, which control the sea

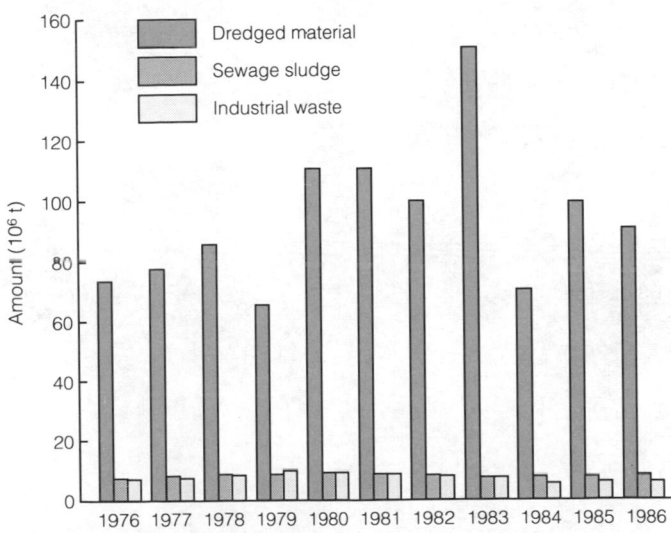

Figure 8.4 Total amounts of waste dumped at sea by Oslo Convention signatory countries, 1976–1986
Source: Oslo Commission, 1989

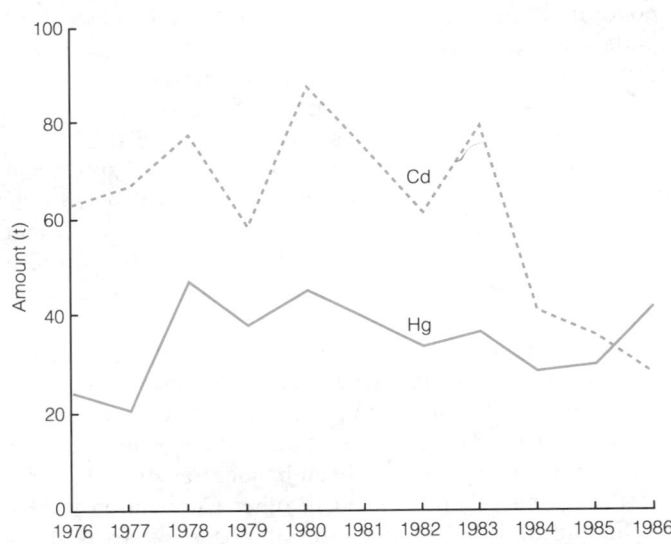

Figure 8.5 Amounts of Hg and Cd in wastes dumped at sea by Oslo Convention signatory countries, 1976–1986
Source: Oslo Commission, 1989

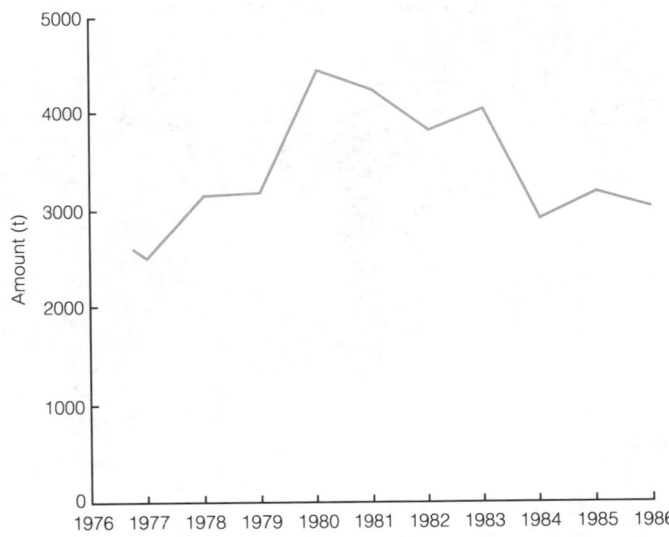

Figure 8.6 Amounts of Pb in wastes dumped at sea by Oslo Convention signatory countries, 1976–1986
Source: Oslo Commission, 1989

disposal of wastes. Contracting Parties to the Oslo Convention, which entered into force in 1974, are Belgium, Denmark, Finland, France, Germany, Fed. Rep., Iceland, Ireland, the Netherlands, Norway, Portugal, Spain, Sweden and the UK; ocean regions covered by the convention are the north-east Atlantic, the North Sea and the Baltic Sea. Data on sewage sludges, industrial wastes and dredged soils dumped at sea by signatory countries in these regions are given in Tables 8.8–8.10. Approximately 80–90 per cent of all wastes dumped at sea (by weight) are dredged spoils; it is estimated that about 215×10^6 t a^{-1} of dredged spoils were dumped between 1980–1985, compared with 15×10^6 t a^{-1} of sewage sludges during the same period.

Figure 8.4 shows the total amount of wastes dumped by Oslo Convention signatories between 1976 and 1986. Each of the waste streams – sewage sludges, dredged spoils and industrial wastes – contains heavy metals which are thus introduced into the marine environment. Figures 8.5 and 8.6 illustrate trends in the amounts of lead (Pb), mercury (Hg) and cadmium (Cd) entering the marine environment each year via this route.

At the present time, sewage sludges are dumped at sea by only a few countries. Under the Oslo Convention only Ireland and the UK are permitted to dump sewage sludges at sea (Table 8.8); dumping of hazardous and industrial wastes in the North Sea has been banned (as of 31 December 1989) and will be banned in other Convention waters by the end of 1995. Incineration of wastes at sea is scheduled to terminate by 1994.

Since 1946 variable amounts of packaged low-level radioactive waste have been disposed of at more than 50 sites in northern parts of the Atlantic and Pacific Oceans. Table 8.11 presents data on the activity of low-level packaged waste dumped at sea by individual countries between 1949–1982. During this period an estimated 46 PBq of radioactive waste from research and medical establish-

ments, the nuclear industry and military activities were disposed of at sea. Beta and gamma emitters account for more than 98 per cent of the total radioactivity of the dumped waste; tritium alone represents more than one-third of the total radioactivity disposed of at the north-east Atlantic sites (IAEA, 1990). Figure 8.7 shows the location of disposal sites for wastes in the Pacific and Atlantic oceans and the relative contributions of various countries to the total amount of low-level packaged wasted dumped between 1949–1982.

Data on the sea disposal of low-level packaged radioactive wastes have been compiled by the International Atomic Energy Agency (IAEA). This effort is the first in a series of three studies designed to generate a comprehensive inventory of inputs of anthropogenic radionuclides to the marine environment. Further investigations will consider inputs from low-level radioactive liquid effluents and marine accidents involving radioactive materials.

Disposal to Agricultural Land

The application of organic wastes to agricultural land is a widespread practice. In the European Community, for example, it is estimated that 30 per cent of sewage sludges are used in this way (Petruzzelli, 1989). Large quantities of animal slurries and silage effluents are also sprayed on fields as a fertilizer.

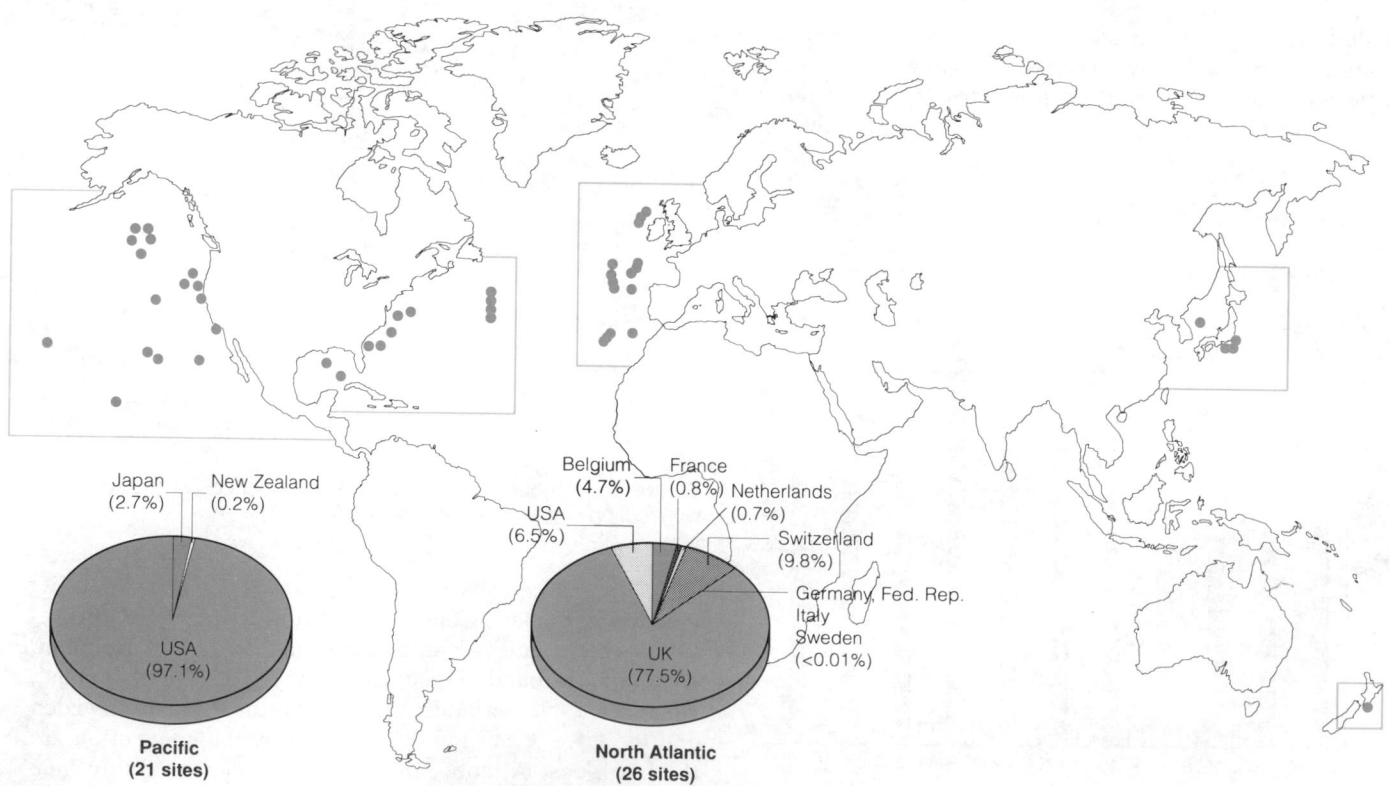

Figure 8.7 Disposal of low-level packaged radioactive wastes at sea, 1949–1982
Source: IAEA, 1990

Careless storage, handling and improper application of farm organic wastes can represent serious sources of water pollution (Beck, 1989). Sewage sludges may contain relatively high levels of potentially toxic trace metals; application of sludges to agricultural land may thus lead to soil and crop contamination (see Part 1: Environmental Pollution, Soils and Sediments).

Oil Spills

Statistics on oil spills and tanker accidents are compiled by a number of organizations, among them the International Tanker Owners Pollution Federation Limited. Established in 1974, in response to the recognition of the need for reliable data on oil spills, the Federation now maintains a data base of comprehensive information relating to oil spills. Data are obtained from Federation members and also from published sources.

Figure 8.8 shows that both the number of oil spills and the quantity of oil spilt as a result of transportation accidents have declined during the period 1974–1989. A small number of large spills have been responsible for a high percentage of the total oil spilt. Since 1981, there have been 360 spills of over 50 billion barrels (bbl), releasing some 945×10^3 t of oil into the marine environment; 509×10^3 t of oil (56 per cent of the total) were spilt in just 10 incidents (1 per cent of the total number). Figure 8.9 shows the distribution of tanker spills over 10,000 bbl since 1974. Not surprisingly, these are concentrated in areas of heaviest oil tanker traffic (see Part 7: Transport/Tourism). More detailed information on individual oil spills that occurred between 1975 and 1985 was included in the second edition of this report (UNEP, 1989).

Oil spills and their resultant effects on the flora and fauna where they occur are generally well reported and

Figure 8.9 Distribution of tanker spills greater than 10,000 bbl since 1974
Source: figure supplied by the International Tanker Owners Pollution Federation Limited, London

documented. Although a major oil spill can seriously damage the environment, the effects are typically quite localized. Oil spills account for only a small proportion of the total input of hydrocarbons to the marine environment. Other sources include atmospheric deposition, river run-off and seepage effluents. Estimates of total inputs of petroleum hydrocarbons to the North Sea and the global marine environment were reported in the 1989 edition of this report (UNEP, 1989).

References

Beck, L. 1989 A review of farm waste pollution, *Journal of the Institution of Water and Environmental Management* 3(5), 467–477.

Biswas, A. 1989 Environmental aspects of hazardous waste management for developing countries: problems and prospects. In: *Proceedings of the UNIDO Hazardous Waste Management Workshop*, Vienna, 22–26 June 1987, S. Maltezou, A. Biswas and H. Sutter (Eds), Tycooly International, Dublin.

IAEA 1990 *Inventory of Radioactive Material Entering the Marine Environment: Part 1 Sea Disposal of Low-level Packaged Radioactive Waste*, International Atomic Energy Agency, Vienna.

Oslo Commission 1989 *Thirteenth Annual Report*, Oslo Commission, London.

Petruzzelli, G. 1989 Recycling wastes in agriculture: heavy metal bioavailability, *Agriculture Ecosystems and Environment* 27, 493–507.

Suess, M. J. (Ed.) 1985 *Solid Waste Management: Selected Topics*, World Health Organization Regional Office for Europe, Copenhagen.

UNEP 1989 *United Nations Environment Programme Environmental Data Report*, Basil Blackwell, Oxford.

WHO 1989 *Polychlorinated Dibenzo-para-dioxins and Dibenzofurans*, Environmental Health Criteria 88, World Health Organization, Geneva.

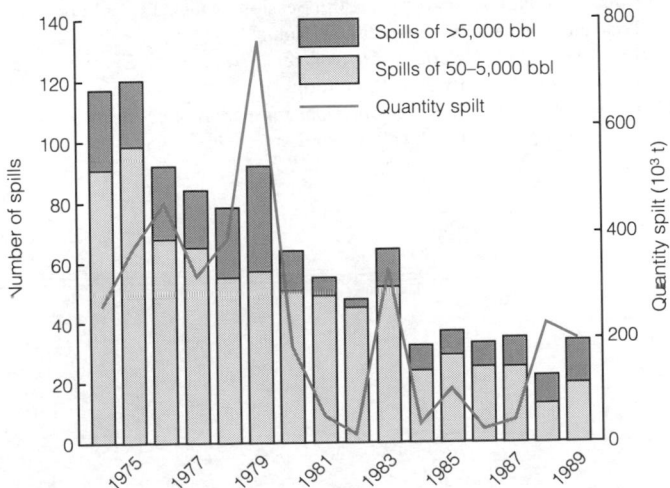

Figure 8.8 Oil spills resulting from accidents involving tankers, combination carriers and barges, 1974–1989
Source: International Tanker Owners Pollution Federation Limited, 1990 Unpublished data

Resource Recovery

Many waste streams contain useful materials which can be reclaimed and reused. In many industries, for example, steel production, a certain amount of recovery of "in-house" scrap already occurs. Although significant amounts of valuable materials in bulky consumer goods, such as cars and "white goods" are recovered, it is clear that many more discarded consumer items, particularly packaging materials, could be reclaimed and reused. Many governments, faced with a rapid growth in the volume of municipal wastes, are actively encouraging recycling of materials from domestic or municipal waste streams.

A number of environmental benefits, other than savings on the costs of waste disposal, can accrue by substituting secondary materials for virgin resources. The table inset below illustrates the percentage reduction in energy and water use, in mining wastes and in air and water pollution that can be achieved when specific materials are recycled:

	Potential saving (%)			
	Aluminium	Steel	Paper	Glass
Energy use	90–97	47–74	23–74	4–32
Air pollution	95	85	74	20
Water pollution	97	76	35	–
Mining wastes	–	97	–	80
Water use	–	40	58	50

Source: Bartone, 1990

Waste Paper Recovery

National statistics on waste paper recovery (expressed as a percentage of paper consumption) are given in Table 8.12. Data, which span the period 1960–1988, have been extracted from a number of sources (UNEP 1987, 1989). The most recent data, for 1986–1988, have been compiled by the Food and Agriculture Organization (FAO, 1989). The countries for which recent information is provided comprise about 83 per cent of the world's paper and paperboard capacity; the data thus provide a fair representation of the level of waste paper recovery and use world-wide.

During the past two decades, many countries have shown a significant increase in their waste paper recovery rate; in 1988, 60 per cent of the countries surveyed by the FAO reported recovery rates of over 30 per cent (Table 8.12). The success of paper recycling depends on favourable market conditions. In some countries these have been created by government regulations which stipulate the proportion of recycled paper to be used in the production of some paper goods.

Aluminium Recycling

Data on aluminium recycling are derived from annual statistics published by the Aluminium Association and are presented in Table 8.13 for the period 1972–1988. The total amount of aluminium recycled, as a percentage of consumption, has increased globally from 21 per cent in 1972 to 30 per cent in 1988. However, whilst one or two countries have matched or exceeded that rate of increase, many others have shown a fall in the rate at which aluminium is recycled.

Glass Recycling

Statistics on the level of glass recycling in European countries are routinely compiled and published by the European Glass Container Federation (FEVE). National data on both the total quantity of glass recycled and the glass recycled as a percentage of consumption, are given in Table 8.14 for the period 1980–1989. Data for non-European countries, obtained from other sources, have been added where possible. During the 1980s, there has been a substantial increase in both the total quantity recovered and an increase in its ratio to consumption in most European countries. In 1989, five European countries obtained over half of their glass requirements from recycled sources (Table 8.14).

References

Bartone, C. 1990 Economic and policy issues in resource recovery from municipal solid wastes, *Resources Conservation and Recycling* **4**, 7–23.

FAO 1989 *Waste Paper Data 1986–88*, Report of the FAO Advisory Committee on Pulp and Paper, 30th Session, Rome, 17–19 May 1989, Food and Agriculture Organization, Rome.

UNEP 1987 *United Nations Environment Programme Environmental Data Report*, Basil Blackwell, Oxford.

UNEP 1989 *United Nations Environment Programme Environmental Data Report*, Basil Blackwell, Oxford.

Table 8.1 Quantities of solid waste generated in selected countries by source category, 1985 (10^3 t a^{-1})

Region/country	Municipal	Industrial	Agricultural	Mining/quarrying	Sewage sludge
NORTH AMERICA					
Canada	16,000	61,000[a]	48,000	910,213	500
USA	178,000[b]	628,000[c]	1,400,000	1,300,000[d]	8,400[e]
ASIA					
Cyprus			3	190	
Japan	41,530	312,000	90,544	26,017	2,003
EUROPE					
Austria	2,052[e]	31,000[b,e]		466[e]	1,350[e]
Belgium	3,082[a]	8,000[a]	53,000[a]	7,069[a]	18[a]
Bulgaria	6,773		6,271	21,872	
Czechoslovakia				452,360[d]	
Denmark	2,161	1,317			82[f]
Finland	2,000	15,000	23,200	17,700	137[g]
France	15,000	50,000	399,400	60,160[h]	600
Germany, Fed. Rep.	19,387[g]	55,932[g]		3,454[g]	1,591[e]
Greece	2,500[a]	3,904		3,900	
Hungary	5,500	101,000	54,237	5,200	
Iceland	93				
Ireland	1,270[g]	1,580[g]	22,000[g]	1,930[g]	570[g]
Italy	15,000	35,000[b]	29,830[a]	57,000[a]	
Luxembourg	190	135			11
Netherlands	7,242[g]	3,942[i,j]	100,501[g]	162[g]	250
Norway	1,970	2,186[a,k]	18,500[g]	9,000[g]	70[g]
Poland	7,900		107	101,400	
Portugal	2,246	11,200[a]		3,900[a]	
Spain	10,600	5,108[i]	47,600	180,000	10,000
Sweden	2,650	4,000[a]	17,000	28,000	372
Switzerland	2,500				255[i]
UK[l]	16,700	50,000	250,000	230,000	30,000
USSR			2,300		
OCEANIA					
Australia	10,000[a]	20,000[a,b]			
New Zealand	2,106[d]	300[d,j]			45[d]

[a] 1980.
[b] Estimate.
[c] Includes waste waters which meet the US definition of solid wastes.
[d] 1982.
[e] 1983.
[f] 1977.
[g] 1984.
[h] Includes demolition waste.
[i] 1986.
[j] Non-chemical wastes only.
[k] Chemical industry wastes only.
[l] England and Wales only.

Data for sewage sludge refer to dry weight, with the exception of the UK for which data are in terms of wet weight.

Sources:
OECD 1989 OECD Environmental Data Compendium 1989, Organisation for Economic Co-operation and Development, Paris.
UN-ECE 1987 Environment Statistics in Europe and North America: An Experimental Compendium, United Nations, New York.

Table 8.2 Composition of municipal wastes in selected countries, 1975–1985

Region/country	Paper and cardboard (%)			Plastics (%)			Glass (%)		
	1975	1980	1985	1975	1980	1985	1975	1980	1985
NORTH AMERICA									
Canada		36.5	36.5					6.6	6.6
USA	32.5	29.7[a]	34.7[b]	3.0	5.3	6.7[b]	10.0	10.3	9.0[b]
ASIA									
Israel	20[c]			12[c]			3[c]		
Japan[d]	30.9	27.4	38.3[b]	8.9	12.3	7.7[b]	6.1[e]	8.0[e]	1.3[b]
Pakistan[f]			10.1			9.9			1.2
EUROPE									
Austria	27.2[g]	30.7[a]	33.6[h]	6.0[g]	6.1[a]	7.0[h]	11.1[g]	10.4[a]	10.0[h]
Belgium	30[j]	35.0		5[j]	5.8		8[j]	8.2	
Denmark	35[j]	34[k]		4[j]	7[k]		8[j]	6[k]	
Finland			40			8			4
France	35[j]	28	27.5	5[j]	6	4.5	8[j]	11	7.5
Germany, Fed. Rep.	25	19.9	17.9	8[l]	6.1	5.4	15	11.6	9.2
Greece		19.6			7.0			2.7	
Ireland	33[j]	35[k]	24.5	4[j]	11[k]	14	8[j]	8[k]	7.5
Italy	20.4	22.5	22.3[h]	5.3	6.8	7.2[h]	6.4	6.7	6.2[m]
Luxembourg	25[j]		17.2	4.5[j]		6.4	5[j]		7.2
Netherlands	23.0	21.0	22.8	5.6	6.5	6.8	12.0	11.9	7.2
Norway[n]	31	31	31	4	4	4	3	3	3
Portugal		18.9	19		3.2	3		2.9	3
Spain		15	15		6	6		6	6
Sweden		43	35–45		10	8–10		5	6–8
Switzerland		30[o]			13[o]			9[o]	
UK[p]	30	29		4	7		10	10	
OCEANIA									
Australia[q]		26.0			6.1			15.1	
New Zealand		33.6			3.0			2.5	

[a] 1978.
[b] 1984.
[c] 1976.
[d] 1975 and 1980 data are average values for four cities: 1985 data refer to Tokyo only.
[e] Glass and ceramics.
[f] Data refer to Karachi only.
[g] 1973.
[h] 1986.
[i] 1983.
[j] 1977.
[k] 1979.

[l] Includes textiles.
[m] OECD Secretariat estimate.
[n] 1975 and 1980 data refer to surveys conducted during 1973–1974 and 1979–1981, respectively.
[o] 1982.
[p] England and Wales only.
[q] Data are based on sample figures for Sydney (1982) and Melbourne (1980–1981).

The composition of municipal wastes is described here in terms of the percentage contribution of "Paper and cardboard", "Plastics", "Glass", "Metals" and "Other" to the total mass. These five categories total 100 per

Metals (%)			Other (%)			Organic (%)			Putrescible (%)		
1975	1980	1985	1975	1980	1985	1975	1980	1985	1975	1980	1985
	6.6	6.6		45.7	45.7		57.6	74.3			
9.0	9.6a	8.8b	45.5	45.1	40.8b		37.5a				
4.5c			60.5c			54c					
3.7	4.7	1.4b	50.4	47.3	51.3b	78	85				
		0.7			78.1			77.5			
8.0g	8.2a	3.7h	47.7g	44.6a	48.0h	65.4g	61.7a	60.5i			
4.5j	5.1		51.5j	45.9		40j	35		43j		
4j	5k		49j	47k					15j		
		3			45			85			
5j	5	6.5		50	54		59		20j		
5	3.9	3.2	47	58.8	64.3		63.4		16		
	4.2			66.5			92	82	60		
4j	3k	3	51j	43k	51			56	28j		
3.0	2.9	3.1h	64.9	61.4	61.6m	68.9	67.2	64.4h	39		
3.5j		2.6	62j		66.6			44	56j		
3.3	3.1	3.4	56.1	57.5	59.8	82.8	83.7	87.9	48		
7	7	7	55	55	55	77	77	77			
	3.6	3.5		71.4	71.5		74.7	74.5			
	2.5	2.5		70.5	70.5		52.5	52.5			
	6			36			89				
	6o			42o			70o				
8	8		48	46		54	58		21		
	7.0			45.8			41.4				
	7.6			53.3			37				

cent (In some cases, totals may not tally to exactly 100 per cent due to rounding). The category "Other" may include organic materials, kitchen waste, ash and grit, textiles, sweepings and garden refuse.

Estimates of the contribution of "Organic" and "Putrescible" materials to the total mass of municipal wastes are expressed as percentages and are given as separate categories.

Sources:

Haley, C. 1990 Energy recovery from burning municipal solid wastes: a review, *Resources Conservation and Recycling* **4**, 77–103.

Khatib, N., Uomani, N., and Husan, N. 1990 Evaluation of recyclable materials in municipal waste in Karachi, *Biological Wastes* **31**, 113–122.

Ministro dell'Ambiente 1989 *Relazione sullo Stato dell'Ambiente*, Vol. 1, Ministry of the Interior, Rome.

OECD 1987 *OECD Environmental Data Compendium 1987*, Organisation for Economic Co-operation and Development, Paris.

Statistics Sweden 1990 *Naturmiljön i Siffror*, 3rd edition, Statistics Sweden, Stockholm.

Whitman, J. (Ed.) 1988 *The Environment in Israel 1988*, Environmental Protection Service, Jerusalem.

Table 8.3 Percentage of population with access to municipal waste services in selected countries, 1975–1985

Region/country	1975	1980	1985	Increase in % population served, 1975–85
NORTH AMERICA				
Canada		99	99	
USA	100	100	100	0
ASIA				
Japan	92	95	98	6
EUROPE				
Austria	86[a]	96	99	13
Belgium	95	100		
Finland[b]			75[c]	
France	80	95	98	18
Germany, Fed. Rep.	98	100	100[d]	2
Greece		69[a]		
Ireland[b]	70	75	77[d]	7
Luxembourg	100	100	100	0
Netherlands	95[e]		99	4
Norway		76		
Portugal		64	75[f]	
Spain			85	
Sweden	95	100	100	5
Switzerland	85	96	97	12
UK[g]	100[h]	100	100	0
OCEANIA				
New Zealand	90	91[i]		

a 1979.
b Percentage of municipal waste collected nationally by local authorities; towns and cities, however, have 100 per cent collection.
c 1983.
d 1984.
e 1977.
f OECD Secretariat estimate.

g England and Wales only.
h 1976.
i 1982.

Source:
OECD 1989 *OECD Environmental Data Compendium 1989*, Organisation for Economic Co-operation and Development, Paris.

Table 8.4 Production and movement of hazardous and special wastes in selected countries, mid-1980s (10^3 t a^{-1})

Region/country	Year	Total production	Exports	Imports
NORTH AMERICA				
Canada	1982	3,280	70	70
Puerto Rico	1987	50	12.5[a]	
USA	1985	265,000	150[b]	40[b]
ASIA				
China, Taiwan	Annual[c]	2,900		
India	1980	36,000[d]		
Israel	1988	25[e]		
Japan	1986	666		
Korea	Annual[c]	733		
Malaysia	1985	419[f]		
EUROPE				
Austria	1983	200	1.5	
Belgium	1980	915		
Denmark	1985	125	20	
Finland	1985	124	2.8	
France	1987	2,000	25	250
Germany, Fed. Rep.	1984	5,000	700	50–100
Hungary	1986	5,000[g]	0	0
Ireland	1984	20	20	
Italy	1985	1,000–3,000		
Luxembourg	1986	6	1.3	0
Netherlands	1986	1,500	155	
Norway	1987	120	0.4	
Portugal	1986	1,049		
Spain	1987	1,708		
Sweden	1980	500	15	3
Switzerland	1987	120	68	
UK[h]	1987	2,000	0	80
OCEANIA				
Australia	1980	300[i]	0.7	
New Zealand	1982	36–60		

[a] All exports to USA.
[b] 1987.
[c] Annual average figure: does not refer to any specific 12-month period.
[d] Figure refers to selected industries only; these include pesticides, dyes and pigments, pharmaceuticals, organic chemicals, fertilizers, steel production, non-ferrous metals and caustic soda.
[e] Figure is for wastes transferred to the Ramat Hovav disposal site. It is estimated that this amount constitutes only half of all hazardous waste production in Israel.
[f] Data expressed as m^3 a^{-1}.
[g] Includes 3×10^6 t of red mud from aluminium production.
[h] England and Wales only.
[i] 1985.

Hazardous wastes are not consistently defined from country to country.

Sources:
Narkis, Y. N. and Kornberg, Y. 1989 The problem of hazardous wastes in Israel. In: *Environmental Quality and Ecosystem Stability*, Proceedings of the 4th International Conference of the Israel Society for Ecology and Environmental Quality Sciences, Jerusalem, 4–8 June 1989.

OECD 1989 *OECD Environmental Data Compendium 1989*, Organisation for Economic Co-operation and Development, Paris.
Sundaresan, B. B., Subrahmanyam, P. and Bhide, A. 1987 An overview of toxic and hazardous waste in India. In: *Technical Manual for the Safe Disposal of Hazardous Wastes with Special Emphasis on the Needs of Developing Countries*, Vol. 4, World Health Organization, Geneva, United Nations Environment Programme, Nairobi, and the World Bank, Washington DC.
Szenes, E. 1990 Managing mountains of waste. In: *State of the Hungarian Environment*, D. Hinrichsen and G. Enyedi (Eds), Hungarian Academy of Sciences, Budapest, Ministry for Environment and Water Management, Budapest, and Hungarian Statistical Office, Budapest, 135–137.
UN-ECE 1987 *Environment Statistics in Europe and North America: An Experimental Compendium*, United Nations, New York.

Table 8.5 Activity of liquid effluents from nuclear power reactors, 1980–1985

Region/country	1980	1981	1982	1983	1984	1985
NORTH AMERICA						
Canada						
Tritium, H^3 (TBq)	1,369.4	1,026.0	1,332.1	2,023.9	1,346.6	1,846.2
Total (GBq)[a]	178.0	91.0	96.6	129.7	147.1	59.3
USA						
Tritium, H^3 (TBq)	522.4	701.7	645.4	705.2	850.4	484.4
Total (GBq)[a]	3,051.2	3,240.2	5,608.4	7,037.7	9,251.7	4,695.6
SOUTH AMERICA						
Argentina						
Tritium, H^3 (TBq)	290	410	310	240	414	436
Total (GBq)[a]	81	51	37	51	77	53
EUROPE						
Belgium						
Tritium, H^3 (TBq)	37.2	49.2	58.5	70.9	61.8	96.0
Total (GBq)[a]	154	351	55			
Finland						
Tritium, H^3 (TBq)	4.3	11.8	10.5	10.3	8.1	10.6
Total (GBq)[a]	29.2	19.8	23.3	31.1	35.2	31.9
France						
Tritium, H^3 (TBq)	233	394	364	456	619	684
Total (GBq)[a]	1,684	2,034	1,249	1,622	1,640	1,450
Germany, Fed. Rep.						
Tritium, H^3 (TBq)	63.8	61.3	83.3	103.6	114.3	131.6
Total (GBq)[a]	48.8	23.6	23.2	20.4	26.1	12.6
Italy						
Tritium, H^3 (TBq)	37.6	2.6	10.7			
Total (GBq)[a]	60.1	111.4	193.8			
Netherlands						
Tritium, H^3 (TBq)	6.9	6.5	7.8	6.4	4.8	
Total (GBq)[a]	22.2	31.8	42.9	25.5	32.9	
Sweden						
Tritium, H^3 (TBq)	17.3	25.4	22.2	28.9	49.4	48.0
Total (GBq)[a]	376.4	491.3	795.0	819.5	2,812.3	692.6
UK						
Tritium, H^3 (TBq)	295.7	384.6	519.8	601.1	708.5	474.8
Total (GBq)[a]	28,807	23,375	24,668	16,877	15,874	13,700
USSR						
Tritium, H^3 (TBq)	7.4					

[a] Excluding tritium.

Source:
UNSCEAR 1988 *Sources, Effects and Risk of Ionizing Radiation*, 1988
Report to the General Assembly, United Nations, New York.

Table 8.6 Disposal of municipal wastes in selected countries, mid-1980s (10^3 t a^{-1})

Region/country	Year	Landfill	Incineration Total	Incineration With energy recovery	Other
NORTH AMERICA					
Canada	1985	14,880	960	580	160
USA	1984	110,000	15,000		
ASIA					
Cyprus[a]	1985	32	0		0
Japan	1986	10,588	30,860		1,409
EUROPE					
Austria	1983	1,308	329		411[b]
Belgium	1980	1,530	720	215	832
Bulgaria[a]	1985	9,408	0		0
Denmark	1985	1,361	700		100[b]
Finland	1985	1,735	50	50	215
France	1985	7,080	5,385	3,420	2,535
Germany, Fed. Rep.	1984	13,396	5,467		523
Greece	1980	2,500	0		0
Ireland	1984	1,100	0		0
Italy	1980	5,286	2,794	595	5,886
Luxembourg	1985	35	124	124	0
Netherlands	1985	3,595	2,347	1,666	568
Norway	1985	1,535	275	145	160
Poland	1985	58,900	0		0
Portugal	1985	1,392			280[b]
Spain	1986	7,984	542	296	2,042[b]
Sweden	1985	1,100	1,400	1,200	250[c]
Switzerland	1985	450	2,000	1,360	50[b]
UK[d,e]	1984	25,510	2,233		6,787
OCEANIA					
Australia	1980	9,800	200	0	0
New Zealand	1980	2,005	0		35

[a] All non-hazardous wastes.
[b] Composting only.
[c] Mechanical sorting and composting only.
[d] England and Wales only.
[e] Includes small amounts of industrial and commercial wastes disposed of by waste disposal authorities.

"Other" disposal options for municipal wastes may include composting and animal feed.

Sources:
OECD 1989 *OECD Environmental Data Compendium 1989*, Organisation for Economic Co-operation and Development, Paris.
UN-ECE 1987 *Environment Statistics in Europe and North America: An Experimental Compendium*, United Nations, New York.

Table 8.7 Treatment and disposal of hazardous wastes, 1980s (10^3 t a^{-1})

Region/country	Year	Phys./chem. treatment	Incineration	Landfill	Biological treatment	Sea disposal[a]	Recycling	Storage/ containment	Other
NORTH AMERICA									
Canada	1985					76			
USA[b]	1981	54,000	2,700	3,000				32,000	
ASIA									
Korea[c]	1984		12	29			89		23
EUROPE									
Finland[d]	1985	3	17						
France[e]	1982	220	276	700					
Germany, Fed. Rep.	1984	280	362	384					
Hungary	1988			400[f]			600	3,340[g]	660[h]
Ireland	1984			80					
Luxembourg	1986	1.1	0	3.6	0	0	0		
Netherlands	1984								
Norway	1987					8[i]			49[j]
Sweden	1980		98	195			117		
UK[k]	1988–89	260	80	1,300	0	160			78

a   Includes incineration at sea.
b   Physical/chemical treatment refers only to treatment in tanks and possible additional treatment in surface impoundments. Data for storage/containment refer to underground injection of hazardous wastes.
c   Values in all categories (except "Other") refer to amounts treated by generators. "Other" refers to the amount passed on for disposal; a breakdown of the final disposal route is not available. Data were originally reported in tons per day and have been converted to tons per year by multiplying by 365.
d   Data refer to the Ekokem plant only.
e   Data are for physical/chemical treatment and incineration at public installations only.
f   After neutralization.
g   Includes 3×10^6 t of red mud transferred to special disposal sites for storage without treatment.
h   Final disposal route not known.
i   Incinerated at sea.
j   Includes 28,000 t disposed of in industry; 13,000 t exported; and 8,000 t for unspecified disposal.
k   England and Wales only; data refer to special wastes.

Sources:

Appelberg, M. 1985 Hazardous waste in Sweden, Paper presented at the World Commission on Environment and Development Meeting, Oslo, June 1985. Unpublished paper.

CBS 1988 *Environmental Statistics 1988, Natural Resources and the Environment*, Central Bureau of Statistics of Norway, Oslo (in Norwegian with English titles).

Hyung-Cheull, K. and Yun-Hwa, K. 1987 Hazardous industrial solid wastes management in Korea. In: *Technical Manual for the Safe Disposal of Hazardous Wastes with Special Emphasis on the Needs of Developing Countries*, Vol. 4, World Health Organization, Geneva, United Nations Environment Programme, Nairobi, and the World Bank, Washington DC.

Szenes, E. 1990 Managing mountains of waste. In: *State of the Hungarian Environment*, D. Hinrichsen and G. Enyedi (Eds), Hungarian Academy of Sciences, Budapest, Ministry for Environment and Water Management, Budapest, and Hungarian Statistical Office, Budapest, 135–137.

UN-ECE 1987 *Environment Statistics in Europe and North America: An Experimental Compendium*, United Nations, New York.

Table 8.8 Sewage sludge dumped at sea, 1976–1986 (10^3 t a^{-1})

Region/country	1976	1977	1978	1979	1980	1981	1982	1983	1984	1985	1986
NORTH AMERICA											
USA	527[a]	5,134[a]	5,535[a]	5,932[a]	7,546[b]	6,094					
ASIA											
Hong Kong		1.4[b,c]									
EUROPE											
Germany, Fed. Rep.	299	272	272	236	217	15[d]	17[d]	5[d]	0	0	0
Ireland	108	114	124	94	97	132	83	139	190	179	220
UK	7,224	7,791	8,254	8,469	8,907	8,485	8,144	7,297	7,458	7,522	7,990
OCEANIA											
New Zealand	1,482[e]										

[a] Data expressed in tons.
[b] Amount licensed for disposal.
[c] Night soil.
[d] Dry solids.
[e] Data expressed in m^3 a^{-1}.

No sewage sludge is dumped at sea by the following European countries: Belgium, Denmark, Finland, France, Netherlands, Norway, Portugal and Sweden.
No data are currently available for countries not listed here.
Germany, Fed. Rep. ceased sludge dumping et sea in 1982.

Sources:
CEQ 1980 Environmental Quality – 1980, Council on Environmental Quality, Washington DC.
IMCO 1979 Convention on the Prevention of Marine Pollution by Dumping of Wastes and Other Matter 1972: Report of Permits Issued in 1977, Inter-governmental Maritime Consultative Organization, London.
IMO 1983 Seventh Consultative Meeting of Contracting Parties to the Convention on the Prevention of Marine Pollution by the Dumping of Wastes and Other Matter: Summary Report of Permits Issued in 1980, International Maritime Organization, London.
OECD 1985 OECD Environmental Data Compendium 1985, Organisation for Economic Co-operation and Development, Paris.

Oslo Commission 1984 Eighth Annual Report, Oslo Commission, London.
Oslo Commission 1984 Ninth Annual Report, Oslo Commission, London.
Oslo Commission 1985 Tenth Annual Report, Oslo Commission, London.
Oslo Commission 1986 Eleventh Annual Report, Oslo Commission, London.
Oslo Commission 1987 Twelfth Annual Report, Oslo Commission, London.
Oslo Commission 1989 Thirteenth Annual Report, Oslo Commission, London.

Table 8.9 Industrial wastes dumped at sea, 1976–1986 (10^3 t a^{-1})

Region/country	1976	1977	1978	1979	1980	1981	1982	1983	1984	1985	1986
NORTH AMERICA											
Canada	110	<1[a]	3.6[a]	7.2[a]	8.5[a]	140					
USA	2,734[b]	1,844[b]	2,548[b]	2,577[b]	3,154[b]	2,049[b]					
EUROPE											
Belgium	280	288	299	702	534	671	588	648	618	618	614
Denmark	22	6	6	12	9	5	4	1			
Finland					0	0	0	0			
France	1,691	1,978	2,557	3,076	3,257	2,855	2,571	1,596	1,644	842	645
Germany, Fed. Rep.	691	759	728	740	1,676	1,757	1,339	1,265	1,313	1,271	1,070
Iceland					0	0	0	0			
Ireland	811	811	854	704	751	370	530	727	779	684	785
Italy					–	1,000[a]					
Netherlands	1,381	1,256	1,501	1,671	16	14	11	7	6	2	1
Norway	0[a]	0[a]			10	0	0	0			
Portugal	0[a]	0[a]	0[a]	–	0	0	0	0			
Spain	525[a]	525[a]	525[a]	453	304	518	513	549	527	539	496
Sweden	0[a]	0[a]	0[a]	–	0	0	0	0			
UK	2,666	2,386	2,469	2,886	2,500	2,495	2,249	2,506	686	1,968	2,157
OCEANIA											
Australia			432[a]	425[a]							

a Amount licensed for disposal.
b Data expressed in tons.

Industrial wastes consist mainly of liquid wastes, sludges, TiO_2 wastes, phosphogypsum, fly-ash and colliery wastes.

Sources:
IMCO 1979 *Convention on the Prevention of Marine Pollution by Dumping of Wastes and Other Matter 1972: Report of Permits Issued for Dumping in 1976*, Inter-governmental Maritime Consultative Organization, London.
IMCO 1979 *Convention on the Prevention of Marine Pollution by Dumping of Wastes and Other Matter 1972: Report of Permits Issued in 1977*, Inter-governmental Maritime Consultative Organization, London.
IMCO 1980 *Convention on the Prevention of Marine Pollution by Dumping of Wastes and Other Matter 1972: Report of Permits Issued in 1978*, Inter-governmental Maritime Consultative Organization, London.
IMCO 1981 *Convention on the Prevention of Marine Pollution by Dumping of Wastes and Other Matter 1972: Report of Permits Issued in 1979*, Inter-governmental Maritime Consultative Organization, London.
IMO 1983 *Seventh Consultative Meeting of Contracting Parties to the Convention on the Prevention of Marine Pollution by Dumping of Wastes and Other Matter: Summary Report of Permits Issued in 1980*, International Maritime Organization, London.

OECD 1985 *OECD Environmental Data Compendium 1985*, Organisation for Economic Co-operation and Development, Paris.
Oslo Commission 1984 *Eighth Annual Report*, Oslo Commission, London.
Oslo Commission 1984 *Ninth Annual Report*, Oslo Commission, London.
Oslo Commission 1985 *Tenth Annual Report*, Oslo Commission, London.
Oslo Commission 1986 *Eleventh Annual Report*, Oslo Commission, London.
Oslo Commission 1987 *Twelfth Annual Report*, Oslo Commission, London.
Oslo Commission 1989 *Thirteenth Annual Report*, Oslo Commission, London.

Table 8.10 Dredged spoils dumped at sea, 1976–1986 (10^3 t a^{-1})

Region/country	1976	1977	1978	1979	1980	1981	1982	1983	1984	1985	1986
NORTH AMERICA											
Canada	5,829[a,b]	7,071[a,b]	79,040[a,b]	25,480[a,b]	36,277[a,b]	19,000[a,b]		8,450[a,b]			
USA	65	47	45	71	45	53		37,146[a,b]			
ASIA											
Hong Kong		6,018[a,c]	7,254[a,b]	8,268[a,b]	13,351[a,b]						20,830[a,c]
EUROPE											
Belgium	26,972	25,660	26,909	30,484	43,359	52,505	47,745	64,577	25,417	28,256	36,991
Denmark	507	34	202[a,b]	230	483	818	345[a]	565[a]	417	713	401
Finland					0	0		0			
France			15,739	1,430[b]	8,500	6,800	16,949	26,974	12,151	17,793	9,858
Germany, Fed. Rep.					6,500	0	5,200	650	750	3,632	
Iceland					0	0	0	0			
Ireland	149	714	446		653	153	942	225	504	136	1,752
Italy						1,800					
Netherlands	21,186	26,109	25,565	2,166	30,557	37,200	21,351	29,583	28,340	24,297	26,576
Norway	0[b]	0[b]			0	0	0	0			
Portugal	0[b]	0[b]	3,334	37	1,667	789	1,703	8,894	885	6,661	641
Sweden	53[b]	6.5[b]				0	0	3,132[b]		48[b]	
UK	13,341	12,232	12,607	12,124	16,044	12,786	12,906	13,604	20,200	12,581	15,233
OCEANIA											
New Zealand	5,962[a,b]	2,766[a,b]	3,351[a,b]	2,344[a,b]	2,623[a,b]	2,200		1,577[a,b]			

a Converted from m³ to t by a factor of 1.3.
b Amount licensed for disposal.
c 1987.

Dredged spoils are the materials which are periodically removed from waterways (mainly harbours and estuaries) to keep navigation channels open.

Sources:
DoE 1987 *Digest of Environmental Protection and Water Statistics*, Department of the Environment, Her Majesty's Stationery Office, London.
Environmental Protection Department 1988 *Environment Hong Kong: A Review of 1987*, Environmental Protection Department, Hong Kong.
IMCO 1979 *Convention on the Prevention of Marine Pollution by Dumping of Wastes and Other Matter 1972: Report of Permits Issued for Dumping in 1976*, Inter-governmental Maritime Consultative Organization, London.
IMCO 1979 *Convention on the Prevention of Marine Pollution by Dumping of Wastes and Other Matter 1972: Report of Permits Issued in 1977*, Inter-governmental Maritime Consultative Organization, London.
IMCO 1980 *Convention on the Prevention of Marine Pollution by Dumping of Wastes and Other Matter 1972: Report of Permits Issued in 1978*, Inter-governmental Maritime Consultative Organization, London.
IMCO 1981 *Convention on the Prevention of Marine Pollution by Dumping of Wastes and Other Matter 1972: Report of Permits Issued in 1979*, Inter-governmental Maritime Consultative Organization, London.
IMO 1983 *Seventh Consultative Meeting of Contracting Parties to the Convention on the Prevention of Marine Pollution by Dumping of Wastes and Other Matter: Summary Report of Permits Issued in 1980*, International Maritime Organization, London.
OECD 1987 *OECD Environmental Data Compendium 1987*, Organisation for Economic Co-operation and Development, Paris.
Oslo Commission 1984 *Eighth Annual Report*, Oslo Commission, London.
Oslo Commission 1984 *Ninth Annual Report*, Oslo Commission, London.
Oslo Commission 1985 *Tenth Annual Report*, Oslo Commission, London.
Oslo Commission 1986 *Eleventh Annual Report*, Oslo Commission, London.
Oslo Commission 1987 *Twelfth Annual Report*, Oslo Commission, London.
Oslo Commission 1989 *Thirteenth Annual Report*, Oslo Commission, London.

Table 8.11 Activity of low-level packaged radioactive wastes dumped at sea, 1960–1982 (TBq)

Region/country	1960	1961	1962	1963	1964	1965	1966	1967	1968	1969	1970
NORTH AMERICA											
USA											
ASIA											
Japan	0.6		1.0	2.4	2.6	1.0		2.9	1.5	2.8	
EUROPE											
Belgium				2.3							
France								7.0		18.0	
Germany, Fed. Rep.								219.0		134.4	
Italy								0.2			
Netherlands								0.7		1.0	
										0.2	
Sweden										3.2	
Switzerland										12.6	
UK	10.8[a]	93.3	9.7[a]	277.0	574.8	513.1	104.3	65.6	2,796.0	665.3	756.9
OCEANIA											
New Zealand			–								

[a] Includes waste from Belgium.

Source:
IAEA 1990 *Inventory of Radioactive Material Entering the Marine Environment: Part 1 Sea Disposal of Low-level Packaged Radioactive Waste*, International Atomic Energy Agency, Vienna.

1971	1972	1973	1974	1975	1976	1977	1978	1979	1980	1981	1982	Total 1949–82
												3,500
												15.4
91.1	71.5	66.2		121.8	77.9		169.4	41.9	858.6	346.0	246.4	2,120
												353
												0.2
												0.2
0.8	2.0	1.9	21.0	18.2	36.4	22.2	57.1	31.3	20.0	68.8	55.4	336
												3.2
13.2	22.2		79.0	43.4	27.4	35.3	166.1	63.7	1,904.0	1,405.6	646.8	4,420
330.8	729.8	458.8	3,497.4	1,967.8	1,870.9	2,803.1	2,594.5	3,051.1	3,991.2	3,949.4	3,802.7	35,100
	1.2	0.4			0.5							2.1

Table 8.12 Waste paper recovery and consumption, 1960–1988

Region/country	Paper recovery as a percentage of paper consumption									Apparent consumption (10^3 t)
	1960	1965	1970	1975	1980	1984	1986	1987	1988	1988
AFRICA										
Algeria						21				
Egypt						7	28	30	29	530
Kenya						54				
Madagascar							15	35	29	8
Morocco						28	27	28	25	215
South Africa						27				
Tunisia						4	6	6	8	122
Zimbabwe						31	27	29	30	86
NORTH AMERICA										
Canada	16	15	19	19[a]	19	20	19	19	21	5,950
Mexico					50[b]	41				
Panama						43				
USA				15	26[b]	27	28	28	30	77,057
SOUTH AMERICA										
Argentina						36	34	37	43	971
Bolivia							14	16	17	26
Brazil					29[b]	35	34	34	39	3,710
Chile							54	53	54	370
Colombia							31	35	37	584
Uruguay						34				
Venezuela						26				
ASIA										
China							18	19	22	13,200
China, Taiwan						45				
Hong Kong						67				
India						30				
Indonesia						13				
Iran						16				
Iraq						14				
Israel						19	23	21	21	470
Japan		37	39	39	47	49	50	50	48	24,940
Jordan						11	18	18	11	59
Korea					38[b]	33	36	37	39	3,300
Malaysia						3				
Myanmar q.v. Burma							14	16	14	20
Pakistan						23	5	4		
Philippines					16[b]	10				
Singapore						13				
Sri Lanka						9	16	15	22	75
Thailand						24	37	35	35	811
Turkey						26	27	27	24	979
EUROPE										
Austria	22	25	30	30[a]	33	39	46	49	49	1,083
Belgium				9	15	32			36	1,943
Czechoslovakia							47	48	49	

Continued opposite

Table 8.12 Continued

Region/country	Paper recovery as a percentage of paper consumption									Apparent consumption (10^3 t)
	1960	1965	1970	1975	1980	1984	1986	1987	1988	1988
Denmark	21	13	18	28[a]	27	29	31	31	31	1,085
Finland					29	38[c]	45	36	33	34	1,115
France	27	27	28	32	30	28	33	34	33	7,934
Germany, Fed. Rep.	27	27	30	34	35	38	42	42	41	12,346
Greece						16				
Hungary					37[b]		29	30	29	680
Iceland						5				
Ireland				22	15					
Italy	15	17	21	28[a]	30	26			27	
Netherlands	34	34	40	42	44	45	46	53	54	2,800
Norway	16	20	17	21[a]	22	21				662
Portugal						45	39	44	41	
Spain	25	28	28	32[a]	38	41	40	38	37	3,897
Sweden	26	21	22	30	33	38	47	46	48	2,050
Switzerland	33	33	31	40[a]	35	44	40	57	61	1,005
UK	28	29	29	28[a]	34	29	30	30	30	9,286
OCEANIA										
Australia		16		23[a]	28	22	24	28	30	2,570
New Zealand					17[d]	20	18	17	18	561

[a] 1974.
[b] Three-year average (1978–1980).
[c] 1983.
[d] 1978.

Apparent consumption is derived from estimates of national production of paper and paperboard, plus imports minus exports.

Sources:
BIR 1990 Personal communication, Bureau International de la Récuperation, Brussels, Belgium.

Chandler, W. U. 1983 *Materials Recycling: The Virtue of Necessity*, Worldwatch Paper 56, The Worldwatch Institute, Washington DC.
FAO 1989 *Waste Paper Data 1986–88*, Report of the FAO Advisory Committee on Pulp and Paper, 30th Session, Rome, 17–19 May 1989, Food and Agriculture Organization, Rome.
Ministry of the Environment 1985 *Survey of Waste Re-use*, Publication A:36, Environmental Protection and Nature Conservation Department, Helsinki.
OECD 1987 *OECD Environmental Data Compendium 1987*, Organisation for Economic Co-operation and Development, Paris.

Table 8.13 Aluminium recycling, 1972–1988

Region/country	Aluminium recycled as a percentage of aluminium consumed								
	1972	1973	1974	1975	1976	1977	1978	1979	1980
WORLD	21	19	20	21	21	23	23	23	24
Recycled (10³ t)	2,052	2,157	2,527	2,501	2,429	3,040	3,273	3,446	3,530
Consumed (10³ t)	10,306	13,203	12,756	10,325	12,866	13,334	14,336	14,911	14,477
AFRICA									
South Africa	9	9	8	8	7	15	16	22	25
NORTH AMERICA									
Canada	11	12	10	13	13	15	20	21	17
El Salvador	50	33	56	75	36	100	48	45	80
Mexico	10	10	10	10	10	10	10	10	10
Panama	14	15	13	14	18	35	21	21	20
USAb	19	18	20	26	24	25	23	24	27
SOUTH AMERICA									
Argentina	17	17	19	17	20	13	14	9	11
Brazil	8	10	10	8	11	11	16	16	13
Venezuela			5	2	4	2	15	16	10
ASIA									
China	12	24	17	12	10	11	10	12	18
Japan	17	14	14	15	16	21	23	21	25
Koreaa						8	7	8	10
EUROPE									
Austria	10	13	10	7	11	13	12	10	15
Belgiuma	3	3	3	3	3	3	1	1	
Finlanda	20	22	12	14	16	22	28	20	19
France	22	22	22	23	22	24	26	24	23
Denmarka									
Germany, Fed. Rep.	27	27	29	30	27	30	33	31	31
Greecea									
Italy	36	37	35	41	37	39	38	35	36
Netherlands				30	21	26	30	28	31
Norway	9	11	8	9	5	4	5	4	4
Portugala	6	8	6	17	8	7	12	13	8
Spain									
Sweden	22	21	23	23	16	19	20	17	19
Switzerland	17	18	17	23	22	25	21	22	18
UK	30	27	27	30	30	27	26	29	27
USSR									
OCEANIA									
Australia	14	16	18	15	14	12	12	12	15
New Zealand	10	6	6	6	5	7	7	7	8

a Percentage calculated based on apparent aluminium consumption.
b Consumption of secondary aluminium plus direct use of scrap by manufacturers.
c Super purity aluminium from scrap is excluded.
d Estimated.

e 1987.

Data for the world are estimates only.

1981	1982	1983	1984	1985	1986	1987	1988	Aluminium consumption, 1988	
								Total (10³ t)	Per capita (kg a⁻¹)
28	28	28	29	29	30	30	30	17,485	
3,771	3,858	4,137	4,255	4,255	4,355	4,470	5,237		
13,708	13,582	14,563	14,711	15,238	15,132	16,506	17,485		
24	25	29	25	22	23		19	145	5
16	12	16	16	15	16	14	12	691	27
43	50[a]	20[a]	50[a]		11[a]	38[a]	7[a]	2	–
10	17	18	17	15	14	8	5	96	1
27	38[a]	20[a]	13[a]	39[a]	39[a]	33[a]	39[a]	3	2
32	31	29	28	28	28	30	31	6,758	28
10	10	10	10	10	10	10	10	71	2
13	14	15	16	11	11	11	17	383	3
16	11	17	14	25	18				
14									
27	25	29	31	31	34	36	35	3,443	28
9	9	8	10	10					
15	16	19	22	22	22	18	21	138	18
		1	2	2	2	4		103	10
19	29	52	102	127	76	98		19	4
27	21	23	26	24	23	25	30	897	16
	16	15	20	24	28	31		53	10
33	34	32	32	30	31	31		1,701	28
		4	4	14	6				
41	35	37	37	36	36	36	36	1,034	18
42	31	38	33	42	45	47	45	258	18
4	2[c]	1[c]	3[c]	2[c]	3[c]	3[c]	8[c]	87[c]	21[c]
4	4	5	6	5	4[d]				
	17	18	24	24	22	28		248[e]	6[e]
19	18	17	18	18	19	17	26	191	23
21	19	22	20	21	19	21	23	125	19
28	24	24	24	23	20	19	15	651	11
10									
16	16	16	16	16	20	13	14	335	20
10	12	11	12	12	12	10	9	34	10

Sources:
Aluminium Association 1982 *Aluminium Statistical Review for 1981*, The Aluminium Association Inc., Washington DC.
Aluminium Association 1987 *Aluminium Statistical Review for 1987*, The Aluminium Association Inc., Washington DC.
Aluminium Association 1988 *Aluminium Statistical Review for 1988*, The Aluminium Association Inc., Washington DC.
Chandler, W. U. 1983 *Materials Recycling: The Virtue of Necessity*, Worldwatch Paper 56, The Worldwatch Institute, Washington DC.

Table 8.14 Glass recycling, 1981–1989

Region/country	Total quantity recovered (10^3 t a^{-1})									
	1980	1981	1982	1983	1984	1985	1986	1987	1988	1989
NORTH AMERICA										
Canada				61						
USA										
ASIA										
Japan										
EUROPE	1,500	1,960	2,170	2,530	2,720	2,670	3,340	3,565	3,861	4,560
Austria		43	43	44	48	48	77	85	98	115
Belgium	100	100	100	100	120		140	127	166	208
Bulgaria						153				
Czechoslovakia			393							
Denmark	12	20	22	23	25		33	35	46	58
Finland						14			2	18
France	336	416	478	522	540	540	621	646	676	760
Germany, Fed. Rep.	500[b]	673	750	832	884	1,290	1,076	1,102	1,176	1,538
Greece									14	14
Hungary						189				
Ireland		6	7	6	6	9	7	7	9	11
Italy	320	350	356	400	428		523	580	610	670
Luxembourg						57				
Netherlands	170[b]	175	200	180	230		245	320	261	279
Norway									3	11
Portugal				28	23	27	27	29	31	34
Spain				123	124	133	232	261	278	287
Sweden									31	42
Switzerland		92	106	127	127		131	140	156	164
Turkey									40	47
UK[d]	55	85	110	112	161	210	228	233	264	310
USSR						980				
OCEANIA										
Australia										
New Zealand										

[a] Based on glass industry estimates.
[b] Approximate value.
[c] Derived from domestic sales of glass packaging with no adjustments for imports/exports.
[d] Great Britain only.

As there are data for fewer than 10 European countries in 1980 and 1985 the quantity of glass recycled as a percentage of glass consumption has not been calculated for Europe as a whole for those two years.

Sources:
FEVE 1980 *Glass Gazette*, Spring issue, European Glass Container Federation, Brussels.
FEVE 1981 *Glass Gazette*, No. 4, European Glass Container Federation, Brussels.
FEVE 1982 *Glass Gazette*, No. 6, European Glass Container Federation, Brussels.
FEVE 1983 *Glass Gazette*, No. 7, European Glass Container Federation, Brussels.

Percentage of national glass consumption

1980	1981	1982	1983	1984	1985	1986	1987	1988	1989
12					10				
3									
				17					
	20	21	23	24		29	35	33	39
	20	20	20	30	38	39	44	50	54
40	33	32	32	36		44	39	50	60
	8	10	10	20		32	32	27	36
	20							3	36[a]
11	20	20	24	25		28		34	38
27	24	28	30	31	39	37	37	39	53[c]
								16	13
	8	8	8	7	8	8		10	13[a]
	20	21	22	24	25	26	38	40	42
	41	47	48	53	53	48	62	53	57
								6	24[a]
			12	10		13	14	13	14
			12	13		20	22	23	24
					20			22	34
	36	42	42	45	46	46	47	55	56
								23	27
	5	6	8	9	12	14	13	15	17

17
53

FEVE 1984 *Glass Gazette*, No. 8, European Glass Container Federation, Brussels.

FEVE 1985 Glass Gazette, No. 9, European Glass Container Federation, Brussels.

FEVE 1988 Glass Gazette, No. 14, European Glass Container Federation, Brussels.

Glass Manufacturers Federation 1986 *Recycling: The Way Forward*, Glass Manufacturers Federation, London.

OECD 1987 *OECD Environmental Data Compendium 1987*, Organisation for Economic Co-operation and Development, Paris.

Pollock, C. 1987 *The Potential for Recycling*, Worldwatch Paper 76, The Worldwatch Institute, Washington DC.

UN-ECE 1987 *Environment Statistics in Europe and North America: An Experimental Compendium*, United Nations, New York.

Part 9
Natural Disasters

Natural disasters, with far-reaching and severe physical, ecological and socio-economic consequences, can occur suddenly like earthquakes, floods, tsunamis, volcanic eruptions, cyclones and landslides. They can also occur slowly, like drought and desertification which are caused by natural phenomena, or by natural phenomena coupled with overt effects of human actions. Natural disasters are becoming increasingly significant both in terms of numbers of events and magnitude of impact. Evidence suggests that the frequency of natural disasters has increased in recent decades (Figure 9.1) although there has also been a marked increase in awareness of phenomena such as earthquakes, volcanic eruptions, hurricanes, cyclones, floods and landslides due to direct and thorough reporting in the mass media. The description of natural events as disasters can be applied to those which have a major effect on populated areas or on those of economic importance to humankind.

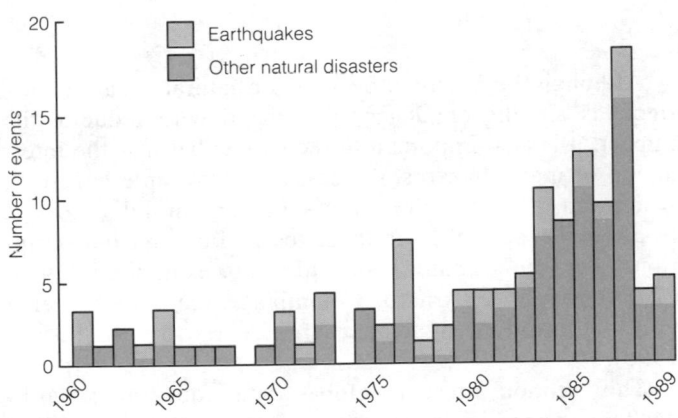

Figure 9.1 Frequency of major natural disasters, 1960–1989
Source: Munich Reinsurance Company, 1990; reproduced in Borz, 1990

The most widely accepted reason for the rise in number of natural disasters over the last few decades is that the "hit rate" has increased considerably due to the continuing growth of the world population. This population growth has led to an increase in building density caused by the increasing concentration of people and economic assets in urban areas and by the large-scale migration of populations throughout the world into coastal regions that are generally more highly exposed to natural disasters. Already more than a third of the world's largest and fastest

growing cities are located in regions of high seismic risk of natural disasters (Tyler, 1990). Many of these are in developing countries where poor construction methods exacerbate the risk. There is also some concern that global change throughout this century may be changing climatic conditions and increasing the severity and frequency of phenomena such as windstorms and floods (Berz, 1990). Figure 9.2 shows the regions of the world at highest risk from natural disasters.

Until relatively recently, there has been little collective response to the threat of natural disasters. One of the most effective means of reducing the adverse consequences of natural disasters is to ensure that communities are prepared for them. UNEP continues to promote the adoption of environmentally-based measures to develop community preparedness further. However, there is now a growing awareness of the need for documentation and data to supplement progress in science and technology and so aid political and economic decision-making leading to a significant reduction in disaster losses. At the present time, there are only a few global data bases for natural disasters. Of them, UNINET, the computer network for disaster-related information developed by the Office of the United Nations Disaster Relief Co-ordinator (UNDRO) has been one of the most comprehensive and includes a facility for direct communication to aid disaster management. However, UNINET was suspended in 1988. UNDRO released, in 1990, a 'Preliminary Study on the Identification of Disaster-prone Countries Based on Economic Impact' (UNDRO, 1990). The United Nations Educational, Scientific and Cultural Organization (UNESCO) and the World Meteorological Organization (WMO) also support relevant data gathering and research into an understanding of the basic phenomena causing disasters.

Another global data base containing data on major disasters since 1900 is held by the Office of US Foreign Disaster Assistance (AID/OFDA, 1989). It is also recognized that there is a need for more accurate predictions of natural disaster events and, in view of this, UNEP has made the development of an early warning system for forecasting environmental disasters a priority for the 1990s; this approach will be addressed in the next edition of the 'UNEP Environmental Data Report'.

Quantifying the scale of natural disasters is not easy and is the cause of some debate. Almost all data bases concentrate on three main criteria: the number of people killed, the number of people affected, and the damage

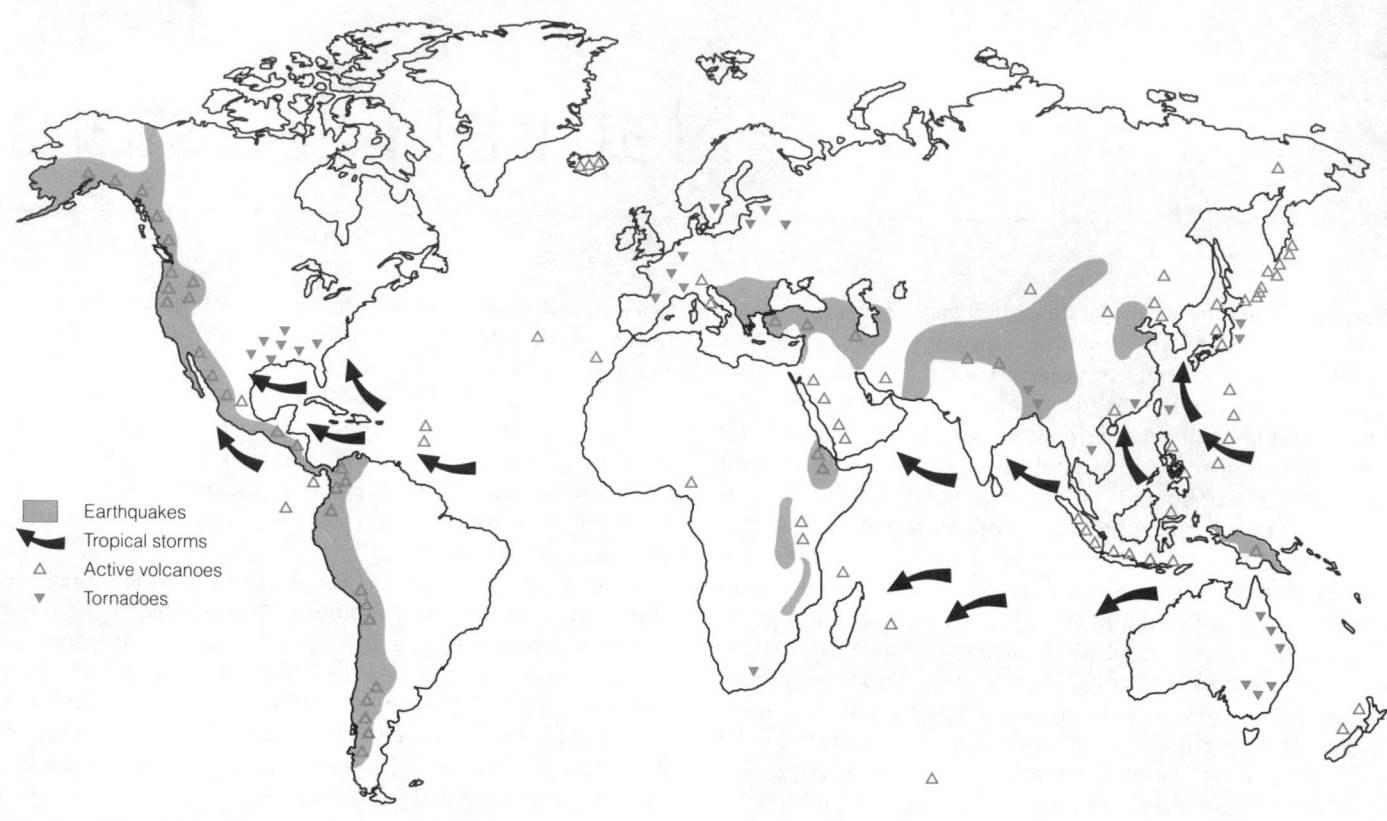

Figure 9.2 Natural disasters – regions of highest risk
Source: Wijkman and Timberlake, 1984

caused, estimated in financial terms (usually in US dollars). The last of these three has been subjected to the criticism that exchange and inflation rates render the figures meaningless and that they are particularly irrelevant when listed against numbers of dead, injured and homeless (Cruden, 1990). Published listings of disasters are often restricted to those in which at least 10 deaths were reported or property damage exceeded US$ 1 million. This approach necessarily results in the omission of numerous events which occur in remote regions but which can be recorded by global monitoring networks, such as those for seismic activity, and by satellite measurements.

The designation of the 1990s as the International Decade for Natural Disaster Reduction (IDNDR) by the General Assembly of the United Nations is a positive response to the increased susceptibility of populations throughout the world. The principal aim of IDNDR is to capitalize on existing knowledge of the ways whereby the effects of natural disasters can be mitigated. Although much of this knowledge is available in the developed world, it is in the developing world that the increased frequency of natural disaster occurrence is often more severely felt. Therefore, IDNDR aims to encourage the transfer of relevant knowledge to those countries recognizably most at risk from the effects of natural disasters and to enhance its application within them.

Although the nature of each major natural hazard is distinct, as are the challenges associated with reducing its impact, it is also important to recognize that it is the interaction of major hazards, the so-called "multiple hazards", which cause some of the world's worst natural disasters. It is often the case that earthquakes and/or volcanic eruptions cause floods and/or landslides. For example, in 1985, 22,000 people in Arnero, Colombia, were killed after a volcanic eruption triggered a large debris flow (Schuster, 1990).

This section presents global data concerning earthquakes, tsunami, windstorms, floods and landslides. Information on volcanic eruptions, natural dams, wildfires and droughts can be found in the previous editions of this report (UNEP 1987, 1989).

References

AID/OFDA 1989 *Disaster History: Significant Data on Major Disasters World-wide, 1900–Present*, Office of US Foreign Disaster Assistance, Washington DC.

Berz, G. 1990 Natural disasters and insurance/reinsurance, *UNDRO News*, January/February 1990, 18–19.

Cruden, D. M. 1990 Personal communication, Department of Civil Engineering, University of Alberta, Edmonton, Canada.

Schuster, R. L. 1990 Personal communication, Branch of Geologic Risk Assessment, US Geological Survey, Denver, Colorado, USA.

Tyler, C. 1990 Earth-moving events, *Geographical Magazine* **62**(3), 28–31.

UNDRO 1990 *Preliminary Study on the Identification of Disaster-prone Countries Based on Economic Impact*, Office of the United Nations Disaster Relief Co-ordinator, Geneva.

UNEP 1987 *United Nations Environment Programme Environmental Data Report*, Basil Blackwell, Oxford.

UNEP 1989 *United Nations Environment Programme Environmental Data Report*, Basil Blackwell, Oxford.

Wijkman, A. and Timberlake, L. 1984 *Natural Disasters*, Earthscan, International Institute for Environment and Development, London and Washington DC.

Earthquakes

An earthquake, a sudden motion of the earth caused by an abrupt release of slowly accumulating stress, is a potent natural hazard. Although more infrequent than other types of natural disasters (see Figure 9.1), an earthquake can cause devastation and loss of life on a scale far greater than any other individual natural hazard and is, therefore, generally regarded as the most destructive of the various forces of nature.

Seismic activity is well monitored and documented throughout the world by a number of national and international recording networks. Comprehensive listings of seismic events are held by several agencies such as the International Seismological Centre (ISC) in Newbury, UK, and the National Earthquake Information Center at the World Data Center A in Boulder, Colorado, USA. Much research has also been conducted on areas of the world particularly prone to earthquakes with a view to improving predictive capabilities; today, earthquake prediction on a scientific basis is making slow but steady progress (Tyler, 1990).

At least 35 countries face a high probability of being struck by earthquakes (NAS, 1987). Although there are thousands of relatively small earthquakes around the world each year, it is those of magnitudes 6–8 on the Richter scale which generally cause the greatest damage. Table 9.1 gives an indication of the regions and countries of the world which are particularly at risk by listing the major earthquake events since 1980 along with their magnitude and human and economic losses. Data for earthquakes since 1966 were included in the second edition of this report (UNEP, 1989).

References

NAS 1987 *Confronting Natural Disasters: An International Decade for Natural Hazard Reduction*, US National Academy of Sciences, Washington DC.

Tyler, C. 1990 Earth-moving events, *Geographical Magazine* **62**(3), 28–31.

UNEP 1989 *United Nations Environment Programme Environmental Data Report*, Basil Blackwell, Oxford.

Tsunami

Tsunami, or seismic sea waves, are large ocean waves generated by impulses from geophysical events occurring on the ocean floor or along the coastline, such as earthquakes, landslides and volcanic eruptions. Mostly occurring in the Pacific Ocean, tsunami, although hardly noticeable at sea, can reach gigantic proportions as they reach shallow, coastal waters. In Hawaii and Japan, for example, tsunami have been known to reach 30 m in height. At least 22 countries along the rim of the Pacific are estimated to be at risk from potential tsunami (NAS, 1987).

The fact that tsunami can travel 10,000 km at velocities exceeding 900 km per hour with little loss of energy and are therefore capable of hitting areas not directly affected by the inducing event, has led to the establishment of a tsunami early warning service for the whole circum-Pacific area (Munich Reinsurance Company, 1988). However, only a few of the 22 countries most at risk are considered to have standard operating procedures for immediate evacuation or reliable, rapid communication systems capable of receiving real-time warnings from the Pacific Tsunami Warning Centre.

About 6,000 people have been killed by tsunami in the last decade alone (NAS, 1987). Table 9.2, extracted from the data base of historic and recent tsunami held by the National Oceanic and Atmospheric Administration (NOAA) at the National Geophysical Data Center, World Data Center A in Boulder, lists tsunami events arising in the Pacific Ocean since 1980. Probably the best documented of these events is the occurrence at Noshiro, Japan, in 1983 which caused approximately 100 deaths and extensive property damage and flooding.

References

Munich Reinsurance Company 1988 *World Map of Natural Hazards*, Munich Reinsurance Company, Munich.

NAS 1987 *Confronting Natural Disasters: An International Decade for Natural Disaster Reduction*, US National Academy of Sciences, Washington DC.

Windstorms

Judged by the frequency with which they cause damage and by the surface area of the regions they strike, windstorms can be said to be the most significant of all natural hazards (Munich Reinsurance Company, 1988). Windstorms influence precipitation systems, floods and, most importantly, cause severe destruction to crops and properties. Severe tropical cyclones (called "hurricanes" in the Atlantic, Caribbean and north-eastern Pacific; "typhoons" in the western Pacific; and "cyclones" in the Indian Ocean and in the sea around Australia), tornadoes, monsoons and thunderstorms between them affect every country in the world.

Today, increasing attention is being paid to windstorms, particularly tropical cyclones, as some scientists see their incidence as being a possible indicator of global climatic change and predict an increase in their frequency. Have tropical cyclone frequencies or their intensities increased with global changes throughout this century? At present, available evidence does not support this idea, perhaps because the warming is not yet large enough to make its impact felt (WMO/UNEP, 1990). Table 9.3 provides a global summary of windstorm occurrence from 1980 to 1985.

Global information on major windstorms and their impact is collated by organizations such as UNDRO, UNEP and AID/OFDA. However, global listings of disasters rarely include those which occur in small states such as island states, which in areas such as the Caribbean, Indian Ocean and South Pacific, are particularly prone to tropical cyclones (Lewis, 1990). This is because listings often set a criteria based on magnitude of impact with which small states cannot compete against larger countries. However, the proportional impact upon small states is often far greater in terms of population, housing and economics. Table 9.4 presents data on natural disasters (especially tropical cyclones) suffered by island states during the 1980s.

References

Lewis, J. 1990 Personal communication, Datum International, Marshfield, UK.

Munich Reinsurance Company 1988 *World Map of Natural Hazards*, Munich Reinsurance Company, Munich.

WMO/UNEP 1990 *Scientific Assessment of Climate Change*, Report prepared for the Intergovernmental Panel on Climate Change by Working Group I, World Meteorological Organization, Geneva, and the United Nations Environment Programme, Nairobi.

Floods

The potential for major floods has increased in recent decades. Floods are not only caused by high amounts of precipitation, but also by man-made changes to the earth's surface. Poor management of agricultural land, increased deforestation and urbanization all alter the retention properties of surface soil layers, resulting in greater run-off and increased erosion. Further human contributions to the causes of floods, particularly in developing countries, include reckless building, poor watershed management and failure to control flooding. Promotion of co-operation on flood management, with special attention to early warning systems and practical measures for flood prevention and control, is the strategy necessary to mitigate and to prevent the occurrence of floods.

Major floods are generally reported with reference to their direct impact on human life and property. However, due to the interactive nature of floods with other natural hazards such as monsoons, landslides and the failure of natural dams, it is very difficult to identify and isolate the impact of the flood alone. Evaluation of the after effects of floods, such as food shortages and the spread of disease, are also difficult to quantify. However, the World Health Organization (WHO) has recorded that, in 1988, 300 people were killed in Brazil when an epidemic of leptospirosis spread as a result of serious flooding (see Part 5: Human Health, Table 5.12).

The principal information source for agencies compiling global data on floods are press reports. UNESCO and the International Association of Hydrological Sciences (IAHS) have produced data compilations of floods (UN-

ESCO, 1976; IAHS, 1984). The information on floods presented in Table 9.5 updates that given in the previous edition of this report (UNEP, 1989) and shows the extent of death and destruction caused by floods.

References

IAHS 1984 *World Catalogue of Maximum Observed Floods*, J. A. Rudier and M. Roche (Eds), International Association of Hydrological Sciences, Wallingford, UK.

UNEP 1989 *United Nations Environment Programme Environmental Data Report*, Basil Blackwell, Oxford.

UNESCO 1976 *World Catalogue of Very Large Floods*, United Nations Educational, Scientific and Cultural Organization, Paris.

Landslides

Landslides are movements of large masses of rock, earth or debris down slopes (Cruden, 1990). They may vary widely in size and occur in virtually every country of the world as well as on the ocean floor. The extent of landslide impacts throughout the world is not well known as very few countries keep records of landslide damage.

The compilation of data on the global occurrence of landslides is a much more onerous task than the documentation of other natural disasters as much of the damage caused by landslides is masked by the more spectacular events such as earthquakes, volcanic eruptions, windstorms and floods from which they often result. However, casualties and damage from landslides may exceed those from other causes. In addition, landslides cannot be recorded by remote sensing as can earthquakes or tsunamis, nor are there particular government agencies charged with the collection of global statistics on landslides (Cruden, 1990).

Detailed national compilations of events suggest that in some countries landslides are the principal cause of death from natural disasters. Unfortunately, no systematic global compilations of these data exist although some national reports have been collected by Brabb and Harrod (1989).

Successful landslide studies in Austria, Canada, France, Italy, Japan, New Zealand, Scandinavia, Switzerland, the UK and the USA have shown that the first step in coping with landslides on a regional basis is to use aerial photography to map or "inventory" all existing landslides (Brabb, 1989). In view of this, the International Geotechnical Societies/UNESCO Working Party on World Landslide Inventories has sought to provide the means (using standardized terminology) to build a global data network based on local and national inventories.

The information in Table 9.6 relates to major landslides which have been reported to international agencies from 1981 to 1989. The table also documents multiple hazards, with particular reference to the association between landslides and floods, where appropriate.

References

Brabb, E. E. 1989 Personal communication, International Landslide Research Group, Palo Alto, California, USA.

Brabb, E. E. and Harrod, B. L. 1989 *Landslides: Extent and Economic Significance*, Balkema, Rotterdam.

Cruden, D. M. 1990 Personal communication, Department of Civil Engineering, University of Alberta, Edmonton, Canada.

China: A National Example of Collated Data

Natural disasters may be very widespread in terms of land area affected. Table 9.7 illustrates this by comparing land area affected by all natural disasters, floods and droughts in China during the latter half of this century. Areas of arable land affected are also included in the table giving an indication of the economic extent of the disasters. In 1987, 48.5 per cent of the 42×10^6 ha of land affected by natural disasters consisted of cultivated arable land. This represents 4.4 per cent of the total land area of China (State Statistical Bureau of the People's Republic of China, 1988).

Table 9.7 also shows that floods and droughts affect more cultivated and total land area than other types of natural disaster phenomena. The consistently high percentage of arable land affected by both floods and droughts between 1950 and 1965 may be related to the decrease in population in China during this period (see Part 4: Population/Settlements, Figure 4.3).

Reference

State Statistical Bureau of the People's Republic of China 1988 *China Statistical Yearbook 1988*, China Statistical Information and Consultancy Service Centre, Beijing.

Table 9.1 Principal destructive earthquakes, 1980–1990

Year	Region	Country	Magnitude	Deaths	Damage
1980	AFRICA	Algeria	7.4	5,000	Severe
	NORTH AMERICA	Guatemala	5.3	0	Moderate
		Mexico	6.8	65	Severe
			6.4	2	Moderate
		USA	5.2	0	Moderate
			5.9	1	Moderate
			7.0	5	Moderate
	SOUTH AMERICA	Ecuador	5.6	8	Severe
		Peru	5.2	7	Moderate
		Venezuela	4.7	0	Moderate
	ASIA	India	5.2	13	Limited
			6.5	150	Severe[a]
		Indonesia	5.9	0	Severe
		Iran	5.4	1	Moderate
			5.7	26	Severe
			5.5	4	Moderate
		Japan	6.2	2	Moderate
		Nepal	6.5	150	Severe[a]
	EUROPE	Greece	6.4	1	Severe
		Italy	4.5	0	Moderate
			6.9	3,105	Severe
		Portugal	6.7	60	Severe
		Yugoslavia	5.8	0	Severe
	USSR	USSR	4.5	87	Severe
	OCEANIA	Solomon Is.	8.0	0	Limited[b]
		Vanuatu	8.0	0	Limited[b]
1981	NORTH AMERICA	Mexico	7.4	1	Severe
	SOUTH AMERICA	Peru	5.2	10	Severe
		Venezuela	5.5	15	Severe
	ASIA	China	6.9	150	Severe
		India	6.1	212	Severe
		Indonesia	6.8	306	Severe
		Iran	6.9	3,000	Severe
			7.3	1,500	Severe
		Pakistan	4.7	6	Moderate
	EUROPE	Greece	6.8	22	Moderate
		Italy	4.9	12	Limited
		Yugoslavia	5.5	0	Severe
1982	NORTH AMERICA	El Salvador	4.8	3	Moderate[c]
			6.9	20	Severe[d]
		Guatemala	6.9	20	Severe[d]
			4.8	3	Moderate[c]
		Honduras	4.8	3	Moderate[c]
	SOUTH AMERICA	Peru	6.1	3	Severe
	ASIA	Afghanistan	6.6	500	Moderate
		China	6.5	1	Moderate
			5.6	10	Moderate
		India	6.2	0	Moderate
		Indonesia	5.5	0	Moderate
			5.6	13	Moderate

Continued opposite

Table 9.1 Continued

Year	Region	Country	Magnitude	Deaths	Damage
		Japan	6.9	110	Moderate
		Yemen, Dem.	6.0	2,800	Extreme
	EUROPE	Albania	5.6	1	Severe
		Italy	4.5	0	Extreme
1983	NORTH AMERICA	Costa Rica	7.2	10	Moderate
			6.1	2	Severe
		USA	6.7	0	Severe
			7.3	2	Severe
			6.5	0	Extreme
	SOUTH AMERICA	Chile	7.3	5	Moderate
		Colombia	5.3	350	Severe
		Peru	6.7	10	Limited
	ASIA	Afghanistan	5.2	0	Severe[e]
			7.2	24	Severe[f]
			7.0	12	Moderate
		China	5.7	34	Severe
			5.6		Moderate
			6.2	0	Moderate
		Indonesia	6.5	36	Moderate
		Iran	5.1	30	Severe
			5.5	3	Severe
		Japan	7.8	104	Extreme
		Pakistan	7.2	24	Severe[f]
			6.5	24	Moderate
		Philippines	6.7	21	Moderate
		Turkey	6.1	5	Moderate
			6.9	1,400	Extreme
	EUROPE	Belgium	4.7	2	Extreme
		Italy	5.2	0	Moderate
		Yugoslavia	4.8	12	Limited
	USSR	USSR	5.2	0	Severe[e]
	OCEANIA	Papua New Guinea	7.9	0	Moderate
			6.3	443	Severe
1984	NORTH AMERICA	USA	6.1	0	Extreme
	ASIA	Afghanistan	5.8	4	Severe[g]
		Indonesia	6.4	2	Moderate
				0	Moderate
		Japan	6.3	24	Severe
		Pakistan	5.8	4	Severe[g]
		Turkey	5.4	3	Moderate
	EUROPE	Italy	5.3	0	Severe
			5.6	0	Extreme
			5.4	3	Severe
			5.8	3	Severe
		Yugoslavia	5.3	0	Moderate
	USSR	USSR	7.1	0	Severe
	OCEANIA	Papua New Guinea	6.8	0	Moderate
		Solomon Is.	7.7	0	Moderate
1985	AFRICA	Algeria	5.9	30	Moderate

Continued over

Table 9.1 Continued

Year	Region	Country	Magnitude	Deaths	Damage
	NORTH AMERICA	Guatemala	4.6		Moderate
		Mexico	8.1	10,000	Extreme
			7.6		Moderate
		Nicaragua	6.0		Moderate
	SOUTH AMERICA	Argentina	5.8	6	Severe
	ASIA	China	6.0	67	Severe
			5.8	22	Moderate
	EUROPE	Yugoslavia	5.2		Moderate
	USSR	USSR	6.1	29	Severe
	OCEANIA	Papua New Guinea	7.2		Moderate
1986	NORTH AMERICA	El Salvador	5.4	1,100	Severe
		USA	7.7		Limited
			6.2		Moderate
			6.0		Moderate
	SOUTH AMERICA	Brazil	5.0	1	Severe
		Peru	5.3	1	Moderate
			5.3	16	Severe
		Venezuela	6.2	2	Moderate
	ASIA	China	7.8	14	Moderate
		India	5.6	3	Severe
		Indonesia	5.0		Severe
		Iran	5.0	1	Moderate
			5.7		Moderate
		Turkey	5.9	15	Severe
			5.6	2	Severe[h]
	EUROPE	Bulgaria	5.1	3	Severe
		Greece	5.9	20	Severe
		Romania	6.9	2	Severe
		Yugoslavia	5.5		Moderate
	USSR	USSR	5.6	2	Severe[h]
	OCEANIA	New Zealand	8.3	0	Limited
		Papua New Guinea	7.1		
1987	AFRICA	Algeria	4.9	1	Moderate
	NORTH AMERICA	USA	6.6		Moderate
			7.6		Limited
			5.9	8	Extreme
			5.2	1	Moderate
	SOUTH AMERICA	Chile	7.5	1	Limited
			7.0	4	Moderate
		Colombia	6.9	1,000	Severe[i]
		Ecuador	6.9	1,000	Severe[i]
	ASIA	China	6.0		Moderate
			4.9		Moderate
		Indonesia	6.5	2	Moderate
			6.5	125	Severe
		Japan	6.7	1	Severe

Continued opposite

Table 9.1   Continued

Year	Region	Country	Magnitude	Deaths	Damage
	OCEANIA	New Zealand	6.6	1	Severe
		Papua New Guinea	7.4	3	Moderate
			7.4	1	Moderate
			7.5	0	Moderate
1988	ASIA	Myanmar q.v. Burma	7.1	3	Moderate[j]
			6.1	730	Extreme[k]
		China	6.1	730	Extreme[k]
		India	7.1	3	Moderate[j]
			7.0	382	Severe
		Iran	6.1	1	Moderate
		Nepal	6.5	1,000	Severe
		Turkey	7.6	25,000	Extreme[l]
	EUROPE	Albania	5.7	0	Limited
	USSR	USSR	7.6	25,000	Extreme[l]
1989	AFRICA	Algeria	6.0	30	Severe
		Malawi	6.2	9	Severe
	NORTH AMERICA	Costa Rica	6.3	0	Moderate
		USA	7.1	67	Extreme
			6.1		Moderate
	ASIA	Myanmar q.v. Burma	5.6	1	Moderate[m]
		China	5.6	1	Moderate[m]
			6.2	4	Severe
			6.2		Severe
			5.3	29	Severe
		Indonesia	5.9	120	Moderate
			6.1	0	Moderate
			5.9		Moderate
		Iran	6.2		Severe
		Philippines	7.3	2	Moderate
	USSR	USSR	5.3	274	
	OCEANIA	Australia	5.4	11	Severe
		Fiji	7.5		None
1990	NORTH AMERICA	USA	4.6		Moderate
	SOUTH AMERICA	Peru	5.8	67	Moderate
	ASIA	China	6.9	115	Moderate
		Iran	7.3	50,000	Extreme
		Pakistan	6.1	11	Moderate
		Philippines	7.7	100	Severe
	EUROPE	Romania	6.5	7	Moderate
	OCEANIA	Fiji	7.5		None

Notes a–m indicate that the earthquake was recorded in more than one country: the same event is denoted by the same superscript. Entries in the deaths and damage columns are the combined totals for countries affected by each event, although the major effects may have been in one country only.

Magnitude refers to surface waves, expressed as points on the Richter scale. The extent of damage, as estimated in US dollars at the time of the event, is categorized as limited (less than 1 million), moderate (1–5 million), severe (5–25 million) or extreme (25 million or more). Earthquakes listed are those which caused at least moderate damage, and/or at least 10 deaths, and/or were of magnitude 7.5 or greater. The source data base includes information on the detailed location and time of occurrence for each event and multiple references for events where individual information sources differ in their estimate of impacts; information from only one reporting source has been selected for the above table.

Source:
World Data Center A 1990 Earthquake Data Base, National Oceanic and Atmospheric Administration, Boulder, Colorado, USA.

Table 9.2 Tsunami events arising in the Pacific Ocean, 1980–1990

Year	Region of Pacific	Source	Magnitude	Run-up
1980	NORTH-WEST PACIFIC	Honshu Island, Japan	6.7	0.6
		S. Kuril Islands, USSR	6.8	0.2
	SOUTH-WEST PACIFIC	New Hebrides Islands	7.7	0.3
1981	NORTH-WEST PACIFIC	E. Honshu Island, Japan	7.0	0.4
	SOUTH-WEST PACIFIC	Samoa Islands	7.3	0.3
1982	NORTH-WEST PACIFIC	Hokkaido Island, Japan	7.1	0.8
		Ibaraki, Japan	7.0	0.4
		S. Honshu, Japan	6.4	0.4
	SOUTH-WEST PACIFIC	Kermadec Islands	7.7	0.1
	WEST PACIFIC	Java Trench	5.4	
1983	EAST PACIFIC	N. Central Chile	7.4	0.4
	NORTH-WEST PACIFIC	N. Honshu Island, Japan	6.9	0.5
		Noshiro, Japan	7.7	14.5
	WEST PACIFIC	Banda Sea, Indonesia	6.5	3.0
		Luzon Island, Philippines	6.5	
		New Britain	7.6	0.3
1984	NORTH-WEST PACIFIC	Honshu, Japan	6.9	0.1
		Kuril Islands	7.1	0.2
		Kyushu, Japan	6.9	0.2
		Tori Shima, Okinawa	5.5	1.5
1985	EAST PACIFIC	Mexico	7.6	1.4
			8.1	3.0
		Valparaiso, Chile	7.8	1.1
1986	NORTH PACIFIC	Aleutian Islands	7.9	1.7
	SOUTH-WEST PACIFIC	Kermadec Islands	8.3	0.2
1987	EAST PACIFIC	Antofagasta, Chile	7.3	
	NORTH PACIFIC	Gulf of Alaska	7.5	0.5
			7.0	0.1
	NORTH-WEST PACIFIC	E. coast Honshu, Japan	6.1	
		Kyushu, Japan	6.7	0.1
	SOUTH-WEST PACIFIC	Solomon Islands	6.9	
		Tonga Islands	7.3	0.2
		Vanuatu	6.6	
	WEST PACIFIC	Papua New Guinea	7.5	0.1
			7.4	2.0
1988	NORTH PACIFIC	Gulf of Alaska	7.6	0.2
	SOUTH-WEST PACIFIC	Solomon Islands	7.4	
	WEST PACIFIC	Papua New Guinea	6.7	
1989	NORTH PACIFIC	Alaska	6.9	0.1
		Hawaii	6.1	0.3
		California	7.1	0.1

Continued opposite

Table 9.2 Continued

Year	Region of Pacific	Source	Magnitude	Run-up
	NORTH-WEST PACIFIC	Japan	7.3	0.6
	SOUTH-WEST PACIFIC	Macquarie Island	8.3	0.3
1990	WEST PACIFIC	Marianas Trench	7.4	0.2

Tsunami listed are those described as probable or definite (validity 3 and 4) in the source document. Magnitude of earthquakes which were the sources of tsunami are expressed as points on the Richter scale. Run-up refers to the maximum height, in metres, above sea level in the area where the tsunami was observed or measured.
Source region was listed directly from the NOAA data base. Additional information included in the source data base relates to details of the location and time at which the events occurred and sources of records.

Source:
World Data Center A 1990 Tsunami Data Base, National Oceanic and Atmospheric Administration, Boulder, Colorado, USA.

Table 9.3 A global summary of windstorms, 1980–1985

Year	Number of events	Dead	Injured	Affected	Homeless	Damage (10^6 US$)
1980	24	1,374	697	5,206,100	1,194,500	1,585.4
1981	30	3,954	12,795	3,305,565	2,392,840	1,127.2
1982	42	3,931	1,641	8,092,000	1,720,100	4,007.5
1983	37	4,716	13,744	2,324,042	6,28,901	5,029.8
1984	30	3,175	2,631	4,947,654	1,045,240	4,477.6
1985	45	13,361	3,681	4,406,541	1,052,650	3,712.1
TOTAL	208	30,468	35,189	28,281,902	8,034,231	19,939.6
Average per year	34	5,078	5,865	4,713,650	1,339,038	3,323.3

Source:
Zupka, D. 1988 Economic impact of disasters, *UNDRO News*, January/February 1988, 19–22.

Table 9.4 Natural disasters in Commonwealth island states, 1980–1990

Year	Month	Region	Country	Type/name	Homeless	Damage estimates
1980	August	CARIBBEAN	Barbados	Hurricane Allen	5,000	7 injured 25 fishing boats destroyed US$ 1.5 million
	August		St Lucia	Hurricane Allen	10,000	18 dead 400 dwellings destroyed and 1,100 seriously damaged US$ 88 million
	August		St Vincent	Hurricane Allen	500	US$ 16.3 million
	August		Jamaica	Hurricane Allen	4,000	8 dead, 9 injured entire banana crop destroyed US$ 6.4 million
	March	INDIAN OCEAN	Sri Lanka	Drought		150,000 acres of tea plantation destroyed
	January	SOUTH PACIFIC	Fiji	Cyclone Penni		
	April		Fiji	Cyclone Wally	7,000	20 dead, 250 injured US$ 2.5 million
	June		Tonga	Earthquake (magnitude 6.3)		
	July		Solomon Is.	Earthquake (magnitude 7.3)		
	July		Vanuatu	Earthquake (magnitude 8.0)		
	October		Vanuatu	Earthquake (magnitude 7.2)		
1981	January	SOUTH PACIFIC	Fiji	Cyclone Arthur	4,700	
	February		Vanuatu	Cyclone Cliff		
			Papua New Guinea	Frost and drought		4,000 people affected
	December		Vanuatu	Cyclone Gyan		US$ 1 million
1982	January	SOUTH PACIFIC	Fiji	Cyclone Hettie		
	March		Tonga	Cyclone Isaac	46,500	6 dead, 150 injured 22% of housing destroyed year's foodcrops destroyed US$ 21.2 million
	April		Solomon Is.	Cyclone Bernie	1,000	
1983	March	SOUTH PACIFIC	Fiji	Cyclone Oscar	50,000	9 dead 10,000 houses destroyed US$ 85 million
	March		Fiji	Cyclone Sarah		US$ 851,000
	September		Papua New Guinea	Floods	13,000	6 dead US$ 12 million
1984	January–August October November	CARIBBEAN	Antigua Barbados Dominica	Drought Floods Hurricane Klaus	250	2 dead US$ 2 million

Continued opposite

Table 9.4 Continued

Year	Month	Region	Country	Type/name	Homeless	Damage estimates
	January–May	INDIAN OCEAN	Sri Lanka	Floods	250,000	3 dead 50,000 homes destroyed 21% of the rice harvest destroyed
	March	SOUTH PACIFIC	Fiji	Cyclone Cyril		
	September		Western Samoa	Fire		US$ 31.6 million
1985	November	CARIBBEAN	Turks & Caicos Is.	Hurricane Kate		154 houses damaged port facilities damaged US$ 5,000
	November		Jamaica	Hurricane Kate	300	7 dead US$ 5.2 million
	January	SOUTH PACIFIC	Fiji	Cyclones Eric and Nigel	30,000	28 dead 21,000 houses destroyed US$ 45 million
	January		Vanuatu	Cyclones Eric and Nigel		9 dead 75% of the copra crop destroyed
	March		Fiji	Cyclone Gavin	1,000	2 dead
	March		Solomon Is.	Cyclone Hina	650	131 houses destroyed
			Papua New Guinea	Earthquake (magnitude 7.2)		US$ 1million
1986	May–June	CARIBBEAN	Jamaica	Floods	6,400	54 dead 8,320 ha agricultural land destroyed US$ 76 million
	September		St Vincent	Tropical storm	142	10 injured 63 houses destroyed and 147 damaged US$ 147,900
	September		Grenada	Tropical storm		
	January and April	INDIAN OCEAN	Sri Lanka	Floods and dam bursts		168 dead
	April	SOUTH PACIFIC	Fiji	Cyclone Martin	9,000	19 dead 1,822 houses destroyed US$ 15.4 million
	May		Solomon Is.	Cyclone Namu	60,000	102 dead 3,400 houses destroyed and 4,000 severely damaged 90,000 people dependent on aid for 6 months
	December		Fiji	Cyclone Raja	3,000	1 dead US$ 20 million
	December		Wallis & Futuna	Cyclone Raja		
1987	September	CARIBBEAN	Bermuda	Hurricane Emily		40 injured US$ 50 million
	September		Barbados	Hurricane Emily		46 houses destroyed US$ 100,000
	September		St Vincent	Hurricane Emily	200	36 houses destroyed and 238 damaged 45% of the banana production destroyed US$ 5.3 million

Continued over

Table 9.4 Continued

Year	Month	Region	Country	Type/name	Homeless	Damage estimates
	September		St Lucia	Hurricane Emily		15% of the banana production destroyed
	October		Jamaica	Floods	1,138	4 dead, US$ 30.8 million
	October		Bahamas	Hurricane Floyd		
	March	INDIAN OCEAN	Sri Lanka	Drought		
	April		Maldives	Floods	300	US$ 6 million
	January	SOUTH PACIFIC	Cook Is.	Cyclone Sally	2,000	5 injured 80% of buildings in Avarua and 100% of the banana crop in Aitutaki destroyed US$ 25 million
	February		Vanuatu	Cyclone Uma		48 dead 905 buildings in Port Villa destroyed US$ 200 million
	February		Tokelau	Cyclone Tusi	30	5,000 coconut and breadfruit trees uprooted US$ 500,000
	February		Tuvalu	Cyclone		
	February		Papua New Guinea	Earthquake (magnitude 7.4)	5,000	1 dead 1,051 houses destroyed US$ 2.6 million
1988	September	CARIBBEAN	St Lucia	Hurricane Gilbert		45 dead 25% of housing destroyed US$ 1,000 million
	September		Jamaica	Hurricane Gilbert	810,000	49 dead 100,000 homes destroyed and 300,000 severely damaged US$ 455,000
	January	SOUTH PACIFIC	Vanuatu	Cyclone Anne	1,600	
	August		Solomon Is.	Earthquake		40 houses destroyed
			Vanuatu	Cyclone Bola	2,000	
1989	September	CARIBBEAN	Dominica	Hurricane Hugo		80% of bananas and 50% of all tree crops destroyed
	September		Montserrat	Hurricane Hugo	12,000	10 dead, 40 injured 90% of houses destroyed or damaged US$ 150 million
	September		Antigua & Barbuda	Hurricane Hugo		106 houses destroyed and 1,500 damaged 30 vessels sunk US$ 2.09 million
	September		St Kitts & Nevis	Hurricane Hugo		30 injured 20% of sugar production lost US$ 7.28 million
	September		Br. Virgin Is.	Hurricane Hugo		US$ 21.8 million
	January	INDIAN OCEAN	Mauritius	Cyclone Firinga	4,000	1 dead, 507 injured 844 houses destroyed US$ 50 million
	June		Sri Lanka	Floods and landslides	200,000	315 dead US$ 200 million

Continued opposite

Table 9.4 Continued

Year	Month	Region	Country	Type/name	Homeless	Damage estimates
	December		Mauritius	Cyclone Alibera		
	January	SOUTH PACIFIC	Western Samoa	Cyclones Fili and Gina		US$ 15.5 million
1990	February	SOUTH PACIFIC	Tuvalu	Cyclone Ofa	400	
	February		Tokelau	Cyclone Ofa		80% of breadfruit and coconut trees destroyed US$ 2.4 million
	February		Western Samoa	Cyclone Ofa		12 dead 100% of food crops and 50% of livestock destroyed 80% of telecommunications lost US$ 200 million
	February		Tonga	Cyclone Ofa	1,000	US$ 2.2 million
	February		Niue	Cyclone Ofa		Hospital and hotel destroyed

Source:
Lewis, J. June 1990 Personal communication, Datum International, Marshfield, UK.

Table 9.5 Major floods, 1981–1989

Year	Region	Country	Deaths	Comment
1981	AFRICA	Somalia		>60,000 homeless
	NORTH AMERICA	USA	30	
	ASIA	China	1,500	1,130,000 homeless
		India	3,000	500,000 homeless
	EUROPE	France		Extensive damage, US$ 166 million
		Portugal	30	900 homeless; floods also affected western Spain
	USSR	USSR		Thousands homeless
	OCEANIA	Australia		Extensive damage, US$ 230 million
1982	NORTH AMERICA	USA	30	
	SOUTH AMERICA	Peru	2,500	5,000 homeless
	ASIA	China	447	4,643 injured; 210,000 homeless
		China	75	
		India	932	
		Japan	332	347 injured; 27,000 homeless
	EUROPE	France	18	Extensive damage, US$ 152 million
		Spain	43	1,600 injured; 225,000 affected
		UK		Extensive damage, US$ 174 million
1983	NORTH AMERICA	USA	11	
	SOUTH AMERICA	Ecuador	307	700,000 affected
	ASIA	India	1,600	
		Japan	100	88 injured; typhoon and debris flow
	EUROPE	France		Extensive damage, US$ 604 million
		Portugal	10	2,000 homeless
		Spain	45	6,000 homeless
1984	NORTH AMERICA	USA	>10	
	SOUTH AMERICA	Argentina	30	12,000 affected
	ASIA	Korea	166	>200,000 homeless
	OCEANIA	New Zealand		Extensive damage, US$ 22 million
1985	AFRICA	Benin	61	200,000 homeless
		Ethiopia	9	8,000 homeless
	NORTH AMERICA	Puerto Rico	50	
	SOUTH AMERICA	Argentina	14	50,000 evacuated; >6 million ha farmland flooded
		Brazil	100	600,000 affected; 30 inches of rain in less than one month
		Brazil	1	10,000 evacuated
		Venezuela	38	15,000 homeless
	ASIA	China	422	
		China	283	14,000 homeless
		China	50	24,000 homes destroyed
		China	200	100 missing; thousands homeless
		India	237	Monsoon
		India	130	400,000 homeless; heavy damage to crops and infrastructure

Continued opposite

Table 9.5 Continued

Year	Region	Country	Deaths	Comment
		India	741	Extensive damage, >US$ 500 million
		Philippines	25	5,000 homeless
		Saudi Arabia	32	
1986	AFRICA	Tanzania		6,000 homeless
	NORTH AMERICA	Haiti	69	45,000 affected; extensive damage to crops and infrastructure
		Jamaica	54	11,000 homeless; >16,000 ha farmland flooded
		USA		Thousands evacuated; US$ 25 million damage
		USA		10,000 evacuated
	SOUTH AMERICA	Bolivia	29	2,000 homes destroyed; 8,000 ha farmland flooded
		Brazil	>28	6,500 homeless
		Chile	15	8 missing; 54,000 affected; serious damage to infrastructure
		Colombia	13	>250,000 evacuated
		Peru	12	25,000 homeless
	ASIA	Bangladesh	4	>30,000 homeless; >100,000 affected
		Bangladesh	120	>1 million homeless; >6 million affected;
		China	172	>1,200 injured; 4 million affected after typhoon
		China	80	>5 million affected
		India	18	650,000 homeless
		India	14	>150,000 homeless
		India	>200	
		India	230	Winter storms
		Indonesia	7	>19,000 evacuated; >1,000 ha crops destroyed
		Indonesia	1	30,000 evacuated
		Indonesia	1	60,000 homeless
		Indonesia		12,000 evacuated
		Iran	>230	40,000 homeless; extensive damage, US$ 1,500 million; heavy damage to tree plantations
		Japan	14	>54,000 homes affected
		Malaysia	11	25,000 evacuated
		Philippines	21	20,000 affected by floods after typhoon
		Sri Lanka	168	554,000 affected; >300,000 evacuated
1987	AFRICA	Egypt	11	11 injured; flood and landslide
		Madagascar		Crop and property damage from floods after cyclone
		Somalia		several hundred affected; crop and property damage
		South Africa	>400	Extensive property damage
	NORTH AMERICA	Guatemala	84	125 missing; 15 injured; 6,500 affected; extensive damage
		Haiti	13	20 missing; 150 injured
		Mexico	>7	Dozens injured; hundreds homeless
	SOUTH AMERICA	Argentina	11	Thousands homeless
		Bolivia	20	13 missing; 20,000 affected
		Brazil	95	
		Brazil	12	1,500 homeless
		Chile	54	>80,000 affected
		Chile	55	18 missing; >116,000 affected
		Colombia	5	16 missing
		Ecuador		10,000 evacuated
		Peru	15	10 missing; flood, landslide and dam rupture
		Peru	40	500 missing; severe crop and property damage
		Peru	100	3,000 affected; flood and debris flow
		Venezuela	104	255 missing; 230 injured; flood and debris flow
		Venezuela	23	26 missing; 40 injured
	ASIA	Bangladesh	2,055	3 million affected; severe crop damage; 34,162 cattle killed
		Bangladesh	550	600,000 affected; floods and epidemic disease
		China	86	860 injured; 400,000 ha farmland damaged
		China	42	120 injured; >1 million ha farmland flooded

Continued over

Table 9.5 Continued

Year	Region	Country	Deaths	Comment
		China	>130	900,000 affected; >60,000 ha farmland flooded
		China	22	200,000 affected; >80,000 ha farmland flooded
		China	92	>1 million affected; >300,000 ha farmland flooded
		India	150	1 million affected
		India	>1,200	several million affected; 4 million ha farmland flooded
		Indonesia	38	>84 injured
		Indonesia	92	Flood and landslide
		Indonesia	3	>60,000 evacuated
		Indonesia	>130	>650 affected; floods and landslide
		Iran	40	Flood and landslide; storms
		Iran	196	346 injured
		Iran	147	
		Korea, Dem.	231	71 injured; tens of thousands affected
		Korea, Dem.	32	52 missing; 85,000 ha farmland flooded after typhoon
		Nepal	188	351,000 affected; severe crop and property damage; flood and landslide
		Nepal	137	27 missing; several thousand affected
		Thailand	24	Villages evacuated; 137,000 ha farmland flooded
	EUROPE	France	30	flood and debris flow
		Italy	50	189 injured; US$ 1,000 million damage; flood and landslide
		Spain	15	Extensive damage; thousands evacuated
		Switzerland	1	US$ 40 million damage; floods, debris flow and storms
	USSR	USSR	138	>16,000 homeless; 80,000 ha arable land destroyed after flood and debris flow
		USSR	31	21 missing; 500 affected
1988	AFRICA	Mozambique	>100	>4,500 homeless after cyclone caused floods
		Rwanda	48	>21,000 homeless; extensive structural damage
		South Africa	25	Hundreds homeless; damage to communications
		Sudan	96	1.5 million affected; 100,000 homes destroyed; severe damage to urban infrastructure
	NORTH AMERICA	El Salvador	33	39,000 affected; heavy seasonal rains destroyed hundreds of homes and 9,500 ha of farmland
		Mexico	48	25,000 homeless after a series of tropical storms
	SOUTH AMERICA	Argentina	25	4.5 million affected; 200,000 homes damaged; crops destroyed
		Brazil	251	11,000 homeless after floods and debris flows
		Brazil	277	95 missing; extensive damage after flood and deris flow
		Brazil	300	>1,000 injured
	ASIA	Bangladesh	>2,000	45 million affected; 28 million homeless; worst floods of the century
		China		280,000 affected; 33 villages inundated
		China	577	22 million affected
		China	54	Thousands of mud and cave homes collapsed
		China	170	110,000 homeless
		China	204	30,000 homeless; 30,000 ha farmland destroyed
		China	158	2,800,000 affected; 167,000 homes and 350,000 ha farmland destroyed
		China	22	>7,000 homes destroyed
		China	58	505 injured; 300,000 affected; >1 million ha farmland damaged
		India	>1,000	Late monsoon rains triggered floods
		Indonesia	49	Monsoon
		Iran		150,000 affected; severe damage to 90 villages and farmland; total loss US$ 150 million
		Iran	90	Number of deaths include injured and missing
		Nepal	106	Floods and landslides following monsoon rains and the bursting of a debris dam
		Thailand	457	1,000 missing; >1million affected; 500,000 head of livestock killed
		Turkey	10	5,00 homes affected; roads and bridges collapsed

Continued opposite

Table 9.5   Continued

Year	Region	Country	Deaths	Comment
	EUROPE	Germany, Fed. Rep.	6	1,400 evacuated after rivers burst banks
	OCEANIA	Australia	10	Floods caused by cyclone; major losses of livestock
		New Zealand	4	5 missing; 3,000 evacuated after cyclone
		Vanuatu	1	3,000 homeless; floods and landslides
1989	AFRICA	Malawi	7	137,000 affected; thousands evacuated from refugee camps
		Somalia		40,000 affected; 30,000–50,000 ha farmland flooded
		Tanzania	10	300,000 affected
		Tanzania	12	Extensive damage
	NORTH AMERICA	El Salvador	10	
		Guatemala	10	
	SOUTH AMERICA	Brazil	20	Flood and landslide
		Brazil	36	Flood and landslide
		Brazil	40	Flood and landslide
		Ecuador	35	30,000 homeless; US$ 15 million damage
		Peru	38	100 families displaced after flood and debris flow
	ASIA	Bangladesh	200	
		China	197	
		China	>250	>3,500 injured; >100,000 homeless; 1.28 million ha farmland flooded
		China	>2,500	>10,000 injured; 100 million affected
		India	16	Thousands displaced
		India	1,040	550 missing; Bombay seriously affected
		India	38	
		Indonesia	18	32,000 affected; thousands evacuated
		Japan	10	
		Korea	>100	49 injured; 75,000 affected
		Philippines	33	Flood and landslide caused by typhoon
		Philippines	72	Flood and landslide
		Sri Lanka	305	Flood and landslide caused by monsoon; 250,000 homeless
	EUROPE	Spain	12	Floods after storm; extensive damage; US$ 375 million
	USSR	USSR	20	Floods after cyclone
	OCEANIA	Australia	0	US$ 1.2 million damage
		Fiji	10	
		New Zealand	0	US$ 2.2 million damage

Major floods listed are those which have caused 10 or more deaths and/or 1,000 people to be evacuated and/or extensive property damage. Estimates of damage costs cited in the "Comment" column are given in US dollars.

Sources:
Heinemann/George Philip Publishers 1984 *Geographical Digest* (and earlier editions), Heinemann, Oxford, and George Philip Publishers, London.

OECD 1985 *OECD Environmental Data Compendium 1985,* Organisation for Economic Co-operation and Development, Paris.
UNDRO 1988 *Disaster Briefs – Summary UNINET Data Base* (and earlier editions), United Nations Disaster Relief Organization, Geneva.
UNEP 1987 Environmental Events Record, supplements in *UNEP News* (and earlier editions), United Nations Environment Programme, Nairobi.

Table 9.6 Major landslides, 1981–1989

Year	Region	Country	Deaths	Comment
1981	NORTH AMERICA	Puerto Rico	26	
	SOUTH AMERICA	Colombia	65	14,000 homeless
		Peru	>70	
	ASIA	Indonesia	23	
		Indonesia	500	3,300 evacuated; landslides following volcanic eruption
		Japan	>40	
1982	SOUTH AMERICA	Bolivia	25	Landslide after earth tremor
		Colombia	~30	
	ASIA	China	19	
		Indonesia	~50	
1983	NORTH AMERICA	Mexico	32	
	SOUTH AMERICA	Brazil	13	
		Colombia	~150	
		Peru	232	300 missing, presumed dead
		Peru	13	
	ASIA	China	277	Landslide caused by underground streams
		India	67	
		Indonesia	21	
		Japan	>70	
		Lebanon	20	Landslide caused by leakage from water tank
		Nepal	~21	
	EUROPE	Italy	17	Mountain landslide; 3,000 evacuated; 4,000 homeless
	OCEANIA	Papua New Guinea	45	
1984	SOUTH AMERICA	Argentina	10	
		Peru	13	
	ASIA	China	~100	
		Indonesia	11	11 missing
		Japan	14	
1985	SOUTH AMERICA	Peru	>150	4,000 homeless after successive landslides
	ASIA	Japan	>20	
		Philippines	300	Debris flows
1986	SOUTH AMERICA	Peru	13	
	ASIA	Sri Lanka	40	
1987	AFRICA	Egypt	11	Landslide and flood
	SOUTH AMERICA	Chile	15	Debris flow; 17 missing
		Colombia	355	Debris flow; 2,436 injured
		Colombia	13	
		Ecuador	~1,000	6,000 affected
		Peru	34	Snow avalanche; many missing
		Peru	15	Flood, landslide and dam rupture; 10 missing
		Peru	100	3,000 affected; debris flow and flood
		Venezuela	96	15,000 affected; 1,700 homeless; 300 injured; debris flow caused by torrential rain
		Venezuela	104	255 missing; 230 injured; debris flow and flood
	ASIA	China	102	Landslide caused by severe natural erosion; 20 missing

Continued opposite

Table 9.6 Continued

Year	Region	Country	Deaths	Comment
		Indonesia	132	653 affected; landslide and flood
		Indonesia	44	50 missing
		Indonesia	92	Landslide and flood
		Iran	40	Landslide and flood; storms
		Korea, Dem.	73	Tens of thousands affected; severe damage
		Nepal	188	Landslide and flood; 351,000 affected
		Nepal	137	Several thousand affected; 27 missing
	EUROPE	France	30	Debris flow and flood
		Italy	50	189 injured; US$ 1,000 million damage; landslide and flood
		Switzerland	1	US$ 40 million damage; debris flow after storms and floods
	USSR	USSR	138	16,000 homeless; 80,000 ha arable land destroyed by flood and debris flow
1988	AFRICA	Morocco	52	Several homes destroyed
	SOUTH AMERICA	Brazil	277	95 missing; extensive damage after debris flow and flood
		Brazil	>250	Thousands evacuated after series of debris flows
		Peru	80	10 villages isolated by major debris flows
		Peru		50 missing, presumed dead; many homes destroyed
		Peru	30	Debris flow; 70 missing; homes destroyed
	ASIA	India	160	Damage to roads and communications
		Nepal	106	Major landslide caused by heavy rains and the bursting of a debris dam
		Turkey	19	Houses crushed by rock avalanche
	EUROPE	Switzerland		US$ 7 million damage
		Switzerland		2,000 evacuated; villages isolated by snow avalanche
	OCEANIA	Vanuatu	1	3,000 homeless after landslide caused by floods
1989	NORTH AMERICA	Honduras	10	Debris flow
	SOUTH AMERICA	Brazil	69	Landslide caused by heavy rains; 78,000 affected
		Brazil	36	Landslide and flood
		Brazil	20	Landslide and flood
		Brazil	17	
		Brazil	15	
		Brazil	40	Landslide and flood
		Colombia	10	
		Peru	38	100 families displaced after debris flow caused by floods
	ASIA	China	800	Landslide and floods
		China	84	
		Japan	18	
		Nepal	38	
		Philippines	72	Landslide and flood
		Philippines	13	Landslide caused by heavy rains; gold mine collapsed trapping 1,000 and injuring 200
		Philippines	33	Landslide and floods caused by typhoon
		Philippines	15	
		Sri Lanka	305	Landslide and floods caused by monsoon; 250,000 homeless
	USSR	USSR	46	Landslide caused dam burst

Landslides listed are those which have caused 10 or more deaths and/or major evacuation of populations and/or damage estimated at US$ 1 million or more.

Sources:
Heinemann/George Philip Publishers 1984 *Geographical Digest* (and earlier editions), Heinemann, Oxford, and George Philip Publishers, London.

OECD 1985 *OECD Environmental Data Compendium 1985*, Organisation for Economic Co-operation and Development, Paris.
UNDRO 1988 *Disaster Briefs: Summary*, UNINET data base (and earlier editions), United Nations Disaster Relief Organization, Geneva.
UNEP 1988 Environmental Events Record, supplements in *UNEP News* (and earlier editions), United Nations Environment Programme, Nairobi.
AID/OFDA 1989 *Disaster History*, Office of US Foreign Disaster Assistance Agency for International Development, Washington DC.

Table 9.7 Land area affected by natural disasters in China, 1949–1987

	All natural disasters[a]			Floods			Droughts		
		Arable land affected			Arable land affected			Arable land affected	
Year	Total land area affected (10⁴ ha)	Area[b] (10⁴ ha)	% of total land area affected	Total land area affected (10⁴ ha)	Area[b] (10⁴ ha)	% of total land area affected	Total land area affected (10⁴ ha)	Area[b] (10⁴ ha)	% of total land area affected
1949		853			853				
1952	819	443	54.1	279	184	65.9	424	259	61.1
1957	2,915	1,498	51.4	808	603	74.6	1,721	740	43.0
1962	3,718	1,667	44.8	981	632	64.4	2,081	869	41.8
1965	2,080	1,122	53.9	559	281	50.3	1,363	811	59.5
1970	997	330	33.1	313	123	39.3	572	193	33.7
1975	3,538	1,024	28.9	682	347	50.9	2,483	532	21.4
1976	4,250	1,144	26.9	420	133	31.7	2,749	785	28.6
1977	5,202	1,516	29.1	910	499	54.8	2,985	701	23.5
1978	5,079	2,180	42.9	285	92	32.3	4,017	1,797	44.7
1979	3,937	1,512	38.4	676	287	42.5	2,465	932	37.8
1980	4,453	2,232	50.1	915	503	54.9	2,611	1,249	47.8
1981	3,979	1,874	47.1	862	397	46.1	2,569	1,213	47.2
1982	3,313	1,612	48.7	836	446	53.3	2,070	997	48.2
1983	3,471	1,621	46.7	1,216	575	47.3	1,609	759	47.2
1984	3,189	1,526	47.9	1,063	540	50.8	1,582	702	44.4
1985	4,437	2,271	51.2	1,420	895	63.0	2,299	1,006	43.8
1986	4,714	2,366	50.2	916	558	60.9	3,104	1,476	47.6
1987	4,209	2,039	48.5	869	410	47.2	2,492	1,303	52.3

[a] Includes floods, droughts, frost-freezing, typhoons and hailstorms.
[b] Areas where crop production was reduced by 30 per cent compared with normal years as a result of the disaster.

Source:
State Statistical Bureau of the People's Republic of China 1988 *China Statistical Yearbook 1988*, China Statistical Information and Consultancy Service Centre, Beijing.

Part 10

International Co-operation

Our knowledge about the world's environment is expanding rapidly. Governments and the public alike in all regions of the world are becoming increasingly aware of the need for reliable, consistent information upon which to base the management policies and programmes which will determine the future state of our environment. This section examines current activities in the field of international co-operation and agreements, information availability and exchange, and public awareness and participation which are contributing to environmental protection and to the preservation of our natural resources.

International Agreements

During the past several decades growing environmental awareness has encouraged national governments to legislate for better protection and management of the environment. In addition, recognition of the global nature of problems such as ozone layer depletion and climate change has resulted in co-operation between governments in negotiating international treaties and agreements.

The UNEP Environmental Law and Institutions Unit in Nairobi maintains a 'Register of International Treaties and Other Agreements in the Field of the Environment' (UNEP, 1989a). This listing is submitted annually to the General Assembly of the United Nations, which has expressed concern that many existing international agreements have not yet received the wide acceptance and application they deserve. UNEP continues to urge all states entitled to become parties to existing conventions and protocols to do so as soon as possible. A comprehensive listing of existing international treaties and agreements on the environment was provided in the 1989 edition of this report (UNEP, 1989b).

The late 1980s saw the signing of several important conventions and protocols concerned with the environment. Agreements covering air pollution, endangered wildlife (see Part 3: Natural Resources), Antarctica, depletion of the ozone layer (see Part 1: Environmental Pollution, Atmosphere), and hazardous wastes (see Part 8: Wastes) have set the stage for further international negotiation and co-operation on environmental issues. The following sections provide an overview of the status of three major conventions and protocols: the Convention on Long-range Transboundary Air Pollution and its related Protocols, the Montreal Protocol on the Substances that Deplete the Ozone Layer and the Basel Convention on the Control of Transboundary Movements of Hazardous Wastes and their Disposal.

References

UNEP 1989a *Register of International Treaties and Other Agreements in the Field of the Environment*, United Nations Environment Programme, Nairobi.

UNEP 1989b *United Nations Environment Programme Environmental Data Report*, Basil Blackwell, Oxford.

Convention on Long-range Transboundary Air Pollution and its related Protocols

The Convention on Long-range Transboundary Air Pollution was adopted in 1979 and came into force in 1983. The Convention is open for accession to countries which are members of the United Nations Economic Commission for Europe (UN-ECE), as well as to countries having consultative status with the Commission and to regional economic integration organizations constituted by sovereign State members of the Commission. The 32 countries which are signatories to the Convention have committed themselves to adopting national policies for controlling air pollution; this is defined in the Convention as "the introduction by man, directly or indirectly, of substances or energy into the air resulting in deleterious effects of such a nature as to endanger human health, harm living resources and ecosystems and material property, and impair or interfere with amenities and other legitimate uses of the environment" (DocTer, 1987). The objective of the Convention and its Protocols is to provide for the control or reduction of nitrogen oxide and sulphur dioxide emissions.

Three Protocols have been admitted to the Convention. The first, the European Monitoring and Evaluation Programme (EMEP) Protocol, dealt with the implementation and financing after 1984 of the EMEP programme. EMEP co-ordinates data collection and assessment of acidic deposition within the European region (see Part 1: Environmental Pollution, Atmospheric Deposition). The second Protocol, the SO_2 Protocol, was admitted in Helsinki in July 1985. This Protocol binds signatory countries to reducing their sulphur dioxide emissions by 30 per cent of 1980 values by 1993. The third Protocol, the NO_x Protocol, was admitted in November 1988 in Sofia. This Protocol states that as from 1994 nitrogen oxide emissions should not exceed 1987 levels. A second stage of the NO_x Protocol is stipulated to take place within six months after the Protocol comes into force. In the second stage the aim of negotiations will be to initiate further action to reduce emissions by 1996 at the latest (Agren, 1988). Table 10.1 lists the signatories and status of ratification of the Convention and its related Protocols as of 17 December 1990.

Montreal Protocol on the Substances that Deplete the Ozone Layer

The Montreal Protocol on the Substances that Deplete the Ozone Layer operates within the framework of the Vienna Convention for the Protection of the Ozone Layer. The Vienna Convention was adopted in March 1985 and came into force in September 1988. Its objectives are to encourage co-operation in research and in the formulation and implementation of measures to protect human health and the environment against adverse effects resulting from modifications of the ozone layer (UNEP, 1989). The Montreal Protocol, which was adopted in September 1987 and came into force in 1989, has as its objective the protection of the ozone layer by taking precautionary measures to control global emissions of the substances that deplete it (UNEP, 1989). The Montreal Protocol bound industrialized nations to reduce their consumption of five chlorofluorocarbons (CFCs) and three halons by 20 per cent of their 1986 level by 1994 and by 50 per cent of their 1986 level by 1999. Developing countries consuming less than 0.3 kg per capita of the eight halocarbons controlled by the Protocol are permitted to delay compliance for ten years, provided that they do not exceed a per capita consumption of 0.3 kg in that time (UNEP, 1989). Under the terms of the Protocol, Parties are required to submit data concerning their levels of consumption, production and trade of the controlled substances (see Part 1: Environmental Pollution, Atmosphere).

Table 10.2 lists the signatories and the status of ratification of the 1987 Montreal Protocol as of 12 October 1990. The 64 states and the European Economic Community (EEC) that have to date deposited their instruments of ratification, acceptance, approval or accession account for approximately 90 per cent of the estimated global consumption of ozone-depleting substances (UNEP, 1990).

Basel Convention on the Control of Transboundary Movements of Hazardous Wastes and their Disposal

The Basel Convention is designed to reduce the generation of hazardous and other wastes, and to guarantee the environmentally sound management of the disposal of wastes. The Convention specifies that where the generation of hazardous wastes is unavoidable they must be disposed of as close as possible to the source of their generation. It restricts the transboundary movements of hazardous and other wastes to a minimum, allowing export only if the country of origin does not have the technical capacity and facilities to dispose of the wastes in an environmentally sound manner (IMO, 1989).

In recognition of the concerns expressed by developing nations regarding their lack of technical capacity and expertise in handling hazardous wastes, the Convention strongly emphasizes the need for co-operation between nations in order to develop and promote technologies for the environmentally sound disposal of wastes. Nations are encouraged to participate in the harmonization of technical standards and guidelines, and in monitoring the effects of waste management on human health and the environment (IMO, 1989).

Table 10.3 lists the status of signature and ratification of the Basel Convention on the Control of Transboundary Movements of Hazardous Wastes and their Disposal as at 30 September 1990. As of that date 53 countries and the EEC had signed the Convention and five had ratified it. Twenty more countries informed UNEP that they were in the process of ratification or accession (UNEP, 1990).

References

Agren, C. 1988 Nitrogen oxides freeze, *Acid Magazine* **7**, 18–19.

DocTer 1987 *European Environmental Yearbook 1987*, DocTer Institute for Environmental Studies, Milan.

IMO 1989 *Transboundary Transport of Hazardous Wastes: Summary of the Main Provisions of the Basel Convention Submitted by the United Nations Environment Programme*, International Maritime Organization, London.

UNEP 1989 *Register of International Treaties and Other Agreements in the Field of the Environment*, United Nations Environment Programme, Nairobi.

UNEP 1990 Personal communication, United Nations Environment Programme Environmental Law and Institutions Unit, Nairobi.

Information Sources

UNEP's Global Environment Monitoring System (GEMS) is responsible for the monitoring and assessment of the state of the global environment. GEMS is focused on the monitoring and collection of reliable global environmental data, and on publishing technical assessments of a range of environmental issues. GEMS works in close co-operation with leading UN agencies and national and international institutions involved in monitoring programmes. Another useful source of environmental information is UNEP's Global Resource Information Database (GRID). GRID has developed regional and global environmental data bases using image-analysing and Geographical Information Systems technology (GIS). Its main task is to provide reliable data handling and analytical capabilities for the assessment of deforestation, climate change, desertification, ozone depletion and many other important environmental issues.

The International Referral System for Sources of Environmental Information (INFOTERRA) was established in 1974 with the aim of identifying sources of relevant environmental expertise and information. It exists as a decentralized network of national and international institutions and experts linking 137 countries, and covers a wide range of topics including natural resources, climate, pollution and waste management, energy sources and supplies, agriculture and land use, and human settlements and health. The INFOTERRA data base is co-ordinated through the Programme Activity Centre in Nairobi, and processes more than 12,000 queries per year (UNEP, 1989). INFOTERRA publishes a listing of information sources in its 'International Directory of Sources' (INFOTERRA, 1987). In addition, an increasing number of publications provide syntheses of environmental data and emerging trends on regional and global levels. UNEP, for example, prepares annual "state of the environment" reports which focus on specific issues, and periodically, more general overviews of global environmental trends are produced. The next overview is scheduled for publication in 1992.

Collection and dissemination of information on cleaner industrial production technologies is the function of the International Cleaner Production Information Clearing House (ICPIC), developed by UNEP's Industry and Environment Office (IEO), Paris, in conjunction with the US Environmental Protection Agency. As a computerized information exchange system, the ICPIC facilitates the transfer of technical, policy, legislative and financial expertise on cleaner production. Information is available on-line to research institutions, industry and trade organizations, national and local governments, international organizations, and to non-government groups. In addition to the computerized network, the ICPIC publishes technical reviews, a quarterly newsletter and other information material, and runs seminars on cleaner production.

The comparability of available data is still a major concern in assembling and reporting national and international information relating to the environment. UN agencies such as the World Health Organization (WHO), the Food and Agriculture Organization (FAO) and the UN Statistical Office (UNSO) play an important part in assembling and publishing internationally comparable data within their respective fields.

Efforts are being made to develop standardized international classifications for environmental data, through programmes such as GEMS Harmonization of Environmental Measurement (HEM). Established in 1989, HEM aims to develop methods for the harmonization of data collection and of ongoing and planned programmes and projects (HEM, 1990). Other organizations active in this field include the International Standards Organization (ISO), which provides information on validated analytical techniques and standard reference materials, and CODATA (the International Council of Scientific Unions Committee on Data for Science and Technology), which deals with the compilation, critical evaluation and management of data of relevance to science and technology.

During the 1980s, growing awareness of the need for reliable data on environmental quality and natural resources has resulted in an increase in the publication of state of the environment reports and environmental statistics reports. National state of the environment reports provide a baseline against which future changes in the environment can be judged, document progress made in dealing with environmental problems and may identify areas where further efforts can be made. A directory of UN information sources relating to the environment, compiled by the UN Advisory Committee for the Co-ordination of Information Systems (ACCIS) in collaboration with INFOTERRA, is also available in published form (ACCIS, 1988).

Table 10.4 provides a bibliography of national state of the environment reports, environmental statistical reports and international publications dealing with the state of the world environment. Publications covering specific environmental issues, programmes or policies have been excluded from this listing, as have general statistical yearbooks unless these contain detailed information on the environment. Reports dealing with individual regions within a country have also been excluded.

UNEP, as the lead organization within the UN system with responsibility for environmental issues, promotes through various programmes the generation of information and data on all aspects of the environment. In recognition of the difficulty faced by developing countries in data compilation, UNEP is assisting a number of governments with the preparation of a series of national state of the environment reports. Environmental country profiles for several developing countries have been prepared by the US Agency for International Development (USAID), often in conjunction with other organizations. The World Conservation Monitoring Centre (WCMC), similarly, has produced Biological Diversity Profiles for many developing countries.

References

ACCIS 1988 *ACCIS Guide to United Nations Information Sources on the Environment*, No. 2, United Nations, New York.

HEM 1990 *A Survey of Environmental Monitoring and Information Management Programmes of International Organizations*, United Nations Environment Programme-Harmonization of Environmental Measurement, Munich.

INFOTERRA 1987 *International Directory of Sources, International Referral System for Sources of Environmental Information*, United Nations Environment Programme, Nairobi.

UNEP 1989 *United Nations Environment Programme Environmental Data Report*, Basil Blackwell, Oxford.

Satellite Remote Sensing

Remote sensing techniques are based on an understanding of the way in which various parts of the electromagnetic spectrum are reflected or emitted from the surface of the earth (US Department of State, 1986). Remote sensing can be used to produce inventories and undertake long-term monitoring of forest, mineral, energy and water resources. Satellite remote sensing is also widely applied to meteorological and climate monitoring (see Part 2: Climate). When data gathered from remote sensing are combined with those gathered by other means, such as Geographical Information Systems (GIS) and conventional land research on specific sites, a detailed picture of a particular area or problem can be formulated.

Since the launch of the first earth-survey satellite series, LANDSAT, by the USA in 1972, remote sensing satellites have become increasingly important for earth resources monitoring. Table 10.5 lists all artificial satellites involved in remote sensing launched in 1988 and 1989. The list is compiled from the 'Telecommunication Journal' (ITU 1989, 1990), which publishes a list of all satellites launched in a specific year from information provided by telecommunication administrations of International Telecommunication Union (ITU) member countries, the Committee on Space Research (COSPAR), national space research organizations, the International Frequency Registration Board (IFRB) of the ITU, and from details published in the specialized press. The 1989 edition of this report provided a listing of all meteorological and earth resources monitoring satellites launched since 1959 (UNEP, 1989).

References

ITU 1989 Table of artificial satellites launched in 1988, *Telecommunication Journal* **56**(V), Supplement.

ITU 1990 Table of artificial satellites launched in 1989, *Telecommunication Journal* **57**(V), Supplement.

UNEP 1989 *United Nations Environment Programme Environmental Data Report*, Basil Blackwell, Oxford.

US Department of State 1986 *Coupling of Ecological Studies with Remote Sensing*, US Man and the Biosphere Programme/US Department of State, Washington DC.

Environmental Awareness

In recent years environmental concerns have been at the forefront of public attention. Public awareness of environmental issues is a major driving force leading to calls for the development of national and international policies to protect the environment. Growing public participation in community organizations, lobbying groups and local action groups also reflects an increasing environmental awareness.

Public Opinion

Between February 1988 and June 1989 a survey of public and leadership attitudes towards environmental issues was conducted in 16 countries by Louis Harris and Associates on behalf of UNEP. The results of the survey pointed to deep public concern about the quality of the environment, coupled with the belief that environmental protection should be a major governmental priority. In all countries but one, most members of the public and leaders surveyed believed that their environments had become worse over the past 10 years (Table 10.6).

Figure 10.1 shows the level of public concern over various environmental issues, both local and global in scale, in 10 or more European countries surveyed at intervals between 1982 and 1988. The figure shows that levels of concern on the majority of issues have been increasing. It is evident, though perhaps surprising, that higher levels of concern are expressed over global environmental issues than for local issues.

Membership of Non-government Organizations

Since the 1970s non-government organizations (NGOs) have played an increasingly important role in promoting environmental awareness. It is difficult to estimate how

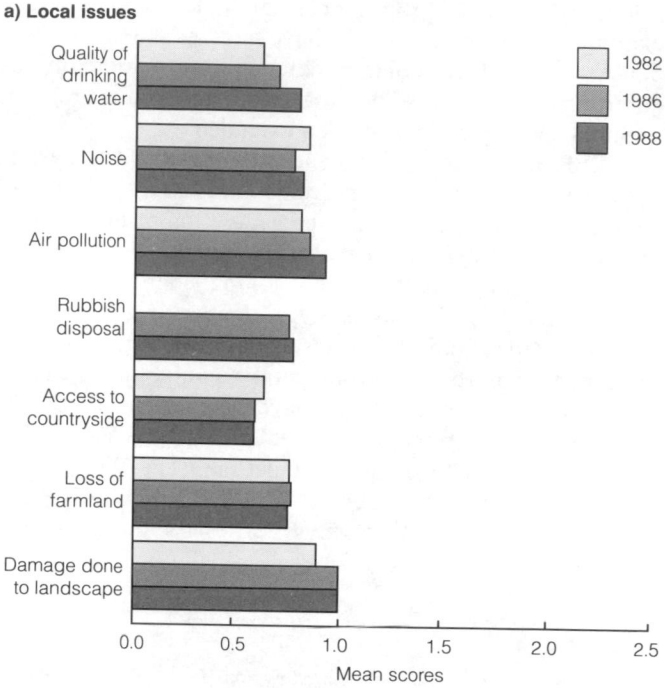

a) Local issues

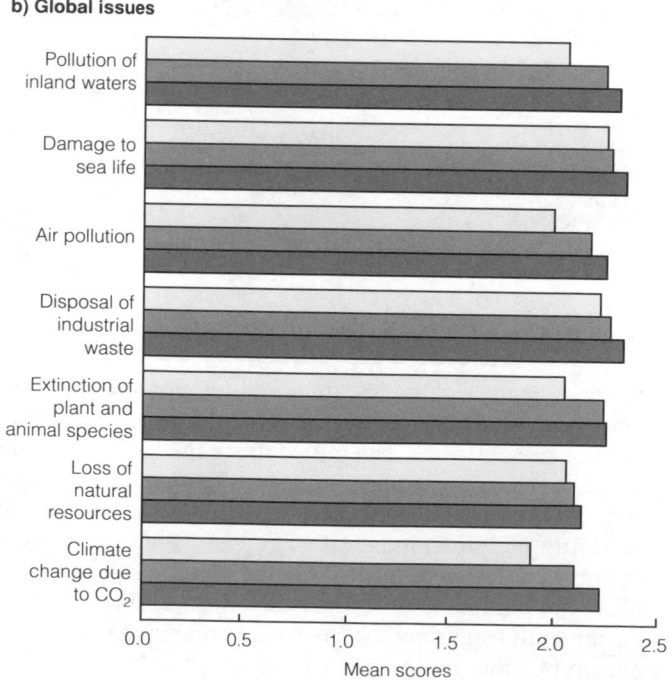

b) Global issues

Figure 10.1 Public opinion on local, national and global environmental issues, 1982, 1984 and 1988 (values are mean scores for replies weighted as follows: "a great deal" (3), "a fair amount" (2), "not very much" (1), "not at all" (0))
Source: EUROSTAT, 1990

many people world-wide are members of environmental organizations. Non-government organizations are as varied as the issues they confront, ranging from small groups organized in response to a particular issue of local concern to large organizations spanning several countries and working on global issues. This latter category includes the World Conservation Union (IUCN), the World Resources Institute (WRI) and the International Institute for Environment and Development (IIED). Many NGOs have similar interests and co-ordination of activities is seen to be increasingly important. A number of NGO liaison centres have been established including, for example, the Environment Liaison Centre in Nairobi which is supported by UNEP. Additional information relating to both regional and global NGO liaison centres can be found in the previous edition of this report (UNEP, 1989).

Table 10.7 gives membership numbers for two international environmental NGOs, Friends of the Earth and Greenpeace. Figure 10.2 shows the growth of membership in the UK of the World Wide Fund for Nature (WWF) and Friends of the Earth. A survey by 'The Times' newspaper in June 1989 found that membership in the environmental movement in the UK was beginning to rival that of the largest sectional interest group in the UK – trade unions (McCarthy, 1989).

The more developed, western nations are not alone in experiencing a rise in the number of, and participation in, NGOs. Developing regions have a history of action by non-government groups in environmental and development issues. Often based around local communities, these groups are having an increasingly important impact on environmental outcomes. In Indonesia, for example, there are an estimated 600 independent development groups working in environmental protection. In Colombia, farmers have organized themselves into local "green councils". In Eastern Europe there has also been growing environmental awareness; an estimated 62 independent environmental groups have been organized in Poland since 1980, focusing mainly on air and water pollution and forest destruction (Durning, 1989).

The public opinion poll conducted by Louis Harris and Associates referred to above, found that 74 per cent of people surveyed felt that voluntary and community organizations which are not a part of government could play a major part in solving environmental problems (Louis

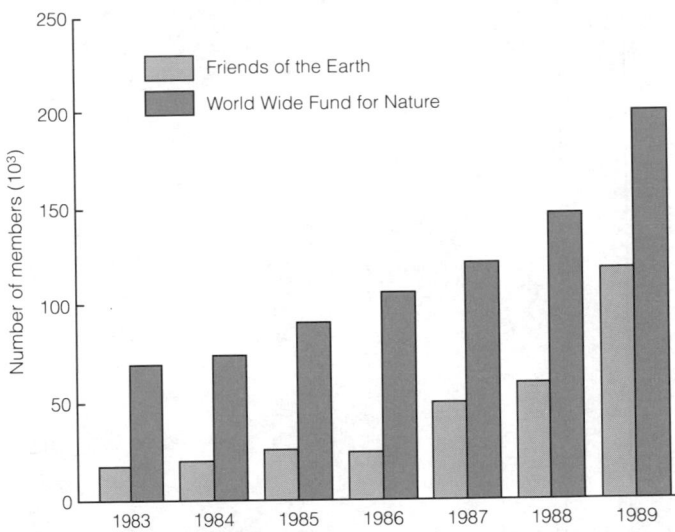

Figure 10.2 Membership of selected environmental groups in the UK, 1983–1989
Sources: Friends of the Earth, 1990; WWF, 1990

Harris and Associates, 1990). The poll found that 81 per cent of leaders surveyed agreed that NGOs had an important role to play. From these responses it can safely be assumed that NGOs will continue to be a major driving force in solving both local and global environmental problems.

References

Durning, A. 1989 *Action at the Grassroots: Fighting Poverty and Environmental Decline*, Worldwatch Paper 88, Worldwatch Institute, Washington DC.
EUROSTAT 1990 *Environment Statistics 1989*, Statistical Office of the European Communities, Luxembourg.
Friends of the Earth 1990 Personal communication, Friends of the Earth, Amsterdam, Netherlands.
Louis Harris and Associates 1989 *Public and Leadership Attitudes to the Environment in Four Continents: A Report of a Survey in 16 Countries*, Louis Harris and Associates, New York.
McCarthy, M. 1989 Green power becoming force to rival unions, *The Times*, 5 June 1989.
UNEP 1989 *United Nations Environment Programme Environmental Data Report*, Basil Blackwell, Oxford.
WWF 1990 Personal communication, World Wide Fund for Nature, Godalming, UK.

Table 10.1 Status of the UN-ECE Convention on Long-range Transboundary Air Pollution and its Related Protocols, as of 17 December 1990

Region/country	Convention[a] Signature	Convention[a] Ratification	EMEP Protocol[b] Signature	EMEP Protocol[b] Ratification	SO$_2$ Protocol[c] Signature	SO$_2$ Protocol[c] Ratification	NO$_x$ Protocol[d] Signature	NO$_x$ Protocol[d] Ratification
ASIA								
Turkey	13-Nov-79	18-Apr-83	3-Oct-84	20-Dec-85				
NORTH AMERICA								
Canada	13-Nov-79	15-Dec-81	3-Oct-84	4-Dec-84	9-Jul-85	4-Dec-85	1-Nov-88	
USA	13-Nov-79	30-Nov-81	28-Sep-84	29-Oct-84			1-Nov-88[e]	13-Jul-89
EUROPE								
EEC	14-Nov-79	15-Jul-82	28-Sep-84	17-Jul-86				
Austria	13-Nov-79	16-Dec-82		4-Jun-87	9-Jul-85	4-Jun-87	1-Nov-88	15-Jan-90
Belgium	13-Nov-79	15-Jul-82	25-Feb-85	5-Aug-87	9-Jul-85	9-Jun-89	1-Nov-88	
Bulgaria	14-Nov-79	9-Jun-81	4-Apr-85	26-Sep-86	9-Jul-85	26-Sep-86	1-Nov-88	30-Mar-89
Czechoslovakia	13-Nov-79	23-Dec-83		26-Nov-86	9-Jul-85	26-Nov-86	1-Nov-88	
Denmark	14-Nov-79	18-Jun-82	28-Sep-84	29-Apr-86	9-Jul-85	29-Apr-86	1-Nov-88	17-Aug-90
Finland	13-Nov-79	15-Apr-81	7-Dec-84	24-Jun-86	9-Jul-85	24-Jun-86	1-Nov-88	
France	13-Nov-79	3-Nov-81	22-Feb-85	30-Oct-87	9-Jul-85	13-Mar-86	1-Nov-88	1-Feb-90
German Dem. Rep.	13-Nov-79	7-Jun-82	17-Dec-86		9-Jul-85		1-Nov-88	20-Jul-89
Germany, Fed. Rep.	13-Nov-79	15-Jul-82[f]	26-Feb-85	7-Oct-86[f]	9-Jul-85	3-Mar-87[f]	1-Nov-88	16-Nov-90
Greece	14-Nov-79	30-Aug-83		24-Jun-88	9-Jul-85		1-Nov-88	
Holy See	14-Nov-79							
Hungary	13-Nov-79	22-Sep-80	27-Mar-85	8-May-85	9-Jul-85	11-Sep-86	3-May-89	
Iceland	13-Nov-79	5-May-83						
Ireland	13-Nov-79	15-Jul-82	4-Apr-85	26-Jun-87			1-May-89	
Italy	14-Nov-79	15-Jul-82	28-Sep-84	12-Jan-89	9-Jul-85	5-Feb-90	1-Nov-88	
Liechtenstein	14-Nov-79	22-Nov-83	21-Nov-84	1-May-85	9-Jul-85	13-Feb-86	1-Nov-88	4-Oct-90
Luxembourg	13-Nov-79	15-Jul-82	28-Sep-84	24-Aug-87	9-Jul-85	24-Jun-87	1-Nov-88	
Netherlands	13-Nov-79	15-Jul-82[g]	28-Sep-84	22-Oct-85[g]	9-Jul-85	30-Apr-86[g]	1-Nov-88	11-Nov-89
Norway	13-Nov-79	13-Feb-81		12-Mar-85	9-Jul-85	4-Nov-86	1-Nov-88	11-Nov-89
Poland	13-Nov-79	19-Jul-85[f]		14-Sep-88	9-Jul-85		1-Nov-88	
Portugal	14-Nov-79	29-Sep-80						
Romania	14-Nov-79[e]			10-Jan-89				
San Marino	14-Nov-79							
Spain	14-Nov-79	15-Jun-82		11-Aug-87	9-Jul-85		1-Nov-88	4-Dec-90
Sweden	13-Nov-79	12-Feb-81	28-Sep-84	12-Aug-85	9-Jul-85	31-Mar-86	1-Nov-88	27-Jul-90

Continued below

Table 10.1 Continued

Region/country	Convention[a] Signature	Convention[a] Ratification	EMEP Protocol[b] Signature	EMEP Protocol[b] Ratification	SO$_2$ Protocol[c] Signature	SO$_2$ Protocol[c] Ratification	NO$_x$ Protocol[d] Signature	NO$_x$ Protocol[d] Ratification
Switzerland	13-Nov-79	6-May-83	3-Oct-84	26-Jul-85	9-Jul-85	21-Sep-87	1-Nov-88	18-Sep-90
UK	13-Nov-79	15-Jul-82[h]	20-Nov-84	12-Aug-85			1-Nov-88	15-Oct-90[h]
Yugoslavia	13-Nov-79	18-Mar-87		28-Oct-87				
USSR	13-Nov-79	22-May-80	28-Sep-84	21-Aug-85	9-Jul-85	10-Sep-86	1-Nov-88	21-Jun-89
Byelorussian SSR	14-Nov-79	13-Jun-80	28-Sep-84	4-Oct-84	9-Jul-85	10-Sep-86	1-Nov-88	8-Jun-89
Ukranian SSR	14-Nov-79	5-Jun-80	28-Sep-84	30-Aug-85	9-Jul-85	2-Oct-86	1-Nov-88	24-Jul-89

a Convention on Long-range Transboundary Air Pollution.
b Protocol to the 1979 Convention on Long-range Transboundary Air Pollution on Long-term Financing of the Co-operative Programme for Monitoring and Evaluation of the Long-range Transmission of Air Pollutants in Europe (EMEP).
c Protocol to the 1979 Convention on Long-range Transboundary Air Pollution on the Reduction of Sulphur Emissions or their Transboundary Fluxes by at least 30 per cent.

d Protocol to the 1979 Convention on Long-range Transboundary Air Pollution concerning the Control of Emissions of Nitrogen Oxides or their Transboundary Fluxes.
e With a declaration upon signature.
f With a declaration upon ratification.
g For the Kingdom in Europe only.
h Including the Bailiwick of Jersey, the Bailiwick of Guernsey, the Isle of Man, Gibraltar, the United Kingdom Sovereign Base Areas of Akrotiri and Dhekelia in the Island of Cyprus.

Ratification is the generic term for the process by which national parliaments agree to be bound by a Convention or Protocol. Individual countries may use the terms "ratification", "accession", "acceptance" or "approval".

Source:
UN-ECE 1990 Personal Communication, United Nations Economic Commission for Europe, Geneva, Switzerland.

Table 10.2 Status of Ratification of the 1987 Montreal Protocol on the Substances that Deplete the Ozone Layer[a], as of 12 October 1990

Region/country	Signature	Ratification	Entry into force	Region/country	Signature	Ratification	Entry into force
AFRICA				Singapore		5-Jan-89	5-Apr-89
				Sri Lanka		15-Dec-89	15-Mar-90
Burkina Faso	14-Sep-88	20-Jul-89	18-Oct-89	Syria		12-Dec-89	12-Mar-90
Cameroon		30-Aug-89	28-Nov-89	Thailand	15-Sep-88	7-Jul-89	5-Oct-89
Congo	15-Sep-88			Turkey	b		
Gambia		25-Jul-90	23-Oct-90	United Arab Em.		22-Dec-89	22-Mar-90
Ghana	16-Sep-87	24-Jul-89	22-Oct-89				
				EUROPE			
Kenya	16-Sep-87	9-Nov-88	7-Feb-89				
Morocco	7-Jan-88[b]			EEC	16-Sep-87	16-Dec-88	16-Mar-89
Nigeria		31-Oct-88	29-Jan-89				
Senegal	16-Sep-87			Austria	29-Aug-88	3-May-89	1-Aug-89
South Africa		15-Jan-90	15-Apr-90	Belgium	16-Sep-87	30-Dec-88	30-Mar-89
				Czechoslovakia		1-Oct-90	
Togo	16-Sep-87			Denmark[e]	16-Sep-87	16-Dec-88	1-Jan-89
Tunisia		25-Sep-89	24-Dec-89	Finland	16-Sep-87	23-Dec-88	1-Jan-89
Uganda	15-Sep-88	15-Sep-88	1-Jan-89				
Zambia		24-Jan-90	24-Apr-90	France	16-Sep-87	28-Dec-88	1-Jan-89
				German Dem. Rep.		25-Jan-89	25-Apr-89
NORTH AMERICA				Germany, Fed. Rep.[f]	16-Sep-87	16-Dec-88	1-Jan-89
				Greece	29-Oct-87	29-Dec-88	29-Mar-89
Canada	16-Sep-87	30-Jun-88	1-Jan-89	Hungary		20-Apr-89	19-Jul-89
Guatemala		7-Nov-89	5-Feb-90				
Mexico	16-Sep-87	31-Mar-88	1-Jan-89	Iceland		29-Aug-89	27-Nov-89
Panama	16-Sep-87	3-Mar-89	1-Jun-89	Ireland	15-Sep-88	16-Dec-88	1-Jan-89
Trinidad & Tobago		28-Aug-89	26-Nov-89	Italy	16-Sep-87	16-Dec-88	1-Jan-89
USA	16-Sep-87	21-Apr-88	1-Jan-89	Liechtenstein		8-Feb-89	8-May-89
				Luxembourg	29-Jan-88	17-Oct-88	15-Jan-89
SOUTH AMERICA							
				Malta	15-Sep-88	29-Dec-88	1-Jan-89
Argentina	29-Jun-88			Netherlands[g]	16-Sep-87	16-Dec-88	1-Jan-89
Brazil		19-Mar-90	17-Jun-90	Norway	16-Sep-87	24-Jun-88	1-Jan-89
Chile[c]	14-Jun-88	26-Mar-90	24-Jun-90	Poland		13-Jul-90	11-Oct-90
Ecuador		30-Apr-90	29-Jul-90	Portugal	16-Sep-87	17-Oct-88	15-Jan-89
Venezuela	16-Sep-87	6-Feb-89	7-May-89				
				Spain	21-Jul-88	16-Dec-88	1-Jan-89
ASIA				Sweden	16-Sep-87	29-Jun-88	1-Jan-89
				Switzerland	16-Sep-87	28-Dec-88	1-Jan-89
Bahrain[d]		27-Apr-90	26-Jul-90	UK[h]	16-Sep-87	16-Dec-88	1-Jan-89
Bangladesh		2-Aug-90	31-Oct-90				
Egypt	16-Sep-87	2-Aug-88	1-Jan-89	USSR	29-Dec-87	10-Nov-88	1-Jan-89
Indonesia	21-Jul-88						
Iran		3-Oct-90	1-Jan-90	Byelorussian SSR	22-Jan-88	31-Oct-88	1-Jan-89
				Ukrainian SSR	18-Feb-88	20-Sep-88	1-Jan-89
Israel	14-Jan-88						
Japan	16-Sep-87	30-Sep-88	1-Jan-89	**OCEANIA**			
Jordan		31-May-89	30-Aug-89				
Libya		11-Jul-90	9-Oct-90	Australia	8-Jun-88	19-May-89	17-Aug-89
Malaysia		29-Aug-89	27-Nov-89	Fiji		23-Oct-89	21-Jan-90
				New Zealand[i]	16-Sep-87	21-Jul-88	1-Jan-89
Maldives	12-Jul-88	16-May-89	14-Aug-89				
Philippines	14-Sep-88						

Continued opposite

Table 10.2 Continued

^a Adopted in Montreal on 16 September 1987 and entered into force on 1 January 1989.

^b Formal indication received by UNEP that the ratification, acceptance, approval or accession procedures are in progress.

^c Upon ratification, the Government of Chile made the following declaration: (Chile) rejects the declaration made by the United Kingdom of Great Britain and Northern Ireland upon ratification, as it concerns the Chilean Antarctic Territory, including the corresponding maritime zones, (Chile) reaffirms once more its sovereignty over the said territory including its maritime areas, as defined by Supreme Decree No. 1747 of 6 November 1940.

^d The accession shall in no way constitute recognition of Israel or be a cause for establishment of any relations of any kind therewith.

^e Decision reserved as concerns the Faeroe Islands and Greenland.

^f With application to West Berlin.

^g For the Kingdom in Europe, the Netherlands Antilles and Aruba.

^h On behalf of the United Kingdom of Great Britain and Northern Ireland, the Bailiwick of Jersey, the Isle of Man, Anguilla, Bermuda, British Antarctic Territory, British Indian Ocean Territory, British Virgin Islands, Cayman Islands, Falkland Islands, Gibraltar, Hong Kong, Montserrat, Pitcairn, Henderson, Ducie and Oeno Islands, Saint Helena and dependencies, South Georgia and the South Sandwich Islands, and the Turks and Caicos Islands.

ⁱ The Protocol shall not apply to the Cook Islands and Niue.

Ratification is the generic term for the process by which national parliaments agree to be bound by a Convention or Protocol. Individual countries may use the terms "ratification", "accession", "acceptance" or "approval".

Source:
UNEP 1990 Personal communication, United Nations Environment Programme Environmental Law and Institutions Unit, Nairobi, Kenya.

Table 10.3 Signatories and status of the Basel Convention on the Control of Transboundary Movements of Hazardous Wastes and their Disposal, as of 30 September 1990

Region/country[a]	Signature Final Act	Signature Convention	Ratification Convention
AFRICA			
Algeria	22-Mar-89		
Angola	22-Mar-89		
Benin	22-Mar-89		
Burkina Faso	22-Mar-89		
Burundi	22-Mar-89		
Cameroon	22-Mar-89		
Cape Verde	22-Mar-89		
Cent. African Rep.	22-Mar-89		
Comoros	22-Mar-89		
Congo			
Côte d'Ivoire	22-Mar-89		
Djibouti	22-Mar-89		
Egypt	22-Mar-89		
Ethiopia			
Gabon			
Gambia	22-Mar-89		
Ghana	22-Mar-89		
Guinea	22-Mar-89		
Kenya	22-Mar-89		
Libya	22-Mar-89		
Madagascar	22-Mar-89		
Malawi	22-Mar-89		
Mali	22-Mar-89		
Mauritania	22-Mar-89		
Morocco	22-Mar-89		
Mozambique	22-Mar-89		
Niger	22-Mar-89		
Nigeria		15-Mar-90	
Rwanda	22-Mar-89		
Senegal	22-Mar-89		
Seychelles	22-Mar-89		
Sierra Leone	22-Mar-89		
Somalia			
Swaziland	22-Mar-89		
Tanzania			
Togo			
Tunisia	22-Mar-89		
Uganda			
Zaire	22-Mar-89		
Zambia	22-Mar-89		
Zimbabwe	22-Mar-89		
NORTH AMERICA			
Canada	22-Mar-89	22-Mar-89	
Cuba	22-Mar-89		
El Salvador		22-Mar-90	
Guatemala	22-Mar-89	22-Mar-89	
Haiti	22-Mar-89	22-Mar-89	
Mexico	22-Mar-89	22-Mar-89	
Panama	22-Mar-89	22-Mar-89	
USA	22-Mar-89	22-Mar-90	
SOUTH AMERICA			
Argentina	22-Mar-89	22-Mar-89	
Bolivia	22-Mar-89	22-Mar-89	
Brazil	22-Mar-89		
Chile	22-Mar-89	31-Jan-90	
Colombia	22-Mar-89	22-Mar-89	
Ecuador	22-Mar-89	22-Mar-89	
Peru	22-Mar-89		
Uruguay	22-Mar-89	22-Mar-89	
Venezuela	22-Mar-89	22-Mar-89	
ASIA			
Afghanistan	22-Mar-89	22-Mar-89	
Bangladesh	22-Mar-89		
Bahrain	22-Mar-89	22-Mar-89	
Brunei			
China	22-Mar-89	22-Mar-89	
Cyprus	22-Mar-89	22-Mar-89	
India	22-Mar-89	15-Mar-90	
Indonesia	22-Mar-89		
Iraq	22-Mar-89		
Israel	22-Mar-89	22-Mar-89	
Japan	22-Mar-89		
Jordan	22-Mar-89	22-Mar-89	22-Jun-89
Korea	22-Mar-89		
Korea, Dem.	22-Mar-89		
Kuwait	22-Mar-89	22-Mar-89	
Lebanon	22-Mar-89	22-Mar-89	
Malaysia	22-Mar-89		
Maldives	22-Mar-89		
Mongolia	22-Mar-89		
Pakistan	22-Mar-89		
Philippines	22-Mar-89	22-Mar-89	
Saudi Arabia	22-Mar-89	22-Mar-89	7-Mar-90
Sri Lanka	22-Mar-89		
Syria	22-Mar-89	11-Oct-89	
Thailand		22-Mar-90	
Turkey	22-Mar-89	22-Mar-89	
United Arab Em.	22-Mar-89	22-Mar-89	
Viet Nam	22-Mar-89		
Yemen			
Yemen, Dem.	22-Mar-89		
EUROPE			
EEC	22-Mar-89	22-Mar-89	

Continued opposite

Table 10.3 Continued

Region/country[a]	Signature Final Act	Signature Convention	Ratification Convention	Region/country[a]	Signature Final Act	Signature Convention	Ratification Convention
Albania	22-Mar-89			Netherlands	22-Mar-89	22-Mar-89	
Austria	22-Mar-89	19-Mar-90		Norway	22-Mar-89	22-Mar-89	2-Jul-90
Belgium	22-Mar-89	22-Mar-89		Poland		22-Mar-90	
Bulgaria	22-Mar-89			Portugal	22-Mar-89	26-Jun-89	
Czechoslovakia	22-Mar-89			Romania	22-Mar-89		
Denmark	22-Mar-89	22-Mar-89		Spain	22-Mar-89	22-Mar-89	
Finland	22-Mar-89	22-Mar-89		Sweden	22-Mar-89	22-Mar-89	
France	22-Mar-89	22-Mar-89		Switzerland	22-Mar-89	22-Mar-89	31-Jan-90
German Dem. Rep.	22-Mar-89	19-Mar-90		UK	22-Mar-89	6-Oct-89	
Germany, Fed. Rep.	22-Mar-89	23-Oct-89		Yugoslavia	22-Mar-89		
Greece	22-Mar-89	22-Mar-89		USSR	22-Mar-89	22-Mar-90	
Hungary	22-Mar-89	22-Mar-89	21-May-90	OCEANIA			
Ireland	22-Mar-89	19-Jan-90					
Italy	22-Mar-89	22-Mar-89		Australia	22-Mar-89		
Liechtenstein	22-Mar-89	22-Mar-89		New Zealand		18-Dec-89	
Luxembourg	22-Mar-89	22-Mar-89		Samoa	22-Mar-89		
Malta	22-Mar-89						

[a] Attended Basel Convention.

Ratification is the generic term for the process by which national parliaments agree to be bound by a Convention or Protocol. Individual countries may use the terms "ratification", "accession", "acceptance" or "approval".

Source:
UNEP 1990 Personal communication, United Nations Environment Programme Environmental Law and Institutions Unit, Nairobi, Kenya.

Table 10.4 State of the environment reports, by country

Region/country	Year	Title	Issuing agency
		National Reports	
AFRICA			
Kenya	1987	Kenya: National State of the Environment	United Nations Environment Programme, Nairobi
Madagascar	1987	Madagascar: an Environmental Profile	IUCN/WCMC, Cambridge
Mauritius	1985	Annual Digest of Statistics 1984	Central Statistical Office, Mauritius
Morocco	Under preparation	State of the Environment Report	United Nations Environment Programme, Nairobi
Mozambique	1985	Informacao Estatistica 1975–1984	Direccao Nacional de Estatistica, Maputo
Zimbabwe	1990	State of the Environment Report	United Nations Environment Programme, Nairobi
NORTH AMERICA			
Canada	1986	State of the Environment Report for Canada	Environment Canada, Ottawa
Canada	1986	Human Activity and the Environment: A Statistical Compendium	Statistics Canada, Ottawa
Costa Rica	1988	Desarrollo Socioeconómico y el Ambiente Natural de Costa Rica	Fundación Neotrópica, San Jose
Mexico	1986	Informe Sobre El Estado del Medio Ambiente en Mexico	Secretario de Desarrollo Urbano y Ecología, Mexico City
Panama	1985	National Environment Statistical Report	The Technical Secretariat of the National Commission of the Environment, Panama
USA	1988	Environmental Quality	Council of Environmental Quality, Washington DC
USA	1988	State of the Environment: a View Towards the Nineties	The Conservation Foundation, Washington DC
SOUTH AMERICA			
Brazil	1984	Relatõrio da Qualidade do Meio Ambiente	Ministerio do Interior, SEMA, Brasília
Brazil	1985	Anuário Estatístico do Brazil 1984	Fundaçáo Instituto Brasileiro de Geografia e Estatística, Rio de Janeiro
Chile	1984	Comendio Estadístico 1984	Instituto Nacional de Estadisticas, Santiago
Chile	1985	Diagnóstico Preliminar de la Situatión Ambiental del País	República de Chile Ministerio de Salud Depto. de Planificación, Santiago
ASIA			
Bahrain	1988	Bahrain: National State of the Environment Report	United Nations Environment Programme, Nairobi
China	1988	China: Statistical Yearbook, 1988	China Statistical Information and Consultancy Service Centre, Beijing
Cyprus	1989	Cyprus National Report on Issues Relating to Sustainable Economic Development	Republic of Cyprus, Nicosia
Hong Kong	1988	Environment Hong Kong 1988: A review of 1987	Environmental Protection Department, Hong Kong
India	1985	The State of India's Environment 1985: a Citizen's Report	Centre for Science and Environment, New Dehli
Indonesia	1990	Statistik Lingkungan Hidup Indonesia 1989	Biro Pusat Statistik, Jakarta
Israel	1988	The Environment in Israel	Environmental Protection Service, Jerusalem
Japan	1988	Quality of the Environment in Japan	International Affairs Division, Environment Agency, Government of Japan, Tokyo
Kuwait	1987	National State of the Environment Report, Kuwait	Environmental Protection Department, Kuwait
Malaysia	1987	Environmental Quality Report 1985–1986	Ministry of Science, Technology and the Environment, Kuala Lumpur
Nepal	In press	State of the Environment	United Nations Environment Programme, Nairobi
Qatar	1987	Qatar: National State of the Environment Report	United Nations Environment Programme, Nairobi

Continued opposite

Table 10.4 Continued

Region/country	Year	Title	Issuing agency
Saudi Arabia	1989	The State of the Environment in the Kingdom of Saudia Arabia	Meteorological & Environmental Protection Administration (MEPA), Jeddah
Thailand	In press	State of the Environment Report	United Nations Environment Programme, Nairobi

EUROPE

Region/country	Year	Title	Issuing agency
Austria	1989	Umwelt Bericht	Österreichisches Bundesinstitut für Gesundheitswesen, Vienna
Belgium	1989	Annuaire Statistique de la Belgique	Institut National de Statistique, Ministère des Affaires Economiques, Brussels
Finland	1988	Environmental Protection in Finland: National Report 1987	Ministry of the Environment, Helsinki
France	1988	State of the Environment 1987 Report	Ministry of the Environment of the French Republic, Paris
German Dem. Rep.	1990	Umweltbericht der DDR	Institut für Umweltschutz, Berlin
Germany, Fed. Rep.	1989	Daten zur Umwelt 1988/89	Erich Schmidt Verlag Gmblt & Co., Berlin
Greece	1983	Environmental Policies in Greece	Organisation for Economic Co-operation and Development, Paris
Hungary	1990	State of the Hungarian Environment	Hungarian Academy of Sciences, the Ministry for Environment and Water Management and the Hungarian Central Statistical Office, Budapest
Ireland	1987	Irish Environmental Statistics 1986	An Foras Forbartha, Dublin
Italy	1987	Nota Preliminare alla Relazione Sullo stato dell'Ambiente	Ministero dell'Ambiente, Rome
Italy	1989	Relazione sullo stato dell'ambiente, Vols 1 & 2	Instituto Centrale di Statistica, Rome
Liechtenstein	1984	Statistisches Jahrbuch 1984	Amt für Volkswirtschaft, Vaduz, Furstentum Liechtenstein
Luxembourg	1984	Livre Blanc sur l'Environment	Comité National pour la Protection de l'Environment de Luxembourg
Luxembourg	1988	Rapport d'activité 1987	Ministère de l'Environment, Luxembourg
Netherlands	1987	Environmental Statistics of the Netherlands 1987	Netherlands Central Bureau of Statistics, The Hague
Netherlands	1989	Concern for Tomorrow, a National Environmental Survey 1985–2010	National Institute of Public Health and Environmental Protection, The Hague
Netherlands	1989	To Choose or to Lose: National Environmental Policy Plan	Second Chamber of the States General, The Hague
Netherlands	1989	Kwartaalbericht milieustatistieken	Centraal Bureau voor de Statistiek, The Hague
Norway	1988	Yearbook of Nordic Statistics, 1988	Nordisk Statisktisk Sekretariat, Copenhagen
Poland	1989	Ochrona Srodowiska	Glówny Urzad Statystyczny, Statystyka Polski, Warsaw
Portugal	1989	Relatório do Estado do Ambiente e Ordenamento do Território	Ministerio do Planeamento e da Administração, do Território, Lisbon
Sweden	1990	The Natural Environment in Figures: Yearbook of Environmental Statistics	Statistics Sweden, Stockholm
Switzerland	1989	Survey of the Present State and Recent Evolution of the Swiss Environmental Policy	Swiss Federal Office for the Protection of the Environment, Federal Department of the Interior, Bern
UK	1989	Digest of Environmental Protection and Water Statistics	Environmental Protection Statistics and Economics Division, Department of Environment, London
Yugoslavia	1987	The State of and Policies for the Protection and Promotion of the Human Environment	Commission for the Environment, Belgrade

OCEANIA

Region/country	Year	Title	Issuing agency
Australia	1986	State of the Environment in Australia 1986	Department of Arts, Heritage and Environment, Canberra

Continued over

Table 10.4 Continued

Region/country	Year	Title	Issuing agency
Publisher		*International Reports*	
Oxford University Press	1990	World Resources 1990–91	World Resources Institute, Washington DC
Basil Blackwell	1991	United Nations Environment Programme Environmental Data Report	United Nations Environment Programme, Nairobi
CEC	1990	The State of the Environment in the European Community 1989	Commission of the European Communities, Luxembourg
DocTer Int. UK	1991	European Environmental Yearbook	DocTer Institute for Environmental Studies, Milan
ESCAP	1985	State of the Environment in Asia and the Pacific	UN Economic and Social Commission for Asia and the Pacific, Bangkok
EUROSTAT	1990	Environment Statistics	Statistical Office of the European Communities, Brussels
OECD	1991	The State of the Environment	Organisation for Economic Co-operation and Development, Paris
OECD	1989	OECD Environmental Data Compendium 1989	Organisation for Economic Co-operation and Development, Paris
Tycooley Int.	1982	The World Environment 1972–1982	United Nations Environment Programme, Nairobi
UN-ECE	1988	Environmental Statistics in Europe and North America: An Experimental Compendium	United Nations-Economic Commission for Europe, New York
UNEP	1990	Children and the Environment: The State of the Environment 1990	United Nations Environment Programme, Nairobi
W. W. Norton	1990	State of the World 1990	Worldwatch Institute, Washington DC

As far as can be ascertained, the reports listed are the most recent at the time of this compilation.

Source:
GEMS MARC 1991 GEMS MARC Environmental Data Base, Global Environment Monitoring System, Monitoring and Assessment Research Centre, London.

Table 10.5 Remote sensing satellites launched in 1988 and 1989

Code name/ spacecraft description	Country	Date of launch	Recovery date	Observations
Meteor-2 (17)	USSR	30-Jan-88		Meteorology
Cosmos-1920	USSR	18-Feb-88	9-Mar-88	Exploration of earth's natural resources
IRS-1A	India	17-Mar-88		Remote sensing
San Marco-D	Italy	25-Mar-88		Research on upper atmosphere
Cosmos-1951	USSR	31-May-88	14-Jun-88	Earth resources studies
Meteostat-P2	Europe (ESA)	15-Jun-88		Meteorology
Okean-1	USSR	5-Jul-88		Optical scanning and radio-physical equipment to obtain oceanographic information and data on ice conditions
Meteor-3 (2)	USSR	26-Jul-88		Meteorology and geophysical exploration
Cosmos-1965	USSR	23-Aug-88	22-Sep-88	Earth resources exploration
Cosmos-1968	USSR	9-Sep-88	23-Sep-88	Earth resources exploration
NOAA-11	USA (NOAA)	24-Sep-88		Meteorology
Cosmos-1990	USSR	12-Jan-89	11-Feb-89	Earth resources exploration; photography of seismically active regions of the USSR, including Armenia
Cosmos-2000	USSR	10-Feb-89	3-Mar-89	Earth resources exploration
Meteor-2 (18)	USSR	28-Feb-89		Meteorology; instruments for obtaining global data on cloud layers and for the constant observation of the streams of penetrating radiation in circum-terrestrial space
MOP-1	International (EUMETSAT)	6-Mar-89		Meteorology
GMS-4 (Himawari-4)	Japan	5-Sep-89		Meteorology
Meteor-3 (3)	USSR	24-Oct-89		Meteorology
COBE	US	18-Nov-89		Monitoring of cosmic background radiation

Sources:
ITU 1989 Table of artificial satellites launched in 1988, *Telecommunications Journal* **56**(V), Supplement.
ITU 1990 Table of artificial satellites launched in 1989, *Telecommunications Journal* **57**(V), Supplement.

Table 10.6   Public opinion on perceived change in the environment over the last 10 years, 1989

Region/country	No. of people interviewed	Response (percentage distribution)			
		Better	Worse	Stayed the same	Not sure
TOTAL					
Public	7,072	22	55	21	2
Leaders	761	19	69	12	1
AFRICA					
Kenya					
Public	300	39	44	13	4
Leaders	50	14	82	4	0
Nigeria					
Public	600	46	46	7	2
Leaders	50	24	70	6	0
Senegal					
Public	300	14	60	23	4
Leaders	50	12	70	16	2
Zimbabwe					
Public	300	39	40	16	5
Leaders	50	14	68	18	0
NORTH AMERICA					
Jamaica					
Public	300	14	63	17	6
Leaders	50	32	54	12	2
Mexico					
Public	399	12	61	28	0
Leaders	52	12	88	0	0
SOUTH AMERICA					
Argentina					
Public	400	10	76	13	1
Leaders	50	4	92	4	0
Brazil					
Public	500	16	52	31	1
Leaders	50	8	82	10	0
ASIA					
China					
Public	509	36	49	15	–
Leaders	50	32	58	4	6
India					
Public	538	20	63	16	1
Leaders	50	2	98	0	0
Japan					
Public	510	28	39	33	0
Leaders	52	27	52	21	0
Saudi Arabia					
Public	398	45	41	9	5
Leaders	52	44	38	17	0
EUROPE					
Germany, Fed. Rep.					
Public	513	7	59	32	2
Leaders	54	28	50	20	2

Continued opposite

Table 10.6 Continued

Region/country	No. of people interviewed	Response (percentage distribution)			
		Better	Worse	Stayed the same	Not sure
Hungary					
Public	499	10	68	20	2
Leaders	51	14	69	14	4
Norway					
Public	1,006	7	62	28	3
Leaders	50	10	64	26	0

The question asked was "Do you feel that the environment where you live has become better or worse in the last 10 years, or has it stayed about the same?".

The sample was designed to be representative of all persons aged 16 and over. In most developing countries the sample was limited to major metropolitan areas and urban centres, because of the impracticality of surveying rural populations. In Saudi Arabia the survey was limited to men. Leaders interviewed included politicians, senior civil servants, editors or policymakers of major news media, business leaders, industrial managers, religious leaders, medical and health care experts, labour union leaders and academics. The number of each type of leader interviewed varied from country to country.
Totals may not add up to 100 per cent due to rounding.

Source:
Louis Harris and Associates 1989 *Public and Leadership Attitudes to the Environment in Four Continents: A Report of a Survey in 16 Countries*, Louis Harris and Associates, New York.

Table 10.7 Membership of selected environmental organizations, 1989

Region/country	Greenpeace	Friends of the Earth	Region/country	Greenpeace	Friends of the Earth
AFRICA			**EUROPE**		
			Austria	144,000	300
Ghana		1,500	Belgium	44,000	a
Sierra Leone		1,058	Denmark	48,000	400
Tanzania		3,000	France	10,000	5,000
			German Dem. Rep.		200
NORTH AMERICA					
			Germany, Fed. Rep.	640,000	170,000
Canada	200,000	15,000	Ireland		1,500
Neth. Antilles		45	Italy	21,000	5,000
Nicaragua		800	Luxembourg	9,000	
USA	1,529,000	8,000	Netherlands	618,000	20,000
SOUTH AMERICA			Poland		a
			Spain	25,000	9,300
Argentina		83	Sweden	184,000	1,450
Brazil		400	Switzerland	98,000	200
Ecuador		300	UK	282,000	183,200
Uraguay		32			
			USSR		
ASIA					
			Estonia		4,500
Bangladesh		4,000			
Cyprus		200	**OCEANIA**		
Hong Kong		500			
Indonesia		600	Australia	40,000	600
Japan		100	New Zealand	48,500	1,300
			Papua New Guinea		a
Malaysia		500			
Pakistan		47	**OTHER**	11,000	

[a] Membership figures not supplied.

Membership includes supporters, who are people who have made donations or purchased goods from the organization.

Sources:
Friends of the Earth 1990 Personal communication, Friends of the Earth, London, UK.
Greenpeace 1990 Personal communication, Greenpeace International, Amsterdam, Netherlands.

Appendix 1
List of Contributors

UNEP Environmental Data Report

Produced on behalf of the United Nations Environment Programme by the staff of GEMS MARC in London with the co-operation of the World Resources Institute, Washington DC and the Department of the Environment, London, UK.

A. D. Willcocks, GEMS MARC, London: Editor
P. J. Peterson, UNEP/GEMS MARC, London: Assistant Editor

Steering Committee

M. D. Gwynne, UNEP/GEMS, Nairobi
P. J. Peterson, UNEP/GEMS MARC, London
A. D. Willcocks, GEMS MARC, London
A. L. Hammond, WRI, Washington DC
E. Rodenberg, WRI, Washington DC
P. S. MacCormack, UK DoE, London
C. Ogden, UK DoE, London

Compilers

P. S. Burgess, GEMS MARC: Water Quality, Biological Monitoring, Natural Disasters
J. A. Carless, GEMS MARC: Human Exposure, Human Health
N. Henninger, WRI: Natural Resources
C. Ogden, UK DoE: Wastes
C. A. Owen, GEMS MARC: Population/Settlements, Energy, Transport/Tourism, International Co-operation
P. J. Peterson, UNEP/GEMS MARC: Soils and Sediments, Historical Monitoring, Protected Areas and Wildlife
E. Rodenberg, WRI: Natural Resources
A. D. Webster, GEMS MARC: Atmosphere
A. D. Willcocks, GEMS MARC: Atmosphere, Atmospheric Deposition, Climate, Historical Monitoring, Protected Areas and Wildlife

Typesetting and Layout

I. Stewart, GEMS MARC, London

Editorial and Production Assistance

M. Bremner, GEMS MARC, London
C. J. Meads, GEMS MARC, London
F. Preston, GEMS MARC, London
Words and Publications, Oxford (figures)

Contributors/Reviewers

G. G. Akland, Environmental Monitoring Systems Laboratory, US EPA, Research Triangle Park, North Carolina, USA
D. H. M. Alderton, Royal Holloway and Bedford New College, Egham, UK
J. Allen, EUROSTAT, Luxembourg
J. Aloisi de Larderel, UNEP/IEO, Paris, France
M. Ando, ILEC, Shiga, Japan
A. Bakar Jaafar, Ministry of Science, Technology and Environment, Kuala Lumpur, Malaysia
F. Balkau, UNEP/IEO, Paris, France
M. Barke, Newcastle-Upon-Tyne Polytechnic, Newcastle-Upon-Tyne, UK
T. P. Barnett, Scripps Institution of Oceanography, La Jolla, California, USA
G. Berz, Natural Hazards Research Group, Munich Reinsurance Company, Munich, Germany
V. Boldirev, WMO, Geneva, Switzerland
E. E. Brabb, US Geological Survey, Palo Alto, California, USA
J. C. Bruce, CDSC, London, UK
W. Bulski, UNEP consultant, Nairobi, Kenya
I. D. Chivers, King's College London, London, UK
J. Christensen, UNEP Collaborating Centre on Energy and Environment, Risø National Laboratory, Roskilde, Denmark
D. M. Clark, World Data Center A, NOAA, Boulder, Colorado, USA
K. Clark, Greenpeace International, Amsterdam, Netherlands
J. A. Clubb, British Scrap Federation, Huntingdon, UK
A. Cooper, Tourism Concern, Tyne and Wear, UK
D. M. Cruden, University of Alberta, Edmonton, Canada
U. Dabholkar, UNEP/DPCU, Nairobi, Kenya
B. E. Davies, University of Bradford, Bradford, UK
M. Depraz, WWF, Amsterdam, Netherlands

F. Dixon, World Energy Council, London, UK

E. J. Dlugokencky, NOAA/CMDL, Boulder, Colorado, USA

H. Dovland, EMEP, Norwegian Institute for Air Research, Lillestrøm, Norway

R. Duffield, NWRI/CCIW, Burlington, Ontario, Canada

T. W. Elkins, NOAA/CMDL, Boulder, Colorado, USA

G. Evans, Environmental Monitoring Systems Laboratory, US EPA, Research Triangle Park, North Carolina, USA

A. Faiz, The World Bank, Washington DC, USA

M. Friesen, IARC, Lyon, France

S. Gabbay, Ministry of Environment, Jerusalem, Israel

H. Galal-Gorchev, WHO, Geneva, Switzerland

R. Garland, Transnet, London, UK

N. Gebremedhin, UNEP/EM, Nairobi, Kenya

H. Genot, UNEP/IEO, Paris, France

K. Grey, International Tanker Owners Pollution Federation Ltd, London, UK

D. Guha-Sapir, Centre for Research on the Epidemiology of Disease, Brussels, Belgium

M. D. Gwynne, UNEP/GEMS, Nairobi, Kenya

W. Haeberli, WGMS, Zurich, Switzerland

J. Harrison, WCMC, Cambridge, UK

D. Hart, King's College London, London, UK

R. Helmer, WHO, Geneva, Switzerland

N. V. Hicks, WHO, Geneva, Switzerland

J. Huismans, UNEP/IRPTC, Geneva, Switzerland

T. Iverson, EMEP, Norwegian Meteorological Institute, Oslo, Norway

T. M. Jaansoo-Boudreau, FAO, Rome, Italy

J. A. Jackson, GEMS MARC, London, UK

K. C. Jones, University of Lancaster, Lancaster, UK

P. D. Jones, University of East Anglia, Norwich, UK

A. Kahnert, Statistical Division, UN-ECE, Geneva, Switzerland

C. Kerpelman, UNDRO, Geneva, Switzerland

T. Kjellström, WHO, Geneva, Switzerland

R. J. Kim-Farley, WHO, Geneva, Switzerland

D. King, Office of US Foreign Disaster Assistance, Washington DC, USA

L. Kristoferson, Stockholm Environment Institute, Stockholm, Sweden

P. J. Lamb, Illinois State Water Survey, Champaign, Illinois, USA

P. M. Lang, NOAA/CMDL, Boulder, Colorado, USA

R. J. Law, Ministry of Agriculture, Fisheries and Food, Fisheries Laboratory, Burnham-on-Crouch, UK

P. Lamont, Australian Conservation Foundation, Melbourne, Australia

D. H. Landers, National Surface Water Survey, EPA, Corralis, Oregon, USA

A. Lees, Friends of the Earth, London, UK

J. Lewis, Datum International, Marshfield, UK

G. A. Mackenzie, UNEP Collaborating Centre on Energy and Environment, Risø National Laboratory, Roskilde, Denmark

D. Mage, WHO, Geneva, Switzerland

S. Matsui, ILEC, Shiga, Japan

B. Mendonca, NOAA/CMDL, Boulder, Colorado, USA

J. Mes, Health and Welfare Canada, Ottawa, Ontario, Canada

B. Mitchell, Statistics Canada, Ottawa, Ontario, Canada

D. Mitchell, UNEP/GEMS, Nairobi, Kenya

F. Mitchelmore, UNEP/EEC consultant, Nairobi, Kenya

C. S. Muir, WHO, Geneva, Switzerland

F. Murray, Murdoch University, Murdoch, Australia

J. P. Neale, WWF, Godalming, UK

S. A. M. Nicholas, CDSC, London, UK

M. Norton-Griffiths, UNITAR, GEMS PAC, Nairobi, Kenya

E. D. Ongley, NWRI/CCIW, Burlington, Ontario, Canada

G. Ozolins, WHO, Geneva, Switzerland

K. F. Panzer, Bundesforschungsanstalt für Forst- und Holzwirtschaft, Hamburg, Germany

D. M. Parkin, IARC, Lyon, France

D. B. Peakall, Canadian Wildlife Service, Environment Canada, Ottawa, Ontario, Canada

D. Piekarz, Environment Canada, Toronto, Ontario, Canada

A. Pradilla, WHO, Geneva, Switzerland

S. A. Ramadan, Royal Scientific Society, Amman, Jordan

G. Robyns, FEVE, Brussels, Belgium

C. F. Ropelowski, NOAA-CAC, Washington DC, USA

F. Rosillo Calle, King's College London, London, UK

Å. Rühling, University of Lund, Sweden

I. Rummel-Bulska, UNEP/ELIU, Nairobi, Kenya

F. Ya. Rovinsky, Natural Environment and Climate Monitoring Laboratory, LAM, Moscow, USSR

N. Sadik, UNFPA, New York, USA

L. J. Saliba, Mediterranean Action Plan, WHO, Geneva, Switzerland

P. Sand, UN-ECE, Geneva, Switzerland

R. Sarin, National Environmental Engineering Research Institute, Nagpur, India

A. Semb, Norwegian Institute for Air Research, Lillestrøm, Norway

R. L. Schuster, US Geological Survey, Denver, Colorado, USA

H. Soud, IEA Coal Research, London, UK

S. de Souza Hacon, Financiadora de Estudos E Projetos, Rio de Janeiro, Brazil

G. Stephens, NOAA-NESDIS, Washington DC, USA

Tan Jianan, Institute of Geography, Chinese Academy of Science, Beijing, People's Republic of China

P. P. Tans, NOAA/CMDL, Boulder, Colorado, USA

V. Vandeweerd, UNEP/GEMS, Nairobi, Kenya

C. C. Wallén, Senior Adviser, UNEP, Nairobi

M. Wattam, UN Information Service, London, UK

G. Watters, WHO, Geneva, Switzerland

S. Whyte, British Glass Manufacturers Association, Sheffield, UK

C. P. Wild, IARC, Lyon, France

B. O. Wilen, US Fish and Wildlife Service, US Department of the Interior, Washington DC, USA

World Tourist Organization, Madrid, Spain

Xu Jialin, Institute of Environmental Science, Beijing, People's Republic of China

Appendix 2
List of Country Names

The description and classification of countries and territories in this study and the arrangement of the material do not imply the expression of any opinion whatsoever of the Secretariat of the United Nations concerning the legal status of any country, territory, city or area, or of its authorities, or concerning the delimitation of its frontiers or boundaries, or regarding its economic system or degree of development.

Since the publication of the previous edition of this report in 1989, several country name changes have occurred. The Socialist Republic of the Union of Burma is now known as the Union of Myanmar. Democratic Kampuchea is now Cambodia. Furthermore, a number of countries have united. In May 1990 the People's Democratic Republic of Yemen and the Yemen Arab Republic merged to form the Republic of Yemen. In October 1990 the Federal Republic of Germany and the German Democratic Republic united to form the Federal Republic of Germany. Since the information presented in the data tables of this report refer to years prior to unification, these countries have been listed according to their former names.

Short name below refers to the abbreviated name used within the body of this report.

Short name	Full name
Afghanistan	Democratic Republic of Afghanistan
Albania	People's Socialist Republic of Albania
Algeria	People's Democratic Republic of Algeria
American Samoa	American Samoa
Andorra	Andorra
Angola	People's Republic of Angola
Anguilla	Anguilla, UK Dependency
Antarctic	Antarctic
Antigua & Barbuda	Antigua and Barbuda
Arctic	Arctic
Argentina	Argentine Republic
Australia	Commonwealth of Australia
Austria	Republic of Austria
Bahamas	Commonwealth of the Bahamas
Bahrain	State of Bahrain

Short name	Full name
Bangladesh	People's Republic of Bangladesh
Barbados	Barbados
Belgium	Kingdom of Belgium
Belize	Belize
Benin	People's Republic of Benin
Bermuda	Bermuda
Bhutan	Kingdom of Bhutan
Bolivia	Republic of Bolivia
Botswana	Republic of Botswana
Br. Ind. Oc. Tr.	British Indian Ocean Territory
Br. Virgin Is.	British Virgin Islands
Brazil	Federative Republic of Brazil
Brunei	Brunei
Bulgaria	People's Republic of Bulgaria
Burkina Faso	Burkina Faso
Burundi	Republic of Burundi
Byelorussian SSR	Byelorussian Soviet Socialist Republic
Cameroon	United Republic of Cameroon
Cambodia qv Kampuchea	Cambodia
Canada	Canada
Canton Is.	Canton and Enderbury Islands
Cape Verde	Republic of Cape Verde
Cayman Is.	Cayman Islands
Cent. African Rep.	Central African Republic
Chad	Republic of Chad
Chile	Republic of Chile
China	People's Republic of China
China, Taiwan	Chinese Province of Taiwan
Christmas Is.	Christmas Island
Cocos Is.	Cocos (Keeling) Islands
Colombia	Republic of Columbia
Comoros	Federal and Islamic Republic of Comoros
Congo	People's Republic of the Congo
Cook Is.	Cook Island
Costa Rica	Republic of Costa Rica
Côte d'Ivoire	Republic of Côte d'Ivoire
Cuba	Republic of Cuba
Cyprus	Republic of Cyprus

Short name	Full name	Short name	Full name
Czechoslovakia	Czech and Slovak Federal Republic	Jamaica	Jamaica
		Japan	Japan
		Jordan	Hashemite Kingdom of Jordan
Denmark	Kingdom of Denmark		
Djibouti	Republic of Djibouti	Kenya	Republic of Kenya
Dominica	Commonwealth of Dominica	Kiribati	Kiribati
Dominican Rep.	Dominican Republic	Korea	Republic of Korea
		Korea, Dem.	Democratic People's Republic of Korea
East Timor	East Timor		
Ecuador	Republic of Ecuador	Kuwait	State of Kuwait
Egypt	Arab Republic of Egypt		
El Salvador	Republic of El Salvador	Laos	Lao People's Democratic Republic
Equatorial Guinea	Republic of Equatorial Guinea		
Ethiopia	Socialist Republic of Ethiopia	Lebanon	Lebanese Republic
		Lesotho	Kingdom of Lesotho
Faeroe Is.	Faeroe Islands	Liberia	Republic of Liberia
Falkland Is.	Falkland Islands	Libya	Socialist People's Libyan Arab Jamahiriya
Fiji	Fiji		
Finland	Republic of Finland	Liechtenstein	Principality of Liechtenstein
France	French Republic	Luxembourg	Grand Duchy of Luxembourg
French Guiana	French Guiana		
French Polynesia	French Polynesia	Macau	Macau
French Southern Tr.	French Southern Territory	Madagascar	Democratic Republic of Madagascar
Gabon	Gabonese Republic	Malawi	Republic of Malawi
Gambia	Republic of Gambia	Malaysia	Malaysia
Gaza Strip	Gaza Strip	Maldives	Republic of Maldives
German Dem. Rep.	German Democratic Republic	Mali	Republic of Mali
Germany, Fed. Rep.	Federal Republic of Germany	Malta	Republic of Malta
Ghana	Republic of Ghana	Martinique	Martinique
Gibraltar	Gibraltar	Mauritania	Islamic Republic of Mauritania
Greece	Hellenic Republic		
Greenland	Greenland	Mauritius	Mauritius
Grenada	Grenada	Mexico	United Mexican States
Guadeloupe	Guadeloupe	Monaco	Principality of Monaco
Guam	Guam	Mongolia	Mongolian People's Republic
Guatemala	Republic of Guatemala	Montserrat	Montserrat
Guinea	Revolutionary People's Republic of Guinea	Morocco	Kingdom of Morocco
		Mozambique	People's Republic of Mozambique
Guinea-Bissau	Republic of Guinea-Bissau		
Guyana	Republic of Guyana	Myanmar qv Burma	The Union of Myanmar
Haiti	Republic of Haiti	Namibia	Namibia
Honduras	Republic of Honduras	Nauru	Republic of Nauru
Hong Kong	Hong Kong	Nepal	Kingdom of Nepal
Hungary	Hungarian People's Republic	Neth. Antilles	Netherlands Antilles
		Netherlands	Kingdom of the Netherlands
Iceland	Republic of Iceland	New Caledonia	New Caledonia
India	Republic of India	New Zealand	New Zealand
Indonesia	Republic of Indonesia	Nicaragua	Republic of Nicaragua
Iran	Islamic Republic of Iran	Niger	Republic of the Niger
Iraq	Republic of Iraq	Nigeria	Federal Republic of Nigeria
Ireland	Ireland	Niue	Niue
Israel	State of Israel	Norfolk Is.	Norfolk Island
Italy	Italian Republic	Northern Marianas Is.	Northern Marianas Islands, Commonwealth of Islands

Short name	Full name	Short name	Full name
Norway	Kingdom of Norway	Sweden	Kingdom of Sweden
		Switzerland	Swiss Confederation
Oman	Sultanate of Oman	Syria	Syrian Arab Republic
Pacific Is. Tr. Tr.	Pacific Islands Trust Territory	Tanzania	United Republic of Tanzania
Pakistan	Islamic Republic of Pakistan	Thailand	Kingdom of Thailand
Panama	Republic of Panama	Togo	Togolese Republic
Papua New Guinea	Papua New Guinea	Tokelau	Tokelau
Paraguay	Republic of Paraguay	Tonga	Kingdom of Tonga
Peru	Republic of Peru	Trinidad & Tobago	Republic of Trinidad and Tobago
Philippines	Republic of the Philippines		
Poland	Polish People's Republic	Tunisia	Republic of Tunisia
Portugal	Portuguese Republic	Turkey	Republic of Turkey
Puerto Rico	Puerto Rico	Turks & Caicos Is.	Turks and Caicos Islands
		Tuvalu	Tuvalu
Qatar	State of Qatar		
		Uganda	Republic of Uganda
Réunion	Réunion	UK	United Kingdom of Great Britain and Northern Ireland
Romania	Socialist Republic of Romania		
Rwanda	Rwandese Republic	Ukranian SSR	Ukranian Soviet Socialist Republic
Samoa	Independent State of Western Samoa	United Arab Em.	United Arab Emirates
		Uruguay	Eastern Republic of Uruguay
San Marino	Republic of San Marino	USA	United States of America
São Tomé & Príncipe	São Tomé and Príncipe	USSR	Union of Soviet Socialist Republics
Saudi Arabia	Kingdom of Saudi Arabia		
Senegal	Republic of Senegal	US Virgin Is.	United States Virgin Islands
Seychelles	Republic of Seychelles		
Sierra Leone	Republic of Sierra Leone	Vanuatu	Republic of Vanuatu
Singapore	Republic of Singapore	Venezuela	Republic of Venezuela
Solomon Is.	Solomon Islands	Viet Nam	Socialist Republic of Viet Nam
Somalia	Somalia Democratic Republic		
South Africa	Republic of South Africa		
Spain	Spanish State	Wallis Is.	Wallis and Futuna Islands
Sri Lanka	Democratic Socialist Republic of Sri Lanka	Western Sahara	Western Sahara
		Windward Is.	Windward Islands
St Christopher & Nevis	Saint Christopher and Nevis		
St Helena	Saint Helena	Yemen	Yemen Arab Republic
St Lucia	Saint Lucia	Yemen, Dem.	People's Democratic Republic of Yemen
St Pierre & Miquelon	Saint Pierre and Miquelon		
St Vincent & Grenadines	Saint Vincent and the Grenadines	Yugoslavia	Socialist Federal Republic of Yugoslavia
Sudan	Democratic Republic of the Sudan		
		Zaire	Republic of Zaire
Suriname	Republic of Suriname	Zambia	Republic of Zambia
Swaziland	Kingdom of Swaziland	Zimbabwe	Republic of Zimbabwe

Appendix 3
List of Abbreviations

APELL	Awareness and Preparedness for Emergencies at Local Level (IEO)
ARTEMIS	African Real Time Environmental Monitoring Using Imaging Satellites (FAO)
AVHRR	Advanced Very High Resolution Radiometers
BAPMoN	Background Air Pollution Monitoring Network (WMO/EPA/UNEP(GEMS))
CAC	Climate Analysis Center
CCC	Chemical Co-ordinating Centre
CCIW	Canada Centre for Inland Waters
CDD	Control of Diarrhoeal Diseases Programme (WHO)
CDIAC	Carbon Dioxide Information Analysis Center
CDSC	Communicable Disease Surveillance Centre
CEC	Commission of the European Communities
CFCs	Chlorofluorocarbons
CITES	Convention on International Trade in Endangered Species
CLICOM	Transfer of Technology in Climate Data Management and User Services (WMO)
CMA	Chemical Manufacturers Association
CMDL	Climate Monitoring and Diagnostics Laboratory (formerly Climate Monitoring for Climate Change (GMCC))
CMR	Child Mortality Rate
COADS	Comprehensive Ocean-Atmosphere Data Set
CVD	Cardiovascular Disease
DDE	1,1'-(2,2-dichlorethenylidene)-bis[4-chloro benzene]
DDT	Dichlorodiphenyltrichloroethane
EEC	European Economic Community
ELIU	Environmental Law and Institutions Unit (UNEP)
EMEP	European Monitoring and Evaluation Programme (UN-ECE/UNEP/WMO)
EPI	Expanded Programme on Immunization (WHO)
ETH	Swiss Federal Institute of Technology
FAO	Food and Agriculture Organization
FEVE	European Glass Container Federation
FEWS	Famine Early Warning System (US AID)
GAGE	Global Atmospheric Gases Experiment (CMA)
GAW	Global Atmosphere Watch (WMO)
GEMS	Global Environment Monitoring System (UNEP)
GIS	Geographic Information Systems
GLASOD	Global Assessment of Soil Degradation (ISRIC/UNEP)
GNP	Gross National Product
GO$_3$OS	Global Ozone Observing System (WMO)
GOS	Global Observing System (WWW)
GRID	Global Resource Information Database (UNEP(GEMS))
GTS	Global Telecommunications System (WWW(WMO))
HCB	Hexachlorobenzene
HCH	Hexachlorocyclohexane
HEALs	Human Exposure Assessment Locations (WHO/UNEP)
HEM	Harmonization of Environmental Measurement (UNEP(GEMS))
IAEA	International Atomic Energy Agency
IAHS	International Association of Hydrological Sciences
IARC	International Agency for Research on Cancer
IATA	International Air Transport Association
ICAO	International Civil Aviation Organization
ICES	International Council for the Exploration of the Sea
ICP	International Co-operative Programme
ICPIC	International Cleaner Production Information Computer System (IEO)
ICSI	International Commission on Snow and Ice
ICSU	International Council for Scientific Unions
IDNDR	International Decade for Natural Disaster Reduction
IEA	International Energy Agency
IEO	Industry and Environment Office (UNEP)
IGBP	International Geosphere-Biosphere Programme (ICSU)
IHD	Ischaemic Heart Disease
ILEC	International Lake Environment Committee

ILO	International Labour Organization	OECD	Organisation for Economic Co-operation and Development
IMCO	Inter-governmental Maritime Consultative Organization	OFDA	Office of the US Foreign Disaster Assistance
IMO	International Maritime Organization	ORT	Oral Rehydration Therapy
IMR	Infant Mortality Rate	PAHs	Polyaromatic Hydrocarbons
INFOCLIMA	World Climate Data and Information Referral Stytem (WMO)	PCBs	Polychlorinated Biphenyls
INFOTERRA	International Referral System for Sources of Environmental Information (UNEP)	PSMSL	Permanent Service for Mean Sea Level
		RSL	Relative Sea Level
		SFT	Norwegian State Pollution Control Authority
INPE	Instituto de Pesquisas Espaciais	SST	Sea-surface Temperature
IPCC	Intergovernmental Panel on Climate Change (WMO/UNEP)	TBT	Tributyltin
		UIC	Union Internationale des Chemins de Fer
IPCS	International Programme on Chemical Safety (UNEP/WHO/ILO)	UN	United Nations
		UNDIESA	United Nations Department of International Economic and Social Affairs
IRF	International Road Federation		
IRPTC	International Register of Potentially Toxic Chemicals (UNEP)		
ISC	International Seismological Centre	UNDP	United Nations Development Programme
ISO	International Standards Organization	UNDRO	Office of the United Nations Disaster Relief Co-ordinator
ISRIC	International Soil Reference and Information Centre		
		UN-ECE	United Nations Economic Commission for Europe
ITU	International Telecommunications Union		
IUCN	The World Conservation Union (formerly the International Union for Conservation of Nature and Natural Resources)	UNEP	United Nations Environment Programme
		UNESCO	United Nations Educational, Scientific and Cultural Organization
		UNFPA	United Nations Fund for Population Activities
IWC	International Whaling Commission		
JECFA	Joint FAO/WHO Expert Committee on Food Additives	UNHCR	United Nations High Commissioner for Refugees
MAP	Mediterranean Action Plan (OCA-PAC)	UNICEF	United Nations Children's Fund
MED POL	Monitoring and Research Programme of the Mediterranean Action Plan	UNIDO	United Nations Industrial Development Organization
MMR	Maternal Mortality Rate	UNINET	The computer network for disaster-related information developed by UNDRO
MONICA	Multilateral Monitoring of Trends and Determinants in Cardiovascular Diseases (WHO)		
		UNSCEAR	United Nations Scientific Committee on the Effects of Atomic Radiation
MSC	Meteorological Synthesizing Centre		
NAPAP	National Acid Precipitation and Assessment Program	UNSO	United Nations Statistical Office
		US AID	United States Agency for International Development
NAS	US National Academy of Sciences		
NCAR	National Center for Atmospheric Research	USCR	United States Committee for Refugees
		US EPA	United States Environmental Protection Agency
NDVI	Normalized Difference Vegetation Index		
NESDIS	National Environmental Satellite, Data and Information Service (formerly National Earth Satellite Service)	WCMC	World Conservation Monitoring Centre
		WCRP	World Climate Research Programme (WMO/ICSU/UNESCO)
NGL	Natural Gas Liquid	WEC	World Energy Council (formerly World Energy Conference)
NGO	Non-government Organization		
NILU	Norwegian Institute for Air Research	WGI	World Glacier Inventory (ICSI/UNESCO ETH/UNEP(GEMS))
NIVA	Norwegian Institute for Water Research		
NOAA	National Oceanic and Atmospheric Administration	WGMS	World Glacier Monitoring Service
		WHO	World Health Organization
		WMO	World Meteorological Organization
NSWS	National Surface Water Survey	WTO	World Tourism Organization
NWRI	National Water Research Institute	WWF	World Wide Fund for Nature (formerly World Wildlife Fund)
OCA-PAC	Oceans and Coastal Areas-Programme Activity Centre (UNEP)	WWW	World Weather Watch (WMO)